Integrated Models for Information Communication Systems and Networks:

Design and Development

Aderemi A. Atayero
Covenant University, Nigeria

Oleg I. Sheluhin
Moscow Technical University of Communication & Informatics, Russia

Managing Director:	Lindsay Johnston
Production Manager:	Jennifer Yoder
Publishing Systems Analyst:	Adrienne Freeland
Acquisitions Editor:	Kayla Wolfe
Typesetter:	Erin O'Dea
Cover Design:	Jason Mull

Published in the United States of America by
Information Science Reference (an imprint of IGI Global)
701 E. Chocolate Avenue
Hershey PA 17033
Tel: 717-533-8845
Fax: 717-533-8661
E-mail: cust@igi-global.com
Web site: http://www.igi-global.com

Library of Congress Cataloging-in-Publication Data

Integrated models for information communication systems and networks : design and development / Aderemi A. Atayero and Oleg I. Sheluhin, editors.
pages cm
Summary: "This book explores essential information and current research findings on information communication systems and networks and aims to assist professionals in the desire to enhance their knowledge of modeling at systems level with the aid of modern software packages"-- Provided by publisher.
Includes bibliographical references and index.
ISBN 978-1-4666-2208-1 (hardcover) -- ISBN 978-1-4666-2209-8 (ebook) -- ISBN 978-1-4666-2210-4 (print & perpetual access) 1. Wireless communication systems--Design and construction. 2. Mobile communication systems--Design and construction. 3. Integrated services digital networks. 4. System analysis. I. Atayero, Aderemi A., 1969- editor of compilation. II. Shelukhin, O. I. (Oleg Ivanovich), editor of compilation.
TK5103.2.I518 2013
621.382--dc23

2012039669

British Cataloguing in Publication Data
A Cataloguing in Publication record for this book is available from the British Library.

Editorial Advisory Board

List of Reviewers

Table of Contents

Preface xv

Section 1
Network and Information Proccesses

Chapter 1
Principles of Modeling in Information Communication Systems and Networks 1
Oleg I. Sheluhin, Moscow Technical University of Communication and Informatics, Russia
Aderemi A. Atayero, Covenant University, Nigeria

Chapter 2
Numerical Methods of Multifractal Analysis in Information
Communication Systems and Networks 16
Oleg I. Sheluhin, Moscow Technical University of Communications and Informatics, Russia
Artem V. Garmashev, Moscow Technical University of Communications and Informatics, Russia

Chapter 3
The Switched Local Area Networks' Delay Problem: Issues and a
Deterministic Solution Approach.. 47
Monday O. Eyinagho, Covenant University, Nigeria
Samuel O. Falaki, Federal University of Technology Akure, Nigeria

Chapter 4
A Voice-Enabled Framework for Recommender and Adaptation Systems in E-Learning 71
A. A. Azeta, Covenant University, Nigeria
C. K. Ayo, Covenant University, Nigeria
N. A. Ikhu-Omoregbe, Covenant University, Nigeria

Chapter 5
Signals with an Additive Fractal Structure for Information Transmission 97
M. V. Kapranov, Moscow Power Engineering Institute, Russia
A. V. Khandurin, Moscow Power Engineering Institute, Russia

Chapter 6
TCP/IP Protocol-Based Model for Increasing the Efficiency of Data Transfer in Computer Networks 116
S.N. John, Covenant University, Nigeria
A.A. Anoprienko, Donetsk National Technical University, Ukraine
C.U. Ndujiuba, Covenant University, Nigeria

Chapter 7
Validating the INTERPRETOR Software Architecture for the Interpretation of Large and Noisy Data Sets 135
Apkar Salatian, American University of Nigeria, Nigeria

Chapter 8
Modeling Maintenance Productivity Measurement 149
Christian A. Bolu, Federal University Oye-Ekiti, Nigeria

Section 2
Information Communication and Engineering

Chapter 9
Modeling of Packet Streaming Services in Information Communication Networks 166
Aderemi A. Atayero, Covenant University, Nigeria
Yury A. Ivanov, Elster Vital Connections, Russia

Chapter 10
Mathematical Models of Video-Sequences of Digital Half-Tone Images 207
E.P. Petrov, Vyatka State University, Russia
I.S. Trubin, Vyatka State University, Russia
E.V. Medvedeva, Vyatka State University, Russia
S.M. Smolskiy, Moscow Power Engineering Institute, Russia

Chapter 11
Performance Analysis of Multi-Antenna Relay Networks over Nakagami-m Fading Channel 242
E. Soleimani-Nasab, K. N. Toosi University of Technology, Iran
A. Kalantari, K. N. Toosi University of Technology, Iran
M. Ardebilipour, K. N. Toosi University of Technology, Iran

Chapter 12
A Generic Method for the Reliable Calculation of Large-Scale Fading in an Obstacle-Dense Propagation Environment 256
Theofilos Chrysikos, University of Patras, Greece
Stavros Kotsopoulos, University of Patras, Greece
Eduard Babulak, EU CORDIS, Belgium

Chapter 13
Development of Nonlinear Filtering Algorithms of Digital Half-Tone Images 278
E. P. Petrov, Vyatka State University, Russia
I. S. Trubin, Vyatka State University, Russia
E. V. Medvedeva, Vyatka State University, Russia
S. M. Smolskiy, Moscow Power Engineering Institute, Russia

Chapter 14
Performance Analysis of Traffic and Mobility Models on Mobile and Vehicular
Ad Hoc Wireless Networks 305
Lawal Bello, University of Greenwich, UK
Panos Bakalis, University of Greenwich, UK

Chapter 15
Modeling of Quantum Key Distribution System for Secure Information Transfer 314
K. E. Rumyantsev, Taganrog Institute of Technology, Russia
D. M. Golubchikov, Southern Federal University, Russia

Chapter 16
ANFIS Modeling of Dynamic Load Balancing in LTE 343
Matthew K. Luka, Modibbo Adama University of Technology, Nigeria
Aderemi A. Atayero, Covenant University, Nigeria

Chapter 17
Neural Network Control of a Laboratory Magnetic Levitator 361
J. Katende, Botswana International University of Science and Technology, Botswana
M. Mustapha, Bayero University, Nigeria

Chapter 18
Constitutive Modeling of Wind Energy Potential of Selected Sites in Nigeria:
A Pre-Assessment Model.. 375
O. O. Ajayi, Covenant University, Nigeria
R. O. Fagbenle, Obafemi Awolowo University, Nigeria
J. Katende, Botswana International University of Science and Technology, Botswana

Chapter 19
Cross-Layer Optimization in OFDM Wireless Communication Network 390
Babasanjo Oshin, Covenant University, Nigeria
Adeyemi Alatishe, Covenant University, Nigeria

Compilation of References 411

About the Contributors 435

Index... 444

Detailed Table of Contents

Preface xv

Section 1
Networks and Information Processes

Chapter 1
Principles of Modeling in Information Communication Systems and Networks 1
Oleg I. Sheluhin, Moscow Technical University of Communication and Informatics, Russia
Aderemi A. Atayero, Covenant University, Nigeria

The authors present in this entry chapter the basic rubrics of models, modeling, and simulation, an understanding of which is indispensible for the comprehension of subsequent chapters of this text on the all-important topic of modeling and simulation in Information Communication Systems and Networks (ICSN). A good example is the case of analyzing simulation results of traffic models as a tool for investigating network behavioral pattarns as it affects the transmitted content (Atayero, et al., 2013). The various classifications of models are discussed, for example classification based on the degree of semblance to the original object (i.e. isomorphism). Various fundamental terminologies without the knowledge of which the concepts and models and modeling cannot be properly understood are explained. Model stuctures are highlighted and discussed. The methodological basis of formalizing complex system structures is presented. The concept of componential approach to modeling is presented and the necessary stages of mathematical model formation are examined and explained. The chapter concludes with a presentation of the concept of simulation vis-à-vis information communication systems and networks.

Chapter 2
Numerical Methods of Multifractal Analysis in Information
Communication Systems and Networks 16
Oleg I. Sheluhin, Moscow Technical University of Communications and Informatics, Russia
Artem V. Garmashev, Moscow Technical University of Communications and Informatics, Russia

In this chapter, the main principles of the theory of fractals and multifractals are stated. A singularity spectrum is introduced for the random telecommunication traffic, concepts of fractal dimensions and scaling functions, and methods used in their determination by means of Wavelet Transform Modulus Maxima (WTMM) are proposed. Algorithm development methods for estimating multifractal spectrum are presented. A method based on multifractal data analysis at network layer level by means of WTMM is proposed for the detection of traffic anomalies in computer and telecommunication networks. The chapter also introduces WTMM as the informative indicator to exploit the distinction of fractal dimensions on various parts of a given dataset. A novel approach based on the use of multifractal spectrum parameters is proposed for estimating queuing performance for the generalized multifractal traffic on the input of a buffering device. It is shown that the multifractal character of traffic has significant impact on queuing performance characteristics.

Chapter 3
The Switched Local Area Networks' Delay Problem: Issues and a Deterministic Solution Approach 47
Monday O. Eyinagho, Covenant University, Nigeria
Samuel O. Falaki, Federal University of Technology Akure, Nigeria

A large number of installed local area networks are sluggish in terms of speed of uploading and downloading of information. Researchers have, therefore, proposed the need for such networks to be designed with specified maximum end-to-end delay. This is because, if the maximum packet delay between any two nodes of a network is not known, it is impossible to provide a deterministic guarantee of worst case response times of packets' flows. Therefore, the need for analytic and formal basis for designing such networks becomes very imperative. In this regard, this chapter has discussed the switched local area networks' delay problem and related issues. It compared the two principal approaches for determining the end-to-end response times of flows in communication networks – stochastic approach and deterministic approach. The chapter goes on to demonstrate the superiority of the latter approach by using it to develop and validate the goodness of a general maximum delay packet switch model.

Chapter 4
A Voice-Enabled Framework for Recommender and Adaptation Systems in E-Learning 71
A. A. Azeta, Covenant University, Nigeria
C. K. Ayo, Covenant University, Nigeria
N. A. Ikhu-Omoregbe, Covenant University, Nigeria

With the proliferation of learning resources on the Web, finding suitable content (using telephone) has become a rigorous task for voice-based online learners to achieve better performance. The problem with Finding Content Suitability (FCS) with voice E-Learning applications is more complex when the sight-impaired learner is involved. Existing voice-enabled applications in the domain of E-Learning lack the attributes of adaptive and reusable learning objects to be able to address the FCS problem. This study provides a Voice-enabled Framework for Rrecommender and Adaptation (VeFRA) Systems in E-learning and an implementation of a system based on the framework with dual user interfaces – voice and Web. A usability study was carried out in a visually impaired and non-visually impaired school using the International Standard Organization's (ISO) 9241-11 specification to determine the level of effectiveness, efficiency and user satisfaction. The result of the usability evaluation reveals that the prototype application developed for the school has "Good Usability" rating of 4.13 out of 5 scale. This shows that the application will not only complement existing mobile and Web-based learning systems, but will be of immense benefit to users, based on the system's capacity for taking autonomous decisions that are capable of adapting to the needs of both visually impaired and non-visually impaired learners.

Chapter 5
Signals with an Additive Fractal Structure for Information Transmission 97
M. V. Kapranov, Moscow Power Engineering Institute, Russia
A. V. Khandurin, Moscow Power Engineering Institute, Russia

This chapter is devoted to a new class of wideband signals with an additive fractal structure. Properties and characteristics of the new type of signals are studied. It is shown that such signals possess a high level of an irregularity and unpredictability at simple technical implementation. It is shown that an incommensurability of frequencies of fundamental high-stable oscillations leads to the high level of an irregularity of such signals. For an estimation of a level of signal complexity, authors offer to use the fractal dimensionality of their temporal implementations calculated by means of creation of the structural function. Methods of modification of the signal spectrum with the additive fractal structure are offered, permitting to increase the efficiency of the frequency resource application. For reduction of the high low-frequency signal power the authors suggest using signals with the additive fractal structure, centered in a moving average window. Methods of masking of the voice messages by means of signals of a new type are offered. The results of a computer experiment of secretive sound transmission are described.

Chapter 6
TCP/IP Protocol-Based Model for Increasing the Efficiency of Data
Transfer in Computer Networks 116
S.N. John, Covenant University, Nigeria
A.A. Anoprienko, Donetsk National Technical University, Ukraine
C.U. Ndujiuba, Covenant University, Nigeria

This chapter provides solutions for increasing the efficiency of data transfer in modern computer network applications and computing network environments based on the TCP/IP protocol suite. In this work, an imitation model and simulation was used as the basic method in the research. A simulation model was developed for designing and analyzing the computer networks based on TCP/IP protocols suite which fully allows the exact features in realizing the protocols and their impact on increasing the efficiency of data transfer in local and corporate networks. The method of increasing efficiency in the performance of computer networks was offered, based on the TCP/IP protocols by perfection of the modes of data transfer in them. This allows an increased efficient usage of computer networks and network applications without additional expenditure on infrastructure of the network. Practically, the results obtained from this research enable significant increase in the performance efficiency of data transfer in the computer networks environment. An example is the "Donetsk National Technical University" network.

Chapter 7
Validating the INTERPRETOR Software Architecture for the Interpretation
of Large and Noisy Data Sets 135
Apkar Salatian, American University of Nigeria, Nigeria

In this chapter, the authors validate INTERPRETOR software architecture as a dataflow model of computation for filtering, abstracting, and interpreting large and noisy datasets with two detailed empirical studies from the authors' former research endeavours. Also discussed are five further recent and distinct systems that can be tailored or adapted to use the software architecture. The detailed case studies presented are from two disparate domains that include intensive care unit data and building sensor data. By performing pattern mining on five further systems in the way the authors have suggested herein, they argue that INTERPRETOR software architecture has been validated.

Chapter 8
Modeling Maintenance Productivity Measurement 149
Christian A. Bolu, Federal University Oye-Ekiti, Nigeria

Modeling and simulation of industrial information communication systems and networks is one of the major concerns of productivity engineers for the establishment of productivity standards in virtually all functional areas of an industrial organization. Maintenance function is one of such areas that have always engaged the attention of engineering productivity practitioners. However, one of the basic problems is the difficulty in setting up integrated but easy and practical measurement schemes. Even where the measures are set up, the approaches to measurement sometimes are conflicting. Therefore the need for an integrated approach to optimize the basket of parameters measured remains. In this chapter the author attempts to identify approaches in integrated and systematic maintenance productivity measurement and create models for optimising total productivity in maintenance systems. Visual yardstick, utility, queuing systems and simulations approaches for measurement of maintenance productivity are all discussed with a particular focus on markov chain approach for stochastic breakdowns in repairable systems.. The chapter also shows how understanding the impact of plant failure and repair/service distributions assists in providing measures for maintenance productivity using discrete event system simulation.

Section 2
Information Communication and Engineering

Chapter 9
Modeling of Packet Streaming Services in Information Communication Networks 166
Aderemi A. Atayero, Covenant University, Nigeria
Yury A. Ivanov, Elster Vital Connections, Russia

Application of the term video streaming in contemporary usage denotes compression techniques and data buffering, which can transmit video in real time over the network. There is currently a rapid growth and development of technologies using wireless broadband technology as a transport, which is a serious alternative to cellular communication systems. Adverse effect of the aggressive environment used in wireless networks transmission results in data packets undergoing serious distortions and often getting lost in transit. All existing research in this area investigate the known types of errors separately. At present there are no standard approaches to determining the effect of errors on transmission quality of services. Besides, the spate in popularity of multimedia applications has led to the need for optimization of bandwidth allocation and usage in telecommunication networks. Modern telecommunication networks should by their definition be able to maintain the quality of different applications with different Quality of Service (QoS) levels. QoS requirements are generally dependent on the parameters of network and application layers of the OSI model. At the application layer QoS depends on factors such as resolution, bit rate, frame rate, video type, audio codecs, and so on. At the network layer, distortions (such as delay, jitter, packet loss, etc.) are introduced.

Chapter 10
Mathematical Models of Video-Sequences of Digital Half-Tone Images 207
E.P. Petrov, Vyatka State University, Russia
I.S. Trubin, Vyatka State University, Russia
E.V. Medvedeva, Vyatka State University, Russia
S.M. Smolskiy, Moscow Power Engineering Institute, Russia

This chapter is devoted to Mathematical Models (MM) of Digital Half-Tone Images (DHTI) and their video-sequences presented as causal multi-dimensional Markov Processes (MP) on discrete meshes. The difficulties of MM development for DHTI video-sequences of Markov type are shown. These difficulties are related to the enormous volume of computational operations required for their realization. The method of MM-DHTI construction and their statistically correlated video-sequences on the basis of the causal multi-dimensional multi-value MM is described in detail. Realization of such operations is not computationally intensive; Markov models from the second to fourth order demonstrate this. The proposed method is especially effective when DHTI is represented by low-bit (4-8 bits) binary numbers.

Chapter 11
Performance Analysis of Multi-Antenna Relay Networks over Nakagami-m Fading Channel 242
E. Soleimani-Nasab, K. N. Toosi University of Technology, Iran
A. Kalantari, K. N. Toosi University of Technology, Iran
M. Ardebilipour, K. N. Toosi University of Technology, Iran

In this chapter, the authors present the performance of multi-antenna selective combining decode-and-forward (SC-DF) relay networks over independent and identically distributed (i.i.d) Nakagami-m fading channels. The outage probability, moment generation function, symbol error probability and average channel capacity are derived in closed-form using the Signal-to-Noise-Ratio (SNR) statistical characteristics. After that, the authors formulate the outage probability problem, optimize it with an approximated problem, and then solve it analytically. Finally, for comparison with analytical formulas, the authors perform some Monte-Carlo simulations.

Chapter 12
A Generic Method for the Reliable Calculation of Large-Scale Fading in an Obstacle-Dense Propagation Environment 256
Theofilos Chrysikos, University of Patras, Greece
Stavros Kotsopoulos, University of Patras, Greece
Eduard Babulak, EU CORDIS, Belgium

The aim of this chapter is to summarize and present recent findings in the field of wireless channel modeling that provide a new method for the reliable calculation of the statistical parameters of large-scale variations of the average received signal (shadow fading). This algorithm is theoretically based on a path loss estimation model that incorporates losses due to walls and floors. This has been confirmed to be the most precise mathematical tool for average signal strength prediction for various frequencies of interest and propagation environments. The total path loss is estimated as a sum of two independent attenuation processes: free space loss and losses due to obstacles. This solution allows for a direct and reliable calculation of the deviation of the fluctuations of the average received signal in an obstacle-dense environment.

Chapter 13
Development of Nonlinear Filtering Algorithms of Digital Half-Tone Images 278
E. P. Petrov, Vyatka State University, Russia
I. S. Trubin, Vyatka State University, Russia
E. V. Medvedeva, Vyatka State University, Russia
S. M. Smolskiy, Moscow Power Engineering Institute, Russia

This chapter is devoted to solving the problem of algorithms and structures investigations for Radio Receiver Devices (RRD) with the aim of the nonlinear filtering of Digital Half-Tone Images (DHTI) representing the discrete-time and discrete-value random Markovian process with a number of states greater than two. At that, it is assumed that each value of the DHTI element is represented by the binary g-bit number, whose bits are transmitted via digital communication links in the presence of Additive White Gaussian Noise (AWGN). The authors present the qualitative analysis of the optimal DHTI filtering algorithm. The noise immunity of the optimal radio receiver device for the DHTI filtering with varying quantization and dimension levels is investigated.

Chapter 14
Performance Analysis of Traffic and Mobility Models on Mobile and Vehicular
Ad Hoc Wireless Networks 305
Lawal Bello, University of Greenwich, UK
Panos Bakalis, University of Greenwich, UK

Advances in wireless communication technology and the proliferation of mobile devices enable the capabilities of communicating with each other even in areas with no pre-existing communication infrastructure. Traffic and mobility models play an important role in evaluating the performance of these communication networks. Despite criticism and assumption from various researches on Transmission Control Protocols (TCP), weaknesses on Mobile Ad Hoc Network (MANET), and Vehicular Ad Hoc Network (VANET). A simulation was carried out to evaluate the performance of Constant Bit Rate, Variable Bit Rate and Transmission Control Protocol on MANET and VANET using DSR routing protocol. CBR, VBR, and TCP have different manufacturer operation mechanisms and these differences lead to significant performance of CBR and VBR over TCP with better throughput and less average maximal end-to-end delay. DSR was able to respond to link failure at low mobility which led to TCP's performance in packets delivery.

Chapter 15
Modeling of Quantum Key Distribution System for Secure Information Transfer 314
K. E. Rumyantsev, Taganrog Institute of Technology, Russia
D. M. Golubchikov, Southern Federal University, Russia

This chapter is an analysis of commercial quantum key distribution systems. Upon analysis, the generalized structure of QKDS with phase coding of a photon state is presented. The structure includes modules that immediately participate in the task of distribution and processing of quantum states. Phases of key sequence productions are studied. Expressions that allow the estimation of physical characteristics of optoelectronic components, as well as information processing algorithms impact to rate of key sequence production, are formed. Information security infrastructure can be utilized, for instance, to formulate requirements to maximize tolerable error level in quantum channel with a given rate of key sequence production.

Chapter 16
ANFIS Modeling of Dynamic Load Balancing in LTE 343
Matthew K. Luka, Modibbo Adama University of Technology, Nigeria
Aderemi A. Atayero, Covenant University, Nigeria

Modelling of ill-defined or unpredictable systems can be very challenging. Most models have relied on conventional mathematical models which does not adequately track some of the multifaceted challenges of such a system. Load balancing, which is a self-optimization operation of Self-Organizing Networks (SON), aims at ensuring an equitable distribution of users in the network. This translates into better user satisfaction and a more efficient use of network resources. Several methods for load balancing have been proposed. While some of them have a very buoyant theoretical basis, they are not practical. Furthermore, most of the techniques proposed the use of an iterative algorithm, which in itself is not computationally efficient as it does not take the unpredictable fluctuation of network load into consideration. This chapter proposes the use of soft computing, precisely Adaptive Neuro-Fuzzy Inference System (ANFIS) model, for dynamic QoS aware load balancing in 3GPP LTE. The use of ANFIS offers learning capability of neural network and knowledge representation of fuzzy logic for a load balancing solution that is cost effective and closer to human intuition. Three key load parameters (number of satisfied user in the network, virtual load of the serving eNodeB, and the overall state of the target eNodeB) are used to adjust the hysteresis value for load balancing.

Chapter 17
Neural Network Control of a Laboratory Magnetic Levitator 361
J. Katende, Botswana International University of Science and Technology, Botswana
M. Mustapha, Bayero University, Nigeria

Magnetic levitation (maglev) systems are nowadays employed in applications ranging from non-contact bearings and vibration isolation of sensitive machinery to high-speed passenger trains. In this chapter a mathematical model of a laboratory maglev system was derived using the Lagrangian approach. A linear pole-placement controller was designed on the basis of specifications on peak overshoot and settling time. A 3-layer feed-forward Artificial Neural Network (ANN) controller comprising 3-input nodes, a 5-neuron hidden layer, and 1-neuron output layer was trained using the linear state feedback controller with a random reference signal. Simulations to investigate the robustness of the ANN control scheme with respect to parameter variations, reference step input magnitude variations, and sinusoidal input tracking were carried out using SIMULINK. The obtained simulation results show that the ANN controller is robust with respect to good positioning accuracy.

Chapter 18
Constitutive Modeling of Wind Energy Potential of Selected Sites in Nigeria:
A Pre-Assessment Model 375
O. O. Ajayi, Covenant University, Nigeria
R. O. Fagbenle, Obafemi Awolowo University, Nigeria
J. Katende, Botswana International University of Science and Technology, Botswana

In this chapter, the authors present the result of a study carried out to develop a pre-assessment model that can be used to carry out a preliminary study on the availability of wind energy resources of a site. 21 years' (1987 – 2007) monthly average wind speeds for 18 locations in Nigeria were used to create the simple constitutive model. The locations span across the six geopolitical zones of the nation with three stations from each zone. Various statistical procedures were employed in the development of the model. The outcome gave an empirical model, which if employed, will lead to determining the modest range of wind energy potential of a site. Further, the results from this model were compared with those from the well-established two-parameter Weibull statistical distribution function and found to be reasonably adequate. Thus with this model, decision on site selection for complete assessment can be made without much rigour.

Chapter 19
Cross-Layer Optimization in OFDM Wireless Communication Network 390
Babasanjo Oshin, Covenant University, Nigeria
Adeyemi Alatishe, Covenant University, Nigeria

The wide use of OFDM systems in multiuser environments to overcome problem of communication over the wireless channel has gained prominence in recent years. Cross-layer Optimization technique is aimed to further improve the efficiency of this network. This chapter demonstrates that significant improvements in data traffic parameters can be achieved by applying cross-layer optimization techniques to packet switched wireless networks. This work compares the system capacity, delay time and data throughput of QoS traffic in a multiuser OFDM system using two algorithms. The first algorithm, Maximum Weighted Capacity, uses a cross-layer design to share resources and schedule traffic to users on the network, while the other algorithm (Maximum Capacity) simply allocates resources based only on the users channel quality. The results of the research shows that the delay time and data throughput of the Maximum Weighted Capacity algorithm in cross layer OFDM system is much better than that of the Maximum Capacity in simply based users channel quality system. The cost incurred for this gain is the increased complexity of the Maximum Weighted Capacity scheme.

Compilation of References 411

About the Contributors 435

Index 444

Preface

The text is divided into two broad sections. Section 1 deals with Networks and Information processes, while Section 2 is dedicated to chapters on Information Communication and Engineering. The first section consists of chapters one (1) through eight (8), with chapter one serving as an introductory piece. The second section is made up of the remaining eleven chapters from chapter nine to nineteen. Most of the chapters in this second part are in the field of communications with two in the area of artificial intelligence.

In *Chapter One*, the principles of modeling are visited with a special bias to Information Communication Systems and Networks (ICSN). The basic rubrics of models, modeling, and simulation; an understanding of which is indispensible for the comprehension of subsequent chapters are expoused. Various fundamental terminologies, the knowledge of which is necessary for underntding the concepts of models, modeling, and simulation, are explained. The contributing authors also shed some light on model structures and the methodological basis of formalizing complex system structures is discussed. The chapter concludes with recommendations from the authors on how to avoid the most common errors usually made by researchers in the process of model design which is that of losing track of the original problem statement as well as by embarking on actual model design without having enough requisite information about the modeled system.

Chapter two reports on the numerical methods of multifractal analysis as it affects ICSN. In this very compelling chapter, the contributing authors present the theory of fractals and multifractals. A method based on multifractal data analysis at network layer level by means of *Wavelet Transform Modulus Maxima* (WTMM) is proposed for the detection of traffic anomalies in computer and telecommunication networks. Algorithm development methods for estimating multifractal spectrum are presented. The chapter also introduces WTMM as an informative indicator necessary to exploit the distinction of fractal dimensions on various parts of a given dataset. A novel approach based on the use of multifractal spectrum parameters is proposed for estimating queuing performance for the generalized multifractal traffic on the input of a buffering device, which shows that the multifractal character of traffic has significant impact on queuing performance characteristics.

The contributing authors in *Chapter three* present the results of an extensive doctoral research thesis on a deterministic approach for resolving the switched LAN's delay problem. In this interesting chapter, that actually challenges some basic assumptions met frequently in the literature, the authors assert the need for networks to be designed with specified maximum End-To-End delay since, if the maximum packet delay between any two nodes of a network is not known, it is impossible to provide a deterministic guarantee of worst case response times of packets' flows. They then go on to compare the two principal approaches for determining the end-to-end response times of flows in ICSN and submitted on the superiority of the deterministic rather than stochastic approach.

Chapter four presents yet another doctoral thesis research findings on the specific area of e-Learning. This rather educative research was conducted in Western Africa with the participation of a specialized school for the blind. The contributing authors contend that finding suitable content via a mobile phone has become a rigorous task for voice-based online learners to achieve better performance. They opine that this is more acute for sight-impaired learners because existing voice-enabled applications in the domain of e-Learning lack the attributes of adaptive and reusable learning objects. As a *panacea* for this obvious deficiency in eLearning infrastructure, the authors propose a *Voice-Enabled Framework for Recommender and Adaptation Systems in E-Learning* (*VeFRA*). In their submission, they present a usability study result based on ISO 9241-11 specification of 4.13 on a scale of 5, which translates to *Good Usability*. This they assert offers a ubiquitous e-Learning platform for the visually impared to learn, granted the availability of telephony, without the necessity of Internet services.

In *Chapter five,* the subject of *fractality* is revisited albeit from a slightly different angle. In this very informative chapter that cannot but appeal to a specialized set of researchers, the contributing authors present their research findings on *Signals with an Additive Fractal Structure for Information Transmission.* They propose a new class of wideband signals with an additive fractal structure. A detailed study of this novel class of wideband signals possessing a high level of irregularity and unpredictability at the level of simple technical implementation is presented. Exhaustive methods of modifying the signal spectrum with additive fractal structure for increased efficiency of the frequency resource application are given. The authors submit in their conclusion that complex wideband signals with an additive fractal structure can be employed in radioengineering applications such as speech transmission over channels with AWGN.

Chapter six presents a model developed for increasing the efficiency of data transmission in ICSNs based on the TCP/IP protocol suite. Complex simulation models were proposed and simulated for analysis and multilevel modeling processes of data transfer in computer networks based on the protocols of TCP/IP, which fully and accurately allow for determining co-existing exchange factors such as formation of dataflow, network topology, network protocols function, and internet support, which influence efficiency of data transfer. The contributing authors lay claim to an increase in network efficiency of between 10% and 15% when their developed model is deployed.

In *Chapter seven*, the contributing authors present the validation of a software architecture they call the *INTERPRETOR* as a dataflow model of computation for filtering, abstracting, and interpreting large and noisy datasets. They submit in their conclusion to the chapter on the non-triviality of the interpretation of large and noisy data. They contend that their developed architecture can be tailored and applied to different domains, which have the same issues associated with the interpretation of data. For future work, they suggest the development of a generic and reusable tool for proposed architecture.

In *Chapter eight*, the problem of modeling maintenance productivity measurement is addressed. This has been identified as a major area of concern for productivity engineers, based on the need for the establishment of productivity standards in virtually all functional areas of an industrial organization. This chapter identifies the approaches in integrated and systematic maintenance productivity measurement and creates models for optimizing total productivity in maintenance systems. It likewise discusses visual yardstick, utility, queuing systems, and simulations approaches for measurement of maintenance productivity and highlights Markov chain approach for stochastic breakdowns in repairable systems. This chapter effectively concludes the first part of this text.

The second part of this text commences with *Chapter nine*. It essentially addresses issues concerned with the modeling of packet streaming services in ICSN. The chapter presents the result of researches into this very interesting and contemporary domain of study. The chapter gives a detailed discussion on the fundamental concepts of video streaming over wireless broadband access networks (BWAN). The contributing authors assert that all existing research in this area investigate the known types of errors separately. The lack of standard approaches to determining the effect of errors on transmission quality of services is mentioned. This very informative chapter promises to serve as a veritable reference material for those carrying out research in the area of quality estimation of video traffic over BWAN.

In *Chapter ten*, an investigation into the problem of mathematical modeling of video-sequences of digital half-tone images (DHTI) is visited. The fact that the computational rigor necessary for development of DHTI video-sequences of Markov type contributes in no small measure to the difficulty of their realization is particularly highlighted. It is postulated that the realization of a method of Markov Model DHTI construction and their statistically correlated video-sequences on the basis of the causal multi-dimensional multi-value MM is not computationally intensive. The authors submit that their proposed method is particularly effective when DHTI is represented by low-bit (4–8 bits) binary numbers. They conclude among others that the approach for MM construction of several statistically correlated DHTI video-sequences can be reduced to a formalized procedure of sequential elimination of the statistical redundancy between vicinity elements of the simulating image element belonging to the independent coordinates and all others. The results presented in this chapter are quite cutting-edge and should appeal to a specialized set of researchers in the domain of DHTI modeling.

Chapter eleven presents quite a fascinating contribution on the subject of Performance Analysis of Multi-Antenna Relay Networks over Nakagami-m Fading Channel. The performance of multi-antenna selective combining decode-and-forward (SC-DF) relay networks over independent and identically distributed (i.i.d) Nakagami-m fading channels is presented. The authors formulate the outage probability problem, optimize it with an approximated problem, and subsequently provide an analytic solution. They submit in their conclusion that the complexity of double antenna case versus single antenna case is not high and instead of increasing the number of relays, increasing the number of antennas is a practically better option.

A generic method for the reliable calculation of large-scale fading in obstacle-dense propagation environments is presented in *Chapter twelve*. The authors' aim in this chapter is to make an attempt at summarizing recent findings in the field of wireless channel modeling that provide a new method for reliable estimation of the statistical parameters of large-scale variations of the average received signal (shadow fading). They present an algorithmic solution that is theoretically based on pathloss estimation model and allows for a direct and reliable calculation of the deviation of the fluctuations of the average received signal in an obstacle-dense environment.

Chapter thirteen extends the concept of DHTI introduced in chapter ten by presenting the results of works in the *development of nonlinear filtering algorithms of digital half-tone images*. In this chapter, the authors are more concerned with solving the problem of algorithms and structures investigations for radio receiver devices with the aim of nonlinear filtering DHTI representing the time-discrete and value-discrete random Markovian process with more than two states. The contributing authors submit in their conclusion that qualitative and quantitative analysis of developed algorithms for nonlinear filtering of static and dynamic DHTI show that filtering effectiveness increases with reduction in the SNR and with increase in the dimension of filtering process.

The contributing authors of *Chapter fourteen* present the results of performance analysis of traffic and mobility models on Mobile (MANET) and Vehicular Ad Hoc Wireless Networks (VANET). They established the importance of traffic and mobility models in evaluating the performance of communication networks, despite criticism and assumption from various works reported in the literature on transmission control protocol's weaknesses vis-à-vis MANET and VANET. The contributing authors submit based on simulation results that CBR and VBR performed better than TCP at both low and high mobility with high throughput of receiving bits, less end-to-end delay, and less packets dropped. In their informed opinion, most dropped packets were due to high end-to-end delay, time-to-live expiration of the routing protocol, and end of simulation time.

In *Chapter fifteen*, the rather specialized topic of quantum cryptography (QC) is presented. This cutting-edge approach to information security proposes a new method of generation random private key for quantum communication line users. The authors present Quantum Key Distribution (QKD)–a technology based upon quantum principles for generation random bit string used as privacy key between two remote users. They present salient concepts of quantum physics as they are employed vis-a-vis QC (e.g. the *Heisenberg uncertainty principle)* according to which measurement of a quantum system state changes its initial state. They maintain that the main advantage of QC is that legal users will know about eavesdropping activities. A generalized structure of the QKD systems with phase coding of photon states is proposed based on analysis of what is commercially available.

Chapter sixteen presents research results on load balancing in 3GPP LTE systems. The chapter reveals the research efforts of the contributing authors in resolving load-balancing issues of next generation mobile networks (NGN) through the instrumentation of soft computing. They contend that most available models have relied heavily on conventional mathematical models which does not adequately track some of the multifaceted challenges of NGNs. They thus propose in this chapter the use of soft computing, precisely the ANFIS model for dynamic QoS-aware load balancing in 3GPP LTE. They state that the adoption of ANFIS offers learning capability of neural network and knowledge representation of fuzzy logic for a load balancing solution that is cost effective and closer to human intuition. Results obtained from model validation using testing and checking datasets show that the ANFIS model is a robust tool for a dynamic load balancing scheme in 3GPP LTE.

In *Chapter seventeen*, the use of artificial intelligence (AI) for the resolution control problems is presented. Specifically, the contributing authors present the use of artificial neural network (ANN) for the control of a laboratory MAGnetic LEVitator (MAGLEV) system. They present a mathematical model for MAGLEV using the Lagrangian approach. They submit in the conclusion to the chapter that in terms of positioning accuracy, the ANN is very hearty but the dynamic accuracy was found to be inadequate.

In the penultimate *Chapter eighteen*, the contributing authors present a pre-assessment model of constitutive modelling of wind energy potential of selected sites in Nigeria. The chapter presents the result of a study on the availability of wind energy resources of a site using 21 years' (1987 - 2007) monthly average wind speeds for 18 locations in Nigeria to create a constitutive model. The resulting empirical model can be employed for determining the range of wind energy potential of a site and making a less rigorous decision on site selection for complete assessment.

In this concluding chapter of the text, *Chapter nineteen,* the contributing authors present a comparative framework of two algorithms for resource allocation in a wireless system with multiple users vying for wireless network resources. A means of improving system resource sharing indices using cross-layer optimization techniques is proposed. The results show that while the MC has a higher system capacity, the MWC reliably transmits realtime and non-realtime traffic within the requirements for this traffic class. The authors submit that the resource allocation scheme and scheduling done using cross-layer optimization in MWC has reduced the delay time for realtime and non-realtime traffic and done the same at least partially for best-effort traffic.

Aderemi A. Atayero
Covenant University, Nigeria

Oleg I. Sheluhin
Moscow Technical University of Communication and Informatics, Russia

Section 1
Networks and Information Processes

Chapter 1
Principles of Modeling in Information Communication Systems and Networks

Oleg I. Sheluhin
Moscow Technical University of Communication and Informatics, Russia

Aderemi A. Atayero
Covenant University, Nigeria

ABSTRACT

The authors present in this entry chapter the basic rubrics of models, modeling, and simulation, an understanding of which is indispensible for the comprehension of subsequent chapters of this text on the all-important topic of modeling and simulation in Information Communication Systems and Networks (ICSN). A good example is the case of analyzing simulation results of traffic models as a tool for investigating network behavioral pattarns as it affects the transmitted content (Atayero, et al., 2013). The various classifications of models are discussed, for example classification based on the degree of semblance to the original object (i.e. isomorphism). Various fundamental terminologies without the knowledge of which the concepts and models and modeling cannot be properly understood are explained. Model stuctures are highlighted and discussed. The methodological basis of formalizing complex system structures is presented. The concept of componential approach to modeling is presented and the necessary stages of mathematical model formation are examined and explained. The chapter concludes with a presentation of the concept of simulation vis-à-vis information communication systems and networks.

FUNDAMENTALS OF MODELS AND MODELING

A model is essentially the *re*presentation of an object, system or concept in a form different from that in which it occurs naturally. A model may likewise be defined as a tool, which helps in the explanation, understanding or perfection of a system. Modeling can be described as the process of substituting a test object (the original) for its image, description, or substitute object known as a model and providing a behavior close to that of the original within certain reasonable limits of assumptions and uncertainties. Simulation is

DOI: 10.4018/978-1-4666-2208-1.ch001

usually performed in order to gain knowledge of the properties of the original object by studying its model, rather than the object itself.

The use of models is justified in cases when they are simpler in comparison with the option of creating the original object, or when the original object is better left uncreated for whatever reason. In the words of D.K. Nordstrom (2012), "Models are one of the principal tools of modern science and engineering…" Scientists and engineers devote a lot of time to design, build, test, compare, and revise models (Frigg and Hartmann, 2009).

A model may be the exact replica of an object (*albeit* on a different scale and from a different material) or depict certain characteristic properties of the object in an abstract form; i.e. a representation of a real system or process (Konikow and Bredehoeft, 1992). A model is thus essentially an instrument for forecasting the effect of input signals on a given object, while *modeling* is a method of improving the reasoning efficiency and intuitive capacity of specialists.

All models are but simplified *re*presentations or abstractions of the real world. An *abstraction* contains within itself the major behavioral traits of an object, but not necessarily in the same form or as detailed as in the object. Usually a large portion of the real characteristics of the object of study is disregarded, while such peculiarities that idealize a real event version are chosen. As a result, most models are abstract in nature.

The degree of semblance of a model to its object is called *isomorphism.* Two conditions must necessarily be satisfied for a model to be considered *isomorphic* (or similar in form) to the original object:

1. Existence of exclusive correspondence between elements of the model and the modeled object;
2. Maintaining the exact relationships or interactions between these elements.

From the foregone, we see that a model is essentially a physical or abstract object, with properties similar to those of the original object under study in certain defined ways. The specification of models depends on the particular problem of study as well as the available resources. The general requirements for models are as listed below:

1. **Adequacy:** This refers to the level of accuracy in replicating the properties of the original object.
2. **Completeness:** The ability of the model to deliver to the receiver all necessary information about the original object.
3. **Flexibility:** The ability to playout different situations in the whole range of conditions and parameters.
4. The *complexity* of developing the model must agree with the existing time and software constraints.

According to Tedeschi (2006), the design of the tests for adequacy for a particular model should of necessity evaluate weaknesses to be addressed. He further contends that a combination of several statistical analyses vis-à-vis the original conceptual purpose of the model is essential for determining its adequacy.

Since modeling s the process of creating a replica of an object and the subsequent study of the object's properties through the created replica (a.k.a. model), entails two major stages:

1. Model design;
2. Model evaluation/validation and conclusion derivations.

Model validation is concerned with ascertaining that a model performance in satisfactorily accurate vis-a-vis model design objectives; it is all about building the model right (Balci, 1997). It is pertinent to note here that a uniform procedure for validation does not exist, and as such no model has ever been (or will ever be) fully validated (Greenberg et al., 1976).

At each level of modeling, different tasks are resolved using means and methods that differ in context. In practice, different modeling methods are adopted. Depending on the method of their realization, all models belong to one of two classes: *physical* or *mathematical*.

Mathematical modeling is generally considered as a means of investigating processes and events via their mathematical models.

A good majority of models are *homomorphic* i.e. similar in form though with different basal structures. In this case, the semblance between different groups of elements and the object is only superficial. Homomorphism in models is a result of simplification and abstraction. In the design of homomorphic models, the system is first subdivided into smaller parts to allow for ease of required analysis. To this end, it is necessary to identify parts that are independent of each other in first approximation.

This type of analysis is linked to *real system simplification process* (i.e. discarding unimportant components or adopting assumptions of simpler relationships). For example, it may be assumed that there is a linear relationship between a certain set of variables. In control, it is common practice to assume that processes are either deterministic or their behavior can be described using known probability distribution functions.

Sequel to the analysis of the parts of a system their synthesis is embarked upon, this must be done accurately taking into consideration all available interconnections.

As the basis of a successful modeling methodology must be a thorough test of the model. It is common practice to start with a simple model and move towards a more perfect form, that depicts difficult situations more accurately. There is direct interaction between model modification and the data analysis process.

The Modeling Process consists of the following steps:

1. Decomposition of overall system investigation task into a series of easier tasks;
2. Concise formulation of aims;
3. Search for analogy;
4. Consideration of special numerical examples related to current task;
5. Choice of specific symbolism;
6. Documentation of obvious relationships;
7. Expansion of derived model if it can be described mathematically, conversely it is further simplified.

Hence, the development of a model is not limited to a single basic version. New tasks constantly emerge with the aim of improving the degree of *isomorphism*.

MODEL CLASSIFICATIONS

There is a myriad of ways for classifying models. In this section, typical model groups that can serve as basis for classification are mentioned. In the context of information systems, *physical* and *information* environments can be distiguished. Each of these environments can in turn either be described by *physical* or *theoretical* models.

Physical models are often called *natural* since in appearance they remind one of the system under study. They can be either a scaled-down (e.g. model of the solar system) or scaled-up (e.g. model of the atom) version of the system i.e. they are *scalable models*. Hereafter, only theoretical models of information systems will be considered.

Theoretical models can be subdivided into *mathematical* and *graphical models*.

Mathematical Models (MM): This is a compendium of mathematical objects and the relationships between them, which adequately depict certain properties of the object. In this category are models that employ symbols for the description of processes (e.g. differential equations *et cetera*), as opposed to physical properties. Hence, a mathematical model is the simplification of a real situation and can be considered as the abstract, formal description of an object that can be studied mathematically.

Graphical Models (GM): These show the relationship between different quantitative characteristics and are capable of forecasting the change in a set of quantities as a result of changes in others. Depending on the character of the selected properties of an object, *MM* is subdivided into *functional* and *structural* models.

Functional models depict processes concerned with the functioning of the object. They are usually in the form of a system of equations.

Structural models can take the form of matrices, graphs, lists of vectors, *et cetera* and express the spatial orientation of objects. These models are usually employed in cases when structural synthesis tasks can be defined and resolved by abstracting physical processes contained in the object. They reflect the structural properties of studied object.

So-called *schematic models* can be used for obtaining static representation of the modeled system, i.e. models containing graphical representation of the system *modus operandi* (e.g. technological maps, diagrams, multifunctional operational diagrams and schematic diagrams).

Considering the method of obtaining functional *MM*, they are subdivided into *theoretical* and *formal* models. *Theoretical MM* are obtained by studying physical laws. Equation structure and model parameters have a definitive physical interpretation. *Formal MM* are obtained on the basis of the effect of the property of the modeled object on the external medium, i.e. the object is considered a cybernetic 'black box'.

The theoretical approach allows for obtaining more universal models representative of a wider range of change of eternal parameters, while the formal *MM* are more accurate relative to the parameters used for measurement.

Depending on the linearity or otherwise of equations, *MM* are classified as *linear* and *nonlinear.*

In the context of set of values of variables, *MM* can either be *continuous* or *discrete.*

MM can be either *stochastic* or *deterministic* when the criterion for classification is method of description.

Using the form of connection between output, internal and external parameters as classification criterion, *MM* can be *algorithmic* (as a system of equations); *analytic* (in the form of dependence of output parameters on internal and external parameters); and *numerical* (in the form of numerical sequences).

Using the consideration of presence of inertia of physical processes in the model as classification criterion, there are *dynamic MM* and *static MM.*

In general, the type of mathematical model depends not only on the nature of the real object, but also on those tasks, for the resolving of which it is being developed as well as the required accuracy of their resolution.

MODEL STRUCTURES

Knowledge of the structural elements making up a model is necessary before its design is embarked upon. Though mathematical and physical models can be very complex, as a rule the basis of their makeup is always simple.

The general model's structure may be presented in the form of a mathematical formula

$$E = f\left(X_i, Y_i\right) \quad (1)$$

where E – result of systemic action*;* X_i – controllable variables and parameters*;* Y_i – uncontrollable variables and parameters*; fn* of dependence of X_i on Y_i that determines the magnitude of E.

In the case of dynamic systems (Figure 1) an established way of representing their models exists. A complex system functions in a given external medium, the properties and states of which are characterized at every moment in time by a set of parameters forming a vector z (*disturbance*).

The systemic state and properties at every moment *k* is characterized by a group of internal parameters that are subdivided into *state vector* x and *control vector* u.

Dynamic model as a rule contains the following:

1. Description of all possible system states;
2. Description of the system state transition law;

$$x_{k+1} = F\left(x_k, u, z_k\right) \quad (2)$$

where F – vector function.

The set of all possible states of a system is otherwise known as the *state space* of the system. The *state space* can be either continuous or discrete.

The system state transition law is also known as *transition function* or *transitions operator*.

In the general case, a model is a combination of the following:

- Components
- Parameters
- Functional dependences limitations
- Objective functions

Components are parts that under right connections form a system. Components are sometimes regarded as *elements* or *subsystems* of a system.

A *system* is defined as a group of objects joined by a certain form of regular external action or interaction for the purpose of executing a given task.

Parameters are quantities that may be selected arbitrarily unlike *variables,* that can only take values predetermined by the given function type. Once defined, parameters become constants.

In a model, there are *exogenic* (input) variables emanating from outside the system or resulting from external actions on the system as well as *endogenic* variables occurring in the system either as a result of internal interactions (state variables), or under the influence of output variables.

Functional dependences describe the behavior of variables and parameters. They express the following relationships between system components: *deterministic* – this is a definition that sets the relationship between given systemic parameters and variables in cases when the system output process is definitely known; *stochastic* relationships when given input information results in undefined results.

Limitations are a set range of change of value for variables or conditions limiting the spread of certain resources. They can be introduced by either the system designer (artificial limitations), or by the system itself as a result of its inherent properties (natural limitations).

Figure 1. Dynamic model of a system in "input – output" terms

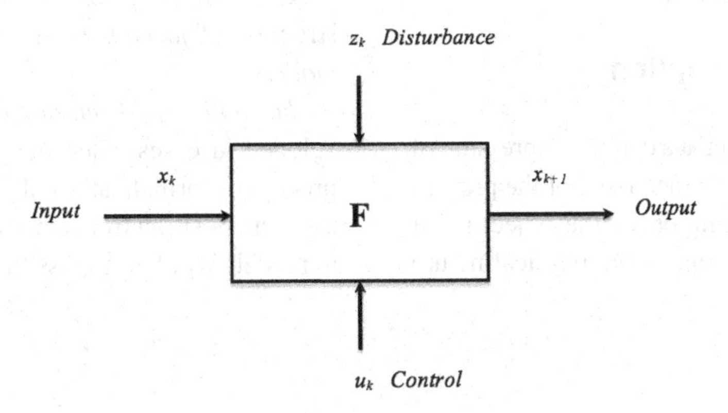

Objective function (criterion function) is an outline of systemic aims and objectives and the necessary rules for measuring their achievement. Aims can be divided into *preservation aims* directed towards the preservation or sustenance of certain resources (energy) or states (safety), and *acquisition aims* connected with the acquisition of new resources or attainment of a defined state, to which the leader aspires.

The most general requirements on a model can be formulated as follows: a model must be *simple* and *understandable* to the user; *aims-oriented*, *reliable* i.e. guaranteed against production of absurd outputs; *user friendly; complete* from the view point of meeting main objective; *adaptive*, allowing for easy transition to other modifications or data reset; *allowing for incremental change*, i.e. starting out as simple, the model should have inherent capacity to become incrementally complex as a result of user interaction.

METHODOLOGICAL BASIS OF FORMALIZING COMPLEX SYSTEMS STRUCTURES

Any model of a real system is an abstract formally described object. A model describing the formalized process of a system's operation is able to encompass only its main characteristic *operational laws*, neglecting unimportant secondary factors.

The formalization of any real process precedes a study of the structures making up its occurrence, as a result of which a componential description of the process is obtained.

Component Description

This is the first attempt at a concise expression of the operational laws characteristic of the process under study and definition of the objective. It provides information on: 1) the physical nature and quantitative characteristics of elementary occurrences of the process, 2) the character of interconnections among them, 3) the position of each occurrence in the process as a whole. Component description can be written only after a detailed study of the process.

In addition to the description of the process proper the aims of modeling the process under study are also included in the componential description, which should contain a list of input quantities and their required accuracy respectively. This part of the formalization process can be executed without the input of mathematicians or corresponding specialist in modeling.

In this case, while creating the static representation of a system the following indicators of the existence of subsystems are analyzed:

1. Which components are to be included in the model,
2. Which elements will be excluded or considered part of the surrounding environment,
3. Which structural interconnections will be setup between them.

The definition of objectives should contain an exact description of the main idea of the proposed study, list of interrelations to be evaluated from the result of modeling, and stipulate those factors that must be considered in the design of the model. Data necessary for research are also included here: numerical values of known characteristics and parameters of the process (as tables, graphs), as well as values for initial conditions.

Componential description enables the construction of *formalized schematics* and *process models*.

Formalized schematics of a process is developed in cases when due to difficulty of the process or formalization of some of its elements a direct transition from componential description to models is either impossible or unjustified. Development of formalized schematics is carried out in conjunction with specialists in the applied area of technology and modeling (or mathematicians). Though the form of description may remain textual, it must be a formal description of the process.

In order to develop formalized schematics it is imperative to select process characteristics; setup a system of parameters defining the process; define all interrelations between characteristics and parameters, while taking into consideration factors considered during formalization. In addition, a concise mathematical formulation of the research objective must be stated.

In the process of developing a model it is necessary:

1. To identify factors influencing the flow or the results of the process under study,
2. To select those that are susceptible to formalized representation (i.e. those that can be expressed quantitatively),
3. To group identified factors by common indicators, thus reducing their list,
4. To define quantitative relationships among them.

Usually, the most difficult stage of the modeling process is the translation of identified germane factors to mathematical language and the defining the relationships between these quantities. The crux of the matter lies in the contradiction inherent in the requirement for a componential and deductive model. In order to satisfy the componential requirement it becomes necessary to consider in the model as many real process factors as possible. The model naturally becomes more complex, leading to difficulty of its study and consequently obtaining componential results. However, the desire to obtain results through simpler methods invariably leads to a need for model simplification, hence reducing its componential nature. Reaching a sensible compromise is important; such that will guarantee neutral results and at the same time maintain the substance of the real process. To this end, an accurate set of all input data, known parameters and starting conditions is employed.

Componential description may not give all the necessary information for the development of formalized schematics, in which case additional experiments and observations of the process under study become necessary. In this case however, obtained results must be used completely in the development of formalized schematics.

Subsequent transformation of formalized schematics into a model is carried out without the input of any additional information.

In mathematical modeling, for the transformation of formalized schematics to mathematical model it is necessary to present in analytical form all relationships yet to be presented, express conditions as a system of inequalities, as well as give analytical form to other contents of the formalized schematics (e.g. numerical characteristics in the form of tables and graphs).

Numerical material is usually used in the form of approximating expression in Personal Computers (PC). Probability Flux Density (*pfd*) of typical probability distribution laws is selected as values for random quantities.

COMPONENT MODELING

Consider a simple system consisting of three basic objects (Figure 2): *input;* the *system;* and the *response (output)*. In order to model the system, two of these three objects must be known (given).

In the process of modeling individual components (elements, subsystems) of a complex system, different kinds of tasks are encountered. These can be divided into direct and reverse tasks.

Direct task: with the control describing a system as given, the response on an input signal can be determined. This task can be easily modeled.

Figure 2. Model of a system

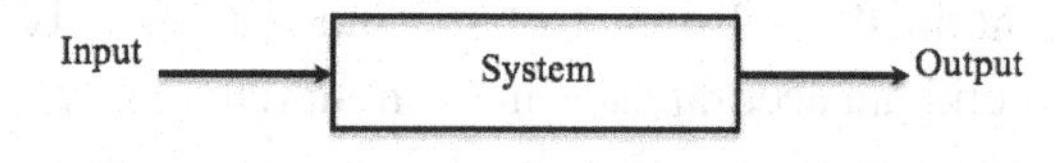

Control may be removed in the process of system development or on the basis of investigating similar systems.

Reverse task: This entails the use of system response and mathematical description of the system to determine the input signal. This belongs in the class of control tasks.

A more difficult task is one obtained if the input and output signals of a system are given and it is required to determine the mathematical description of the system. This is an *identification* or *system structural synthesis* task. The difficulty entails in the fact that one and the same state between the inputs and outputs of a system can be described by different mathematical expressions.

In the general case of component designation for converting input to output signals, there are three types of components (Figure 3):

1. **Conversion:** One or more input signals are converted into one or more output signals,
2. **Sorting:** One or more input signals are *distributed* (*sorted*) over two or more output signals,
3. **Feedback:** Input signals changes with a corresponding change in the output signal.

The difficulty level of system component structure is a function of the knowledge of the system *a priori*. If the nature of the process under investigation is known either partially or wholly, then the identification task is presented as <*black box*>. In this case, the system is described by means of linear or nonlinear equations with transfer characteristics. In certain cases it is possible to know a lot about the nature of a process and not know the values of only a few parameters, such an identification task is known as <*gray box*>.

The basic methods of developing mathematical models are: *axiomatic method, element equating method,* and *identification method.*

Axiomatic Method

This entails the *ab initio* postulation (formulation) of certain submissions relative to the real process expressed in the form of a set of mathematical expressions – *axioms*. Subsequently, definitive conclusions are made based on the axioms. The advantage of this method is that it allows for non-contradictory deductions in relation to the existing properties of the object within the limits of the adopted axioms. A major disadvantage of this method is the fact that the axioms are not tested in the course of the experiment.

Element Equating Method

A method used when it is required to develop the mathematical model of an object based on the properties of its components or when given a group of elements and it is required to develop a complex object and determine its properties. As a rule, complex objects are disintegrated into subsystems and elements so as to be able to re-

Figure 3. Types of system components: a) conversion, b) sorting, and c) feedback

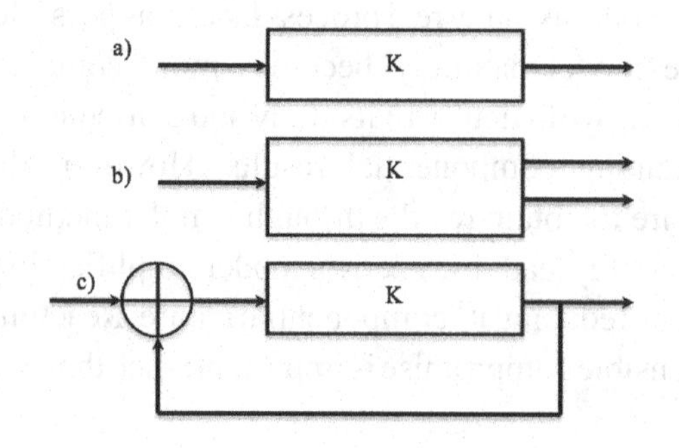

alize the formalization of each element and the relationship between them.

Depending on the character of system elements (deterministic, stochastic, continuous-time, discrete-time, etc.) typical mathematical schemes: differential equations, probabilistic automata, network switches, graphic models etc. employed for the description of elements.

Deterministic objects functioning in continuous time are usually described by differential equations.

Markov random processes or large-scale service systems are used to describe mathematical models of stochastic objects with continuous time. This method gives a false impression that all is taken into consideration. In reality however, the modeled object displays series of properties, which do not obtain from the set of properties of its elements.

Identification Method

Under this method, data collated by observing an object's input and output signals over limited time interval is used to create a mathematical model that optimally describes the studied object relative to given criteria.

If no conditions on the structure of the model are given *a priori*, then the task is one of *identification in the broad sense of the word.* A general method of solving this task does not exist at time of this writing. Under *identification in the narrow sense of the word*, an *a priori* form of the structure of certain mathematical model is added. In this case only the parameters of the adopted mathematical model need be defined.

STAGES OF MATHEMATICAL MODEL FORMATION

A generalized block diagram of the stages of forming a mathematical model is as shown in Figure 4.

Stage 1

Definition of model's objective function. Since a singular meaning for the term *"system model"* does not exist, it may be modeled in any way depending on the desired outcome. For this reason the elements of a model and their interactions should be selected based on the specifications of the task a system is required to perform. Using the example of a house, a builder sees it as the object of difficult tasks, while a sociologist sees it as just an element of the environment. Stage 1 delivers the most appropriate mathematical model, for example, with the use of block diagrams, employing system of equations and other mathematical methods.

Stage 2

At this stage, the block diagram of the discrete process is developed as well as *linking a system of equations to the discrete form.* This stage ends with the mathematical description and block diagram of all discrete systems.

Stage 3

At this stage it is imperative to *abide strictly by the time relationships* in the mathematical model being synthesized.

Figure 4. Block diagram of formation of a mathematical model

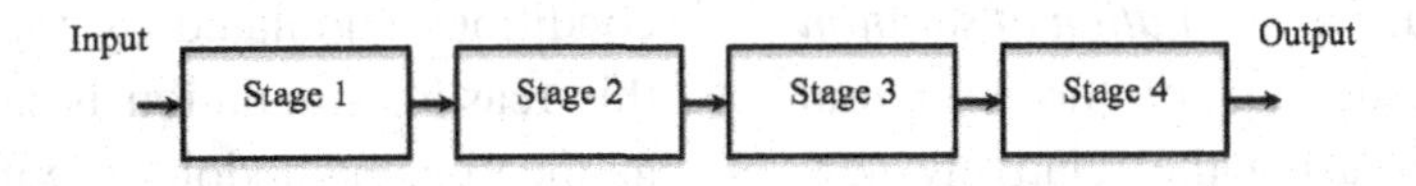

Stage 4

This stage is for experimenting, testing, and correcting of the model under synthesis.

After a model has been developed, it is necessary to test its adequacy for the task it was created to perform. There exists a number of aspects of *adequacy evaluation*: the mathematical basis of the model must be non-contradictory and satisfy all laws of mathematical logic; the verity of a model is determined by its ability to adequately describe the starting situation.

Depending on the complexity of the mathematical description of a system, the following basic *ways of mathematical model usage* are identified: analytic research; qualitative research; research using numerical methods; simulation on digital computers (the opposite of analogue modeling).

Analytic Research

Presupposes the availability of a sufficiently complete and accurate analytical description of a whole system. As a rule, a mathematical model in its initial form is unsuitable for direct research (for example, it may not present required quantities in obvious enough form). In this case, it is necessary to transform the initial model *vis-à-vis* the input quantities in a manner that makes it possible to obtain results by analytic methods. This gives the possibility of obtaining sufficiently complete information on the functionality of the research objects. Suffice it to note here that practical application of this type of research is relatively rare.

Qualitative Research

This is embarked upon in cases when an obvious solution is absent, but certain *properties of the solution* can be found, e.g. *evaluation of solution robustness* etc. Investigation of the structural robustness of models using the relatively new methods of the mathematical theory of catastrophe falls under this category.

Numerical Methods-Based Research

This is employed sequel to the transformation of the model into a system of equations relative to input quantities. A solution is obtained by realizing a corresponding numerical method. However, problem solution is usually less complete in this case compared to the analytical scenario, since it doesn't show the structure and character of system functionality as a whole, but merely allows for the evaluation of its state at selected numerical values of the parameters.

The use of numerical methods has become very effective with the use of contemporary PC processing power. The use of PC however, is not the principal factor since all it does is limited to computational automation.

Expert opinion and *intuition* play a decisive role in the process of model formation (in the case of simulation). Expert opinion is engaged in choosing the most productive approach in resolving which elements to include in a model while it is under development.

SIMULATION

Shannon (1998) defines simulation as "the process of designing a model of a real system and conducting experiments with this model for the purpose of understanding the behavior of the system and/or evaluating various strategies for the operation of the system."

This is not limited to machine models alone. Results can also be obtained via paper, pen and desktop calculator. Imitation models are incapable of providing solutions in the form they are produced by analytical models. They only serve as a means of analyzing system behavior under conditions stipulated by the experimenter. For this reason, simulation is an experimental and application methodology, with an aim to describing the behavior of a system; develop theories and hypotheses, capable of explaining observed systemic behavior; engage the theories in the prognosis of future systemic behavior.

Simulation is one of the few methods at the disposal of a researcher for solving problems. Since the choice of method must be tailored towards the solution of a problem, the question of when it is useful to employ simulation arises. Simulation can be employed if one of the following conditions is present:

1. A complete mathematical description of the problem does not exist (e.g. models of large-scale service system with queue consideration).
2. Complex and difficult analytical methods exist, but simulation gives a simpler solution.
3. Analytical solution exists, but they cannot be realized due to the low expertise level of available personnel. In this case, the cost implication of working with an imitation model is weighed against that of inviting a specialist.
4. In addition to evaluating certain parameters, there is the need to observe the process flow within a given period.
5. Simulation maybe the only possible option as a result of the difficulty of experimental setup and observing the process under real conditions (e.g. observing the behavior of space ships).
6. It may be necessary to record time scale (both slowing down and accelerating).

Advantages of simulation are: possibility of use in education and professional training; possibility of playing out scenarios of real processes in situations that help the researcher understand as well as have a feel of the problem leading to innovative ideas.

As a result, simulation is widely used, accounting for about 30% of all employed methods. This is irrespective of the fact that people with high level of mathematical training consider the imitation approach rough or the last means to be considered.

Imitation computation has a host of difficulties that boil down to the following:

- Development of a good imitation model is often expensive and time consuming, requiring the input of highly qualified specialists;
- Simulation is not accurate and its level of accuracy is not easily measurable. This can be resolved in part by analyzing the model's sensitivity to changes in certain parameters;
- Simulation in reality does not depict the real situation of things and this must be noted;
- The result of simulation is usually numerical, and its accuracy is a function of the number decimal places.

If it is possible to reduce a task (problem) to a simple model and solved analytically, then there should be no need for imitation since it is a last resort option. Besides, with each increase in available information on the problem at hand, the choice of employing imitation should be reassessed.

Imitation requires the use of powerful computers and a large set of data, which accounts for the high cost of this type of modeling in comparison with analytic models. The imitation process is as shown in Figure 5.

Since imitation is used for investigating real systems, the following stages of this process may be identified:

1. **System definition:** Boundary definition, limitations and evaluators of efficiency of system under investigation;
2. **Model formation:** Transition from real system to logical schematics (abstraction);
3. **Preparation of data:** Selection of data necessary for development of model, and their representation in the appropriate form;
4. **Model translation:** Description of model in a language acceptable for computer usage;

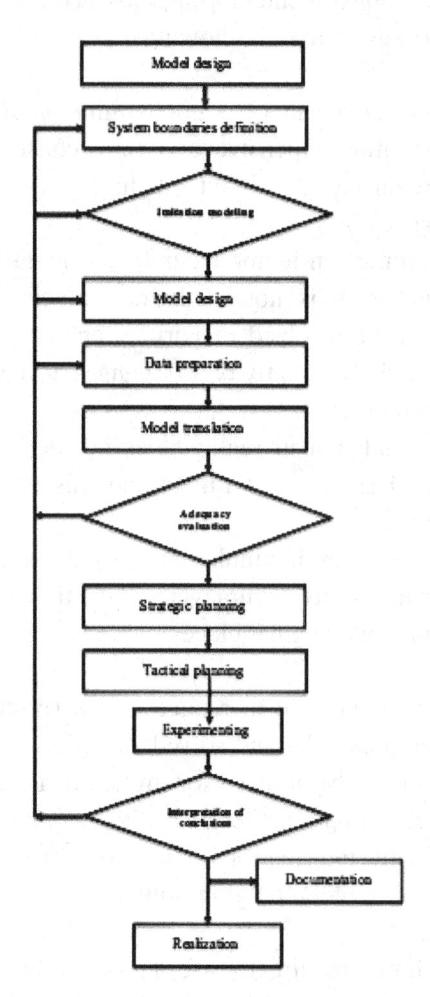

Figure 5. Flowchart of imitation modeling

5. **Evaluation of adequacy:** Raising certainty to acceptable level, at which a judgment may be made about the accuracy of conclusions about the real system;
6. **Strategic planning:** Planning of the experiment that should generate necessary information;
7. **Tactical planning:** Definition of method of executing each series of experiments, as contained in the experiment plan;
8. **Experimenting:** Process of executing imitation with a view to obtaining desired results (data);
9. **Interpretation:** Deduction of conclusions based on data generated from imitation;
10. **Realization:** Practical use of model and modeling results;
11. **Documentation:** Registration of project execution steps and its results, as well as recording of process development and usage.

For qualitative evaluation of a complex system, it is desirable to employ random process theory results. Experience of monitoring objects shows that they operate under the influence of a large quantity of random factors; this is why predicting the behavior of a complex system makes sense only within the limits of the probabilistic category.

In the study of the process of operation of each complex system considering random factors, it is necessary to have an exact understanding of the sources of the random interactions as well as reliable data on their quantitative characteristics. This is the reason for experimental collation of statistical material characterizing the behavior of independent elements as well as the system as a whole in real conditions, at the onset of any calculation or theoretical analysis in connection with investigating complex systems.

The main sources of random interaction are external factors and deviations from normal operating regimes (errors, noise, etc.) occurring within the system.

From the foregone, it becomes obvious that in the investigating of complex systems, consideration of random factors must be given utmost priority.

The effect of random factors on process flow is imitated with the aid of random numbers with predefined probability characteristics. Even then, the results obtained from a single modeling process should be considered as only the realization of a random process. Each of such realizations in isolation cannot serve as an objective characteristic of the system under study. Initial quantities are usually defined from averages and statistical processing of data from a large number of realizations, hence the common name of *statistical modeling method* for this approach. However, simulation can also be employed in deterministic cases, there are no statistical tasks whatsoever.

Statistical modeling method allows for the computing of the value of any functional element defined for the set of realizations of the process under study. For example, given the possibility of determining the value of efficiency indicator of a system by means of statistical experiments, a host of complex system analysis tasks become solvable, tasks such as: evaluation of effect of parameter (or initial value) changes on system efficiency; evaluation of the efficiency of various control principles.

Modeling results are also useful in system synthesis for the evaluation of various modes of its structure as well as perspective planning.

The statistical modeling method has a disadvantage inherent in any numerical method. Results obtained by this method evaluate system efficiency only in those situation for which modeling was done.

This serious disadvantage notwithstanding, simulation is currently the most effective method of investigating complex systems. At times, it is the only practically available means of obtaining information of interest on system behavior (especially during its development and modernization).

ANALYTIC MODELS (AM)

Presuppose the availability of mathematical description of processes, flowing in the original. They are usually developed under strict limitations on the parameters of the original and eternal medium. AM allow for obtaining relationships of the form:

$$P_i = f\left(\alpha_1, \ldots, \alpha_j\right) \quad (3)$$

IMITATION MODELS (IM)

These are the most universal and can be developed in the absence of a mathematical model of the original. The simulation idea is a simple one; it entails the development of an algorithm of the behavior of subsystems and individual elements of the system in time. During the productivity analysis, only the state of the subsystem is of interest (functional or not). The algorithm may be realized in the form of a computer program. By repeating the execution of the IM algorithm in the presence of random events at the system input and within the system statistical information on the dynamics of change of important variables of the IM states can be collated. The statistical processing of this information allows for obtaining the statistical indicator of efficiency. Unlike AM, IM exhibits a strong medical error, depending to a large extent on sample size and consequently, on IM observation time.

CONCLUSION

The role played by mathematical modeling depends on a number of factors, including but not limited to: the character of task at hand, level of expertise of the investigator, amount of time and resources available for research, as well as the choice of model. It is important to always keep the original task in view all through the process of modeling.

The most common error is related to the fact that investigators often lose track of the original task and main aim. The other and not less important mistake stems from moving on to the modling stage without sufficient data on the systems past behavior.

A systematic method comprising of the following stages is available in the literature:

1. Problem statement,
2. Aggregation of experimental data,
3. Determination of the effect of system's working paramenters,
4. Setting up of experimental methodology (e.g. changing of parameters with a view to determining factual effect on observed results),
5. Reducing the number of working parameters (by eliminating those parameters to which the system is least sensitive),
6. Determination of method's characteristic limitations.

One of the major mistakes usually committed by researchers during modeling is the perceived notion of a need to try and change real conditions, i.e. the conditions observed in real-world or technical systems. This perceived need often arises in their bid to employ specific models that were developed for other purposes. Such an approach is definitely not sensible even if it appears to be justifiable.

The researcher's task is not limited to just model development. Upon a successful development of the model, it is imperative to populate it with necessary information, in order to determine how accurately it mimicks the modelled system by a comparison with previously obtained experimental empirical data. In conclusion, the onus rests on scientists and engineers to always keep in mind that perhaps the simplest and most concise definition of a model is – A model is a simplification of reality (National Research Council, 2007).

REFERENCES

Atayero, A. A., Sheluhin, O. I., & Ivanov, Y. A. (2013). Modeling, simulation and analysis of video streaming errors in wireless wideband access networks. In *Proceedings of IAENG Transactions on Engineering Technologies* (pp. 15-28). Springer.

Balci, O. (1997). Verification, validation and accreditation of simulation models. In *Proceedings of the 29th Conference Winter, Simulation*, (pp. 47–52). IEEE.

Frigg, R., & Hartmann, S. (2009). Models in science. In Zalta, E. N. (Ed.), *The Stanford Encyclopedia of Philosophy*. Palo Alto, CA: Metaphysics Research Lab, Center for the Study of Language and Information, Stanford University.

Greenberger, M., Crenson, M., & Crissey, B. (1976). *Models in the policy process: Public decision making in the computer era*. New York: Russel Sage Foundation.

Kirk Nordstrom, D. (2012). Models, validation, and applied geochemistry: Issues in science, communication, and philosophy. *Applied Geochemistry*. doi:10.1016/j.apgeochem.2012.07.007.

Konikow, L. F., & Bredehoeft, J. D. (1992). Ground-water models cannot be validated. *Advances in Water Resources*, *15*(1), 75–83. doi:10.1016/0309-1708(92)90033-X.

National Research Council. (2007). *Models in environmental regulation decision making*. Washington, DC: The National Academies Press.

Shannon, R. E. (1998). Introduction to the art and science of simulation. In *Proceedings of the Simulation Conference* (Vol. 1, pp. 7-14). IEEE.

Tedeschi, L. O. (2006). Assessment of the adequacy of mathematical models. *Agricultural Systems*, *89*(2), 225–247. doi:10.1016/j.agsy.2005.11.004.

ADDITIONAL READING

Anderson, M. P., & Woessner, W. W. (1992). The role of the postaudit in model validation. *Advances in Water Resources*, *15*(3), 167–173. doi:10.1016/0309-1708(92)90021-S.

Brately, P., Fox, B. L., & Schrage, L. E. (1987). *A guide to simulation* (2nd ed.). Berlin: Springer-Verlag. doi:10.1007/978-1-4419-8724-2.

Ogorodnikov, V. A. (1996). *Numerical modelling of random processes and fields: Algorithms and applications*. VSP.

Sargent, R. (1996). Verifying and validating simulation models. In *Proceedings of the 1996 Winter Simulation Conference*. IEEE.

Shannon, R., & Johannes, J. D. (1976). Systems simulation: the art and science. *IEEE Transactions on Systems, Man, and Cybernetics*, (10): 723–724. doi:10.1109/TSMC.1976.4309432.

Shannon, R. E. (1977). Simulation modeling and methodology. *ACM SIGSIM Simulation Digest*, *8*(3), 33–38. doi:10.1145/1102766.1102770.

Shannon, R. E. (1984). Keynote address-Artificial intelligence and simulation. In *Proceedings of the 16th Conference on Winter Simulation* (pp. 3-9). IEEE Press.

Shannon, R. E. (1992). Introduction to simulation. In *Proceedings of the 24th Conference on Winter Simulation* (pp. 65-73). ACM.

Chapter 2
Numerical Methods of Multifractal Analysis in Information Communication Systems and Networks

Oleg I. Sheluhin
Moscow Technical University of Communications and Informatics, Russia

Artem V. Garmashev
Moscow Technical University of Communications and Informatics, Russia

ABSTRACT

In this chapter, the main principles of the theory of fractals and multifractals are stated. A singularity spectrum is introduced for the random telecommunication traffic, concepts of fractal dimensions and scaling functions, and methods used in their determination by means of Wavelet Transform Modulus Maxima (WTMM) are proposed. Algorithm development methods for estimating multifractal spectrum are presented. A method based on multifractal data analysis at network layer level by means of WTMM is proposed for the detection of traffic anomalies in computer and telecommunication networks. The chapter also introduces WTMM as the informative indicator to exploit the distinction of fractal dimensions on various parts of a given dataset. A novel approach based on the use of multifractal spectrum parameters is proposed for estimating queuing performance for the generalized multifractal traffic on the input of a buffering device. It is shown that the multifractal character of traffic has significant impact on queuing performance characteristics.

INTRODUCTION

Often in telecommunication applications, the measured characteristics of traffic datasets display stochastic self-similar properties (i.e. *fractality*). Here it is assumed that a measure of similarity is the traffic type with appropriate amplitude normalization. Accurate structural observation is complicated for datasets, self-similarity however allows for considering the stochastic nature of many network devices and events, which jointly influence the network traffic. One value suffices

DOI: 10.4018/978-1-4666-2208-1.ch002

for the quantitative description of fractals (i.e. the *Hausdorff dimension* or a scaling index) describing an invariance of geometry or statistical performances at a given level of rescaling. However in the fields of physics, chemistry, biology, and telecommunications, there are many appearances, which demand propagation of the fractal concept on complicated structures with more than one scaling index. Such structures are often characterized by a whole spectrum of indices and *Hausdorff dimension* is only one of them. Complex fractals, also known as *multifractals,* are important because they as a rule occur in nature, whereas simple self-similar objects represent idealization of real appearances. Actually, employment of the multifractal approach means that the studied object somehow can be divided into parts, each having its own self-similar properties.

Thus multifractals are *non-homogeneous fractal* objects, for which complete description is required, unlike the regular fractals, there is not enough information in any one value of fractal dimension, but a whole spectrum of such dimensions is required, the number of which, generally speaking, is infinite. The distinctive feature of the latter consists in the fact that they, along with the global characteristics of stochastic processes (obtained as a result of the procedure of averaging on large time intervals), allow for considering singularities of their local structure. Their versatility is in important techniques based on fractal representations and wavelet transforms.

The material in this chapter is divided into three parts. The first part sets out the basic theory of fractals and multifractals, as well as methods of determining the basic parameters of multifractal processes using wavelet transforms. The other two parts deal with specific technical tasks, where investigation of multifractal properties of the processed sequences yield innovative solutions and algorithms. The second part is devoted to the use of fractal analysis for problems of detection of traffic anomaly, which allows for a fundamentally new approach to algorithms development. In the third part, for the generalized multifractal traffic the new practical evaluation method of telecommunication networks queuing performance is offered.

THEORY OF FRACTALS AND MULTIFRACTALS

The term *"fractal"* was used for the first time in Benoît Mandelbrot's work (Mandelbrot, 1982). The word fractal is derived from the Latin *fractus* meaning "fractured" or "broken." Mandelbrot used the term "fractals" for geometric objects that have strongly fragmented shape and can possess the property of *self-similarity*. It is possible to generalize the concept of fractal to any object (image, speech, telecommunication traffic, etc.) some parameters of which are remain invariant with change in scale or time. Thus, the principal property of such objects (i.e. self-similarity) implies that at augmentation, its parts are similar (in some specified sense) to its total shape.

The property of exact self-similarity is a characteristic of the regular fractals only. If an element of randomness is to be included in the algorithm of their creation instead of the determined method of construction (as it happens, for example, in many processes of diffusion growth of clusters, voltage failure, etc.), then the so-called incidental fractals appear. Their basic difference from regular ones is that the property of self-similarity holds true only after a corresponding averaging on the base of all statistically independent realizations of the object. For quantitative description of fractals, a single value is enough - a fractal dimension (Hausdorff dimension) or the index of scaling which is determined as follows

$$D_f = -\lim_{\varepsilon \to 0} \frac{lnM\left(\varepsilon\right)}{\ln\left(\frac{1}{\varepsilon}\right)} \tag{1}$$

Here D_f is fractal dimension of set occupying area by volume of L^{D_f} in D-dimensional space, covered with a number of cubes with a volume of ε^{D_f}. The minimum number of such nonempty cubes occupying the set is $M(\varepsilon) = L^{D_f}(1/\varepsilon)^{D_f}$. Apart from regular fractals there is a special class of fractal objects, within which the distribution of points of set is heterogeneous. The reason of heterogeneity is different occupation probabilities of geometrically identical elements of the fractal, or in the general case, a disparity of occupation probabilities with geometrical sizes of the corresponding areas. Such heterogeneous fractal objects are known as multifractals. For their complete description, unlike the case of regular fractals introducing only one value, its fractal dimension D_f, is not enough, and the whole spectrum of such dimensions, infinite in their number, is required. It can be accounted for by the fact that such fractals also possess some statistical properties along with the purely geometrical descriptions determined by D_f dimension.

General definition of a multifractal: we consider a fractal object occupying a certain limited area L of the size L in Euclidean space with dimension d. We divide the whole area under L into cubic cells having a length of size $\varepsilon << L$ and a volume ε^d. We will hereafter be interested only in the occupied cells containing at least one point. Let the number of the occupied cells *i* change within the range of $1,2,\ldots,N(\varepsilon)$, where $N(\varepsilon)$ is the general number of the occupied cells, defined naturally, by the size of the cell ε. Let $n_i(\varepsilon)$ be the quantity of points in the ith cell, then the value

$$p_i(\varepsilon) = \lim_{N\to\infty} \frac{n_i(\varepsilon)}{N} \tag{2}$$

represents the probability of a point taken at random from our set being in the cell *i*. In other words, probabilities *p* characterize the relative filing of the cells. It follows from the normalizing condition of probability that

$$\sum_{i=1}^{N(\varepsilon)} p_i(\varepsilon) = 1 \tag{3}$$

We now consider the generalized statistical sum $S(q,\varepsilon)$ (henceforth called the *decomposition function*), characterized by an exponent *q*, which can take any values in the range of $-\infty < q < +\infty$

$$S(q,\varepsilon) = \sum_{i=1}^{N(\varepsilon)} p_i(\varepsilon) \tag{4}$$

The spectrum of generalized fractal dimensions D_q characterizing the given distribution of points in area L, is defined by the following correlation:

$$D_q = \frac{\tau(q)}{q-1} \tag{5}$$

where the function $\tau(q)$ is defined as

$$\tau(q) = \lim_{\varepsilon\to 0}\left(\frac{\ln S(q,\varepsilon)}{\ln \varepsilon}\right) \tag{6}$$

If $D_q = D = const$ (i.e. it does not depend on *q*) then the given set of points represents a regular fractal (*monofractal*), characterized only by one value – the fractal dimension D. On the contrary, if the function D_q somehow varies with change in q, then the considered set of points is a multifractal. Thus, the multifractal is generally characterized by some nonlinear function τ_q (hereafter called the scaling function) defining the behavior of the statistical sum $S(q,\varepsilon)$ at $\varepsilon \to 0$.

$$S\left(q,\varepsilon\right)=\sum_{i=1}^{N}p_i^q\left(\varepsilon\right)\approx\varepsilon^{\tau(q)} \quad (7)$$

Bozhokin and Parshin (2001) showed what physical meaning the spectrum of generalized fractal dimensions D_q has at various values of q. Thus, at $q=0$

$$N\left(\varepsilon\right)\approx\varepsilon^{-D_0} \quad (8)$$

It means that the value D_0 represents the usual *Hausdorff Dimension* of the set L. It is the roughest characteristic of a multifractal and does not provide any information on its statistical properties.

At $q=1$

$$D_1=-\lim_{\varepsilon\to0}\frac{Z\left(\varepsilon\right)}{\ln\varepsilon} \quad (9)$$

where $Z\left(\varepsilon\right)=-\sum_{i=1}^{N(\varepsilon)}p_i\ln p_i$ represents the entropy of a fractal set.

This definition of the entropy of a set is completely identical to the one used in thermodynamics where p_i is the probability of detecting a system in a quantum condition *i*. *Claude E. Shannon* generalized the concept of entropy *Z* known in thermodynamics, in his epochal work on the mathematical theory of communication (Shannon, 1948). For such problems, entropy became a measure of the information quantity required for defining a system in some position *i*. In other words, it is *a measure of our ignorance of the system*, i.e. a measure of uncertainty about the system. Coming back to initial problem of distribution of points in the fractal set L, it is possible to say, that since from (9) it follows that

$$Z\left(\varepsilon\right)\approx\varepsilon^{-D_1} \quad (10)$$

then the value D_1 characterizes the information necessary for the definition of the location of a point in some cell. This is why the generalized fractal dimension D_1 is often called *information dimension*. It shows how the information necessary for the definition of location of a point increases when the size of the cell ε tends to zero.

At $q=2$, we have

$$D_2=\lim_{\varepsilon\to0}\frac{\sum_{i=1}^{N(\varepsilon)}p_i^2}{\ln\varepsilon} \quad (11)$$

the paired correlation integral is defined as

$$I\left(\varepsilon\right)=\lim_{N\to\infty}\frac{1}{N^2}\sum_{n,m}\theta\left(\varepsilon-\left|r_n-r_m\right|\right) \quad (12)$$

where summation is done for all pairs of points in our fractal set with radius-vectors r_n and r_m; $\theta\left(x\right)-$ is the Heaviside's step function. $\theta\left(x\right)=1$, if $x\geq0$ and $\theta\left(x\right)=0$, if $x<0$.

The sum in the expression (12) defines the number of pairs of points *n, m*, with the distance between them less than ε. Divided by N^2, it defines the probability of two randomly chosen points to be separated by a distance smaller than ε^{12}. The same probability can be defined in another way. The value p_i, according to its definition in (2), represents the probability of a point being in the cell *i* having size ε. Hence, the value p_i can be defined as the probability of two points being in this cell. By finding the sum of p_i^2 for all occupied cells, we will get the probability of any two randomly chosen points from set L falling in a cell with size ε. Consequently, the distance between these points will be less than or of an order of ε. Thus taking Equation (11) into consideration, we have

$$I(\varepsilon) \approx \sum_{i=1}^{N(\varepsilon)} p_i^2 \approx \varepsilon^{D_2} \qquad (13)$$

It is possible to draw the conclusion that the generalized dimension D_2 defines the dependence of the correlation integral $I(\varepsilon)$ on ε. It is for this reason that the value D_2 is known as the correlation dimension. However, the values of D_q are not, strictly speaking, fractal dimensions in the generally accepted sense. Therefore, along with them, the so-called function of multifractal spectrum (multifractal singularities spectrum) is often used to characterize the multifractal set. One of the main characteristics of a multifractal is a set of probabilities p_i, showing the relative filling of cells ε, covering the set. The smaller the cell is, the smaller its filling. For self-similar sets, the dependence of p_i, on the size of the cell has an exponential character

$$p_i(\varepsilon) \approx \varepsilon^{\alpha_i} \qquad (14)$$

where α_i is some exponent (different for different cells *i*).

Let $n(\alpha)d\alpha$ be the probability of α_i being in a range from $\alpha\, to\, d\alpha$. In other words, $n(\alpha)d\alpha$ represents the relative number of cells *i*, with the same measure of p_i with α_i, lying in this range. In the case of a monofractals, for which all α_i are the same (and equal to the fractal dimension *D*), this number is obviously proportional to the total number of cells $N(\varepsilon) \approx \varepsilon^{-D}$, dependent by extension on the size of the cell ε. The fractal dimension of the set D determines the index in this ratio. However, it is not accurately true for multifractals, and different values of α_i occur with a probability that is characterized not by one and the same value of *D*, but by different values (according to α) of the exponent $f(\alpha)$,

$$n(\alpha) \approx \varepsilon^{-f(\alpha)} \qquad (15)$$

Thus the physical meaning of the function $f(\alpha)$ is that it represents the Hausdorff dimension of a homogeneous fractal subset L_α, from the original set *L*, characterized by equal probabilities of filling of the cells $p_i \approx \varepsilon$. Since the fractal dimension of a subset is clearly always less than or equal to the fractal dimension of the original set D_0, there is an important inequality for the function $f(\alpha)$:

$$f(\alpha) \le D_0 \qquad (16)$$

The conclusion is that a set of different values of the function $f(\alpha)$ (for different α) represents a spectrum of fractal dimensions of homogeneous subsets of L_α into which the original set of L can be divided. This explains the term of a multifractal. It can be understood as a kind of incorporation of the various homogeneous fractal subsets L_α of the original set of *L*, each of which has its own value of the fractal dimension $f(\alpha)$. Since any subset contains only a fraction of the total number of cells $N(\varepsilon)$, into which the initial set of L is divided, normalization condition of probability (3), is obviously not fulfilled in the case of summation for this subset only. Since the sum of the probabilities is less than one. Therefore, the probabilities p_i with the same value of α_i are obviously less than or at least are of the same order as the value $\varepsilon^{f(\alpha_i)}$, which is inversely proportional to the number of cells, covering the given subset (in the case of a monofractal

$p_i \approx 1/N(\varepsilon)$). As a result, we have the following important inequality for the function $f(\alpha)$. For all possible values of α

$$f(\alpha) \leq \alpha \tag{17}$$

With equality *iff* the fractal is completely homogeneous in which case $f(\alpha) = \alpha = D$.

Researches reported in the literature have shown that the multifractal spectre of real data $f_G(\alpha)$ is difficult to calculate directly (Sheluhin, Smolskiy, & Osin, 2007). It can however be easily calculated by means of the Legendre transformation, giving the Legendre's spectrum $f_L(\alpha)$. $f_L(\alpha)$ is the same as $f_G(\alpha)$ provided that $\tau(q)$ exists and is differentiable for all valid values of q. The following expressions define the Legendre transformation from variables $\{q,\tau(q)\} to \{\alpha, f(\alpha)\}$:

$$\tau(q) = q^{2}\alpha(q) - f(\alpha(q)) \tag{18}$$

$$\alpha = \frac{d\tau}{dq} \tag{19}$$

$$f(\alpha) = q\frac{d\tau}{dq} - \tau \tag{20}$$

where $\tau(q)$ is the scaling index or the scaling function.

The inverse Legendre transformation is defined by the following formulas:

$$q = \frac{df}{d\alpha} \tag{21}$$

$$\tau(q) = \alpha\frac{df}{d\alpha} - f \tag{22}$$

For a homogeneous fractal $D_q = D = const.$ Which is the reason why $\alpha = d\tau / dq = D$, and $f(\alpha) = q\alpha - \tau(q) = qD - D(q-1) = D$. In this case, plot of the function $f(\alpha)$ on the plane $\{\alpha, f(\alpha)\}$ consists of one point only (i.e. $\{D, D\}$).

The authors consider more interesting cases when the graph of the function $f(\alpha)$ consists not of discrete points, but represents a continuous line. Since $f'(\alpha) = q$, then for $q = 0$ the derivative of the function turns to zero. This means that at some point $\alpha_0 = \alpha(0)$ the function $f(\alpha)$ has a maximum (keeping in mind that the function $f(\alpha)$ is convex). The function's value at the maximum $f(\alpha_0) = D_0$, i.e. the maximum value of $f(\alpha)$, is equal to the Hausdorff dimension of the multifractal D_0 (see Figure 1).

Now consider the case when $q = 1$. As $\tau(1) = 0$, then $\alpha(1) = f(\alpha(1))$. On the other hand, the derivative of the function $f(\alpha)$ at this point equals 1: $f'(\alpha(1)) = 1$. Differentiating the

Figure 1. Function maximum is equal to the fractal dimension of DO

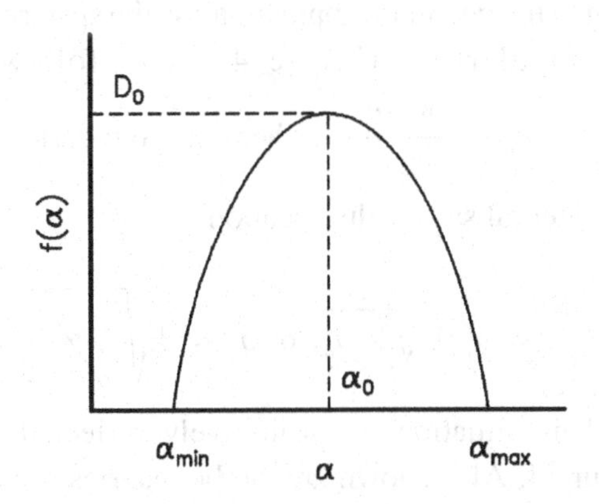

reference $\tau(q) = (q-1)D_q$ on $q\frac{d\tau}{dq} = D_q + (q-1)D'_q = \alpha(q)$ and supposing that $q = 1$, we find that $\alpha(1) = D_1$. Thus, $D_1 = \alpha(1) = f(\alpha(1))$. i.e. the informational dimension D_1 lies on the curve $f(\alpha)$ at the point, where $\alpha = f(\alpha)$ and $f'(\alpha(1)) = 1$. This gives us a graphic way to determine the informational dimension on the curve $f(\alpha)$ (see Figure 2). Now let's consider the case when $q = 2$. We have $D_2 = 2\alpha(2) = f(\alpha(2))$ or $f(\alpha(2)) = 2\alpha(2) - D_2$, which corresponds with the geometric construction on the Figure 3.

The multifractal dimension of the qth order is determined by Equation (23)

$$D_q = \frac{1}{q-1}\left[q(\alpha(q)) - f(\alpha(q))\right] \tag{23}$$

Using numerical methods of estimating the scaling function we can find an analytic expression for the spectrum of singularities. For example, if the scaling function is described by the formula

$$\tau(q) = -a_0 + a_1 q - a_2\frac{q^2}{2!} + a_3\frac{q^3}{3!} = \sum_{i=0}^{3} a_i q^i,$$

then in the quadratic approximation the spectrum of singularities (Figure 4) is as follows: $f(\alpha) = a_0 - \frac{(\alpha - a_1)^2}{2a_2}$, where the boundaries of the interval satisfy the equation :

$$\alpha_{\min,\max} = a_1 \pm \sqrt{2a_2 a_0}, \text{ or } q_{\pm}^{*} = \pm\sqrt{2a_0 / a_2}.$$

This situation is qualitatively reflected in Figure 4. Also shown are the boundaries of the interval $(\alpha_{min}, \alpha_{max})$, in which the function *f(α)* is set. It is necessary to specify that the conversion of the function $f(\alpha)$ to zero in this range (as shown in the figure) does not always occur and in some other cases $f(\alpha)$ in one of these points (or in both) may differ from zero. A prerequisite, however, is the conversion of the derivative $f'(\alpha)$ to infinity at these two points.

Figure 2. Finding the information dimension $D_1 = \alpha(1) = f(\alpha(1))$

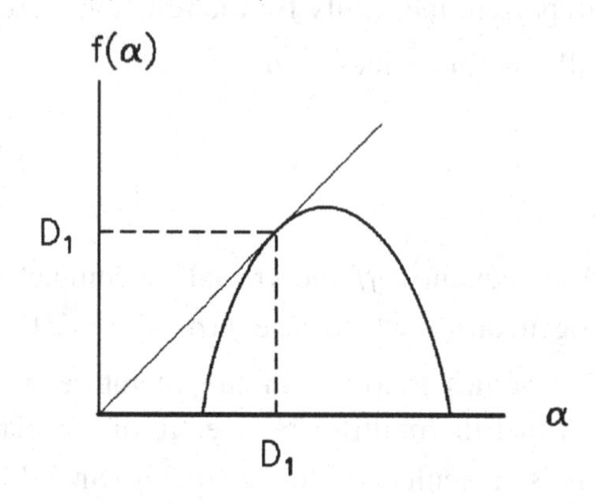

Figure 3. Geometric definition of the correlation dimension D_2

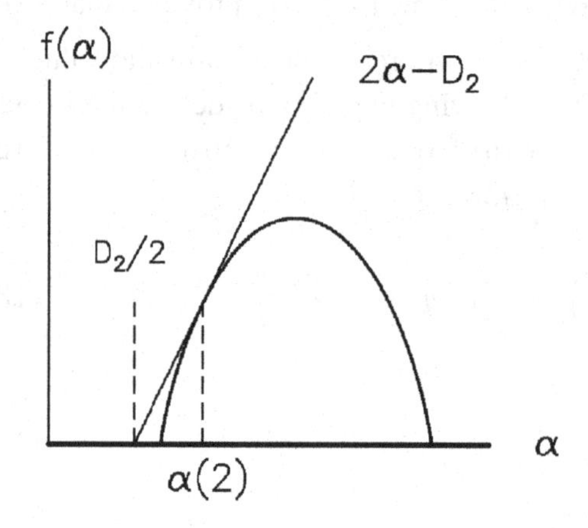

Figure 4. Singularity spectrum of the multifractal process

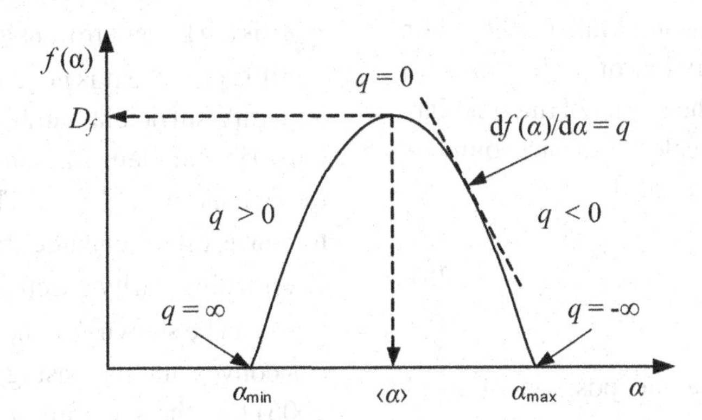

WAVELET TRANSFORM MODULUS MAXIMA METHOD

The method of Wavelet Transform Modulus Maxima (WTMM) was been proposed for the estimation of multifractal spectrum parameters by Hwang and Mallat (1994). The WTMM method has a number of essential advantages: a capacity for the analysis of a wide class of singularities-not only signals, but also their derivatives-the smaller inaccuracy of scaling characteristics evaluation, and so forth. WTMM technique, which can be successfully applied in examination of non-homogeneous structure of processes of a various nature, is based on the wavelet analysis named mathematically "microscope" in view of its ability to save good resolution on different scales.

Attractiveness of the given method consists in its possibility to analyze both singular measures, and singular functions. The method is a more general-purpose means of examining the multi-scaling properties of objects in comparison with earlier developed approaches.

In spite of the fact that in WTMM at the intermediate stages the wavelet-transform is used, it represents a combination of two different theories namely – the wavelet theory and the theory of multifractals. For the analysis of the input signal $s(t)$ we execute n continuous wavelet-transforms ($n = log_2 N$, where N – is length of the signal) with the mother wavelet $\psi(t)$ on a scale level (or octave) of j:

$$W_s(u,j) = (s(t), \psi_{u,j}(t)) = 2^{-j/2} \int_{-\infty}^{\infty} s(t)\psi\left(\frac{t-u}{2^j}\right) dt, \tag{24}$$

As shown by Mallat (2005), if function $s(t)$ is self-similar then its wavelet-transform $W_s(u,j)$ also has the property of self-similarity. The concept of self-similarity in wavelet-transform presupposes that the positions and magnitudes of its modulus-maxima are also self-similar.

S. Mallat in (Mallat, 2005) proved that the singularity of non-stationary signals (e.g. multifractal signals) can be detected using WTMM global partition function. By employing WTMM in the computation of the global partition function, deviations engendered by the oscillation of wavelet-coefficients when $q < 0$ may be avoided. WTMM is a more accurate and correct approach to detecting the singularity of a signal. Hence, it is possible to measure the spectrum of the peculiarities of a multifractal signal from local maxima of the wavelet-transform, using the global partition function introduced by Muzy et al. in (Muzy, Bacry, & Arneodo, 1994).

Let ψ be a wavelet with n zero moments. It is proven that if s has smooth *Lipschitz* points $\alpha_0 < n$ at point ν, then wavelet-transform $W_s(u,j)$ has a sequence of modulus-maxima that converges to ν on small scales (Hwang and Mallat, 1994). For this reason, a set of maxima of scale *j* may be interpreted as covering the carrier of the singularity *s* with wavelets of scale 2^{j} at the points of occurrence of these maxima.

$$\left|W_s(u,j)\right| \sim 2^{j(\alpha_0+1/2)} \quad (25)$$

Let $\{u_p(j)\}_{p\in Z}$ – be the position of local maxima of $\left|W_s(u,j)\right|$ on a fixed scale *j*. Partition function *S* measures the sum of all these maxima of wavelet-modulus raised to power *q*:

$$S(q,j) = \sum_{P} \left|W_s(u_p,j)\right|^q \quad (26)$$

For each scale *s*, it is assumed that any two consecutive maxima u_p and u_{p+1} are located at distance $|u_{p+1} - u_p| > \varepsilon s$ for a given $\varepsilon > 0$. If this is not so then at intervals with size $\varepsilon 2^j$, the sum expressed in (26) will consist of only the maxima with the highest amplitudes. This concept protects the partition function from superposition of close maxima that are consequences of fast oscillations. For each $q \in R$, the scaling function $\tau(q)$ measures the asymptotic decrease of $S(q,j)$ at small scales of *j*:

$$\tau(q,j) = \liminf_{j\to 0} \frac{\ln S(q,j)}{\ln 2^j} \quad (27)$$

This usually implies that $S(q,j) \sim 2^{j\tau(q)}$.

Function $\tau(q)$ is connected to the Legendre transform for self-similar signals through expression (28). This result has been discovered (Bacry, Muzy, Arneodo, 1993) for a private class of fractal signals and generalized by Zhaffar (1997).

$$\tau(q,j) = \min_{\alpha\in\Lambda}(q(\alpha) - f_L(\alpha,J)) \quad (28)$$

This theorem proves that the scaling function $\tau(q)$ is the Legendre transform of function $f_L(\alpha)$. For this purpose it is necessary to use only wavelet with a sufficient number of zero moments. At numerical implementations $\tau(q)$ is estimated via the evaluation of $S(q,\varepsilon)$. Therefore it is necessary to convert the Legendre transform in (28) to recover a singularity spectrum $f_L(\alpha)$.

It can be shown that the scaling function $\tau(q)$ is a convex and increasing function of *q* (Mallat, 2005) that the spectrum $f(\alpha)$ of the self-similar signals is convex, while the Legendre transform in Equation (28) is reversible *iff* $f(\alpha)$ is a convex function. In this case Equation (29) holds.

$$f_L(\alpha,j) = \min_{q\in R}(q(\alpha) - \tau(q,j)) \quad (29)$$

This formula holds for a wide class of multifractals. For example, it may be applied in the case of statistical self-similar signals such as in the realization of Fractional Brownian Motion (FBM). The multifractals having some stochastic self-similarity have a spectrum, which can be often calculated as reversal of Legendre transform (29). However, we pay special attention that this formula is not exact for any function *s*, because its spectrum of singularities $f_L(\alpha)$ is not mandatorily convex. Generally, it was proved in (Zhaffar, 1997) that Legendre transform (28) gives only upper bound of $f_L(\alpha)$.

WTMM ALGORITHM FOR ESTIMATING MULTIFRACTAL SPECTRAL PARAMETERS

Algorithm of the method applied in the estimation of multifractal spectral parameters is presented below.

Step 1: With the aid of continuous dyadic wavelet-transform of the mother wavelet $\psi(t)$, decompose input signal $s(t)$ into its coefficients:

$$W_s(u,j) = (s(t), \psi_{u,j}(t)) = 2^{-j/2} \int_{-\infty}^{\infty} s(t)\psi\left(\frac{t-u}{2^j}\right) dt,$$

Step 2: In the resulting array of wavelet coefficients, find the position of local maxima and their absolute values $\{u_p(j)\}_{p \in Z}$, thus forming an array of local maxima $|W_s(u_p, j)|$

Step 3: Calculate the partition function:

$$S(q,j) = \sum_P |W_s(u_p, j)|^q$$

Step 4: Calculate the scaling function $\tau(q)$ for each $q \in R$:

$$\tau(q,j) = \liminf_{j \to 0} \frac{\ln S(q,j)}{\ln 2^j}$$

Step 5: Using the Legendre transform, compute the multifractal spectrum $f_L(\alpha)$

$$f_L(\alpha, j) = \min_{q \in R}(q(\alpha) - \tau(q,j))$$

Step 6: For each octave *j*, compute multifractal dimension of order *q*:

$$D_{q,j} = \frac{1}{q-1}[q(\alpha(q,j) - f(\alpha(q), j)]$$

For $q < 0$ the value of $S(q,j)$ depends mainly on small maxima of the amplitude $|Wf(u_p, j)|$. It is for this reason that the computation maybe unstable. To avoid false modulus-maxima created by computational errors in areas where *s* is almost constant, wavelet-maxima are chained together to form a scale-dependent curve of maxima.

If $\psi = (-1)^P \theta^{(p)}$, where $\theta = \frac{1}{\sqrt{2\pi}} e^{=t^2/2}$ is the Gaussian function, then all the lines of maxima $u_p(j)$ define curves that spread up to the limit $j=0$. Therefore, all maxima lines, that do not spread up to the smallest scale are removed in the calculation of $S(q,j)$.

MULTIFRACTAL ANALYSIS IN THE DETECTION OF TELECOMMUNICATION TRAFFIC ANOMALIES

Researches (Sheluhin, Smolskiy, & Osin, 2007; Bacry, Muzy, & Arneodo, 1993; Jaffard, 1997; Riedi, Crouse, Ribeiro, & Baraniuk, 1997; Meyer, 1997; Feldmann, Gilbert, & Willinger, 1998) abound which show that the network traffic is self-similar in time scales of the order of some hundreds of milliseconds and more. At the same time, it also shows multifractal properties in smaller time scales (the order of milliseconds). It is possible to tell that self-similarity reflects long-range behavior of a measured signal, and multifractal properties reflect its instant behavior. The search for singularity distribution (peculiarity) in a multifractal signal is very important for the analysis of its properties. A number of methods have been advanced in the literature for the determination of the singularity spectrum of a multifractal signal based on wavelet transform (Riedi, Crouse, Ribeiro, & Baraniuk, 1999; Muzy, Bacry, & Arneodo, 1999).

Datasets made available by the Lincoln Laboratory of MIT - 1999 DARPA Intrusion Detection Evaluation (MIT, 2012) were analyzed as the experimental test sequence. The datasets are network traffic collected by the end router of the institute's network. Figure 5a shows a realization of pure network traffic without attack for 72,700 s (~20 hours) sampled at 1s intervals, while Figure 5b depicts the same realization with different types of anomalies relating to attacks such as Denial of

Service (DoS) and different types of unauthorized network sniffing. DoS attacks also incorporate Distributed DoS attacks (DDoS) which entail the enslavement of a number of host computers for the purposes of unleashing attack on a single victim. Various anomalous network *sniffings* are indicative of hacker events as well as acts of harmful programs (worms). Suffice it to note here that network traffic with different types of attack differed significantly in comparison with the normal scenario. This difference affected the throughput at both the packet and bit level as well as the connection usage and consequently the volume of transmitted data. The change in network traffic characteristic can be observed visually. But a visual observation alone cannot suffice, since the manner in which the changes occur and their representations in the form of mathematical models are problems that must be studied with the instrumentation of mathematical tools.

In considering the features of WTMM method used for the detection of anomalies in the traffic with DoS attacks, $n = \log_2 72{,}700 = 16$ continuous wavelet-transforms of the input realization was performed. The spectrograms for selected octaves are shown in Figure 6 (Sheluhin, Atayero, & Garmashev, 2011).

The spectrograms clearly reveal a frequency-time localization of all the features of the signal. For example, the abnormal spike in the region of $n = 6{\cdot}10^4$ s (Figure 6 a, b, c) manifests as abrupt disturbances in the spectrogram, this is evidently absent in the same region of Figure 5a.

It is appreciable at decomposition levels approximately from 1 to 11 (Figure 6a). As the mother wavelet scale becomes more than anomaly time period, it ceases to be fixed on the spectrogram. The mother wavelet scale at 16th level of decomposition (Figure 6c) is proportionate to all length of the implementation, therefore actually any time-and-frequency singularities is not watched. Therefore, spectrogram analysis suggests that some features of the signal can manifest themselves at some level of decomposition, but not at other levels, therefore to identify all the features of the signal it is analyzed on all octaves.

Figures 7a through 7d show the partition functions $S\left(q,j\right) = \sum_{P}\left|W_S\left(u_p,j\right)\right|^q$ for an octave j=16 are represented.

Partition functions for implementations with anomalies and without have considerable differences. Figure 7b and 7d, show that the statistical sum at $q < 0$ is characterized by the presence of specific peaks, at $q > 0$, the partition function is much more smooth. To analyze differences, we consider partition functions for the positive and negative values q separately (Figure 8a, 8b).

Figure 8a shows that though differences are available, they are insignificant and cannot serve as criteria for anomalous activity determination. It is possible to tell that partition functions at

Figure 5. Implementation of network traffic: a) network without anomaly and b) network with abnormal activity

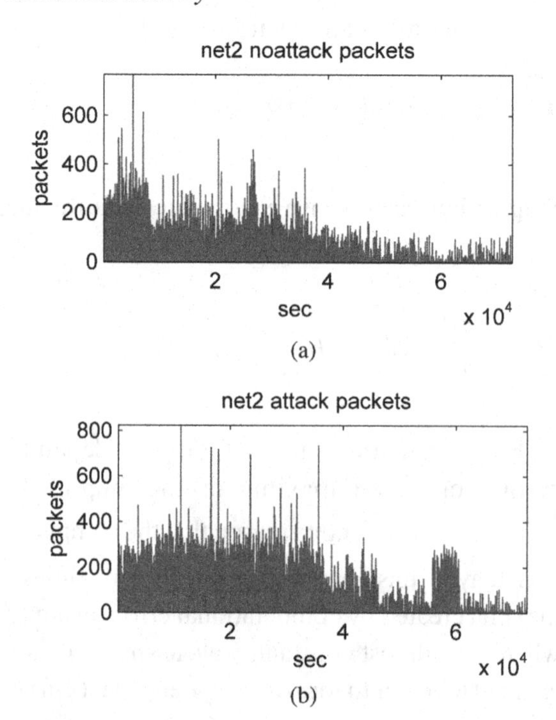

Figure 6. Spectrograms of wavelet-transform: at the left - for network without attacks, at the right – for network with anomalies and rejections a) octave j=11, b) j=13, c)j=15

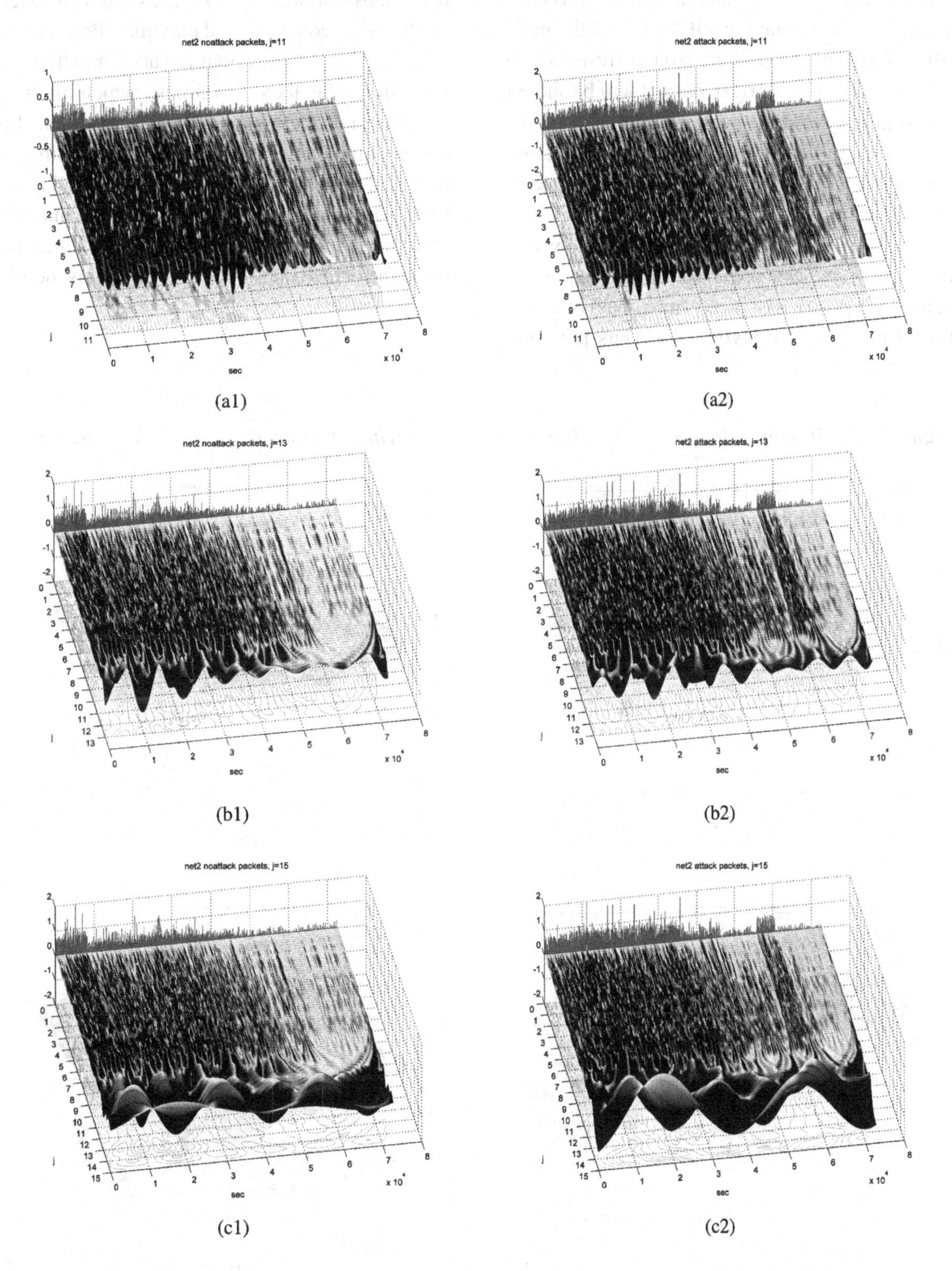

(a1) (a2)

(b1) (b2)

(c1) (c2)

$q > 0$ responsible more likely for similarity, than for differences of two implementations. It is necessary to remind that the left "wing" of the multifractal spectrum function $f(\alpha)$ corresponds to values $\alpha\, at\, q > 0$. Furthermore, it will be shown that similarity of some implementations is exhibited in this part of a singularities spectrum. Now we consider a partition function for values $q < 0$ (Figure 8b).

On this figure differences are accurately visible. They are characterized by distinction of values and position of peaks (maximas) of a partition function on an axis of scales. Thus, presence of peaks at a partition function at $q > 0$ at some decomposition scale level *j* speaks about presence on its high-frequency local maximas. Presence of peaks at $q < 0$ talks about the accumulations of low-amplitude local maximas, which in turn speaks about local singularities of a signal decomposition on the given octave. It is possible to make a conclusion that various values and positions of peaks on decomposition scale axis indicate various frequency characteristics of a signal on the same octave that speaks about their principle distinction.

Figure 7. Partition function for j=16: a, b) implementation without anomalies, c-d) with anomalies

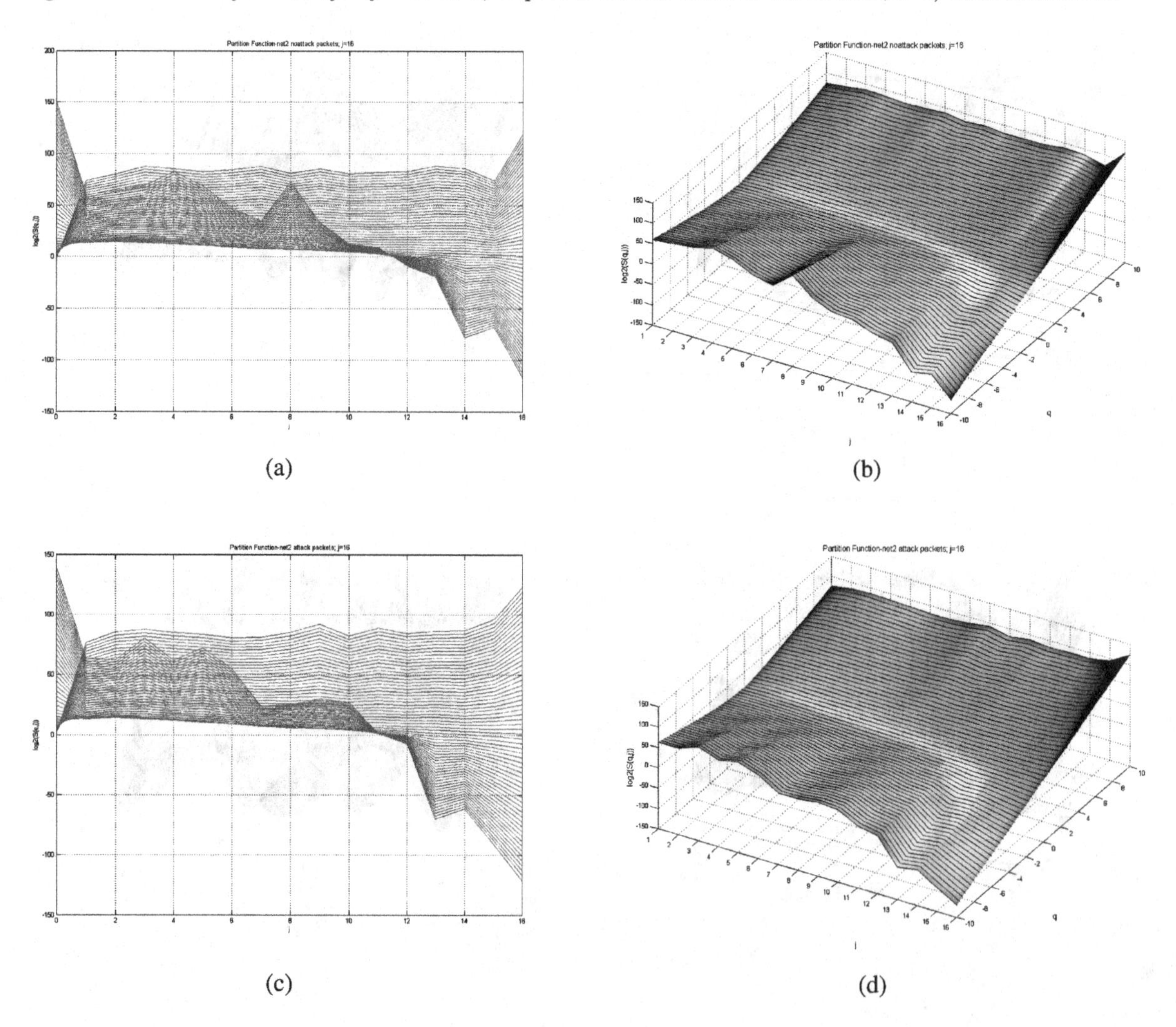

Figure 8. a) Partition functions at q> 0, j=16: on top implementation without anomalies, from below - with anomalies; b) partition functions at q <0, j=16: on top implementation without anomalies, from below - with anomalies

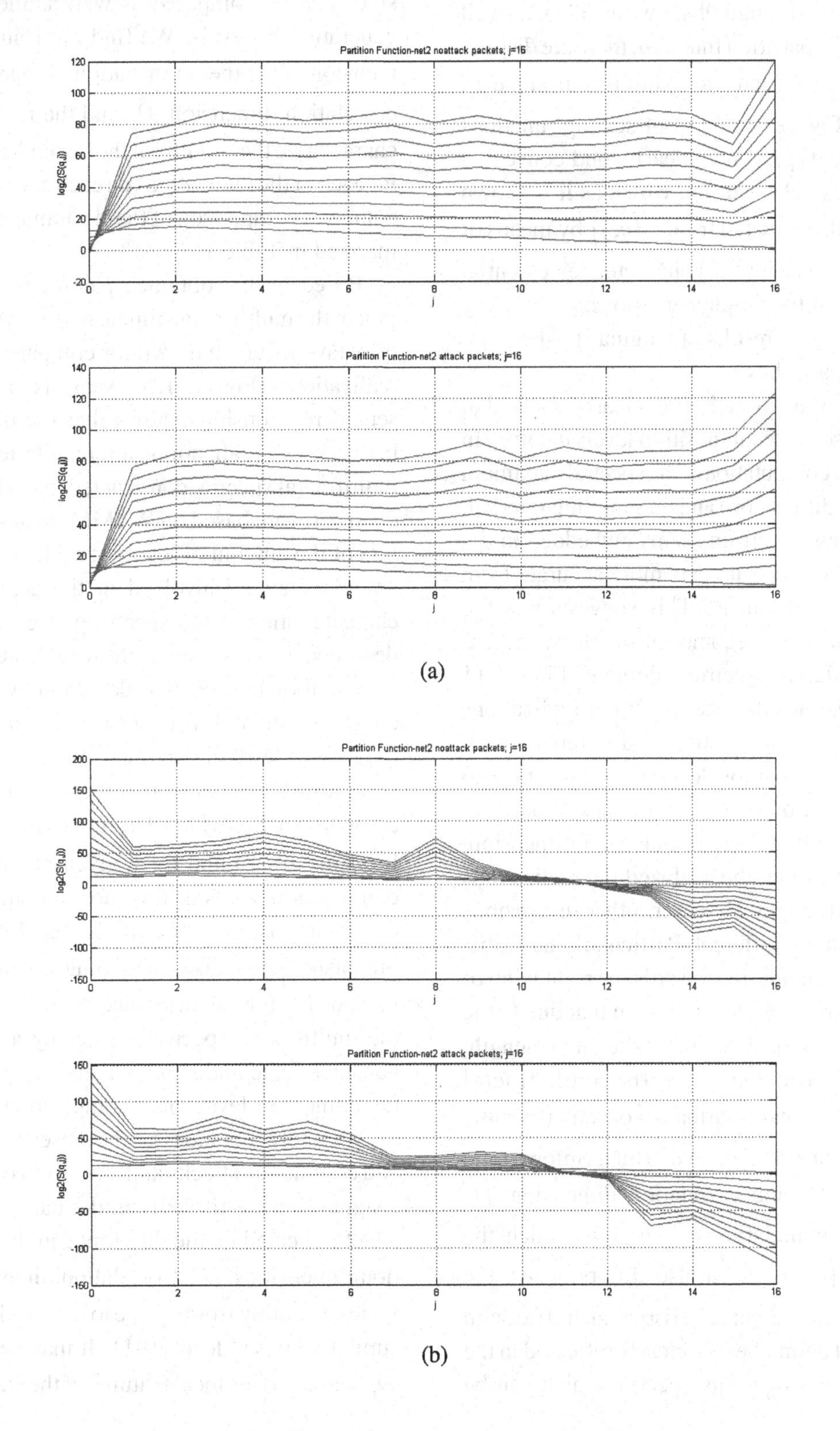

On Figure 9-a-d results of the scaling function $\tau(q,j)$ evaluation are shown.

Figures 9a through 9f show that also, as well as in case of a partition function, there are distinctions in $\tau(q,j)$, and are exhibited in slope of functions. Figure 9e and 9f of scaling functions illustrate the typical nonlinearity and convexity. The multifractal spectrum, which as it is shown in Figure 10, estimated from $\tau(q,j)$ by means of Legendre transform (28) characterizes essential differences of two implementations.

On Figure 10 results of singularity spectrum evaluations are shown.

Figures 10a through 10d clearly show that increasing scale decomposition levels involved in the analysis, computation of the spectral maximum (Hausdorff dimension) and its sampling interval, each previous spectrum seems embedded in the next, (i.e. the spectrum gets more accurate from one octave to the next). This suggests that the higher the level of decomposition, the more features the signal spectrum depicts. Figure 11 clearly illustrates that the spectra of realizations with and without anomalies are different for each scaling decomposition level j. From octave to octave spectra of normal and attacked network have practically the same Hausdorff dimension, due to the fact that the analyzed the realizations are of equal length. However, other dimensions are significantly different. Particularly large differences are manifested towards the right wing of the spectrum for $q < 0$. It is seen that due to the fact that the sequences have the same length, Hausdorff dimension of the multifractal $f(\alpha_0) = D_0$ remains virtually constant (maxima of the functions are the same). But its information dimension D_1 and correlation dimension D_2 differ. The boundaries $\alpha_{min}, \alpha_{max}$ in which the function $f(\alpha)$ is given also differs. Thus, the differences in the characteristics of traffic with and without anomalies are clearly reflected in the plots of their singularity spectra, which can be found using the WTMM method. Formalizing how spectra differ from each other, these dimensions can be compared as well as the function generation intervals. We find the Hausdorff dimension D_0, the information dimension D_1, correlation dimension D_2 and the intervals that characterize the "width" of the Legendre spectrum for each of the realizations on each decomposition octave. A comparison of these parameters is summarized in Table 1.

Based on the obtained parametric values, a plot of the multifractal dimensions *D* as a function of octave *j*, can be drawn for comparing the two realizations (Figure 12). Analysis of the presented relationships shows that the differences between two realizations are manifested in their multifractal spectra, constructed using the developed software based on WTMM method, regardless of the amount of levels of scaling decomposition (octave) j involved in the analysis. The characteristics of the spectrum at each level of decomposition can reveal the local features of the signal, allowing for their detection by means of analyzing the multifractal spectra of realizations for a given level of decomposition.

Hausdorff dimension of the realization under comparison D_0, which determines the number of local maxima found for a given number of decomposition levels differs most for small values of decomposition (octave) levels. Information dimension of realizations being compared D_1, responsible for the difference in the left slopes of the multifractal spectrum differ by a small but constant value and is practically independent of the number of levels of decomposition.

We safely conclude that the presence of diverse and continuous attacks and anomalous activity in a signal changes the self-similar nature of traffic a fact indicated by the difference in the information dimensions D_1. Correlation dimension D_2 varies smoothly from octave to octave, displaying similar values at levels 9-11. It may be said that D_1 characterizes local features of the signals over

Figure 9. Functions $\tau(q, j)$: for scale levels $j=0 \ldots 16$ a-d) at the left - for a network without attacks, on the right - for a network with anomalies; e)-for an octave 13 in comparing; f)-for an octave 15 in comparing

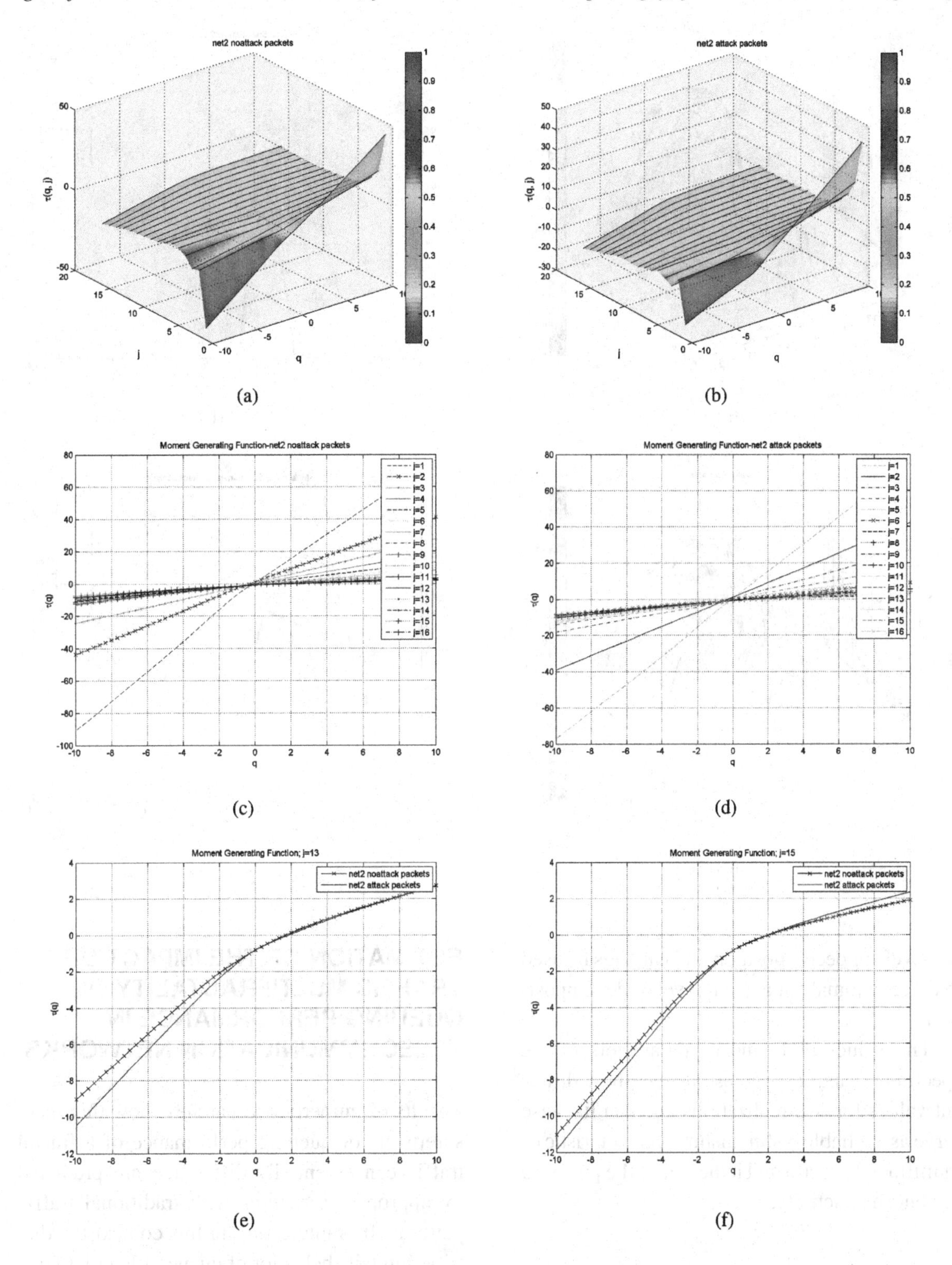

Figure 10. Dependence of a multifractal spectrum on an amount of scale levels involved in the analysis j, j=0...16. a, b) for a network without anomalies, c, d) - for a network with anomalies

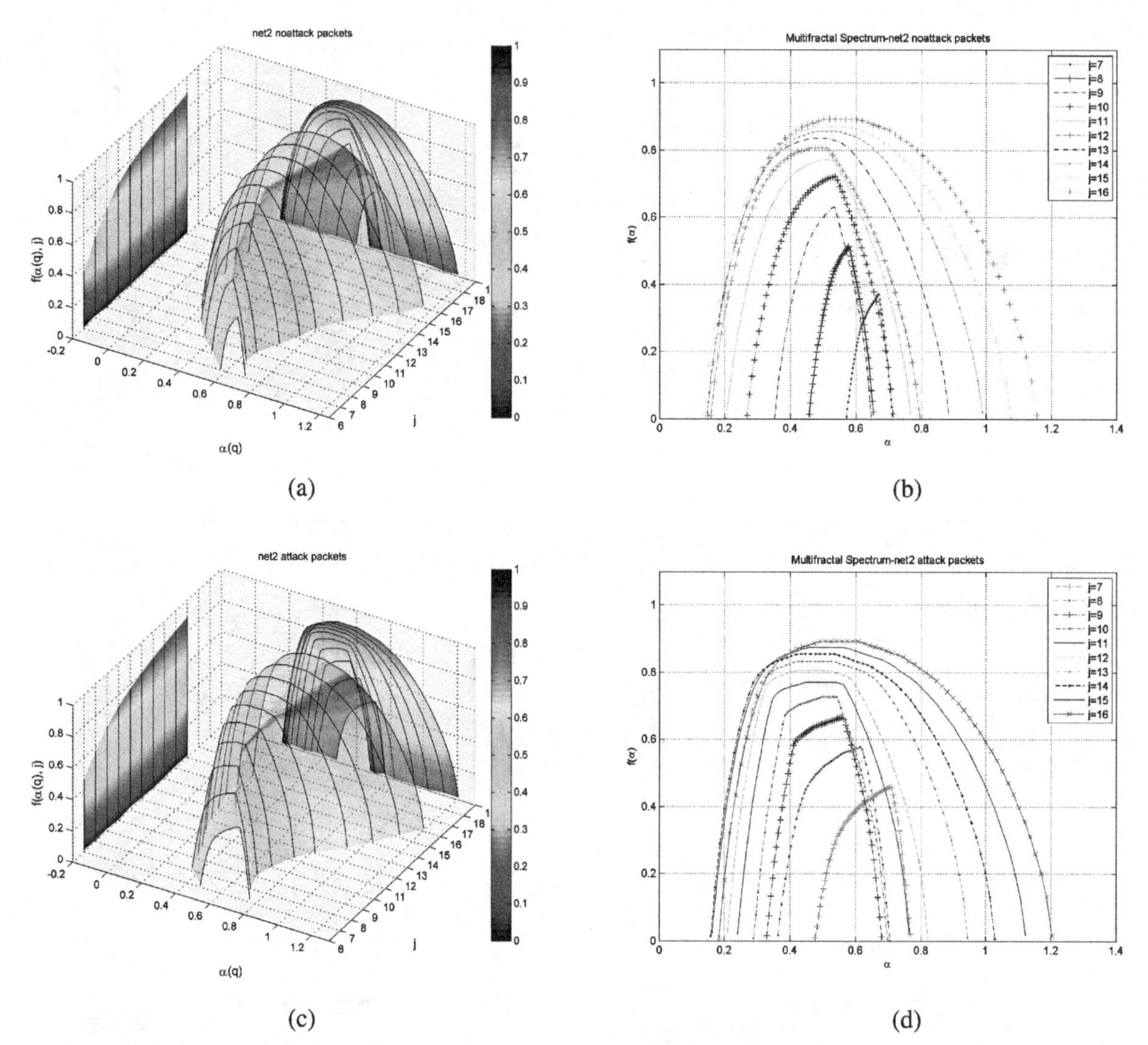

the levels of decomposition and can thus be used to detect anomaly at a given level of decomposition.

The values of boundary parameters of the spectra α_{min} and α_{max} almost always show different values for two realizations and can likewise serve as a reliable distinguishing characteristic of multifractal spectra and indicator of the presence of abnormal activity.

ESTIMATION OF THE IMPACT OF TRAFFIC MULTIFRACTALITY ON QUEUING PERFORMANCE IN TELECOMMUNICATION NETWORKS

Results of numerous researches show that measurements of queuing performance of a fractal traffic can essentially differ that are predicted by appropriate systems with traditional traffic patterns. It is interesting in this context the distribution tails behavior of queue of length Q in a stable condition for one server with infinite queue

Figure 11. Multifractal spectra in comparing, black - without anomalies, white - with anomalies

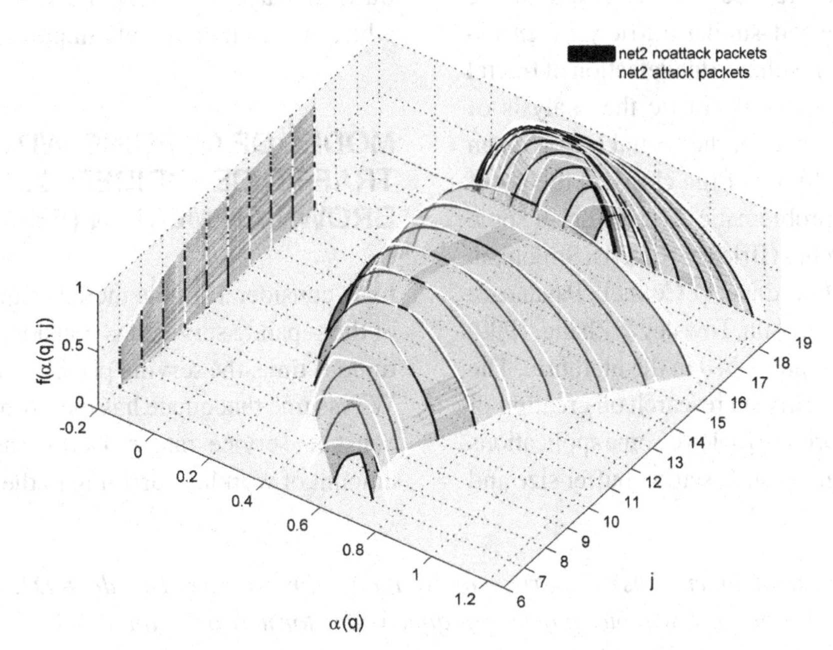

buffer capacity. For the Markov traffic processed in such queue, distribution of tails is approximately exponential (Park & Willinger, 1999).

$$P\{Q > B\} \sim e^{-\eta B} \text{ ,as } B \to \infty \tag{30}$$

where $\eta > 0-$ asymptotic decay rate.

Expression (30) is taken as a principle concept of effective transmission capacity, where access control or the arranged capacity of the service channel is based on a tails probability distribution of a random variables choice. Unlike (30) traffic flows with long-range dependence (in particular, the models based on fractal Brownian motion) lead to tail queue distribution that decays asymptotically with a Weibullian law, that is

$$P\{Q > B\} \sim e^{-\gamma B^{\beta}} \text{ ,as } B \to \infty \tag{31}$$

where $\gamma-$ is a constant, and $\beta = 2 - 2H \in (0\ ;1]$.

Formulas 30 and 31 strongly differ. The first on comparing with the second gives rather optimistic predictions. The question about, whether other traffic models lead to correct, in comparison with experimental data, prognoses of network productivity, till now remains open. The general analytical results of queuing performance, or influences of traffic self-similarity and long-range dependence on Quality of Service (*QoS*) do not exist at present. Only separate analytical results for special cases are known. At the same time the most effective method of an overall performance estimation of telecommunication networks remains, obviously, simulation-modeling methods. From these positions problems of influence of a traffic self-similarity level on telecommunication systems efficiency will be considered in the following section.

THE MONOFRACTAL TRAFFIC

When designing any telecommunication network one has is faced with restrictions on transmission capacity of channels. In these conditions the estimation of effective band pass range becomes one of the key problems. Calculations on the basis of classical methods of queuing theorems oriented on uncorrelated request flows in the conditions of the self-similar traffic yield excessively optimistic results. After detection of fractal structure in the network traffic the analysis of queuing performance for the fractal traffic on an input within the limits of the classical theory of queues become problematic. The results of some important researches (Brichet, Roberts, Simonian, & Veitch, 1996; Giordano, O'Connell, Pagano, & Procissi, 1999; Lui, Nain, Towsley & Zhang, 1999; Norros, 1994) are published in the literature. The influence of fractality on research on creation of queues is an important problem. Some applications of network design, such as setting buffer size and traffic management are connected to this problem, which makes it extremely important.

MODEL OF QUEUING WITH TRAFFIC DESCRIBED BY FRACTAL BROWNIAN MOTION (FBM)

Let's consider a simple model of queuing: queue of the separate server. It is considered in the continuous time, the serving principle is set to FIFO. We assume that queue has the infinite buffer and constant service rate *r*. Denote as *A(t)* a total amount of workload arriving to the queue from a

Figure 12. Multifractal dimensions comparison of two realizations (circle– D0 , dots–D1, triangle–D2): blue–dimensions for network without attack; red–dimensions for network with attack

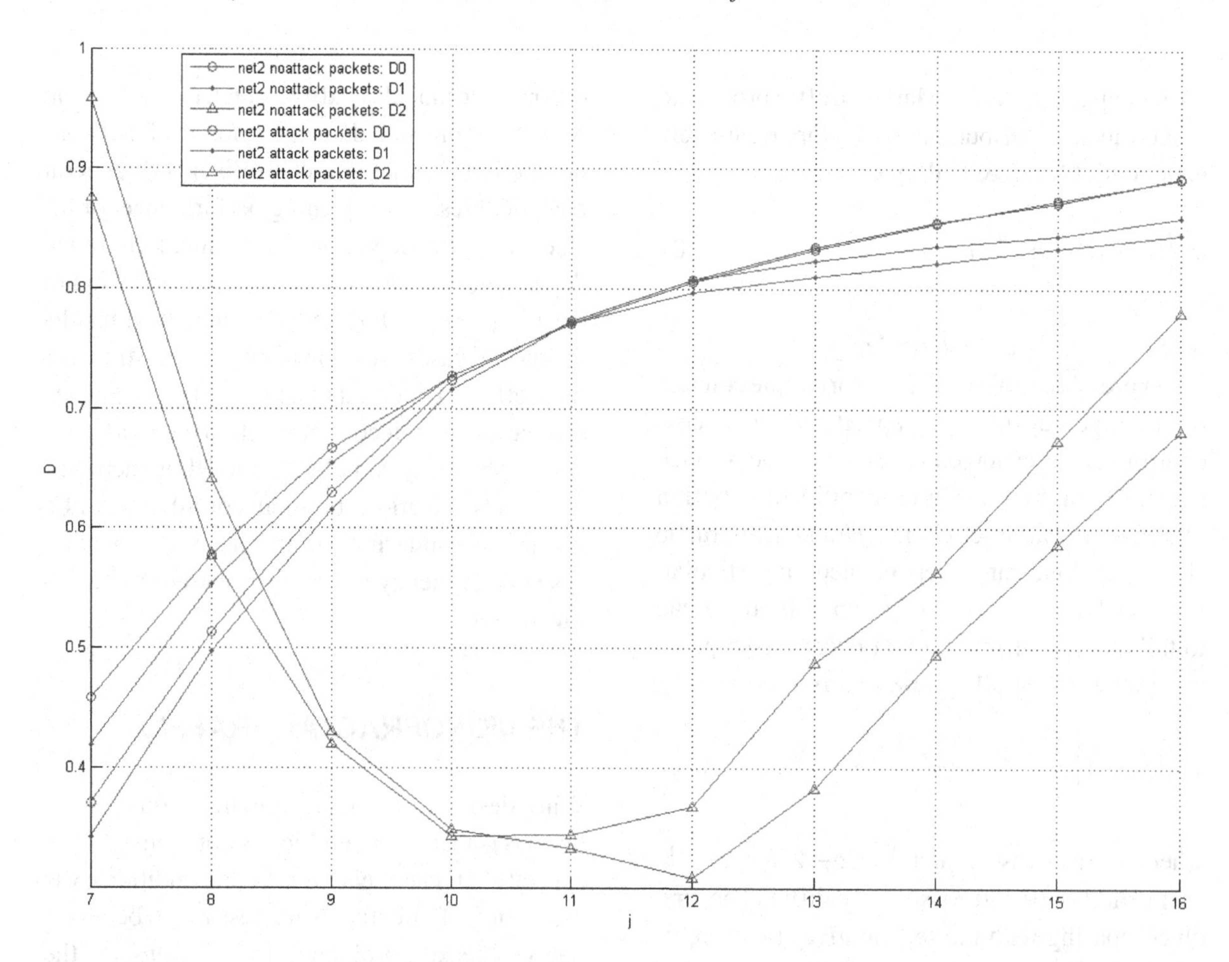

Table 1. Characteristics of the multifractal spectrum: (Realizations without anomalies (N) and those with anomalies (A))

Par.	j = 7		j=8		j=9		j=10		j=11		j=12		j=13		j=14		j=15		j=16	
	N	*A*	*N*	*A*	*N*	*A*	*N*	*A*	*N*	*A*	*N*	*A*	*N*	*A*	*N*	*A*	*N*	*A*	*N*	*A*
D_0	0.370	0.458	0.513	0.577	0.630	0.666	0.723	0.727	0.773	0.771	0.807	0.806	0.835	0.833	0.856	0.854	0.872	0.874	0.893	0.892
D_1	0.342	0.419	0.497	0.553	0.615	0.655	0.715	0.727	0.773	0.771	0.807	0.797	0.823	0.810	0.836	0.821	0.844	0.834	0.859	0.846
D_2	0.959	0.876	0.641	0.576	0.430	0.420	0.348	0.343	0.332	0.344	0.308	0.368	0.383	0.488	0.495	0.564	0.587	0.673	0.682	0.780
α_{min}	0.572	0.478	0.458	0.364	0.352	0.330	0.268	0.290	0.206	0.242	0.158	0.210	0.146	0.184	0.146	0.158	0.136	0.162	0.150	0.184
α_{max}	0.712	0.768	0.654	0.706	0.648	0.680	0.714	0.698	0.766	0.764	0.794	0.822	0.884	0.944	0.988	1.028	1.076	1.122	1.156	1.204

time moment *-t* in the past until a moment in present *t=0*. The so-called workload process $Q(t)$ is the total amount storable in buffer at the interval $(-t\ ;0)$.

Let's define current length of the queue buffer as $Q(t,r)$ which is the queue length in an equilibrium state when the system has been running for a long time and initial queue length has no influence. If such state of system exists (i.e. the supposition of stationarity and ergodicity of workload process is valid) and the state of system stability also satisfied, then

$$Q(t;r) = \sup_{0 \le S \le t} \left(A(t) - A(s) - r(t-s)\right) \quad (32)$$

Here $\left(A(t) - A(s)\right)$ – is the value of workload, received for processing during time interval $\left[s,t\right]$; $r(t-s)$ – is the value of workload processed in the same time interval.

Input process $A(t)$ is considered a fractal process of the type given in (33)

$$A(t) = \lambda^2 t + \sqrt{a^2 \lambda^2 Z(t)} \quad ; t \in (-\infty\ ;+\infty) \quad (33)$$

where $Z(t)$ – is the normalized fractal Brownian motion,

$H \in [1/2;1)$ – is Hurst parameter of process $Z(t)$;

$\lambda > 0$ – is average input intensity;

$a > 0$ – is modification coefficient and

$r > \lambda$ – is service rate.

Equations system (32) and (33) are completely characterized by four parameters: λ, a, H and r. The self-similarity of process $Z(t)$ allows for obtaining more exact ratios between network parameters - buffer length *L*, channel transmission capacity *C* and traffic parameters *r*, *a* and *H* for boundary values from Equation (33).

The analysis of queuing performance with *fBm* input traffic was presented for the first time by Norros (1994), where it was shown that the distribution of queue length can be approximated by Weibull distribution. In was particularly reported by Norros (1994) that the queue tail distribution in the case of a *fBm* input satisfies the equation:

$$\log\left(P\left[Q > L\right]\right) \approx -\frac{1}{2} L^{2(1-H)} r^{2H} \left(1-H\right)^{-2(1-H)} H^{-2H} \quad (34)$$

for sufficiently large values of *L*.

On Figure 13 dependencies of a queue tail approximation on a queue size L in log-log scale are presented at fixed H and r.

$$\log\left(P\left[Q > L\right]\right) = f\left(L\right) = -\log\left[\frac{1}{2}{}^{2} L^{2(1-H)} r^{2H}\left(1-H\right)^{-2(1-H)} H^{-2H}\right]$$

Observable linearity of the graph illustrates probability decay under the Weibull law.

Supposing that the probability $P\left(Q > L\right) = \varepsilon$ and $\rho = r / C$ it is possible to solve (34) *wrt C* and to discover that QoS is roughly reached, when Equation (35) holds

$$C = r + \left\{k\left(H\right)\sqrt{-2\cdot\ln\varepsilon}\right\}^{1/H}\cdot a^{1/2H}\cdot L^{-(1-H)/H}\cdot r^{1/2H} \quad (35)$$

where $k\left(H\right) = H^{H}\cdot\left(1-H\right)^{1-H}$

For practical applications of Equation (35) as the formula determining the size of a channel, considering its sensitivity to a and H becomes something of interest. On Figure 14 channels characteristics with various values of a and H at $r = 2Mb / s, \varepsilon = 10^{-3}$ and for two buffer sizes $L = 100KB and 1MB$. Certainly, the same reservation as well as in the previous figure should be done at strict independence of modification of

Box 1.

$$\log\left(P\left[Q > L\right]\right) \approx \min_{q>0}\log\left\{c\left(q\right)^{2}\frac{\left[\dfrac{L^{2}\tau_0\left(q\right)}{r\left(q-\tau_0\left(q\right)\right)}\right]^{\tau_0(q)}}{\left[\dfrac{L^{2}q}{q-\tau_0\left(q\right)}\right]^{q}}\right\} \quad (36)$$

for sufficiently large values of L, where $\tau_0\left(q\right) = \tau\left(q\right) + 1.$

Figure 13. Dependence of queue tail approximation on a queue size L at a) r = 1 and fixed H, b) r = 5 and fixed H

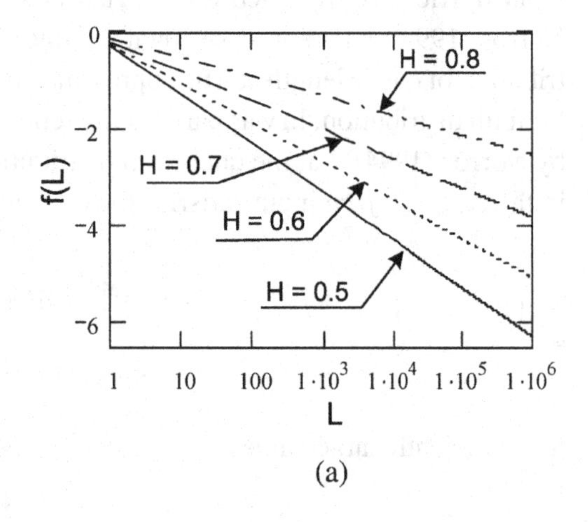

(a)

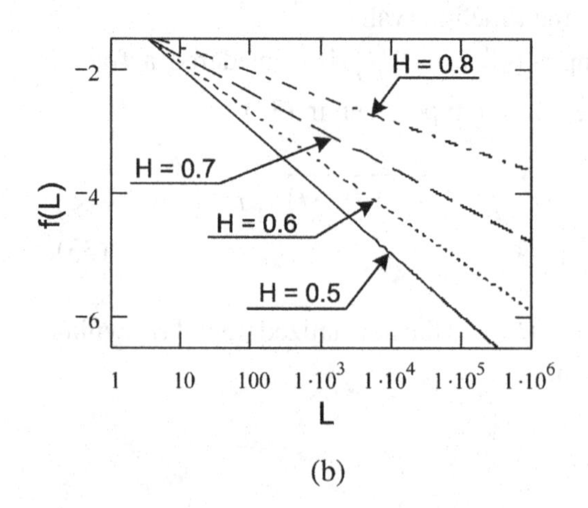

(b)

a and *H*. It is visible however, that when the buffer is small, requirements of the channel depend less on *H* than when the buffer is large. The observable outcome illustrates a well-established fact, that for short-range dependent traffic it is very difficult to fill big buffer sizes.

The obtained results show that queue distribution with *fBm* on an input has much smaller decay than in an exponential case. However, this approach is based on the Gaussian property of input process and cannot be spread to other processes with scale properties. There are only some analytical results for queuing performance for cases when the traffic has more complicated scale behavior. For example, there is a result when the input traffic is asymptotically self-similar and is described by the Pareto distribution, and for the case when Levi's distribution is used to describe the traffic.

TRAFFIC MULTIFRACTAL INFLUENCE ESTIMATION ON QUEUING PERFORMANCE

Queuing performance formulas in cases of Gaussian inbound processes lead to results that conform to the theory. For the generalized multifractal traffic a new practical method is proposed for queuing performance estimation.

APPROXIMATION OF QUEUE'S TAIL PROBABILITY

Researchers in (Dang, 2002) showed that probabilities of queue tail distribution asymptotes for queue construction model with single server and generalized multifractal inbound process are approximated correctly with Equation 36 (see Box 1).

As previously noted, scaling functions $\tau(q)$ and $c(q)$ are functions, which determine the multifractal inbound process. Considering Equation (36) it is evident it has an exact form, and

Figure 14. Transmission capacity of the channel as function of a at r = 2 Mbit\s and fixed; a) for L = 100Kbytes, b) for L = 1 MB

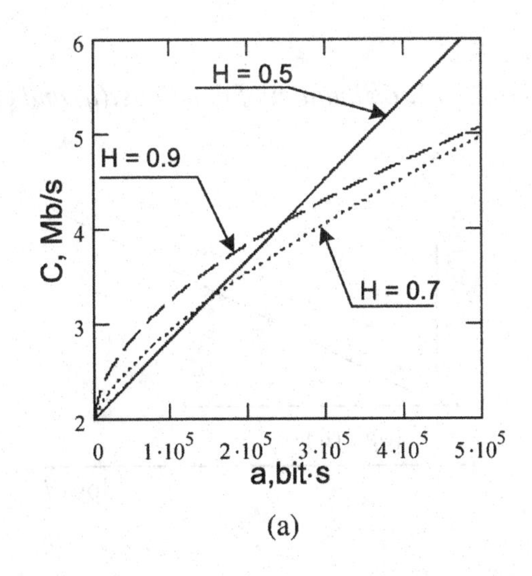

(a)

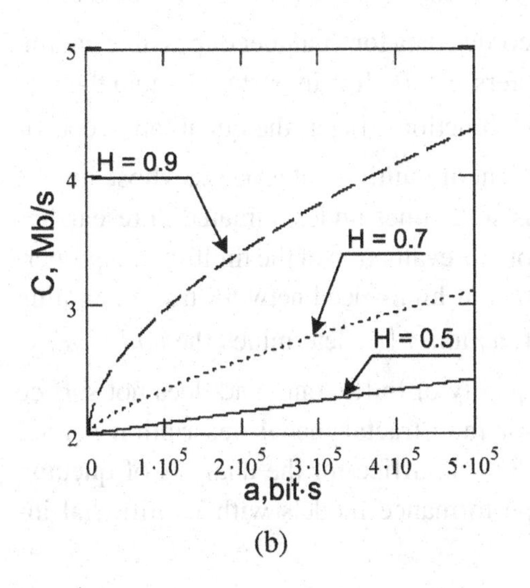

(b)

only determined form of scaling function $\tau_0(q)$ and moment coefficient $c(q)$ could provide a final result. The reason for this consists in the definition of multifractal process class, that doesn't impose any restrictions on functions $c(q)$ and $\tau_0(q)$ (except that $\tau_0(q)$ is a convex function). Investigation of queuing performance systems with summarized multifractal traffic shows that it can provide some similarity with monofractal inbound process generalized results. Equation (36) shows that the queue distribution characteristic in case of multifractal traffic input is completely characterized by the scaling function $\tau_0(q)$ and scale coefficient $c(q)$ of the input traffic.

ESTIMATION METHODOLOGY FOR FUNCTIONS $c(q)$ AND $\tau_0(q)$ IN THE CASE OF ARBITRARY MULTIFRACTAL INBOUND PROCESS

Phase 1: High definition measurement of inbound entry process $X(t)$. Assume that inbound process shows multifractal scaling properties. Then scaling function $\tau(q)$ and function $c(q)$ can be estimated on the basis of recorded data for a number of possible parameters $q > 0$. It is important to note the role of function $c(q)$ as the quantitative coefficient of multifractal process, whose import is sometimes underestimated in researches on the evaluation of the multifractal properties of high-speed network traffic. Scaling function $\tau(q)$ determines the *multiscaling* quality of traffic only and does not suffice for multifractal model description neither does it suffice for the analysis of queuing performance models with multifractal inbound processes. Scaling behavior can be examined by means of wavelet representation methods.

Advantages of wavelet analysis follow from the fact that function of the basal wavelet itself shows a scaling property and consequently composes an optimal *coordinate system*, where it is possible to observe the scaling phenomenon. It likewise provides a stable scale behavior, detection and accurate measurement of parameters that describe this scaling behavior.

We execute the wavelet decomposition of a sequential sample given by

$$X(t):\{x(t_0),x(t_1),\dots,x(t_{N-1})\}$$

of size $n_0 = 2^{Jmax}$,$(n_0 \le N)$, to a scale varying detail function. Here $J_{max} = \log_2 N$ – maximal number of decomposition scales, $\log_2 N$ – integer part of $\log_2 N$.

Scale index value $j = 0$ conforms to a maximum resolution case i.e. the most exact approximation achievable. It equals the original series $X(t)$ consisting of n_0 samples. Conversion to coarser resolution occurs with increase in $j(0<j\le J_{max})$. In accordance with the rules of

Figure 15. Estimation of functions$\tau(q)$ and $c(q)$

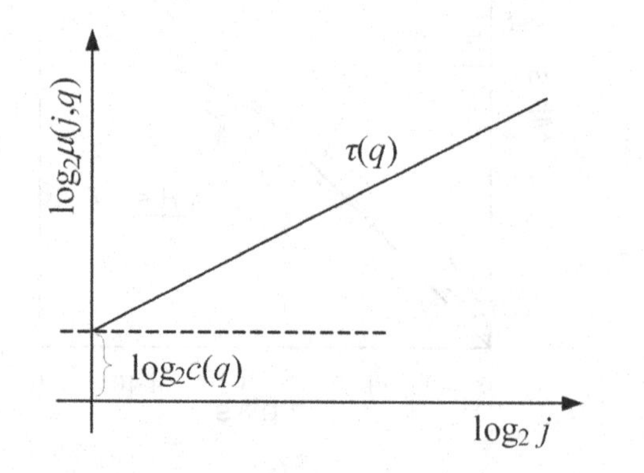

Table 2. Approximation coefficients

Function $\tau(q)$				Function $\log_2 c(q)$			
a_0	a_1	a_2	a_3	c_0	c_1	c_2	c_3
-0.8260	0.4249	-0.0296	0.0012	11.8325	3.9479	0.3873	-0.0160

wavelet analysis, we represent the time series $X(t)$ as follows:

$$X(t) = X_J(t) + \sum_{j=1}^{J} D_j(t)$$

where $X_J(t) = \sum_{k=0}^{n_0/2^J-1} S_{J,k}\,{}^{2}\varphi_{J,k}(t)$ – initial approximation function, conforms to scale J ($J \leq J_{max}$);

$S_{J,k} = < X(t), \varphi_{j,k} >$ – scale coefficient, equals to scalar product of initial series $X(t)$ and scaling function with "*roughest*" scale J, shifted

Figure 16. Traffic data for analysis

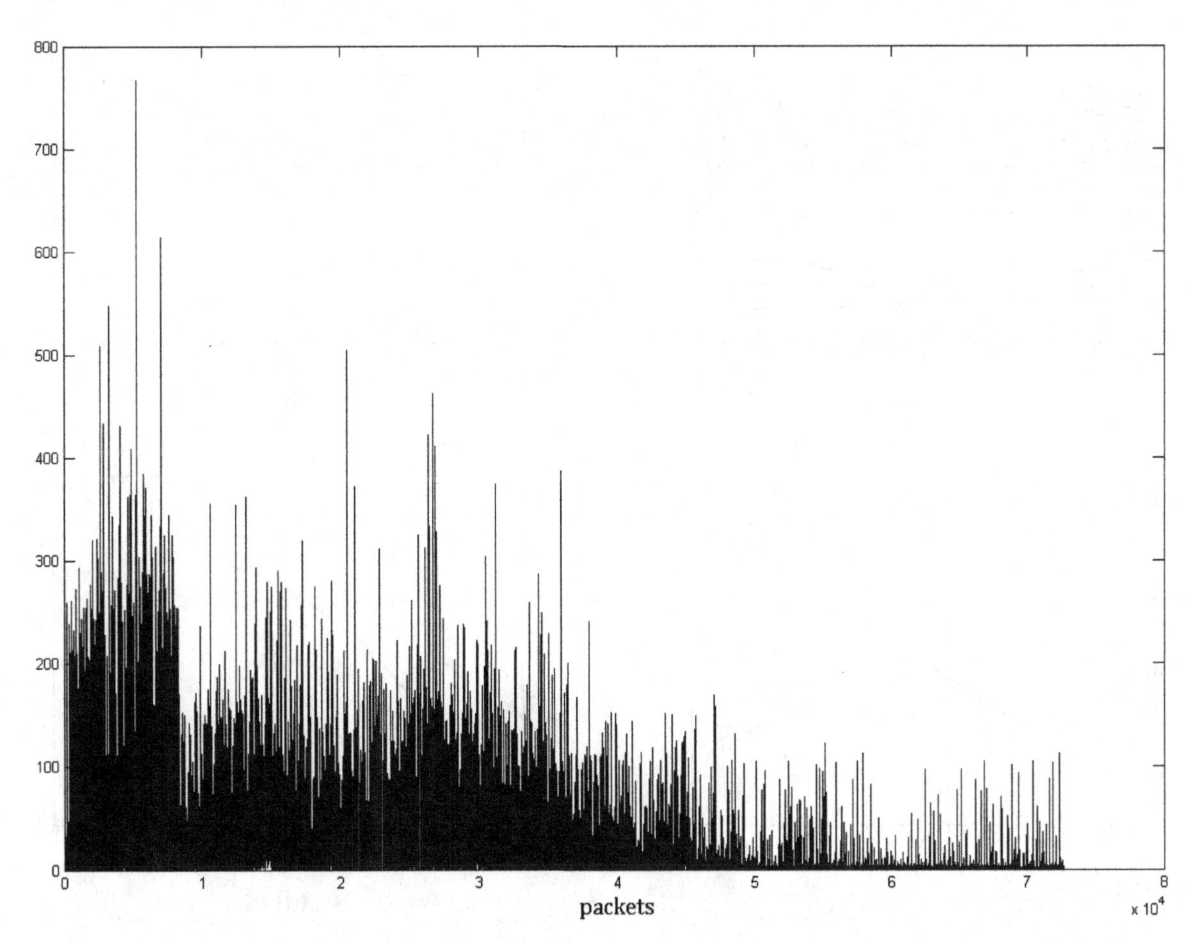

to the right by k scale units from origin of the coordinate system; $D_j(t) = \sum_{k=0}^{n_0/2^j-1} d_{j,k}\,{}^2\psi_{j,k}(t)$ – j-scale order detailed function; $d_{j,k} = < X(t), \psi_{j,k} >$ – wavelet coefficient of scale j, equals scalar product of initial series $X(t)$ and wavelet of scale j, shifted to the right by k scale units from origin of the coordinate system.

The resultant discrete wavelet transform presents a series X of size n on scale j, derived by the means of wavelet coefficients set $d_X(j,k), k=1,2,\ldots,n_j$, where $n_j = 2^{-jn}$ and n – accessible number of wavelet coefficients in octave j.

Phase 2: Definition of qth logarithmic order diagram of the qth moment of octave j:

$$\mu(j,q) = 1 / n_j \sum_{k=1}^{n_j} \left|d_X(j,k)\right|^q \qquad (37)$$

The sum in expression (37) is taken of points in space, where the wavelet transform modulus can take maximum values (i.e. on local maxima

Figure 17. Results of multifractal analysis of sampled data: a) decomposition function $\mu(j,q)$; b) function $\tau(q)$; c) dependence $\log_2 c(q)$; d) multifractal spectra $f(\alpha)$ at $q > 0$

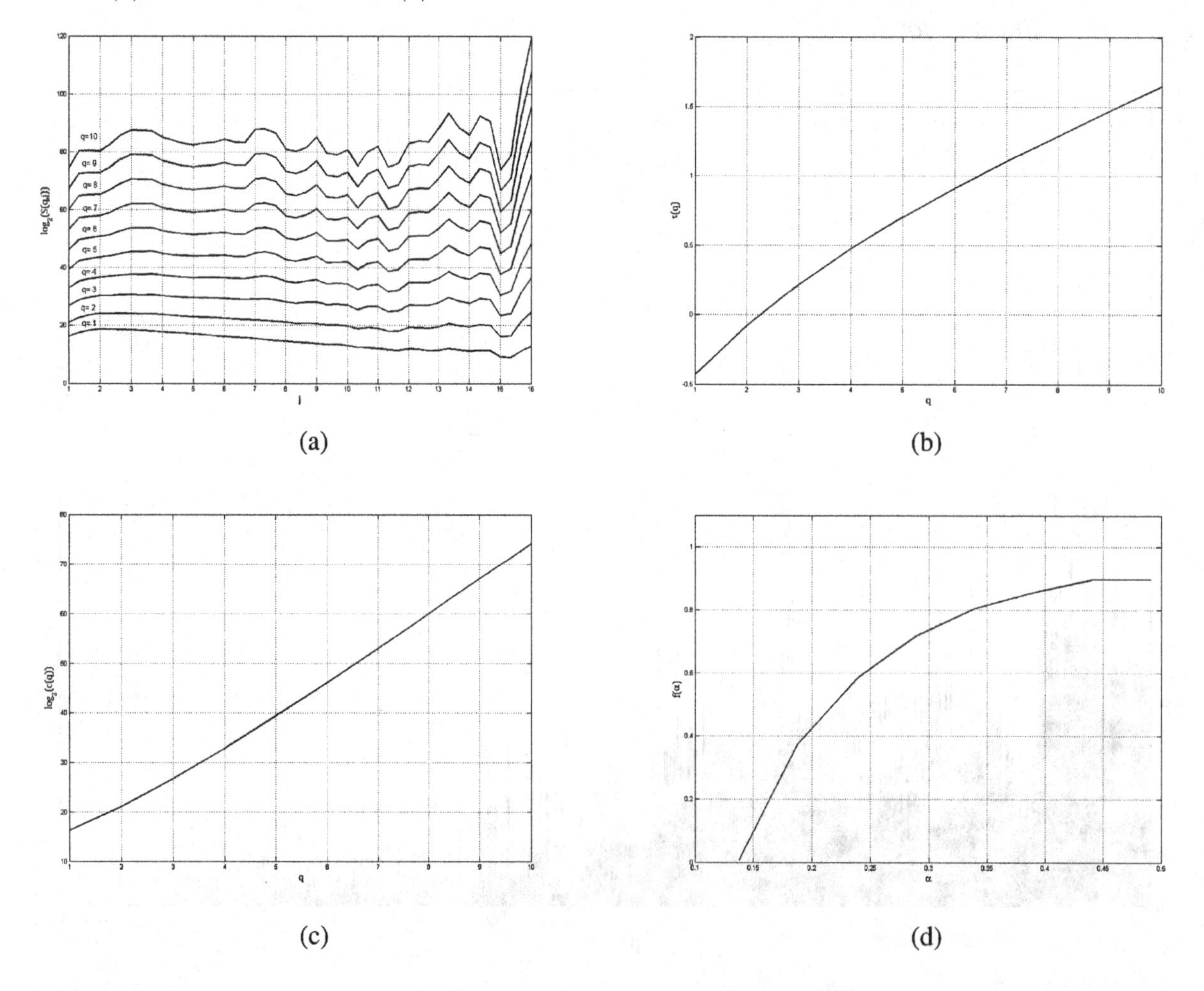

of modulus). Calculations of decomposition function (Renyi's function) allow for a trace of the scaling for large $(q > 0)$ and small $(q < 0)$ fluctuations.

We note once again that the sum of the second moments $\mu(j,q) = 2$ represents a variation of wavelet coefficients at their average value equal to zero. At $q > 0$ function $\mu(j,q) > 0$ describes a scaling of large fluctuations and strong singularities. At negative values of q, it is responsible for scaling of small fluctuations and weak features, thereby showing the sensitivity to different aspects of the dynamics underlying the investigated signal. Linearity of logarithmic diagrams at various orders of the moment q informs on the scaling property of the series, that is

$$\log_2 \mu(j,q) = \tau(q)\ {}^{2}\log_2 j + \log_2 c(q) \tag{38}$$

where $\tau(q)$ is a scaling function, and $c(q) = const.$

The estimation method of $\tau(q)$ and $c(q)$ for the fixed value q is illustrated on Figure 15

This figure shows that the line slope characterises the scaling function $\tau(q)$, and the cut piece on the axis of ordinates is $\log_2 c(q)$. From Figure 15 and expression (38) we have that:

$$\tau(q) = \lim_{j\to\infty} \frac{\log_2 \mu(j,q)}{\log_2 j} \tag{39}$$

Figure 18. Dependences lnP[Q>L] from lnL at r =2 and r = 5

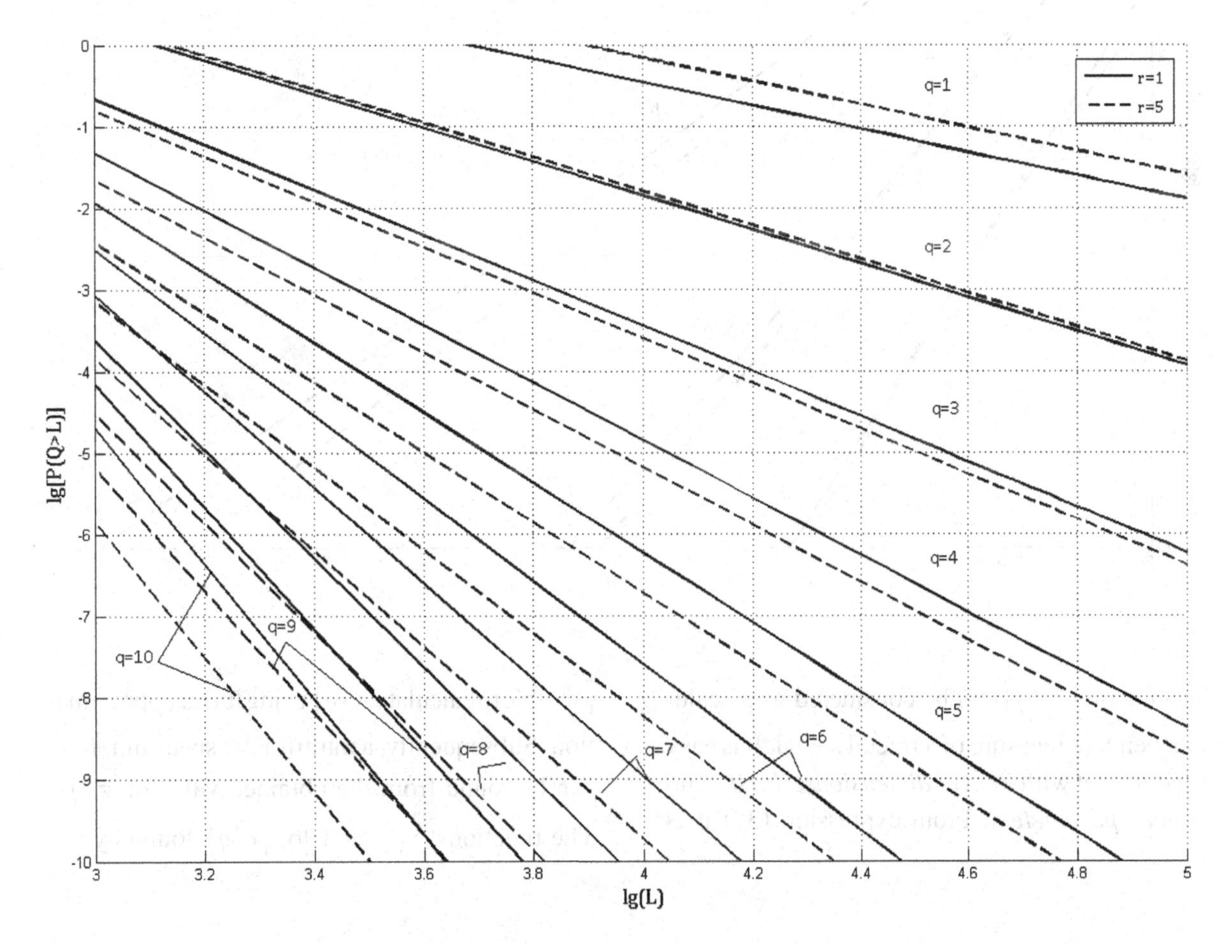

Box 2.

$$\log\left(P\left[Q > L\right]\right) \approx \min_{q>0} \log\left\{\sum_{i=0}^{3} c_i q^i + \tau_0\left(q\right)\log\left[\frac{b^{2}\tau_0\left(q\right)}{s\left(q-\tau_0\left(q\right)\right)}\right] - q\log\left[\frac{b^{2} q}{q-\tau_0\left(q\right)}\right]\right\} \quad (42)$$

where $\tau_0\left(q\right) = \sum_{i=0}^{3} a_i q + 1$

Figure 19. Dependences lnP[Q>L] from q at r =2 and r = 5

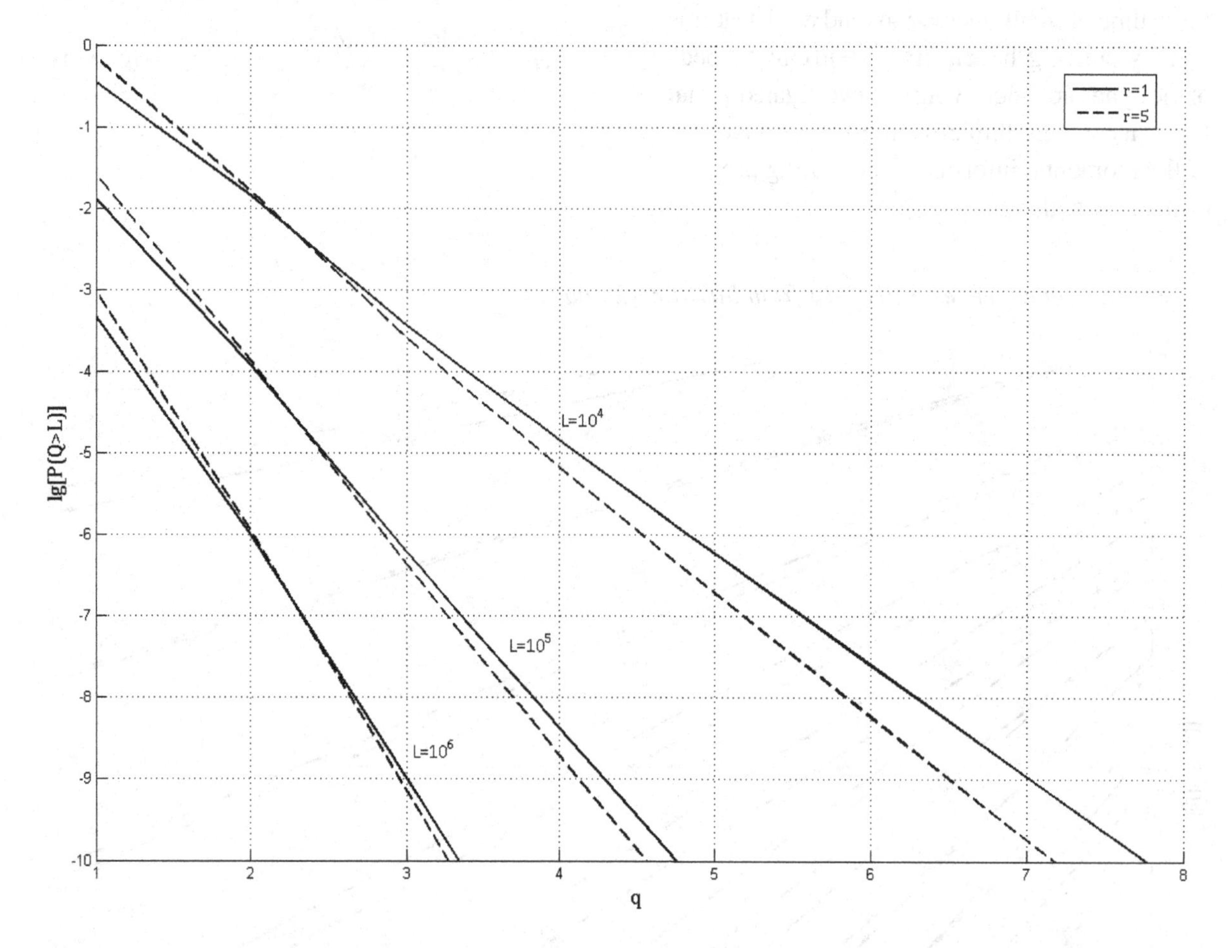

Function $\tau\left(q\right)$ can be considered as a scale-independent measure of a fractal signal. It is easy to connect it with *Renyi's dimensions*, *Hurst's* and *Holder parameters*. From expression (39) it is possible to calculate $\tau\left(q\right)$ using linear approximation. Subsequently, a multifractal spectrum $f(\alpha)$ can be found from the obtained value of $\tau\left(q\right)$. The functions $\tau\left(q\right)$ and $\log_2 c\left(q\right)$ found by numerical estimation can be approximated by the following types of polynomials:

$$\tau\left(q\right) = a_0 + a_1 q + a_2 q^2 + a_3 q^3 \qquad (40)$$

and

$$\log_2 c\left(q\right) = c + cq + cq^2 + c_3 q^3 \qquad (41)$$

Substituting into expression (36), we obtain formulas for estimating the probability of queue "tail" rejection with any kind of multifractal traffic on input (see Box 2).

NUMERICAL RESULTS

Consider the dataset taken from Internet traffic archive (MIT, 1999). The data structure is presented in Figure 16

The raw data was sampled at 1s intervals. The preliminary analysis of these implementations reveals their scaling properties; therefore they have been used as input process for the analysis of queuing performance. A plot of decomposition function of an investigated trace depending on decomposition level on *log-log* graph is shown in Figure 17 for some values of the qth order moment.

Nonlinear scaling function $\tau\left(q\right)$ obtained according to the technique stated above is presented on Figure 17b, it reveals the scaling property of this dataset. After applying the estimation method stated above, functions $\tau_0\left(q\right)$ and $\log_2 c\left(q\right)$ have been calculated. The graph of function $\tau_0\left(q\right) = \tau\left(q\right) + 1$ is a convex curve; this speaks about the multifractal character of the investigated dataset. Parameters of a multifractal spectrum can be estimated from expression $f\ (\alpha)\, at\, q > 0$, and are presented on Figure 2c. Approximation coefficients of functions $\tau\left(q\right)$ and $\log_2 c\left(q\right)$, corresponding to the resulting experimental data are presented in Table 2.

Substituting obtained values of approximation coefficients in expression (42), we obtain the analytical relationships illustrating efficiency of queue service in case of multifractal character of the processed traffic.

Figure 18 and 19 show the probability of exceeding the buffer length at an intensity of service $r = 2$ and $r = 5$ for the studied traffic with moment coefficient q taking values from 1 to 10. From these graphs it follows that the probability of dropping the "tail" for the traffic studied is much higher than the similar probability in the case of a fractional Brownian motion.

The conclusion, which follows from the presented relationships, is that the multifractal nature of traffic at the input buffer device has a significant influence on the characteristics of queuing. The largest component of the influence of multifractal traffic is observed for a moment coefficient value of $q = 2$, with increasing q its impact on quality of service decreases. In actual use, it is sufficient to restrict the values of $q = 2\ \ldots 5$.

CONCLUSION

For detection of traffic anomalies in computer and telecommunication networks the method based on multifractal data analysis at network layer is proposed. As the informative indicator, the use of distinction of fractal dimensions on various parts of a given dataset is introduced, and also parameters of a singularity spectrum estimated by means of Legendre transform.

A new method based on usage of multifractal spectrum parameters is proposed for the estimation of queuing performance for the generalized multifractal traffic on an input of buffer device. It is shown that multifractal character of the traffic has essential impact on queuing performance characteristics. The greatest influence is caused by a component of the multifractal traffic with moment coefficient $q = 2$. With increasing q its impact on quality of service decreases. In actual use, it is sufficient to restrict the values of $q = 2 \ldots 5$.

REFERENCES

Bacry, E., Muzy, J. F., & Arneodo, A. (1993). Singularity spectrum of fractal signals: Exact results. *Journal of Statistical Physics*, *70*(3/4), 635–674. doi:10.1007/BF01053588.

Bozhokin, S. V., & Parshin, D. A. (2001). *Fractals and multifractals* [Regularnaya i haoticheskaya dinamika]. Izhevsk, Russia: NIC.

Brichet, F., Roberts, J., Simonian, A., & Veitch, D. (1996). Heavy traffic analysis of a storage model with long range dependent on/off sources. *Queueing Systems*, *23*, 197–215. doi:10.1007/BF01206557.

Dang, T. D. (2002). *New results in multifractal traffic analysis and modeling*. (Ph.D. Dissertation). Budapest, Hungary.

Feldmann, A., Gilbert, A. C., & Willinger, W. (1998). Data networks as cascades: Investigating the multifractal nature of internet WAN traffic. *ACM SIGCOMM Computer Communication Review*, *28*(4), 42–55. doi:10.1145/285243.285256.

Giordano, S., O'Connell, N., Pagano, M., & Procissi, G. (1999). A variational approach to the queuing analysis with fractional brownian motion input traffic. In *Proceedings of the 7th IFIP Workshop on Performance Modelling and Evaluation of ATM Networks*. Antwerp, Belgium: IFIP.

Hwang, W. L., & Mallat, S. (1994). Characterization of self-similar multifractals with wavelet maxima. *Journal of Applied and Computational Harmonic Analysis*, *1*, 316–328. doi:10.1006/acha.1994.1018.

Jaffard, S. (1997). Multifractal formalism for functions parts I and II. *SIAM Journal on Mathematical Analysis*, *28*(4), 944–998. doi:10.1137/S0036141095282991.

Lui, Z., Nain, P., Towsley, D., & Zhang, Z. L. (1999). Asymptotic behavior of a multiplexer fed by a long-range dependent process. *Journal of Applied Probability*, *36*, 105–118. doi:10.1239/jap/1032374233.

Mallat, S. (2005). *A wavelet tour of signal processing: The sparse way* (3rd ed.). New York: Academic Press.

Mandelbrot, B. (1982). *The fractal geometry of nature*. San Francisco, CA: Freeman.

Meyer, Y. (1997). *Wavelets, vibrations, and scalings*. Montreal, Canada: Universite de Montreal.

MIT Lincoln Laboratory. (2012). *1999 DARPA intrusion detection evaluation dataset*. Retrieved from http://www.ll.mit.edu/mission/communications/ist/corpora/ideval/data/index.html

Muzy, J. F., Bacry, E., & Arneodo, A. (1994). The muitifractal formalism revisited with wavelets. *International Journal of Bifurcation and Chaos in Applied Sciences and Engineering*, *4*, 245. doi:10.1142/S0218127494000204.

Muzy, J. F., Bacry, E., & Arneodo, A. (1999). Wavelets and multifractal formalism for singularity signals: Application to turbulence data. *Physical Review Letters*, *67*(25), 3515–3518. doi:10.1103/PhysRevLett.67.3515.

Norros, I. (1994). A storage model with self-similar input. *Queueing Systems*, *16*, 387–396. doi:10.1007/BF01158964.

Park, K., & Willinger, W. (Eds.). (1999). *Self-similar network traffic and performance evaluation*. New York: Wiley-Interscience.

Riedi, R. H., Crouse, M. S., Ribeiro, V. J., & Baraniuk, R. G. (1999). A multifractal wavelet model with application to network traffic. *IEEE Transactions on Information Theory*, *45*(3). doi:10.1109/18.761337.

Shannon, C. E. (1948). A mathematical theory of communication. *The Bell System Technical Journal*, *27*, 379–423, 623–656.

Sheluhin, O. I., & Atayero, A. A. (2012). Detection of DoS and DDoS attacks in information communication networks with discrete wavelet analysis. *International Journal of Computer Science and Information Scurity*, *10*(1), 53–57.

Sheluhin, O. I., Atayero, A. A., & Garmashev, A. V. (2011). Detection of teletraffic anomalies using multifractal analysis. *International Journal of Advancements in Computing Technology*, *3*(4), 174–182. doi:10.4156/ijact.vol3.issue4.19.

Sheluhin, O. I., Smolskiy, S. M., & Osin, A. V. (2007). *Self-similar processes in telecommunications*. New York: John Wiley & Sons. doi:10.1002/9780470062098.

ADDITIONAL READING

Bakhoum & Toma. (2010). Mathematical transform of traveling-wave equations and phase aspects of quantum interaction. *Mathematical Problems in Engineering*. doi: doi:10.1155/2010/695208.

Beran. (1994). Statistics for long-memory processes. In *Monographs on Statistics and Applied Probability*. New York, NY: Chapmand and Hall.

Cattani & Kudreyko. (2008). On the discrete harmonic wavelet transform. *Mathematical Problems in Engineering*.

Cattani & Kudreyko. (2010). Application of periodized harmonic wavelets towards solution of eigenvalue problems for integral equations. *Mathematical Problems in Engineering*.

Cattani. (2009). Harmonic wavelet analysis of a localized fractal. *International Journal of Engineering and Interdisciplinary Mathematics, 1*.

Gong, Liu, Misra, & Towsley. (2005). Self-similarity and long range dependence on the internet: A second look at the evidence, origins, and implications. *Computer Networks*, *48*(3), 377–399. doi:10.1016/j.comnet.2004.11.026.

He & Leung. (2008). Network intrusion detection using CFAR abrupt-change detectors. *IEEE Transactions on Instrumentation and Measurement*, *57*(3), 490–497. doi:10.1109/TIM.2007.910108.

Leland, Taqqu, Willinger, & Wilson. (1994). On the self-similar nature of ethernet traffic. *IEEE/ACM Transactions on Networking*, *2*(1), 1–15. doi:10.1109/90.282603.

Li, Li, & Zhao. (2009). Experimental study of DDOS attacking of flood type based on NS2. *International Journal of Electronics and Computers*, *1*(2), 143–152.

Li & Lim. (2008). Modeling network traffic using generalized Cauchy process. *Physica A*, *387*(11), 2584–2594. doi:10.1016/j.physa.2008.01.026.

Li & Zhao. (2008). Detection of variations of local irregularity of traffic under DDOS flood attack. *Mathematical Problems in Engineering*.

Li & Zhao. (2010). Representation of a stochastic traffic bound. *IEEE Transactions on Parallel and Distributed Systems*, *21*(9), 1368–1372. doi:10.1109/TPDS.2009.162.

Li & Zhao. (2010). Variance bound of ACF estimation of one block of fGn with LRD. *Mathematical Problems in Engineering*.

Li. (2004). An approach to reliably identifying signs of DDOS flood attacks based on LRD traffic pattern recognition. *Computers and Security, 23*(7), 549–558.

Li. (2006). Change trend of averaged Hurst parameter of traffic under DDOS flood attacks. *Computers and Security, 25*(3), 213–220.

Li. (2010). Fractal time series: A tutorial review. *Mathematical Problems in Engineering*.

Paxson & Floyd. (1995). Wide area traffic: The failure of Poisson modeling. *IEEE/ACM Transactions on Networking*, *3*(3), 226–244. doi:10.1109/90.392383.

Rohani, M. Selamat, & Kettani (Eds.). (2008). *Proceedings from ICCCE '08: Continuous LoSS detection using iterative window based on SOSS model and MLS approach: International Conference on Computer and Communication Engineering*. Kuala Lumpur, Malaysia: ICCCE.

Sastry, Rawat, Pujari, & Gulati. (2007). Network traffic analysis using singular value decomposition and multiscale transforms. *Information Sciences*, *177*(23), 5275–5291. doi:10.1016/j.ins.2006.07.007.

Schleifer & Mannle. (2001). Online error detection through observation of traffic self-similarity. *IEE Proceedings. Communications*, *148*(1), 38–42. doi:10.1049/ip-com:20010063.

Sheluhin, & Atayero. (2012). Detection of DoS and DDoS attacks in information communication networks with discrete wavelet analysis. *International Journal of Computer Science and Information Security, 10*(1), 53-57.

Song, Ng, & Tang. (2004). Some results on the self-similarity property in communication\networks. *IEEE Transactions on Communications*, *52*(10), 1636–1642. doi:10.1109/TCOMM.2004.833136.

Tickoo & Sikdar. (2003). On the impact of IEEE 802.11 MAC on traffic characteristics. *IEEE Journal on Selected Areas in Communications*, *21*(2), 189–203. doi:10.1109/JSAC.2002.807346.

Toma. (2010). Specific differential equations for generating pulse sequences. *Mathematical Problems in Engineering*.

Wang & Yang. (2008). An intelligent method for real-time detection of DDoS attack based on fuzzy logic. *Journal of Electronics (China)*, *25*(4), 511–518. doi:10.1007/s11767-007-0056-6.

Chapter 3
The Switched Local Area Networks' Delay Problem:
Issues and a Deterministic Solution Approach

Monday O. Eyinagho
Covenant University, Nigeria

Samuel O. Falaki
Federal University of Technology Akure, Nigeria

ABSTRACT

A large number of installed local area networks are sluggish in terms of speed of uploading and downloading of information. Researchers have, therefore, proposed the need for such networks to be designed with specified maximum end-to-end delay. This is because, if the maximum packet delay between any two nodes of a network is not known, it is impossible to provide a deterministic guarantee of worst case response times of packets' flows. Therefore, the need for analytic and formal basis for designing such networks becomes very imperative. In this regard, this chapter has discussed the switched local area networks' delay problem and related issues. It compared the two principal approaches for determining the end-to-end response times of flows in communication networks – stochastic approach and deterministic approach. The chapter goes on to demonstrate the superiority of the latter approach by using it to develop and validate the goodness of a general maximum delay packet switch model.

INTRODUCTION

The rapid establishments of standards relating to Local Area Networks (LANs), coupled with the development by major semi-conductor manufacturers of inexpensive chipsets for interfacing computers to them has resulted in LANs forming the basis of almost all commercial, research and university data communication networks. As the applications of LANs have grown, so are the demands on them in terms of throughput and reliability. (Halsall, 1992, p. 308) The literature on LANs

DOI: 10.4018/978-1-4666-2208-1.ch003

is almost in a flux. However, a common challenge that has been confronting researchers for a long time now, is, how to tackle the problem of slow response of local area networks. Slow response of such networks means packets' flows from one host (origin host) to another host (destination host) takes longer time than is necessary for comfort at certain times of the day. In this regard, switched networks were quite recent developments by the computer networking community in attempts at solving this slow response challenge. While the introduction of switched networks have reduced considerably this slow response (and, hence, long delay) problem, it has not completely eliminated it. This has elicited researches into switched networks in efforts at totally eliminating this problem. These researches have been said to be important in the present dispensation because of the deployment and/or the increased necessity to deploy real-time applications on these networks. In the next and succeeding sections, theoretical concepts that are important for an understanding of the switched LANs' delay problem, and of some aspects of the solutions approaches that has been adopted by our research team are discussed. In this regard, the network calculus and traditional queuing approaches to modeling network traffic are compared and contrasted, and some elementary network components, which were proposed and characterized by Cruz (1991) are described. The chapter then went on to describe a maximum delay model of a packet switch, which, was shown to be good for the practical engineering of local area networks that meets specified maximum end-to-end delay constraints.

BACKGROUND

The design of switched networks has largely been based on experience and heuristics. Experience has shown that, the network is just installed, switches randomly placed as the need arises, without any load analysis and load computation; there are usually no performance specifications to be met. This approach, frequently leads to expensive systems that fail to satisfy end users in terms of speed in uploading and downloading of information (Kanem et al., 1999; Torab and Kanem, 1999). In other words, this approach, usually leads to long networks' delays. According to Gallo and Wilder (1981), in a network, the arrival of information in real-time to the destination point at a specified time is a critical issue. In the view of Fowler and Leland (1991), there are times when a network appears to be more congestion-prone (incurring long packets' delays) than at other times. Falaki and Sorensen (1992) has also once averred that, there have always been a need for a basic understanding of the causes of communication delays in distributed systems on a Local Area Network (LAN).

THE DELAYS IN COMPUTER NETWORKS

One fundamental characteristics of a packet-switched network is the delay required to deliver a packet from a source to a destination. (Bolot, 1993) Each packet generated by a source is routed to the destination via a sequence of intermediate nodes; the end-to-end delay is, thus, the sum of the delays experienced at each hop on the way to the destination. (Bolot, 1993) Each such delay in turn consists of two components (Ming-Yang et al., 2004; Bolot, 1993; Bertsekas and Gallager, 1992, p. 150);

1. A fixed component which includes:
    a. The transmission delay at the node,
    b. The propagation delay on the link to the next node,
2. A variable component which includes:
    a. The processing delay at the node,
    b. The queuing delay at the node.

Transmission delay is the time required to transmit a packet (Gerd, 1989, p. 110), it is the time between when the first bit and the last bit are transmitted. (Bertsekas and Gallager, 1992, p. 150) Propagation delay is the time between when the last bit is transmitted at the head node of a link and the time when the last bit is received at the tail node. (Bertsekas & Gallager, 1992, p. 150) Processing delay is the time required for nodal equipment to perform the necessary processing and switching (Comer, 2004, p. 244) of data (packets in packet switched networks) at a node. (Bertsekas & Gallager, 1992, p. 150; Gerd, 1989, p. 110) Included here are error detection and address recognition, and transfer of packet to the output queue. (Gerd, 1989, p. 110) Queuing delay is the time between when the packet is assigned to a queue for transmission and when it starts being transmitted; during this time, the packet waits while other packets in the transmission queue are transmitted. (Bertsekas & Gallager, 1992, p. 150) The queuing delay has the most adverse effect on packet delay in a switched network (Song, 2001).

Two other types of delays identified by Gerd (1989, p. 240), are, the waiting time at the buffers associated with the source and destination stations and the processing delays at these stations; this was called thinking time in (Jasperneite & Ifak, 2001). But these are usually not part of end-to-end delay (see previous definition of end-to-end delay), since in a way, by simply having hosts of high buffer and processing capacities, delays associated with the host stations can be minimized. Moreover, the capacities of host stations are not part of the factors that are put into consideration when engineering local area networks. As argued by Costa et al. (2004), the message processing time consumed in source and destination hosts is not included in the calculation of end-to-end delay because these times are not directly related to the physical conditions of the network. Access delays occur when a number of hosts share a medium and hence may wait in turns to use the medium (Comer, 2004, p. 244); but this delay does not apply to switched networks.

While propagation and switching delays are often negligible, queuing delay is not (Bertsekas & Gallager, 1992, p. 150; Ersoy & Panwar, 1993; Georges et al., 2005). Inter-nodal propagation delay is negligible for local area networks (Mann & Terplan, 1999, p. 247; Gerd, 1989, p. 110), propagation delays are neglected in delay computations even in wide area networks because of its negligibility. (Bertsekas & Gallager, 1992, p. 15) It is, therefore, reasonable to neglect propagation delays when computing end-to-end delays.

SWITCHED LOCAL AREA NETWORKS AND THE NETWORK DELAY PROBLEM

Local Area Networks made a dramatic entry into the communications scene in the late 1970s and early 1980s. (Bertsekas & Gallager, 1992, p. 2; Gerd, 1989, p. 13) The manner in which the nodes of a network are geometrically arranged and connected is known as the topology of the network and local area networks are commonly characterized in terms of their topology. (Bertsekas & Gallager, 1992, p. 146; Gerd, 1989, p. 50) A family of standards for LANs was developed by IEEE to enable equipment of a variety of manufacturers to interface to one another; this is called the IEEE 802 standard family. This standard defines three types of media-access technologies and the associated physical media, which, can be used for a wide range of particular applications or system objectives. (Bertsekas & Gallager, 1992, p. 54) The standards that relate to baseband LANs are the IEEE-802.3 standard for baseband CSMA/CD bus LANs, and IEEE 802.5 token ring local area networks. Several variations on IEEE 802.3 now exist. The original implementation of the IEEE 802.3 standard is the Ethernet system; this operates at 10Mb/sec. This original Ethernet, referred to as Thicknet, is also known as the IEEE 802.3 Type 10-Base-5 standard. A more limited abbreviated version of the original Ethernet is known as Thinnet or Cheapernet or IEEE 802.3 Type 10-Base-2 standard. Thinnet also operates at 10Mb/sec, but uses a thinner, less expensive coaxial cable for interconnecting stations such as personal computers and workstations. A third variation originated from Star LAN, which was developed by AT&T and uses unshielded, twisted-pair cable which is often already installed in office buildings for telephone lines (Bertsekas & Gallager, 1992, p. 364; Michael & Richard, 2003, p. 220), and the first version was formally known as IEEE 802.3 Type 10-Base-T. There has been other versions of the twisted pair Ethernet – Fast Ethernet (100-Base-T or IEEE 802.3u), Gigabit Ethernet (1000-Base-T or IEEE 802.3z). Instead of a shared medium, twisted pair Ethernet wiring scheme uses an electronic device known as a hub in place of a shared cable; electronic components in the hub emulate a physical cable, making the entire system operate like a conventional Ethernet.

Ethernet, in its original implementation, is a branching broadcast communication system for carrying data packets among locally distributed computing stations. The thicknet, thinnet and hub-based twisted-pair Ethernet are all shared-medium networks. (Song, 2001) That is, traditional Ethernet (which these three types of Ethernet represent), in which all hosts compete for the same bandwidth is called shared Ethernet. Because access to the shared medium by the attached hosts' are random in nature, packets' collisions in the medium are inevitable. The Carrier Sense Multiple Access with Collision Detection (CSMA/CD) protocol was therefore, developed to control access of the interconnected stations to the shared medium; but this result in a non-deterministic access delay, since, after every collision, a station waits a random delay before it retransmits. (Bolot, 1993) The probability of collision depends on the number of stations in a collision domain and the network load. (Georges et al., 2005; Song, 2001) Moreover, the number of stations attached to a shared-medium Ethernet LAN cannot be increased indefinitely; as eventually, the traffic generated by the stations will approach the limit of the shared transmission medium. (Alberto & Widjaja, 2004, p. 433) One traditional way to decrease the collision probability is to reduce the size of the collision domain by forming micro-segments separated by bridges (Song, 2001). This is where switches come in, as functionally, switches can be considered as multi-port bridges. (Bejerano, et al., 2003; Song, 2001)

A Switched Ethernet, therefore, is an Ethernet/802.3 LAN that uses switches to connect individual nodes or segments. On switched Ethernet networks where nodes are directly connected to switches with full-duplex links, the communications become point-to-point. That is, a switched Ethernet/802.3 LAN isolates network traffic between sending and receiving nodes. In this configuration, switches break up collision domains into small groups of devices, effectively reducing the number of collision (Georges et al., 2005; Song, 2001) Furthermore, with micro-segmentation with full-duplex links, each device is isolated in its own segment in full-duplex mode and has the entire port throughput for its own use; collisions are therefore, eliminate (Jasperneite & Ifak, 2001) The CSMA/CD protocol does not therefore, play any role in switched Ethernet networks (Anurag et al., 2004, p. 102). The collision problem is thus shifted to congestion in switches. (Georges et al., 2005; Song, 2001; Kanem et al., 1999) This is, because, switched Ethernet transforms traditional Ethernet/802.3 LAN from broadcast technology to a point-to-point technology. The congestion in such switches is a function of their loading (number of hosts connected) (Georges et al., 2005); in fact, loading increases as more people log on to a network (Falaki & Sorensen, 1992), and congestion occurs when the users of the network collectively demand more resources than the network can offer. (Bertsekas & Gallager, 1992, p. 27).

According to Trulove (2000, p. 143), LAN switching has done much to overcome the limitations of shared LANs; however, despite the vast increase in bandwidth provision per user that this represents over and above a shared LAN scenario, there is still contention in the network leading to unacceptable delay characteristics. For example, multiple users connected to a switch may demand file transfers from several servers connected via 100 Mb/sec Fast Ethernet to the backbone. Each Server may send a burst of packets that temporarily overwhelms the Fast Ethernet uplink to the wiring closet. A queue will form in the backbone switch that is driving this link and any voice or video packet being sent to the same wiring closet will have to wait their turn behind the data packets in this queue. The resultant delays will compromise the perceived quality of the voice or video transmission.

MITIGATING THE EFFECTS OF THE SWITCHED LOCAL AREA NETWORKS' DELAY PROBLEM

The path transversed by a packet through a network can be modeled as a sequence of queuing system (Alberto & Widjaja, 2004, p. 539; Torab & Kanem, 1999); this is illustrated in Figure 1. The dashed arrows show packets from other flows that may 'interfere' with the packet of interest in the sense of contending for buffers and transmission along the path. It should be noted that these interfering flows may enter at one node and depart at some later node, since they belong to different origin-destination pairs and follow different paths through the network.

The performance experienced by a packet along the path is the accumulation of the performances experienced along the N queuing systems; for example, the total end-to-end delay is the sum of the individual delays experienced at each system. (Alberto & Widjaja, 2004, p. 539) If we can guarantee that the delay at each system can be kept below some upper bound, then the end-to-end delay can be kept below the sum of the upper bounds. (Alberto & Widjaja, 2004, p. 540)

It is easy to see from Figure 1 that, a reasonable way to mitigate the effects of network delay problem on a switched LAN is to upper bound the end-to-end packet delay of each origin-destination path. The reason for this is that, if the end-to-end packet delay of a given network is upper bounded, then under no network loading condition will a packet's end-to-end delay exceed the upper bound. Therefore, to determine the maximum end-to-end delays from all origins to all destinations of a switched communication system (a path is illustrated in Figure 1), we must add the different maximum delays at each switch from all origins to all destinations if we know the number of switches on each route from origin to destination. (Alberto & Widjaja, 2004, p. 539; Torab & Kanem, 1999) Therefore, all we need to do in order to make this to be possible, is, to develop a maximum packet delay model for an arbitrary N-port packet switch.

Figure 1. The end-to-end QoS of a packet switch along a line transversing N queuing systems (source: Alberto & Widjaja, 2004, p. 539)

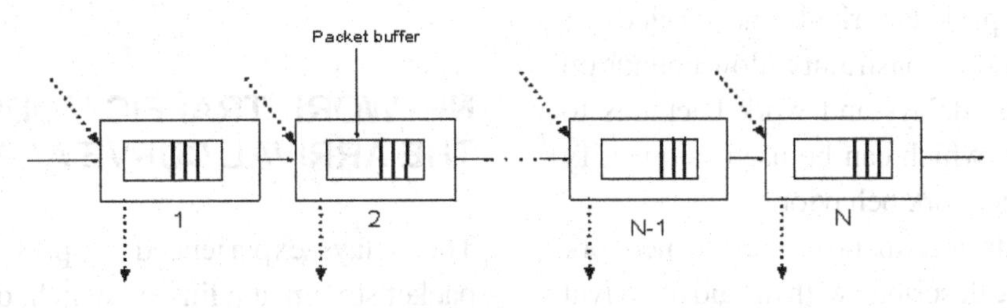

MODELING OF TRAFFIC FLOWS IN COMMUNICATION NETWORKS FOR NETWORK DELAY COMPUTATION PURPOSES: NETWORK CALCULUS VERSUS TRADITIONAL QUEUING THEORY

To determine the end-to-end response time of flows in a communication network two general approaches can be used: stochastic approaches or deterministic approaches. Stochastic approaches consist in determining the mean behavior of the considered network, leading to mean statistical or probabilistic end-to-end response times; while deterministic approaches are based on a worst-case analysis of the network behavior, leading to worst-case end-to-end response times. (Georges et al., 2005; Martin et al., 2005) This is because, stochastic processes are processes with events that can be described by probability functions; while a deterministic process is a process whose behavior is certain and completely known. Network calculus is a deterministic approach to modeling network entities and flows, while, queuing theory has traditionally been used for the same purpose. The advantages of the Network Calculus over the Traditional Queuing Theory can be put in the following compact form (Jasperneite et al., 2002; Bertsekas & Gallager, 1992, p. 149; Reiser, 1982):

NETWORK CALCULUS

1. Network calculus basically considers networks of service nodes and packets' flows between the nodes.
2. Network calculus involves bounded constraints on packets arrivals and services.
3. These bounded constraints allow bounds on the packets' delays and work backlogs to be derived, which can be used to quantify real-time network behavior.
4. The packets arrival processes in network calculus are described with the aid of arrival curves, which quantify constraints on the number of packets or the number of bits of a packet flow in a time interval at a service node.

TRADITIONAL QUEUING THEORY

1. Traditional queuing theory deals with stochastic processes and probability distributions.
2. Traditional queuing theory normally yields mean values and perhaps quantiles of distributions.
3. The derivations of these mean values and quantiles of distributions are often difficult.
4. Upper bounds on end-to-end delays may not exist or be computable.

Generally, the deterministic methodology which the network calculus represents considers the worst case performance of the network and, therefore, yields conservative results. (Anurag et al., 2004, p. 127) Network calculus has traditionally been used for scheduling and traffic regulation problems in order to improve Quality of Service (QoS); but it is now more and more being used to study switched Ethernet networks. (for example, Georges et al., 2005, 2003, 2002; Jasperneite et al., 2002) Network calculus can be used to engineer Internet networks. (Jasperneite et al., 2002) In end-to-end deterministic network calculus approach, input processes are characterized via envelops, network elements are characterized via service curves, and it is useful for the engineering of networks if worst-case guarantees are required. (Anurag et al., 2004, p. 252)

NETWORK TRAFFIC MODELING: THE ARRIVAL CURVE APPROACH

The delays experienced by packets of a given packet stream at a link or switch, depends on the pattern of arrivals in the stream (arriving instants and the number of bits in the arriving packets) and in the case of a link, on the way the link transmits packets from the stream (the link may be shared in some way between two or more packet streams). To analyze such situations, we use mathematical models that are variously called traffic models, congestion models, or queuing models. (Anurag et al., 2004, p. 120)

The modeling of network traffic is traditionally done using stochastic models (Georges et al., 2005; Bertsekas & Gallager, 1992, p. 149); for example, Bernoulli arrival process was assumed in (Song, 2001). But in order to guarantee bounded end-to-end delay for any traffic flow, the traffic itself has to be bounded. (Georges et al., 2003) This is where the arrival curve concept of traffic arrivals to a system is important. In integrated service networks (ATM and other integrated service internet), the concept of arrival curves is used to provide guarantees to data flows. (Le Boudec & Thiran, 2004) In this approach (arrival curve), the traffic is unknown, but it is assumed that its arrival satisfies a time constraint. Generally, this means that the quantity of data that has arrived before time t will not be more than the arrival curve value at time t. The constraints are normally specified by a regulation method; for example, the leaky bucket controller (regulation).

LEAKY BUCKET CONTROLLER

The arrival curve concept can be viewed as an abstraction of the regulation algorithm, and the most common example of traffic regulation algorithm is the leaky bucket algorithm, which has an arrival curve given by Equation (1) (Krishna et al., 2004);

$$b(t) = \sigma + \rho t \text{ for } t > 0, \quad (1)$$

which means that, no more than σ data units can be sent at once and the long-term rate is ρ. The arrival curve, therefore, bounds traffic and denotes the largest amount of traffic allowed to be sent in a given time interval. (Krishna et al., 2004; Bertsekas & Gallager, 1992, p. 512) A leaky bucket controller according to Le Boudec and Thiran (2004, p. 10) is a device that analyses the data on a flow as follows. There is a pool (bucket) of fluid of size σ. The bucket is initially empty. The bucket has a hole and leaks at a rate, ρ units of fluid per second when it is not empty. Data from the flow R(t) has to pour into the bucket an amount of fluid equal to the amount of data that will make the bucket to be full. Data that would cause the bucket to overflow is declared as non-conformant (it would not pour into the bucket) otherwise, the data is declared as conformant. The leaky bucket scheme is used to regulate the burstiness of transmitted traffic. (Bertsekas & Gallager, 1992, p. 911) Figure 2 is an illustration of the operation of the leaky bucket regulator, while Figure 3 illustrates it graphically.

Figure 2. Illustration of the leaky bucket controller concept

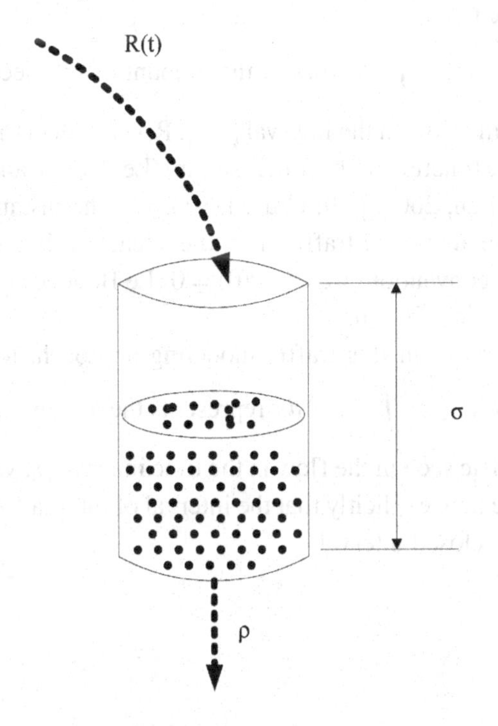

In ATM systems, non-conformant data is either discarded, tagged with low priority for loss ("red" cells) or can be put in a buffer (buffered leaky bucket controller); with the Integrated Services Internet, non-conformant data is in principle, not marked, but simply passed as 'best effort' traffic (namely, normal IP traffic). (Le Boudec & Thiran, 2004, p. 10) A similar concept to the leaky bucket concept is the token bucket controller. While the leaky bucket algorithm shapes bursty traffic into fixed-rate traffic by averaging the data rate, the token bucket algorithm allows bursty traffic at a regulated maximum rate (Forouzan, 2008, p. 779).

TRAFFIC STREAM CHARACTERIZATION

In the network calculus approach for describing network traffic, a traffic stream (which is a collection of packets that can be of variable length [Cruz, 1991]) or flow is described by a wide-sense increasing function r(t). The function r is wide-sense increasing if and only if $r(s) \leq r(t)$ for all $s \leq t$. We represent a traffic stream as follows: for any $t > 0$,

$r(t) = \int_0^t R(s)\,ds$ is the amount of bits seen in the flow in the interval [0, t]. R(s) is called the rate function of the traffic stream (Le Boudec and Thiran, 2004, p. 9; Cruz, 1991); it is the instantaneous rate of traffic from the stream at time s. By convention, we take $r(0) = 0$ (Le Boudec and Thiran, 2004, p. 4).

Also, in this traffic modeling approach, for any $y \geq x$, $\int_x^y R(s)\,ds$ represents the amount of traffic seen in the flow in the time interval [x, y]. We note explicitly that the interval of integration is a closed interval.

DEFINITION OF BURSTINESS CONSTRAINT

According to Cruz (1991), given any $\rho \geq 0$ and $\sigma \geq 0$, $R \sim (\sigma, \rho)$ if and only if for all x, y satisfying $y \geq x$, there holds;

$$\int_x^y R \leq \sigma + \rho(y - x) \qquad (2)$$

Thus, if $R \sim (\sigma, \rho)$, there is an upper bound on the amount of traffic contained in any interval [x, y] that is equal to a constant σ plus a quantity that is proportional to the length of the interval. The constant of proportionality ρ determines an upper bound to the long-term average rate of traffic flow, if such an average rate exists. For a fixed value of ρ, the term σ allows for some burstiness. (Cruz, 1991) From (2), another interpretation of the constraint $R \sim (\sigma, \rho)$ is that;

$$\int_x^y R - \rho(t - s) \leq \sigma \qquad (3)$$

or

$$\sigma \geq \int_x^y R - \rho(t - s) \qquad (4)$$

Therefore, a useful interpretation of the constraint $R \sim (\sigma, \rho)$ is as follows (Cruz, 1991): for any function R and a constant $\rho > 0$, define the function $W\rho(R)$ for all times by Equation (5).

$$W\rho(R)(t) = \max_{s \leq t}\left[\int_s^t R - \rho(t - s)\right], \; -\infty < t < \infty \qquad (5)$$

Figure 3. Graph of $y = \rho t + \sigma$

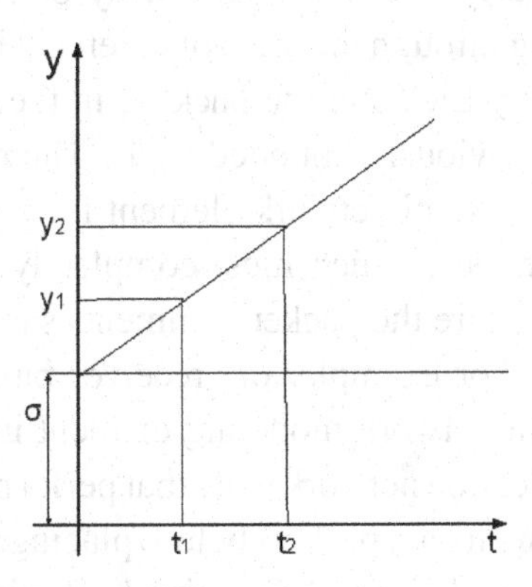

Clearly, from (3) and (4), $W\rho(R)(t) \leq \sigma$ for all t if and only if $R \sim (\sigma, \rho)$; $W\rho(R)(t)$ is the size of the backlog; that is, the amount of unfinished work at time t in a work-conserving system which accepts data at a rate described by the rate function R and transmits the data at rate ρ while there is data to be transmitted (work to be done). (Cruz, 1991)

BURSTY TRAFFIC AND NETWORK DELAYS

The class of message flows that satisfies the condition that, the amount of traffic in an interval is upper bounded by an affine function of the length of the interval has been found to be a useful class of models for traffic on internal links in networks that have to handle bursty traffic (Anantharam, 1993), and bursty traffic is one of the causes of congestion in a network.. (Forouzan, 2008, p.763) Congestion in a network may occur if the load on the network (the number of packets sent to the network) is greater than the capacity of the network (the number of packets a network can handle). (Forouzan, 2008, p. 763) Fundamentally, congestion occurs when the users of a network collectively demand more resources than the network (including the destination sites) has to offer (Bertsekas & Gallager, 1992, p. 27), and congestion leads to delays. (Bertsekas & Gallager, 1992, p. 27) Bursty traffic sessions, therefore, generally lead to large delays in networks (Bertsekas & Gallager, 1992, p. 511); the delay suffered in a switch by an arriving packet increases as the burstiness of the traffic going into the switch increases (Georges et al., 2003).

ELEMENTARY NETWORK COMPONENTS THAT CAN BE USED TO MODEL A PACKET SWITCH

This section discusses some elementary network components that can be used for the modeling of packet switches and is based on the work of Cruz (1991).

1. The Constant Delay Line

The constant delay line is a network element with a single input stream and a single output stream. The operation is defined by a single parameter D. All data which arrive in the input stream exit on the output stream exactly D seconds later; that is, each packet is delayed a fixed constant time before it is moved out. Thus, if Rin represents the rate of the input stream, then, Rout the rate of the output stream is given by Equation (6).

$$R_{out}(t) = R_{in}(t - D) \text{ for all } t \tag{6}$$

The maximum delay of a delay line is obviously D. The delay line can be used in conjunction with other elements to model devices that do not process data instantaneously. The constant delay line is illustrated in Figure 4.The routing latency in a packet switch could be modeled by applying a burst-delay service curve $\delta T(t)$, which is equivalent to adding a constant delay T. (Georges et al., 2005) Figure 5a shows the input and output curves of the guaranteed delay element, while Figure 5b shows the curve of the burst-delay function.

2. The Receiver Buffer

The receiver buffer is a network element with a single input stream and a single output stream. The input stream arrives on a link with a finite transmission, rate, say C. The output stream exits on a link with infinite transmission rate. The receiver buffer simply outputs the data that arrives on the input link in First-Come-First-Served (FCFS) order. The data packet exits the receive buffer instantaneously at the time instant when it is completely transmitted to the receive buffer on the input link. That is, the receive buffer does not output a packet until the last bit of the packet has been received; at which time, it now outputs the packet. The receive buffer is employed to model situations in which cut-through switching is not used; but, in which store-and-forward switching is used.

If Lk = length in bits of packet k that starts transmission on the input link at time Sk, then tk, the time at which the kth packet starts exiting the receive buffer is given for all k by Equation (7).

$$t_k = S_k + L_k \, / / \, C \quad (7)$$

Figure 4. Illustration of a constant delay line

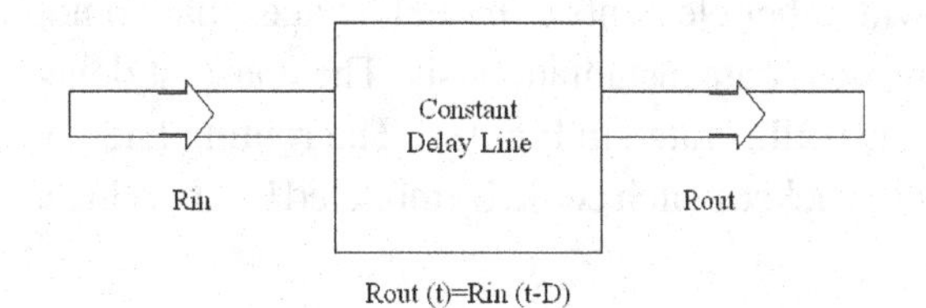

Obviously, the maximum delay of any data bit passing through this network element is upper bounded by L/C, and the backlog in the receive buffer is obviously bounded by L. The receiver buffer is a useful network element for modeling network nodes, which must completely receive a packet before the packet commences exit from the node. For example, the receiver buffer is a convenient network-modeling element in a data communication network node that performs error correction on data packets before placing them in a queue. In addition, the receive buffer is useful for devices in which the input links have smaller transmission rates than the output links. The receive buffer is illustrated in Figure 6.

3. The First-Come-First-Served Multiplexer (FCFS MUX)

The multiplexer (FCFS MUX) has two or more input links and a single output link. The function of the FCFS MUX is to merge the streams arriving on the input links onto the output link. That is, it multiplexes two or more input streams together onto a single output stream. The output link has maximum transmission rate Cout and the input links have maximum transmission rates Ci, i = 1,2,3,...,N. It is normally assumed that Ci ≥ Cout, for i = 1, 2, 3,...,N. An illustration of the FCFS MUX is shown in Figure 7.

4. First-In-First-Out (FIFO) Queue

The FIFO queue can be viewed as a degenerate form of FCFS multiplexer. The FIFO queue has one input link and one output link. It is illustrated in Figure 8. The input link has transmission capacity Cin and the output link has transmission capacity Cout. The FIFO is defined simply as follows. Data that arrives on the input link is transmitted on the output link in FCFS order as soon as possible at the transmission rate Cout. For

Figure 5. Illustration of arrivals delayed for at most T seconds before departure (input/output curves of guaranteed delay elements) (a) and the burst-delay function δ, (b) Source: LeBoudec & Thiran (2004, p. 107)

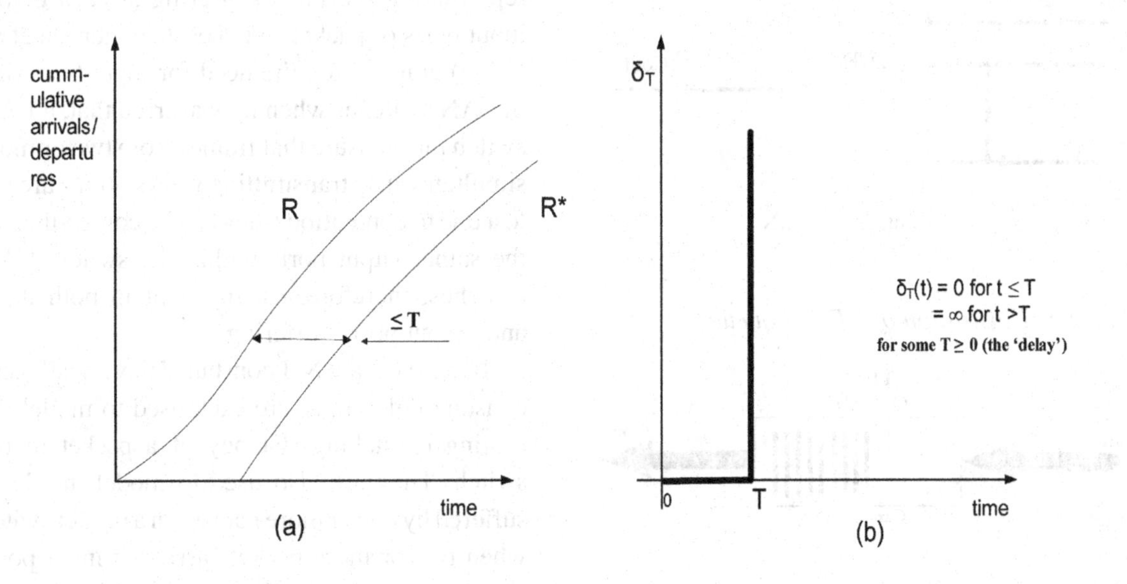

example, if a packet begins to arrive at time t0 and if no backlog exists inside the FIFO at time t0, then the packet also commences transmission on the output link at time t0. It is assumed that Cin ≥ Cout so that this is possible. If Cin were less than Cout, then this would be impossible to do, as the FIFO would 'run out' of data to transmit immediately following time t0 before the packet could be transmitted at rate Cout. Suppose that the rate of the input stream to the FIFO queue is given as Rin(t), if the size of the backlog inside the FIFO at time t is given by WCout (Rin)(t). The jth packet which arrives at time Sj must wait for all, the, current backlog and this backlog gets

Figure 6. Illustration of a receive buffer

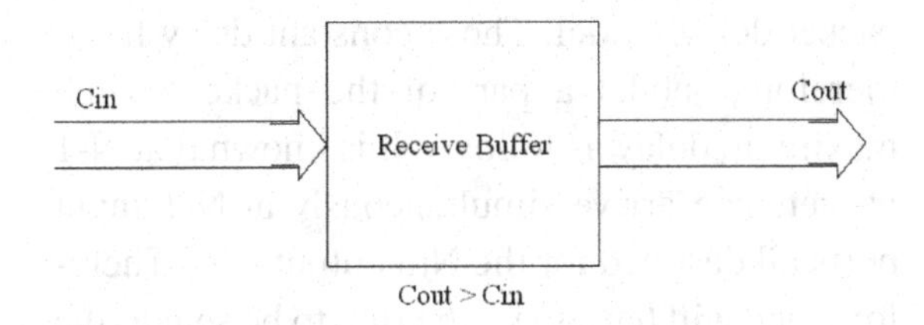

transmitted at rate Cout. It follows that the jth packet commences exit from the FIFO queue at time tj = Sj + dj, where,

$$d_j = \frac{1}{Cout} W_{Cout}(R_0)(S_j) \tag{8}$$

= time spent by the jth packet in the FIFO queue before being transmitted at rate Cout.

MAXIMUM DELAY MODEL OF A PACKET SWITCH

A switch is a complex system which introduces different mechanisms and different technologies. (Georges et al., 2005, 2003) Some researchers have modeled a packet switch as a black box (for example Jasperneite et al., 2002); the service curve notion defined in (Le Boudec & Thiran, 2004, p. 18) was also used in (Jasperneite et al., 2002) to describe the service offered by a switch to packets that are arriving to it. We now proceed

Figure 7. Illustration of a FCFS MUX

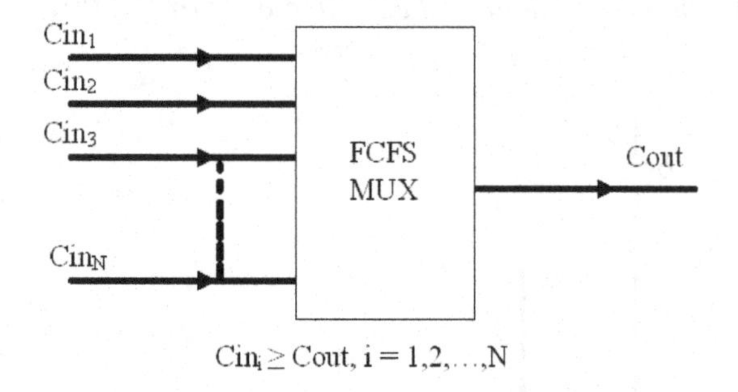

Figure 8. Illustration of a FIFO queue

in the next few sections to describe a maximum delay model of a packet switch developed by using the elementary components whose operations were explained in paragraph titled "The Receiver Buffer" and to derive its mathematical equivalent. The model is shown in Figure 9.

DESCRIPTION OF THE MAXIMUM DELAY MODEL

The maximum delay packet switch model is based on the following delays/latencies: (1) packet (frame) forwarding latency, (2) packet (frame) routing latency, (3) queuing delay, (4) packet (frame) transmission delay and, (5) concurrent arrival of packets (frames) delay. So the maximum delay, which a packet will suffer in a packet switch is given by:

Maximum Packet Delay = Maximum Forwarding (Store and Forward) Latency + Maximum Routing (Switching) Latency + Maximum Delay as a result of concurrent arrival of packets + Maximum Queuing Delay + Maximum Transmission Delay (9)

In the model, there, are, N-1 (where N is the number of ports in the switch) receive buffers, representing the input buffering at each of the input ports of packet switches. Christensen et al. (1995) emphasized the need for input buffering in LAN switches when they averred that, a LAN switch must ensure that frames from two or more simultaneously transmitting workstations are not lost due to contention (they can be contending for the same output port) within the switch; LAN switches, therefore, usually contain both input and output ports buffering.

Next, there are N-1 constant delay lines. These constant delay lines are each used to model the routing (switching) latency of a packet in the switch. They are also used to model the delay suffered by one or more packets in a packet switch when two or more packets arrive at input ports simultaneously, and all of these arriving packets are destined for the same output port. When two packets arrive simultaneously at two input ports, but both of them are destined for the same output port, one of them is delayed for a fixed constant time (T seconds) before it is sent to the output port.

Then, there are a set of constant delay lines between the first set of constant delay lines and the FCFS MUX (first-come, first-serve multiplexer). The first port (port 1) has no other constant delay line (except the constant delay line that is used to model routing or switching latency). The second port (port 2) has one constant delay line, the third port has two constant delay lines, and so on up to the (N-1)th port that has N-2 constant delay lines between the constant delay line that models the routing (switching) latency and the FCFS MUX. These set of constant delay lines are necessary because, the switch model is a maximum packet delay model. These constant delay lines, therefore, model a part of the packet switch maximum delay as follows. It is known that N-1 packets can arrive simultaneously at N-1 input ports all destined for the Nth output port. Therefore, one will have to be the first to be sent to the output port. It is assumed that the data packet that

Figure 9. Maximum delay model of a packet switch

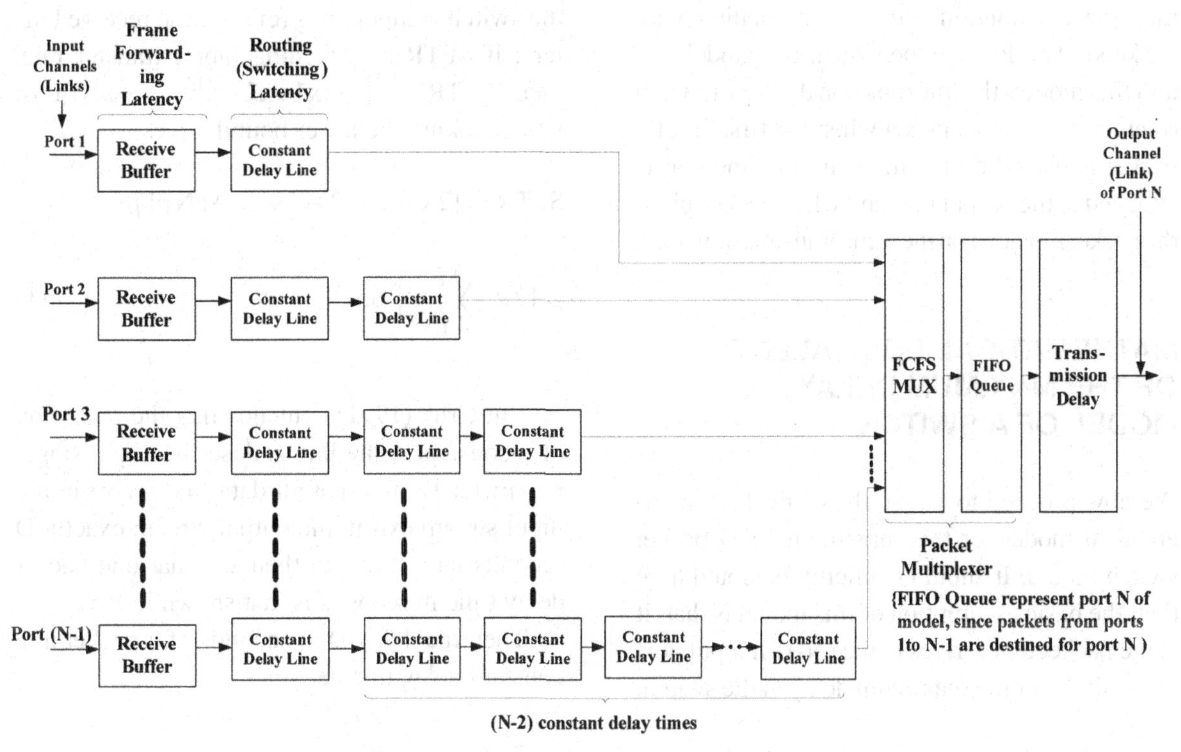

arrived at port 1 is the first to be sent to the port N; therefore, it suffers no delay. Then the packet that arrived at port 2 is the next to be sent to the output port N, therefore, it suffers one delay (represented by the one constant delay line). The packet that arrived at port 3 is the next to be sent to output port N, therefore, it suffers two delays (represented by the two constant delay lines), and so on up to the packet that arrived at port N-1 being the next to be sent to output port N, therefore, it suffers N-2 delays (which is represented by N-2 constant delay lines).

The next component in this model is the FCFS MUX (first come, first serve multiplexer).The multiplexer has two or more input links and a single output link. The function of the MUX is to merge the streams arriving on the input links onto the output link. It is included in the model to indicate the fact that, packets can arrive at different input ports (represented by the inputs of the multiplexer), but all of them are destined for the same output port (the output of the multiplexer).

FIFO (first-in, first-out) Queue is the next component in the model. It is used to model the output queuing in packet switches. If a data packet arrives at the input port, after the packet header has been checked to know its destination address, it is switched (routed) to the output port corresponding to the destination address by the switching fabric. If there are other packets waiting in the queue of the output port to be transmitted on the transmission line, it has to wait for the transmission of these other data packets before being transmitted. The FCFS MUX together with the FIFO queue is called packet multiplexer (this is because, apart from multiplexing data packets from multiple inputs onto a single output, data multiplexers contain buffers for queuing data packets). The last component in the model is a unit that models the transmission delay in a switch (that is, the delay between when the first bit of a packet is placed on the transmission line that is attached to the output port and when the last bit of the packet is placed on the same transmission line).

MATHEMATICAL EQUIVALENT OF THE MAXIMUM DELAY MODEL OF A SWITCH

We now proceed to obtain the equivalent mathematical model for this maximum delay packet switch model. It should explicitly be noted here that, the basic assumption of this model is that, it is the packet that arrives at the (N-1)th input port that will suffer the maximum delay in the switch.

RECEIVE BUFFER

A packet of length L-bits arriving over a link of bit rate Ci, has a maximum delay given by Equation (10). (Anurag et al., 2004, p. 121; Cruz, 1991)

$$\text{Dbuffer} = \frac{L}{C_i}\,(\text{secs}) \qquad (10)$$

CONSTANT DELAY LINE

This switch model is assumed to be based on the shared-memory switching fabric, which is the most commonly implemented switching fabric for local area network switches (Georges et al., 2005). In this type of switch, the packets transfer rate of the switching fabric is usually at least twice the sum of the input line rates. (Anurag et al., 2004, p. 600; Song, 2001) Therefore, assuming that there are N ports with input line rates x1, x2, x3,…,xN in bps (bits per second) = speeds of the connected mediums to input ports 1, 2, 3,…,N of the switch = input rates (ci's) of the receive buffers; if SFTR = switching fabric transfer rate, then, SFTR $\geq$ [2×(x1+x2+x3+ …+xN)]bps; which, taking the lower bound, gives;

SFTR = [2× (c1+c2+c3+ …+cN)]bps

$$= [2\times (\sum_{i=1}^{N} c_i)]\ \text{bps} \qquad (11)$$

But Cruz (1991) contends that the operation of a constant delay line is described by a single parameter D, and that all data that arrive in the input stream exit in the output stream exactly D seconds later. We can then say that one packet delay time in seconds is that shown in Box 1.

Then the delay D in seconds of a packet in a constant delay line becomes:

$$D(\text{secs}) = \left(\frac{L}{2\times\sum_{i=1}^{N} C_i} \right) \qquad (12)$$

Since the arriving (N-1)th packet will suffer N-2 constant delay times in this model, we then have:

$$D_{CDT}(\text{secs}) = (N-2)\times\left(\frac{L}{2\times\sum_{i=1}^{N} C_i} \right) \qquad (13)$$

where, DCDT = maximum delay suffered by a data packet in the switch as a result of N-1 constant delay times,

N = the number of I/O ports in the switch,

L = maximum length in bits of a data packet.

The ci's are the input rates of the receive buffers.

FIRST-COME-FIRST-SERVED MULTIPLEXER (FCFS MUX)

The multiplexer is assumed to be bufferless. We adopt the notion in this presentation that, output contention resolution (packet scheduling policy) along with output buffering (used for output queuing), both in the switch is called packet multiplexer. (Anurag et al., 2004, p. 120). Packets, therefore, do not suffer delay in the FCFS MUX. The delay that is supposed to be suffered by packets in the FCFS MUX is represented by the succeeding FIFO Queuing delay.

FIRST-IN-FIRST-OUT (FIFO) QUEUE

Wρ(R)(t), the size of the backlog (amount of unfinished work) at time t in a work-conserving system which accepts data at a rate described by the rate function R, and transmits data at the rate ρ while there is work to be done (data to be transmitted) was defined by Cruz (1991) as:

$$W_{\rho}\left(R\right)\left(t\right) = \max_{s \leq t}\left[\int_{s}^{t} R - \rho(t-s)\right] \tag{14}$$

where, ρ is an upper bound on the long-term average rate of traffic flow, and σ is the burstiness constraint of the traffic flow (and also the maximum amount of data that can arrive in a burst). Since an arriving packet to a FIFO queue has to wait for the backlog in the queue to be zero before it will be forwarded on the output link at rate Cout, Equation (14) becomes:

$$W_{Cout}\left(R\right)\left(t\right) = \max_{s \leq t}\left[\int_{s}^{t} R_{in}(t)dt - C_{out}(t-s)\right] \tag{15}$$

where, Wcout(R)(t) = backlog inside the queue and Rin(t) = rate function of the incoming traffic at time t. Putting (8) into (15), we have:

$$d_{j} = \frac{1}{C_{out}} \max_{s \leq s_{j}}\left[\int_{s}^{s_{j}} R_{in}(t)\,dt - C_{out}(s_{j} - s)\right] \tag{16}$$

Since our intention in this model is to provide a maximum bound on the queuing delay (that is, dj), how then do we determine the interval [s, sj] for which dj is maximum? This will have to correspond to the maximum burst traffic arrival period of the incoming traffic. But Cout is fixed, this is because, the FIFO queue is a degenerate FCFS MUX (Cruz, 1991), and we assume that the FCFS MUX is work-conserving; that is, if B(t) is the backlog at time t and B(t)>0 at any instant of time t, then, Rout(t) = Cout (Cruz, 1991). So definitely, the interval [s, sj] where dj is maximum only depends on the arrival process of the traffic Rin(t). This is illustrated in Figure 10. We now proceed to determine a possible traffic arrival interval where dj would be maximum by following the procedure developed by Georges et al., (2005). Recall that Rin is the rate function of the incoming traffic stream;

$$\forall s_{j} \geq s$$

$\int_{S}^{S_j} R_{in}(t)\,dt$ is the amount of traffic that have arrived in the closed interval [s, sj].

Given σ ≥ 0, and ρ ≥ 0, we write Rin ~ (σ, ρ), if and only if for all s, sj satisfying sj ≥ s, there holds:

$$\int_{S}^{S_j} R_{in}(t)dt \leq \sigma + \rho\left(s_{j} - s\right) \tag{17}$$

Similarly, if b is any function defined in the non-negative reals, and Rin ~ b, we can write (Georges et al., 2005; Cruz, 1991):

$$b(t) = \sigma + \rho t \quad (18)$$

where, b(t) is an affine arrival curve. In consonance with the description of the physical layer switch system in (US Patent No. 5889776, 2008); that the switching circuit of a switch establishes a link between two ports specified by the source address and the destination address that is received from the status look-up table, we can then take into account, the internal bus (the bus connecting the receive buffer to the output buffer) capacity (transfer rate). If this is C bits/sec, then the affine function (Equation [18]) can be completed with an inequality constraint as:

$$b(t) \leq Ct \quad (19)$$

This inequality constraint idea was introduced by Georges et al. (2005) in relation to the communication link feeding a switch. The inequality relationship represented by (19) means that, the arrival of data to the output buffers cannot be greater than the internal bus capacity through which the data will flow. Equation (18) can now be completed with the inequality constraint (19) as:

$$b(t) = \min\left\{Ct, \sigma + \rho t\right\} \quad (20)$$

We can now write out the amount of data that have arrived in the interval [sj, s] for all sj ≥ s as:

$$\int_{s}^{s_j} R_{in}(t)dt \leq \min\left\{C(s_j - s), \sigma + \rho(s_j - s)\right\} \quad (21)$$

From Equation (20), if $Ct < \sigma + \rho t$, then

$$b(t) = Ct \, and \quad (22)$$

$$\frac{db(t)}{dt} = C \quad (23)$$

and if $\sigma + \rho t < Ct$, then

$$b(t) = \sigma + \rho t \text{ and } t > \quad (24)$$

$$\frac{db(t)}{dt} = \rho \quad (25)$$

Equations (23) and (25) then give us two possible arrival rates: C, the internal bus capacity and ρ, a long term average rate (both are in bits/sec). But the maximum burst size has been defined as the maximum length of time that a data traffic flows at the peak rate. (Forouzan, 2008, p.762; Alberto & Widjaja, 2004, p. 551) We, therefore, ignore Equation (25) which deals with average rate. Equation (21) can now be written (taking the upper bound of the inequality) as:

$$\int_{s}^{s_j} R_{in}(t)\,dt = C\,(s_j - s) \quad (26)$$

Equation (16) now becomes:

$$d_j = \frac{1}{C_{out}} = \max_{s \leq s_j} \left[C(s_j - s) - C_{out}(s_j - s)\right] \quad (27)$$

To determine the maximum length of time or max [sj – s] that the incoming traffic flows at the peak rate, we note that, the upper bound of the inequality of (21) implies, either

$$\int_{s}^{s_j} R_{in}(t)\,dt = C\,(s_j - s) \quad (28)$$

or

$$\int_{s}^{s_j} R_{in}(t)\,dt = \sigma + \rho\,(s_j - s) \quad (29)$$

Box 1.

$$D\left(\text{secs}\right) = \frac{packet\ length\ (bits)}{packet\ transfer\ rate\ (bits\ /\ \sec s)} = \frac{L\ (bits)}{packet\ transfer\ rate\ (bits\ /\ \sec s)}$$

that is

$$C(sj-s)=\sigma+\rho(sj\ -s) \quad (30)$$

or

$$S_j - S = \frac{\sigma}{C-\rho} \quad (31)$$

= maximum length of time at which the traffic flows at the peak rate.

We can now re-write Equation (27) as Equation (32) in Box 2.

We note here again that σ is the maximum amount of traffic (in bits) that can arrive in a burst to the FIFO Queue. But we had earlier stated that ρ is the rate at which a work-conserving system that accepts data at a rate described by the rate function R, transmits the data while there is data to be transmitted (Cruz, 1991). We can explain this concept in this simple way. Consider a work-conserving system as shown in Figure 11, which receives data at a rate described by R(t) and issues out the data at a constant rate Cout. Consider also, a communication session between the traffic source and the work-conserving system. It is easy to see that the traffic that arrives to the work-conserving system during the communication session (including burst traffic arrivals) would eventually be issued out by the system over time, at, rate Cout. It is easy to see also, that, Cout represents the average rate of traffic arrivals to the work-conserving system during the communication session.

This idea (output port issuing rate equals average rate of traffic arrivals) was amply illustrated by Sven et al. (2008) as shown in Figure 12.

Figure 10. An example of traffic arrival pattern to a queuing system

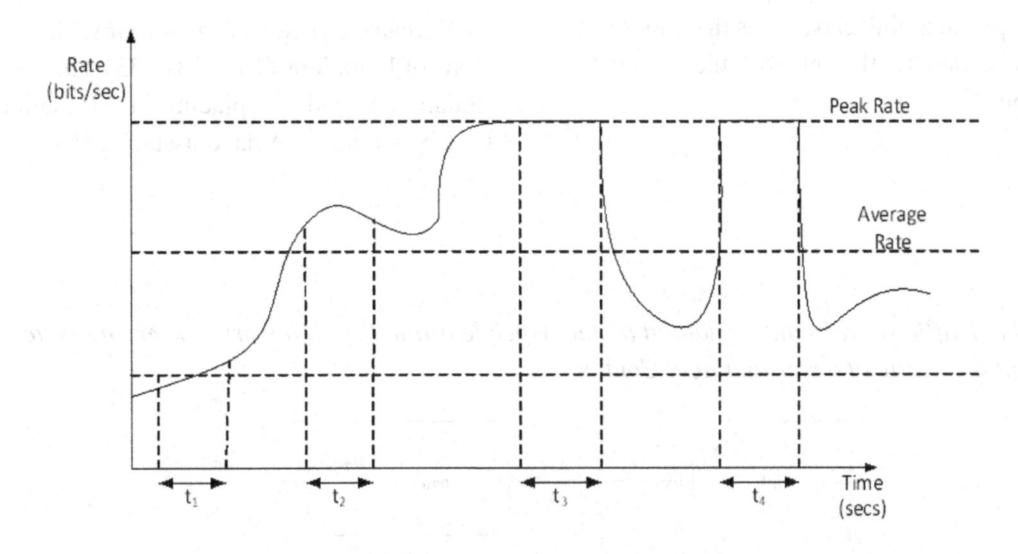

Box 2.

$$d_j = \frac{1}{C_{out}}\left[C\left(\frac{\sigma}{C-\rho}\right) - C_{out}\left(\frac{\sigma}{C-\rho}\right)\right] = \frac{1}{C_{out}}\left[\frac{(C-C_{out})\sigma}{C-\rho}\right] \quad (32)$$

= maximum delay in seconds incurred by the jth packet in crossing the FIFO queue.

Therefore, taking ρ as Cout, Equation (32) becomes:

$$d_j = \frac{\sigma}{C_{out}} \quad (33)$$

where,

d j = maximum delay in seconds incurred by the jth packet in crossing the FIFO Queue,
σ = maximum amount of data traffic that can arrive in a burst in bits,
Cout = bit rate of the output link (switch port) in bits per second (bps).

Equation (33) is in agreement with the assertion (with respect to a router) by Sven et al. (2008), that since the output queue of a router is emptied at the nominal link capacity, an hypothesis can be made that, the size of a packet burst in bits measured on a router's output port divided by the nominal physical link capacity is the upper limit of delay added to the queue build-up by the packet burst.

TRANSMISSION DELAY

According to Kanem et al. (1999), Bersekas and Gallager (1992, p. 149), Gerd (1989, p. 169) Reiser (1982), for all arriving instants, the delay experienced by a message upon arrival at a queuing system is composed of the message's own service time plus the backlog 'seen' upon arrival. The maximum transmission delay that can be suffered by an arriving packet is obviously the ratio of the maximum size that can be assumed by the packet to the transmission speed of the output port (channel). Therefore, if L = maximum length of a packet in bits, Cout = transmission speed of the output port (link) in bits/sec, Dmaxtrans, the maximum transmission delay of the packet in the switch in seconds is given by Equation (34).

$$D_{maxtrans} = \frac{L}{C_{out}} \text{ secs} \quad (34)$$

We can then insert the maximum delay expressions of Equations (10), (13), (33), and (34) into Equation (9) and by replacing Ci in Equation (10) by CN-1 (since we have assumed that the data

Figure 11. Traffic source sending data at a time dependent rate R(t) to a work conserving system, that issues out the traffic at a constant rate, Cout

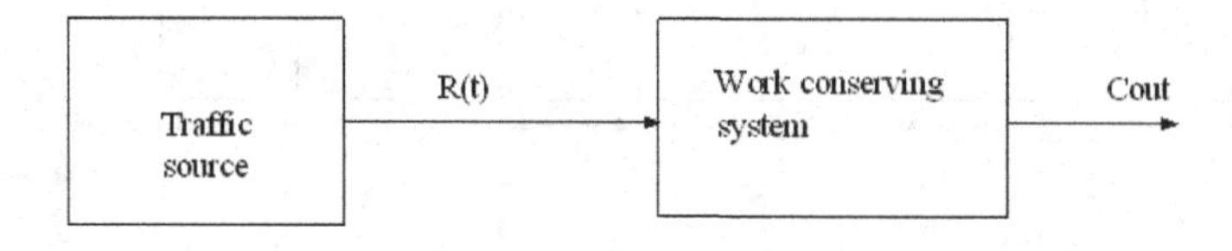

Figure 12. Illustration of traffic arrivals to, and departures from, a queuing system with constant output rate, C (Source: Sven, et al., 2008)

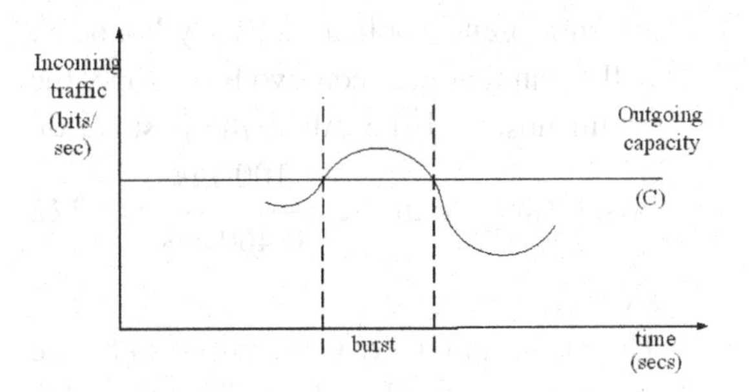

packet that arrived in port N-1 will suffer the maximum delay – it is the last to be forwarded to the output port N), we have Equation (35) in Box 3.

PRACTICAL IMPLICATIONS OF THE MAXIMUM DELAY MODEL OF A PACKET SWITCH

It is easy to see from Figure 1 that, if one can guarantee that the delay of a packet in any of the switches in an origin-destination path can be kept below an upper bound, then the end-to-end delay of the path can be kept below the sum of the upper bounds delays of the switches on that path. If we are able to know all the origin-destination paths in any switched LAN (this can be done with a methodology that we have developed in our research work), with our maximum delay model of a packet switch, we can calculate all the origin-destination paths maximum delays. We can then go ahead to compare these maximum delays with the maximum delay constraints of the applications to be deployed in the LAN. If the origin-destination paths maximum delays are all below the maximum delay constraints of the applications to be deployed in the LAN, then the network is well designed; if otherwise, then the network has to be redesigned so as to have maximum paths end-to-end delays that are below the maximum delay constraints of the applications. Consequently, the maximum delay packet switch model was validated to be good for practical network engineering by comparing its maximum delay value to values that were obtained

Box 3.

$$D_{\max}\left(\text{seconds}\right) = \frac{L}{C_{N-1}} + \left(\frac{L}{2\times\sum_{i=1}^{N} C_i}\right) + \left(N-2\right)\times\left(\frac{L}{2\times\sum_{i=1}^{N} C_i}\right) + \frac{\sigma}{C_{out}} + \frac{L}{C_{out}}$$

$$= \frac{L}{C_{N-1}} + \left(N-1\right)\times\left(\frac{L}{2\times\sum_{i=1}^{N} C_i}\right) + \frac{\sigma}{C_{out}} + \frac{L}{C_{out}} \qquad (35)$$

where,
Dmax = maximum delay in seconds for a packet to cross any N-port packet switch,
N = No of input/output ports,
Ci, i = 1, 2, 3,…,N = bit rates of ports 1, 2, 3,…,N in bps,
= channel (for example, Ethernet) rates of input ports in bps,
Cout = bit rate of the Nth output link in bps,
= output port (line) rate of the Nth port (the destination of the other N-1 input traffics)
CN-1 = bit rate of the (N-1)th input port in bps,
L = maximum length in bits of a data (for example, Ethernet) packet,
σ = maximum amount of traffic in bits that can arrive in a burst.

from literature. We now give a simple explanation of the validation that was carried out.

Assume we are dealing with a switched Ethernet LAN (which is almost the only type of switch LAN that is deployed by organizations). We use also, the maximum packet size of an Ethernet packet (the extended Ethernet packet), which is 1530 bytes (8-bytes preamble + 18-bytes header + 1500 data bytes + 4-bytes CRC). The maximum packet size is used, because, we are seeking to establish an upper bound delay, and hence, there is the need to maximally load the switch.

Assume also, that, $\sigma =$ Ethernet frames = 340 Ethernet frames. This is the average of IETF (Internet Engineering Task Force). RFC (Request for Comments) 2544 (see RFC 2544, (2009)) recommended values for Device under Test (DUT) to switching devices manufacturers. With these values of L (1530 bytes × 8 bits) and σ (340 × 1530 bytes × 8 bits) inserted into Equation (35) with appropriate C's and N, the maximum delay value of the model is 42 milliseconds (42 ms).

Georges et al. (2005) reported that the maximum delay value obtained with the maximum delay Ethernet packet switch model reported in the paper is $3080\mu s$ or $3.080 ms$; while the COMNET 111 simulation software package gave a maximum delay value of 450 µs or 0.450 ms. Using 100 ms which is the upper delay bound for IEEE 802 networks as recommended in IETF's RFC 2815: Integrated Services Mappings on IEEE 802 Networks (see RFC 2815, (2009)), we make the following simple comparisons.

1. The maximum delay value obtained by Georges et al. (2005). This value is 3.080 ms. Using 100 ms end-to-end application delay bound, it will mean that between two hosts (one, the origin host and the other, the destination host) there can be $\frac{100\ ms}{3.080\ ms} =$ 32.5 $\cong$ 33 switches.
2. The maximum delay value provided by COMNET 111 as reported by Georges et al. (2005). This value is 0.450 ms. Using 100 ms end-to-end application delay bound, it will mean that between two hosts (one, the origin host and the other, the destination host) there can be $\frac{100\ ms}{0.450\ ms} = 222$ switches.
3. The maximum delay value provided by the model represented by Equation (35). This value is 42 ms. Using 100 ms end-to-end application delay bound, it will mean that between two hosts (one, the origin host and the other, the destination host) there can be $\frac{100\ ms}{42\ ms} = 2.4 \cong 3$ switches.

Square D's (2009) specifications for the installation of the Model SDM 5DE 100, Class 1400 Ethernet packet switch is: 'switches can be concatenated between devices (hosts) as long as the path between hosts does not exceed four (4) switches and five (5) cable runs.' From the information provided by this manufacturer, it can be seen that in practical terms, the model represented by Equation (35) is close to reality, unlike, the values provided by the models obtained from literature (and it is therefore, validated).

CONCLUSION

This work has highlighted the switched LANs' delay problem. It has also discussed briefly, the evolution of switched Ethernet LANs, and, has discussed the two principal approaches of determining the end-to-end delays of computer communication networks (the stochastic approach and the deterministic approach), bringing out the fact that the latter has obvious advantages over the former. The work then took a brief excursion in to the deterministic approach, and demonstrated its application by using it to model a packet switch using the network components that were proposed and specified by Cruz (1991). The packet switch model was shown to be good for the practical engineering of local area networks that meets specified maximum end-to-end delay constraints.

FUTURE RESEARCH DIRECTIONS

Some problems' areas have been discovered in the course of our research work. The most pressing of these, is, the determination of a value for the maximum amount of traffic that can arrive to a network (or switch) in a burst. This parameter is termed σ in our chapter. This is presently an area of very intense research activity. In fact, it is the, believe here that, coming out with an empirically validated value for σ (or how to determine σ) will be a major breakthrough to the Internet and Networking research community.

REFERENCES

Alberto, L., & Widjaja, I. (2004). *Communications networks: Fundamental concepts and key architectures*. New York: McGraw Hill.

Anantharam, V. (1993). An approach to the design of high-speed networks for bursty traffic. In *Proceedings of the 32nd IEEE Conference on Decision and Control*. San Antonio, TX: IEEE.

Anurag, K., Manjunath, D., & Kuri, J. (2004). *Communication networking: An analytical approach*. San Francisco, CA: Morgan Kaufmann Publishers.

Bejerano, Y., Breithart, Y., Garofalakis, M., & Rastogi, R. (2003). Physical topology discovery for large multi-subnet networks. *IEEE Transactions on Networking*, *3*(6), 342–352.

Bertsekas, D., & Gallager, R. (1992). *Data networks*. Englewood Cliffs, NJ: Prentice Hall.

Bolot, J. (1993). Characterizing end-to-end packet delay and loss in the internet. *Journal of High-Speed Networks*, *2*(3), 305–323.

Christensen, K., Hass, L., Noel, F., & Stole, N. (1995). Local area networks: Evolving from shared to switched access. *IBM Systems Journal*, 347–374. doi:10.1147/sj.343.0347.

Comer, D. (2004). *Computer networks and intranets with internet applications*. Englewood Cliffs, NJ: Pearson Prentice Hall.

Costa, P., Netto, J., & Pereira, C. (2004). Analysis of traffic differentiation on switched ethernet. In *Proceedings of the International Workshop on Real-Time Networks*. Retrieved August 20, 2009 from http://www.ieeta.pt/lse/rtn2004/preprints

Cruz, R. (1991). A calculus for network delay, part 1: Network elements in isolation. *IEEE Transactions on Information Theory*, *37*(1), 114–131. doi:10.1109/18.61109.

Ersoy, C., & Panwar, S. (1993). Topological design of interconnected LAN/MAN networks. *IEEE Journal on Selected Areas in Communications*, *11*(8), 1172–1182. doi:10.1109/49.245906.

Falaki, S., & Sorensen, S. (1992). Traffic measurements on a local area computer network. *Butterworth Heinemann Computer Communications Journal*, *15*(3), 192–197. doi:10.1016/0140-3664(92)90080-X.

Forouzan, B. (2008). *Data communications and networking*. New Delhi: Tata McGraw-Hill.

Fowler, H., & Leland, W. (1991). Local area network traffic characteristics, with implications for broadband network congestion management. *IEEE Journal on Selected Areas in Communications*, *9*(7), 1139–1149. doi:10.1109/49.103559.

Freepatentonline.com. (n.d.). Physical layer switch system for ethernet local area communication system. *US Patent No. 5889776.* Retrieved November 10, 2008 from http://www.freepatentsonline.com/5889776

Gallo, A., & Wilder, R. (1981). Performance measurement of data communication systems with emphasis on open system interconnections. In *Proceedings 8th IEEE Annual Symposium on Computer Architecture,* (pp. 149-161). Minneapolis, MN: IEEE.

Georges, J., Divoux, T., & Rondeau, E. (2002). Evaluation of switched ethernet in an industrial context using the network calculus. In *Proceedings of the 4th IEEE International Workshop on Factory Communication Systems,* (pp. 19-26). Vasteras, Sweden: IEEE.

Georges, J., Divoux, T., & Rondeau, E. (2003). Comparison of switched ethernet architecture models. In *Proceedings IEEE Conference on Emerging Technologies and Factory Automation,* (pp. 375-382). Lisbon, Portugal: IEEE.

Georges, J., Divoux, T., & Rondeau, E. (2005). Confronting the performances of a switched ethernet network with industrial constraints by using network calculus. *International Journal of Communication Systems, 18,* 877–903. doi:10.1002/dac.740.

Gerd, K. (1989). *Local area networks.* New York: McGraw-Hill.

Halsall, F. (1992). Data communications. In *Computer Networks and Open Systems.* Reading, MA: Addison-Wesley.

Ietf.org. (n.d.a). *Request for comments 2544.* Retrieved August 20, 2009 from http://www.ietf.org/rfc/rfc2544

Ietf.org. (n.d.b). *Integrated services mappings on IEEE 802 networks.* Retrieved August 20, 2009 from http://tools.ietf.org/html/rfc2815

Jasperneite, J., & Ifak, N. (2001). Switched ethernet for factory communication. In *Proceedings 8th IEEE International Conference on Emerging Technologies and Factory Automation (ETFA 2001),* (pp. 205-212). Antibes, France: IEEE.

Jasperneite, J., Neumann, P., Theis, M., & Watson, K. (2002). Deterministic real-time communication with switched ethernet. In *Proceedings of the 4th IEEE International Workshop on Factory Communication Systems,* (pp. 11-18). Vasteras, Sweden: IEEE.

Kanem, E., Torab, P., Cooper, K., & Custodi, G. (1999). Design and analysis of packet switched networks for control systems. In *Proceedings 1999 IEEE Conference on Decision and Control,* (pp. 4460-4465). Phoenix, AZ: IEEE.

Krishna, P., Jens, S., & Ralf, S. (2004). Network calculus meets queuing theory: A simulation-based approach to bounded queues. In *Proceedings of the 12th IEEE International Workshop on Quality of Service (IWQoS 2004),* (pp. 114-118). Montreal, Canada: IEEE.

Le Boudec, J., & Thiran, P. (2004). *Network calculus: Theory of deterministic queuing systems for the internet.* Berlin: Springer.

Mann, R., & Terplan, K. (1999). *Network design: Management and technical perspectives. New-York.* CRC Press.

Martin, S., Minet, P., & George, L. (2005). End-to-end response time with fixed priority scheduling: Trajectory approach versus holistic approach. *International Journal of Communication Systems, 18,* 37–56. doi:10.1002/dac.688.

Micheal, D., & Richard, R. (2003). *Computer communications and data networks for computer scientists and engineers*. Essex, UK: Pearson Prentice Hall.

Ming-Yang, X., Rong, L., & Huimin, C. (2004). Predicting internet end-to-end delay: An overview. In *Proceedings of the IEEE 36th South Eastern Symposium on Information Systems Theory,* (pp. 210 – 214). IEEE.

Reiser, M. (1982). Performance evaluation of data communications systems. *Proceedings of the IEEE, 70*(2), 171–194. doi:10.1109/PROC.1982.12261.

Song, Y. (2001). Time constrained communication over switched ethernet. In *Proceedings IFAC International Conference on Fieldbus Systems and their Application,* (pp. 152-169). Nancy, France: IFAC.

Square D® ethernet switch model SDM 5DE 100 installation and illustration bulletin. (n.d.). Retrieved February 03, 2009 from www.us.squareD

Sven, U., Ales, F., & Stanislav, H. (2008). Quantification of traffic burstiness with MAPI middleware. In *Proceedings 2008 CESNET (Czech Educational and Scientific Network) Conference,* (pp. 13-22). Prague, Czech Republic: CESNET.

Torab, P., & Kanem, E. (1999). Load analysis of packet switched networks in control systems. In *Proceedings 25th Annual Conference of the IEEE Industrial Electronics Society,* (pp. 1222-1227). San Jose, CA: IEEE.

Trulove, J. (2000). *Broadband networking*. Boca Raton, FL: CRC Press.

ADDITIONAL READING

Cruz, R. (1991). A calculus for network delay, part 2: Network analysis. *IEEE Transactions on Information Theory, 37*(1), 132–141. doi:10.1109/18.61110.

Eyinagho, M. O., Atayero, A. A., & Falaki, S. O. (2011). Characterizing the maximum queuing delay of a packet switch. *Journal of Computing and ICT Research, 5*(2), 32–37.

Eyinagho, M. O., Falaki, S. O., & Atayero, A. A. (2009). Enhancement in the identities-exchange process during the authentication process. *International Journal of Computer Network And Security, 1*(1), 43–48.

Eyinagho, M. O., Falaki, S. O., & Atayero, A. A. (2011). Revisiting the notion of origin-destination traffic matrix of the hosts that are attached to a switched local area network. *International Journal of Distributed and Parallel Systems, 2*(6), 227–235. doi:10.5121/ijdps.2011.2620.

Eyinagho, M. O., Falaki, S. O., & Atayero, A. A. (2012). *Determination of end-to-end delays of switched local area networks: Designing upper delay-bounded switched LANS*. Berlin: Lambert Academic Publishing GmbH & Co. KG.

Fortier, P., & Desrochers, G. (1999). *Modeling and analysis of local area networks*. New York: CRC Press.

Ingvaldsen, T., Klovning, E., & Wilkins, M. (2000). Determining the causes of end-to-end delay in CSCW applications. *Computer Communications, 23*(3), 219–232. doi:10.1016/S0140-3664(99)00176-0.

Krommenacker, N., Rondeau, E., & Divoux, T. (2001). Study of algorithms to define the cabling plan of switched ethernet for real-time applications. In *Proceedings of the 8th IEEE International Conference on Emerging Technologies and Factory Communications,* (pp. 223-230). Antibes, France: IEEE.

Wollingger, B., Wolf, J., & Le Grand, G. (2005). Improving node behaviour in a QoS control environment by means of load-dependent resource redistributions in LANs. *International Journal of Communication Systems*, *18*, 373–394. doi:10.1002/dac.710.

KEY TERMS AND DEFINITIONS

σ: The maximum amount of traffic that can arrive to a system in a burst.

ρ: The long-term average rate of traffic flow to a system.

~: Roughly similar, or poorly approximates.

ATM: Asynchronous Transfer Mode.

CSMA/CD: Carrier Sense Multiple Access with Collision Detection.

LAN: Local Area Network.

QoS: Quality of Service.

Chapter 4
A Voice-Enabled Framework for Recommender and Adaptation Systems in E-Learning

A. A. Azeta
Covenant University, Nigeria

C. K. Ayo
Covenant University, Nigeria

N. A. Ikhu-Omoregbe
Covenant University, Nigeria

ABSTRACT

With the proliferation of learning resources on the Web, finding suitable content (using telephone) has become a rigorous task for voice-based online learners to achieve better performance. The problem with Finding Content Suitability (FCS) with voice E-Learning applications is more complex when the sight-impaired learner is involved. Existing voice-enabled applications in the domain of E-Learning lack the attributes of adaptive and reusable learning objects to be able to address the FCS problem. This study provides a Voice-enabled Framework for Recommender and Adaptation (VeFRA) Systems in E-learning and an implementation of a system based on the framework with dual user interfaces – voice and Web. A usability study was carried out in a visually impaired and non-visually impaired school using the International Standard Organization's (ISO) 9241-11 specification to determine the level of effectiveness, efficiency and user satisfaction. The result of the usability evaluation reveals that the prototype application developed for the school has "Good Usability" rating of 4.13 out of 5 scale. This shows that the application will not only complement existing mobile and Web-based learning systems, but will be of immense benefit to users, based on the system's capacity for taking autonomous decisions that are capable of adapting to the needs of both visually impaired and non-visually impaired learners.

DOI: 10.4018/978-1-4666-2208-1.ch004

INTRODUCTION

Over the last decade, there has been a change of focus from Web-based learning systems that merely turn pages of content to systems, which present learning materials in such a way as to satisfy the needs of learners. This change of focus is especially important in modern learning methods, which places strong emphasis on learners' previous knowledge. The uniqueness of a learner is met by making the Web-based learning content adaptive (Oboko et al., 2008). The increasing number of Learning Management Systems (LMS) for online teaching, quiz, assignment delivery, discussion forum, email, chat, et cetera, means that dynamic educational online services will be needed for efficient management of all educational resources on the Web. Selecting and organizing learning resources based on learner's interest is cumbersome (Gil and García-Penalvo, 2008). The process of selection may be easier with the normal users, but for certain category of learners with a visual impairment, navigating a Voice User Interface (VUI) for the desired learning content is a strenuous task. Web-deployed VUI applications for educational purposes provide user accessibility to content via telephone. One of the tools used for developing VUI applications is Voice eXtensible Mark-up Language (VoiceXML or VXML).

VUI applications are primarily developed to cater for the visually impaired (Raghuraman, 2004), to address the problem of Web accessibility associated with the use of m-Learning. The major problem of Web access is that the services of reusable learning objects currently available to Internet-connected users are not available for the visually impaired (Holzinger et al., 2006), for reasons of constraint in their navigation abilities. Thus, the voice-based Web applications mainly designed for the visually impaired lack adequate quality of using recommender and adaptable system for learning, which is a major requirement for this category of users as a result of their visual impairment. Recommender systems are software agents that recommend options for users. These agents can be very useful in an E-Learning environment to recommend actions, resources or links (Zaiane, 2005). The services provided by recommender systems are generally referred to as recommendation services. Adaptive Web system monitors particular user's behavior and characteristics. Based on them, the system compiles document from larger universal source document and then produce adapted document to users (Bures & Jelinek, 2004).

The goal of adaptive voice-based Web learning is to adjust the content of the learning objects to suit user's knowledge level, whereas recommendation services provide the most appropriate learning objects to users through voice. The inability of existing E-Learning voice applications to meet these requirements has some far reaching implications such as limited accessibility for certain users especially the visually impaired, and usability issues as a result of lack of features for reasoning, adaptation and recommendation. A significant contribution would be to introduce the concept of reusing learner's previous experiences which is often neglected in existing voice-based E-Learning systems, to make them more adaptable and provide recommendation services to users' needs. Thus, we have to further take into account that the reference guidelines for developing existing voice-based E-Learning applications, which although important, lack intelligent component services to approach the problem. One of the ways of enhancing existing voice-based E-Learning applications is to adapt their content to the needs of each student.

The needs of users differ when accessing learning content, such needs may require the ability of the system to reason, make decisions, be flexible and adapt to divers requests during interaction. These needs have placed new requirements in voice application development such as the use of advanced models, techniques and methodologies which take into account the needs of different users and environments. The ability of a system to behave close to human reasoning for adaptability support is often mentioned as one of the major requirements for the development of intelligent voice applications. Intelligent systems belong to the domain of Artificial Intelligence (AI). AI is a branch of computer science concerned with creating or mimicking intelligent behaviours or thoughts in computers (Gloss, 2004). A system can also be said to be intelligent if it is able to improve its performance or maintain an acceptable level of performance in the presence of uncertainty. The main attributes of intelligence are learning, adaptation, fault tolerance and self-organisation (Jain and Martin, 1998). If adaptability services must exist as a feature of voice-based E-Learning system, then an intelligent agent will be required to power the application.

From the foregoing, it becomes obvious that there exists a need to provide a framework for recommender and adaptation system in E-learning. This study aims at addressing the needs as identified, and employing the framework so obtained for the development of a prototype voice-enabled framework for recommender and adaptation system (*VeFRA*). The prototype application developed was tested in a school for the blind, and the result of evaluation reported. The framework suffices as a reference model for implementing intelligent voice applications in the domain of E-Learning. Applications developed based on this framework would exhibit the necessary attributes of Case Based Reasoning (CBR), including adaptation and recommendation during interaction resulting in intelligence such as the ability of the system to take autonomous decision that will adapt to learners' requests based on requirements. The application will therefore be helpful for people with physical access difficulties engendered by their visual impairment.

The objective of this study is to provide a Voice-enabled Framework for Recommender and Adaptation (*VeFRA*) Systems and adapt the framework for the development of *VeFRA* that has the capability to improve learning processes using telephone and Web-based technologies.

BACKGROUND

This section discusses existing frameworks and systems in the area of E-Learning. A framework provides reference guideline for developing applications. Existing framework for developing voice-based E-Learning system such as VoiceXML application development life-circle (VoiceXML, 2007) does not have an intelligent component services and it was modeled after the conventional software development life-circle model. However, VoiceXML applications developed using such framework serve as an alternative platform for non-visually impaired users.

REVIEW OF EXISTING SYSTEMS

In addition to the provision of alternative platform for normal users, voice-enabled E-Learning systems can be helpful for people with physical access difficulties (e.g. repetitive strain injury, arthritis, high spinal injury) that make writing difficult (Donegan, 2000). It can also be effective for students with reading, writing or spelling difficulties, such as dyslexia (Husni & Jamaludin, 2009) and for those with visual impairment (Nisbet & Wilson, 2002). Paul (2003) described some important factors to be considered when introducing and using speech recognition for students with disabilities. It was reported by Paul (2003) that speech recognition programs have been used successfully by students with a range of disabilities. The programs have been shown to provide an effective means of writing and recording work, and in some cases, they produced significant improvements in basic reading, spelling and writing skills. Chin et al.,

(2006) recommended that one can actually make use of VoiceXML technology to build speech applications that can serve educational purposes or in other words, to build an online learning system that provide better accessibility to users. One of the E-Learning applications that can be provided using speech technology are those that deliver basic teaching by simply listening. For example, students can check their scores or other information by simply calling a particular number and get the information they want. Several schemes for providing E-Learning system have been proposed in literature. Chin et al., (2006) went further to develop an E-Learning prototype based on VoiceXML concepts. However, the prototype was not deployed on the real telephone environment. Instead, a microphone and a speaker were used to simulate the telephone environment.

Gallivan et al. (2002) developed a voice-enabled Web-based absentee system on TellMe voice portal (TellMe Voice Portal, 2002). It was tested by the class of software engineering students; students who intended to miss a class called the VoiceXML telephone number and were led through an automated dialog to record their names, the date and time of the call, the courseID, and the date they would miss class in a database. The system provides the instructor and other administrators with a permanent record of absentees that can be accessed and displayed in various forms through a Web interface. The absentee system application was developed basically for Pace University students to report class absences. The VoiceXML absentee system has been designed to include record keeping of absentee calls from students, faculty and university staff. This system made use of the general VoiceXML platform architecture in Figure 1.

Likewise, Raghuraman (2004) designed, implemented and deployed a voice-enabled application called V-HELP system. In the V-HELP system, a portion of the Computer Science and Engineering (CSE) department website was voice enabled using VoiceXML to enable the visually impaired student population to access the information on it. The website also provides easy access to the information through voice, while the user is on the go, and if the user does not have a handheld with sufficient screen size or is constrained by the bandwidth to browse through the visual content. It can be used by visually impaired student population of the school to access information about the Computer Science and Engineering department. Though the primary purpose of this project is to utilize information technology in the area of assistive technology, it can also serve students, who do not have Internet connection to browse the text based website or who do not have access to a computer. Since this Web portal can be accessed through a phone call, students will also be able to access CSE department information while they are on the go.

Similarly, Kolias et al., (2004) described the design and implementation of an audio wiki application accessible via the Public Switched Telephone Network (PSTN) and the Internet for educational purposes. The application exploits World Wide Web Consortium standards such as VoiceXML, Speech Synthesis Markup Language (SSML) and Speech Recognition Grammar Specification (SRGS). The purpose of the application was to assist visually impaired, technologically uneducated, and underprivileged people in accessing information originally intended to be accessed visually via a Personal Computer. Users access wiki content via wired or mobile phones, or via a Personal Computer using a Web Browser or a Voice over IP service. In its current form, the application supports pronunciation of the content of existing articles via synthetic speech. It does not support editing or creation of new articles due to the incapability of existing recognition engines to provide full speech recognition instead of recognition of words from a predefined set.

Motiwalla and Qin (2007) explored the integration of speech or voice recognition technologies into m-Learning applications to reduce access barriers. An educational online forum accessible

Figure 1. Architecture for voice-enabled web-based absentee system (source: Gallivan et al., 2002)

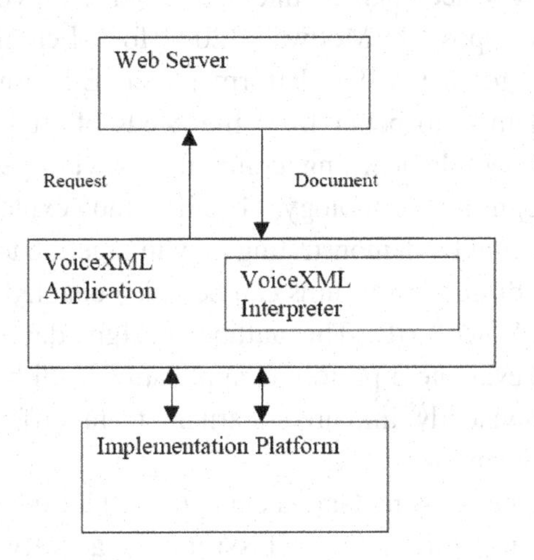

through mobile devices was built, based on an m-Learning framework proposed in Motiwalla and Qin's previous work. A customized Interactive Voice Response (IVR) and Text-To-Speech (TTS) technologies to allow users to interact with the forum through voice commands was also developed. This voice-enabled discussion forum application does not only help normal users to avoid the cumbersome task of typing using small keypads, but also enables people with visual and mobility disabilities to engage in online educations. The prototype forum was tested in two different blind institutions in Massachusetts with 10 users. The results from this study provide insights into how to improve accessibility of m-Learning. The research utilizes the framework in Figure 2 to develop a set of mobile phone accessible applications that can be used for the m-Learning environment.

The architecture in Figure 3 utilises the m-Learning framework in Figure 2. The architecture contains three layers: back-end layer, middle-ware layer, and user interface layer. The back-end layer consists of core Web applications such as forums, Web blogs, Wikis, as well as E-Learning applications such as WebCT, Blackboard, etc. The back-end also consists of the Web/application server that supports those applications. The back-end provides source materials and basic services of the whole m-Learning system. The middle-ware layer consists of components that enable the users to access back-end E-Learning applications through various means. For example, the speech engine may contain customized IVR and TTS technologies or commercial speech recognition software that allow users to interact with the E-Learning applications through voice commands. The mobile application server component enables users to interact with the E-Learning applications through WAP or SMS on their mobile devices. Finally, the user interface layer resides on user devices. Users can access the E-Learning applications on their PCs, telephones, or mobile devices. They can do so by typing messages in text browsers or issuing voice commands.

Also, Azeta et al. (2008c) carried out a preliminary study of the *VeFRA* project on the design and development of a prototype telephone-based E-Learning portal for course registration and

Figure 2. An m-learning framework (source: Motiwalla, 2007)

	Personalized Content	**Collaborative Content**	
PUSH Mechanism	*Pedagogical Agents & Mentors*	*Communication Aids*	*SMS, IM, Alerts, Scheduling Calendars*
PULL Mechanism	*System Tools & Resources*	*Simulated Classrooms*	*WML websites, Discussion Boards & Chat Forums*
	Alerts, Scheduling Calendars, WML websites	*SMS, IM, Discussion Boards & Chat Forums*	**M-learning Applications**

Figure 3. M-learning architecture with speech recognition enhancement (source: Motiwalla & Qin, 2007)

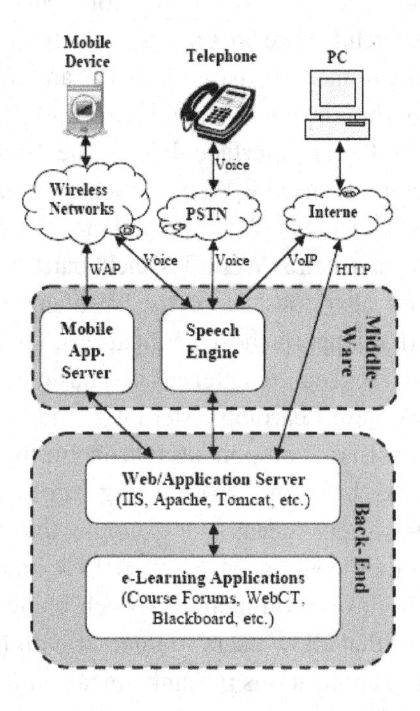

examination by the students. Jianhua et al., (2009) employed the technology of VoiceXML to construct an open VoiceXML-based Mobile Learning System (VMLS). The hardware and software system structure design was achieved. The research results could not only be used in VMLS, but could also be used in other voice-based application system. Peter et al., (2008) presented an architecture to enable multi-channel interaction (Web, SMS/MMS and voice) with services that support collaboration on a blog server. The use of blogs to support learning can be found in some works by Lin et al. (2006) and Divitini et al. (2005). The motivation for this work was to enable learners to access collaborative learning services regardless of their situation and location. Kondratova (2009) discusses issues associated with improving usability of user interactions with mobile devices in mobile learning applications. The focus is on using speech recognition and multimodal interaction in order to improve usability of data entry and information management for mobile learners.

A Voice-enabled Interactive Service (VoIS) was proposed by Motiwalla (2009) for E-Learning. The goal of VoIS platform for an E-Learning system is to better meet the needs of students and mobile learning communities via speech recognition technology. The pilot study explored this goal by demonstrating how interaction tools like discussion forums can be voice-enabled using VoiceXML. The authors design, develop, and evaluate a prototype application with blind and visually impaired learners from different organizations.

The study by Garcia et al., (2010) introduced "Voice Interactive Classroom," a software solution that proposes a middleware approach to provide visual and auditory access to Web-based learning. The approach has successfully enabled the integration of visual interfaces to voice dialogues and to provide auditory access to functionalities already present in various learning management systems such as Segui, Moodle and Sakai.

The educational contents and the framework in these systems lack support for intelligence such as the ability to take decisions that will adapt to users' request. Thus, we believe that if finding suitable content of learning resources can be introduced into a voice-based E-Learning system, including CBR and ontology-based properties, then the voice-based E-Learning system will have the capabilities of providing adaptable and intelligent learning to users.

This study also addresses some of the concerns expressed by Devedzic (2004), where it was noted that there are several challenges in improving Web-based education, such as providing for more intelligence, and that a key enabler of this improvement will be the provision of ontological support. Other studies such as Holohan et al., (2005); Aroyo and Dicheva, (2004); Aroyo et al., (2003) have used ontology to provide E-Learning

Content Generation based on Semantic Web Technology. Meanwhile these approaches were not based on voice architecture.

MOTIVATION FOR THE STUDY

The equipment used as assistive technology for learning in school for the blind like Slate and Stylus, Mathematics board and Figures, Braille, Typewriters, Abacus, and so on are expensive to procure and maintain (Azeta et al., 2009b). As a result of the pace of technological revolution, these pieces of equipment are gradually being replaced by the numerous applications developed to run on the Internet.

The Internet, certainly has received significant attention in recent years, but verbal communication is still the most natural form of interaction amongst human. Therefore the human speech is a very good medium of communication using telephone access. Given the naturalness and expressive power of speech, speech input and output have the potential for becoming key modalities in future interactive systems (Niels, Ole, & Bernsen, 2000). There is an effort to use this kind of communication also in human–computer interaction and for data access on the Web (Ondas, 2006). Mobile phone is one of the media for accessing Web content. The limitations of mobile phones such as small screen size, small keypad, and limited battery power to effectively hold and display information does not pose any constraint to telephone calls and conversation, compared to when using it to access the Web through Wireless Application Protocol (WAP). Typing on the tiny keyboards of WAP-enabled phones or pointing with stylus is very uncomfortable and prone to errors. Another issue is that mobile devices are often used when a person is really "on the move". Operating in such conditions is either impeded or even prohibited, e.g. in the case of car driving (Zaykovskiy, 2006).

The natural way to overcome this problem is the use of voice technology. The possibility of using spoken language to interact with computers has generated wide interest in spoken language technology. Many universities and research laboratories have put their efforts to a development of the spoken language technology (Lerlerdthaiyanupap, 2008). However, voice technology is limited to only one form of input and output – human voice (Kondratova, 2009).

The high popularity and wide spread use of telephone globally, with an estimate of about four billion active telephone lines (fixed and mobile phone) prompted the World Wide Web Consortium (W3C) speech interface framework (Larson, 2000) to create an avenue for users to interact with Web-based services via key pads, spoken commands, prerecorded speeches, synthetic speeches and music. The interface framework led to the massive convergence of Web and voice technologies to provide solutions in the areas of E-Health, E-Stock, E-Democracy, E-Learning and a lot more.

Majority of the present day E-Learning applications have support for the Web user interface (WUI) through the use of PC, while others are based on mobile devices such as Wireless Application Protocol (WAP) phones and Personal Digital Assistants (PDAs). Given the limited input/output capabilities of mobile devices, speech presents an excellent way to enter and retrieve information either alone or in combination with other access modes. Furthermore, people with disabilities should be provided with a wide range of alternative interaction modalities other than the traditional screen-mouse based desktop computing devices. People who suffer disability whether temporary or permanent, either in reading difficulty, visual impairment, or any difficulty using a keyboard, or mouse can rely on speech as an alternate approach for information access (Farinazzo et al., 2010).

The need to reduce access barriers for the visually impaired has necessitated this research in the education domain with mobile and land phones as access point. The problems with the various conventional learning systems such as face to face, telephone, electronic mail, chat room, instant messaging, etc, are numerous, since using them becomes a more difficult task for those with disabilities.

Lack of accessibility in the design of E-Learning courses continues to hinder students with vision impairment. Despite significant advances in assistive technologies, blind and visually impaired Internet users continue to encounter barriers when accessing Web content (Gerber & Kirchner, 2001; Williamson et al., 2001). E-Learning materials are predominantly vision-centric, incorporating images, animation, and interactive media, and as a result students with low or acute vision impairment do not have equal opportunity to gain tertiary qualifications or skills (Armstrong, 2009). A blind person cannot see or communicate through mail or electronic means that require the ability to see the screen. Lack of provision for voice in the conventional learning methods has restricted support for people with limited capabilities such as the visually and mobility impaired that affect either data entry, or ability to read (thus check) what they have entered, since these applications are visual in nature and require the ability sight to see the blackboard or computer screen and manipulate the computer keyboard. More so, it excludes people who have medical history of Repetitive Strain Injury (RSI) as a result of their sedentary lifestyle using a peripheral device such as a keyboard. The Web-based and mobile learning system does not have support for people with textual interpretive problems (e.g. dyslexia) to enter text verbally, and others who have problems of identification of characters and words.

An obvious limitation in providing Information Technology access to learners with low vision is the difficulty that these learners have in reading text. This difficulty is compounded when a visually impaired user is faced with computer technologies and concepts, as a first time user. Voice technology is a possible solution to this problem as it can enable students to learn literacy skills using a more natural human-computer interface (Walsh & Meade, 2003). However, existing voice-based learning application have not been able to adequately proffer solution to the problem of providing suitable learning content in the midst of numerous learning resources available on the Web for both normal and visually impaired learners.

STATEMENT OF THE PROBLEM

In some Educational Institutions, particularly public schools in the developing nations, there is growing shortage of academic staff and the demand for teachers has continued to increase. Demand for access to education remains much higher than the system's physical capacity to accommodate students in public schools (NUC, 2004). As a result, the ratio of teachers to students is constantly unbalanced with students having an increasing number. The process involved in conducting course registration, lecture delivery, examination and result is tedious, since many students are attended to by few teachers. More so, no adequate attention is given to students by their teachers in the areas of counseling, teaching, invigilation, etc. Currently, several Universities and Colleges are overcrowded with inadequate facilities to match the upsurge, thus resulting in deviation from the approved carrying capacity accomplished with poor academic performance (Bobbie et al., 2008).

While trying to address the aforementioned problems, many studies have shown the value of existing platforms such as Web and m-Learning, but lack access to such applications for the large number of students through virtual learning. The number of E-Learning Web portal has continued to rise as a result of the advancement in Web technologies. Some of the popular Web portal available for learning includes: Moodle, WebCT,

Blackboard and Claroline (Ermalai et al., 2009). Voice-based learning (Motiwalla & Qin, 2007) evolved to address the problems of accessibility associated with m-Learning, arising from the limitation in using mobile phone to access learning content on the Web.

With the proliferation of Web learning resources, finding suitable content (using telephone) has become a rigorous task for voice-based online learners to achieve better performance. The biggest disadvantage of voice-based technologies is the rigid structure that they impose on the end user. While it is convenient to use mobile telephony application, it can be extremely slow when the user is forced to drill through several layers of options before finding exactly what he/she wants (Raghuraman, 2004). The Finding Content Suitability (FCS) problem with voice E-Learning applications is more complex when the visually impaired learner is involved. Thus, existing voice-enabled E-Learning applications lack the necessary attributes of reasoning and adaptability during interaction to be able to address the FCS problem.

To solve the FCS problem and enhance voice-based learning, recommending and adapting the contents to the needs of each student is required. It is a necessity that spoken dialogue system performance be enhanced through adaptation (Pakucs, 2003). More so, the adoption of artificial intelligence methodologies using CBR and domain ontology to provide recommendation services to the different needs of students is essential (Abdel-Badeeh and Rania, 2005). Generally, there is dearth of voice application in the domain of E-Learning and the few existing voice-based E-Learning application are not intelligent to provide recommendation services beyond student's queries and request.

Thus, we take cognizance of the fact that there is no reference model containing intelligence upon which the existing voice-based E-Learning applications were developed. Although the approach employed for developing some of them are the general software development life-cycle model, they do not constitute a framework to provide intelligence for voice E-Learning applications.

THE VEFRA FRAMEWORK

This section presents requirement elicitation and *VeFRA* framework. The components of *VeFRA* framework including adaptation and recommendation services are discussed. An Education Ontology was designed using Protégé 3.4.1 and developed with Web Ontology Language (OWL).

ELICITATION OF REQUIREMENTS

The development of a framework requires domain information from the potential users of the system. A school for visually impaired and non-visually impaired were visited to enabled us acquire the required information. The investigation carried out in the visually impaired school shows that the conventional assistive equipment used are expensive to acquire and maintain. It is also difficult to organize the visually impaired learners into classes from their hostel without the assistance of attendants, and this make the entire learning process to be cumbersome.

From investigation carried out in schools attended by the normal learners (i.e. students from non-visually impaired institutions), the existing learning methods in most public institutions in Nigeria are yet to sufficiently provide E-Learning access to students to enable them learn independently (i.e. on their own or on the move) irrespective of location. Students have to be physically present in the classroom to participate in class lectures. This does not favor most of the working class students who have to constantly leave the office for lectures, tutorial and examination. It is the opinion of students and management of one of the campuses/centers that a system that allows the students to learn on their own through distance learning would minimize the problem of over-enrollment of students and scarcity of teachers, among others in the centers.

The collated requirements and specification for the system include: registration of courses, audio streaming of lecture notes, tutorial questions and answers, course examination and checking of examination results. In order to activate the intelligent component services of the system, discussions were held with some students and teachers involved in the learning process to gather the required information that is relevant for CBR paradigm. The system requirement is presented in Figure 4, in which the outer circle is the actual needs of the learners. The inner circle is the platform upon which the framework was developed and deployed.

THE VOICE-ENABLED FRAMEWORK

A user-centric design approach is adopted in order to develop a framework that is based on voice interaction. A survey was conducted to find out the requirements of an E-Learning systems, and in particular that of the visually impaired. From the data collated from the survey questionnaire, significant differences were found between expert users, beginners and intermediate users. Expert users can do most of the typical tasks that users would normally do on the E-Learning application, participate in tutorials and check examination results. As was expected, beginners have little or no knowledge of some particular learning content. Based on the information gathered, the following points were identified as major requirements for the framework and application: 1) Ability to provide users with services involving course registration, voice lecture, tutorial, examination and result; 2) ability to accommodate different types of users based on their respective learning profile; 3) ability to differentiate the course contents into different levels such as expert, intermediate and beginners; and 4) selection of different course contents based on users' profile. The proposed framework for *VeFRA* is shown in Figure 5. The framework comprises of interaction and intelligent layer.

Learner's knowledge level is subdivided into three categories: beginner, intermediate and expert. Learner profile determines whether a learner should receive beginner, intermediate or expert content of lecture, tutorial, examination and result module. The system navigation process is contained in the interaction management. The classification as beginner, intermediate or expert level is done through content adaptation and recommendation using score allocation and result evaluation services. The intelligent information retrieval (IR) involving CBR and stemming is engaged to provide recommended answers to tutorial questions using previous experience of learners, and also to expand the search for answers using stemming algorithm. Learning objects consist of chunks of course materials in text format which allow information to be presented in several ways to users. Tutorial questions asked by previous learners and E-Learning data are stored in case knowledge and domain ontology respectively.

Figure 4. The system requirement for VeFRA framework

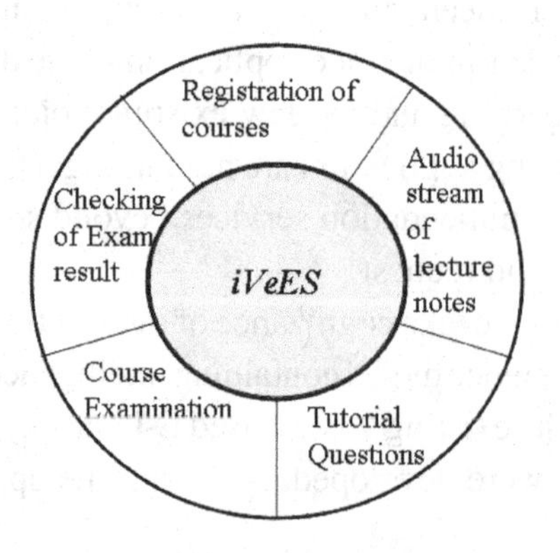

Figure 5. Voice-enabled framework for recommender and adaptation (VeFRA) systems

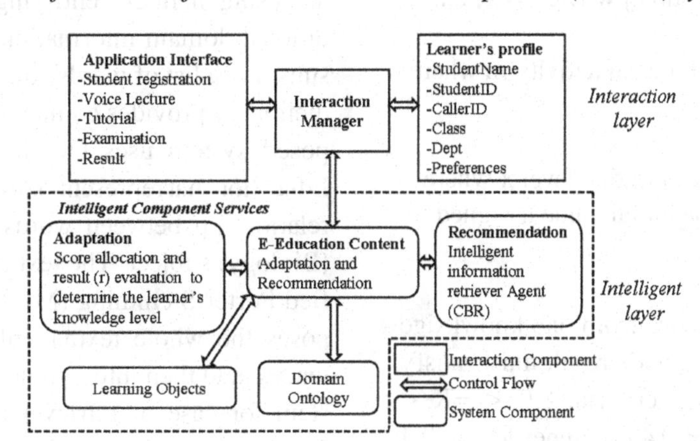

The Adaptation Component Service

The adaptation component service uses the auto score allocation and result (r) evaluation model to determine the learner's knowledge level. The model is expected to create the most suitable course content for each learner and control the passage from one knowledge level to another. There is within a particular knowledge level, an activity (quiz) containing at least one question. Before moving from one knowledge level to another, the system must evaluate the learner's performance through set of evaluations. The evaluation criteria are represented in Figure 6.

Score allocated for each question:

$$Q = \sum_{k=1}^{q} Q_k \text{ and } S = \frac{Max(r)}{Q} \tag{4.1}$$

Evaluation result for each Activity:

Figure 6. A model of score evaluation criterion

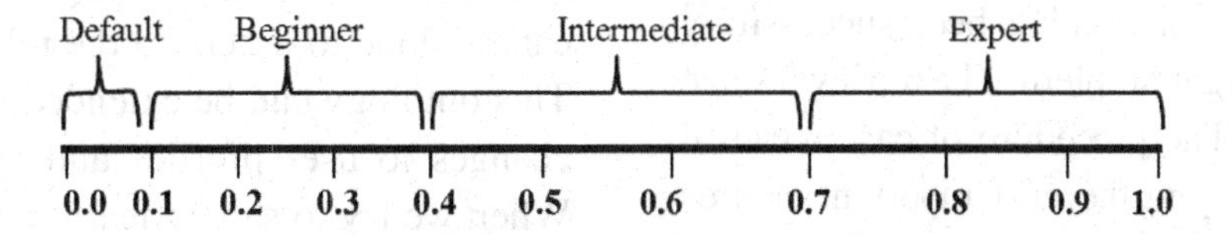

$$Y = \left(\sum_{j=1}^{s} S_j\right) + W \tag{4.2}$$

Evaluation result for each knowledge level:

$$R = \sum_{m=1}^{y} Y_m \tag{4.3}$$

The following assumptions were made in formulating Equations 3.1, 3.2 and 3.3.

r = Expected result for score evaluation criteria (see Figure 14).

Max(r) = The largest value of r.

R = evaluation result for each knowledge level t where t = 1, 2..,r.

Q = total number of questions for each activity k where k = 1, 2,.., q.

S = score for each question j where j = 1, 2,.., s.

Y = evaluation result for each activity m where m = 1, 2,.., y.

W = weight for each knowledge level x where x = 1, 2, …, r. W is the initial value assigned to each knowledge level.

To be allowed to move from one knowledge level to another, the learner's result must satisfy the following transition criteria: 0.0 < =R < 0.1(default), 0.1 < R < 0.4 (beginner level), 0.4 < R < 0.7 (intermediate level), and 0.7 < R <= 1.0 (expert level). The learner's experiences and situation were captured in the learner's profile. By using this experience, the system is able to offer to the current learner the best suited learning content. This experience was captured and provided using CBR.

The Recommendation Component Service

The recommendation service was designed using CBR, stemming and domain ontology. One of the main challenges is to establish structures with which data can be represented as cases. This structure is presented in Figure 7. Alphanumeric data are stored as *text,* numeric data as *number* and date as *date* attribute. A typical data entry for the structure would be 011122, BIO200, "Introduction to Biology", "BiologyCase", "What is Biology", "Biology is the study of life and a branch of the natural sciences", "09-04-2010", "partial".

CBR may be viewed as a cycle involving four steps (Spasic et al., 2005): *retrieve* the most similar case, *reuse* the case to solve the new problem, *revise* the suggested solution and *retain* the useful information obtained during problem solving, after the solution has been successfully adapted to the target problem. The retrieval stage is the first step. The procedure of case retrieval begins with identifying the most important features and using them in identifying cases to reuse. Additional domain information often improves results, i.e. a list of words and their synonyms or a dictionary provides comparable words. Our proposed system uses Ontology for Voice-based Education that represents specific knowledge, i.e., relationship between words used in Education (Biology) subject. The text tokenizer and Modified Porter Stemming (MPS) algorithm decomposes the whole textual information into sentences, and then into individual words with their stem for ease of retrieval of its synonyms. A Computation of the weight for every word and enhancement of term using ontology are required to improve retrieval effectiveness due to the huge amount of words.

A UML sequence diagram for the recommendation service is shown in Figure 8. The learner initiates voice response for tutorial questions and the learners' characteristics are updated. The request for tutorial question is executed using search agent, which then provides the recommended answer using some rules. Thereafter, the recommended answer is passed to the leaner through voice response.

ONTOLOGY-BASED MODEL OF VEFRA FRAMEWORK

Domain ontology is a detailed description about an application specific domain including concepts, entities, attributes and processes related to a given application domain. In this research, our domain is *Education Ontology*. The proposed ontology consists of E-Learning objects and their relationships. Therefore via these ontological relationships, the required learning resources can be located and their metadata can be retrieved. Then matching of user profiles and learning resource metadata can be done to ascertain the relevance of them. This ontology can be extended according to the changes to user profiles and learning content. When we try to satisfy learner requirements we

Figure 7. A case structure for VeFRA

Case field	Attribute
StudentID:	number
CourseID:	text
CourseTitle :	text
CaseName:	text
Query:	text
Solution:	text
Date:	date
SearchMethod:	text

need to match the user profiles with the learning objects in the system (Heiyanthuduwage et al., 2006). However, a direct matching between the learning objects and user profiles is not efficient enough and it will take lot of memory.

THE EDUCATION ONTOLOGY DEVELOPMENT

Our first goal was to collect and structure the available information related to the use of ontologies in the field of education. In this study, we have to deal with subject domain ontology and not structure ontology. The *domain ontology* represents the basic concepts of the domain under consideration along with their interrelations and basic properties. The *structure ontology* defines the logical structure of the content. The Web Ontology Language (OWL) was used to design our ontology. We created an ontology named Education.owl and three classes that model separately the different components of the system. The ontology is encoded in OWL using Protégé 3.4.1. In the ontology there are classes, relationships and attributes related to the domain. New classes, relationships and attributes can be entered to the ontology e.g. by using Protégé 3.4.1. Each model can be extended to include as many relationships and classes as possible. The knowledge base resides in Apache HTTP Server. Figure 9 shows a snapshot of our Education ontology with the classes and properties. It has three classes; Learner, LearningContent and Assessment. A child node is an instance of a father node i.e. Course and Tutorial are instances of LearningContent. All the instances of Enumeration applies to all the classes. The ontology can be used for adaptive learning to retrieve the content of a course. The architecture of Education Ontology model is presented in Figure 10, with the three classes and the relationships between the classes.

Once a class of the ontology is selected, the application delivers the instances related to that class. Figure 11a and 11b presents Classes in Education.owl Ontology and the properties/rela-

Figure 8. A UML sequence diagram for recommendation service

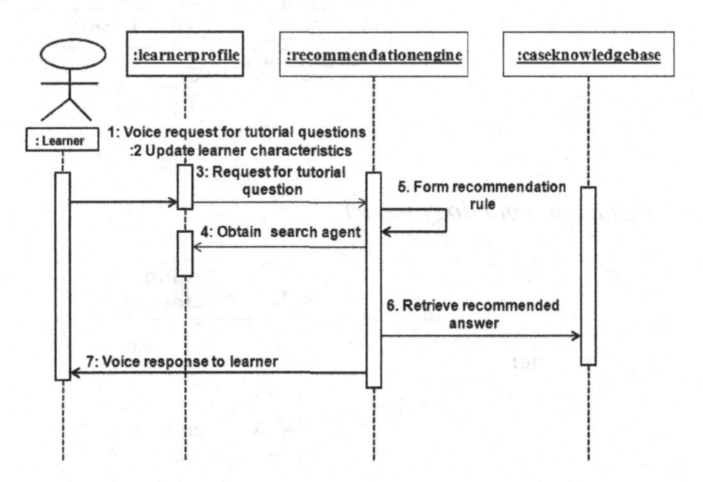

tions respectively using Protégé 3.4.1. The development of the Education ontology involves the creation of the classes, properties and relationship between deferent classes.

VEFRA APPLICATION ARCHITECTURE

The VoiceXML *VeFRA* architecture (see Figure 19) consists of some VoiceXML software suites including Registration, Voice lecture, Tutorial, Examination and Results. For this prototype implementation, we used free Voxeo hosting service to provide a quick way to get started in order to eliminate huge capital expenses in subscription.

The *VeFRA* application architecture shown in Figure 12 was drawn using modular architectural design. The description of the architecture is presented as follows:

1. The learner connects through a telephone and PSTN to the VoiceXML interpreter through Voxeo Speech gateway.
2. The VoiceXML interpreter execute the call interaction with a caller using the instructions of a VoiceXML script supplied by the voice commands in application server.
3. The interpreter calls TTS and ASR as plugins to complete its tasks.
4. The VoiceXML interpreter communicates via Web protocols (HTTP) to VoiceXML application server.
5. The VoiceXML application server delivers the application including VoiceXML text pages.
6. The Web application server queries the database via apache to dynamically retrieve information and the VoiceXML interpreter TTS speak with the caller.

Figure 9. Main classes of the education.owl ontology

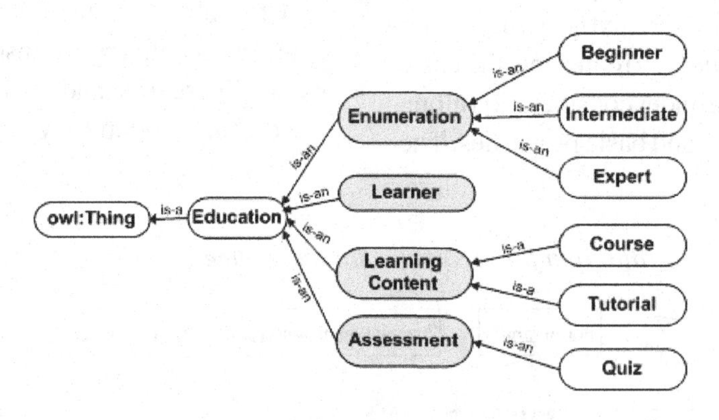

Figure 10. Architecture of education ontology model

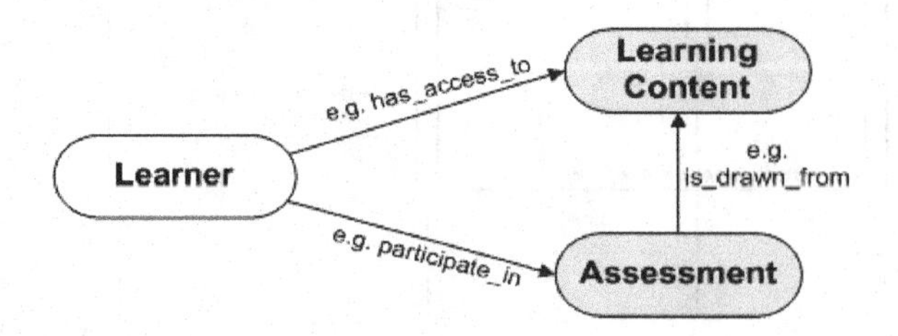

Figure 11. A screenshot of education ontology design using Protégé 3.4.1

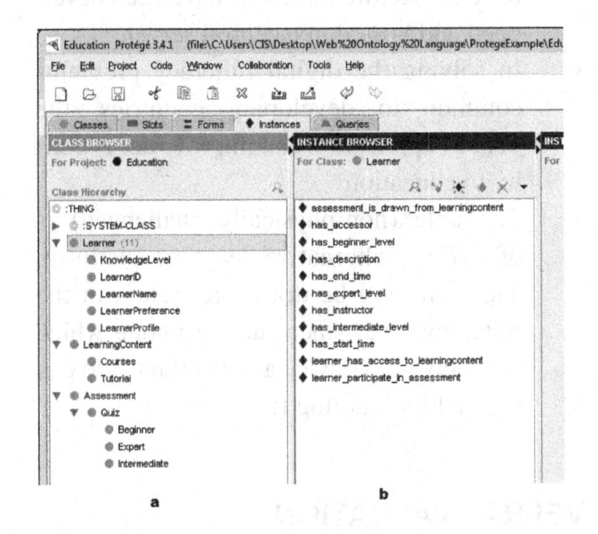

SYSTEMS IMPLEMENTATION

A prototype application has been developed using the *VeFRA* framework. The components of the application comprising design, implementation and development have been reported in Azeta et al., (2009b) and Azeta et al., (2009c). Figure 13 contains screen shot of a sample tutorial question used to demonstrate the recommendation component service of the application. The faculty or course lecturer select course code, course title, and type tutorial question for which answers are sought. The date is automatically selected by the system. It is the responsibility of the faculty to select the search method as either partial of perfect. Partial means displayed answers will include both the exact match and matches that are similar, whereas perfect search showcased answers that are exact. The WUI is developed for system administration purposes such as upload of tutorial questions and lecture notes. Voxeo speech platform (Voxeo, 2003) was engaged as the speech server while CBR and Modified Porter Stemming (MPS) algorithm were used to provide intelligent services.

A prototype part of the VoiceXML application (voice user interface) was deployed on a Voxeo voice server (Voxeo, 2003) on the Web and accessed from a mobile phone and land phone using the format: <source country int. dial out #> <destination country code><destination area code><generated voice network 7 digit #>. Figure 14 shows a model of mobile phone interaction with the system. A user dial a telephone number in Figure 14a. Once a connection is established

Figure 12. VeFRA application architecture

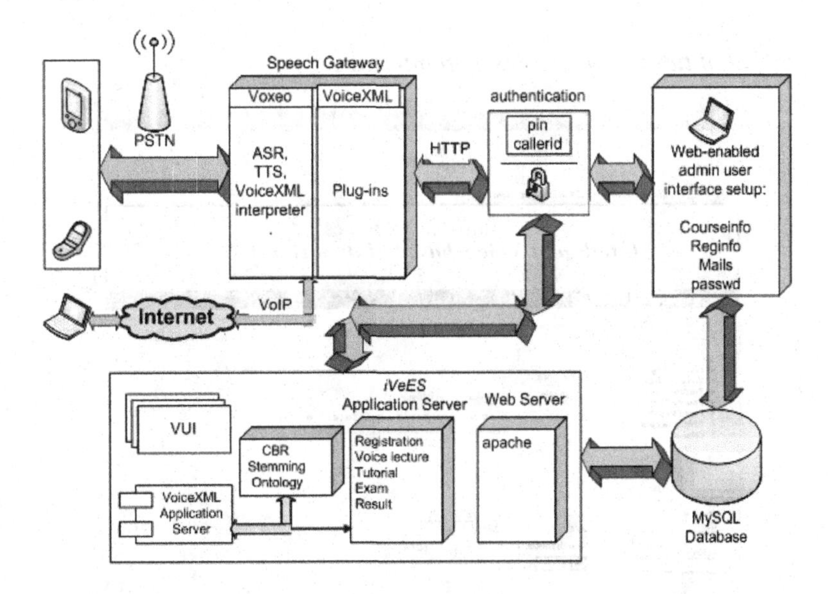

(Figure 14b), the user can then commence conversation (Figure 14c) with *VeFRA*.

Similarly, a prototype part of the Web application (Web user interface) was deployed on a Web server on the Internet and can be accessed using an Internet ready desktop PC by visiting the URL - http://www.emma.byethost24.com/eEducation. After deploying the application, the teachers and students went through some training session to guide them on how to use the prototype application. One of the information given to the students and teachers was that *VeFRA* allows only multiple choice questions.

BENEFITS OF VEFRA

The *VeFRA* system offers numerous benefits:

- The *VeFRA* application can reduce the related expenses for the traditional face-to-face learning method which is common in most developing countries such as lecture halls and other learning delivery facilities associated with physical presence between the students and teachers.
- The *VeFRA* application can provide economies of scale at tertiary institutions, as cost of each additional learner is negligible once the lecture materials have been developed and hosted in a central server.
- In solving the digital illiteracy problems common to developing countries, the *VeFRA* application can improve accessibility to education.
- The able (non-physically challenged) is offered an alternative learning platform; and there will be drastic reduction in the illiteracy level since mobile phone which is widely used device all over the world can be used for learning (m-Learning).

VEFRA EVALUATION

The *VeFRA* application was evaluated for usability to determine the level of effectiveness, efficiency and users' satisfaction. The evaluation of a product is a fundamental requirement in determining the practical usability of a product (Ikhu-Omoregbe, 2010). The usability of the E-Learning application was measured to specify the features and attributes required to make the product usable using ISO's standard of usability (ISO 9241-11, 1998).

Figure 13. A screen shot of tutorial questions web interface

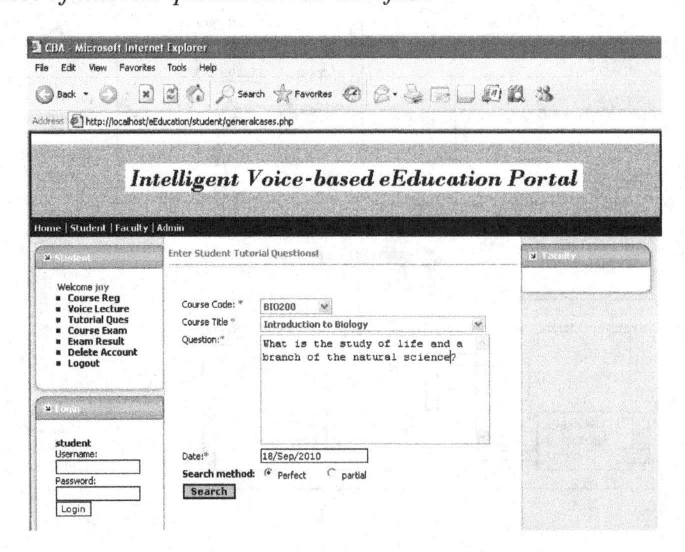

Figure 14. A model of mobile phone interaction with VeFRA

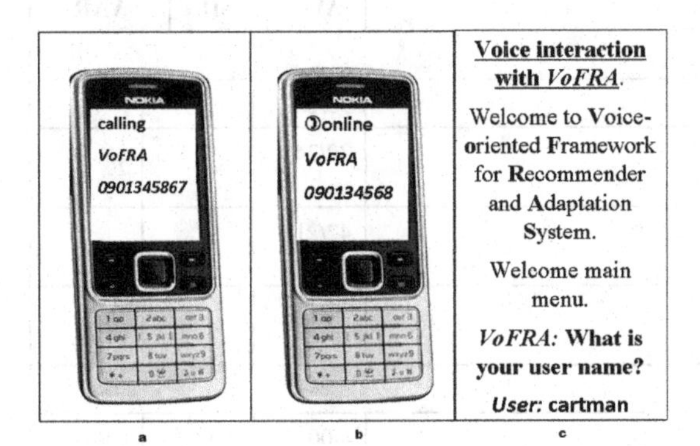

RESEARCH DESIGN

In conducting the usability evaluation, questionnaire were designed and administered. The teachers and students from a school for the blind and partially sighted in Lagos, Nigeria were some of the respondents. The survey questionnaire was divided into five sections namely: background information, user experience with mobile phone and the system, effectiveness of the system, efficiency of the system and user satisfaction with the system.

Each section of Effectiveness, Efficiency and User satisfaction contains five Questions represented by Q1, Q2, Q3, Q4 and Q5. The questionnaire aims at eliciting information from the school in order to measure the usability of the voice-based E-Learning application provided. A total of 70 questionnaires were administered on teachers and students but only 63 responses were received, analyzed and reported (see Table 1). The questions were designed using five-point likert-scale where 1= strongly disagree, 2 = disagree, 3= undecided, 4 = agree and 5= strongly agree.

EVALUATION RESULTS

An overall score of all the learners was computed for each of the usability dimensions by averaging all the ratings on the questionnaire that was used. With the assistance of some of the non-visually impaired teachers, the respondents were taken through a short training on how to use a mobile phone to dial a number that will connect the learners to the application and show how to navigate within the application. In terms of ownership/ usage of mobile phones, users in our sample own/use mobile phones for almost 6 years which resulted to 35 as those having and 28 as those not having experience. In the area of acquiring ICT training to be able to use the application, 51 out of 63 said they would need training. The average effectiveness is 3.98, average efficiency is 4.29 and average users' satisfaction is 4.13.

Some learners were concerned with the time it took for *VeFRA* to recognize a human voice as a result of noise distortion, and that accounted for the low score of 3.98 out of 5 in the question that say "*The voice request & response I got from the*

Table 1. Descriptive statistical analysis of questionnaire data

Summary of Study Variable						
Usability Measures	**Responses from Teachers**		**Responses from Students**		**Total # of Respondents**	**Total Mean Rating**
	Visually Impaired Teachers	**Normal Teachers**	**Visually Impaired Students**	**Normal Students**		
Effectiveness	5	5	47	6	63	3.98
Efficiency	6	6	47	6	63	4.29
Satisfaction	6	6	47	6	63	4.13

Table 2. User survey results (N=63)

	Survey Questions	AVG	SD	VAR
Background Information				
Do you own/use a mobile phone? [yes] [no]		35/28		
Would you be able to afford a mobile phone to call the e-Learning application? [yes] [no]		39/24		
Would you support the use of mobile phone for e-Learning in your school? [yes] [no]		42/21		
Do you need more computing skills/training/time to be able to use the system? [yes] [no]		51/12		
Effectiveness				
Q1	I was able to complete my task successfully and correctly using the application	4.00	0.92	0.84
Q2	The system did not show error message(s) while using it.	4.02	0.85	0.73
Q3	I was able to recover from my mistakes easily.	4.16	0.83	0.68
Q4	I feel comfortable using the application.	4.21	0.83	0.68
Q5	The voice request & response I got from the system was clear	3.49	0.56	0.32
Average Effectiveness		3.98	0.80	0.65
Efficiency				
Q1	Using the system saves me time of learning	4.08	0.81	0.65
Q2	I was able to complete my task on time	4.21	0.72	0.52
Q3	I was well able to navigate the voice user interface on time when using the system	4.41	0.74	0.55
Q4	I didn't have to carry out too many/difficult steps before completing my Task	4.35	0.74	0.55
Q5	The learning content I requested for suited my needs	4.38	0.77	0.59
Average Efficiency		4.29	0.75	0.57
User Satisfaction				
Q1	The system was easy to learn	4.05	0.83	0.69
Q2	The system was easy to use and user friendly	4.13	0.75	0.56
Q3	I am satisfied using the system	4.11	0.84	0.71
Q4	I feel the system met my need	4.21	0.79	0.62
Q5	I am satisfied with the performance of the system in accomplishing my tasks	4.13	0.79	0.62
Average User Satisfaction		4.13	0.80	0.64
Learnability				
Q1	The system provides clarity of wordings.	4.10	0.82	0.67
Q2	The grouping and ordering of menu options is logical for easy learning.	4.06	0.76	0.58
Q3	The command names are meaningful.	4.05	0.83	0.69
Q4	I could perform tasks on a proficient level as a first time user	4.13	0.81	0.66
Q5	As new user, I was able to orient myself with the system	4.02	0.79	0.63
Average Learnability		4.07	0.80	0.65

continued on following page

Table 2. Continued

	Survey Questions	AVG	SD	VAR
Memorability				
Q1	I gain the same level of skill as the last time I used the system	4.02	0.81	0.66
Q2	I was able to remember the commands I performed last time	4.13	0.73	0.53
Q3	I was able to reestablish my skills after a long time of using the system	4.11	0.76	0.58
Q4	I could recall every commands I performed moments earlier	4.14	0.76	0.58
Q5	I could remember the ordering of menu structure after a long time of using the system	4.13	0.73	0.53
Average Memorability		4.11	0.76	0.58
Resultant Average Rating		4.12	0.78	0.62

system was clear". The recognition rate of Voxeo ASR engine was ineffective some of the times arising from noise interference. The VoiceXML interpreter for TTS had problems compiling strings stored in the database with single and double quotes ('and"). The quotes were edited out of the text to record success in TTS translation. Notwithstanding, the user survey results were encouraging, particularly, the Question two (Q2) under efficiency in Table 2 that asked '*I was able to complete my task on time*' resulting to 4.21.

FREQUENCY DISTRIBUTION OF VEFRA USABILITY EVALUATION

In the five questions that make up the efficiency questionnaire category, question five (Q5) contains the question "*The learning content I requested for suited my needs*". This section presents the statistical analysis of Q5 as shown in Figure 15, 16 and 17.

The usability attributes analysis of the evaluation for Effectiveness, Efficiency and User Satisfaction is shown in Figure 18.

USABILITY EVALUATION

Several usability studies suggest the system with "Very Bad Usability" should have 1 as mean rating, "2 as Bad Usability", 3 as Average Usability, "4 as Good Usability" and "5 as Excellent Usability". Sauro et al., (2005) proposed that "Good Usability" should have a mean rating of 4 on a 1-5 scale and 5.6 on a 1-7 scale. Therefore, it can be concluded that the prototype application developed for the school has "Good Usability" based on the average (AVG) total rating of 4.13.

Figure 15. Mean rating for Q5 (efficiency)

N	Valid	63
	Missing	0
Mean		4.3810
Std. Deviation		.77102
Variance		.594

Figure 16. Frequency distribution for Q5 (efficiency)

Q5_Efficiency

		Frequency	Percent	Valid Percent	Cumulative Percent
Valid	2.00	1	1.6	1.6	1.6
	3.00	8	12.7	12.7	14.3
	4.00	20	31.7	31.7	46.0
	5.00	34	54.0	54.0	100.0
	Total	63	100.0	100.0	

Figure 17. Frequency data for Q5 (efficiency) histogram

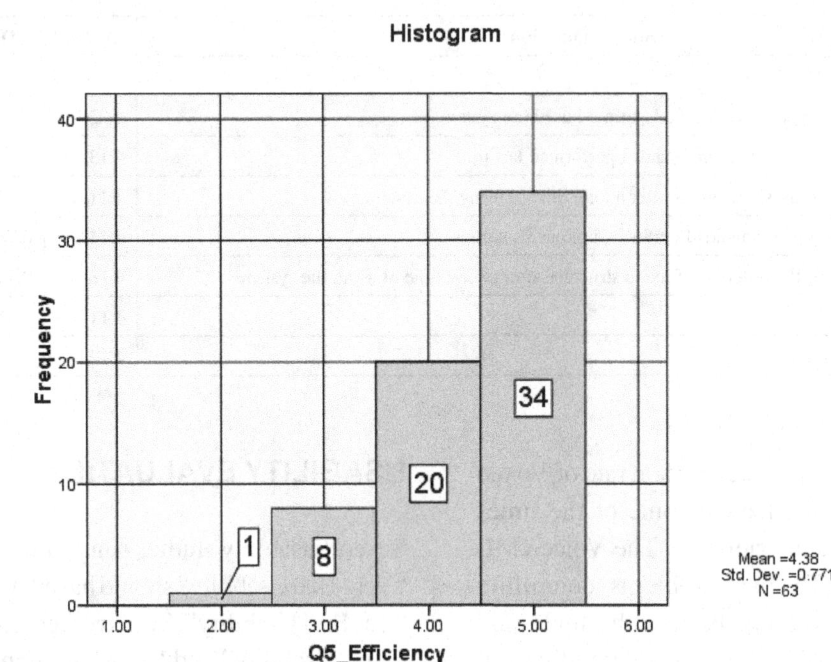

FUTURE RESEARCH DIRECTIONS

The future research direction, for this study is two-fold. First, evaluation of the system using PARAdigm for Dialogue System Evaluation (PARADISE), and second voice biometric techniques based on speech data will be added as additional means of security mechanism to enhance the authentication of candidates for examination. One key identification technique is the use of voiceprint of the caller. An improved system should therefore be provided as further research to combine the conventional pin/telephone number authentication and biometric to increase security of the system.

With these additional features, the voice learning application will be able to provide a more participatory and secured voice-based educational experience for the students.

Figure 18. Usability attributes analysis of VeFRA

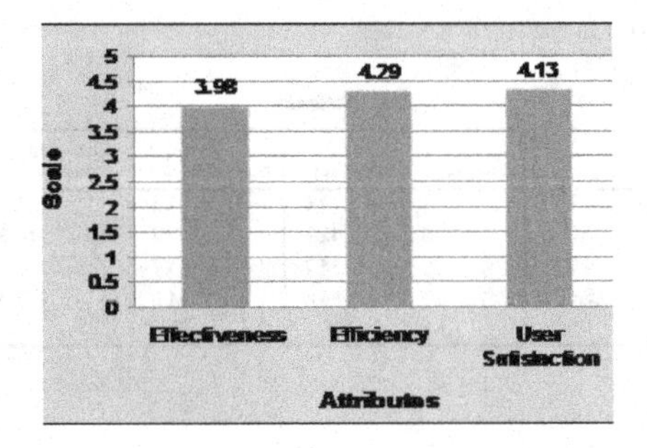

CONCLUSION

In this thesis, a voice-enabled famework for recommender and adaptation system has been provided to offer solution to the problem encountered by learners who use telephone to access Web learning content. This study attempts to solve the problem of using telephone access to find content suitability (FCS) among the numerous learning resources on the Web. The *VeFRA* framework was used as a generic work guideline to develop a prototype intelligent voice-based E-Learning application for the *VeFRA* project. The intelligent component services of the application were realized using CBR, Modified Porter Stemming (MPS) algorithm and ontology. The prototype application was tested in a school for the blind, and the result of evaluation shows that the prototype application developed for the school has "Good Usability" rating of 4.13 out of 5 scale. The findings show that the users are enthusiastic about using a voice-based telephone learning as another form of assistive technology to compliment the conventional learning methods for the visually impaired.

The framework would serve as a reference model for implementing telephone-based E-Learning applications for normal and visually impaired learners. The application will also assist people with physical access difficulties (e.g. repetitive strain injury, arthritis, high spinal injury) that make writing difficult. It could equally be useful to students with reading or spelling difficulties (e.g. dyslexia). It is also vital in the area of ubiquitous learning. The E-Learning application will be useful especially for students who are physically challenged such as the visually impaired. It will also be useful for people who have medical history of reacting to Repetitive Strain Injury (RSI) as a result of their sedentary lifestyle using the keyboard. Therefore this system gives every learner equal right and access to quality education irrespective of his or her physical disability.

The E-Learning system offers an alternative platform of learning for learners without disability. It complements the existing E-Learning systems such as Web-based learning, m-Learning, etc. The E-Learning system offers the possibility to learn anytime and anywhere there is telephone access, regardless of the availability of Internet services.

REFERENCES

Abdel-Badeeh, M. S., & Rania, A. (2005). A case based expert system for supporting diagnosis of heart diseases, *AIML Journal, 5*(1).

Armstrong, H. (2009). Advanced IT education for the vision impaired via e-learning. *Journal of Information Technology Education, 8*, 244–256.

Aroyo, L., & Dicheva, D. (2004). The new challenges for e-learning: The educational semantic web. *Journal of Educational Technology & Society, 7*(4), 59–69.

Azeta, A. A., Ayo, C. K., Atayero, A. A., & Ikhu-Omoregbe, N. A. (2008c). Development of a telephone-based e-learning portal. In *Proceedings of the 1st International Conference on Mobile Computing, Wireless Communication, E-Health, M-Health and TeleMedicine (FICMWiComTel-Health'08)*, (pp. 141-149). Ogbomosho, Nigeria: FICMWiComTelHealth.

Azeta, A. A., Ayo, C. K., Atayero, A. A., & Ikhu-Omoregbe, N. A. (2009b). Application of voiceXML in e-learning systems. In *Cases on Successful E-Learning Practices in the Developed and Developing World: Methods for the Global Information Economy*. Hershey, PA: IGI Global. doi:10.4018/978-1-60566-942-7.ch007.

Azeta, A. A., Ayo, C. K., Atayero, A. A., & Ikhu-Omoregbe, N. A. (2009c). A case-based reasoning approach for speech-enabled e-learning system. In *Proceedings of 2nd IEEE International Conference on Adaptive Science & Technology (ICAST)*. Accra, Ghana: IEEE. Retrieved from http://ieeexplore.ieee.org/xpl/mostRecentIssue.jsp?punumber=5375737

Bobbie, P. O., Fordjour, I., Aboagye, D. O., Dzidonu, C., Darkwa, O., & Nyantakyi, K. (2008). Technology enablers for collaborative virtual education. In *Proceedings of 3rd International Conference on ICT for Development, Education and Training AICC*. Accra, Ghana: AICC.

Bures, I. M., & Jelinek, I. (2004). Description of the adaptive web system for e-learning. In *Proceedings of IADIS International Conference E-Society 2004*, (Vol. 2). IADIS. Retrieved from http://www.iadis.net/dl/final_uploads/200402C042.pdf

Chin, C. C., Hock, G. T., & Veerappan, C. M. (2006). VoiceXML as solution for improving web accessibility and manipulation for e-education. In *Proceedings of School of Computing and IT, INTI College*. Malaysia: INTI. Retrieved from http://intisj.edu.my/INTISJ/InfoFor/StaffResearch/10.pdf

Cranefield, S., Hart, L., Dutra, M., Baclawski, K., Kokar, M., & Smith, J. (2002). UML for ontology development. *The Knowledge Engineering Review*, (17): 61–64.

Devedzic, V. (2004). Education and the semantic web. *International Journal of Artificial Intelligence in Education, 14*, 9–65.

Dicheva, D., Sosnovsky, S., Gavrilova, T., & Brusilovsky, P. (2005). Ontological web portal for educational ontologies. In *Proceedings of International Workshop on Applications of Semantic Web Technologies for E-Learning (SW-EL)*. Amsterdam: SW-EL. Retrieved from http://www.win.tue.nl/SW-EL/2005/swel05-aied05/proceedings/4-Dicheva-final-full.pdf

Divitini, M., Haugalokken, O., & Morken, E. M. (2005). Blog to support learning in the field: Lessons learned from a fiasco. In *Proceedings of the Fifth IEEE International Conference on Advanced Learning Technologies (ICALT '05)*, (pp. 219- 221). IEEE.

Donegan, M. (2000). BECTA voice recognition project report. *In Proceedings of BECTA*. Retrieved from http://www.becta.org.uk/teachers/teachers.cfm?section=2&id=2142

Ermalai, I. And one, D., & Vasiu, R. (2009). Study cases on e-learning technologies used by universities in romania and worldwide. *WSEAS Transactions on Communications, 8*(8), 785–794. Retrieved from http://www.wseas.us/E-library/transactions/communications/2009/29-640.pdf

Farinazzo, V., Salvador, M., & Luiz, A. S. Kawamoto, & de Oliveira Neto, J. S. (2010). An empirical approach for the evaluation of voice user interfaces. *User Interfaces*. Retrieved from www.intechopen.com/download/pdf/pdfs_id/10804

Gallivan, P., Hong, Q., Jordan, L., Li, E., Mathew, G., & Mulyani, Y. … Tappert, C. (2002). VoiceXML absentee system. In *Proceedings of MASPLAS'02: The Mid-Atlantic Student Workshop on Programming Languages and Systems*. Retrieved from http://csis.pace.edu/csis/masplas/p10.pdf

Garcıa, V. M. A., Ruiz, M. P. P., & Perez, J. R. P. (2010). Voice interactive classroom, a service-oriented software architecture for speech-enabled learning. *Journal of Network and Computer Applications, 33*, 603–610. doi:10.1016/j.jnca.2010.03.005.

Gerber, E., & Kirchner, C. (2001). Who's surfing? Internet access and computer use by visually impaired youths and adults. *Journal of Vision Impairment and Blindness, 95*, 176–181.

Ghaleb, F. F. M., Daoud, S. S., Hasna, A. M., Jaam, J. M., & El-Sofany, H. F. (2006). A web-based e-learning system using semantic web framework. *Journal of Computer Science, 2*(8), 619–626. doi:10.3844/jcssp.2006.619.626.

Gil, A., & García-Penalvo, F. J. (2008). Learner course recommendation in e-learning based on swarm intelligence. *Journal of Universal Computer Science, 14*(16), 2737–2755.

Gloss. (2004). Retrieved from http://www.abc.net.au/pipeline/radio/programs/gloss2.htm

Heiyanthuduwage, S. R., & Karunaratne, D. D. (2006). A learner oriented ontology of metadata to improve effectiveness of learning management systems. In *Proceedings of the Third International Conference on E-Learning for Knowledge-Based Society*. Bangkok, Thailand: IEEE.

Holohan, E., Melia, M., McMullen, D., & Pahl, C. (2005). Adaptive e-learning content generation based on semantic web technology. In *Proceedings of Workshop on Applications of Semantic Web Technologies for E-Learning (SW-EL)*. Amsterdam: SW-EL. Retrieved from http://www.win.tue.nl/SW-EL/2005/swel05-aied05/proceedings/5-Holohan-final-full.pdf

Holzinger, A., Smolle, J., & Reibnegger, G. (2006). Learning objects (LO): An object-oriented approach to manage e-learning content. In *Encyclopedia of Information in Healthcare & Biomedicine*. Hershey, PA: IGI Global.

Ikhu-Omoregbe, N. A. (2010). *Development of a formal framework for usable operations support in e-health-based systems*. (Doctoral dissertation). Covenant University, Ota, Nigeria.

ISO 9241-11. (1998). *Ergonomic requirements for office work with visual display terminals (VDTs) - Part 11: Guidance on usability*. Geneva, Switzerland: ISO.

Jain, L. C., & Martin, N. M. (1998). *Fusion of neural network, fuzzy systems, and genetic algorithms: Industrial applications*. Boca Raton, FL: CRC Press International.

Jianhua, W., Long, Z., Jun, Z., & Xiping, D. (2009). A voiceXML-based mobile learning system and its caching strategy. In *Proceedings of MLearn 2009, 8th World Conference on Mobile and Contextual Learning*. Orlando, FL: IEEE.

Kolias, C., Kolias, V., & Anagnostopoulos, L. (2004). *A pervasive wiki application based on voiceXML*. Retrieved from http://www.icsd.aegean.gr/publication_files/conference/275294916.pdf

Kondratova, I. (2009). Multimodal interaction for mobile learning. In Proceedings *of the 5th International Conference (UAHCI '09)*. San Diego, CA: UAHCI.

KSL. (2005). *KSL software and network services*. Retrieved from http://www.ksl.stanford.edu/sns.shtml

Larson, J. (2000). *Introduction and overview of W3C speech interface framework*. W3C Working Draft. Retrieved from http://www.w3.org/TR/2000/WD-voice-intro-20001204/

Lerlerdthaiyanupap, T. (2008). *Speech-based dictionary application*. (MSc Thesis). University of Tampere, Tampere, Finland.

Lin, W. J., Yueh, H. P., Liu, Y. L., Murakami, M., Kakusho, K., & Minoh, M. (2006). Blog as a tool to develop e-learning experience in an international distance course. In *Proceedings of the Sixth International Conference on Advanced Learning Technologies (ICALT'06)*. ICALT.

Motiwalla, L. F. (2009). A voice-enabled interactive services (VòIS) architecture for e-learning. *International Journal on Advances in Life Sciences, 1*(4), 122–133. Retreived from http://www.iariajournals.org/life_sciences/lifsci_v1_n4_2009_paged.pdf

Motiwalla, L. F., & Qin, J. (2007). Enhancing mobile learning using speech recognition technologies: A case study. In *Proceedings of the Eighth World Congress on the Management of eBusiness (WCMeB'07)*. WCMeB.

Niels, O. B. (2000). *Draft position paper for discussion at the ELSNET brainstorming workshop*. Retrieved from http://www.elsnet.org/dox/rM-bernsen-v2.pdf

Nisbet, P. D., & Wilson, A. (2002). *Introducing speech recognition in schools: Using dragon natural speaking*. Edinburgh, UK: University of Edinburgh.

NUC. (2004). The state of Nigerian universities. *Nigerian University System Newsletter, 2*(1).

Oboko, R., Wagacha, P. W., & Omwenga, E. (2008). Adaptive delivery of an object oriented course in a web-based learning environment. In *Proceedings of 3rd International Conference on ICT for Development, Education, and Training*. Accra, Ghana: IEEE.

Ondas, I. S. (2006). VoiceXML-based spoken language interactive system. In *Proceedings 6th PhD Student Conference and Scientific and Technical Competition of Students of Faculty of Electrical Engineering and Informatics Technical University of Košice*. Košice, Slovakia: IRKR. Retrieved from http://irkr.tuke.sk/publikacie/_vti_cnf/Prispevok_eng.pdf

Pakucs, B. (2003). SesaME: A framework for personalised and adaptive speech interfaces. In *Proceedings of EACL-03 Workshop on Dialogue Systems: Interaction, Adaptation and Styles of Management*. Budapest, Hungary: EACL.

Paul, D. (2003). *Speech recognition for students with disabilities*. Edinburgh, UK: University of Edinburgh.

Peter, Y., Vantroys, T., & Lepretre, E. (2008). Enabling mobile collaborative learning through multichannel interactions. In *Proceedings of 4th International Conference on Interactive Mobile and Computer Aided Learning (IMC'08)*. IMC.

Raghuraman, M. B. (2004). *Design and implementation of V-HELP system–A voice-enabled web application for the visually impaired*. (Unpublished Master Thesis). University of Nebraska, Lincoln, NE.

Sauro, J., & Kindlund, E. (2005). A method to standardize usability metrics into a single score. In *Proceedings of CHI'05*. Portland, OR: ACM.

Spasic, I., Ananiadou, S., & Tsujii, J. (2005). *MaSTerClass: A case-based reasoning system for the classification of biomedical terms*. Retrieved http://qr.net/jzsU, accessed 2005.07.05

TellMe Voice Portal. (2002). Retrieved from http://www.tellme.com

Voice, X. M. L. (2007). *VoiceXML application development life cycle*. Palo Alto, CA: Hewlett Packard Development Company. Retrieved from staff.washington.edu/benroy/ivr/vx_devlifecycle.pdf

Voxeo. (2003). *Voice voice server*. Retrieved from http://community.voxeo.com

Walsh, P., & Meade, J. (2003). Speech enabled e-learning for adult literacy tutoring. In *Proceedings of the 3rd IEEE International Conference on Advanced Learning Technologies (ICALT'03)*. IEEE. Retrieved from http://i-learn.uitm.edu.my/resources/journal/j1.pdf

Williamson, K., Wright, S., Schauder, D., & Bow, A. (2001). The internet for the blind and visually impaired. *Journal of Computer Mediated Communication*. Retrieved from http://jcmc.indiana.edu/vol7/issue1/williamson.html

Zaiane, O. R. (2005). Recommended systems for e-learning: Towards non-intrusive web mining. *Data Mining in E-Learning, 2*.

Zaykovskiy, D. (2006). Survey of the speech recognition techniques for mobile devices. In *Proceedings of Speech and Computer (SPECOM'06)*. St. Petersburg, Russia: SPECOM.

ADDITIONAL READING

Aarnio, T. (1999). *Speech recognition with hidden markov models in visual communication*. (Unpublished Master's Thesis). University of Turku, Turku, Finland.

Abbott, K. (2002). *Voice enabling web applications: VoiceXML and beyond*. Berkeley, CA: Apress. doi:10.1007/978-1-4302-0850-1.

Abraham, A. (2005). *Handbook of measuring system design*. New York: John Wiley & Sons.

Abu-Zaina, H., Kirk, D., & Elmer, A. (1996). A speech recognition system for operation of a visual inspection workstation. In *Proceedings of RESNA'96*. Wichita, KS: RESNA. Retrieved from http://www.dinf.ne.jp/doc/english/Us_Eu/conf/resna96/page143.htm.

Adaptive. (2005). *Adaptive and assistive technologies in e-learning*. Retrieved from http://www.adcet.edu.au/StoredFile.aspx?id=1353&fn=adptve_assstv_techn_elearning.Pdf

Begum, S., Ahmed, M. U., Funk, P., Xiong, N., & Schéele, B. B. (2007). Similarity of medical cases in health care using cosine similarity and ontology. In *Proceedings of The 5th Workshop on CBR in the Health Sciences*. Belfast, Ireland: ICCBR. Retrieved from www.cbr-biomed.org/workshops/ICCBR07/iccbr07wk-Begum.pdf

Belkin, N. J. (2005). *Intelligent information retrieval: Whose intelligence. Understanding and Supporting Multiple Information Seeking Strategies*. Newark, NJ: Rutgers University.

Burke, D. (2007). *Speech processing for IP networks, media resource control protocol (MRCP)*. New York: John Wiley & Sons. doi:10.1002/9780470060599.

Chang, S. E. (2007). An adaptive and voice-enabled pervasive web system. *International Journal of Enterprise Information Systems*, *3*(4), 69–83. doi:10.4018/jeis.2007100105.

Chowdhary, K. R. (2005). *Current trends in information retrieval*. Retrieved from http://ncsi-net.ncsi.iisc.ernet.in/gsdl/collect/icco/index/assoc/HASH014f.dir/doc.doc

Cisco. (2010). *Cisco unified customer voice portal 8.0*. Retrieved from http://qr.net/imicsn4a

Cook, S. (2002). *Speech recognition HOWTO*. Retrieved from http://tldp.org/HOWTO/Speech-Recognition-HOWTO/software.html

Divakaran, D. (2011). *Create and setup a website in 10 mins*. Retrieved from http://www.deepeshmd.com/wp-content/uploads/CreatE-and-Setup-a-WebsitE-in-10-mins.pdf

Ehsani, F., & Knodt, E. (1998). Speech technology in computer-aided language learning: Strengths and limitations of a new call paradigm. *Language Learning & Technology*, *2*(1), 54–73. Retrieved from http://llt.msu.edu/vol2num1/article3/.

Fabbrizio, G. D., Okken, T., & Wilpon, J. G. (2009). A speech mashup framework for multimodal mobile services. In *Proceedings of ICMI-MLMI'09*. Cambridge, MA: ICMI. Retrieved from http://www.difabbrizio.com/papers/icmi174-difabbrizio.pdf

Farinazzo, V. Salvador1, M., Luiz, A. S., Kawamoto, & de Oliveira Neto, J. S. (2010). An empirical approach for the evaluation of voice user interfaces. *User Interfaces*. Croatia: INTECH. Retrieved from www.intechopen.com/download/pdf/pdfs_id/10804

Fiedler, G., & Schmidt, P. (2004). *Developing interactive voice response interfaces for large information systems*. Retrieved from http://www.mgovernment.org/resurces/euromgov2005/PDF/19_S042FG-S04.pdf

Freitas, D., & Kouroupetroglou, G. (2004). Speech technologies for blind and low vision persons. *Technology and Disability*, *20*, 135–156.

Hakulinen, J. (2006). *Software tutoring in speech user interfaces*. (Doctoral Dissertation). Dissertations Inc.

Hisayoshi, I., & Toshio, O. (1999). *Case based reasoning system for information technology education*. Institute of Electronics, Information and Communication Engineers.

HKU. (n.d.). *Development of the HKU campus portal*. University of Hong Kong. Retrieved from http://www.hku.hk/cc_news/ccnews100/portal.htm

Holohan, E., Melia, M., McMullen, D., & Pahl, C. (2005). Adaptive e-learning content generation based on semantic web technology. In *Proceedings of International Workshop on Applications of Semantic Web Technologies for E-Learning (SW-EL)*. Amsterdam: SW-EL. Retrieved from http://www.win.tue.nl/SW-EL/2005/swel05-aied05/proceedings/5-Holohan-final-full.pdf

Howard, S. (2006). *Interactive training on mobile devices: Training using text-to-speech and speech recognition, on pocket PC PDA*. (Unpublished Master's Thesis).

Husni, H., & Jamaludin, Z. (2009). ASR technology for children with dyslexia: Enabling immediate intervention to support reading in Bahasa Melayu. *US-China Education Review*, *6*(6), 64–70.

Jankowska, B. (2007). *Architectural frameworks for automated content adaptation to mobile devices based on open-dource technologies*. (Unpublished Doctoral Thesis). European University Viadrina, Frankfurt, Germany. Retrieved from http://opus.kobv.de/euv/volltexte/2007/23/pdf/PHD_BJankowska.pdf

Jumar, O. Cizmar, & Rusko, M. (2006). Galaxy/VoiceXML based spoken slovak dialogue system to access the internet. In *Proceedings of ICSLP'06, Ninth International Conference on Spoken Language Processing*. Pittsburgh, PA: ICSLP. Retrieved from http://www.ling.uni-potsdam.de/ws-ecai06/pdf/juhar.pdf

Selouani, S., Le, T., Moghrabi, C., Lanteigne, B., & Roy, J. (2006). Online collaborative learning system using speech technology. In *Proceedings of World Academy of Science, Engineering and Technology Volume*. Retrieved from http://www.waset.org/pwaset/v15/v15-11.pdf

The National Center on Accessible Information Technology in Education. (2006). *AccessIT*. Author.

KEY TERMS AND DEFINITIONS

Adaptation: To adjust the content of objects to suit users' request. Adaptive system monitors particular user's behaviour and characteristics.

Case-Based Reasoning (CBR): CBR is a technique for solving new problems based on experiences of previous solutions.

Electronic-Learning (E-Learning): E-Learning is the use of Information and Communication Technology (ICT) to support learning processes.

Framework: A guideline for achieving an objective.

Intelligent: A system is said to be intelligent if it mimics the behavior of human.

Mobile-Learning (M-Learning): M-Learning is also known as mobile learning. It is a type of learning that enables the learner to moves from one place to another and learn using a mobile device.

Recommendation: Recommendation is the process whereby software agents recommend appropriate options for users.

Speech: Speech is used interchangeably with voice. A speech is a sound signal used for language communication. Superficially, the speech signal is similar to a sound produced by a musical instrument, although it is more flexible and varied. When we speak, we push air from our lungs through the vocal chords, sometimes tightening the chords to make them vibrate as the air passes over them.

VoiceXML: VoiceXML is an extension of the Extensible Markup Language (XML) that allows interactive access to the Web through the telephone or a voice browser.

Chapter 5
Signals with an Additive Fractal Structure for Information Transmission

M. V. Kapranov
Moscow Power Engineering Institute, Russia

A. V. Khandurin
Moscow Power Engineering Institute, Russia

ABSTRACT

This chapter is devoted to a new class of wideband signals with an additive fractal structure. Properties and characteristics of the new type of signals are studied. It is shown that such signals possess a high level of an irregularity and unpredictability at simple technical implementation. It is shown that an incommensurability of frequencies of fundamental high-stable oscillations leads to the high level of an irregularity of such signals. For an estimation of a level of signal complexity, authors offer to use the fractal dimensionality of their temporal implementations calculated by means of creation of the structural function. Methods of modification of the signal spectrum with the additive fractal structure are offered, permitting to increase the efficiency of the frequency resource application. For reduction of the high low-frequency signal power the authors suggest using signals with the additive fractal structure, centered in a moving average window. Methods of masking of the voice messages by means of signals of a new type are offered. The results of a computer experiment of secretive sound transmission are described.

INTRODUCTION

In the present time there are some important problems of information transfer through radio channels – the electromagnetic compatibility, an increase of data capacity of carrier oscillations, the security and stealthiness of communication. One of the methods of solution of the mentioned problems is based on the reduction of the power spectral density of the message under transmission, at the expense of the extension of its frequency band. Thus in classical methods of the spectrum

DOI: 10.4018/978-1-4666-2208-1.ch005

extension (Ipatov, 2007), the sophisticated modulation of clean waves (CW) is used that leads to serious complication of transmitters and receivers.

Without application of technology of the spectrum extension the specified problems can be solved using non-sinusoidal waves, but the wideband carrier signals. Nowadays there is a tendency to use signals on the basis of a dynamic chaos (Pecora & Carroll, 1990, pp.821-824; Cuomo & Oppenheim, 1993, pp.65-68; Kuznetsov, 2000) as carrier oscillations. However, application of chaotic signals in communication systems (Dedieu, Kennedy, & Hasler, 1993, pp.634-642; Kapranov & Morozov, 1998, pp.66-71; Murali & Leung & Yu, 2003, pp.432-441; Yang, 2004, pp.81-130) has revealed two large lacks. Firstly, the complex nonlinear mechanisms of dynamic chaos formation are rather sensitive to inevitable, even insignificant, mismatches of parameters on the reception and transmission ends that lead to the impossibility of correlative processing of chaotic signals in the receiver. Secondly, it is impossible to change the structure of the chaotic carrier spectrum for adaptation to a spectrum of the message or to interference in the communication channel – the chaos characteristics are completely predetermined by a structure of the forming dynamic system and a choice of its parameters. Signals with the fractal structure are an alternative of chaotic oscillations. Fractal signals are as irregular as chaotic signals, but can give benefits on reproducibility and flexibility of characteristic change.

The subject of this chapter is a research and performance evaluation of wideband signal application with an additive fractal structure for the stealthiness transmission of analog voice messages. At first, we select the type of fractal functions for the simplest generation of signals with fractal structure on their basis, and the properties of these functions are researched. Further, from mathematical record of fractal functions, we turn to their engineering interpretation for radio signal generation. Shortcomings of fractal radio signals come to light. For the elimination of these lacks we enter signals with the modified fractal structure. In the last paragraph methods of information transmission by means of new fractal signals are offered, and the computer experiment of secured voice message transmission is carried out.

MAIN CHARACTERISTICS OF FRACTAL FUNCTIONS WITH AN ADDITIVE STRUCTURE

Signals with a fractal structure can be divided into some types according to methods of their formation in the transmitter: signals with additive (Wornell, 1996, Falconer, 1997) and multiplicative (Bolotov & Tkach, 2006, pp.91-98) structure, signals on the basis of iterative fractal functions (Kravchenko, Perez-Meana, & Ponomaryov, 2009) (functions of Cantor, Bolzano, Bezikovich, etc.), solution of nonlinear dynamic systems in the reverse time (Tomashevsky & Kapranov, 2006). The main lack of almost all fractal signals is the impossibility of their generation in the form of self-oscillations in devices with the simple structure. However, fractal functions with an additive structure and signals on their basis, which are a sum of stable sinusoidal oscillations with incommensurable frequencies, can be obtained without the expensive equipment. Except fractal properties and simple generation methods, signals with an additive fractal structure demonstrate a high level of reproducibility. These properties can be used for secured telecommunications, therefore, the research of such signals is urgent and this chapter is devoted only to them.

On determination (for example Wornell (1996)), any fractal function should satisfy the following scaling equation:

$$f\left(x\right)=\frac{1}{\mu}f\left(\lambda x\right) \tag{1}$$

Usually (Falconer, 1997, Bolotov & Tkach, 2006, pp.91-98, Kravchenko & Perez-Meana &

Ponomaryov, 2009, Tomashevsky & Kapranov, 2006, Gluzman & Sornette, 2002) for (1) examination one can search the solution in the form of the infinite additive power series:

$$f(x)=\sum_{k=1}^{\infty}\frac{1}{\mu^k}g\left[\lambda^k x\right].$$

It is possible to select any function as *g(x)*, however, from the engineering point of view, the simplest way is to form the harmonic oscillations *g(x)=sin(x)*. For the first time, a scale-invariant function with such a basis was offered by Weierstrass (Du Bois & Reymond, 1875, pp.21-37) at the end of the 19th Century.

Falkoner (1997) investigated the Weierstrass function having selected $\mu=\lambda^{(2-D)}$,

$$W(t)=\sum_{k=1}^{\infty}\lambda^{(D-2)k}\sin\left(\lambda^k t\right), \quad (2)$$

and he has proved that at $1<D<2$, $\lambda>1$ the value of parameter *D* numerically corresponds to box dimension of the *W(t)* graph. Here we obtain:

$$A_k=\lambda^{(D-2)k},\ \nu_k=\lambda^k/2\pi$$

are the amplitude and the frequency of the *k*-th component of the function accordingly.

The fractal function (2) possesses the following characteristics:

- **Nondifferentiability:** The nonregular character of behavior of the temporal implementation does not change at reduction of its scale,
- **Fractal dimension of graphs of temporal implementations:** The higher dimension leads to the higher amplitude of fast-changing components (Figure 1(a)),
- **Scale invariance:** The function completely repeats itself on small and big time scales (Figure 1(b)),
- A spectrum decaying in inverse proportion to frequency (Figure 2).

From Expression (2) it is observable that with increasing of fractal dimension *D* the high-frequency amplitudes of spectral components in-

Figure 1. (a) Change of a type of temporal implementation depending on its fractal dimension and (b) an illustration of self-similarity of graphs of Weierstrass function at λ=1.2

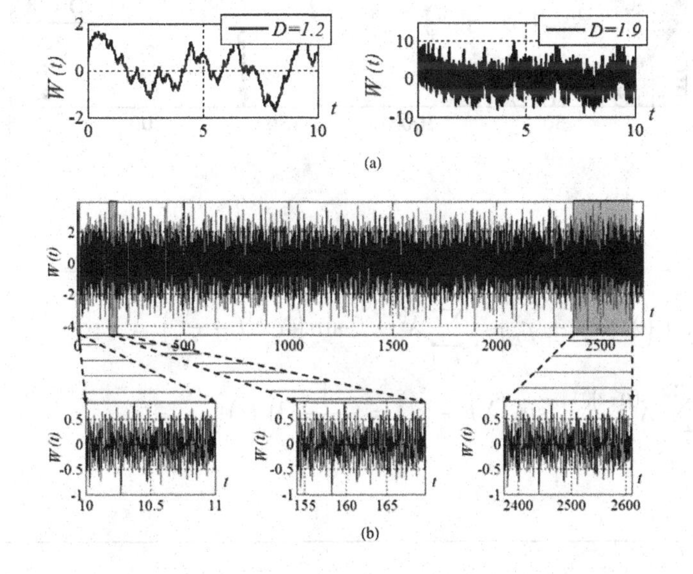

crease as well. In a limit at $D \to 2$ amplitudes of all spectral components are identical (Figure 2).

It is easy to prove the scale invariance of the Weierstrass function (see Box 1).

That is, on an abscissa axis the scale factor is equal to λ, and on an axis of ordinates - $\lambda^{(2-D)}$. The Weierstrass function repeats itself on time intervals $t_0\lambda^n \le t \le (t_0+\Delta t)\lambda^n$, (Figure 1 (b)), where $n=0...\infty$ - a scaling coefficient.

When one speaks about an ergodicity of the temporal process, he implies that its statistical characteristics on the big interval of observation *NT* are equal to averaged characteristics on several implementations *N* in a short interval of time *T*. It means that the equality (for example, concerning assembly average) should be satisfied:

$$\frac{1}{NT}\int_0^{NT} x(t,\varphi_1)dt = \frac{1}{N}\sum_{n=1}^{N}\frac{1}{T}\int_0^{T} x(t,\varphi_n)dt \quad (3)$$

where φ_n is a statistically distributed phase of the process *x(t)*.

According to (3), the assembly average (m_x) of 10 temporal implementations of a signal with an additive fractal structure in the time interval T_c differs from the m_x temporal implementation in the time interval $10T_c$ by $\varepsilon=0.00001$, which is an accuracy from which a series is considered to be ergodic.

For the quantitative estimation of a level of proximity of researched signals *W(t)* to stochastic processes with the normal distribution law we use the fitting criterion of Kolmogorov *q* (Iglin, 2006). This criterion is based on a comparison of histograms of two processes.

Define a significance threshold *q=0.2* and write down in one table all values of reference frequencies at which threshold excess is observed.

From Table 1 we can see that at certain values of the reference frequency by means of the Weierstrass function it is possible to simulate processes with the normal distribution law.

From the analysis it follows that application of the Weierstrass function as a fractal signal is

Figure 2. Spectrum plots of Weierstrass function (2) at λ=1.2

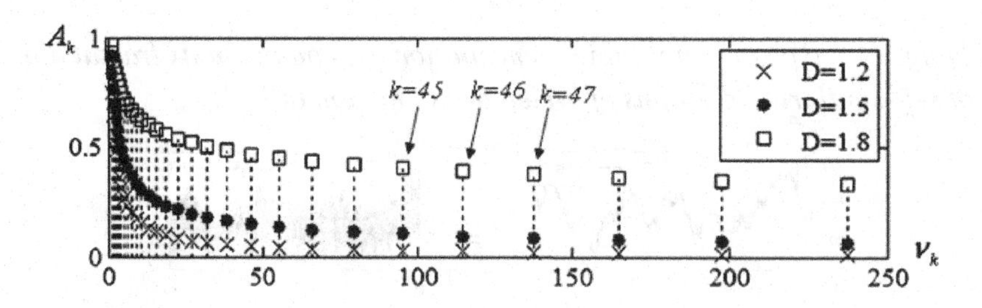

Box 1.

$$W(\lambda t) = \sum_{k=1}^{\infty}\lambda^{(D-2)k}\sin\left(\lambda\cdot\lambda^k t+\varphi_k\right) = \sum_{k=1}^{\infty}\lambda^{(D-2)k}\sin\left(\lambda^{k+1}t+\varphi_k\right) = ...$$

$$... = \begin{Bmatrix} l = k+1 \\ k = l-1 \end{Bmatrix} = \sum_{l=2}^{\infty}\lambda^{(D-2)(l-1)}\sin\left(\lambda^l t+\varphi_l\right) = \frac{1}{\lambda^{(D-2)}}W(t)$$

that gives
$W(\lambda t)= \lambda^{(2-D)}W(t)$.

Table 1. Values of the reference frequencies for which the fitting criterion of Kolmogorov is more than 0.1

1,17	1,175	1,182	1,188	1,192	1,195	1,196	1,203	1,205	1,21
1,235	1,242	1,25	1,262	1,278	1,289	1,299	1,303	1,305	1,342
1,352	1,356	1,358	1,366	1,42	1,425	1,428	1,43		

complicated by two essential lacks following from its self-similarity and non-differentiability:

1. The complete series (2) occupies unfairly big frequency range.
2. The high non-uniformity distribution of energy on frequencies is observed. For example, for a signal on Figure 2 in initial area of frequencies from 0 to 25 Hz, occupying a small part from the general band, are concentrated 87% of all energy of a signal.

In following sections of this chapter the methods of elimination of these lacks are offered.

INCOMMENSURABILITY OF FREQUENCIES OF THE WEIERSTRASS ROW AS THE PRINCIPAL REASON OF AN IRREGULARITY OF ITS TEMPORAL IMPLEMENTATIONS

The important characteristic feature of the Weierstrass series (2) is that its components represent the sinusoidal functions with cyclic frequency λ^k. With k growth, cyclic frequencies of a series increase under the geometrical progression law (Figure 2), i.e. have the exponential growth. Moreover, frequencies of the Weierstrass series will be in an integer ratio extremely rarely (Kapranov & Khandurin, 2011, pp.23-26), only at certain values λ. It is an essential difference of the Weierstrass series from a Fourier series:

$$f\left(t\right)=\sum_{k=1}^{\infty}\omega^{(D-2)k}\sin\left(\omega k\cdot t\right),$$

in which all harmonics consist in an arithmetical progression with respect to ωk and (Figure 4) are multiple to the fundamental frequency.

It is clear that a ratio of frequencies of sinusoidal components of an additive series gives a periodicity of the function, and their exponential growth leads to a self-similarity. It is necessary to be very accurate during the selection of the λ value of the reference frequency. This parameter is responsible for incommensurability and for complexity (the absence of a regularity and periodicity, predictability, recurrence). At that, the incommensurability can be full or partial. At any values of parameter $\lambda \geq 2$ some periodicity is noticeable in behavior of the *W(t)* function. It is important to mark the fact that if λ is an integer then the function (2) becomes completely periodical. This results from the fact that all frequencies of the Weierstrass series become multiple to

Figure 3. Comparison of the normalized histograms of distribution of a signal on the basis of the Weierstrass series W(t) on an observation interval T_c (black trace) and on an interval $10T_c$ (gray background). Parameters: D=1.9, λ=1.21

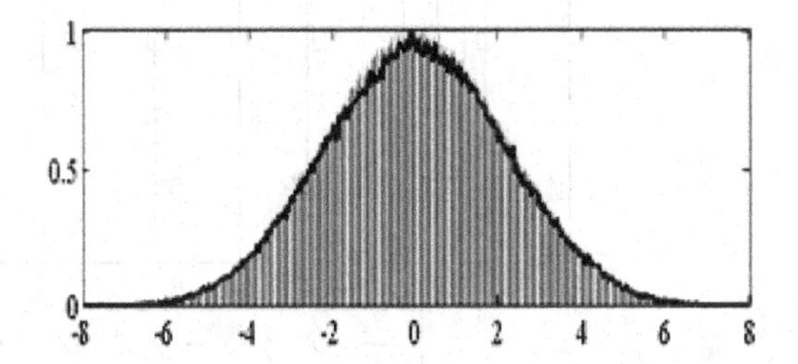

Figure 4. Comparison of additive series of Weierstrass (gray) and Fourier (black) at D=1.9, λ=ω=1.7. Normalized (a) temporal implementations, (b) spectrum plots.

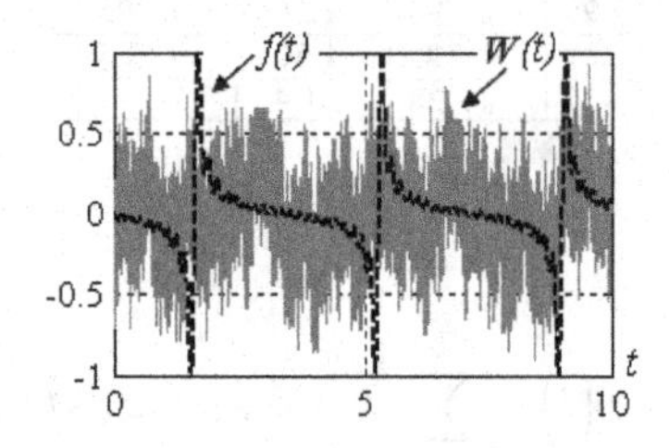

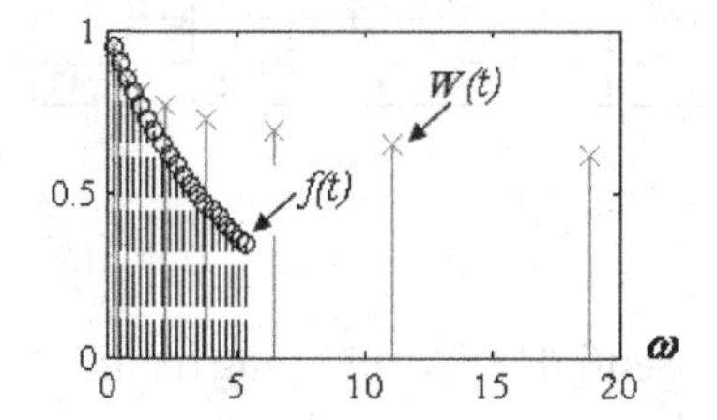

each other, the inherent incommensurability of frequencies disappears.

The forbidden values of the reference frequency are such values of λ_F for which there is a ratio condition (or commensurabilities) of two or more frequencies of the Weierstrass row *W(t)*,

$$m\lambda_F = \lambda_F^n$$

where *n=1,2,3 ..., m=1,2,3, ...* are integer numbers. From here we receive expression:

$$\lambda_F = \sqrt[(n-1)]{m} \quad (4)$$

at *m=1* or *n=1* we have $\lambda_F=1$, and at *n=2* we have $\lambda_F=m$.

If a condition (4) is true, then the values of non-equidistant frequencies of the Weierstrass series can be obtained at an additive combination of several equidistant frequency grids. Number of such grids equals to *(n-1)* and among themselves their frequencies are not intersected (Figure 5). For example, at 11 members of the series *w(t)* and $\lambda_F=1$, we have a composition of two equidistant grids (with a number of frequencies 6 and 5, accordingly), and at $\lambda_F = \sqrt[3]{2}$ the number of such grids becomes three.

On the Figure 5 it can be seen that 12 members of the Weierstrass series with non-equidistant frequencies can be obtained by summation of three series with 8th equidistant frequencies in everyone (at given parameters).

If the condition (4) is not fulfilled, a Weierstrass series with non-equidistant frequencies cannot be made by an additive combination of series with equidistant frequencies. That is, if the reference frequency of the Weierstrass row does not concern the forbidden frequencies λ_F, all frequencies

Figure 5. Arrangement of frequencies on a geometrical and arithmetical progression. Parameters $\lambda = \lambda_R = \sqrt[3]{2}$.

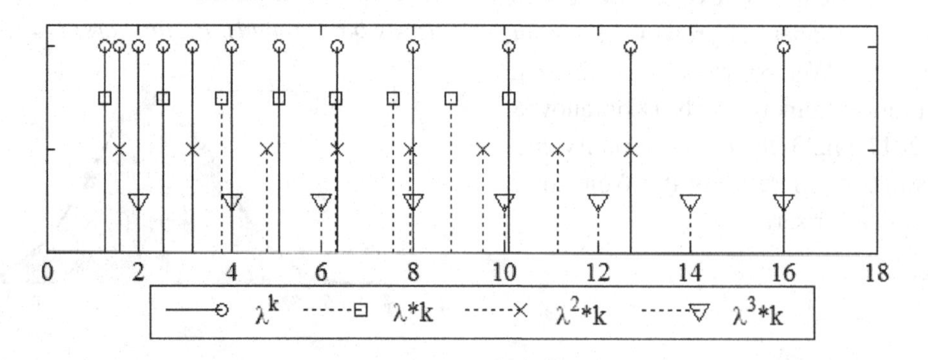

of such series have no general multiple and are completely incommensurable.

The best values for the reference frequency λ_0 need to be selected proceeding from a condition that they are located on the maximum distance from adjacent forbidden values λ_F. Thus, it is necessary to consider an accuracy ε from which we can set values λ_0, i.e.:

$$\lambda_0(n) = \frac{\lambda_F(n+1) + \lambda_0(n)}{2},$$

$$\text{at } \frac{\lambda_F(n+1) - \lambda_0(n)}{2} > \varepsilon. \qquad (5)$$

Proceeding from (5) we can calculate values for the best frequencies (Table 2).

At an increase of the frequency accuracy ε, the number of the best values λ_0 dramatically increases – the more accuracy, the better incommensurability.

Proceeding from the calculated values of the forbidden and best frequencies, it is possible to select values λ under specific engineering tasks. For example, temporal implementations $W(t)$ with rather small number of members equal 4 show such behavior:

- If beat arises between all four frequencies, the full periodicity of temporal implementations is observed,
- If beat arises between two frequencies from four, the signal is quasi-periodical,
- If beat between series components' misses, the period of signal repetition is defined by a level of accuracy of signal's frequencies.

Thus, at already 4 members, but with well-selected value of λ, we obtain the very complicated signal. If the full incommensurability of frequencies is not important, such signal can be formed by means of an additive combination of several equidistant grids of frequencies.

TRUNCATION OF THE FREQUENCY BAND OCCUPIED BY SIGNALS WITH AN ADDITIVE FRACTAL STRUCTURE

To generate a radio signal on the basis of the Weierstrass function (2) it is necessary to pass from its mathematical note to technical interpretation. In other words, it is necessary to truncate a Weierstrass's series as in practice we have a possibility to form the restricted number of its members only. It can be done by different methods proceeding from the set of upper $f_H = \lambda^{k_H}/2\pi$ and lower $f_L = \lambda^{k_L}/2\pi$ boundaries of the selected frequency range:

$$w(t) = \sum_{k=k_L}^{k_H} \lambda^{(D-2)k} \sin\left(\lambda^k t\right), \qquad (6)$$

where numbers of the first and last component of a truncated series $k_H > k_L > 1$. If we have selected a number of members of a series (6) $\Delta k = k_H - k_L$, then the parameter λ turns out equal to $\lambda = \sqrt[\Delta k]{f_H / f_L}$. On the other hand, having selected a specific value of λ, we can find the required number of series members $\Delta k = \ln\left(f_H / f_L - \lambda\right)$.

The relation $f_H / f_L = \lambda^{\Delta k}$ defines a frequency band occupied by a signal. The bandwidth essentially depends on the parameter λ. So at 50 members of a series of Weierstrass and $\lambda = 1.2$ therelationacceptsthegreatvalue $f_H / f_L \approx 7583,7$. At insignificant magnification $\lambda \Rightarrow \lambda = 1.3$ the ratio increases by two orders $f_H / f_L \approx 383022,5$.

A truncated row of Weierstrass (6) possesses fractal properties only in a certain scale range. Besides, at passage from a complete Weierstrass series to the truncated one, there is the smoothing of its temporal implementation, i.e. a loss of complexity, the scale invariance and the dimensionality of the signal. At usage of fractal signals in secure communication systems, it is especially important to generate their as much as possible irregular and complex on the given interval of observation. Therefore, it is necessary to define a minimal number of members of a truncated series of Weierstrass $w(t)$, at which losses in complexity would be minimal.

For an estimation of complexity of full (2) and truncated (6) signals, the numerical general-purpose measure is necessary. To use fractal dimension of oscilloscope patterns of these signals is expediently (Kapranov & Khandurin, 2011, pp.23-26) as such a measure. The method of calculation of the fractal dimension of temporal implementations of signals by means of creation of their structural functions (Korolenko & Maganova & Mesniankin, 2004) is convenient:

$$S_n = \frac{1}{K-n}\sum_{k=1}^{K-n}\left\| f_{k+n} - f_k \right\|,$$

where f_k is the analyzed function, time t is connected with an index $k=1,2,3,\ldots,K$ by a ratio $t = k\Delta t$, Δt is – the time slot between signal samples corresponds to the sampling rate.

Calculations of dimension D_{calc} show (Figures 6 and 7) that at number of members of truncated series (6) smaller than 10 and at the value of the reference frequency $\lambda=1.2$, the calculated dimension of the temporal implementation is almost equal to 1, at a magnification of a number of members of a series the dimension linearly increases and at $k_H>55$ is equal to theoretical dimension $D_{calc}=D=1.6$.

At a specific value of λ, the calculated dimension corresponds to theoretical dimension at a certain number of series members. For example, at $\lambda=1.2$ for achievement of the given dimension D it is necessary to take 55 members of a series minimum (Figure 7), and at $\lambda=1.7$ we need only 21 (Figure 7). However, if it is necessary to generate a signal on the basis of a truncated series of Weierstrass with the actual dimension of the temporal implementation equal to D_{calc} = 1.5, application 10 members of this series only is possible to set $D=1.8$ (Figure 7).

Figure 6. (a) Calculation of the signal dimension on the basis of a truncated series of Weierstrass depending on the number of members of a series for $D=1.6$, $k_L=1$, (b) temporal implementations of a signal at $k_H=20, 30, 50$

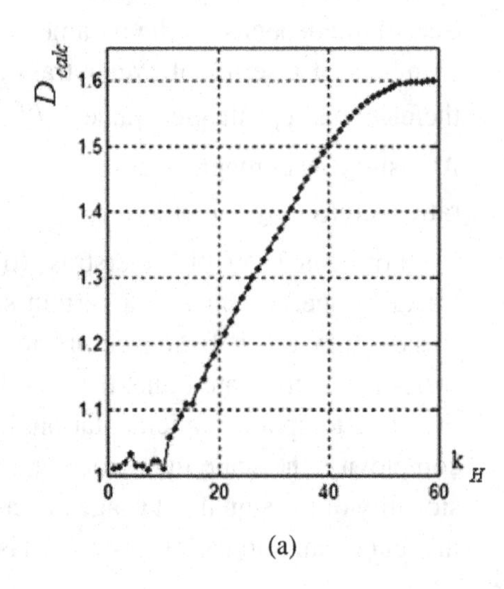

(a)

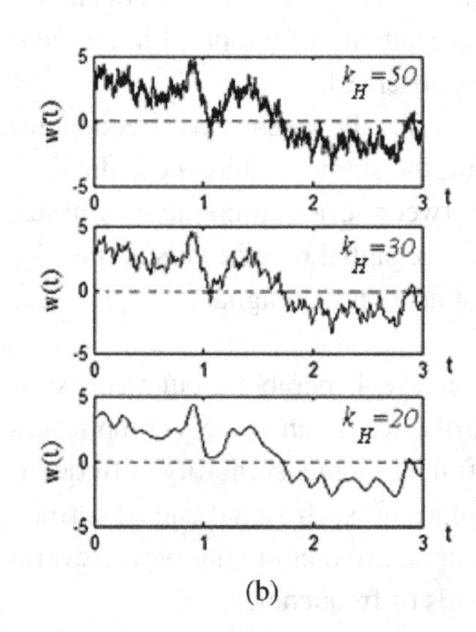

(b)

THE FRACTAL SIGNAL ON THE BASIS OF WEIERSTRASS SERIES WITH A MODIFIED SPECTRUM

As it was shown above, the first lack of a signal on the basis of the truncated Weierstrass series (6) is the unfairly wide spectrum bandwidth. In the range of low frequencies its density is high, and in the range of high ones the spectrum is strongly rarefied (Figure 2). At that, the insignificant magnification of the parameter λ leads to a sharp increase of the frequency band occupied by a signal at an invariable number of its spectral components.

Let us consider the simple method allowing considerably compression of a spectrum, having saved thus the main advantages of a fractal signal structure (unpredictability, functional dependence of dimension of the graph of function *w(t)* from parameter *D*), restriction of growth of the exponent *k* value of parameter *λ* both in the allocation of amplitudes, and in the law of arrangement of frequencies (Kapranov & Khandurin, 2011, pp.23-26). For this purpose we will enter new functional dependence with changeover

$$k \to \chi(m,k), \tag{7}$$

where *χ(m,k)* is some function restricted on top, *m* is a frequency compression parameter. As a result of changeover (7), the initial truncated series (6) saves the formal structure, but there is absolutely other law of arrangement of amplitudes and frequencies $A_k^{\chi} = \lambda^{(D-2)\chi(m,k)}$, $\nu_k^{\chi} = \lambda^{\chi(m,k)} / 2\pi$, than we get an expression:

$$w_{\chi}(t) = \sum_{k=k_{\min}}^{k_{\max}} \lambda^{(D-2)\chi(m,k)} \sin\left(\lambda^{\chi(m,k)} t\right). \tag{8}$$

For example, we will select next limiting function *χ (m, k)*:

$$\chi\left(m,k\right) = m \cdot th\left(k/m\right). \tag{9}$$

From expression (9) it is clear that as *m*→∞, we obtain *χ (m, k)*→*k*.

In the Figure 8 characteristic of the relation of the upper frequency of a signal spectrum on the basis of the series (8) ν^{χ}_{H} to the upper signal frequency on the basis of the initial series (6) ν_H from compression parameter *m* is shown. It can be seen that parameter reduction *m* leads to essential compression of the frequency band occupied by a signal. As the law of compression (9) influences upon amplitudes of components of the series (8), then at a signal on its basis the law of spectrum recession is saved (Figure 8(b)).

Figure 7. Increment of the dimension D_{calc} of temporal implementations of w(t) caused by the growth of the number of its members. Parameters: k_{min}=1, (a) λ=1.2, (b) λ=1.8.

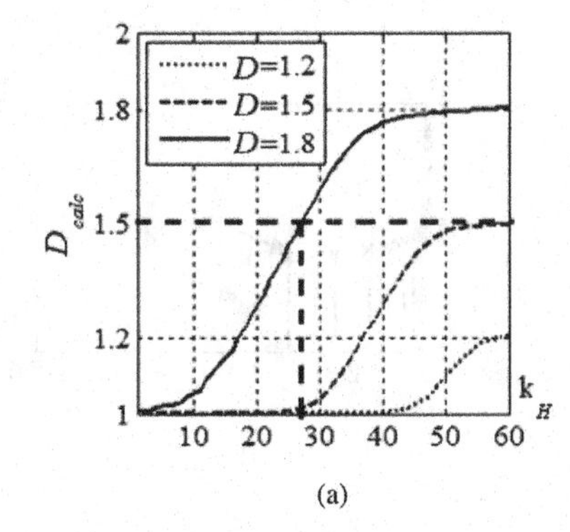

(a)

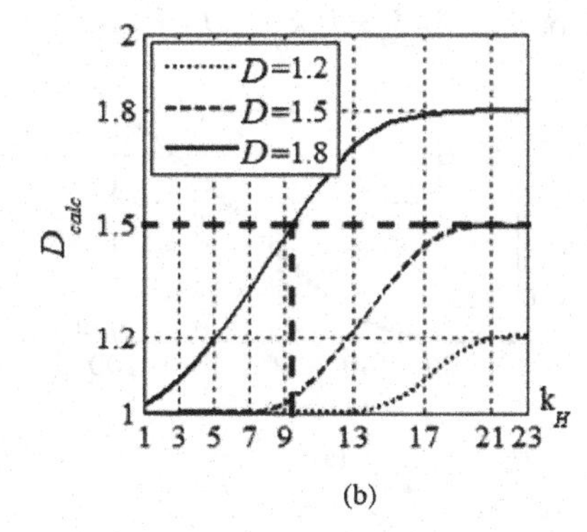

(b)

From Figure 9(a) it is clear that the original signal frequency compression (up to very small m) does not influence on unpredictability of its temporal implementation. It happens because spectral components of the modified series (8) still are not multiple to each other, that is remained incommensurable.

At a limit of m=0 dimension of temporal implementation aspires to a minimum (Figure 9(b)). Comparing Figure 8(a) and Figure 9(b) we see that it is possible to allow frequency compression no more than 10 times at m=50 without reduction of the fractal dimension. The further reduction of the compression parameter m leads to dramatically reduction of the signal dimension at insignificant abbreviation of the frequency range. At technical implementation of the circuit, if it is not planned to use a dimension or self-similarity of a signal, it is possible to resolve the big level of compression.

THE FRACTAL SIGNAL ON THE BASIS OF THE ALIGNED WEIERSTRASS SERIES

The second lack of a concerned fractal signal is that the most part of its capacity is allocated far enough from assembly average. On other words, the mean value of the Weierstrass function strongly changes along an observation interval. In a signal constructed by the Weierstrass series with a truncated spectrum (6), more than 90% of capacity is allocated in less than 10% of the occupied frequency band, i.e. the frequency resource is spent too much ineffectively. To get rid of superfluous capacity and at the same time to extinguish spectral components of the Weierstrass series in the lower part of a spectrum, we will lead its centering concerning a current average.

For determination of the centered value of our series it is necessary to do the following operation:

$$w_C(t,\tau) = w(t) - M(t,\tau), \qquad (10)$$

where $M(t,\tau)$ is a current average from the Weierstrass function in a window with width $\tau = 2\pi / \lambda^{k_H - Z}$ ($Z=1 \ldots k_H$ is a number of high-frequency components of w (t), which are not subject to clearing), which is subtracted from an ordinary Weierstrass function (2). The current average from $w(t)$ is equal (see Box 2).

As a result, it is obtained a current average of the function $w(t)$,

$$M(t,\tau) = \sum_{k=1}^{\infty} \left[\frac{\sin(\tau\lambda^k/2)}{\tau\lambda^k/2} \right] \lambda^{(D-2)k} \sin(\lambda^k t), \qquad (11)$$

Figure 8. (a) The level of frequency compression of a signal depending on m, (b) spectrum plots of signals on the basis of an initial series (6) and a series with frequency compression (8). Parameters for both series: $D=1.8$, $\lambda=1.2$, $k_L=1$, $k_H=50$.

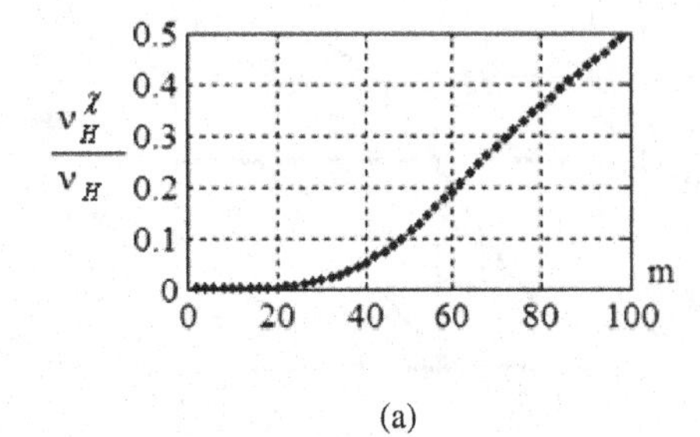

(a)

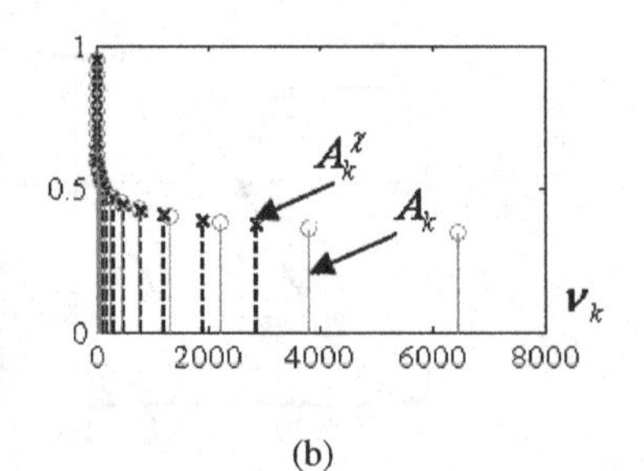

(b)

Figure 9. (a) Comparison of temporal implementations of signals on the basis of the initial truncated Weierstrass series (gray) and the series with modified spectrum (black) (m=40), (b) lowering of dimension of a series at frequency compression. Parameters of the series are similar to Figure 8.

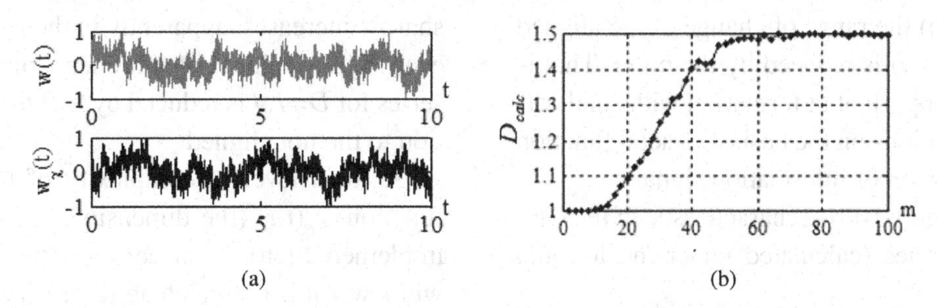

Box 2.

$$M\left(t,\tau\right)=\frac{1}{\tau}\int_{\tau}^{t+\tau} w(t)dt=\frac{1}{\tau}\int_{t-\tau/2}^{t+\tau/2}\sum_{k=1}^{\infty}\lambda^{(D-2)k}\sin(\lambda^{k}t)dt=\frac{1}{\tau}\sum_{k=1}^{\infty}\left\{\lambda^{(D-2)k}\cdot\int_{t-\tau/2}^{t+\tau/2}\sin(\lambda^{k}t)dt\right\},$$

let us calculate expression under integral (weight factors of *k*-th component of a series),

$$\int_{t-\tau/2}^{t+\tau/2}\sin(\lambda^{k}t)dt=\frac{1}{\lambda^{k}}\left(\cos[\lambda^{k}(t-\tau/2)]-\cos[\lambda^{k}(t+\tau/2)]\right)=\frac{\sin(\lambda^{k}\tau/2)}{\lambda^{k}/2}\cdot\sin(\lambda^{k}t).$$

Table 2. The best values of the reference frequencies λ_0 for $\varepsilon=10^{-3}$

1,085	1,097	1,113	1,126	1,139	1,158	1,168	1,180
1,193	1,198	1,210	1,222	1,232	1,244	1,248	1,255
1,268	1,284	1,294	1,301	1,306	1,312	1,325	1,332
1,337	1,343	1,347	1,356	1,363	1,366	1,374	1,381
1,385	1,388	1,393	1,399	1,406	1,412	1,415	1,420
1,428	1,433	1,439	1,444	1,447	1,451	1,456	1,461
1,466	1,474	1,478	1,482	1,490	1,492	1,497	1,501
1,505	1,508	1,518	1,521	1,525	1,528	1,532	1,539
1,543	1,546	1,550	1,556	1,562	1,566	1,569	1,572
1,578	1,583	1,589	1,594	1,597	1,599	1,607	1,612
1,617	1,621	1,624	1,628	1,637	1,652		

Having substituted in (10) expressions for a truncated series *w(t)* (6) and its current average *M(t)* (11), we will obtain a note of the truncated aligned series of Weierstrass:

$$w_{C}(t,\tau)=\sum_{k=k_L}^{k_H}\left(1-\frac{\sin(\tau\lambda^{k}/2)}{\tau\lambda^{k}/2}\right)\lambda^{(D-2)k}\sin(\lambda^{k}t),\qquad(12)$$

where the law of arrangement of amplitudes and frequencies is $A_{k}^{C}=\left(1-\frac{\sin\left(\tau\lambda^{k}/2\right)}{\tau\lambda^{k}/2}\right)\lambda^{(D-2)k}$, $\nu_{k}^{C}=\nu_{k}=\lambda^{k}/2\pi$.

Graphs in the Figure 10 visually show a convenience of usage of the aligned function $w_C(t,\tau)$ instead of an original function of Weierstrass

$w(t,\tau)$. If a dynamic range of an original function is wide (it is noticeable even on a small interval of time of the observation presented on the Figure 10(a)) the range of change of the aligned function $w_C(t,\tau)$ is reduced by the order. That is especially important at formation wideband carrying oscillations on the basis of fractal function for transmission of information signals.

In the Figure 10(b) a characteristic of the relation of energies (calculated under the formula $E_f = \int_0^{Tc} f(t)^2 dt$, where T_c is a duration of temporal implementation) of signals on the basis of the aligned series (12) and the original series (6) from parameter Z defining a width of a window of selection of a current average. It is clear that energy of the aligned function decreases proportionally to Z^{3-D}. So at the high dimension of temporal implementation $D \to 2$ characteristic assumed to be linear (in the Figure 10(b) it is shown by a gray dotted line) and energy of a signal will decay in direct ratio to a number of not aligned components of the series Z. But with reduction of D the scoring from aligning operation sharply increases, apparently in the Figure 10(b) even at great value $Z=40$ the energy of the aligned series for $D=1.4$ is reduced by five times in relation to the not aligned.

As to a level of complexity of the aligned function $w_C(t,\tau)$ (the dimension of its temporal implementation), at correctly selected width of a window τ it is not much above, than complexity of an original function $w(t)$. Principal difference is that oscillations $w_C(t,\tau)$ does not contain slowly changing components as in its spectrum the low-frequency components are removed. Apparently from Figure 10(c) at reduction Z, i.e. at reduction of width of a window of integration τ, the magnification of dimensionality of temporal implementation from set to maximum $D_{calc} \to 2$ is observed. On the graph it is possible to select the critical value Z_{crit}, which indicates that dimension of a signal is always equal 2.

Figure 10. (a) Temporal implementations of signals on the basis of series (6, 11, 12) at D=1.8, λ=1.2, Z=20, (b) reduction of energy and (c) magnification of dimensionality of temporal implementation of a signal on the basis of the aligned series (12) at reduction Z

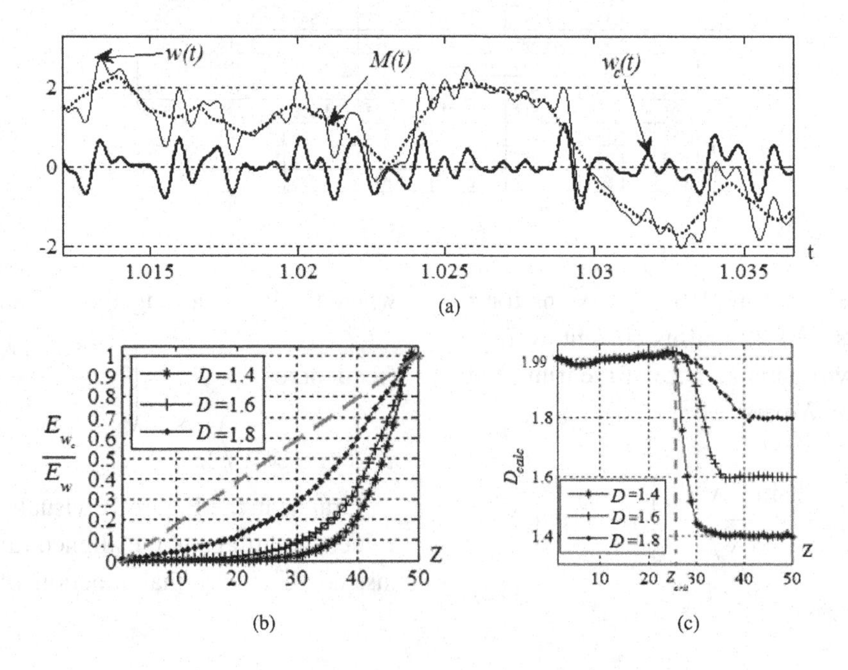

Comparing characteristics of the Figure 10(b) and the Figure 10(c) it is possible to draw an output that application of operation of an aligning to fractal signals with small dimension of temporal implementations $D < 1.5$ leads to the strong reduction of their energy at dimension minor change.

Spectrum plots of signals (Figure 10(a)), are resulted on the Figure 11 at the same values of parameters, as on Figure 10(a). Daggers mark amplitudes of spectral components of an original function $w(t)$, the circles – the aligned function $w_C(t,\tau)$.

In Figure 11 we see the strong suppression of a spectrum of $w_C(t,\tau)$ in the field of low frequencies and its riches in the field of high frequencies. It is possible to tell that oscillations of the aligned function, which are exceeding frequency of the full clearing $1/\tau = \lambda^{kH - Z}/2\pi$, have some power growth.

Having eliminated limitation of fractal signals on the basis of the Weierstrass series, it is possible to pass to experiments on stealthiness transmission of voice messages.

EXPERIMENTS ON TRANSMISSION OF THE VOICE SIGNALS BY MEANS OF FRACTAL SIGNALS ON THE BASIS OF WEIERSTRASS SERIES

In the present chapter we pose a task on secured transmission of the sound message masked by a fractal signal, by means of acoustic waves. For simplification of circuits of the receiver and the transmitter the voice should not be exposed to digitization. Masking and its removal should happen in real time. A level of stealthiness of transmission and quality of signal demodulation is defined as visually, by comparing of oscilloscope patterns of the initial message with demodulated one, and on hearing the results. The first method of cleaning up of the information message from the masking is based on precision of fractal signals on the basis of $w(t)$.

The Coherent Elimination of the Masking Fractal Signal in the Receiver

Thanks to high reproducibility of fractal signals, it is possible to implement a communication system with fractal masking in the transmitter and the coherent elimination of this masking (Figure 12). Here voice message masking was led as a signal on the basis of a truncated Weierstrass series (6), and a signal on the basis of a series with the compressed spectrum (8).

In computational experiments the information voice message $s(t)$ represents a remark "This information is confidential, absolutely confidential" duration 4.004sec and occupies the frequency band from $f_L = 105Hz$ to $f_H = 2000Hz$, a sampling rate has been selected from the computer equal to $f_S = 44100Hz$. As masking oscillations, the signal on the basis of a truncated series of Weierstrass

Figure 11. Spectrum plots of the aligned series of Weierstrass (parameters are similar to Figure 10) (a) Z=3, (b) Z=10

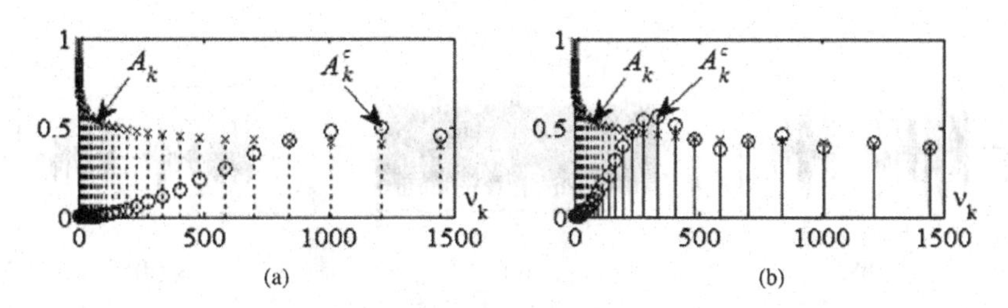

(6), with parameters $D=1.9$, $\lambda=1.15$, $k_L=52$, $k_H=71$, thus the lower signal frequency $f_L=228Hz$ and upper $f_H=3246Hz$ has been used. Frequency bands of information and masking signals were commensurable and were superimposed that was saved and at frequency compression.

It has appeared that quality of masking and demodulation in the given circuit is very high, it has proved to be true in experiment at message listening in the communication channel and on a receiver output. In a vocal range of frequencies humans clearly distinguish the separate spectral components about accuracy to hertz, besides the human ear possesses high sensitivity, i.e. at signal power reduction in 1000 times it seems to us that power level has decreased only 30 times. However, if to mask the sound message a fractal signal on hearing it will cease to be recognized. Probably, it is connected to hearing aid singularities.

In the given circuit implementation of the unit of synchronization of the fractal generator in the receiver appears too difficult. For simplification of the receiver circuit the structure with incoherent removal of a mask from a signal is offered.

Incoherent Elimination of a Masking Fractal Signal in the Receiver

In (Kapranov & Khandurin, 2009, pp.89-92) the system of secured communication FRAMASK with incoherent reception and information message, masking by a fractal signal in the transmitter is offered. This system is similar on the structure to a communication system at chaotic masking (Murali, Leung, & Yu, 2003, pp.432-441), but in it fractal signals are used as difficult carrier oscillations (Figure 13) instead of chaotic. Window operation of the moving average is applied to support a secrecy of transmission on the transmitting and receiving sides. Thanks to application of fractal maskers and the multistage moving average in the receiver for selection of the information message in this circuit, unlike the circuit with chaotic signals, the high secrecy of transmission of the message and high quality of demodulation can be reached, at information transfer through the communication channel with additive noises.

In the transmitter (Figure 13) the analog message $s(t)$ is additive combined with a masking

Figure 12. (a) System of secure communication with fractal masking in the transmitter and the coherent reception. Temporal implementations: (b) the sound message s(t), (c) the disguised message r(t), (d) messages on a receiver output e(t).

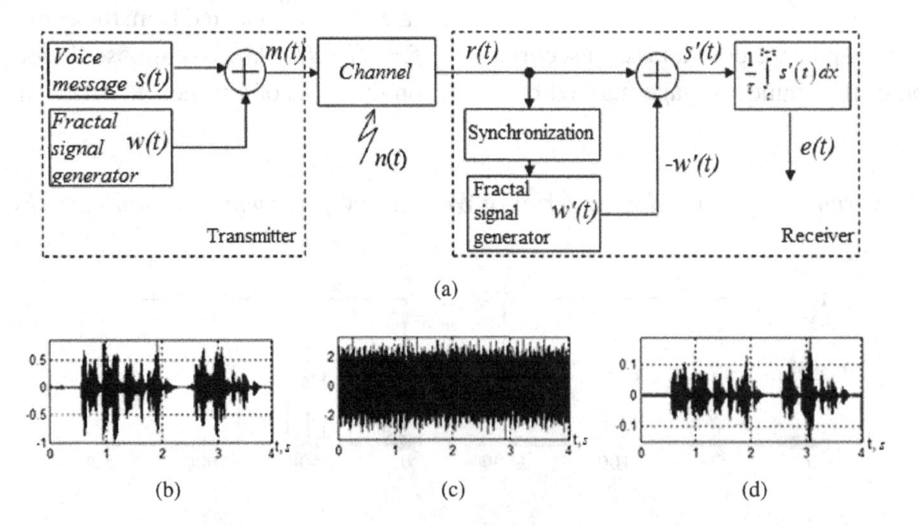

fractal signal on the basis of *w(t)*, processed by centering operation. On the reception side there is a multistage operation of the moving average, permitting at the expense of ergodicity of the aligned series to remove masking and to get rid of noise.

As a result, temporal implementation of a signal on an output of the incoherent receiver (Figure 13) is strongly distorted, however, at hearing the voice message is quite legible.

Low quality of separation of information from masking oscillations in the considered circuit (Figure 13) is caused by necessity of the strong level reduction of the sound message for secure transmission at communication channel, but this reduction degrades a quality of separation of the initial message from masker. To refine the quality of demodulation at high secrecy, the method of change of the circuit on Figure 13 consisting of two stages is developed. The first stage is an adaptation of a spectrum of a fractal signal to a spectrum of the message for improving of its masking properties.

A number of experiments on masking of the sound message by fractal signals with frequency compression of a type (8) have been fulfilled. Functional schemes of systems with such signals are similar to the system shown on Figure 12, but the generator of the fractal signal with a compressed spectrum with parameters was used here: $D=1.9$, $\lambda=1.15$, $k_L=33$, $k_H=52$, thus, the lower signal frequency is $f_L=201Hz$ and upper $f_H=201Hz$. The signal spectrum is compressed under the law $\chi(k,m) = mk\left[1-\left(2k/3k_{\max}\right)^4\right]$, where $m=1.6$. It has been obtained that quality of masking of information for a signal on the basis of $w_\chi(t)$ is better, than for a signal on the basis of an original series *w(t)* at the identical power level *s(t)*. However. In this case, masking is too good, cleaning up of the message from a mask by its multistage window moving average appears to be impossible.

Figure 13. (a) System of secure communication with fractal masking and window moving average in the transferring and receiving sides; temporal implementations: (b) the sound message s(t), (c) the disguised message r(t), (d) messages on a receiver output e(t)

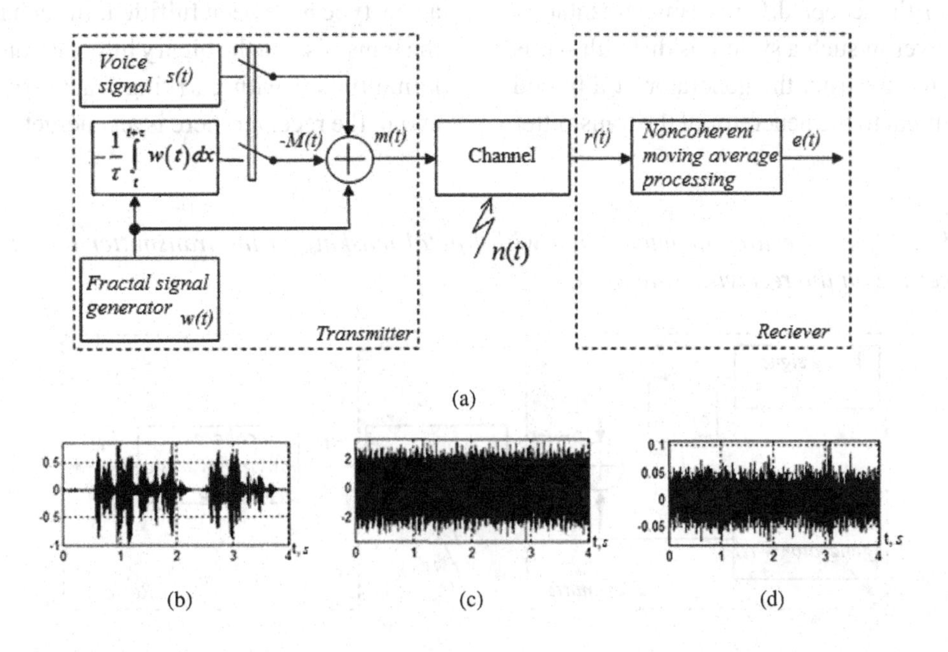

To define a presence of the secured message on an input and a demodulator output is not possible visually and during a hearing.

The second stage of modification of the original circuit (Figure 13(a)) consists in a failure from centering operation on the transmitting end (Figure 14). In the circuit on Figure 14 the parameters of masker are following: $D=1.9$, $\lambda=1.15$, $k_{L1}=52$, $k_{L2}=62$, $k_H=71$, the frequency compression law at an open-ended key the lower signal frequency is $f_{L1}=228Hz$, and at shorted $f_{L2}=923Hz$ and the upper frequency is $f_H=1796Hz$. Signal demodulation was produced similarly as it is in the original circuit. At the appearance of the sound message on a transmitter input, the electronic key is shorted, thus, the generator of a fractal signal ceases to form those components of series $w_\chi(t)$, which were superimposed with a spectrum of the appeared message. At such operation the secrecy of transmission of the message does not decrease, but quality of demodulation increases, temporal implementations are similar Figure 13(b)-(d).

Thus. In the given section two methods of transmission of the voice messages disguised by a fractal signal with additive structure from listening by the third party are developed. The first method is based on the coherent subtraction of masker from the accepted. Circuit implementation of the receiver in such a system is difficult – it is necessary to construct the generator of a fractal signal identical to the generator of the transmitter and to have the unit of its synchronization. However, in this case, there is a quasi-optimal reception of a signal, i.e. their full cleaning up from masking oscillations. The second method is based on incoherent processing of an accepted signal for removal from it the masking fractal oscillations and a white noise. The communication system constructed under such circuit possesses simple implementation of the receiver and does not concede to coherent system on quality of extraction of information.

FUTURE RESEARCH DIRECTIONS

The developed methods of information transfer by means of signals with an additive fractal structure are based only on their high level of reproducibility and wideband. In the further publications we are going to make experiments on usage of self-similarity of these signals, for improvement of quality of demodulation on the receiving side. Also a perspective direction of research is the dimension modulation of temporal implementations of signals with an additive fractal structure.

A number of experiments on direct fractal information transmission by means of signals of a new type have been fulfilled. In such method of the transmission the binary information sequence is multiplied with carrying fractal oscillations, and in the receiver there is an energetic detection

Figure 14. System of secure communication with fractal masking in the transmitter and the window moving average on the receiving side

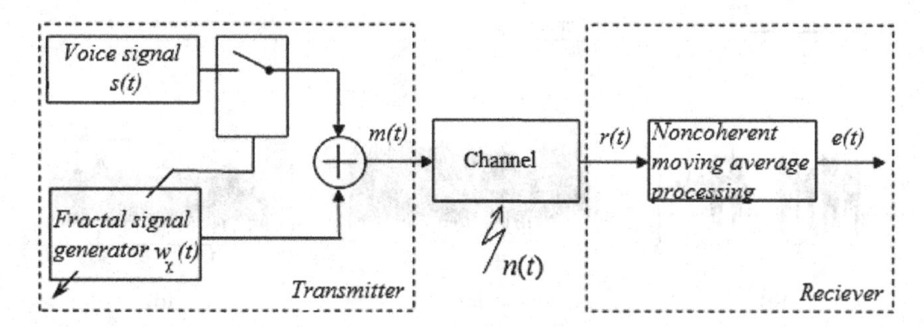

of the received wideband pulses. Researches in the given direction are perspective as such communication systems correspond to the standard of communication IEEE 802.15.4a (UWB).

Besides, it is necessary to develop circuits of generators of offered signals.

CONCLUSION

As a result of this chapter, the following main conclusions are obtained:

- Complex wideband signals with an additive fractal structure on the basis of a series of Weierstrass possess a number of singularities (self-similarity, non-differentiability and precision) and can be used in radio engineering applications.
- Methods of modification of probed fractal signals for more effective expenditure by them of frequency-power resources are offered. Therefore, have been entered into reviewing a fractal signal with a compressed spectrum and the aligned fractal signal. Conditions, at which there is no loss of complexity of original signals at passage to the modified, are found.
- Experiments on reserved transmission of a voice message by means of fractal signals on a communication channel with a white noise are made. Two transmission schemes of the information by means of a new type of signals are developed.

REFERENCES

Bolotov, V. N., & Tkach, Y. V. (2006). Generating of signals with a fractal spectra. *Journal of Technical Physics*, *76*(4), 91–98.

Cuomo, K. M., & Oppenheim, A. V. (1993). Circuit implementation of synchronized chaos with applications to communications. *Physical Review Letters*, *71*(1), 65–68. doi:10.1103/PhysRevLett.71.65 PMID:10054374.

Dedieu, H., Kennedy, M. P., & Hasler, M. (1993). Chaos shift keying: modulation and demodulation of a chaotic carrier using self-synchronizing Chua's circuits. *IEEE Transactions on Circuits and Systems II*, *40*, 634–642. doi:10.1109/82.246164.

Dmitriev, A. S., & Panas, A. I. (2002). *Dynamic chaos: New information carriers for communication systems*. Moscow, Russia: Fizmatlit.

Du Bois, & Reymond, P. (1875). Verch einer classification der willrurlichen functionen reeler argumente nach ihren aenderungen inden beinsten intervallen. *Journal Furder Reine und Angewandte Mathematiques*, *79*, 21–37.

Falconer, K. J. (1997). *Techniques in fractal geometry*. New York: John Wiley & Sons.

Gluzman, S., & Sornette, D. (2002). Log-periodic route to fractal functions. *Physical Review Letters E*, *6503*(3), 418–436.

Iglin, S. P. (2006). *Probability theory and the mathematical statistics on the basis of MATLAB: The manual*. Kharkov, Ukraine: NTU.

Ipatov, V. (2007). *Wideband systems and CDMA: Principles and applications*. Moscow, Russia: Technosphera.

Kapranov, M. V., & Khandurin, A. V. (2009). Information transmission with fractal masking (framask) in communication system [in Russian]. *Vestnik MPEI*, *1*, 89–92.

Kapranov, M. V., & Khandurin, A. V. (2011). Signals with additive fractal structure for information transmission. *Journal of Electromagnetic Waves and Electronic Systems*, *16*(2), 23–36.

Kapranov, M. V., & Morozov, A. G. (1998). Application of chaotic modulation for information transfer. *Radiotechnicheskie Tetrady, 14*, 66–71.

Kapranov, M. V., & Tomashevsky, A. I. (2003). System of secure communication with usage of correlative reception and the synchronous chaotic response. *Journal of Electromagnetic Waves and Electronic Systems, 8*(3), 35–48.

Korolenko, P. V., Maganova, M. S., & Mesniankin, A. V. (2004). *Innovation methods of the analysis of stochastic processes and structures in optics: Fractal and multiracial methods, wavelet-conversions: The manual*. Moscow, Russia: MSU, Nuclear Physics, Scientific Research Institute.

Kravchenko, V. F., Perez-Meana, H. M., & Ponomaryov, V. I. (2009). *Adaptive digital processing of multidimentional signals with applications*. Moscow, Russia: Fizmatlit.

Kuznetsov, S. P. (2000). *Dynamic chaos (lecture course)*. Moscow, Russia: Nauka.

Murali, K., Leung, H., & Yu, H. (2003). Design of noncoherent receiver for analog spread-spectrum communication based on chaotic masking. *IEEE Journal, 50*(3), 432–441.

Pecora, L. M., & Carroll, T. L. (1990). Synchronization in chaotic systems. *Physical Review Letters, 64*, 821–824. doi:10.1103/PhysRevLett.64.821 PMID:10042089.

Tomashevsky, A. I., & Kapranov, M. V. (2006). Fractal properties of chaotic dynamic processes in reverse time. *Nonlinear World*, (4-5), 214–237.

Wornell, G. (1996). *Signal processing with fractals: A wavelet-based approach*. London, UK: Prentice-Hall International.

Yang, T. (2004). A survey of chaotic secure communication systems. *International Journal of Computational Cognition, 2*(2), 81–130.

ADDITIONAL READING

Arnold, V. I., Afraimovich, V. S., Il'yashenko, Yu. S., & Shilnikov, L. P. (1999). *Bifurcation theory and catastrophe theory*. New York: Springer.

Belykh, V. N., & Chua, L. O. (1993). A new type of strange attractor related to the Chua's circuit. *Journal of Circuits. Systems and Computers, 3*(2), 361–374.

Berry, M. V., & Lewis, Z. V. (1980). On the Weierstrass-Mandelbrot fractal function. *Proceedings of the Royal Society of London. Series A, 370*, 459–484. doi:10.1098/rspa.1980.0044.

Bogolyubov, A. N., Koblikov, A. A., & Shapkina, N. E. (2009). Fractal electrodynamics: Analysis and synthesis of fractal antenna radiation pattern. In *Proceedings of PIERS*, (pp. 879-882). PIERS.

Chalice, D. R. (1991). A characterization of the cantor function. *The American Mathematical Monthly, 98*, 255–258. doi:10.2307/2325032.

Falconer, K. J. (1990). *Fractal geometry: Mathematical foundations and applications*. New York: John Wiley & Sons.

Farmer, J. D., Ott, E., & Yorke, J. A. (1983). The dimension of chaotic attractors. *Physica D. Nonlinear Phenomena, 7*(1), 153–170. doi:10.1016/0167-2789(83)90125-2.

Felber, P. (2000). *Fractal Antennas*. Chicago: Illinois Institute of Technology.

Grassberger, P., & Procaccia, I. (1983). Characterization of strange attractors. *Physical Review Letters*, *50*(5), 346–349. doi:10.1103/PhysRevLett.50.346.

Halle, K. S., Wo, C. W., Itoh, M., & Chua, L. O. (1993). Spread spectrum communication through modulation of chaos. *International Journal of Bifurcation and Chaos in Applied Sciences and Engineering*, *2*, 469–477. doi:10.1142/S0218127493000374.

Hardy, G. H. (1916). Weierstrass's non-differentiable function. *Transactions of the American Mathematical Society*, *17*, 302–323.

Hunt, B. R. (1998). The Hausdorff dimension of graphs of Weierstrass Function. *Proceedings of the American Mathematical Society*, *126*(3), 791–800. doi:10.1090/S0002-9939-98-04387-1.

Kocarev, L., Halle, K. S., Eckert, K., Chua, L., & Parlitz, U. (1992). Experimental demonstration of secure communications via chaotic synchronization. *International Journal of Bifurcation and Chaos in Applied Sciences and Engineering*, *3*, 709–713. doi:10.1142/S0218127492000823.

Kolumban, G., & Kennedy, M. P. (1998). The role of synchronization in digital communications using chaos: Part II–Chaotic modulation and chaotic synchronization. *IEEE Transactions on Circuits and Systems. I, Fundamental Theory and Applications*, *45*, 1129–1140. doi:10.1109/81.735435.

Leland, W. E., Taqqu, M. S., Willinger, W., & Wilson, D. V. (1994). On the self-similar nature of ethernet traffic. *IEEE/ACM Transactions on Networking*, *2*(1), 1–15. doi:10.1109/90.282603.

Li, T., & Yorke, J. A. (1975). Period three implies chaos. *The American Mathematical Monthly*, *82*, 985–992. doi:10.2307/2318254.

Lorenz, E. (1963). Deterministic non-periodic flows. *Journal of the Atmospheric Sciences*, *20*, 130–141. doi:10.1175/1520-0469(1963)020<0130:DNF>2.0.CO;2.

May, R. M. (1976). Simple mathematical models with very complicated dynamics. *Nature*, *261*, 459–467. doi:10.1038/261459a0 PMID:934280.

Park, K., & Willinger, W. (2000). *Self-similar network traffic and performance evaluation*. New York: John Wiley & Sons. doi:10.1002/047120644X.

Parlitz, U., Chua, L., Kocarev, L., Halle, K., & Shang, A. (1992). Transmission of digital signals by chaotic synchronization. *International Journal of Bifurcation and Chaos in Applied Sciences and Engineering*, *4*, 973–977. doi:10.1142/S0218127492000562.

Peitgen, H. O., Jurgens, H., & Saupe, D. (1992). Fractals for the classroom. In *Introduction to Fractals and Chaos*. New York: Springer. doi:10.1007/978-1-4757-4740-9.

Potapov, A. A., & German, V. A. (1998). Detection of artificial objects with fractal signatures. *Pattern Recognition and Image Analysis*, *8*(2), 226–229.

Raghavendra, B., & Dutt, D. (2010). Computing fractal dimension of signals using multiresolution box-counting method. *International Journal of Engineering and Mathematical Sciences*, *6*, 50–65.

Rocco, A., & West, B. J. (1998). Fractional calculus and the evolution of fractal phenomena. *Physica A*, 535–546.

Rossler, O. E. (1976). An equation for continuous chaos. *Physical Review Letters*, *57A*(5), 397–398.

Sharkovsky, A. N. (2006). Ideal turbulence. *Nonlinear Dynamics*, *44*, 15–27. doi:10.1007/s11071-006-1931-7.

Voss, R. F., & Clarke, J. (1975). 1/f noise in music and speech. *Nature*, *258*, 317–318. doi:10.1038/258317a0.

Yang, X., & Chiochetti, J., Papadopoulos, & Susman, L. (1999). Fractal antenna elements and arrays. *Applied Microwave & Wireless*, *5*, 34–46.

Chapter 6
TCP/IP Protocol-Based Model for Increasing the Efficiency of Data Transfer in Computer Networks

S.N. John
Covenant University, Nigeria

A.A. Anoprienko
Donetsk National Technical University, Ukraine

C.U. Ndujiuba
Covenant University, Nigeria

ABSTRACT

This chapter provides solutions for increasing the efficiency of data transfer in modern computer network applications and computing network environments based on the TCP/IP protocol suite. In this work, an imitation model and simulation was used as the basic method in the research. A simulation model was developed for designing and analyzing the computer networks based on TCP/IP protocols suite which fully allows the exact features in realizing the protocols and their impact on increasing the efficiency of data transfer in local and corporate networks. The method of increasing efficiency in the performance of computer networks was offered, based on the TCP/IP protocols by perfection of the modes of data transfer in them. This allows an increased efficient usage of computer networks and network applications without additional expenditure on infrastructure of the network. Practically, the results obtained from this research enable significant increase in the performance efficiency of data transfer in the computer networks environment. An example is the "Donetsk National Technical University" network.

DOI: 10.4018/978-1-4666-2208-1.ch006

INTRODUCTION

Intensive development of modern computer networks and programmable device systems realized from them resulted in the sharp increase of load and complexities (Network congestion) based on the stack of TCP/IP protocols. In turn, this results in substantial increase in workload in the operation of such networks. This process causes some difficulties on the hardware of a network, as well as the software applications. Thus, based on the background of intensive expansion of the global Internet infrastructure, both the magnitude of complexities and workload of corporate networks, grow substantially. Accordingly, the task of providing efficiency of the networks based on high-performance of the client-server and the distributed computing systems become more difficult. The only important reservation toward increasing the efficiency and productivity of such networks lies on improving the efficiency of data transfer within them. The Internet has pushed networking technology into the mainstream and it is without doubt the most important network, both in terms of technology advances and social impact, in the world. The number of host computers connected to the Internet continues to increase at an unceasing rate and shows no sign of slowing down (Lottor, 1992). This growth has placed strain on the network infrastructure that was built on what was, at the time ARPANET was created, experimental technology.

The Internet uses packet switching technology to transmit data, i.e. data that is to be transmitted over the Internet is split into small chunks, known as packets. These packets are then transmitted one at a time across the Internet where they are reassembled at the receiver.

The basic building blocks of the Internet are the protocols of TCP/IP suite (Petersen & Davie., 2000), which may be modeled as a stack of protocols split into several layers (Tanenbaum). The underlying protocol at the network layer, Internet Protocol or IP is a connection-less best-effort protocol, meaning it has no established connection or authentication, and it does not provide a guarantee that the data sent will reach their destination (Petersen & Davie, 2000). Reliable delivery is provided by the Transmission Control Protocol, or TCP on which great emphasis will be laid in this chapter.

However, the properties that make the Internet so effective and successful also make it vulnerable to degradation in performance or "Internet Meltdown" or "congestion collapse" (Braden. 1998). Several aspects of the underlying Internet technology are showing their age and reaching the point where other approaches need to be explored if the growth rate and stability of the Internet is to be maintained. These areas include efficiency of data transmission over a network and congestion avoidance control (Nagle, 1984). The accurate operation of TCP/IP protocols brought about the fact that based on the knowledge of complex network projects and increased number of users on a network, noticeably the network traffic grows exponentially to a critical level. Well-founded selection mode of data exchange allows, in many cases, the reduction of workload on a network, increases effective bandwidth and performance efficiency of both network as a whole and separate network hardware-software and programmable systems. The problems related to increasing performance efficiency of computer networks, were looked into and published by many researchers, notably the works conducted at the National Technical Universities in Ukraine, the «Kiev polytechnical institute», the Institute of cybernetics, Ukraine National Academy of Sciences, the Kharkov National University of Radio Electronics and in many other universities of Ukraine. Also, notable are the works of Visheneskoro, Gorodetkovo, Zaborovskovo, Kamera, Menaske, Almeydy, Steven, and many others.

However, literature review of the works carried out in this area showed that questions concerning the perfection in the modes of data exchange and their impacts on the efficiency of data transfer in a modern network application and computing network environments based on the protocol of TCP/IP were insufficiently explored and need further research. As a result of the above stated problems, it becomes necessary and important to conduct a research directed on increasing the efficiency of data transfer with increasing network throughput while maximizing bandwidth usage in modern computer network application and computing network environments. This fact led to the chosen scientific research work, which has scientific and practical importance in developing modern computing network and network application based on the TCP/IP protocols stack. The aim of this paper is to increase the efficiency of data transfer in modern network applications and computer networks based on the protocols of TCP/. In achieving the aim of this research, the following problems were treated:

- The main factors that affect the efficiency of data transfer in computer networks based on TCP/IP protocol and means of improving the efficiency of data exchange.
- Designing simulation models for investigating the efficiency of data transfer on Physical layers, Network layers and Transport layers.
- Determining the basic conformities to changes in effective bandwidth capacity on the network parameters as a result of the workload and the method of data transfer in the LAN.
- Influence of method of data transfer on the performance efficiency of corporate networks.
- Develop method of increasing the efficiency of data transfer based on the result of the research.

ANALYSIS OF THE FEATURES OF NETWORK DATA TRANSFER AND METHODS OF INCREASING THEIR EFFICIENCY

This is based on the research work on factors affecting the efficiency of data transfer in computer networks based on the TCP/IP protocols stack and the basic problems in this area were analyzed. Computer networks play an important and ever increasing role in the modern world. The development of Internet, the corporate intranet, and mobile telephones have extended the reach of network connectivity to places that some years ago would have been unthinkable. This intensive development of modern computer networks and realizing their program-hardware systems results in sharp growth, toward the increase in workload and complexities of computer networks based on TCP/IP protocols (Petersen & Davie, 2000; Tanenbaum, 2003; Lottor, 1992). Many protocols are modeled as finite state machines. The basic means of data transfer in the modern networks is the TCP/IP protocols stack (Camel, D.E., 2003). Regardless of the particular applications, the efficiency of data transfer substantially depends on the performance of the network at Physical, Network, Transport and Application Layers.

Figure 1 shows the basic component problem areas of a network, which results in ineffective realization or ineffective uses, which can negatively affect the network throughput, both in an entire network and/or separate fragments or network applications. The method of data transfer was examined as the main focus of research in this work, as its perfection enables, in many cases, a considerable improvement of network and network application performance without substantial additional expenditures. The main task of analyzing and modeling the modes of data transfer in modern computer networks based on the TCP/IP protocol is to increase the performance efficiency of the network and network application, thereby increasing their productivity. The mathematical representation of the task can be expressed in the following forms.

Find such parameters of data stream block and their sizes, at which the effective bandwidth capacity of network (Q) ➔ (tends to) maximum. Thus,

$$Q = f(Q_N, L, \lambda, n_y), \quad (1)$$

where Q_N is nominal bandwidth capacity of the network; L – size of the transmit data blocks; λ – the parameter of data stream blocks (for every node); n_y – number of active nodes in the networks. However, the properties that make the Internet so effective and successful also make it vulnerable to degradation in performance or "Internet Meltdown" or "congestion collapse" (Braden, 1998; Nagle, 1984). Several aspects of the underlying Internet technology are showing their age and reaching the point where other approaches need to be explored if the growth rate and stability of the Internet is to be maintained. These areas include efficiency of data transmission over a network and congestion avoidance control (Nagle, 1984). Based on this work the factors affecting the efficiency of data transfer in computer networks through TCP/IP protocols and related problems are analyzed.

DESIGNING SIMULATION MODELS FOR INVESTIGATING THE EFFICIENCY OF DATA TRANSFER ON PHYSICAL LAYERS, NETWORK LAYERS AND TRANSPORT LAYERS

This section is devoted to the development of simulation models for research on efficiency of data transfer at physical layer (based on the Ethernet protocol), and also – at network and transport layers (based on the TCP/IP protocols). The dynamics of the process of data exchange in a distributed computer network is so difficult, that to describe it in a comprehensive linear or nonlinear analytic functions with sufficient accuracy are extremely difficult. Therefore the factors that affect the performance of functional communication networks can be described only with the use of algorithmic simulation methods.

The development of the distributed computing environments, based on the modern infrastructure of the Internet, offers useful value in increasing the efficiency of network interaction at all levels of the TCP/IP stack: beginning from a physical level and concluding at the fast-acting of applications at physical level. However, it is on these levels that we have the most significant difficult characteristic dependence of bandwidth capacity on the chosen modes of data transfer. In response to this, multilevel simulation was designed to tackle these level problems. The developed model of link layer allows us to define the basic descriptions of and shows the most critical areas of networks in different working mode. This model was developed and realized as shown in the Simulink blocks model: «nodes» (Host) and «Channel» (Bus) (Figure 2) (John, 2005).

On the side of transport and network interrelation layers, a model was developed and realized in a SIMULINK blocks model of three units: Host, Bus and Gateway – model of data channel between local area networks with the possibility of exit to the global network. In line with this, the basic method of studying the network efficiency is by simulation methods using both specialized tools, and the universal MATLAB to investigate the

Figure 1. The factors that determines the performance of a network

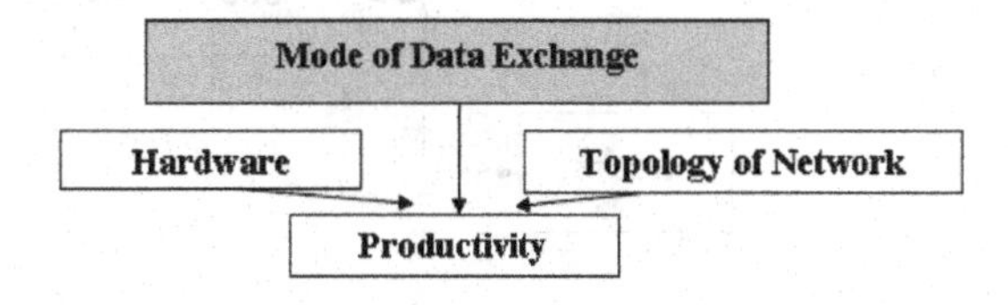

Figure 2. Structural block representation of physical layer models

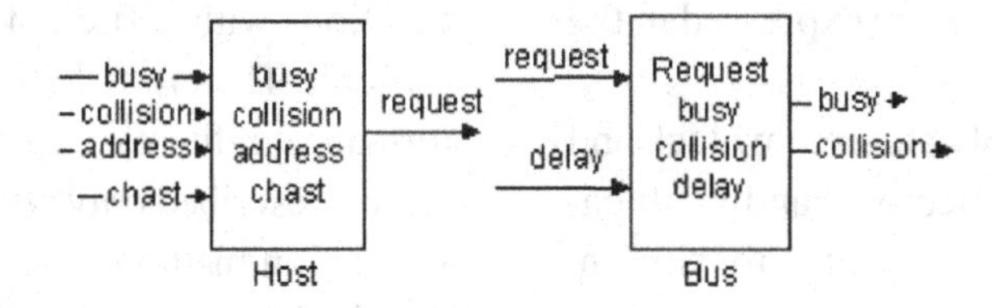

effectiveness of data transfer and maximize their output.

Figure 3 shows a sample model structure of TCP/IP network, consisting of two LANs connected by gateway. The model structures of the network that allows defining the main functional elements are:

- **Host:** Point of network serving the transport layer;
- **Bus:** Medium of transmission in the LAN;
- **Gateway:** Data transmission channel between two LAN.

The model was realized based on the SIMULINK system tools with the use of S-function (Simulink™, 2000) in creating a special blocks of models and control programs. In the simulation model of "object Host", three of its main states were considered: delay, receive frame and send frame. In each state, the state algorithm of the Host unit is different in functions. Host was represented by a system of differential equation shown below:

$$\begin{cases} \overline{x}_{i+1} = \overline{G}(\overline{u}_i, \overline{x}_i, t_i); \\ \overline{y}_{i+1} = \overline{g}(\overline{u}_i, \overline{x}_i, t_i); \\ t_{i+1} = t_i + \Delta t. \end{cases} \tag{2}$$

where $\overline{x}_{i+1}, \overline{x}_i - (i + 1)$ and i are values of variable state vector of Host;

$\overline{y}_{i+1} - (i+1)$ value of variable output vector of Host;

$\overline{u}_i$ $-i$ value of variable input vector of Host;

$\overline{G}, \overline{g}$ – vector-function;

$t_{i+1}, t_i - (i + 1)$ and i values of model time;

Figure 3. Model structure of LAN connection by gateway

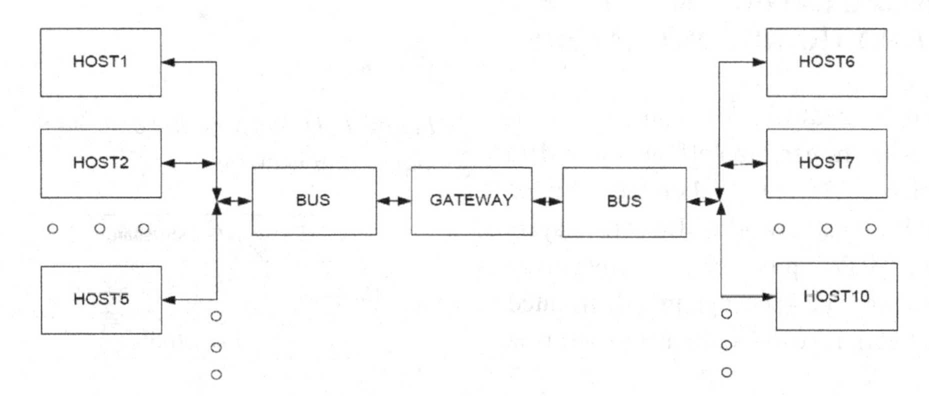

Δt – simulation step.

Figure 4 shows the flowchart of the simulation model of the HOST unit showing the condition of transition from one state to another. Hence, the following values were used in computation:

Average frequency frames:

$$\lambda_{cp} = \frac{Q_T}{n_y \cdot L_{cp}}, \frac{1}{\mathcal{M}\sec} \quad (3)$$

- **Maximum frequency frames:**

$$\lambda_{\max} = 1,5 \cdot \lambda_{cp}, \frac{1}{\mathcal{M}\sec}, \text{ but not more than } Q_N\left(1,2 \cdot L_{cp}\right)^{-1}.$$

- **Minimum frequency frames:**

$$\lambda_{\min} = \left(2 - \frac{\lambda_{\max}}{\lambda_{cp}}\right) \cdot \lambda_{cp}, \frac{1}{m\sec}, \text{ but not less than } Q_N\left(1,2 \cdot L_{cp}\right)^{-1}.$$

- **Average length of frame:**

$$L_{cp} = \frac{L_{\min} + L_{\max}}{2}, \textit{ bit}.$$

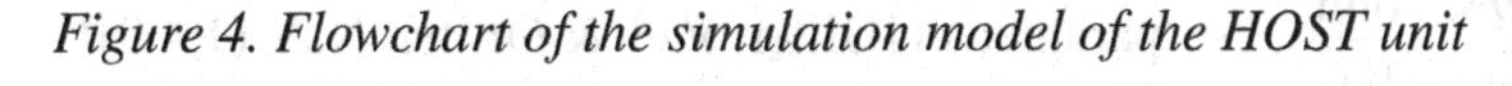

Figure 4. Flowchart of the simulation model of the HOST unit

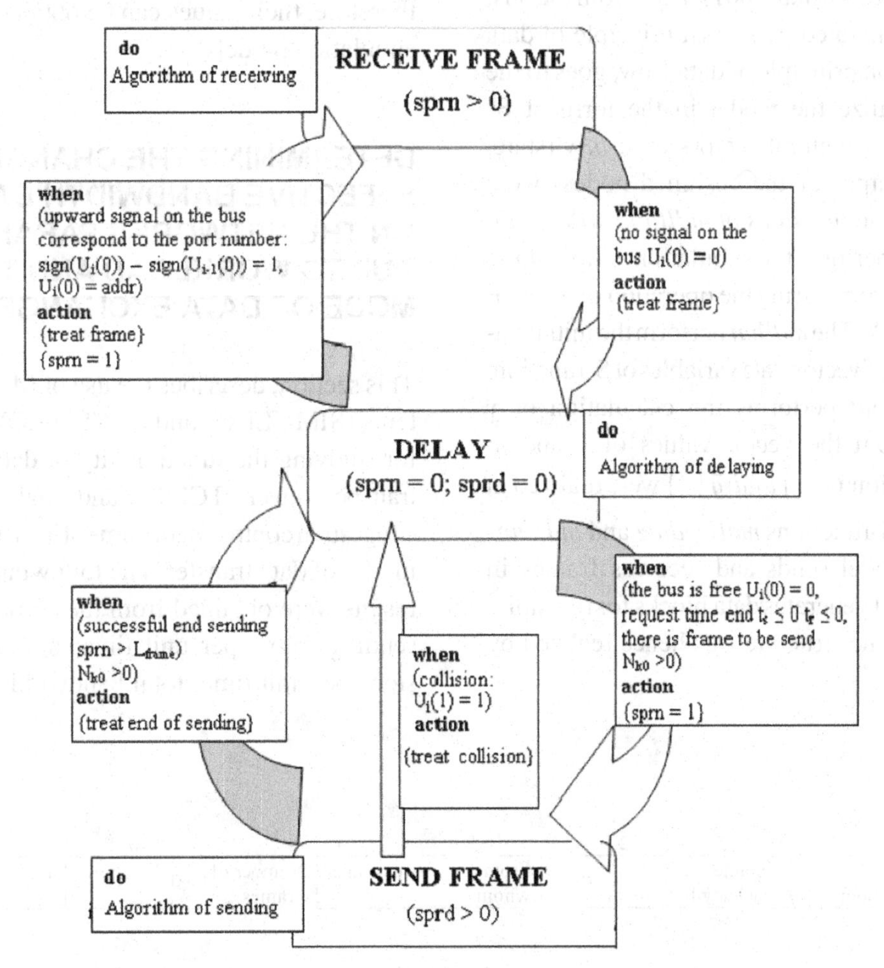

- **Frequency frames for *i* node:** $\lambda_i = \lambda_{min} + \left(\lambda_{max} - \lambda_{min}\right) \cdot d$, where d – variable number, evenly distributed between an intervals of 0 to 1.
- **Minimum interval between frame for *i* -node:** $\Delta t_{min} = \frac{1}{\lambda_i} - \frac{L_{max}}{Q_N}$, мsec.
- **Maximum interval between frame for *i*-node:** $\Delta t_{max} = \frac{1}{\lambda_i} - \frac{L_{min}}{Q_N}$, мsec.

The following procedures were also adopted: displacement in the receiving frame, – displacement in the sending frame. The HOST unit realizes the basic algorithmic functions of the TCP/IP and Ethernet (basic features of CSMA/CD protocol) (Stevens, 1997; Stevens, 1998; John, Anoprienko, & Rishka, 2001). Data from the bus, which are generated by known principle of data flow – Poisson principle of data flow, goes to the Host. To realize the model in the form of S-function, the structural vectors of *x, u, y* (state, input and output of the designed nodes) were developed. The *functions of mdlInit, mdlOutput, mdlUpdate,* perform the simulation action of the Ethernet network during the operation of TCP/IP protocols stack. The *mdlInit* perform the initialization function of vector state variables of S-function. The *mdlOutput* performs the calculation of *y* functions from the vector values of *x* and *u*. Vector-function $\bar{G}(\ )$ *and* $\bar{g}(\ )$ were realized in the form of S-functions *mdlUpdate* and *mdlOutput*. This model sends and receives frames in packages, and generates data blocks for transmission. The frame structure was hence realized by that in Box 1.

The vector *u* consists of two components: busy signal from the bus/channel and signs of collision, which are the internal inputs from the blocks of SIMULINK model. The *y*-vector consists of three components: signal to the bus/channel, number of sending and acknowledgement information, and the delay time. The x vector consists of buffers and state variables as shown in Figure 4.

With the use of the offered simulation models on elements of TCP/IP (Nagle, 1984; Stevens, 1997; John S.N., Anoprienko, A.Y., & Niru, A., 2002) network, Figure 5, it is possible to develop a simulation model of both local and corporate networks. The efficiency of a network data transfer substantially relies on the correct choice of network parameters and this is due to the difficulties in the theoretical estimation of the actual parameters [Olifer, V.G. & OLifer, N.A. (1999)], therefore, their values can be obtained by proper simulation models.

DETERMINING THE CHANGES OF EFFECTIVE BANDWIDTH CAPACITY ON THE NETWORKS PARAMETERS DUE TO WORKLOAD AND THE MODE OF DATA EXCHANGE IN LAN

This section, describes the use of MATLAB systems (SIMULINK and STATEFLOW modules) for studying the functionality of data link layer, transport layer 'TCP/IP' and analysis of some congestion control algorithms of TCP protocol and modes of data transfer. The following significant results were obtained from the work: number of sending frame per unit time; number of collisions per unit time; total bandwidth capacity of

Box 1.

1	2	3	4	5	6		
To whom	N – frame 0 – acknowledgement	From whom	N package	Number of Frames	1	…	1

Figure 5. Model of SIMULINK with two local area networks connected by gateway

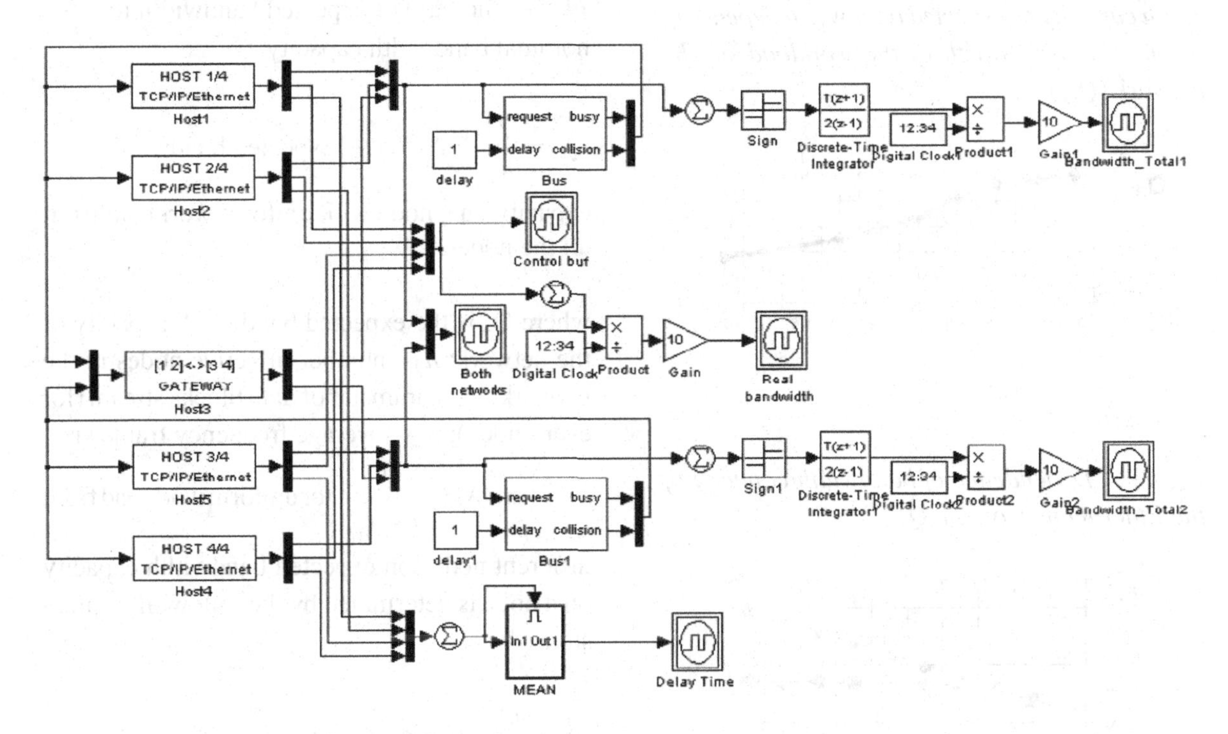

the network; effective bandwidth capacity of the network (without taking into account the unsuccessful attempts of frame transmission) and mean delay time of data block transmission.

The results of the research work, using developed models for investigating the modes of data transfer at link layer are shown in Figures 6 and 7. It is seen from these graphs, how increase in collisions reduces the effective bandwidth capacity of the network. From the simulation results, it is seen that the workload efficiency of the network goes well up to 60% on the Ethernet Technology with the traffic transmission (Olifer, V.G. & OLifer, N.A., 1999; Matloff, 2000; John, S. N., Anoprienko, A. A., Okonigene, R. E., 2010). With further increase of the workload, practically there was no increase in the effective bandwidth capacity. This result agrees with an established fact, which confirms the accuracy of the model for Ethernet Technology traffic. On the quality of the workload, the frequently occurring parameters of file sizes were shown – from 0.1 Kbytes to 2 Mbytes and parameters of data stream block λ, provided by a given file size of intensive network workload.

In a whole from the results of simulation, that during the workload on a network to about 60% of the Ethernet technology (as seen in Figure 7) on the divided segment gets well along with the transmission of traffic generated by the end ports. However, at the growth of intensive generated traffic to such size, when the coefficient use of the network approaches 1, probability of frame collision is so multiplied that most frames, which some station try to send, run into other frames, causing collisions (Olifer, V.G. & Olifer, N.A., 1999; Floyd, 1991; Floyd & Fall, 1999).

During simulation the files for transmission are adopted, on every station generated as Poisson flow (Klienrok, L., 1979; Lebedev, A.I. & Sherniavskovo, E.A., 1986). Amount of files *m*, which is necessary to send at an interval of time ΔT, distributed by the law of Poisson:

$$P_m = \frac{a^m}{m!} e^{-a} \tag{4}$$

Figure 6. Change in the ratio of effective bandwidth capacity to expected bandwidth depending on the relative growth of the workload on the network (Q_{TN})

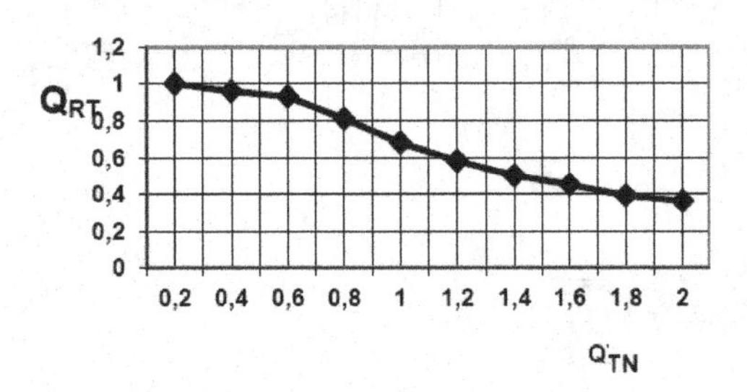

Figure 7. Dependence of bandwidth capacity of the Ethernet network on Q_{TN}

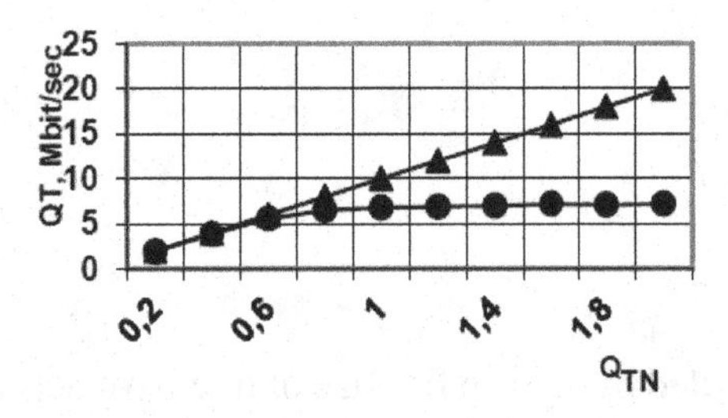

where *a* – average number of files which is necessary to be send at an interval of time ΔT;

Probability that for Poisson flow in a given small area with change in time ΔT occurs an event, i.e. probability of receiving a data block in the TCP buffer, is determined by the below formula:

$$P(\Delta T) \approx \lambda \Delta T.$$

The above formula helps in realizing the principal features of TCP/IP protocol when an event takes place at the transport layer. Files for transmission on every node were generated as poison stream (in general, this may not be the only files, but practically any data blocks, generated in the process of network data exchange).

Thus, the following parameters were used:

Q_{RT} – the ratio of effective bandwidth capacity to expected bandwidth capacity.

Q_{TN} – the ratio of expected bandwidth to nominal bandwidth capacity.

$$Q_1 = \frac{Q_T}{n_y} = \lambda \cdot L_{cp}$$ – expected bandwidth capacity on a node with uniform workload from all the nodes,

where Q_T is the expected bandwidth capacity of the network; n_y – number of active nodes in the network; λ – parameter of data blocks stream (for every node); L_{cp} – average frequency frame size.

Then, $\lambda = \frac{Q_T}{n_y \cdot L_{cp}}$ for uniform workload from different nodes on expected bandwidth capacity on a node is determined by the following expression:

$$Q_1 = \frac{Q_T}{n_y} \cdot b;\ b \in [\,b_{min};\ b_{max}],$$

where b is the random variable, evenly distributed with the expected value equal to one, hence $(b_{max} + b_{min})/2 = 1$.

The ratio of the maximum workload on a node to the minimum is determined by a formula: $k = b_{max}/b_{min}$, then $b_{min} = 2/(1 + k)$; $b_{max} = k \cdot b_{min}$.

Data block length is a random number evenly distributed within a range from L_{min} to L_{max}: $L_{cp} = Q_T/\lambda$; $L = L_{min} + d \cdot (L_{max} - L_{min})$, where d is the random number evenly distributed in an interval between 0 to 1.

The efficient performance of computer network based on obtainable results from simulation of the distributed computer systems and networks can be estimated by the following basic relationships:

Real bandwidth:

$$Q_R = \frac{1}{T}\sum_{i=1}^{n}\sum_{j=1}^{N} L_{ij},\ Mbit/\sec. \qquad (5)$$

where,

- **Q_R:** Effective l bandwidth;
- **L_{ij}:** Data block size;
- **T:** Simulation time;
- **N:** Number of data blocks successfully sent to i-nodes.

Total bandwidth:

$$Q_{Total} = Q_N \frac{T_s}{T}, Mbit / \sec. \quad (6)$$

where

- **Q_{Total}:** Total bandwidth;
- **T_s:** Sending time.

Average delay time:

$$\Delta T = \frac{1}{N_y} \sum_{i=1}^{n} \sum_{j=1}^{N} \frac{\Delta T_{ij}}{N}, \text{ sec}. \quad (7)$$

where ΔT_{ij} – delay time in generating j data block in i node

$$\Delta T_{ij} = T_{send} - (L_{ij} + N_{ij} \cdot S_E)/Q_N \quad (8)$$

where

- **T_{send}:** Time between first and last transmitted data block;
- **S_E:** Length of header frame;
- **N_{ij}:** Number of frames in a packet

Figure 8 shows the simulation results of the dependence of Q_{RT} on expected bandwidth capacity Q_T. It is seen that with L = 0.4 Kbytes, data block size practically has no effect on the effective bandwidth capacity. Analysis of the graph concludes that as Q_T increases to 10 Mbit/s, the effective traffic also increases. Reduction of the effective bandwidth capacity takes place when the standard speed of Ethernet transmission (10 Mbit/s) is exceeded. This shows how an irrational file size affects the network performance in a corporate network. The Q_{RT} correlation in Figure 9 shows that as L > 0.4 Kbyte the coefficient of traffic falls, regardless of the size of data block. From the statistical result, the generalized dependence is shown on the Figure 9.

The result allows the analysis of two regions of Q_{RT} (Q_T) dependence:

- First – with Q_T less than a threshold value (in this case 3,2 Mbit/s), described by $Q_{RT} \approx 1$ regardless of Q_T;
- The second region is described by exponential regressive dependence:

$$Q_{RT} = 1,29 \cdot e^{-0,079 Q_T};$$

Selection of the regressive dependence ΔT (QT, L) allows the following formula to be obtained:

$$\Delta T = 0,00311 \bullet Q_T + 0,000044\, Q_T \bullet L_{cp}, \ sec.$$

The modes of file transfer were analyzed in the following sequence:

1. Data transmission time (T_2);
2. Required bandwidth capacity of a network (workload on a network) (Q_T):

$$Q_T = \frac{I}{T}, \text{ Kbyte/sec},$$

Figure 8. Dependence value Q_{RT} on Q_T for different transmit data block sizes

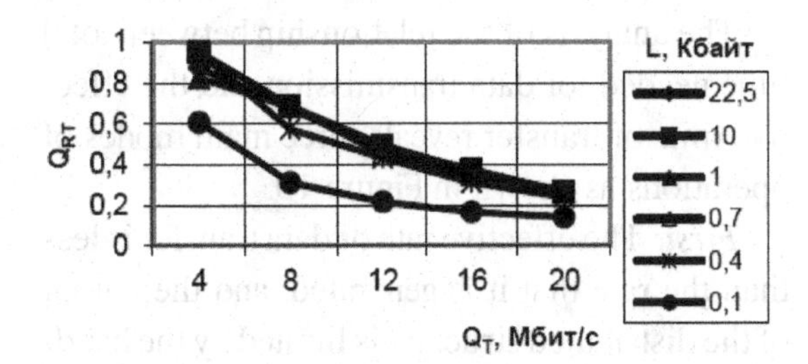

Figure 9. Regressive dependence value of Q_{RT} on Q_T

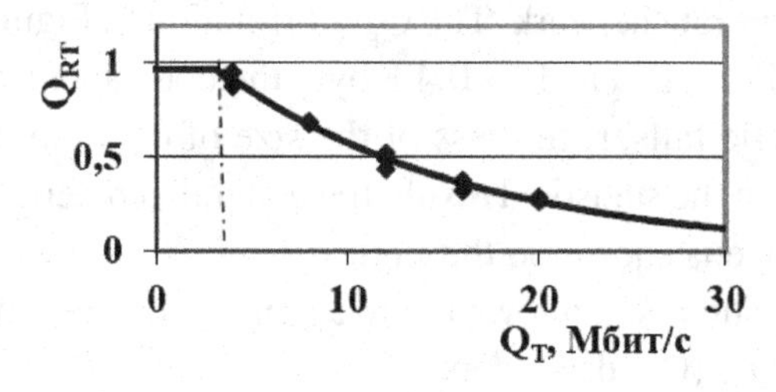

where

- **I:** General information to be transmitted, Kbytes
- **T:** Time of data transfer, sec.

Time of data transfer was determined by the following formula:

$T_2 = (\Delta T + T_{transmission})\, n_f$, sec

where

- $n_f = I/L$: Number of files passed by every network;
- **ΔT:** Time delay in data transfer due to collisions and other problems;
- $T_{transmission}$: Spontaneous time of direct data exchange, $T_{transmission} = I/Q_N$.

Then, the optimum spontaneous condition will be

$$\frac{T_2}{T} = Q_T \left[\frac{1}{Q_N} + \frac{\Delta T}{L} \right] \quad (9)$$

The analysis of the relationship between total time needed for data transmission and the effective time of transfer reveals three main modes of operations as shown in Figure 10.

First: The effective rate of data transfer is less than the rate that it is generated, and the output of the distributed structure is limited by the bandwidth capacity of the network. It results in substantial under-utilization of computing potential of the distributed environment. But in this case, it is possible to select the region of possible workload, for a bandwidth capacity of the network.

Second: The actual rate of data transfer corresponds to the set workload, fulfilling the maximum burst performance of the distributed environment.

Third: Actual rate of data transfer is greater than the rate of generating the data, but due to irrational file size, the operation of the network is not optimum. From well-known simulation results, in a distributed network environment with workload greater than 60% of nominal data rate, the data transfer records substantial loss of efficiency. The achieved dependences allow the execution of concrete estimation of the loss, which is shown in Figure 11.

In the whole analysis, this shows the role of bandwidth usage for efficient data transfer in wireless network in relation to how the method of data exchange affect the efficiency in a corporate network ; the key issue being the Network performance and time delay in file transfer. Based on the shown results, recommendations can be made on the method of increasing the efficiency in data transfer.

THE IMPACT OF METHOD OF DATA TRANSFER ON THE PERFORMANCE EFFICIENCY OF CORPORATE NETWORKS

In this section, specialized means was used in analyzing, modeling and researching of data exchange in large-scale corporate computer network (for example the network infrastructure of DonNTU). Very large corporate intranet networks and the Internet make the development of analytic models very difficult and in such circumstances; simulation models are a viable alternative to understand the behavior of these networks with data

Figure 10. Relationship between send time and the time for generating data file size for different workload on the network

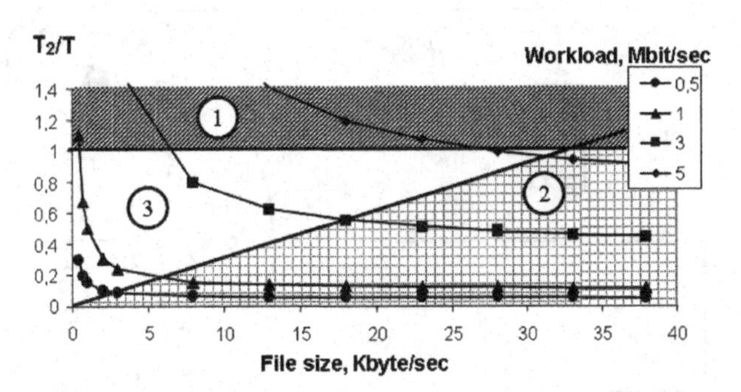

transfer in a corporate intranet. Research work on data transfers (John, S.N., Anoprienko, A.Y., & Rishka, S.V., 2001; John, 2005) in a network using analytical approach allows approximate estimate of the workload of two layer channels in corporate network `as shown in Figure 12. However, large corporate networks such as universities, as a rule, have greater number of levels, which substantially hampers the use of analytical methods and requires application of multilevel simulation design of network infrastructure. As a result, a professional simulation packet, NetCracker, was deployed. Thus a research on workload of an external channel was carried out in a corporate intranet using the following parameters:

- Size of the send files,
- Number of connections,
- Time domain between the transmissions of the files.

Developed in the simulation is a model containing 4 levels that consists of 11 campuses/buildings of 1100 complex networks. Figure 13 shows the obtained result from which it is seen that with increase in transmit file size (at a fixed parameter of data flow), workload on a channel and the effective bandwidth capacity increase toward maximum level (ranging from 128 to 1024 Kbytes for different networks), hence affecting the effective bandwidth capacity and shows a fall in the bandwidth. The obtained relation allows us to show how an increase in transmit file sizes certainly affects the effective bandwidth capacity of a network.

The dependence of bandwidth capacity of external channel of a corporate network using average file sizes from different number of network connections with constant workload on a channel is shown in Figure 14. From the graph it is seen that a change of transmit file size from 128 – 512 Kbytes has no significant impact on the bandwidth capacity of the external channel both with the partial workload of the channel (15 connections, Q_{TN} = 0,61), and actual workload (30 -150 connections, Q_{TN} = 15).

Figure 11. Graph of network throughput/bandwidth of workload on TCP/IP LAN

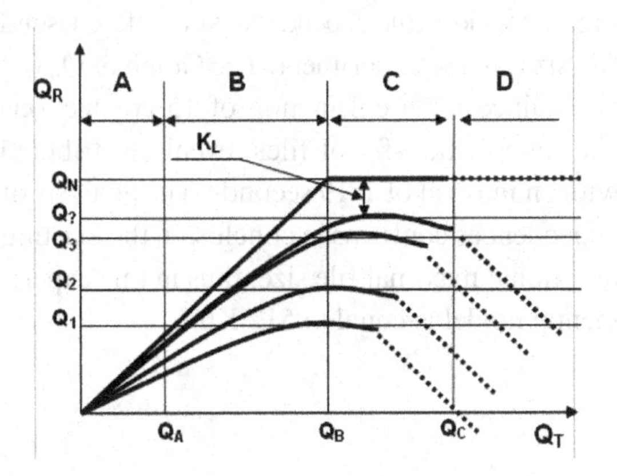

Figure 12. Analytical scheme of network

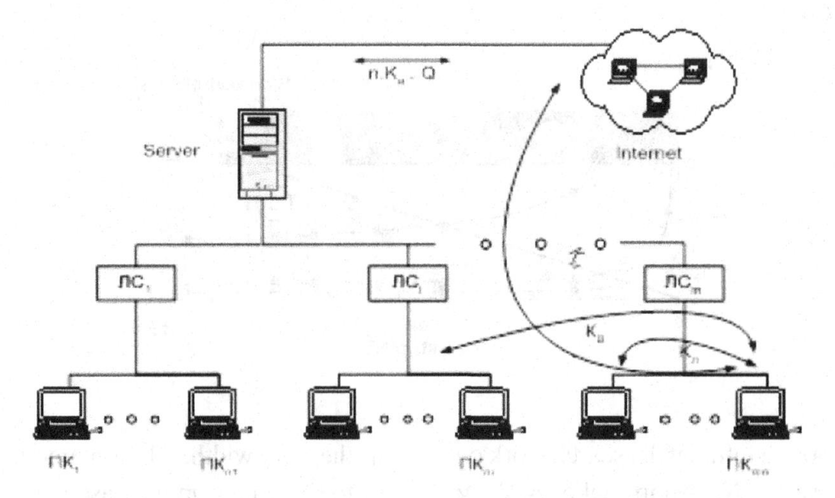

With further increase in workload to the channel the bandwidth capacity of channel begins to decrease (in this case at an average transmit files size of more than 512 Kbytes). Thus, for a corporate network in a given condition, exceeding the maximum transmits file size results in significant reduction in the efficiency of data transfer. For the purpose of verification and authentication of the obtained results, the actual experiment model was conducted, to investigate the impact of transmit file sizes on the efficiency of sent files to the server from one campus to the workstation in another campus.

During the processes of transmission, the transaction time and average bandwidth performance were recorded. The result of the experimental model was compared with the calculated results. Figure 15 shows the dependences on different send file sizes in the experiment. The Graph of Q_R (L) is obtained from calculation of 15 connections and time of transfer of files, evenly distributed with an interval of 1-19 seconds. The analysis of dependences confirms in conclusion the existing of rational maximal file size, thus in this experimental model is equal to 512 Kb.

DEVELOPED METHOD OF INCREASING THE EFFICIENCY OF DATA TRANSFER BASED ON THE RESULT OF THE RESEARCH

This section, describes the method of increasing the efficiency of network data transfer based on using the developed models and corresponding results. Also shown is the corresponding different methodical means of designing and analyzing the network infrastructure with the purpose of providing an increase in the efficiency of data transfer based on the TCP/IP protocols stack.

From the summary of the results of sections 2 – 5, it is possible to conclude that, the method of data transfer can substantially have impact on the performance efficiency of the TCP/IP network as shown in the figures, (Figure 16 and 17). As a whole, summarizing the results of the researches, the three-dimensional dependences represented in Figure 16 and 17, show how the method of data exchange affects the bandwidth capacity of a network. The main source of obtaining all these results was through imitational simulation.

Figure 13. Dependence graph of bandwidth capacity of external channel of a corporate network based on an average file size and different number of network connections

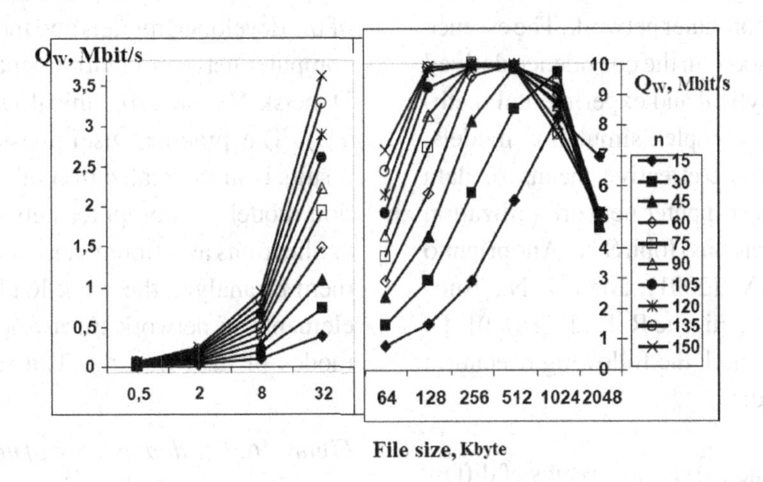

Figure 14. Dependence of bandwidth capacity of external channel on a corporate network based on an average file size, different number of network connections, and workload capacity

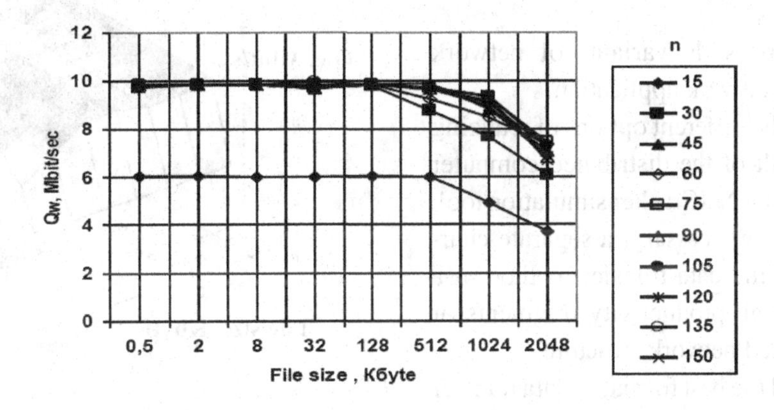

Figure 15. Research result of workload from main computing network system obtained by model and the computer

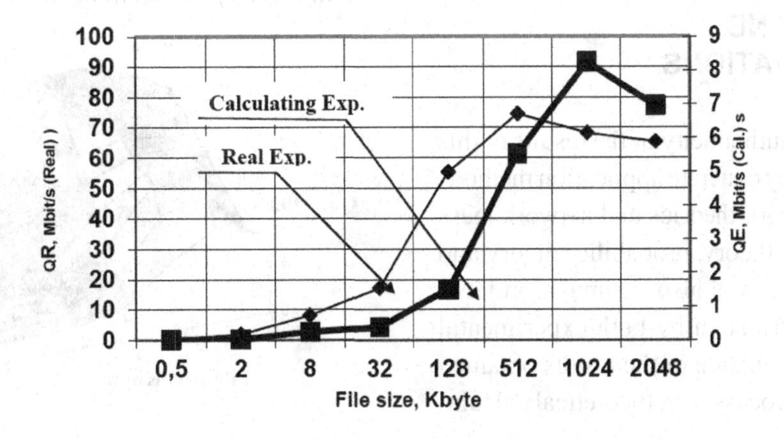

Thus, the achieved results offer a special method of increasing the efficiency of data transfer in a distributed computer network. The essence of the offered method is in the confidence derived from both the analytical and experimental methods, and also from complex simulation models, for deciding the most effective means of data transfer for a given computer network utilization and network applications [John S.N., Anoprienko A.Y. & Rishka S.V. (2001), John S. N., Anoprienko A. A., & Okonigene R. E., 1, (2010)]. To implement this method, the following execution sequence is offered:

1. First determine the characteristics of different means of data transfer and investigate the network structure using the physical and transport level models developed in this research work.
2. Determine possible variants of network structure or network application.
3. Investigate the different options of realizing the key result of the distributed computer networks using NetCracker simulation tool.
4. Clarify, where necessary, a separate characteristic of the data transfer method in a critical through productivity fragments of an investigated network structure.
5. Recommend the best format of data transfer in a computing network within the framework of the investigated network applications.

SOLUTIONS AND RECOMMENDATIONS

The validity and authenticity of the results of this work is provided by concrete application methods of computer network theories and network mass service, automata theory, probability theory and statistical methods, and also – simulation techniques, and confirmation by both experimental models and co-ordination of the results obtained in the modeling process with theoretical calculations. Authenticity of the results is confirmed by the positive results obtained from the application of the developed models and methods in an actual computer network environment, for example, the Donetsk National Technical University (DonNTU). The practical usefulness of the obtained results is in the realization of functional simulation models of computer networks and network applications at different network layers and using them to analyze the work-load per channel and elements of network infrastructure for different modes of data transfer. The result is also use-

Figure 16. The dependence of network bandwidth capacity on the number of connections at different time interval of file transfer

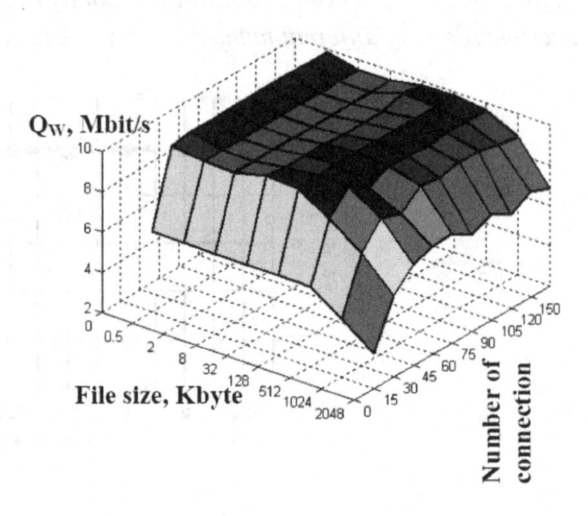

Figure 17. The dependence of network bandwidth on number of connections and transmit file size

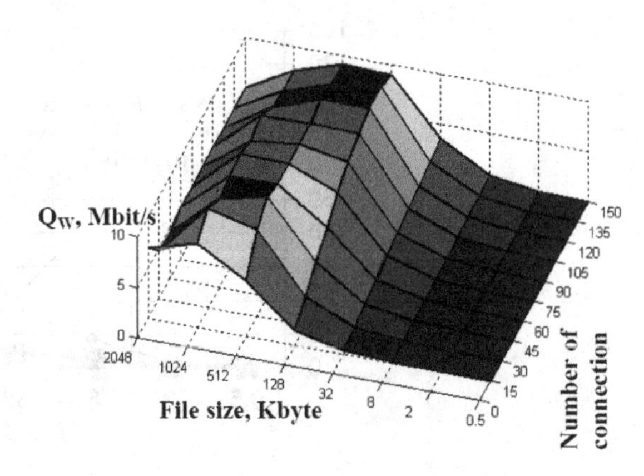

ful in developing multilevel simulation model of corporate network infrastructure that allows effective researching the mode of data rate and search for the most rational variants in the use and development of the networks. The methods and results of this work are novel and have been applied for the first time in complex corporate network infrastructure, such as University and Corporate Network.

FUTURE RESEARCH

We recommend improved high-level method for designing and analyzing the efficiency of computer networks based on a hybrid of different models and analytical methods, adequately taking into account, the influence of mode of data transfer towards in the performance of corporate networks based on TCP/IP protocol. A unified mode of data transfer framing across a network, dynamic bandwidth provisioning on a packet-by-packet basis, and hybrid data-mixing capability that will maximize bandwidth usage and yields major efficiency in wired and wireless equipment and operation of the computer networks.

CONCLUSION

The scientific innovation of the achieved results shows that, for the first time, special complex simulation models were designed for analyzing and for multilevel modeling processes of data transfer in computer networks based on the protocols of TCP/IP, which fully and accurately allows us to determine the co-existing factors exchange such as formation of data flow, network topology, function of network protocols and internet collaboration/support which influence efficiency of data transfer. The characteristic change in effective bandwidth capacity obtained for different modes of data transfer in LAN and WAN, for a given condition of a network utilization agrees with the achieved results. For the first time, based on using the developed simulation models to conduct the complex research on performance efficiency of computer networks (local and corporate network) for different modes of data transfer, which allows obtaining the complex dependences, shows how the real bandwidth capacity and change in the average transmit data block changes the real bandwidth capacity and, accordingly the efficiency performance of networks and network applications. Based on the statistical analysis from the obtained simulation results, an expression to estimate the actual evaluation of the given value of prescribed Q_T, L and other parameters of data stream flow were analyzed. For the first time, a proposed method for increasing efficiency of data transfer in networks based on the use of complex simulation models and improved modes of data transfer and provides an improved efficiency in operation of network by an average of 10 – 15%.

REFERENCES

Arpaci. (2001). *Congestion avoidance in TCP/IP networks*. Retrieved from http://www.csc.gatech.edu/~mutlu/arpaci_thesis.pdf

Braden. (1998). Recommendations on queue management and congestion avoidance in the internet. *RFC 2039*.

Camel, D. E. (2003). *Principles, protocols, and structure*. Networks TCP/IP.

Floyd & Fall. (1999). Promoting the use of end-to-end congestion control in the internet. *ACM/IEEE Transactions on Networking, 7*(4), 458–473.

Floyd. (1991). Connections with multiple congested gateways in packet-switched networks part 1: One-way traffic. *ACM Computer Communication Review, 21*(5), 30–47.

Grossglanster & Bolot. (1996). On the relevance of long range dependence in network traffic. In *Proceedings of ACM SIGCOMM '96*. San Francisco, CA: ACM.

Huang, P., & Heidemann, J. (2000). Capturing TCP burstiness for lightweight simulation. In *Procceedings of Engineering and Networks Laboratory*. Zurich, Switzerland: IEEE.

John, S. N., Anoprienko, A. A., & Okonigene, R. E. (2010). Developed algorithm for increasing the efficiency of data exchange in a computer network. *International Journal of Computers and Applications*, *6*(9), 16–19. doi:10.5120/1103-1446.

John, S.N., Anoprienko, A.Y., & Niru, A. (n.d.). Multilevel simulation of networks on the base of TCP/IP protocols stack using Matlab/Simulink environment. *Cybernetic and Computing Texnika*, *39*, 271–297.

John, S.N., Anoprienko, A.Y., Rishka, S.V. (n.d.). Simulating of university network infrastructure. *Kremeshuk State Technical University*, *2*(11), 271–297.

John. (2005). Increasing the efficiency of data exchange in a computer network based on the protocol of TCP/IP suite. *Information, Cybernetics, and Computing Engineering*, *93*, 256-264.

Klienrok, L. (1979). *Computing systems with queuing*.

Lebedev, A. I., & Sherniavskovo, E. A. (1986). Probability method in computing texnika: Educational manual for institutes of higher learning on special. *Computer*.

Lottor. (1992). Internet growth (1981-1991). *RFC 1296*.

Matloff. (2000). *Some utilization analyses for ALOHA and CSMA protocols*. Davis, CA: University of California at Davis.

Minaev, A., Bashkov, E., Anoprienko, A., Kargin, A., Teslia, V., & Babasyuk, A. (2002). Development of internet infrastructure for higher education in Donetsk region of the Ukraine. In *Proceedings of ICEE 2002 Manchester International Conference on Engineering Education*. Manchester, UK: ICEE.

Nagle. (1984). Congestion control in IP/TCP internetworks. *RFC 896*.

Olifer, V. G., & Olifer, N. A. (1999). Principles of technologies, protocols–SPB. *Computer Networks*.

Petersen & Davie. (2000). *Computer networks: A systems approach*. San Francisco, CA: Morgan Kaufmann.

Simulink™. (2000). *Design and simulate continuous and discrete time systems*. Retrieved from http://www.mathworks.com/products/Simulink™

Stevens, W.R. (1997). TCP slow start, congestion avoidance, fast retransmit, and fast recovery algorithms. *RFC 2001*.

Stevens, W. R. (1998). *The protocols (Vol. 1)*. TCP/IP Illustrated.

Tanenbaum. (2003). *Computer networks*. Upper Saddle River, NJ: Prentice Hall Inc.

Vehel & Sikdar. (2001). A multiplicative multifractal model for TCP traffic. In *Proceedings of IEEE ISCC'01*. IEEE. Retrieved from http://citeseer.ist.psu.edu/vehel01multiplicative.html

ADDITIONAL READING

Ahn, D. Liu, & Yan. (1995). Experience with TCP Vegas: Emulation and experiment. In *Proceedings of ACM SIGCOMM '95*. Boston: ACM.

Allman, Paxson, & Stevens. (1999). TCP congestion control. *RFC 2581*.

Bochmann & Sunshine. (1980). Formal methods in communication protocol design. *IEEE Transactions on Communications*, *28*(4), 624–631. doi:10.1109/TCOM.1980.1094685.

Boggs, M. (1988). Measured capacity of an ethernet: Myths and reality. In *Proceedings of ACM Sigcomm* (pp. 222–234). Kent: ACM.

Braden. (1989). Requirements for internet hosts-Communication layers. *RFC 1122*.

Brakmo & Peterson. (1995). TCP Vegas: End to end congestion avoidance on a global internet. *IEEE Journal on Selected Areas in Communications*, *13*(8), 1465–1480. doi:10.1109/49.464716.

Chiu & Jain. (n.d.). Analysis of the increase and decrease algorithms for congestion avoidance in computer networks. *Computer Networks and ISDN Systems, 17*, 1-14.

Floyd. (1991). Connections with multiple congested gateways in packet-switched networks part 1: One-way traffic. *ACM Computer Communications Review, 21*(5), 30-47.

Heidemann, Obraczka, & Touch. (1997). Modeling the performance of HTTP over several transport protocols. *IEEE/ACM Transactions on Networking*, *5*(5), 616–630. doi:10.1109/90.649564.

Hoe. (1996). Improving the start-up behavior of a congestion control scheme for TCP. In *Proceedings of ACM SIGCOMM'96*. Stanford, CA: ACM.

IEEE. (1998). Carrier sense multiple access with collision detection (CSMA/CD) access method and physical layer specifications. *IEEE*. Retrieved from http://standards.ieee.org/catalog/IEEE802.3.html

IEEE. (1998b). Token ring access method (ISO/IEC 8802-5: 1998 and 8802-5: 1998/Amd 1). *IEEE*. Retrieved from http://www.8025.org/802.5/documents/

Jacobson, Braden, & Borman. (1992). TCP extensions for high performance. *RFC 1323*.

Jacobson. (1988). Congestion avoidance and control. In *Proceedings of ACM SIGCOMM '88*, (pp. 314-329). ACM.

Jain. (1994). *FDDI handbook: High-speed networking using fiber and other media*. Reading, MA: Addison-Wesley.

Kleinrock & Tobagi. (1975). Packet switching in radio channels: Part I -- Carrier sense multiple-access modes and their throughput-delay characteristics. *IEEE Transactions on Communications*, *23*(12), 1400–1416. doi:10.1109/TCOM.1975.1092768.

Lakshman & Madhow. (1994). Performance analysis of window-based flow control using TCP/IP: The effect of high bandwidth-delay products and random loss. *IFIP Transactions*, *26*, 135–150.

Lam. (1980). A carrier sense multiple access protocol for local networks. *Computer Networks, 4*, 21-32.

Mahdavi & Floyd. (1997). *TCP-friendly unicast rate-based flow control*.

Mathis, Mahdavi, Floyd, & Romanow. (1996). TCP selective acknowledgment options. *RFC 2018*.

Metcalfe & Boggs. (1976). Distributed packet switching for local computer networks. *Communications of the ACM*, *19*(7), 395–404. doi:10.1145/360248.360253.

Molle. (1987). Space time analysis of CSMA protocol. *IEEE Journal on Selected Areas in Communications*.

Nielsen, Gettys, Baird-Smith, Prud'hommeaux, Lie, & Lilley. (1997). Network performance effects of HTTP/1.1, CSS1, and PNG. *W3C Document*.

Pickholtz, Schilling, & Milstein. (1982). Theory of spread spectrum communication-A tutorial. *IEEE Transactions on Communications*, *30*(5), 855–884. doi:10.1109/TCOM.1982.1095533.

Postel & Reynolds. (1983). Telnet protocol specifications. *RFC 854*.

RFC 793. (1981).*Transmission control protocol*. IETF.

Rom & Sidi. (1990). *Multiple access protocols: Performance and analysis*. New York: Springer-Verlag.

Shenker, Zhang, & Clark. (1990). Some observations on the dynamics of a congestion control algorithm. *ACM Computer Communications Review, 20*(4), 30-39.

Socolofsky & Kale. (1991). *A TCP/IP tutorial. RFC 1180*. IETF.

Spurgeon. (n.d.). *Charles Spurgeon's ethernet web site*. Retrieved from http://wwwhost.ots.utexas.edu/ethernet/ethernet-home.html

Stevens. (1994). Volume 1: The protocols. In *TCP/IP Illustrated*. Reading, MA: Addison-Wesley.

Sunshine & Dalal. (1978). *Connection management in transport protocols. Computer Networks*. Amsterdam: IOS Press.

Zhang, Shenker, & Clark. (1991). Observations on the dynamics of a congestion control algorithm: The effects of two way traffic. In *Proceedings of ACM SIGCOMM '91*. Zurich, Switzerland: ACM.

KEY TERMS AND DEFINITIONS

Algorithmic Simulation Method: Procedural sequence method of modeling.

Data Transmission Time: Delivery time of the data.

Effective Bandwidth Capacity: Actual data transfer rate per unit time.

Efficiency of Data Transfer: Effective delivery of transmitted/sent data with respect to time and quality.

Internet Meltdown or Congestion Collapse: Degradation in performance of the network.

Modes of Data Transfer: Method and medium of data transfer.

Network Throughput: Measured performance of the network.

Probability of Frame Collision: Chances of frames colliding as a result of intensive growth of generated data.

TCP/IP Protocols Suite: Transport Control Protocol/Internet Protocol Suite (connection-oriented and connection-less transport processes).

Workload: Total number of users on the network.

Chapter 7
Validating the INTERPRETOR Software Architecture for the Interpretation of Large and Noisy Data Sets

Apkar Salatian
American University of Nigeria, Nigeria

ABSTRACT

In this chapter, the authors validate INTERPRETOR software architecture as a dataflow model of computation for filtering, abstracting, and interpreting large and noisy datasets with two detailed empirical studies from the authors' former research endeavours. Also discussed are five further recent and distinct systems that can be tailored or adapted to use the software architecture. The detailed case studies presented are from two disparate domains that include intensive care unit data and building sensor data. By performing pattern mining on five further systems in the way the authors have suggested herein, they argue that INTERPRETOR software architecture has been validated.

INTRODUCTION

In many domains there is a need to interpret high frequency noisy data. Interpretation of such data may typically involve pre-processing of the data to remove noise. Rather than reasoning on a point-to-point basis which is computationally expensive, this filtered data would be processed to derive abstractions which would be interpreted and the results reported. Such a common approach lends itself to the development of a software architecture.

Software architectures involve the description of elements from which systems are built, interactions among those elements, patterns that guide their composition, and constraints on these patterns. In general, a particular system is defined in terms of a collection of components and interactions among these components. Such a system

DOI: 10.4018/978-1-4666-2208-1.ch007

may in turn be used as a (composite) element in a larger system design. Software architectures can act as a model of computation for data flows in a system. Indeed, a good software architecture will involve reuse of established engineering knowledge (Shaw & Garlan, 1996).

In this paper we will describe and validate the *INTERPRETOR* software architecture for interpreting large and noisy data sets. INTEREPRETOR was inspired by the software architecture of ASSOCIATE (Salatian & Oriogun, 2011) for interpreting Intensive Care Unit monitor data and ABSTRACTOR (Salatian, 2010) for interpreting building sensor data - both systems have common features which facilitates a generic architecture. INTERPRETOR consists of 3 consecutive processes: *Filter* which takes the original data and removes noise; Abstraction, which derives abstractions from the filtered data; and Interpretation, which takes the abstractions and provides an interpretation of the original data.

THE INTERPRETOR SOFTWARE ARCHITECTURE

Figure 1 shows the Context Diagram of the INTERPRETOR system. The INTERPRETOR system takes high frequency noisy data and other relevant data to assist in interpretation from various input sources and presents to various output sources an interpretation of the original data.

Figure 2 shows the data flow in the INTERPRETOR system of Figure 1. Data is initially filtered to get rid of noise; rather than reasoning on a point to point basis, the resulting data stream is then converted by a second process into abstractions – this is a form of data compression. A third process to provide an assessment of the original data interprets these abstractions.

We, therefore, derive the overall software architecture of the INTERPRETOR System in form of a Structure Chart as shown in Figure 3.

It can be seen that INTEREPRETOR is a data flow architecture and model of computation. The architecture is decomposed into three processes, which can be changed or replaced independently of the others - this makes INTERPRETOR a loosely coupled system. Indeed, each process of the INTERPRETOR performs one task or achieves a single objective - this makes the INTERPRETOR a highly cohesive system. INTERPRETOR can also be considered a pipe and filter architectural style because it provides a structure for systems that process a stream of data.

We hope to extend our INTERPRETOR design architecture, such that we have a generic design pattern for voluminous and high frequency noisy data, whereby, the data is passed through three consecutive processes: Filter *Data* which takes the original data and removes outliers, inconsistencies or noise; Abstraction which takes the filtered data and abstracts features from the filtered data; and Interpretation which uses the abstractions and generates an interpretation of the original data.

APPLICATIONS OF THE INTERPRETOR SOFTWARE ARCHITECTURE

We will demonstrate the application of the INTERPRETOR software architecture to two case studies from the author's research endeavours: interpreting Intensive Care Unit (ICU) Monitor Data and interpreting building monitor data.

Figure 1. Context diagram of the INTERPRETOR system

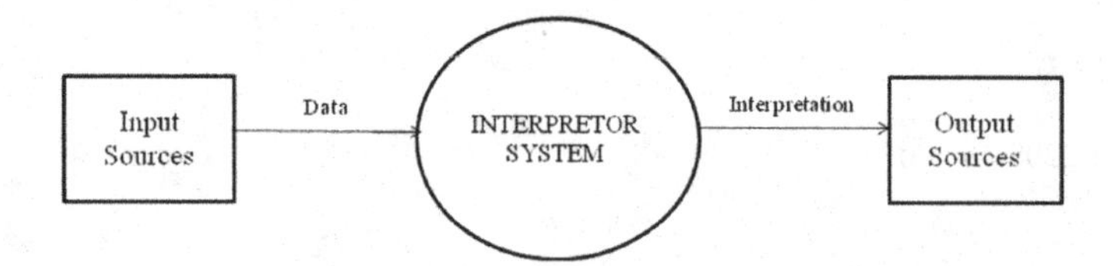

Figure 2. Data flow diagram of the INTERPRETOR system

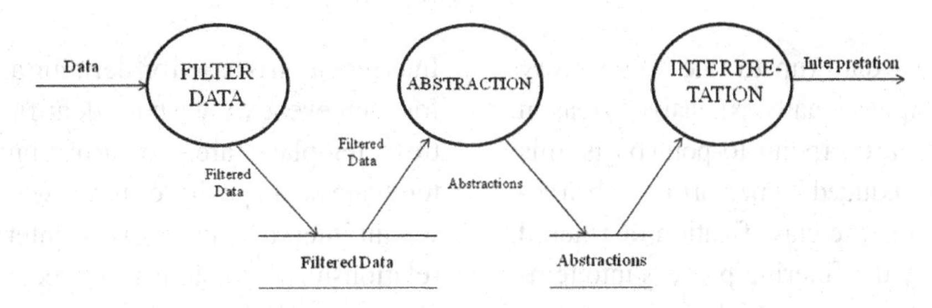

Case Study 1: Interpreting ICU Monitor Data

The ICU bedside monitors confront the medical staff with large amounts of continuous noisy data - this is emphasised when there are many cardiovascular parameters such as the heart rate and blood pressure being recorded simultaneously. The frequency of the data can be higher than 1 value every second which creates information overload for medical staff who need to interpret the data to evaluate the state of the patient.

A system called ASSOCIATE (Salatian, 2003) has been developed using the INTERPRETOR software architecture to interpret the ICU monitor data. We shall describe how ASSOCIATE implemented each of the modules of the INTERPRETOR software architecture.

Filter Module

Filtering is the process of removing certain noise like clinically insignificant events from the physiological parameters. Clinically insignificant events which cannot be removed at this stage will be dealt with by the Interpretation process.

After various investigations of filtering techniques, a median filter was chosen. The median filter involves a moving window which is centred on a point x_n and if the window is of size $2k+1$ the window contains the points x_{n-k} to x_{n+k}. By always choosing the median value in the window as the filtered value, it will remove transient features lasting shorter than k without distortion of the base line signal; features lasting more than that will remain. A summary of the algorithm for applying the median filter to our physiological data is shown in Figure 4.

Figure 3. Overall software architecture of the INTERPRETOR system

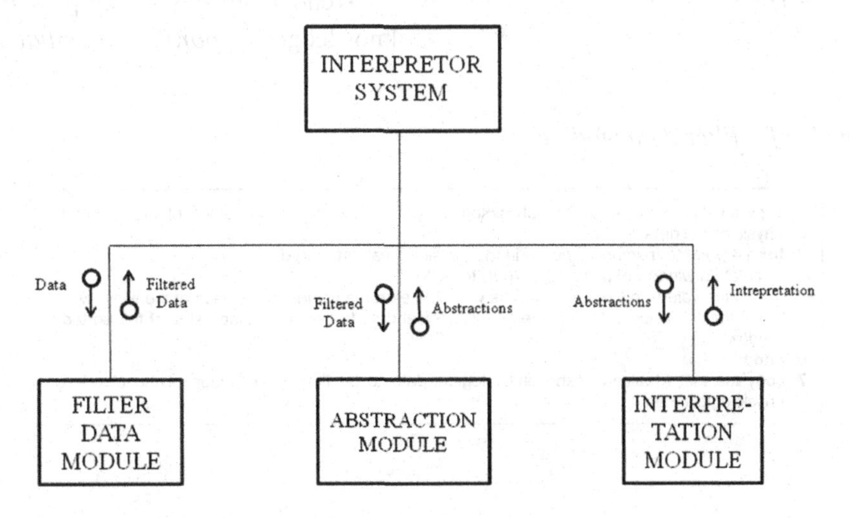

Abstraction Module

Given continuous data (up to one value every second), it is computationally expensive to reason with each data value on a point-to-point basis - this data needs to be reduced by performing abstraction. Abstraction is the classification of filtered data generated by the filtering process into temporal intervals (trends) in which data is *steady, increasing* and *decreasing*. One must decide the beginning and end of an interval since they are not known in advance.

Our algorithm for identifying trends involves following two consecutive sub processes called temporal interpolation and *temporal inferencing*. Temporal interpolation takes the cleaned data and generates simple intervals between consecutive data point. *Temporal inferencing* takes these simple intervals and tries to generate trends - this is achieved using 4 variables: *diff* which is the variance allowed to derive steady trends, *g1* and *g2* which are gradient values used to derive increasing and decreasing trends and *dur* which is used to merge 3 intervals based on the duration of the middle interval. Temporal Inferencing rules to merge 2 meeting intervals (Δ_{H2}) and 3 meeting intervals (Δ_{H3}) use the 4 variables to try to merge intervals into larger intervals until no more merging can take place. The algorithm for abstraction is summarised in Figure 5. For further discussion of the algorithm the reader is advised to read (Salatian & Hunter, 1999).

Interpretation Module

Interpretation is based on defining a *trend template* for each event we wish to identify - examples of trend templates are shown in Figure 6. A trend template will specify criteria, which apply both within intervals and between intervals. The two relationships of interest between intervals are: *meeting* where the end time of one interval matches the start time of the other; and *overlapping* where there exists a time that is common to both intervals.

The algorithm for interpretation involves applying the templates to the temporal intervals. Clinically insignificant event and clinical condition templates initially have the status *absent* and therapy templates initially have the status *working*. The reasoning engine assesses the status of the templates (i.e *hypothesised* or *confirmed*) by evaluating the expressions located in the *HypothesiseConditions* and *ConfirmConditions* slots with the data. Actions to be performed when the templates are hypothesised or confirmed are provided in the *HypothesiseActions* and *ConfirmActions* slots. If we have a template which has a hypothesised status over a number of adjacent segments which are subsequently confirmed then in retrospect we change these hypothesised states to confirmed. This is a way of confirming our initial beliefs. All segments with clinically significant templates that have *confirmed* states represent the interpretation.

Trend templates encompass three types of knowledge: *temporal, differential* and *taxonomi-*

Figure 4. Algorithm for filter data module

1. copy the first k values of the physiological data to be the first k values of the cleaned physiological data
2. **for** n = (k+1) to (number of points in the physiological data - k) **do**
3. create a window of points from (n-k) to (n+k).
4. sort the values in this window - this will force extreme values to the ends of the window
5. set the nth value of the cleaned physiological data to be the median value of the sorted window
6. **end for**
7. copy the last k values of the physiological data to be the last k values of the cleaned physiological data

Figure 5. Algorithm for abstraction module

1. Apply the inferences in Δ_{H2} which derive only increasing or decreasing trends by trying to combine the first two intervals; if this succeeds try to combine this new interval with the next and so on. If combination fails, then we take the interval which failed to be combined, and use it as a new starting point.
2. Apply inferences in Δ_{H2} which derive only steady trends.
3. Set flag *still-to-do* to **true**.
4. **while** *still-to-do* **do**
5. Set *previous* to the number of intervals generated so far.
6. Apply the inferences in Δ_{H3}
7. Apply the inferences in Δ_{H2}
8. Set *still-to-do* to *previous* = current number of intervals.
9. **endwhile**

Figure 6. Possible templates for clinical conditions, insignificant events, and therapies

```
Interpretation respiratory_problem
  Description ("general class of respiratory condition")
  Type_of (clinical_condition)
  Preconditions (NIL)
  HypothesiseConditions(AND (paO2,_,_,steady) (paCO2,_,_,increasing))
  ConfirmConditions(AND(paO2,_,_,decreasing) (paCO2,_,_,increasing))
  HypothesiseActions (ALARM_WARN)
  ConfirmActions (ALARM_TRUE)
end_template

Interpretation transcutenous_probe_off
  Description ("transcutenous probe coming off")
  Type_of (insignificant_event)
  Preconditions (NIL)
  HypothesiseConditions (NIL)
  ConfirmConditions(AND (meeting (paO2,_,>16,increasing)
                                 (paO2,>16,>16,steady)
                                 (paO2, _, >16, decreasing))
                        (meeting (paCO2,<3,_,decreasing)
                                 (paCO2,<3,<3,steady)
                                 (paCO2, <3, _, increasing)))
  HypothesiseActions (NIL)
  ConfirmActions (REMOVE)
end_template

Interpretation pneumothorax
  Description ("pneumothorax")
  Type_of (respiratory_problem)
  Preconditions (NIL)
  HypothesiseConditions(AND (mean_bp,_,_,steady) (heart_rate,_,_,increasing))
  ConfirmConditions (AND (mean_bp _,_,increasing) (heart_rate _,_,increasing))
  HypothesiseActions (ALARM_WARN)
  ConfirmActions (ALARM_TRUE)
end_template

Interpretation digoxin
  Description ("digoxin")
  Type_of (therapy)
  Preconditions (digoxin)
  HypothesiseConditions (heart_rate increased 10)
  ConfirmConditions (heart_rate increased 20)
  HypothesiseActions (ALARM_ALERT)
  ConfirmActions (ALARM_TRUE)
end_template
```

cal. *Temporal knowledge* allows temporal reasoning; interval-based and point-based reasoning. Interval-based temporal reasoning is achieved using the *still_developing* and *together* functions. Given a clinical condition which is described in terms of overlapping intervals, the *still_developing* function operates on the uncertain period between the hypothesised state and the confirmed state of the clinical condition. Here the *still_developing* function is satisfied if there is the correct temporal progression from the hypothesised state to the confirmed state. Similarly the *together* function operates on overlapping temporal intervals which make up clinically insignificant events. Here the *together* function is satisfied if the overall changes in all the individual parameters that make up the event all share a common time interval. Though defined differently, the *together* and *still_developing* functions take into account the expected changes of the individual parameters that make up specific events do not occur at exactly the same time.

Point-based temporal reasoning is used to determine the outcome of therapy. It is known that clinicians expect changes in parameters to be achieved by a lower and upper temporal bound represented as time points in the future. ASSOCIATE expresses point based temporal reasoning within temporal intervals. When therapy is administered at a specific point in time, we compare a (future) interval which contains the therapy's temporal bound (lower and upper) with the interval which contained the time of administration. We are interested in whether parameters have *increased, decreased* or remained the *same* in the future after the time of administration.

Since several clinical conditions may be described by the same patterns, *differential knowledge* can be used to eliminate possibilities and hence prevent unnecessary reasoning. Information such as the patient record which contains the patient's history can be used as differential knowledge.

Also within the trend templates there is *taxonomical knowledge* – since several clinical conditions have similar attributes, this enables us to represent them as a hierarchy of classes and subclasses. Such a representation allows more *abstract* clinical conditions to be identified – if a specific instance of a clinical conditions cannot be identified then the more general class of clinical condition to which it belongs is more likely to describe the data. For further discussion of the algorithm the reader is advised to read (Salatian, 2003).

Results

ASSOCIATE has been tested on three datasets from an adult ICU and six datasets from a neonatal ICU each set covering about 60 hours of data. The data sets were taken in 1995 as part of a research project and the results were validated by a consultant aneasthetist and a consultant neonatologist.

Overall, ASSOCIATE has a false-positive rate of 28.9% and a false-negative rate of 0.3% in identifying clinically insignificant events, a false-positive rate of 10.7% and a false-negative rate of 0.15% in identifying clinical conditions and a false-positive rate of 0% and a false-negative rate of 87.9% in determining the outcome of therapy. Since all have a true positive rate, which is higher than its false positive rate, ASSOCIATE can be seen as a *conservative* system (Fawcett, 2003).

As an example, consider a three day data set taken from an ICU from from 00:01 on 22 April 1995 to 23:59 on 24 April 1995; the frequency of the signal is one data item per minute. The expert or the tester had no prior knowledge of events that occurred within this data set. Figure 7 depicts the physiological data from ICU patient monitors and Figure 8 depicts a graphical summary of the temporal intervals generated for each parameter by the Abstraction Module. Note that in the graphs HR represents the Heart Rate, BP represents the Blood Pressure, PO represents the Partial Pressure of Oxygen and TCO represents the Partial Pressure of Carbon Dioxide.

All clinically insignificant events were correctly identified and removed.

For the clinical condition interpretation, the expert agrees that ASSOCIATE identified all 11 episodes of respiratory problems in the data. Of 2 of these episodes, namely those identified from 11:44 on 23/04/95 to 12:04 on 23/04/95 and from 13:57 on 23/04/95 to 14:32 on 23/04/95 may have been pneumothoraxes. However, ASSOCIATE incorrectly identifies respiratory problems on 5 occasions. ASSOCIATE also incorrectly identifies a pulmonary haemorrhage and a pneumothorax at the same time, though the expert agrees that there is a respiratory problem at this time. ASSOCIATE also identified 3 separate episodes of shock of which the expert agreed with 2 of them. The expert also agrees in ASSOCIATE's identifications of episodes of tachycardia and hypercarbia. However, a few of the episodes of hypoxaemia were incorrectly identified due to noisy data. Indeed, the expert agreed that ASSOCIATE recognised all clinical conditions in the data set i.e no clinical conditions were missed.

For the therapy interpretation, 6 therapies were administered. Of the 5 that worked ASSOCIATE correctly identifies 2 of them as working. ASSOCIATE correctly identifies the therapy that did not work. The incorrect results were because of noisy data and approximate times of administration.

Figure 7. Original physiological data from ICU patient monitor

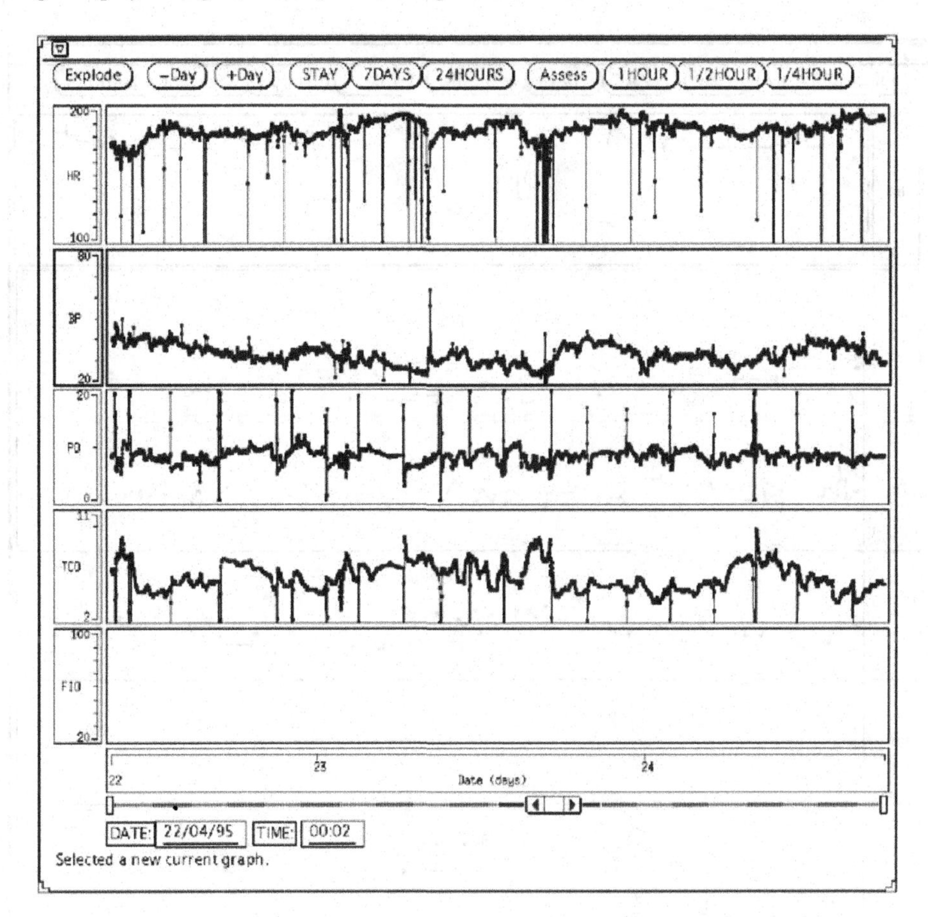

Case Study 2: Interpreting Building Sensor Data

Building operators are confronted with large volumes of continuous data from multiple environmental sensors which require interpretation. The ABSTRACTOR (Salatian & Taylor, 2008, Salatian & Taylor, 2011) system used the INTERPRETOR software architecture to summarise historical building sensor data for interpretation and building performance assessment. We shall describe how ABSTRACTOR implemented each of the modules of the INTERPRETOR software architecture.

Filter Module

Initially data needs to be filtered to get rid of non-significant events in environmental monitoring data. Due to the nature and frequency of the data, an average filter was chosen. The algorithm for the filter module is given in Figure 9

Abstraction Module

This module is exactly the same as the agglomerative approach used for case study 1 - for a discussion of this algorithm applied to building monitor data the reader is advised to read (Salatian & Taylor, 2004)

Figure 8. Graphical summary generated by the abstraction module

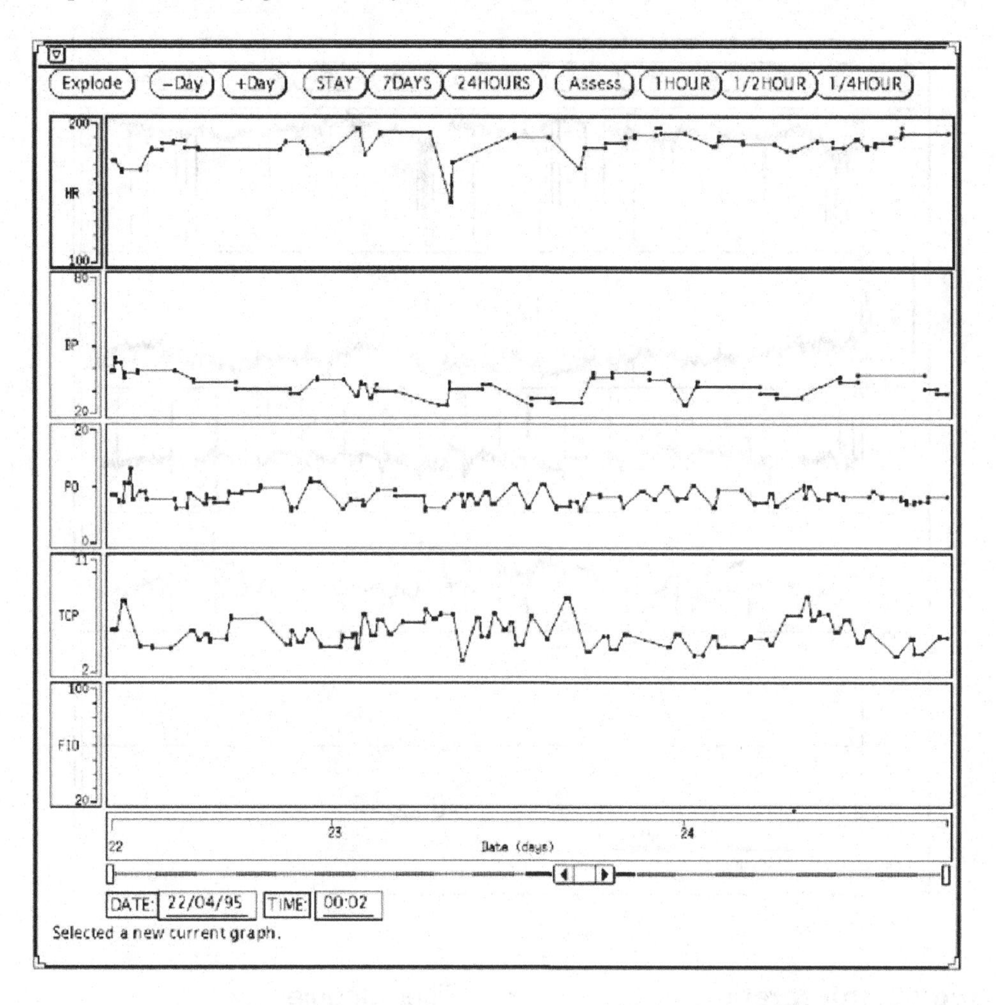

Figure 9. Algorithm for filter data module

1. copy the first k values of the environmental data to be the first k values of the filtered environmental data
2. **for** n = (k+1) to (number of points in the environmental data - k) **do**
3. create a window of points from (n-k) to (n+k).
4. calculate the average of the values in this window
5. set the nth value of the filtered environmental data to be the average value of the window
6. **end for**
7. copy the last k values of the environmental data to be the last k values of the filtered environmental data

Interpretation Module

Given overlapping trends it is proposed, in the spirit of (DeCoste, 1991) they are split into *global segments*. A change in the direction of change of one (or more) channels or a change in the rate of change of one (or more) channels contributes to a split in the trends creating a global segment. A global segment can be considered as being a set of intervals - one for each channel.

The algorithm for interpretation involves applying rules to the global segments. Examples of rules for identifying faults are shown in Figure 10 - here a fault is declared when the heat-flux does not have the same trend as the difference in internal and external temperature (t1-t0). If rules are true over adjacent global segments then one can determine when the fault started and ended.

Results

ABSTRACTOR has been tested on over eight days (12179 minutes) worth of continuous data (see Figure 11a). The data was the heat-flux into a wall and the difference in internal and external temperature (ti-t0) measurements; the sampling frequency of the signals is one data item every 15 minutes. The expert or the tester had no prior knowledge of events that occurred within this data set. The application of the average filter (k=10 filter provides a running five and a quarter hour running average) is shown in the middle graph (b) and the intervals generated are shown in the bottom graph (c).

Overall, ABSTRACTOR has a sensitivity of 56%, specificity of 64%, and predictive value of 43%, a false positive rate of 57% and a false negative rate of 24%. These results mean that when a fault is present ABSTRACTOR is detecting it only 56% of the time but when there is no fault it will correctly identify this 64% of the time. Whilst it would seem that ABSTRACTOR is only slightly better than tossing a coin to decide the presence or absence of a fault it needs to be remembered that the actual fault conditions were derived from an expert's manual abstraction of the raw data that is dependent on the expert's attitude and experience. A direct comparison with the raw data is meaningless because the data is at intervals much shorter than the trends. If ABSTRACTOR were to be incorporated in its present state into a control system it would generate a high number of false alarms (57%) but would fail to detect a fault only 24% of the time. These results are indicating that ABSTRACTOR is a more liberal system than a random system (Fawcett, 2003).

Figure 10. Example of rules to apply to global segments

```
If heat-flux increasing                    If heat-flux decreasing
    and ti-t0 decreasing then                  and ti-t0 steady then
        fault detected                             fault detected
end if                                     end if
If heat-flux increasing                    If heat-flux steady
    and ti-t0 steady then                      and ti-t0 increasing then
        fault detected                             fault detected
end if                                     end if
If heat-flux decreasing                    If heat-flux steady
    and ti-t0 increasing then                  and ti-t0 decreasing then
        fault detected                             fault detected
end if                                     end if
```

Figure 11. Output of ABSTRACTOR

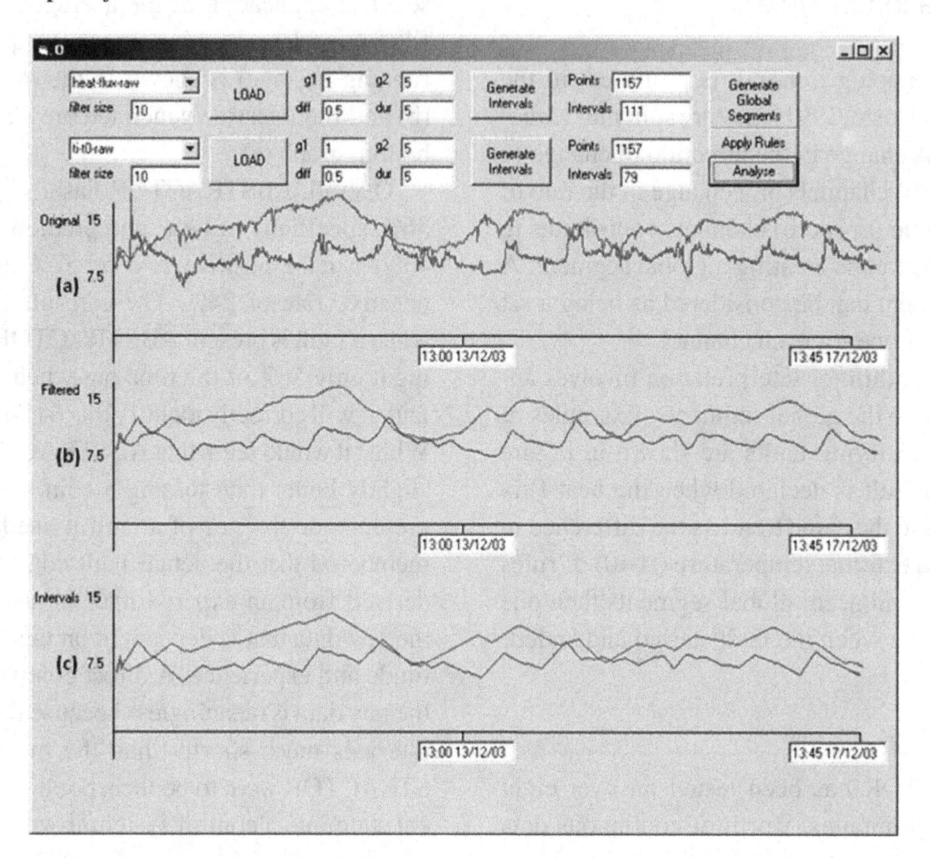

VALIDATION OF THE INTERPRETOR SOFTWARE ARCHITECTURE

By performing pattern mining in the form of tailoring and adapting different systems to perform filtering, abstraction and interpretation we will now further validate the INTERPRETOR software architecture.

BT-45 (Portet et al, 2009) generates natural language textual summaries of continuous physiological signals and discrete events from a Neonatal Intensive Care Unit. BT-45 could be adapted to use the INTERPRETOR software architecture. The first stage of BT-45 is *Signal Analysis, which* extracts the main features of the physiological time series - this fulfils the role of the Filter module of INTERPRETOR. BT-45 then performs *Data* Interpretation, *which* performs some temporal and logical reasoning to infer more abstract medical observations and relations from the signal features which can considered the Abstraction module of INTERPRETOR. The next stages of BT-45 are *Document Planning* which selects the most important events from earlier stages and groups them into a tree of linked events then *Microplanning and Realisation* which translates this tree into coherent text for reporting - collectively they could be considered the Interpretation module of INTERPRETOR.

Sumtime-Mousam (Sripada et al, 2003) is a text generator that produces textual marine weather forecasts for offshore oilrig applications. It uses a subset of the processes of BT-45 and also follows the INTERPRETOR software architecture. The architecture of SUMTIME-MOUSAM follows 3 processes: *Document planning, Micro planning* and *Realization*. Document planning is responsible for selecting the 'important' data points from the input data and to organize them into a paragraph - this is a form of filtering. Micro planning is responsible for lexical selection and ellipsis - this is a form of abstraction of the filtered data. Realization is essentially responsible for ordering of the phrases in the output and also to perform punctuation tasks - this is analogous to the Interpretation module of the INTERPRETOR software architecture.

A similar approach is taken by (Turner et al, 2008) to generate textual summaries of geo-referenced data based on spatial reference frames. From the initial data basic events are generated (filtered out) by a data analysis process which is then abstracted into higher-level concepts. The final stage is to interpret these messages in sentence form for textual summarization.

(Sun et al, 2005) extract extra knowledge from click-through data of a Web search engine to improve web-page summarization. Among the 3,074,678 Web pages crawled, the authors removed those which belong to 'World' and 'Regional' categories, as many of them are not in English - this filtering resulted in 1,125,207 Web pages, 260,763 of which are clicked by Web users using 1,586,472 different queries. Three human evaluators were employed to summarize (abstract) these pages. Each evaluator was requested to extract the sentences which he/she deemed to be the most important ones for a Web page. An interpretation of the precision of the query terms was finally reported.

(Knox et al, 2010) presented a case-based reasoning approach to activity recognition in a smart home setting. An analysis was performed on scalability with respect to case storage, and an ontology-based approach was proposed for case base maintenance - this could also lend itself to the INTERPRETOR software architecture. Firstly to create a cut-down (filtered) case base a reduction was made by firstly using a simple statistical technique, and then by semantically linking the case solutions with corresponding case features - this could be considered a form of abstraction. The case solutions were analysed and some had their accuracy reduced while others had theirs increased - this is considered a form of interpretation. The analysis was then reported in the form of graph.

CONCLUSION

The interpretation of large and noisy data is non-trivial - one approach is to have a software architecture which can be tailored and applied to different domains which have the same issues associated with the interpretation of data.

We have shown that research into trying to interpret large and noisy datasets do not actually follow any particular software architecture or framework - they just tell us about the 'tactics' they have employed in order to process such data. By conducting a detailed empirical study of the author's former research endeavours and pattern mining five further systems, we believe that we have successfully argued that our INTERPRETOR software architecture allows systems to be adapted at a much higher level of abstraction to facilitate the interpretation of large and noisy data leaving the tactics to the individual modules.

Our future work will be towards developing a generic software tool for this software architecture, which should lend itself for reuse.

REFERENCES

DeCoste, D. (1991). Dynamic across-time measurement interpretation. *Artificial Intelligence*, *51*, 273–341. doi:10.1016/0004-3702(91)90113-X.

Fawcett, T. (2003). *ROC graphs: Notes and practical considerations for data mining researchers*. Palo Alto, CA: HP Labs.

Knox, S., Coyle, L., & Dobson, S. (2010). Using ontologies in case-based activity recognition. In *Proceedings of 23rd Florida Artificial Intelligence Research Society Conference*. St. Pete, FL: AIRSC.

Portet, F., Reiter, E., Gatt, A., Hunter, J. R. W., Sripada, S., Freer, Y., & Sykes, C. (2009). Automatic generation of textual summaries from neonatal intensive care data. *Artificial Intelligence*, *173*, 789–816. doi:10.1016/j.artint.2008.12.002.

Salatian, A. (2003). Interpreting historical ICU data using associational and temporal reasoning. In *Proceedings of 15th IEEE International Conference on Tools with Artificial Intelligence*. Sacramento, CA: IEEE.

Salatian, A. (2010). A software architecture for decision support of building sensor data. *International Journal of Smart Home*, *4*(4), 27–34.

Salatian, A., & Hunter, J. R. W. (1999). Deriving trends in historical and real-time continuously sampled medical data. *Journal of Intelligent Information Systems*, *13*, 47–74. doi:10.1023/A:1008706905683.

Salatian, A., & Oriogun, P. (2011b). A software architecture for summarising and interpreting ICU monitor data. *International Journal of Software Engineering*, *4*(1), 3–14.

Salatian, A., & Taylor, B. (2004). An agglomerative approach to creating models of building monitoring data. In *Proceedings of 8th IASTED International Conference on Artificial Intelligence and Soft Computing*. Marbella, Spain: IASTED.

Salatian, A., & Taylor, B. (2008). ABSTRACTOR: An agglomerative approach to interpreting building monitoring data. *Journal of Information Technology in Construction*, *13*, 193–211.

Salatian, A., & Taylor, B. (2011). ABSTRACTOR: An expert system for fault detection in buildings. In *Proceedings of 1st International Conference on Intelligent Systems & Data Processing*. Vallabh Vidya Nagar, India: IEEE.

Shaw, M., & Garlan, D. (1996). *Software architecture: Perspectives on an emerging discipline*. Englewood Cliffs, NJ: Prentice Hall.

Sripada, S., Reiter, E., & Davy, I. (2003). SumTime-mousam: Configurable marine weather forecast generator. *Expert Update*, *6*(3), 4–10.

Sun, J.-T., Shen, D., Zeng, H.-J., Yang, Q., Lu, Y., & Chen, Z. (2005). Web-page summarization using clickthrough data. In *Proceedings of 28th Annual International ACM SIGIR Conference on Research and Development in Information Retrieval*. ACM.

Turner, R., Sripada, S., Reiter, E., & Davy, I. (2008). Using spatial reference frames to generate grounded textual summaries of georeferenced data. In *Proceedings of 5th International Natural Language Generation Conference*. Salt Fork, OH: IEEE.

ADDITIONAL READING

Anthony, T., Babar, M. A., Gorton, I., & Han, J. (2006). A survey of architecture design rationale. *Journal of Systems and Software*, *79*(12), 1792–1804. doi:10.1016/j.jss.2006.04.029.

Anuj, S., Singhal, M., Gibson, T., Sivaramakrishnan, C., Waters, K., & Gorton, I. (2008). An extensible, scalable architecture for managing bioinformatics data and analyses. In *Proceedings of IEEE Fourth International Conference on eScience '08*. Indianapolis, IN: IEEE.

Babar, M. A., & Gorton, I. (2009). Software architecture reviews: The state of the practice. *IEEE Computer*, *42*(7), 26–32. doi:10.1109/MC.2009.233.

Bass, L., Clements, P., & Kazman, R. (2003). *Software architecture in practice* (2nd ed.). Reading, MA: Addison-Wesley Professional.

Bosch, J. (2000). *Design and use of software architecture adopting and evolving a product-line approach*. Reading, MA: Addison-Wesley Professional.

Bosch, J. (2004). Software architecture: The next step. *Lecture Notes in Computer Science*, *3047*, 194–199. doi:10.1007/978-3-540-24769-2_14.

Buschmann, F., Henney, K., & Schmidt, D. C. (2007). *Pattern-oriented software architecture: On patterns and pattern languages*. New York: John Wiley and Sons.

Buschmann, F., Meunier, R., Rohnert, H., & Sommerlad, P. (1996). Pattern-oriented software architecture: *Vol. 1. A system of patterns*. New York: Wiley.

Clements, P., Garlan, D., Bass, L., Stafford, J., Ivers, J., & Little, R. (2002). *Documenting software architectures: Views and beyond*. Upper Saddle River, NJ: Pearson Education.

Clements, P., Garlan, D., Little, R., Nord, R., & Stafford, J. (2003). Documenting software architectures: Views and beyond. In *Proceedings of 25th International Conference on Software Engineering*. Portland, OR: IEEE.

Clements, P., Kazman, R., & Klein, M. (2001). *Evaluating software architectures: Methods and case studies*. Reading, MA: Addison-Wesley Professional.

Dobrica, L., & Niemelä, E. (2002). A survey on sftware architecture analysis methods. *IEEE Transactions on Software Engineering*, *29*(7), 638–653. doi:10.1109/TSE.2002.1019479.

Eeles, P., & Cripps, P. (2009). *The process of software architecting*. Reading, MA: Addison-Wesley Professional.

Fairbanks, G. H. (2010). *Just enough software architecture: A risk-driven approach*. New York: Marshall & Brainerd.

Gorton, I. (2008). Software architecture challenges for data intensive computing. In *Proceedings of 7th Working IEEE / IFIP Conference on Software Architecture*. Vancouver, Canada: IEEE.

Gorton, I. (2011). *Essential software architecture*. Berlin: Springer-Verlag. doi:10.1007/978-3-642-19176-3.

Gorton, I., Cuesta, C. E., & Babar, M. A. (Eds.). (2010). *Proceedings of software architecture, 4th European conference, ECSA 2010*. Copenhagen, Denmark: ECSA.

Hofmeister, C., Kruchten, P., Nord, R. L., Obbink, H., Ran, A., & America, P. (2005). Generalizing a model of software architecture design from five industrial approaches. In *Proceedings of 5th Working IEEE/IFIP Conference on Software Architecture*. Pittsburgh, PA: IEEE.

Hofmeister, C., Nord, R. L., & Soni, D. (1999). *Applied software architecture*. Reading, MA: Addison Wesley.

Jansen, A., & Bosch, J. (2005). Software architecture as a set of architectural design decisions. In *Proceedings of 5th Working IEEE/IFIP Conference on Software Architecture*. Pittsburgh, PA: IEEE.

Kamal, A. W., & Avgeriou, P. (2010). Mining relationships between the participants of architectural patterns. In *Proceedings of 4th European Conference on Software*. Copenhagen, Denmark: IEEE.

Knodel, J., Lindvall, M., & Muthig, D. (2005). Static evaluation of software architectures-A short summary. In *Proceedings of 5th Working IEEE/IFIP Conference on Software Architecture*. Pittsburgh, PA: IEEE.

Qian, K., Fu, X., Tao, L., & Xu, C. W. (2009). *Software architecture and design illuminated*. New York: Jones and Bartlett Publishers.

Schmidt, D. C., Stal, M., Rohnert, H., & Buschmann, F. (2000). Pattern-oriented software architecture: *Vol. 2. Patterns for concurrent and networked objects*. New York: Wiley.

Taylor, R. N., Medvidovic, N., & Dashofy, E. M. (2009). *Software architecture: Foundations, theory, and practice*. New York: Wiley.

KEY TERMS AND DEFINITIONS

Abstraction: This is the process of identifying features such as trends in the data.

Filter: This is the process identifying and retaining or removing outliers, inconsistencies or noise from the data.

Interpretation: An explanation of the data.

Pattern Mining: This is the process of finding or matching systems to a particular architecture or framework.

Software Architecture: This is the structure of a system, which comprises software elements and the relationships among them.

Temporal Inferencing: The process of using rules to merge consecutive intervals into larger intervals.

Temporal Interpolation: The process of creating an interval between 2 consecutive points.

Chapter 8
Modeling Maintenance Productivity Measurement

Christian A. Bolu
Federal University Oye-Ekiti, Nigeria

ABSTRACT

Modeling and simulation of industrial information communication systems and networks is one of the major concerns of productivity engineers for the establishment of productivity standards in virtually all functional areas of an industrial organization. Maintenance function is one of such areas that have always engaged the attention of engineering productivity practitioners. However, one of the basic problems is the difficulty in setting up integrated but easy and practical measurement schemes. Even where the measures are set up, the approaches to measurement sometimes are conflicting. Therefore the need for an integrated approach to optimize the basket of parameters measured remains.

In this chapter the author attempts to identify approaches in integrated and systematic maintenance productivity measurement and create models for optimising total productivity in maintenance systems. Visual yardstick, utility, queuing systems and simulations approaches for measurement of maintenance productivity are all discussed with a particular focus on markov chain approach for stochastic breakdowns in repairable systems.. The chapter also shows how understanding the impact of plant failure and repair/service distributions assists in providing measures for maintenance productivity using discrete event system simulation.

INTRODUCTION

Modeling and simulation of industrial information communication systems and networks is one of the major concerns of productivity engineers for the establishment of productivity standards in virtually all functional areas of an industrial organization. Maintenance function is one of such areas that have always engaged the attention of engineering productivity practitioners. However, the basic problem, and indeed the most important one, is the difficulty in setting up integrated but easy and practical measurement scheme. Even where the measures are set up, the approaches to

DOI: 10.4018/978-1-4666-2208-1.ch008

measurement sometimes are conflicting. There is therefore the need to optimize the basket of parameters measured.

The overall objective of the maintenance function should be to support the operating department by keeping facilities in proper running condition at the lowest possible cost. In judging the productivity of the maintenance department one must consider not only the efficient use of manpower and material, but also how well production losses due to maintenance problems are controlled. The performance of the maintenance department is influenced by various factors such as business condition (e.g low and high profit times), maintenance philosophy (crises maintenance versus planned), extraneous factors (location, availability of skills and spare parts), and so forth.

This chapter discusses approaches in systematic maintenance productivity measurement and creating models for optimising productivity in maintenance systems. It discusses defects accumulation, the manual visual yardstick, queuing systems and simulations approaches and highlights markov chain approach solution for stochastic breakdowns in repairable systems. Also it shows how understanding the impact of plant failure and repair/service distributions assists in providing measures for maintenance productivity using the simulation approach.

APPROACHES TO MODELING MAINTENANCE PRODUCTIVITY

The word productivity is used in a variety of sense some of which are conflicting or very qualitative (namely, "efficiency", "overall effectiveness", etc). Similarly, the definition of "productivity" is varied. Productivity is often confused with "output" or "profitability". Whilst a good total productivity implies profitability, the converse does not hold. Profitability is affected by market prices and accounting practice. Productivity is defined simply as a relationship of output to input.

In sharp contrast to production, the performance of maintenance activity does not lend itself easily to expression in simple or unified figures. However, in the last two decades, the measurement of maintenance performance and productivity has engaged the attention of productivity engineers. (Priel, 1974) has written on maintenance organization particularly on performance ratios. He has identified twenty of such maintenance ratios. Some of the ratios are useful in establishing the basis for incentive scheme for maintenance personnel. (Hamlin, 1979) has shown various methods and (Alli, Ogunwolu, & Oke, 2011) applied same to measure maintenance productivity through their case studies. (Chan, Lau, Ip, Chan, & Kong, 2005), applying total productive maintenance approach to the electronics industry, (Eti, Ogaji, Probert, 2004 to the manufacturing industries in a developing country, (Lilly, Obiajulu, Ogaji, &Probert, 2007) to the petroleum-product marketing company and (Ahn & Abt, 2006), to the sawmills and planning mills industry provides examples of total productivity measurements in industry.

Another interesting point of view is provided by (Nanere, M, Fraser, I, Quazi, A, & D'Souza, C, 2007), who critically examines various methods for estimating productivity incorporating environmental effects and shows that adjusting for environmental impacts can result in higher and lower productivity depending on the assumed form of the damage. Although this was applies to the agriculture sector, this could be applicable to industrial environment, where work place hygiene and design could impact negatively or positively to productivity.

It can be seen that there are several ways of expressing maintenance productivity or performance. The problem is how to model a working measurement scheme that gives good management information in areas critical to increasing productivity as well as being amenable to easy data collection.

GRAPHICAL APPROACH

(Priel, 1974) developed a graphical "instant yardstick" multi-variable chart for assessment of maintenance performance, which clearly identifies the inter-dependence of the various assessment indicators. He also discusses twenty maintenance performance ratios. These can be groups as follows:

1. Operation of the maintenance department determined by manpower utilization, work-order progress and departmental economy.
2. Assessment of the service determined by plant and equipment performance, degree of planning, the amount of service and cost of service provided.
3. Expense justification determined by cost reduction efforts, maintenance intensity and the overall rate of expenditure.

Operations of the maintenance department which deals with manpower efficiency, incentive coverage, utilization of craft hours, work order turnover, completion delays, cost of maintenance hour and department overhead largely affects the repairable systems service rates which impacts on the output side of total productivity measures. On the other hand assessment of the service which deals with downtime due to maintenance, breakdown frequency, routine service workload, breakdown workload, maintenance to production-hours ratio, maintenance mechanization and maintenance cost component largely relate to the input side of the total productivity measurement process.

SYSTEMS DYNAMICS APPROACH

According to (Sterman, 2000) Du Pont organization looked at the result of an in-house benchmarking study documenting a large gap between Du Pont's maintenance record and those of the best-practice companies in the global chemical industry and they developed an interesting defect creation and elimination model. Prior to the modeling work maintenance was largely seen as a process of defect correction (repair of failed equipment) and the maintenance function was viewed as a cost to be minimized. It shifted the views to defect prevention and defect elimination. The model centred on the physics of breakdown rather than cost minimization mentality.

The study postulates the following:

1. Equipment fails when a sufficient number of latent defects accumulate in it. Latent defects are any problem that might ultimately cause a failure. They include leaky oils seals in pumps, dirty equipment that causes bearing wear, pump and motor shaft that are out of alignment and cause vibration. The total number of latent defects in a plant's equipment is a stock (Figure 1).
2. The stock of defects is drained by two flows: reactive maintenance (repair of failed equipment and planned maintenance (proactive repair of operable equipment}. As defects accumulate the chance of breakdown increase. Breakdown leads to more reactive maintenance, and, after repair, the equipment is returned to service and the stock of defects is reduced. Similarly, scheduled maintenance or equipment monitoring may reveal the presence of latent defects. The equipment is then taken out of service and the defects are corrected before breakdown occurs.

Obviously, since accumulation of defects are observable, this thinking can be modeled as a waiting line or queuing system and some of the solution methodologies of queuing theory could be useful in deriving the maintenance productivity, depending on the occurrence pattern (or arrival process) of the defects, the maintenance team service process and queue discipline of the maintenance policy.

THE COMPOSITE APPROACH

This method is an extension of the work done by (Priel, 1974) which were discussed by (Onwugbolu et al, 1988) and (Parida et al, 2009). It starts with a number of performance measures as identified by (Priel, 1974) and then builds a composite number which is a weighted addition of the Utility values of all these performance measures. The approach can be stated as follows:

Let U_t be the utility value of the selected N performance measures, where $t = 1,2 \ldots\ldots N$

Let β_t be the scaling factors for the performance measures

Then the Maintenance Productivity is given by

$$Y_N = \sum_{1}^{N} \beta_t U_t$$

From the case study by (Alli et al, 2009), they selected the following six performance measures mentioned in (Priel, 1974):

$$Equipment\ Availability, U_1 = \frac{Downtime}{Downtime + Uptime} \times 100\%$$

$$Emergency\ Failure\ Intensity, U_2 = \frac{Downtime}{Uptime} \times 100\%$$

$$Cost\ of\ maintenance\ Hour, U_3 = \frac{Total\ Maintenance\ Cost}{Total\ Maintenance\ Hour}$$

Figure 1. System dynamics approach: defects accumulation

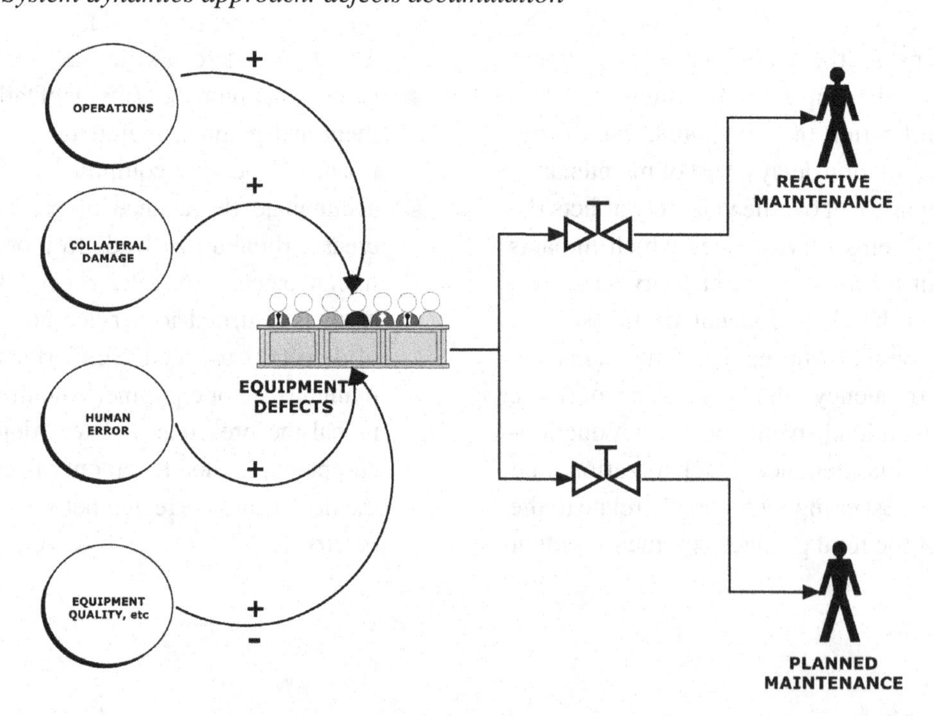

$$Maintenance\ Cost\ Component, U_4 = \frac{Total\ Maintenance\ Cost}{Production\ Output}$$

$$Routine\ Service\ Workload, U_5 = \frac{Planned\ Maintenance\ Hour}{Total\ Maintenance\ Hour}$$

$$Cost\ Reduction\ Ratio, U_6 = \frac{Routine\ Service\ Workload}{Cost\ of\ Maintenance\ Hour}$$

The next step was to obtain the scaling factor, β_i, where $i = 1,2,\ldots.6$

The scaling factor is an index number obtained from the utility values from the plot of the performance measures over a period of years.

According to (Alli, et al, 2009) the utility values for each of the performance measures were derived as follows:

- Determining the best and worst values from the graph of each of the measures used,
- Normalising the values by assigning values of 1.00 and 0.00 for the best and the worst measure respectively,
- Taking five points between the best and the worst performance measure and assign values between 0.00 and 1.0,
- Using the intermediate points with the best and worst measures for each measure to plot a Utility Curve in order to determine the Utility values.

As an example from (Alli, et al, 2009) see Table 1.

This gives a Composite Maintenance Productivity of 63.2% for the period under study

THE QUEUING THEORY APPROACH

Maintenance queuing systems can be classified with the following queuing model characteristics:

1. Defects arrival or breakdowns, λ, which is the distribution of the numbers of defects occurring, the number of defects that exceeds the threshold for plant breakdown. It could also be the distribution of equipment breakdown.
2. The service process, μ, which include the distribution of the time to eliminate or service a defect, the number of maintenance service team, and the arrangement of the maintenance service process (in parallel, series, etc).
3. Queuing discipline such as first come first served (FIFO), last in first served (LIFO), random selection, etc.

Typical maintenance queuing systems are discussed in this chapter.

Table 1.

t	U_t	β_t	$\beta_t y_t$
1	0.66	0.191	0.125
2	0.58	0.181	0.105
3	0.28	0.171	0.048
4	0.89	0.162	0.144
5	0.85	0.152	0.129
6	0.56	0.143	0.081
Composite Number			0.632

Example 1 (Analytical): Single Breakdown Queue and Single Maintenance Team-Poisson Failure Rate and Exponential Maintenance Service Distribution [Infinite Queue – Infinite Source]

Let $X =$ number of breakdowns or failures per week.

Then $f(x) = \frac{e^{-\lambda}\lambda^x}{x!} \quad x = 0,1,2\ldots; \quad \lambda > 0$ and mean $E(X) = \lambda$.

The parameter λ, then is the mean time to failure.

Also, let $T = time\, to\, service\, a\, breakdown$

Then $g(t) = \mu e^{-\mu t} \quad t > 0; \mu > 0$ and $E(T) = \frac{1}{\mu}$. the parameter, μ, mean service time.

From Queuing theory, the following queuing equations can be derived:

Average numbers of breakdowns: $L = \frac{\lambda}{\mu - \lambda}$ (1)

Average number of breakdowns in the queue:

$$L_q = \frac{\lambda^2}{\mu(\mu - \lambda)} \tag{2}$$

Average number of breakdowns in nonempty queues: $L_w = \frac{\mu}{\mu - \lambda}$ (3)

Average time a breakdown stays in the system:

$$W = \frac{1}{\mu - \lambda} \tag{4}$$

Average time a breakdown stays in the queue:

$$W_q = \frac{\lambda}{\mu(\mu - \lambda)} \tag{5}$$

Probability of more than k breakdowns in the system: $P(n > k) = \left(\frac{\lambda}{\mu}\right)^{k+1}$ (6)

Probability of the time in the system is greater than t: $P(T > t) = e^{-\mu\left(1 - \frac{\lambda}{\mu}\right)t}$ (7)

If any one of the quantities $L, L_q, W\, or\, W_q$ can be determined, then others can be determined from the relationships:

$$L = \lambda W \tag{8}$$

$$L_q = \lambda W_q \tag{9}$$

$$W = W_q + \frac{1}{\mu} \tag{10}$$

Figure 2. Single breakdown queue, single-server maintenance service team

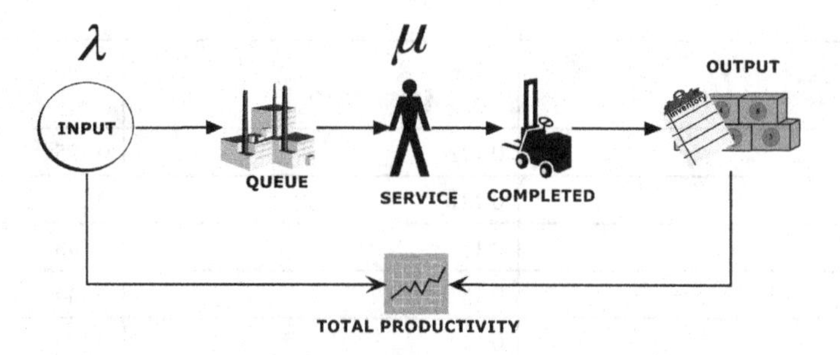

$$L = L_q + \frac{\lambda}{\mu} \quad (11)$$

THE ERLANG MAINTENANCE SERVICE TIME

The *Erlang* distribution is a two-parameter family of distributions, which is a special case of the more general *gamma* distribution. It permits more latitude in selecting a service-time distribution than the one-parameter exponential distribution. In fact, the exponential service time and constant service-time situations are special cases of the Erlang service time. In practical situations, the exponential distribution is unduly restrictive because it assumes that small service times are more probable than large service time, which is unusual for manufacturing plants. On the other hand, the Erlang distribution permits the flexibility of approximating almost any realistic service-time distribution.

We consider two-parameter Erlang distribution

$$f(t;\mu,k) = \frac{(\mu k)^k t^{k-1} e^{-\mu k t}}{(k-1)!}$$

$t > 0;\ \mu > 0;\ k = 1,2,3,\ldots..$

$$E(T) = \frac{1}{\mu} \text{ for every } k = 1,2,3\ldots..$$

With $var(T) = \frac{1}{k\mu^2}$

For $k = 1$, the Erlang reduces to the exponential distribution

The following queuing statistics can be derived:

Average numbers of breakdowns=

$$L = \left(\frac{k+1}{2k}\right)\left(\frac{\lambda^2}{\mu(\mu-\lambda)}\right) + \frac{\lambda}{\mu}\ for\,\lambda < \mu \quad (12)$$

Average number of breakdowns in the queue=

$$L_q = \left(\frac{k+1}{2k}\right)\left(\frac{\lambda^2}{\mu(\mu-\lambda)}\right) for\,\lambda < \mu \quad (13)$$

Average time a breakdown stays in the system=

$$W = \frac{L}{\lambda}\ for\,\lambda < \mu \quad (14)$$

Average time a breakdown stays in the queue=

$$W_q = \frac{L_q}{\lambda}\ for\,\lambda < \mu \quad (15)$$

WEIBULL DISTRIBUTION - MEAN TIME TO FAILURE

The Weibull distribution can be considered as a generalization of the exponential distribution

$$f(t) = \lambda\beta(\lambda t)^{\beta-1} e^{-(\lambda t)^\beta} \quad t > 0; \lambda, \beta > 0 \quad \lambda$$

is on the scale parameter and β the shape factor.

When $\beta = 1$ this yields the exponential distribution.

Defects accumulation in some manufacturing systems approximates to the Weibull distributions.

GENERATION OF SIMULATION DATA

There are several approaches of generating the breakdown data for the system under consideration.

1. Actual data could be used to calculate the desired statistics.
2. Plot the histograms of the cumulative distribution of the breakdown times and the cumulative distribution of the service times and then generate sample breakdown and service times using these distributions.
3. Assume the actual data are values from certain theoretical distribution, and then

sample from the theoretical distribution. To determine a theoretical distribution that would be a good approximation of the actual data, several possible distributions could be considered as candidates, and then the chi-square and/or Kolmogorov-Smirnov test could be used to determine the best distribution to use.

These approaches were used in generating simulation data for the breakdown data from a four-hi Aluminium Rolling Mills collected over three years. Curve fitting was performed using MATLAB version 2011a Statistical Toolkit [3].

Example 2 (Analytical): Single Breakdown Queue and Single Maintenance Team-Poisson Failure Rate and Exponential Maintenance Service Distributions [Finite Queue –Infinite Source]

In practice, breakdowns queues cannot be infinite as this will definitely affect the total productivity of the production plant. When the capacity of the maintenance team is exceeded, service is procured from contract service team, of course, with the increased cost of maintenance and increased logistical effort.

Let $M =$ breakdowns that can be accommodated by the in-house maintenance team. For the case, λ need not be less than the mean service time since the breakdown queue cannot build up without bound.

We have that

$$\mu_n = \mu \qquad for\, n = 1,2,3,\ldots\ldots$$

$$\lambda_n = \begin{cases} \lambda & for\, n = 0,2,3,\ldots..M-1 \\ 0 & for\, n = M,\ M+1,\ldots. \end{cases}$$

We can derive the following queuing characteristics:

Fraction of time that there is no breakdown in the system

$$P_0 = \frac{1-\lambda/\mu}{1-(\frac{\lambda}{\mu})^{M+1}} \; for\, \lambda \neq \mu \tag{16}$$

$$P_0 = \frac{1}{M+1} \; for\, \lambda = \mu \tag{17}$$

Average numbers of breakdowns:

$$L = \frac{(M+1)(\frac{\lambda}{\mu})^{M+1}}{1-(\frac{\lambda}{\mu})^{M+1}} \; for\, \lambda \neq \mu \tag{18}$$

$$L = M/2 \; for\, \lambda \neq \mu \tag{19}$$

Table 2.

Mean Time Between Failure	0.333 Days
Breakdown Distribution	Poisson
Mean Service Time	0.25 days
Mean Service Time Distribution	Exponential
Run Period	365 Days, One Financial Year
Working Hours	00:00a.m to 24:00 hrs, 7 Days

Average number of breakdowns in the queue:

$$L_q = L - (1 - P_0) \quad (20)$$

Example 3 (Simulation Using SIMUL8 Version 2010): Single Breakdown Queue and Single Maintenance Team

The data in Table 2 was used.

For productivity profile, the following data were used:

$$Productivity = \frac{Output}{Input} \quad (21)$$

For $\lambda = 0.33333$ and

$\mu = 0.1, 0.2, \ldots\ldots\ldots\ldots 0.95$

Optimal productivity profile can be obtained by varying breakdown rate, and "s"ervice rate μ.

SINGLE BREAKDOWN QUEUE AND MULTIPLE MAINTENANCE TEAM

We assume

1. *s maintenance teams*
2. Each maintenance team provides service at the same constant average rate μ
3. The average breakdown rate is constant, $\lambda_n = \lambda\, for\, all\, n$
4. $\lambda < s\mu$

With these assumptions, the following queuing equations can be derived.

$$P_n = \frac{1}{n!}\left(\frac{\lambda}{\mu}\right)^n P_0 \quad n = 0, 1, \ldots., s-1 \quad (22)$$

$$P_n = \frac{1}{s!\, s^{n-s}}\left(\frac{\lambda}{\mu}\right)^n P_0 \quad n \geq s \quad (23)$$

$P(n \geq s) = probability\, a\, breakdown\, has\, to\, wait\, for\, service$

= probability of at least $s\, breakdown\, in\, the\, system$

$= \sum_{n=s}^{\infty} P_n$

$$= \frac{\left(\frac{\lambda}{\mu}\right)^s P_0}{s!\left(1 - \frac{\lambda}{\mu s}\right)} \quad (24)$$

$$P_0 = \frac{1}{\left\{\left[\sum_{n=0}^{s-1} \frac{1}{n!}\left(\frac{\lambda}{\mu}\right)^n\right] + \frac{1}{s!\left(1 - \frac{\lambda}{\mu s}\right)}\left(\frac{\lambda}{\mu}\right)^s\right\}} \quad (25)$$

Average number of breakdowns in the queue:

$$L_q = \frac{\left(\frac{\lambda}{\mu}\right)^{s+1} P_0}{s.s!\left(1 - \frac{\lambda}{\mu s}\right)^2} \quad (26)$$

Average numbers of breakdowns: $L = L_q + \frac{\lambda}{\mu}$ (27)

Figure 3. SIMUL8 implementation: single breakdown queue, single maintenance team

Figure 4. SIMUL8 result: single breakdown queue, single maintenance team

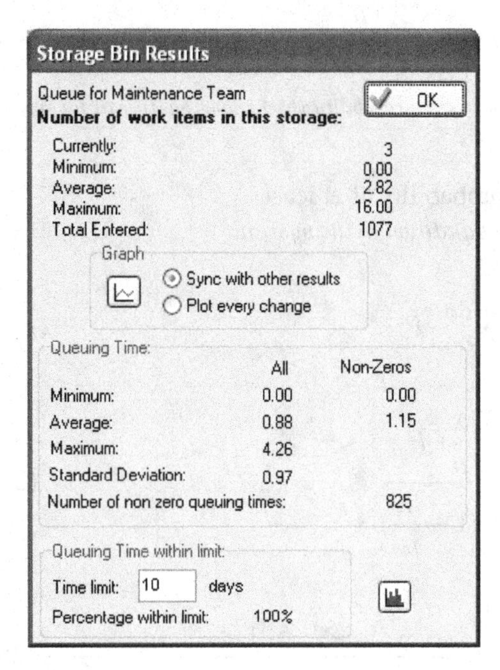

Figure 5. Maintenance productivity: single breakdown queue, single maintenance team

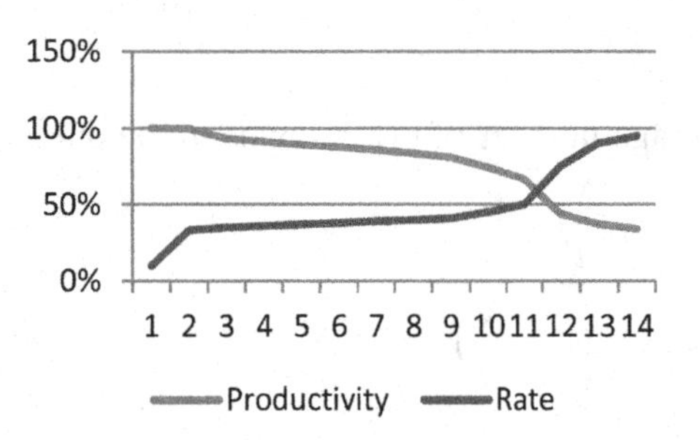

Average time a breakdown stays in the system:

$$W = \frac{L}{\lambda} \tag{28}$$

Average time a breakdown stays in the queue:

$$W_q = \frac{L_q}{\lambda} \tag{29}$$

Probability of the time in the system is greater than t:

$$P\left(T > t\right) = e^{-\mu t}\left\{1 + \frac{\left(\frac{\lambda}{\mu}\right)^s P_0\left[1 - e^{-\mu t\left(s-1-\frac{\lambda}{\mu}\right)}\right]}{s!\left(1 - \frac{\lambda}{\mu s}\right)\left(s - 1 - \frac{\lambda}{\mu}\right)}\right\} \tag{30}$$

Also in practice, breakdowns queues cannot be infinite as this will definitely affect the total productivity of the production plant. When the capacity of the maintenance team is exceeded, service is procured from contract service team, of course, with the increased cost of maintenance and increased logistical effort.

Let

$s =$ number of servers

$M =$ maximum number of breakdowns that can be accommodated by the maintenance service teams

$$\lambda_n = \begin{cases} \lambda & for\, n = 0,1,\ldots\ldots M-1 \\ 0 & for\, n = M, M+1,\ldots\ldots \end{cases}$$

Assume $1 < s < M$

$$\mu_n = \begin{cases} n\mu & for\, n = 0,1,\ldots\ldots s \\ s\mu & for\, n = s+1, s+2,\ldots\ldots \end{cases}$$

Assume $1 < s < M$

Fraction of time that there is no breakdown in the system

$$P_0 = \frac{1}{\sum_{n=0}^{s}\left(\frac{1}{n!}\right)\left(\frac{\lambda}{\mu}\right)^n + \left(\frac{1}{s!}\right)\left(\frac{\lambda}{\mu}\right)^s \sum_{n=s+1}^{M}\left(\frac{\lambda}{\mu s}\right)^{n-s}} \tag{31}$$

Fraction of time that there is nbreakdowns in the system

Figure 6. Single queue, multiple servers model

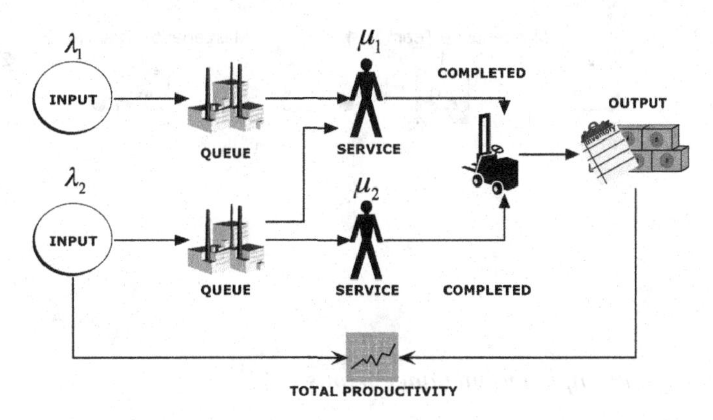

Figure 7. SIMUL8 implementation: single breakdown queue and multiple maintenance team

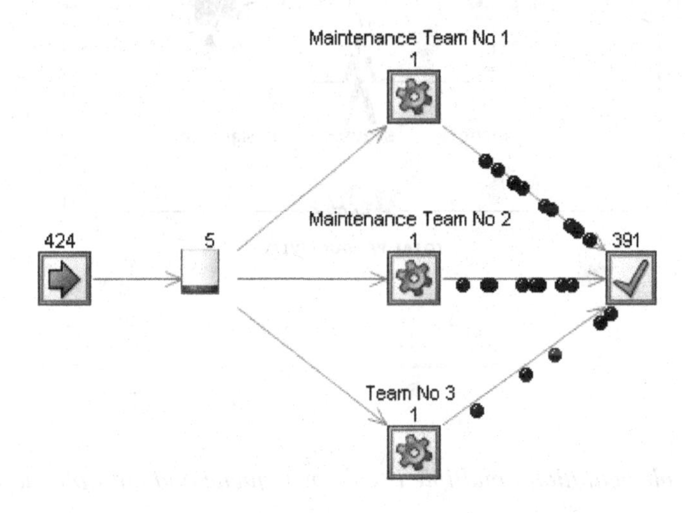

Figure 8. Single breakdown queue, multiple maintenance teams/job shops in series

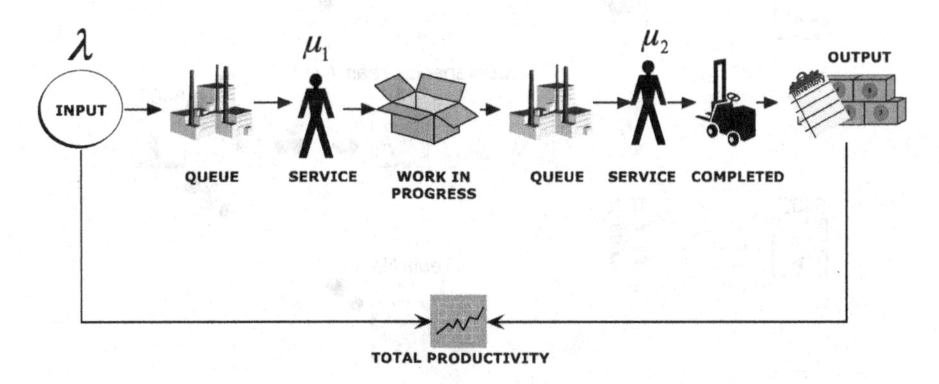

Figure 9. SIMUL8 implementation - single breakdown queue, multiple maintenance job shops in series

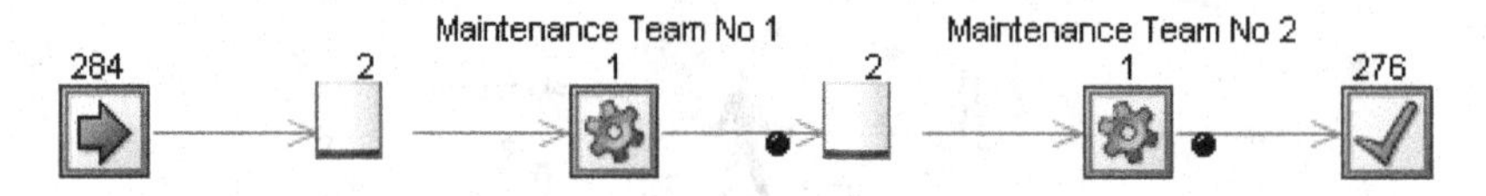

Figure 10. Multiple queues, multiple maintenance teams

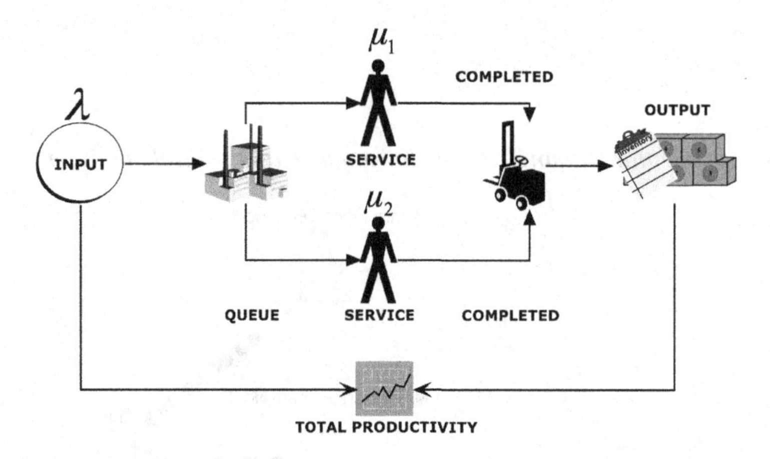

Figure 11. SIMUL8 implementation - multiple breakdown queue and multiple maintenance team

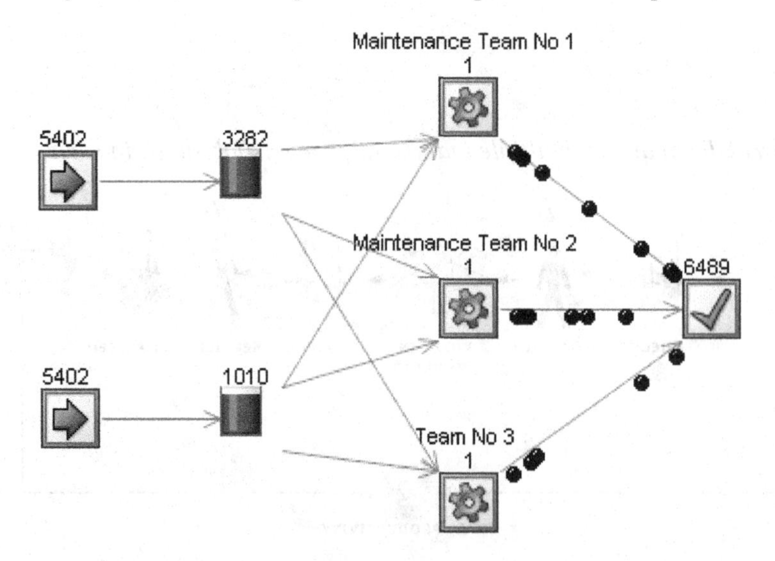

$$P_n = \begin{cases} \frac{1}{n!}(\frac{\lambda}{\mu})^n P_0 & for\, n \le s \\ \frac{1}{s!s^{n-s}}(\frac{\lambda}{\mu})^n P_0 & for\, s < n \le M \\ 0 & for\, n > M \end{cases} \tag{32}$$

Average number of breakdowns in the queue

$$L_q = \frac{P_0 \left(\frac{\lambda}{\mu}\right)^s (\frac{\lambda}{\mu s})}{s!(1-\frac{\lambda}{\mu s})^2} \begin{bmatrix} 1-(\lambda/\mu s)^{M-s} - \\ \left(M-s\right)(\frac{\lambda}{\mu s})^{M-s}(1-\frac{\lambda}{\mu s}) \end{bmatrix} \tag{33}$$

Average numbers of breakdowns

$$L = L_q + s - \sum_{n=0}^{s-1}\left(s-n\right)P_n \tag{34}$$

Example 5 (Simulation): Single breakdown queue and multiple maintenance team (see Figure 7).

Example 6 (Simulation): Single breakdown queue and multiple maintenance team in series (see Figures 8 and 9).

Example 7 (Simulation): Multiple breakdown queue and multiple maintenance team (see Figures 10 and 11).

FUTURE RESEARCH DIRECTION

Formulation of Markov Chains

The service process can be considered for a stochastic process $\left\{X_i\right\}$ with a first order, finite-state *markovian* process, where the conditional probability distribution of X_{i+1} is independent on the states the system is in step 0, 1, 2, 3...., $i-1$ and is dependent only on the state of the system is at step i. It has a finite number of states, a set of stationery transition probabilities, and a set of initial probabilities, $P\left(X_0 = r\right)$, $for\,all\,r$.

The probability of the state of the plant r to state s in n steps (for all states r and s) is given by

$$p_{rs}^{(n)} = P\left(X_{i+n} = s | X_i = r\right) = P(X_n = s \mid X_0 = r) \tag{34}$$

where

$$p_{rs}^{(n)} \ge 0 \quad for\, all\, states\, r\, and\, s; n = 1,2,....... \tag{35}$$

$$\sum_{s=0}^{N} p_{rs}^{(n)} = 1 \quad for\, all\, states\, r; n = 1,2,...... \tag{36}$$

A comparison of the various methods is shown in Table 3.

Table 3. Comparison of methods

Method	Visual Presentation (Priel, 1974)	System Dynamics (Sterman, 2000)	Utility (Alli, et al, 2009)	Queuing Simulation (Inclusive of Environmental Factor)
Ease of Determination	1	4	3	1
Integrated	3	2	3	1
Data Collection	1	4	3	3

1 = Excellent 2 = Good 3 = Fair 4 = Lot of work

CONCLUSION

This chapter attempts at identifying approaches in systematic maintenance productivity measurement and creating models for optimising productivity in maintenance systems. It looked at the following approaches:

1. **The graphical/visual approach:** Using the *'Instant yardstick'* from the ratio analysis maintenance data collected. It can be seen that Operations of the maintenance department which deals with manpower efficiency, incentive coverage, utilization of craft hours, work order turnover, completion delays, cost of maintenance hour and department overhead largely affects the repairable systems service rates which impacts on the output side of total productivity measures. On the other hand assessment of the service which deals with downtime due to maintenance, breakdown frequency, routine service workload, breakdown workload, maintenance to production-hours ratio, maintenance mechanization and maintenance cost component largely relate to the input side of the total productivity measurement process.
2. **The System dynamics approach:** Since accumulation of defects are observable, this thinking can be modeled as a waiting line or queuing system and some of the solution methodologies of queuing theory could be useful in deriving the maintenance productivity, depending on the occurrence pattern (or arrival process) of the defects, the maintenance team service process and queue discipline of the maintenance policy.
3. **The Queuing theory approach:** With adequate assumptions, some of simple industrial maintenance productivity can be estimated using analytical methods; this is impractical for most real life industrial problems. Discrete event simulation approach is very useful in measuring maintenance productivity for several breakdown distributions and maintenance team service distributions subject to maintenance team capacity constraints.
4. The states of the plant after maintenance activities can be incorporated as a *markovian* property of the production system.

REFERENCES

Ahn, S., & Abt, R. C. (2006). Productivity measurement with improved index numbers: Application to the sawmills and planning mills industry of the US: 1947–2000. *Forest Policy and Economics*, *8*, 323–335. doi:10.1016/j.forpol.2005.02.006.

Alli, O. A., Ogunwolu, L., & Oke, O. (2009). Maintenance Productivity Measurement: Case Study of a Manufacturing Company, *Advanced Materials Research, 62-64, 565-570. doi:10.4028/* www.scientifi.net/AMR.62-64.565.

Alsyouf, I. (2007). The role of maintenance in improving companies' productivity and profitability. *International Journal of Production Economics*, *105*, 70–78. doi:10.1016/j.ijpe.2004.06.057.

Bolu, C. A. (2011*)*. Curve fitting breakdown distribution of a 4-high aluminium rolling mills, Ota, Nigeria using MATLAB. (Unpublished Report). Department of Mechanical Engineering, Covenant University, Lagos, Nigeria.

Chan, F. T. S., Lau, H. C. W., Ip, R. W. L., Chan, H. K., & Kong, S. (2005). Implementation of total productive maintenance: A case study. *International Journal of Production Economics*, *95*, 71–94. doi:10.1016/j.ijpe.2003.10.021.

Eti, M. C., Ogaji, S. O. T., & Probert, S. D. (2004). Implementing total productive maintenance in Nigerian manufacturing industries. *Applied Energy*, *79*, 385–401. doi:10.1016/j.apenergy.2004.01.007.

Gillett, B. E. (1979). *Operations research – A computer-oriented algorithmic approach*. New Delhi: Tata McGraw-Hill Publishing Company Ltd..

Hamlin, J. L. (1979).Productivity appraisal for maintenance centre, *Industrial Engineering, 11*(9), September, 1979.

Hauge, J. W., & Paige, K. N. (2004). *Learning Simul8: The complete guide*. Billingham, UK: PlainVu Publishers.

Lilly, M. T., Obiajulu, U. E., Ogaji, S. O. T., & Probert, S. D. (2007). Total-productivity analysis of a Nigerian petroleum-product marketing company. *Applied Energy, 84*, 1150–1173. doi:10.1016/j.apenergy.2007.04.003.

Nanere, M., Fraser, I., Quazi, A., & D'Souza, C. (2007). Environmentally adjusted productivity measurement: An Australian case study. *Journal of Environmental Management, 85*, 350–362. doi:10.1016/j.jenvman.2006.10.004 PMID:17129666.

Onwugbolu, C. A., & Oloruniwo, F. (1988). *Measuring maintenance productivity.(Presented paper.)*. Cincinnati, OH: The Computer Aided Manufacturing Conference.

Parida, A., & Kumar, U. (2009). *Maintenance Productivity and performance measurement. Handbook of Maintenance and Engineering*. London: Springer-Verlag Ltd..

Priel, V. Z. (1974). *Systematic maintenance organisation*. London: MacDonald & Evans Ltd..

Sterman, J. D. (2000). *Business dynamics – Systems thinking and modeling for a complex world*. New York: Irwin McGraw-Hill.

Velten, K. (2009). *Mathematical modeling and simulation: Introduction for scientists and engineers*. Weinheim: Wiley-VCH Verlag GmbH..

Venkataraman, P. (2009). *Applied optimisation with MATLAB programming*. New Jersey: John Wiley & Sons, Inc..

ADDITIONAL READING

Anderson, D. R. Sweeny, & Williams. (2007). Statistics for business and economics. London: Thompson Learning.

Appuu Kuttan, K. K. (2007). *Introduction to mechatronics*. New Delhi: Oxford University Press.

Bhushan, B. (2002). *Introduction to tribology*. New York: John Wiley and Sons Inc..

Birolini, A. (2010). *Reliability engineering: Theory and practice*. Berlin, Heidelberg: Springer-Verlag.

Blischke, W. R. (2003). *Case studies in reliability and maintenance*. New Jersey: John Wiley and Sons Inc..

Boschian, V, Rezg, N., & Chelbi, A. (2009). Contribution of simulation to the optimization of maintenance strategies for a randomly failing production system. *European Journal of Operational Research, 197*(2), 2009, 1142-1149.

Bose, S. K. (2002). *An introduction to queuing systems*. New York: Kluwer Academic/Plenum Publishers.

Budynas, R. G., & Nisbett, K. (2010). *Shigley's mechanical engineering design* (8th ed.). New York: McGraw-Hill Companies Inc..

Fishback, P. E. (2009). *Linear and nonlinear programming with maple–An interactive, application-based approach*. New York: CRC Press Taylor & Francis Group.

Gerhard, C. D. (1998). two-stage generalized age maintenance of a queue-like production system. *European Journal of Operational Research*, *108*(2), 363–378. doi:10.1016/S0377-2217(97)00105-7.

Giambene, G. (2010). *Queuing theory and telecommunications: Networks and applications*. Springer Science and Business Media Inc..

Groover, M. P. (2011). *Principles of modern manufacturing* (4th ed.). John Wiley and Sons Ltd..

Higgins, L. R. (Ed.). (1988). *Maintenance engineering handbook* (4th ed.). New York: McGraw-Hill Book Company.

Huang, S. H., Dismukes, J. P., Shi, J., & Su, Q. (2002). Manufacturing system modeling for productivity improvement. *Journal of Manufacturing Systems*, *21*(4), 249–259. doi:10.1016/S0278-6125(02)80165-0.

Lee, C., & Johnson, A. L. (2012). Two-dimensional efficiency decomposition to measure the demand effect in productivity analysis. *European Journal of Operational Research*, *216*, 584–593. doi:10.1016/j.ejor.2011.08.004.

Lie-Fern, H. (1992). Optimal preventive maintenance policies in an M/G/1 queue-like production system. *European Journal of Operational Research*, *58*(1), 112–122. doi:10.1016/0377-2217(92)90240-A.

Losften, H. (2000). Measuring maintenance performance–in search for a maintenance productivity index. *International Journal of Production Economics*, *63*(1), 47–58. doi:10.1016/S0925-5273(98)00245-X.

Manzini, R. (2010). *Maintenance for industrial systems*. London: Springer-Verlag Ltd. doi:10.1007/978-1-84882-575-8.

Monks, J. G. (1985). *Operations management: Shaum's outline series*. New York: McGraw-Hill Company.

Percy, D., & Kobbacy Khairy, A. H. (2000). Determining economical maintenance intervals. *International Journal of Production Economics*, *67*(1), 87–94. doi:10.1016/S0925-5273(00)00013-X.

Stephens, L. J. (2004). *Advanced statistics demystified*. New York: The McGraw-Hills Companies Inc..

Stidham, S. (2009). *Optimal design of queuing systems*. CRC Press/Taylor & Francis. doi:10.1201/9781420010008.

Stroud, K. A. (2007). *Engineering mathematics* (6th ed.). New York: Industrial Press, Inc..

Stroud, K. A. (2011). *Advanced engineering mathematics* (6th ed.). New York: Industrial Press, Inc..

Sumanth, D. J. (1984). *Productivity engineering and management*. New York: McGraw-Hill.

Sumanth, D. J., & Yavuz, F. P. (1983). A formalized approach to select productivity improvement techniques in organizations. *Engineering Management International*, *1*(4), 259–273. doi:10.1016/0167-5419(83)90003-0.

Valdez-Flores, C., & Feldman, R. (1989). A survey of preventive maintenance models for stochastically deteriorating single-unit systems. *Naval Research Quarterly*, *33*, 419–446. doi:10.1002/1520-6750(198908)36:4<419::AID-NAV3220360407>3.0.CO;2-5.

Wagner, H. M. (1979). *Principles of operations research* (2nd ed.). New Jersey: Prentice-Hall, Inc..

Wang, H. (2002). A survey of maintenance policies of deteriorating systems. *European Journal of Operational Research*, *39*, 469–489. doi:10.1016/S0377-2217(01)00197-7.

Zhang, R., Phillis, Y., & Kouikoglou, V. S. (2005). *Fuzzy control of queuing systems*. London: Springer-Verlag.

Section 2
Information Communication and Engineering

Chapter 9
Modeling of Packet Streaming Services in Information Communication Networks

Aderemi A. Atayero
Covenant University, Nigeria

Yury A. Ivanov
Elster Vital Connections, Russia

ABSTRACT

Application of the term video streaming in contemporary usage denotes compression techniques and data buffering, which can transmit video in real time over the network. There is currently a rapid growth and development of technologie's using wireless broadband technology as a transport, which is a serious alternative to cellular communication systems. Adverse effect of the aggressive environment used in wireless networks transmission results in data packets undergoing serious distortions and often getting lost in transit. All existing research in this area investigate the known types of errors separately. At present there are no standard approaches to determining the effect of errors on transmission quality of services. Besides, the spate in popularity of multimedia applications has led to the need for optimization of bandwidth allocation and usage in telecommunication networks. Modern telecommunication networks should by their definition be able to maintain the quality of different applications with different Quality of Service (QoS) levels. QoS requirements are generally dependent on the parameters of network and application layers of the OSI model. At the application layer QoS depends on factors such as resolution, bit rate, frame rate, video type, audio codecs, and so on. At the network layer, distortions (such as delay, jitter, packet loss, etc.) are introduced.

INTRODUCTION

We present in this chapter simulation results of modeling video streaming over wireless broadband communications networks and the differences in spatial and time characteristics of the different subject groups during transmission over networks. Numerical results of the modeling and analysis of the effect of these parameters on quality of video streaming are presented and discussed. Also presented is the proposal of a completely new approach to modeling errors, based on a developed

DOI: 10.4018/978-1-4666-2208-1.ch009

Markov model with the use of actual statistics of errors in the channels of broadband wireless access networks. We show that discrete Markov processes with the necessary number of states describe the mechanism of transmission of video sufficiently well and an increase in the number of states of the Markov chain allows to observe less divergence between real and simulated data, but this increases the complexity of the model, analysis and processing of data. The chapter effectively summarizes the researches carried out to date by the authors in investigating the effects of video streaming errors on the performance of broadband wireless access networks.

In section 1, we present background information on the features of streaming services: their characteristics, quality parameters, and peculiarities of streaming H.264/AVC video over broadband wireless access networks. The second section presents the design and development of our streaming video software and its use in estimation of the quality of streamed video. In the third section of the chapter, we present our findings on investigating the effect of noise stability on the quality of streaming video. Each section of the chapter ends with a conclusion and relevant recommendations arising from the discussion of research findings.

1. PROPERTIES OF STREAMING SERVICES

1.1. Characteristics of Streaming Traffic and Quality Parameters Characterizing Continuity of Service

Streaming traffic–traffic type, which is characterized by viewing and (or) auditioning information as it becomes available to the user (terminal) equipment.

Traffic in modern computer networks can be divided into two large groups - *elastic traffic,* which generates the traditional services such as email, WWW, FTP, and *real-time traffic,* which generates multimedia services such as IP-telephony or video conferencing. The share of real-time traffic is gradually increasing, due to growing interest in services, which allow for sound and high-quality video to be transmitted over computer networks (with high-speed bit stream and high resolution), such as the Music on Demand (MoD), Video on Demand (VoD) and IP-Television (IPTV).

Transmission of Streaming services (audio and video) over various media (wireless access, Internet, etc) is becoming more popular. This rapid expansion defines a new challenge of maintaining quality of service for each stream. On the other hand, new mobile systems are anticipated that will offer wireless services to a wide variety of portable terminals, ranging from cell phones and personal digital assistants (PDAs) to small portable computers. All these devices are heterogeneous.

They have different processing power, display, memory, and possible data rate. Thus, the rate of decoded data and content resolution need to be adapted to the surrounding network and display device (terminal). This quality is necessary to transfer huge amount of data on heterogeneous networks, and at the same time should find applications where the above-mentioned terminals are not able to display the full image resolution or all of the picture properties. Despite the shift to higher speeds, overload conditions often arise when trying to run resource-intensive services such as IPTV, available to multiple users. As a result, service quality is low, which is especially critical for video streaming - it should be noted that even minor disruptions to the picture on the screen or desync of audio and video tracks will cause a negative viewer reaction.

However, the problem lies not in slow network speed, but rather in the characteristics of the traffic, and more precisely in the peculiarities of the interaction between elastic traffic flows and real-time data.

A characteristic feature of the QoS indicators for data services in broadband wireless access is that it takes into account the classes of data (traffic), as defined by the ETSI TS 123 107 standard: dialogue, *streaming,* interactive and background. The main difference between these classes is their sensitivity to time delay in the network transmitted data streams. Effect of packet delay in the network elements with respect to time manifested in the possibility (or otherwise) of man's perception of a message fragment, for example, whole audio or video fragment. Thus, the subjective estimates of the messages for the maximum packet delay from a sender to a receiver should not exceed 400 ms. Delay constraint is stringent for some services, the inability to provide necessary delay in packets leads to unacceptable quality of service.

The dialogue (speech) traffic class: This is the only class in which delay is strictly determined by human perception and packet transmission is done real-timewith extremely low latency. This traffic class corresponds to voice services and video telephony.

Streaming traffic class: The data is processed as a steady and continuous stream. This class corresponds to the reception/transmission of web-information and receiption/transmission of information on request. This kind of application (transfer methods) are asymmetric and therefore able to withstand longer delay than symmetric dialogue systems, as well as allow for considerable variation, and change the values of the delay.

The interactive traffic class: the type of traffic, which is characterized by a direct interaction (dialogue) of communication service users or terminal equipment user.This traffic class is used to provide services for which the end-user (human or machine) engaged in a dialogue requests in real-time data from a remote source (e.g. servers). Examples of human interaction with a remote source are viewing Web-pages, searching for information in the databases, access to a remote server, interaction with remote sources - measurement data survey and automated queries sent to the database (telemetry system). The classical scheme of data transfer is interactive traffic, which in general is characterized by a form of "end-user query-response." One of the key parameters is the delay associated with the acknowledgement of data reception. These services include: user location determination service, and computer games. However, depending on the nature of the game (i.e. how much data is being actively transmitted), this service can be classified by the degree of acceptable delay to the dialog class (data transfer in real time).

Background traffic class: This class of traffic (e-mail delivery, SMS, download of databases, etc.) can be transmitted with a delay, as this information does not require immediate implementation of any action. The delay in this case may be seconds, tens of seconds or even minutes. At the initial stage of commercial operation of the UMTS traffic classes and streaming dialog are transmitted in real-time switching channels mode. Table 1 shows the main characteristics of data on 3G networks for the described classes of traffic. each of which has its own specific features vis-a-vis QoS. Table 2 and 3 are the main quantitative indicators for certain services with traffic streaming and interactive classes, respectively.

As can be seen from these tables, the main characteristics of traffic streaming and interactive classes are data packets' delay and Frame Error Probability (FEP), which characterizes the data quality.

Data quality can also be assessed based on the reliability information of "soft frame" (a soft decision decoder). Such information may include:

- Error probability of message elements (BER - bit error probability), calculated before the channel decoder - BER in the physical channel;
- Soft (current) information from the Viterbi decoder of the convolutional code;

Table 1. Quantitative indicators for services with traffic streaming and interactive classes

Type of Service	Application	Degree of Symmetry	Data Transfer Rate (kbps)	Main Characteristics and Their Indicators		
				One-Way Delay (ms)	Change in Delay (ms)	Data Loss
Audio Transmission	High-quality direct audio playback	In general, one-sided	16-128	<150	<<1	FER < 3%
Video Transmission	High quality direct video playback	Unidirectional	32-384	<150		FER < 1%
Data Transmission	Array conversion data/search	In general, one-sided		<250	Not applicable	0
Data Transmission	Picture	Unidirectional		<250	Not applicable	0
Data Transmission	Telemetry-monitoring	Unidirectional	<28.8	<250	Not applicable	0

Table 2. Quantitative indicators for voice and data streaming services

Type of Service	Application	Degree of Symmetry	Data Transfer Rate (kbps)	Main Characteristics and Their Indicators		
				Unidirectional Delay	Change in Delay (ms)	Data Loss
Voice transmission	Voice messages	Mostly unidirectional	4.32.	playback <1s Record time <2s	<1	FER < 3%
Data Transmission	Web-search/Web-browsing	Mostly unidirectional		Preferably <2s per page. Allowable <4s per page.	No	0
Data Transmission	Transactions with high priority, E-commerce	Bidirectional		Preferably <2s Allowable <4s	No	0
Data Transmission	E-mail	Mostly unidirectional		Preferably <2s Allowable <4s	No	0

Table 3. Technical standards for average monthly network operation access to be controlled

Indicator	Interactive	Interactive During Usage Satellite Communication Link	Streamed	Data Traffic, Except Interactive and Streaming Traffic
Packet transmission average delay information, (ms)	≤ 100	≤ 400	≤ 400	≤ 1000
Deviation from the average information packet transmission delay (ms)	≤ 50	≤ 50	≤ 50	
Error coefficient of information packets	$\leq 10^{-3}$	$\leq 10^{-3}$	$\leq 10^{-3}$	$\leq 10^{-3}$
Coefficient of information packet loss	$\leq 10^{-4}$	$\leq 10^{-4}$	$\leq 10^{-4}$	$\leq 10^{-4}$

- Soft information from turbo decoder such as the E_b / N_0 ratio in the channel.

However, the choice of using a particular method for determining the quality of the received data has its peculiarities. The quality of the data can be estimated through any of the three methods mentioned above, however, a hybrid (integrated) approach seems to be the most effective. The essence of the integrated approach would be to use the error information received from the decoder, and data on the reception quality of individual elements of the received signal (or the signal-to-noise ratio).

Multimedia stream: In this case, the streaming technology sends information through the network from the server to the user in real time. Tools are not loaded on the viewer hard disk. The media is viewed as long as the client accepts them (it is possible that the buffer is not used). Should the client desire to see the media again, the streaming process is repeated. The streaming system "from end to end" requires the availability of streaming software, a streaming server and a media player at the customer's end. Clips are made with special programs that convert audio, video and animation to MPEG -4 format for streaming. Streaming servers, such as the Apple Inc. server or RealServer (from RealNetworks) can be used to transfer media clips to customers using MP4 Player, RealPlayer or QuickTime Player.

1.2. Transmission of H.264/ AVC Standard Streaming Video over Broadband Wireless Access Networks

During the development and formalization of a new process of video compression the final format was arrived at via multiple organizations (ITU, ISO, etc.) and for this reason, the new standard has five different names: H.264, MPEG-4 Part 10, AVC, H.26L, JVT. Using the new coding standard is possible in many different digital video transmission systems known by several names: Internet TV, IPTV, streaming video, video over IP, IP-Video information system, including transmission of different resolution up to HDTV 1080i (1920x1080). The newest H.264 standard as well as earlier versions of MPEG-4, allow for high compression ratios by exploiting both spatial and temporal redundancy in video frames. Thus, only those elements of the image that has changed compared to the corresponding elements of the previous frame need be procesed.

For ease of use in various applications and a variety of networks, the H.264 codec is divided into layers of video encoding VCL (Video Coding Layers) and network abstraction NAL (Network Adaptation Layer) (Figure 1). Layering allows for being independent of network transmission conditions (Wiegand, Sullivan, Bjntegaard, Luthra, 2003). The VCL level consists of the main compression mechanism, and includes the syntactic level, known as Slice Macroblock (MB), and block (Lee and Kalva, 2008). The NAL H.264/ AVC level defines the interface between the video codec itself and the outside world and is designed for the adaptation of bit sequence generated by the VCL for transmission over various networks (Marpe, Wiegand, Sullivan, 2006).

NAL encapsulation for the various transport networks such as H.320 (ITU-T H320, 1999), MPEG-TS systems (*ISO-IEC* 13818, 1994) and RTP/IP (Wenger, Stockhammer, Hannuksela, 2003) is outside the scope of H.264/AVC standardization. Moreover, all forms of NAL H.264 packaging are called models with a "simple packaging" in which one NAL is placed in one RTP package (Wenger, 2003). Packaging rules for this method are really very simple: NAL (including its header, which also serves as the header for useful information) is placed in the RTP packet, header parameters are defined according to the specification in (Schulzrinne, Casner, Frederick, & Jacobson, 1996) and subsequently sent to the RTP packet transport layer UDP.

The use of hierarchical coding allows for video distribution in complex networks with varying bandwidth allocation for individual segments. Ideally, VCL should not produce NAL of a size larger than the MTU, thereby avoiding fragmentation at the IP level. This is easily achieved by using slices. However, since the NAL is less than 64 kB, IP-level performs the fragmentation and recombination of fragmented packets.

IP networks are a quite convenient environment for streaming video, due to the delay and data rate requirements (Wenger, 2003). As a rule, standard IP networks do not depend on the implementation of the physical and link levels and can work with their different protocols. Therefore, these levels are not discussed. At the network level, IP-based networks use the Internet Protocol. The IP-packet header size is 20 bytes and is protected by a checksum. However, useful information when it is not secure. The maximum size of IP-packet is 64 kB, but this size is rarely used, since the maximum packet size of the network Maximum Transfer Unit (MTU) is limited.

At the transport layer, videodata is usually transmitted via the User Datagram Protocol (UDP) (Postel, 1980), which in contrast to the Transmission Control Protocol (TCP) (Postel, 1981), does not guarantee the successful delivery of packets. Nevertheless, it is widely used for streaming video and video telephony, due to the small delay in transmission. Usually, checksum calculation is used for detecting transmission errors on UDP. At the application level, streaming video transmission is achieved by means of the following core protocols (Dvorkovich, 2005):

- **Real-time Transmission protocol (RTP):** This is a packet-oriented data delivery real-time transport protocol, which includes both video and sound (Schulzrinne, Casner, Frederick, Jacobson, 1996).
- **Real-Time Control Protocol (RTCP):** This is the control protocol designed to work with RTP, it helps to synchronize video and audio, as well as provide quality of service (QoS).
- **Real-Time Streaming Protocol (RTSP):** Management protocol for the initialization and directing of streaming data from video server, realizing the possibility of "remote control" (Schulzrinne, Rao, Lanphier, 1998).
- **Resource Reservation Protocol (RSVP):** A protocol to establish and support the required level of quality of service (QoS), ensuring the availability of adequate network resources (such as sufficient bandwidth).

1.3. Broadband Wireless Access Network Error Models

Error-rates arising from the transmission of digital streams over the physical layer of wireless networks can be divided into two types*: Single-bit errors* and *Bit error packet.*

A single-bit error is expressed as a bit inversion in the transmission, which leads to incorrect recognition bit sequences and bytes as a whole. Bit-error packet is any sequence of errors longer than two inverted bits in a data segment. Bit error packets occur more frequently than single-bit errors. The length of error packets is measured from the first to the last inverted bit.

Bit errors are the most common and easily avoidable distortion of the digital stream. However, in some cases they may lead to the loss of a data segment. Thus, not eliminating bit errors at the physical layer will result in a loss of information (transport) packets at the link layer known as information packet error. Figure 1 presents types of errors in the context of the OSI model.

The following are possible reasons for loss of data packets:

Analog and electromagnetic interference, impulse noise: Usually occur because of external factors, including weather and close proximity to electrical equipment. Error correction mechanisms at the physical layer are not always able to elimi-

Figure 1. Models of errors in the context of the OSI model

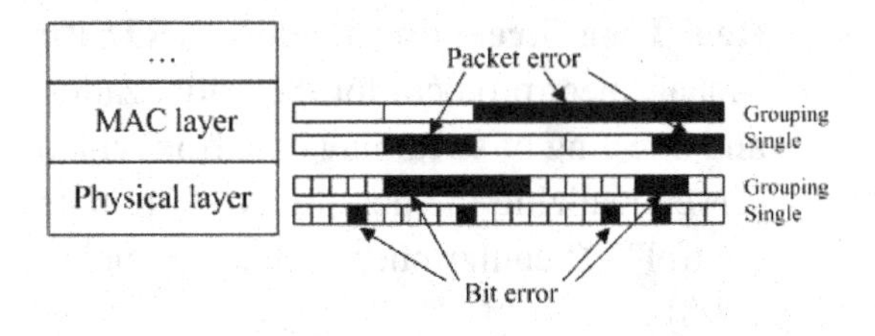

nate error effects, which in turn leads to loss of the transport packet. The use of special means of protection against interference entails a decrease in bandwidth and increases the cost of equipment.

Short-term changes in bandwidth: This is associated with a bad connection of dial-up equipment. QoS constraints necessarily affect the bandwidth limits, going beyond which limit may cause packet loss in the absence of adequate control. Strong jitter, or bursty traffic can overwhelm the buffer and subsequently affect the ability to handle a sequence of packets, resulting in either their loss or late reception and processing.

Equipment problems: This may be caused by malfunctioning devices, the parasitic coupling between components, and untimely processing of packets due to jitter. To simulate the errors, different models have been adopted with different effects on the transmitted information.

Additive White Gaussian Noise (AWGN) Model: Since wireless communication channels are characterized by randomly distributed and independent bit errors, the AWGN is often adopted in the simulation of wireless communication channels, in which a certain bit in a sequence of distorted (inverted) with an *apriori* probability. Adopted value describes the probability of occurrence of bit errors i.e. the Bit Error Rate (BER). The signal received in the AWGN channel can be represented as:

$$r(t) = s(t) + n(t)$$

where *s (t)* - the transmitted signal; *n (t)* - a noise signal having a mean value 0 and noise power spectral density $N_0 / 2WHz^{-1}$ (Telatar, 1999).

The AWGN model cannot simulate a fading channel. The attenuation of the transmitted signal results in packetization (clustering) of errors. Since most modern codecs use variable length code (VLC), differentiating between bit-error and error packets makes little sense, because in any case errors will be displayed as loss or distortion of whole groups of consecutive bits in the decoder (Atayero, Sheluhin, Ivanov, Alatishe, 2011). However, there is a difference in the impact of different types of errors on different parts of the video stream. For example, a single error in the header can cause a greater distortion than the group of errors in several blocks.

Gilbert Model: Another very popular error model is the Gilbert model (Gilbert, 1960). This model presents a channel in the form of two states: the "good" state, and the "bad" state. For the "good" state, bit or packet is received successfully, whereas it is lost for the "bad" state. Hence corresponding to the probability transition states of P_{01} and P_{10}. For the "good" state, the error probability $P_{good} = 0$. While for the "bad" state error occurs with an independent probability P_{bad}. Thus, to fully describe the Gilbert model three parameters are required: P_{01}, P_{10} and P_{bad} however, what is often misunderstood about the Gilbert model is that the "bad" state corresponds to the error/loss state, that is, $P_{bad} = 1$ (Qi, Pei, Modestino, Tian, 2004). This corresponds to a simple two-state Markov model, which takes into account only single errors. It is for this singular reason that error groups or their packets cannot be modeled (Fantacci and Scardi, 1996; Wang and Moayeri, 1995).

Gilbert-Elliot (GE): The Gilbert model was supplemented by Elliot (Elliot, 1963), resulting in what is now known as the Gilbert-Elliott

Box 1.

$$P = \begin{bmatrix} P(S_n = 0 \mid S_{n-1} = 0) & P(S_n = 1 \mid S_{n-1} = 0) \\ P(S_n = 0 \mid S_{n-1} = 1) & P(S_n = 1 \mid S_{n-1} = 1) \end{bmatrix} = \begin{pmatrix} P_{00} & P_{01} \\ P_{10} & P_{11} \end{pmatrix} \quad (1.1)$$

model. This model assumes a small (non-zero) and independent probability of error $P_{good} > 0$, even in the "good" state. Thus, four parameters are required for a complete description of the GE model (Hohlfeld, 2008).

The Gilbert-Elliot model can be described by the matrix *P*. Let s_n be a Markov process corresponding to $s_n = 0$ if the channel is in the "good" state in *the n-th* moment of time, and $s_n = 1$ otherwise. Thus the transition matrix would take the form presented in (1.1) (see Box 1).

Average loss probability and the mean error length is gotten from expression (1.2)

$$P = \frac{P_{01}}{P_{10} + P_{01}},\ L = \frac{1}{P_{10}} \quad (1.2)$$

Both the AWGN model and the Gilbert-Elliot model can be used both on the physical layer with respect to bits, and the link layer, in relation to transport packets. They are often used in the experimental evaluation of simulated channels (Baguda, Fisal, Syed, Yusof, Mohd SA, Mohd A., Zulkarmawan, 2008; Ebert and Willig, 1999), due to their different effects on video stream (Figure 2), but they cannot simulate all the errors.

The most realistic and accurate means of modeling error statistics at the data link and physical layers is by the use of probability data obtained from a real network. In cases of rare occurrence of errors, they cause significant problems in the visual quality of streaming video, while in other types of services they would have remained unnoticed.

1.4. Features of Streaming Video over Broadband Wireless Networks

Application of more sophisticated coding methods does not allow for the complete avoidance of the apperance of characteristic distortions in the real-time transmission of video streams. As a rule, in wired networks with abundant bandwidth, the transmission channel has a low probability of bit error occurrence. However, data transmission over the wireless channel has a number of peculiarities due to the unpredictability of transmission conditions. Specific error protection mechanisms are employed at each layer of the OSI model:

Figure 2. Models of bit errors and their effect on video stream

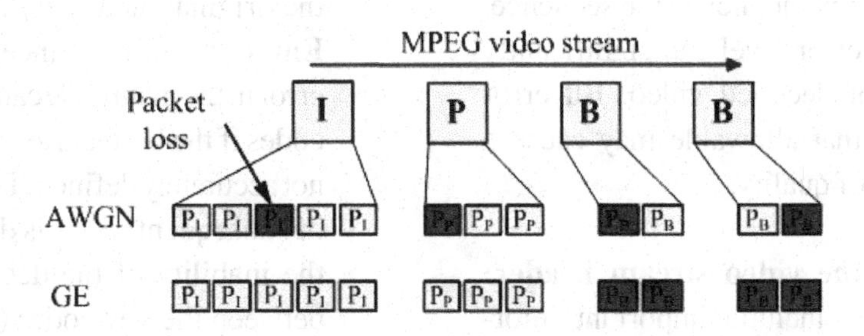

Application Layer (i.e. in the codec): these mechanisms determine the quality of video sequences at the decoding stage. Various forms of frame segmentation (e.g. slice, block) were applied at the onset of coding standards such as H.261, H.263, MPEG-1 and MPEG-2. The properties of the specific decoder in use need be taken into consideration when decoding distorted video sequences. Not all of the MPEG decoders handle stream errors qualitatively (Atayero, Sheluhin, Ivanov, & Alatishe, 2011). Some decoders are capable of processing errors with high probability. Other decoders cannot decode streams with lots of errors effectively, but they will decode with high quality streams with little errors. There are decoders, which decode the streams with errors rather poorly, regardless of the errors and are simply not suitable for use with the particular type of stream. Data partitioning (DP), which is an effective way of increasing system error robustness is already employed in later versions of codecs such as H.263, MPEG-4 Part 2. As at this writing, some mechanisms for protection against errors e.g. a group of parameters such as SPS, PPS, FMO and others are already incorporated in the H.264/AVC standard (Wenger, 2003). The link layer uses changes in the packet size to reduce losses, ensure service discrimination, etc. Uneven error protection is employed at the physical layer.

Bit errors occur during transmission over wireless channels and can affect the quality of received (decoded) video in different ways, some of which are listed below (Romer, 2004):

Bit error in different parts of the bitstream: Since the MPEG-4 compression mechanism employs the removal of redundancy in the sequence, a relatively low bit error level can significantly affect the quality of decoded video. Bit error values higher than that allowable may cause a drastic degradation of quality.

- **Bit error in the video stream header:** Title sequences include important information such as frame resolution, number of frames, and the quantization table.
- **Bit error in the image header:** If an error occurs in the image header, the decoder may fail to detect the beginning of a frame. In the the worst case, the frame will be lost. In other cases, with time prediction, serious degradation of quality may occur.
- **Bit error in GOP frame group:** Error in either the GOP proper or in its header has little or no effect on the proper decoding of video.
- **Bit error in DCT coefficients:** (Richardson, 2003) informs that if part of the DCT coefficients is distorted, it may lead to inaccurate decoding of the variable length codes.

Since codecs process information in blocks, the minimum unit of video stream distortion when exposed to a single errors is a block (4x4 or 16x16) depending on the encoding. Another area of error propagation is macro-block and slice. Thus, a single error message can cause the spread of errors not only in the actual macro-block, but also in the slice and subsequently the frame. It was shown experimentally in that smaller size of the slice encoding significantly improves image quality in the presence of packet loss.

There are three possible sources of error propagation (Rodriguez, 2008):

1. **Spatial prediction:** A macroblock restored during decoding with distorted neighboring macroblocks will also be distorted.
2. **Temporal prediction:** If a frame is distorted, then subsequent frames using it as the original picture will also be distorted.
3. **Entropy coding:** Since VLCs are used, an error in the main code can affect the following codes if the boundaries of the main code are not accurately defined. Thus synchronization of subsequent codes is disturbed, leading to the inability of the decoder to distinguish between the key codes (see Figure 3).

Figure 3. An example of desynchronization of VLC

Encoding:
⇨ C B D B E E F A C
⇨ 1100 10 1101 10 1110 1110 1111 0 1100
Bit error:
⇨ 1100 10 0101 10 1110 1110 1111 0 1100
Decoding:
⇨ 1100 10 0 10 1101 1101 1101 1110 1100
⇨ C B A B D D D E C

Symbol	Codeword
A	0
B	10
C	1100
D	1101
E	1110
F	1111

The use of VLC results in information desynchronization, with the result that part of the information before the next code becomes 'undecodeable'. In some cases, even after synchronization restoration, the decoded signal can not be used correctly, since the necessary additional information on how to use it, such as the type of frame, or the motion vector is lost. Distortion resulting from the impact of transmission errors and subsequent decoding, are defined by the following terms: tiling, blurring, color transmission errors, error blocks, jerkiness, mosquito noise, the quantization noise, blurring, smearing (ETSI TR 102 493; ITU-T P.910 P.920 P.930; Atayero et al., 2011b). In addition, the transmission of video in real time is fraught with other certain problems associated with visual quality control, speed control/delay, error control, and scalability (Lakshman, Ortega, & Reibman, 1998; Stuhlmuller, Farber, Link, & Girod, 2000; Wang, Ostermann, & Zhang, 2001).

2. STREAMING VIDEO QUALITY ESTIMATION SOFTWARE

Most modern communication systems provide real time video transmission services, where the issue of video quality is very important. There are many publications in the literature devoted to the mechanisms of ensuring the required quality of service (QoS) for example (Aguiar et al., 2003; Sanneck et al., 2002; etc), but only some of them were able to achieve satisfactory results of practical import (Hertrich, 2002 and Wolf, 1999), since the effect of QoS parameters on the quality of video cannot be uniquely determined because of the large variety of coding schemes and post-processing and error recovery methods.

In some studies reported in the literature, frame synchronization of the transmitting and the receiving side is often used to assess the quality of video, which implies the inability to assess quality in case of frame loss or decoding errors (Sarnoff Corporation, 2002; EURESCOM Project P905-PF, 2000). There are known methods of assessing the quality of video distorted during transmission, for example (Wu, D., Hou, Y.T., Zhu, W., Lee, H.-J., Chiang, T., Zhang, Y.-Q., & Chao, H.J., 2000; Wolf, S. & Pinson, M., 2002), but their software is not freely available.

2.1. The Hardware-Software Solution for Assessing the Quality of Streaming Video

The main objective of video streaming performance research in wireless networks is optimization of decoding using the *coding Rate–Distortion* criterion. This criterion is characterized by digital video transmission efficiency and the quality of decoding at the receiving end. Various decoding algorithms, which affect the quality of received signals in different ways are employed for correct decoding of video signals transmitted over imperfect data transmission media (Dai, Loguinov, 2005; Feng, 1997; Koutsakis & Paterakis, 2004; Krunz, Sass, & Hughes, 1995; Krunz & Tripathi, 1997).

Generally, video data can be presented in several forms including the following:

- The actual encoded bit stream, usually large, copyrighted and requiring expertise in coding/decoding, making its distribution to users quite difficult;
- Videotraces containing encoded video information in the bit stream (but not the actual encoded information), and freely distributed to users;
- In the form of video traffic models based on videotraces with certain statistical properties, which limit the user's choice of subject (e.g, sports, news).

Videotraces give the opportunity to explore the network without the use of expensive equipment and software. At the same time they are much smaller in volume than an encoded video, and can easily be used in the simulation. Easy videotrace integration into any transmission system forms the basis for the development of hardware and software complex (HSC) based on the *Evalvid* system for assessing the quality of video transmitted over real or simulated communication networks (Klaue, Rathke, & Wolish, 2003).

The HSC modular structure allows for changing the main transmission system as well as codecs at the discretion of the user. This provides a wide range of experimental possibilities. Along with the evaluation of such network QoS parameters as the rate of loss, delay and jitter, assessment of the quality of the video based on the calculation of indicators PSNR and MOS is also possible.

The block diagram of *Evalvid* HSC for assessing the quality of streaming video transmitted in a variety of telecommunication networks is shown in Figure 4. The diagram shows the interaction between modules in the process of transmission of digital video from a source through a network connection to the viewer.

In order to assess video quality, video file data prior to transmission over the network (on the transmit end) and after reception from the network (on the receiving end) are required. The necessary data on the transmit side are: the original unencoded video in YUV format, encoded MPEG-4 format video, as well as time and type of each packet sent to the network.

The following data must be obtained at the receiving end: the reception time and type of each packet received from the network, the encoded video (possibly distorted) in MPEG-4 and the

Figure 4. HSC structure: VP – video transmitter; OT – trace scores; BB – reconstructed video; PSNR – quality estimation

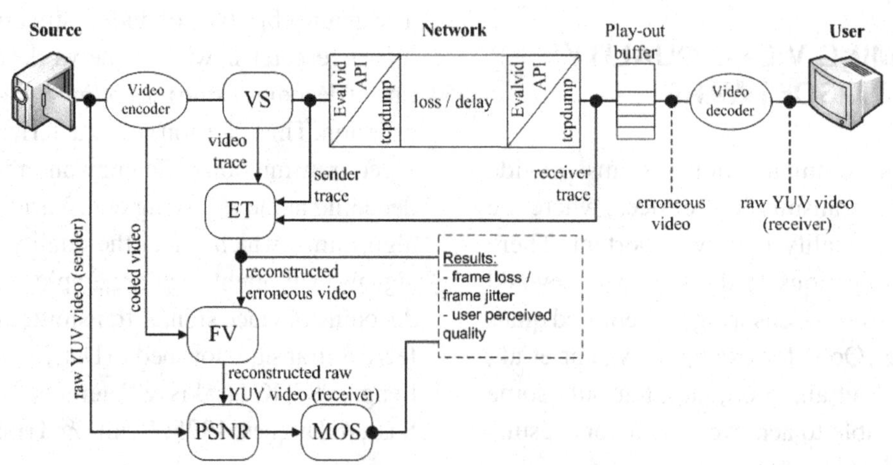

decoded video in YUV for display. Data evaluation is performed by comparing the transmitted information with the received. In practice, uncompressed video can be very large, for this reason, it is advisable to transfer only the additional information in a file with a record receipt time of each packet. It is more convenient than transmitting a full (distorted and converted) video file from the receiving side. Data processing is carried out in three stages as described below:

In the first stage, the time taken to send and receive each packet on both sides as well as the packet type are analyzed. This results in a record of the type of frame and the time elapsed between transmitted and received packets. The distorted video file at the receive end is restored using the originally encoded video file and information about lost packets. Subsequently, the video is decoded for playback to the viewer. Assessment of video quality is done at this stage. Video quality indicators always require a comparison of the received (possibly distorted) video frame and the corresponding source frame. In the case of a total loss of frame in transit, the necessary frame synchronization before and after transmission over the network becomes impossible.

In the second stage, the problem of quality assessment is resolved based on the analysis of information about frame loses. Substituting the last relayed frame for the lost frame restores frame synchronization. This methodology allows for subsequent frame-wise assessment of video quality. At the third stage, the assessment of the quality of decoded video is achieved by means of both the restored and source video files.

The HSC modules interact with the network by using traces containing all the necessary data listed above. Thus, for proper functioning, the HSC requires two traces, the source video and the decoder. The data network can be considered simply as a two-port *black-box* that introduces delay, packet loss, and possibly packet rearrangement. The network was simulated based on the aforementioned assumptions in the NS-2 environment (http://www.isi.edu/nsnam/ns/ns-documentation.html). A more detailed description of the functional modules of the HSC is presented in (Klaue, Rathke, & Wolish, 2003).

2.2. Representation of the Source Files and Video Format

Standard test video in YUV format can be used as initial test video sequences. However, these videos are limited in play time and do not allow for estimating the change in long-term quality of broadcast video, and getting a sufficient amount of experimental data. Thus, with the aid of special software, personal YUV format videos of 30min length and 640x480 resolution with frame rate of 25 frames/sec was recorded. Then the original video file was encoded in format H.264. The encoded video stream is then packaged in an MP4-container for onward transport over the network using the User Datagram Protocol (UDP). After encoding the source video, MP4-file is obtained.

Since it is necessary to evaluate the quality of video transmitted over the network, the need arises to create a spare decoded YUV file from the newly created MPEG layer-4 file, which serves as the control in evaluating the quality of video transmitted over the network, excluding the impact of the codec. It is thus possible to estimate the influence of a wireless network on the received visual video quality, while excluding encoding and decoding losses. For simulation purposes, it is necessary to create a video trace file that contains the following information: frame number, frame type, frame size, and the number of segments in which the frame is divided into packets. This video trace serves as the input to the simulator network, where the sending and reception of video data occurs. As a result of video transmission over the network, it is necessary to obtain transmission trace files and reception trace files, which contain the following packet data: the transmission/reception time, a unique identifier and trace file size. These two traces are used to determine lost packets in the network. In the end, we obtain files of the sent and received packets containing detailed information about the time of sending from the transmitter and the time of reception by the receiver.

2.3. Investigation of Broadband Wireless Access for Streaming Video Using the NS-2 Software

When modeling the wireless communication channel it is necessary to consider many destabilizing factors in the transmission medium, such as the imposition of white Gaussian noise (AWGN), multipath propagation, fading, interference, and many others. One cannot imagine the signal at the receiver end as purely the source signal, undistorted by any effects of the transmission medium. The results and reliability of the model are directly dependent on the construction of the communication channel, hence the need for employing an extremely accurate model, that approximates the real conditions (IEEE 802.16 Broadband Wireless Access Working Group; Deb, S., Jaiswal, S., Nagaraj, K., 2008). An accurate model may be obtained on the example of an extensive network of WiMAX IEEE 802.16e standard with the base and subscriber stations; the general scheme of such connections is shown in Figure 5.

Network Simulator 2 (NS-2) can be used for modeling errors arising in the real network, it allows for providing the desired level of simulation and obtaining the required performance characteristics of the network being modeled. NS-2 is distributed as Free Open Source code Software (FOSS). This category of software is distributed for free of charge without usage restrictions on

Figure 5. Architecture of a WiMAX broadband network

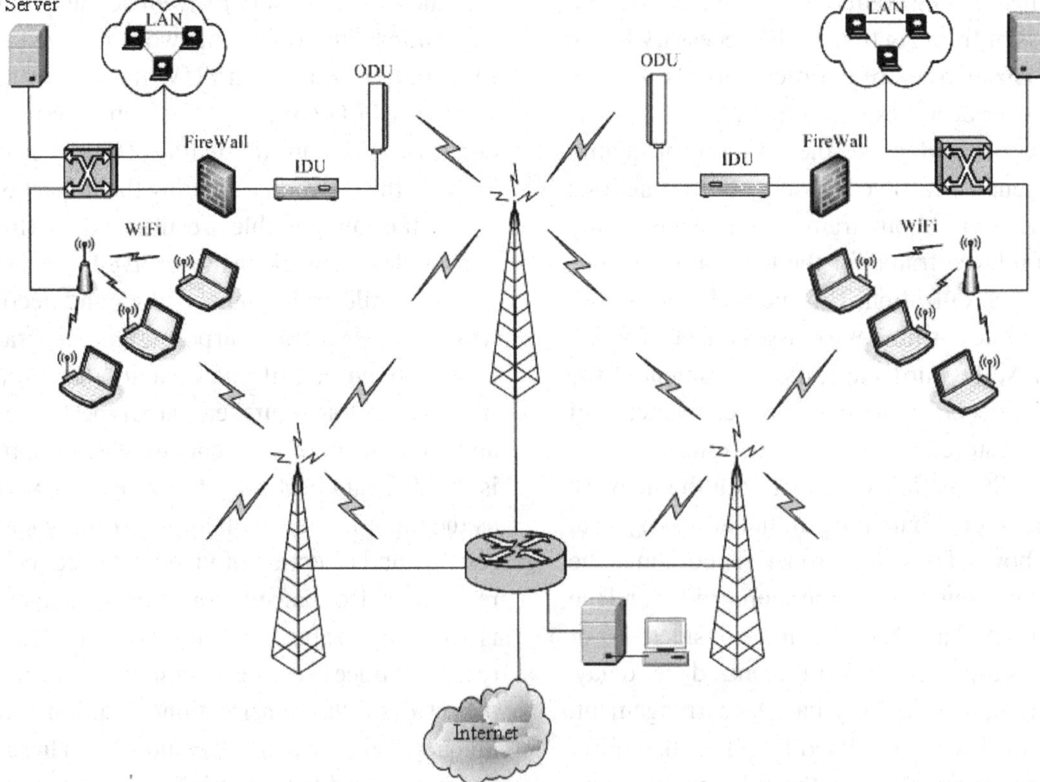

modification and distribution by third parties. Thus, NS-2 is by far the leader in comparison with similar products cost wise. For this reason, its updates are distributed free of charge as well as new libraries, protocols, e.t.c.

Another no less remarkable property of a FOSS is the possibility of modifying the core software and flexibility of configuration in accordance with the requirements of a particular user. NS-2 satisfies the requirements of flexible process modeling, since the language incorporates the ready scripts and C++ programming language, with which modeling objects such as nodes, channels, background traffic generators, etc. are described, parameterized from actual measurements. Figure 6 presents the functional interaction diagram of the SHC with NS-2.

The NS-2 software with several incorporated agents is used to simulate the network. *MyTrafficTrace* agent is used to calculate the type and size of the video-trace frame. In addition, this agent breaks the video into packets and sends them to the UDP in due course, according to user defined simulation settings.

MyUDP: in essence is an agent of the UDP. This agent writes each packet transmission time, packet ID, size and payload to file sent by the trace. *MyUDP* agent function is similarly to those of TCP-dump or Win-dump on real networks.

MyUDPSink agent: this is the object that receives packets of fragmented frames sent by MyUDP. This agent records the time, packet ID, packet size and payload of each received packet in the receiver trace file.

As a result of video transmission over UDP transmission and reception trace files are obtained. These two traces are used to determine the lost packets on the network. In real network scenario, the receiver trace is formed using a network analysis tool such as TCP-dump (http://www.tcpdump.org) or Win-dump (http://www.windump.polito.it). If the network is simulated, the simulation receiver object creates this file. Trace files contain complete information on the transfer of video over a network, necessary for further evaluation SHC. The VI module allows for generating traces for different video with different packet sizes, which can then be transmitted to the network (or simulator). The networking introduces delay and possibly loss and reordering of packets. An example of wideband wireless access IEEE 802.16 standard simulation in NS-2 software package is shown in Figure 7.

A feature of the presented simulation of wireless networks is the evaluation of the transmission

Figure 6. Interaction of SHC with NS-2

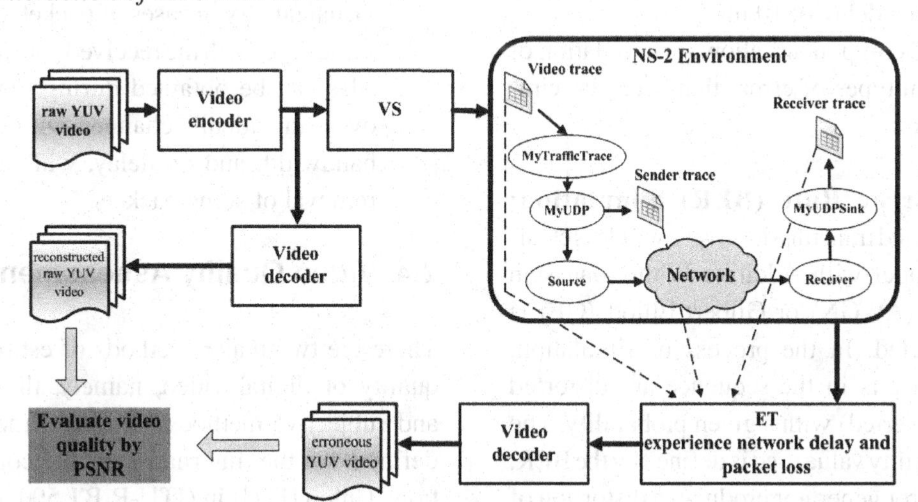

Figure 7. IEEE 802.16 network topology

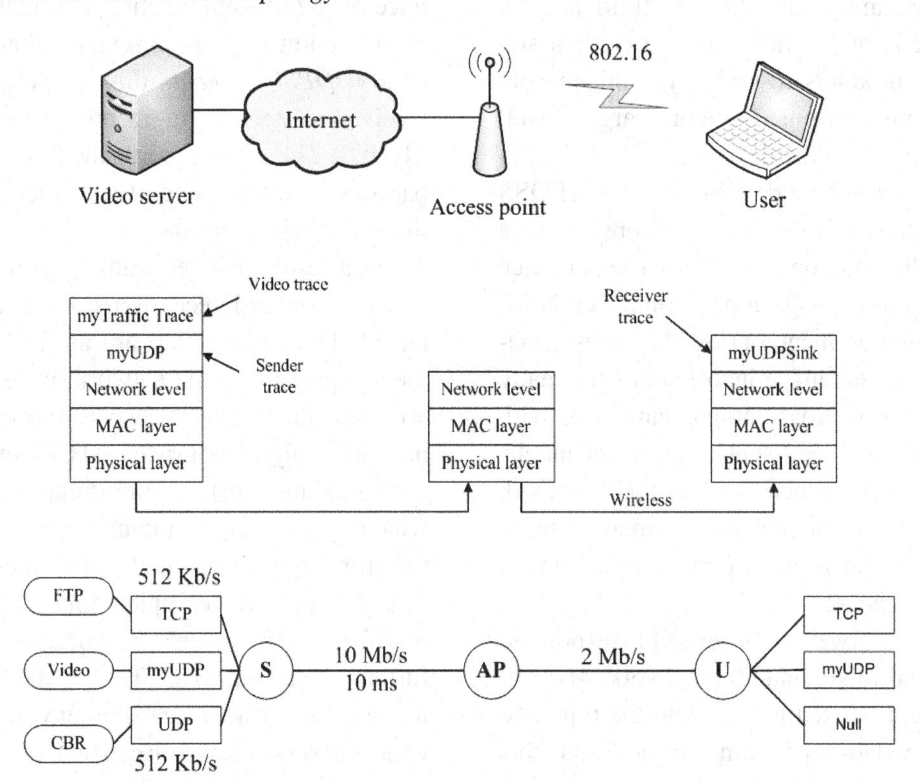

of video streams with (and without) the effect of background traffic. Two types of background traffic; FTP and CBR are employed. FTP traffic is transmitted over TCP protocol at a data transfer rate of 512 kbps. CBR traffic is sent over UDP protocol at a transfer rate of 256 kbps. Bandwidth between the video server and base station equals 2 Mbps with a delay of 10 ms.

The SHC components allow for simulation of the two main types of errors that occur in wireless networks:

1. **Bit Error Rate (BER) Simulation:** Simulated transmission over a wireless channel model with Additive White Gaussian Noise (AWGN) or Gilbert-Elliott (GE) is conducted. In the process of simulation, certain bits in the sequence are distorted (i.e. inverted) with a given probability. The probability value used is defined by the BER. The error generator produces a distortion of the transmit trace file with a given probability and error distribution model. The receiver trace file is thus generated indicating the lost packets.
2. **Packet Error Simulation:** The UDP packets can be manually deleted from the received trace file. This allows for the observation of codec functionality and analysis of change in visual quality in cases of packet loss. At the same time, both the received and undistorted files can be obtained during transmission over an "ideal" channel with unlimited bandwidth and no delay, with subsequent removal of some packets.

2.4. Video Quality Assessment

There are two major methods of estimating the quality of digital video, namely, the objective and subjective methods. Objective methods are defined by the International Telecommunications Union (ITU) in (ITU-R BT.500-11), ANSI in (T1.801.01/02, 1996) and the Motion Picture

Expert Group (MPEG) in (ISO-IEC/JTC1/SC29/WG11, 1996). Subjective quality assessment is always based on viewer impression. It is extremely costly, very time consuming and requires specialized equipment. Traditionally, subjective video quality is determined by expert assessment and calculation of the average Mean opinion Score (MOS), which is assigned a value from 1 to 5 on the ITU scale as prescribed in (ITU P.800; Atayero, 2000), where 1 and 5 represent worst and best received video quality respectively (Table 4).

Traditional signal distortion measures for system quality determination employ the absolute difference between original and processed signal. Objective video quality is usually measured using mean-square error (MSE) and peak signal to noise ratio PSNR, which is calculated from the RMSE and is a logarithmic measure of its inverse. MSE and its derivative indicator PSNR are the traditional metrics that allow for comparing any two images. RMSE can be called a measure of "distortion" and PSNR that of "quality".In comparison with other objective indicators, PSNR can be easily calculated and is best understood by most users.However, both measures do not correlate with the subjective quality of the reconstructed image and do not properly reflect the minute deteriorations in intensity. Equation (1) (see Box 2) is the definition of PSNR between the luminance component Y of source (S) and received (D) image.

Based on the evaluation of PSNR, MOS estimate can be calculated, and the percentage of frames with worse MOS than the that of the original video. Table 4 shows the correspondence of PSNR with the MOS scale.

2.4.1. Estimating PSNR Value

PSNR is the main indicator of quality, which cannot be calculated, if two images are equivalent, i.e. standard error is zero. This is resolved by computing the PSNR between the original and the received video files. This ensures that the difference between the images will always exist, since all modern video codecs are lossy. It is possible to use other indicators, and software modules instead of PSNR/MOS, for example (Berts and Persson,1998). Evaluation of objective video in the HSC module is done by the PSNR module. The result will be the values of PSNR, obtained from formula (1) between the original and distorted frames. Standard deviation of quality on average PSNR value is gotten from (2)

Table 4. PSNR-MOS correspondence

PSNR, dB	MOS,%	ITU Scale Quality	The Deterioration of the Image
> 37	5	Excellent	Not perceptible
31 - 37	4	Good	Perceptible, but not annoying
25 - 31	3	Satisfactory	Slightly irritating
20 - 25	2	Poor	Irritating
< 20	A	Very poor	Annoying

Box 2.

$$PSNR = 20log_{10}\left[\frac{V_{peak}}{\sqrt{\frac{1}{N_{col}N_{row}}\sum_{i=0}^{N_{col}}\sum_{j=0}^{N_{row}}\left[Y_S\left(n,i,j\right)-Y_D\left(n,i,j\right)\right]^2}}\right]dB \quad (1)$$

$$S'_{PSNR} = \sqrt{\frac{1}{N-1}\sum_{n=0}^{N-1}\left(PSNR_n - \overline{PSNR'}\right)^2} \quad (2)$$

The values of PSNR cannot be totally predicted even with the full knowledge of experimental conditions, under which measurement are made. One can only indicate the likelihood of having certain values or the interval of the probable occurrence. However, knowing the probability distribution of this quantity, one can draw conclusions on its properties and characteristics. Thus it is possible to calculate the distribution of PSNR values, so that the quality of transmitted images can be evaluated statistically. Along with the evaluation of other network QoS parameters such as the rate of loss, delay and jitter. The HSC allows us to analyze statistical data under different conditions of video transmission, such as the probability density function, the expectation and variance. The mathematical expectation of PSNR value is given by (3)

$$M = \frac{1}{n}\sum_{i=1}^{n} PSNR_i \quad (3)$$

and the variance is gotten from (4)

$$\sigma^2 = \frac{1}{n-1}\sum_{i=1}^{n}\left(PSNR_i - M\right)^2 \quad (4)$$

where n - number of frames in video sequence.

The probability density is described by Equation (5)

$$W\left(PSNR\right) = N\left(M, \sigma^2\right) + \Delta \quad (5)$$

The distribution function is given by (6)

$$F\left(PSNR\right) = P\left(PSNR_i \leq X_{???}\right) \quad (6)$$

2.4.2. MOS Assessment of Video Quality

The mean opinion score subjective assessment of video quality is evaluated in terms of PSNR. The video quality is determined by computing the average MOS, having a value in the range from 1 to 5 (ITU scale), where 1 corresponds to the worst, and 5 the best video quality according to Table 1. Evaluation of the subjective quality of the video in the HSC is done by the MOS module. As a result a file with a frame by frame MOS value is generated. It is possible to calculate the percentage of frames with MOS values worse than that of the original video based on PSNR estimates. Quality of user experience (user satisfaction) is calculated on the basis of MOS values obtained in the HSC. Thus, network performance can be expressed in terms of user perceived reception quality. For normalization of the PSNR curve across MOS scale, a scale factor a and a shift factor b are required. The optimal scale and shift are defined by Equations (7) and (8) respectively.

$$a = \frac{CoV_{MOS,PSNR}}{\sigma^2_{PSNR}} \quad (7)$$

$$b = \mu_{MOS} - a\mu_{PSNR} \quad (8)$$

where $CoV_{MOS,PSNR}$ – covariance between PSNR and MOS, μ_{PSNR} and μ_{MOS} – average PSNR and MOS, respectively, σ^2_{PSNR} – PSNR variance.

Thus, we can obtain an expression for the evaluation of MOS based on the PSNR (9):

$$MOS_{PSNR} = a * PSNR + b \quad (9)$$

Thus, the quality of streaming video transmitted over any random network is assessed based on the results of the software-hardware complex, by calculating the following quality indicators: PSNR, MSE, and MOS. Assessment of quality of user experience for streaming video is authentic for different network simulations.

3. EFFECT OF NOISE STABILITY ON THE QUALITY OF H.264/AVC STANDARD STREAMING VIDEO

The most important QoS parameters for wireless networks include the probability of bit error occurrence i.e. Bit Error Rate (BER) and that of packet error occurence Packet Error Rate (PER). Fading channels are not capable of simulating single packet loss as well as single-bit errors. Typically, error occurrence are often long-term in nature, since a high probability of packet loss occurs in specific periods of data transmission, such as in the case of poor propagation. Attenuation of the transmitted signal leads to clustering (grouping or packetization) of errors. A group of erroneous packets is a sequence of packets either totally lost in transit (i.e. not received) or received with transmission errors incurred over a communications channel in a stipulated time frame. In this regard, the notion of the length of error burst i.e. Burst Error Length (BEL) was introduced in (Cornaglia and Spini, 1996; Lemmon, 2002). The length of a group of errors is defined as the number of erroneous packets from the very first to the last (inclusively) in a particular group of errors.

Due to the constant changing in the location of sources of transmission and reception of broadband communication systems in urban settings, parts of the information sequence (packet groups) do not reach the subscribers, which leads to distortion of the video signal or any other information transmitted. Markov processes with the necessary number of states describe the mechanism of transmission of information sufficiently well. This is necessary for the analysis of network problems encountered in the process of packet transmission of video. The model parameters allow for the estimation of the quality of transmitted video and the statistical parameters of the network.

3.1. Experimental Studies of the Quality of H.264/AVC Video Standard

In order to assess the impact subscriber mobility, a WiMAX IEEE 802.16e standard network was deployed with the use of a base and subscriber stations. The Base Station (BS) was installed on the roof of a 23-story building. Cross-polarized antenna with a gain of 9 dBi and beam width 90 degrees were used. Antenna directional azimuth was 300^0. The Mobile Subscriber Station (MSS) was installed in a car. Two omni-directional antennas with a gain of 2 dBi were installed on the roof of a car. Images were recorded from a camera carried in a moving car on a laptop and simultaneously broadcast to a remote computer through the WiMAX network. The network architecture of the WiMAX broadband network and the overall connectivity diagram is shown in Figure 8.

The average vehicle speed was 60 kmph. Maximum distance from the BC was equal to 950 m. In most of the route between BC and AC lacked direct line of sight, so the main causes of interference in the broadcast were a reflection, diffraction, scattering, etc. The route of the vehicle and the location of the BS shown in Figure 9.

The following equipments were used for setting up the WiMAX network and subsequent video broadcast:

- **The base station and its specifications:** *RuggedMAX*™ WiN7000|Specifications: operational frequency bands – 1350... 1400 MHz, OFDMA, compression method – Time Division Duplex TDD, the maximum transmit power – 36 dBm);
- **The user station and its specifications:** *RuggedMAX*™ WiN5100|Specifications: operational frequency bands – 1350... 1400 MHz, OFDMA, compression method –

Figure 8. WiMAX broadband network architecture

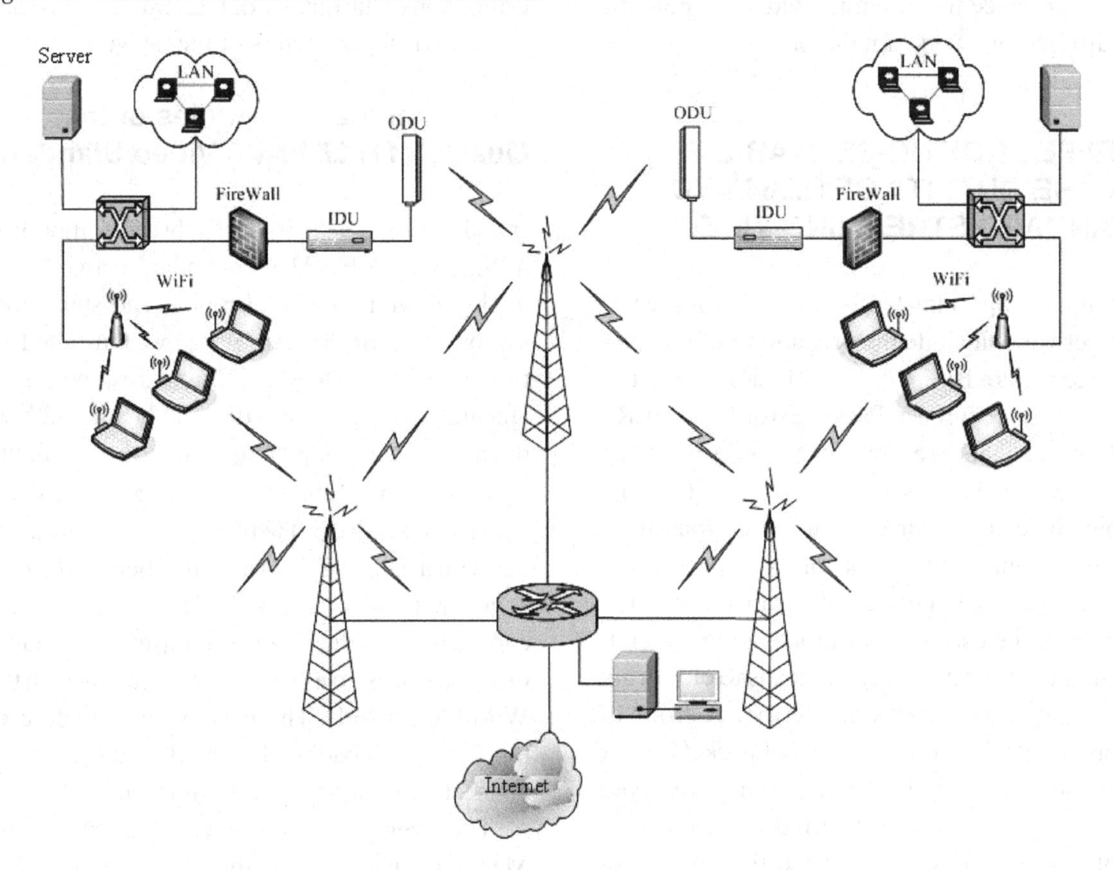

Time Division Duplex TDD, the maximum transmit power – 23 dBm);

- DELL Latitude D430 laptop and a Logitech QuickCam Pro 9000 webcam.

The video broadcast lasted for 30 minutes with the following parameters:

- **Format:** mp4;
- Codec H.264;
- **Constant bitrate:** 1150 kbps;
- **Frame rate:** 25fps;
- Resolution of 640x480;
- **GOP Type:** IBBPBBPBB.

The streaming server *DarwinStreamingServer* was used for broadcasting together with Apple Inc. QuickTime Player (http://www.apple.com). Information about the transmitted and received network packets were processed using the *Wireshark* protocol analyzer (http://www.wireshark.org). The VirtualDub program (http://www.virtualdub.org) was used for synchronizing both the sent and received video sequences. The *Wireshark* software was used to compute the video protocols used during broadcast as well as their statistical parameters (see Figure 10).

A deterioration in the quality of transmitted video was observed as a result of interference. Quality assessment was performed by means of the quality indicators and specifically PSNR and MOS, calculated using the HSC tools. Processing of the RTP-packet files sent and received during video transmission over the WiMAX network showed that a total of 281,720 pieces of RTP-packets was exchanged, of which 2,590 (0.919%)

Figure 9. Base station and mobile subscriber station location in Moscow

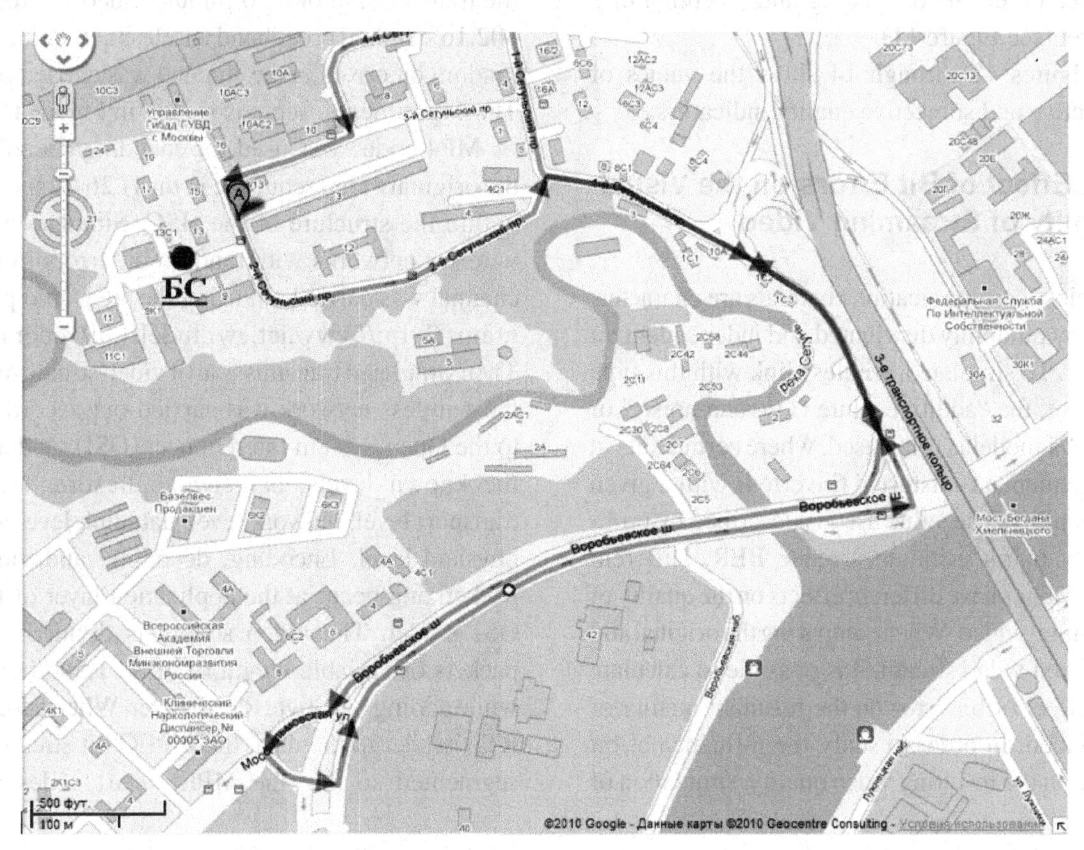

Figure 10. Statistical data of video protocols involved in the broadcast

Protocol	% Packets	Packets	Bytes	Mbit/s	End Packets	End Bytes	End Mbit/s
Frame	100,00 %	320572	120281876	0,530	0	0	0,000
Ethernet	100,00 %	320572	120281876	0,530	0	0	0,000
Internet Protocol	100,00 %	320572	120281876	0,530	0	0	0,000
Transmission Control Protocol	0,01 %	22	6139	0,000	11	2243	0,000
Real Time Streaming Protocol	0,00 %	11	3896	0,000	11	3896	0,000
User Datagram Protocol	99,99 %	320550	120275737	0,530	0	0	0,000
Real-Time Transport Protocol	87,88 %	281720	117658157	0,519	281720	117658157	0,519
Real-time Transport Control Protocol	12,11 %	38830	2617580	0,012	38222	2506100	0,011
Real-time Transport Control Protocol	0,19 %	608	111480	0,000	0	0	0,000
Real-time Transport Control Protocol	0,19 %	608	111480	0,000	608	111480	0,000

was missing. Information about the parameters of the video streams is presented in Figure 11. This illustration shows the distribution of RTP-packets in time, where the white areas (Figure 11b) represents the received packets, while the black region corresponds to lost packets. Real-time estimation of objective video quality obtained at the communication channel output was calculated using the equation (1) (shown on Figure 11a). The delay was calculated as the difference between the time of sending and reception of a packet (see Figure 11).

Figures 12 through 14 show the values of objective and subjective quality indicators.

3.2. Effect of Bit Errors on the Visual Quality of Streaming Video

Wireless communication channels are characterized by randomly distributed and independent bit errors. To simulate a wireless link with this type of error, the "additive white Gaussian noise," or AWGN model is often used, where certain bits in the sequence is distorted (inverted) with a given probability. The value used is described by probability of bit error occurrence BER. Different BER values have different effects on the quality of streaming video. When comparing the original and distorted video stream, it is possible to calculate the effect of bit error on the resultant quality of the video. In order to study the influence of bit error on the resulting video quality, simulation of the transmission of a 30-minute video via IEEE 802.16 standard broadband wireless network with random bit errors in the channel was carried out. The experimental setup is shown in Figure 15.

MP4 codec was used for encoding/decoding the original video sequence in the H.264 standard within the structure of the HSC. Simulation of wireless networks with random bit errors in the channel was carried out using the VCDemo program (http://www.ict.ewi.tudelft.nl/vcdemo). Then simulated transmission of video stream over the wireless network was carried out according to the Open System Interconnect (OSI) model at the known levels, namely: application level, transport level, network level, data link level and physical level. Encoding, decoding, and video packetizing occur at the application layer of the OSI model. The video stream is divided into packets of variable length of up to 1,500 bytes, while adding a 12-byte RTP header. When adding RTP header to the data, the MPEG bit stream is segmented so that the MPEG start codes are

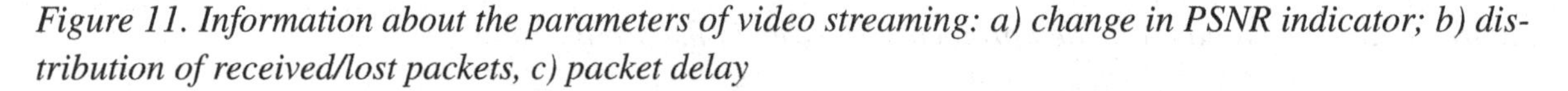

Figure 11. Information about the parameters of video streaming: a) change in PSNR indicator; b) distribution of received/lost packets, c) packet delay

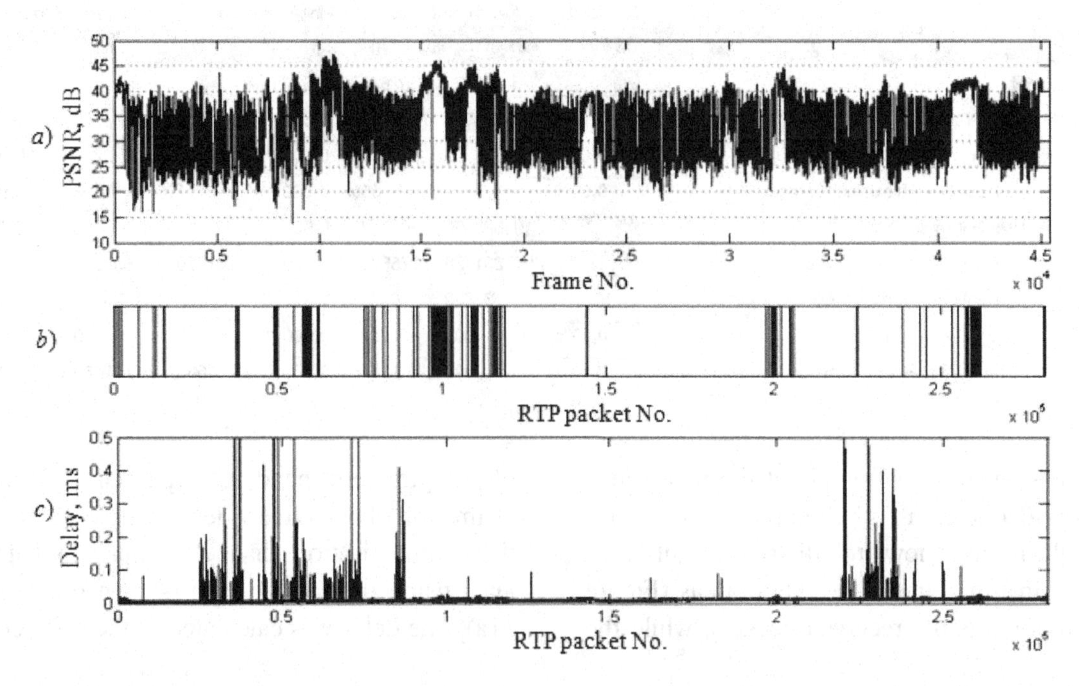

Figure 12. Histogram indicator PSNR for video broadcasting

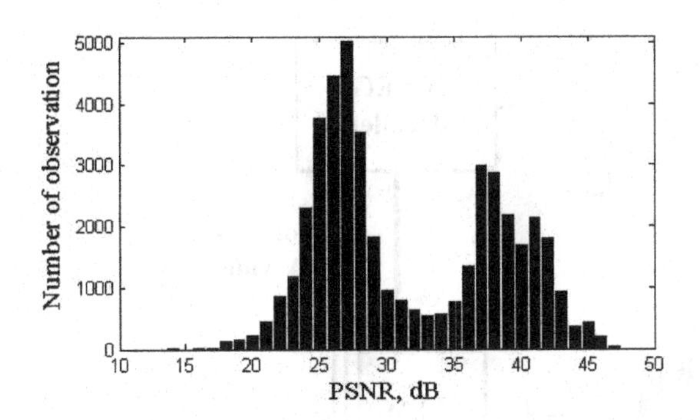

Figure 13. The distribution function of PSNR measure for broadcasting video

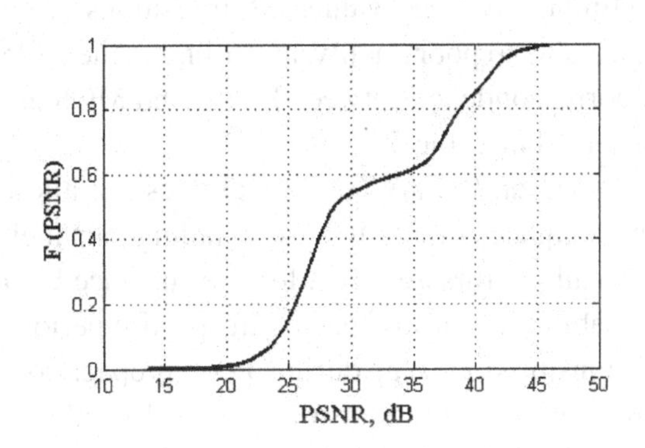

Figure 14. Gradation of MOS quality value for broadcast video

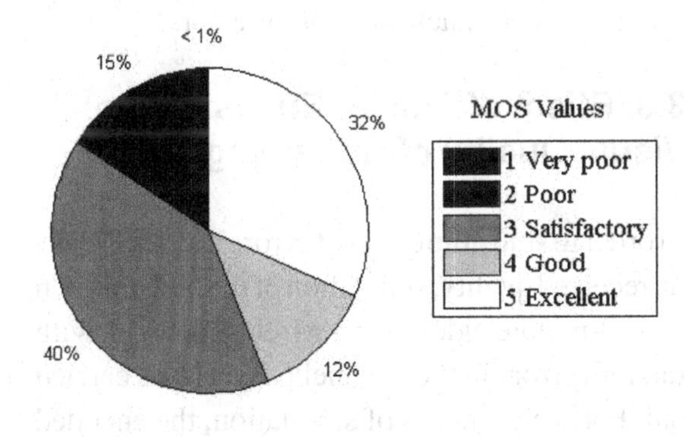

contained in the beginning of the MPEG data packets. The UDP protocol is modeled at the transport layer, respectively, adding a header and a checksum (8 bytes). Subsequently, a 20-byte IP header is added at the network layer. IEEE 802.16 protocol is modeled at the link layer of communication. The channel transmission rate is set to 20 MB/s. Finally, the simulation of random bit error in the channel (Gaussian noise) with a given BER probability is done at the physical layer. For modeling purposes, the encoded video stream was split into RTP/UDP–packets using the HSC tools. Quality assessment was performed by means of PSNR and MOS indicators, calculated using the tools of the HSC. The standard deviation of quality on average PSNR value was gotten from Formula (2). Figure 16 shows the effect of BER indicator on the quality of streaming video.

BER ranges are shown, within which the received video quality is maximal, i.e. equal to the original, and minimal i.e. with maximum difference from the original. It is shown that at $BER \leq 3 \times 10^{-5}$ error does not affect the visual quality and can be easily eliminated using decoders and existing methods of protection against errors. Further changes in quality is of step (sequential) nature and decreases with increasing BER (as expected). At $BER = 4 \times 10^{-3}$ packet loss reaches its maximum value and represents more than 99.9% of the total.

Analyzing the results of streaming video over a simulated wireless network with different values of BER, one can draw the following conclusions:

1. Simulating a wireless channel using AWGN model, and additive, bit errors with a value of $BER \leq 3 \times 10^{-5}$ does not affect the quality of the video. However, when $BER \geq 4 \times 10^{-3}$ packet loss in the network reaches its maximum value ≥ 99,9%.
2. Objectively, excellent quality of video transmission over a channel can be guaranteed for all bit error probabilities less than 1×10^{-4}, good quality is in the range of $10^{-4} to 4 \times 10^{-4}$, satisfactory quality is in the range of $4 \times 10^{-4} to 8 \times 10^{-4}$, poor qual-

Figure 15. Block diagram of the experiment

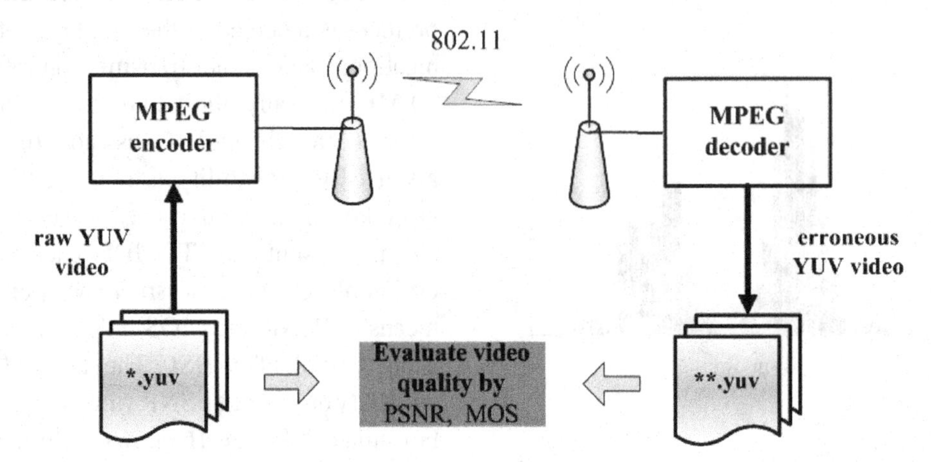

ity is in the range of $8 \times 10^{-4} to 10^{-3}$, while very bad quality is for any $BER > 1 \times 10^{-3}$.

3. The average broadcast video quality on a real wireless network prone to distortion (e.g., when driving in the city) is comparable to the simulation of a AWGN model wireless channel with at $BER = 5 \times 10^{-4}$.
4. Histograms of the distribution of PSNR values both for the simulation, and during broadcast on a real network, in general, have a *twin-peak* form. One of the peaks characterizes the PSNR value of video in the absence of errors (the decoder can correct the bit errors when they are present in a small number in the frame). The second represents the maximum PSNR deterioration due to the large number of distorted video frames in moments of fading (the decoder is unable to fix a large number of bit errors). As the number of errors increases, this maximum increases commensurately with a reduction in the second. During transmission, depending on the error level, the value of a maximum increases. If the errors in the communication channel can be neglected, PSNR distribution has only one maximum.

Empirical BER values of transitions from acceptable to poor quality, according to the table of correspondence between PSNR and MOS are presented in Table 5.

However, the AWGN model does not allow for adequate simulation of a fading channel. Typically, errors are often long term, since high probability of bit loss occurs in specific periods of transmission, e.g. during poor propagation. Attenuation of the transmitted signal results in packetizing (grouping) of errors. Another cause of error grouping can be physical defects of, and failures inherent in the information storage system. When using VLC, bit error occurrence results in group errors or packetization of errors.

3.3. Effect of Packet Errors on the Visual Quality of Streaming Video

In order to study the effect of errors in data packets on received quality, simulation of the transmission of a 30-minute video over a wireless network with random errors in the channel packets was carried out. For the purposes of simulation, the encoded video stream was split into RTP/UDP-packets using the HSC tools. Simulation of packet errors during transmission over a wireless channel was done by removing packets from the receive trace

Figure 16. Values of video sequence quality indicators for different values of wireless channel BER: a) PSNR value distribution histogram; b) PSNR value distribution histogram for certain values of BER; c) quality deviation from average PSNR value; d) quality gradation for MOS values

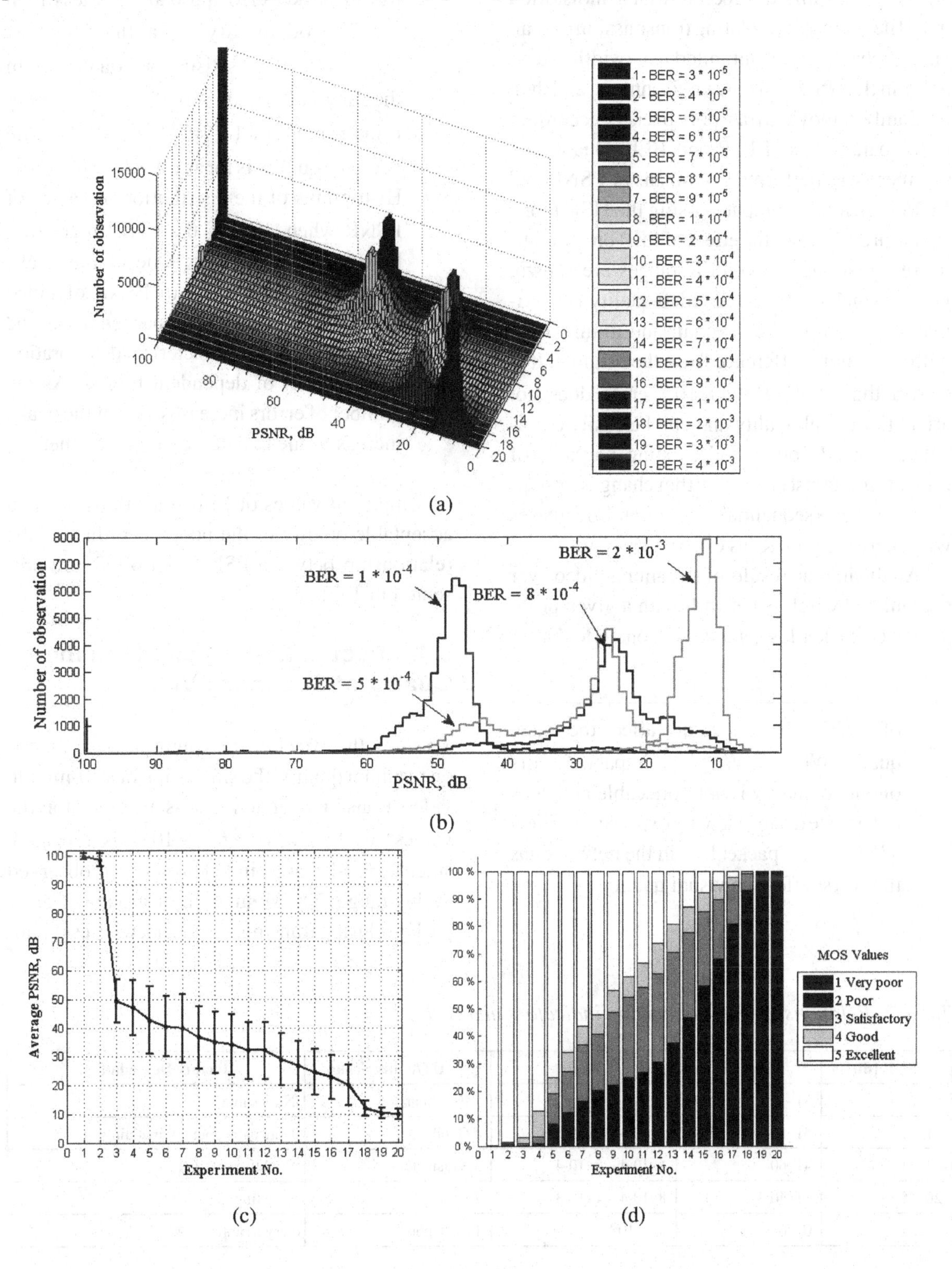

file. This made it possible to investigate and analyze changes in visual quality during packet loss. At the same time the received and undistorted trace file was obtained during transmission over an "ideal" channel with unlimited bandwidth and no delay in the NS-2 software environment, and then randomly removing transport packets according to the parameters of PER and BEL. Quality assessment was performed by means of PSNR and MOS indicators, computed using the HSC tools.

Figure 17 shows the effect of PER on the quality of streaming video. PER ranges are shown, within which the received video quality is maximal, i.e. equal to the original, and minimal i.e. with maximum difference from the original. It is shown that at $PER \leq 1 \times 10^{-4}$ error does not affect the visual quality and can be easily eliminated using decoders and existing methods of protection against errors. Further changes in quality is of step (sequential) nature and decreases with increasing PER (as expected).

Analyzing the results of streaming video over a simulated wireless network with a given probability of packet loss, we safely conclude that:

1. In simulation of a wireless network, a value of $PER \leq 10^{-4}$ does not affect the video quality. When $PER \leq 10^{-3}$ impact of errors on video quality is not noticeable and does not irritate during viewing experience. When $PER \geq 0.1$, packet loss in the network has the worst effect on visual quality.
2. Objectively, excellent quality of video transmission over a channel can be guaranteed for all packet error probabilities less than 10^{-3}, good quality is in the range of $10^{-3}\, to 3 \times 10^{-3}$, satisfactory quality is in the range of $3 \times 10^{-3}\, to 10^{-2}$, poor quality is in the range of $1 \times 10^{-2}\, to 5 \times 10^{-2}$, while very bad quality is for any $PER > 5 \times 10^{-2}$.
3. Histograms of the distribution of values of PSNR when $PER \leq 6 \times 10^{-4}$, in general, have a bimodal shape. One of the peaks characterizes the value of PSNR of video stream distorted due to packet loss. The second maximum characterizes deterioration in the PSNR of dependent frames. As the number of errors increases, one of the peaks increases due to a decrease in the other.

Empirical values of PER transitions from an acceptable quality to the poor, according to the relationship between PSNR and MOS, are presented in Table 6.

3.4. Effect of Errors Length on the Quality of Streaming Video

To study the effect of the length of error groups on resultant quality, the simulation of a 30-minute video transfer over a wireless network for the values of $PER of 10^{-3}\, to 5 \times 10^{-2}$ is repeated, since a visual change in video quality is observed at this range. The simulation of groups of error packets during transmission over a wireless chan-

Table 5. Relationship between quality indicators and BER

PSNR [dB]	MOS [%]	BER	ITU Quality Scale	Picture Degradation
> 37	81–100	< 1x10^{-4}	5 Excellent	Noticeable
31–37	61–80	1x10-4 – 4x10-4	4 Good	Noticeable, but not irritating
25–31	41–60	4x10-4 – 8x10-4	3 Satisfactory	Slightly irritating
20–35	21–40	8x10-4 – 1x10-3	2 Poor	Irritating
< 20	0–20	> 1x10^{-3}	1 Very poor	very irritating

Figure 17. Values of video sequence quality indicators for different values of wireless channel PER: a) PSNR value distribution histogram; b) PSNR value distribution histogram for certain values of PER; c) quality deviation from average PSNR value; d) quality gradation for MOS values

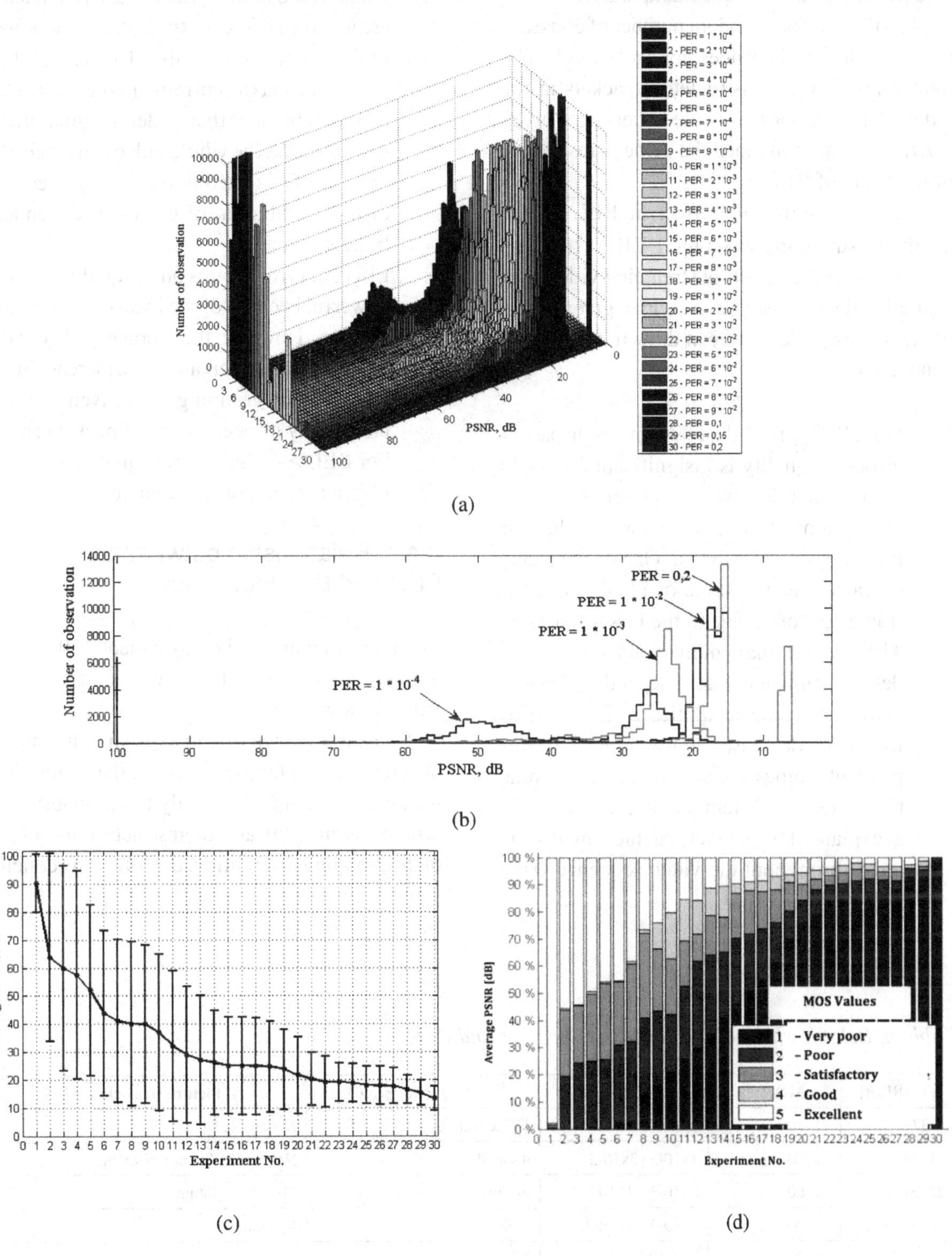

nel was done by means of random deletion of packet groups from the receive trace file with a given BEL. For this particular example $BEL = 100$ implies that the total random number of consecutively deleted packets does not exceed 100. The total sum of erroneous (deleted) packets in the video sequence for the whole experiment given $PER = const.$ remained the same, irrespective of the value of BEL.

Figure 18 shows the effect of BEL on the quality of streaming video for $\text{PER} = 10^{-3}$.

Analyzing the results of streaming video over a simulated wireless network with a given group of erroneous packets we can draw the following conclusions:

1. For $PER \leq 10^{-3}$ the effect of single packet errors on quality is insignificant and does not irritate the viewing experience.
2. Histograms of the distribution of values of PSNR have two maxima. One of the peaks characterizes the value of PSNR of video frames distorted due to the loss of packets. The second maximum characterizes the deterioration of PSNR of dependent frames. With increasing quantities BEL is one of the peaks decreases as the number of dependent frames are also reduced, whereas the second peak remains unchanged. This is explained by the fact that the single scattered throughout the video sequence error number of distorted frames is large due to error propagation to dependent frames.
3. An increase in the BEL value leads to a decrease in one of the maxima, since the number of dependent frames also decreases, while the second maximum remains the same. This is due to the fact that under singular errors spread across the whole video sequence, the number of distorted frames is large because of the distribution of errors on dependent frames.
4. Effect of error groups on the quality is more powerful because of the local concentration of errors. However, the average quality of the video sequence increases with increase in the length of the grouping for a given value of probability of occurrence of packet errors.
5. For BEL ≥ 60 the average quality is almost identical to the original video.

3.4.1. Relationship between the PER and BEL Indicators

The average quality of the experimental 30-minute video sequence for different values of PER and BEL is shown in Figure 19.

Thus, it is shown that in assessing the impact of erroneous packets received on the quality it is necessary to analyze not only the probability of error occurence, but also their structure and length of the grouping. In addition, the following conclusions can be drawn:

Table 6. Relationship between quality indicators and PER

PSNR[dB]	MOS[%]	PER	ITU Quality Scale	Picture Degradation
> 37	81–100	< $1x10^{-4}$	5-Excellent	Noticeable
31–37	61–80	1x10-3– 3x10-3	4-Good	Noticeable, but not irritating
25–31	41–60	3x10-3 – 1x10-2	3-Satisfactory	Slightly irritating
20–35	21–40	1x10-2 – 5x10-2	2-Poor	Irritating
< 20	0–20	> $5x10^{-2}$	1-Very poor	Very irritating

Figure 18. Values of video sequence quality indicators for $PER = 10^{-3}$ and varying values of wireless channel BEL: a) PSNR value distribution histogram; b) PSNR value and RTP/UDP packet distribution (black spaces correspond to lost packets) for certain values of BEL; c) quality deviation from average PSNR value; d) quality gradation for MOS values

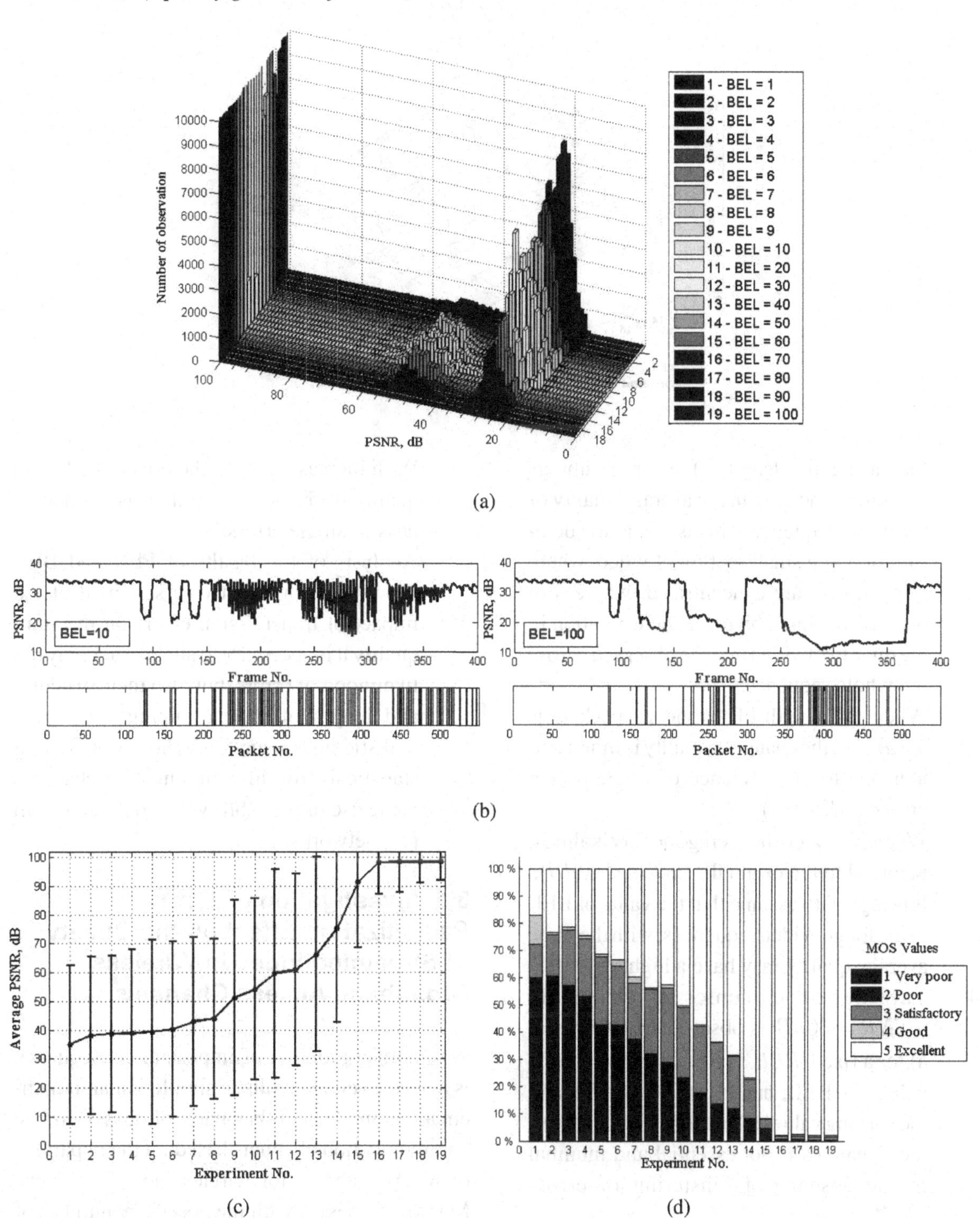

Figure 19. The values of video sequence quality indicators at $PER = 10^{-3}$ and different values of BEL for the wireless channel

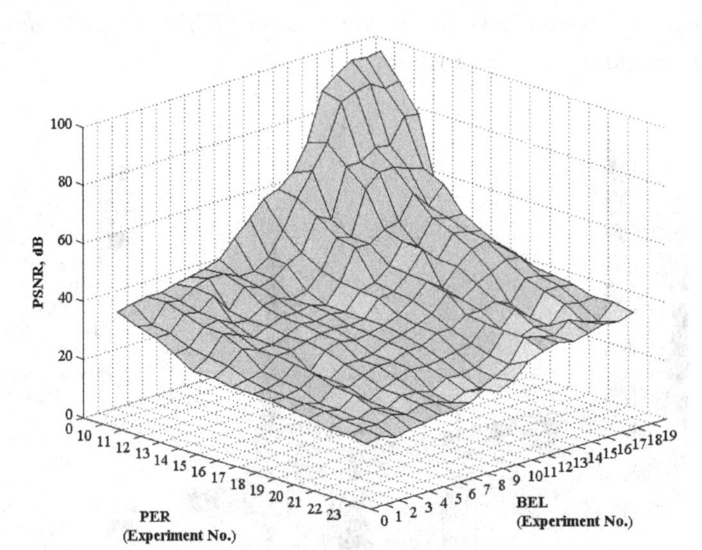

1. Increasing the length of error groupings leads to an increase in the average quality of the video sequence. This is due to the deterioration of a small section of video, where error groups are concentrated, whereas in the case of single bit errors deterioration in the quality of video may be observed across the whole sequence;
2. When the length of erroneous packets is $BEL \leq 6$ the change in quality is minor and identical to the influence of single packet errors $(BEL = 1)$;
3. When BEL ≥ 60 the average quality is almost identical to the original $(PSNR < 90dB)$. It is logical to assume that the value of BEL in the longer video sequences, with the same average quality may have a higher value;
4. The highest dynamics of change in $PSNR = 60dB$ is observed in two cases: a) for a fixed $PER = 10^{-3}$ and the variable values of BEL; and b) at $BEL \geq 80$ and the varying values of the PER. In other cases, the dynamics is not essential and minimal in the absence of clustering of errors $(BEL = 1)$;
5. With increasing PER, the effect of BEL on quality decreases due to increase in denseness of single errors;
6. Analysis of the results of PER and BEL shows that for effective assessment of the impact of transmission errors on resultant quality it is necessary to analyze not only the likelihood of errors, but also their structure and length of their grouping. The most realistic and accurate method of modeling statistical errors in communication channels is the use of probability data obtained from real networks.

3.5. Investigation of Error Packetization Effect on the Quality of Streaming Video in Wireless Broadband Access Channels

A scientific problem of important consequence is a need to create realistic simulation and mathematical models of behavior of losses in the communication channels based on the apparatus of Markov chains for wireless access systems. Markov processes with the necessary number of states sufficiently well describe the mechanism of transmission of information, the knowledge of which is necessary to analyze network problems during packet video transmission. The model parameters allow for determining the quality of transmitted video as well as the statistical parameters of the network. A model decscribing the length of error intervals and error-free reception for streaming video transmission was developed based on the experimental data obtained as a result of streaming video from a moving source on WiMAX network. Based on the graph of packet loss distribution over time (Figure 3.3, *b*), an array was formed in which the lost packet corresponds to a logic zero (0) and received packet corresponds to a logic unit (1). The original array was split into two, one of which contains information about the lost packets and the other contains information about the received packets. The formation of arrays was carried out in accordance with the procedure shown in Figure 20.

3.5.1. Markov Model for Describing the Experimental Data

In accordance with the method presented in (ITU P.800), the available raw data file was divided into two parts, each of which separately contains the duration of ON periods and OFF periods. Variables $y_a[n]$ fall under the ON periods, while variables $y_n[n]$ fall under the OFF peroids.

An approximation of the Distribution Function (DF) of real processes is done. Equation (10) is used for approximating the DF OFF function.

$$F^*(k) = A_i \sum_{i=1}^{3} e^{-\alpha_i k} \quad (10)$$

By using the method of least squares we find the unknown coefficients of the approximation for the expression (10) as presented in Table 7.

Substituting the coefficient values obtained and given in Table 7 into Equation (10), we obtain the approximation of the original additional distribution of the length of OFF periods as equation (11) (see Box 3).

Equation (12) is used for approximating the ON distribution function state.

$$F^*(k) = B_i \sum_{i=1}^{6} e^{-\beta_i k} \quad (12)$$

By using the method of least squares we find the unknown coefficients of the approximation for the expression (12) as presented in Table 8.

Figure 20. Formation of arrays

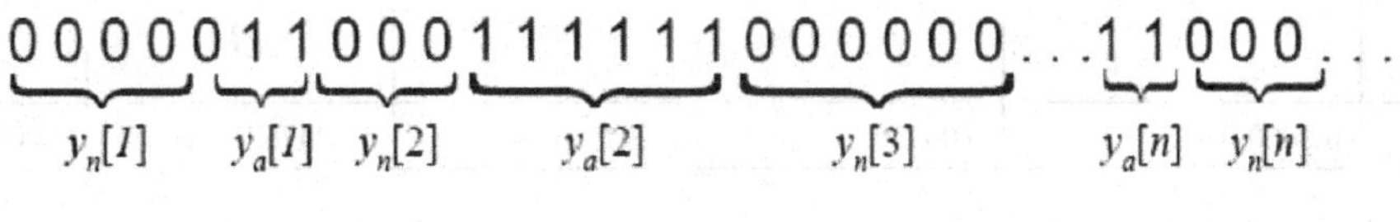

$$\underbrace{00000}_{y_n[1]}\underbrace{11}_{y_a[1]}\underbrace{000}_{y_n[2]}\underbrace{111111}_{y_a[2]}\underbrace{000000}_{y_n[3]}\ldots\underbrace{11}_{y_a[n]}\underbrace{000}_{y_n[n]}\ldots$$

Box 3.

$$F^*(k) = 0.612086 \times e^{-0.072672k} + 0.631933 \times e^{-0.540023k} + 0.073586 \times e^{-0.040006k} \quad (11)$$

Table 7. Approximation coefficients

A_1	α_1	A_2	α_2	A_3	α_3
0.612086	0.072672	0.631933	0.540023	0.073586	0.040006

Substituting the coefficient values obtained and given in Table 8 into Equation (12), we obtain the approximation of the original additional distribution of the length of ON periods as equation (13) (see Box 4).

The approximation of DF ON is shown in Figure 21.

After the normalization of obtained approximating expressions (11) (13) additional distributions of duration of ON-and OFF-processes, the matrix of transition probabilities is created, which is of the form presented in Figure 22.

Substituting the values of the coefficients found in Table 7 and 8 into the matrix of transition probabilities, we obtain the matrix of values (Figure 23).

3.5.2. Software for Error Packetization Simulation

With the probability transition matrix and vector of initial probabilities simulation of the transmission of streaming video traffic over a WiMAX network can be done. The choice of the initial state of the system was carried out using the condition that all states are equiprobable (*i.e.* $p = 1 / N$, where *N-number* of states the system can be in after DF approximation). Description of the block diagram of the simulation algorithm is as given below.

Table 8. Approximation coefficients

B_1	β_1	B_2	β_2	B_3	β_3
0.065836	0.000643	0.107716	0.000708	0.33109	0.007203
B_4	β_4	B_5	β_5	B_6	β_6
0.057449	0.0000618	0.007203	0.291568	0.224767	0.0094038

Box 4.

$$F^*(k) = 0.065836 \times e^{-0.000643k} + 0.107716 \times e^{-0.000708k} + 0.33109 \times e^{-0.007203k} + 0.057449 \times e^{-0.0000618k} + 0.007203 \times e^{-0.291568k} + 0.224767 \times e^{-0.0094038k} \quad (13)$$

Figure 21. DF ON approximation (2), DF ON experiment (1) (embedded graph - reduced scale of DF ON)

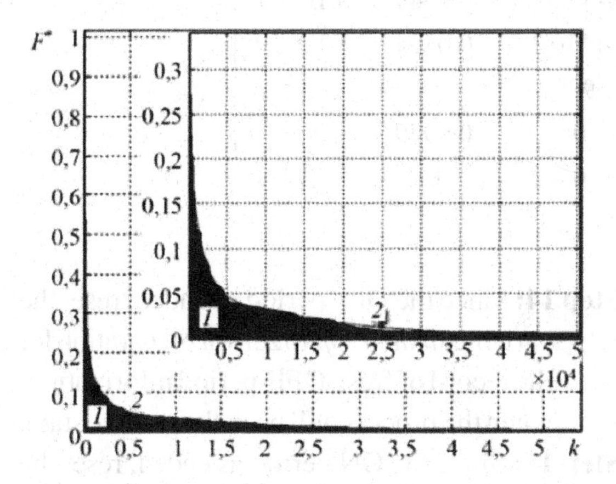

3.5.3. Error Packetization Algorithm

Step 1: Start program (Description of the variables, functions, procedures and modules used).

Step 2: Enter two-dimensional array matrix of transition probabilities. In the developed software, this is matrix was given as an array of constants in the declarations section and named *markov*.

Step 3: Set state from which to begin modeling. Since a 9-state model was chosen, the *state* variable can take integer values on the interval (1 – 9). Also, at this stage of the algorithm the accumulated variables *summa_on* and *summa_off*, which reflect the duration of the ON periods and OFF periods, are reset to zero respectively.

Step 4: Begin cycle with parameter *i*. The number of iterations equals the number of transitions in the simulated system.

Step 5: Instantiate the built-in generator of pseudorandom uniformly distributed sequence, generating a random value in the interval (0, 1). Assign the generated value to *rnd*. At the moment of generating the variable *rnd*, the system moves to the next state. The exact state into which it falls will be determined by the subsequent actions of the algorithm. The variable *summa* is reset to zero.

Step 6: Start the cycle with parameter *k*. The number of iterations in the cycle equals the number of states of the system being modeled. For this case, the number of iterations is eight (8). This loop is used to determine the state into which of the system has moved at the particular time of consideration.

Step 7: Check if the value of *rnd* fell in the kth state of the Markov chain. At the same time the following variables are involved: *summa* - accumulates the probability of all states up to *the* k^{th}; *markov [state, k]* – a two-dimensional array, which contains the transition matrix. If *rnd* falls within a range of probabilities corresponding to the kth state, then goto step *8*, otherwise goto step *9*.

Figure 22. Transition probabilities' matrix

$$\Gamma = \begin{array}{c|cccccc|} & A_1 & A_2 & A_3 & B_1 & B_2 & B_3 \\ \hline A_1 & e^{-\alpha 1} & 0 & 0 & (1-e^{-\alpha 1})B_1 & (1-e^{-\alpha 1})B_2 & (1-e^{-\alpha 1})B_3 \\ A_2 & 0 & e^{-\alpha 2} & 0 & (1-e^{-\alpha 2})B_1 & (1-e^{-\alpha 2})B_2 & (1-e^{-\alpha 2})B_3 \\ A_3 & 0 & 0 & e^{-\alpha 3} & (1-e^{-\alpha 3})B_1 & (1-e^{-\alpha 3})B_2 & (1-e^{-\alpha 3})B_3 \\ B_1 & (1-e^{-\beta 1})A_1 & (1-e^{-\beta 1})A_2 & (1-e^{-\beta 1})A_3 & e^{-\beta 1} & 0 & 0 \\ B_2 & (1-e^{-\beta 2})A_1 & (1-e^{-\beta 2})A_2 & (1-e^{-\beta 2})A_3 & 0 & e^{-\beta 2} & 0 \\ B_3 & (1-e^{-\beta 3})A_1 & (1-e^{-\beta 3})A_2 & (1-e^{-\beta 3})A_3 & 0 & 0 & e^{-\beta 3} \end{array}$$

Figure 23. The matrix of values

$$\Gamma = \begin{vmatrix} 0.999 & 0 & 0 & 2.4*10^{-5} & 8.69*10^{-4} & 1.1*10^{-4} \\ 0 & 0.9944 & 0 & 1.344*10^{-4} & 0.0049 & 6.16*10^{-4} \\ 0 & 0 & 0.965 & 8.4*10^{-4} & 0.0304 & 0.0039 \\ 1.8*10^{-5} & 3.6*10^{-4} & 3.6*10^{-4} & 0.9991 & 0 & 0 \\ 4.2*10^{-5} & 8.4*10^{-4} & 8.4*10^{-4} & 0 & 0.9979 & 0 \\ 2.58*10^{-4} & 0.0052 & 0.0052 & 0 & 0 & 0.9871 \end{vmatrix}$$

Step 8: Check – in which state is the process currently? If in the active state, then goto step 10. If in passive state, then goto step 11.

Step 9: The *summa* variable is increased by the value of the probability of being in state *k*. Then proceed to the next iteration of step 6.

Step 10: Check – was the last state of the matrix passive? If yes, goto step 12. Otherwise, goto step 16.

Step 11: Check – was the last state of the matrix active? If yes, goto step 13. Otherwise, goto step 17.

Step 12: Arrival at this step implies the end of OFF period. Therefore save or print to file *summa_off*.

Step 13: Arrival at this step implies the end of ON period. Therefore save or print to file *summa_on*.

Step 14: Since the OFF period as ended, reset the variable *summa_off* to zero in preparation for the record of fresh OFF-period information, when the process will be in the passive state.

Step 15: Since the ON period as ended, reset the variable *summa_on* to zero in preparation for the record of fresh ON-period information, when the process will be in the active state.

Step 16: Arrival at this step implies either the continuation of the previous ON period, or the start of a new ON period. So increment the variable *summa_on* and assign the value of cycle *k* to the *state* variable.

Step 17: Arrival at this step implies either the continuation of the previous OFF period, or the start of a new OFF period. So increment the variable *summa_off* and assign the value of cycle *k* to the *state* variable.

Figure 24. DF of simulated samples of the length of OFF (a) and ON (b) periods: curve 1 – experiment, curve 2 – simulation

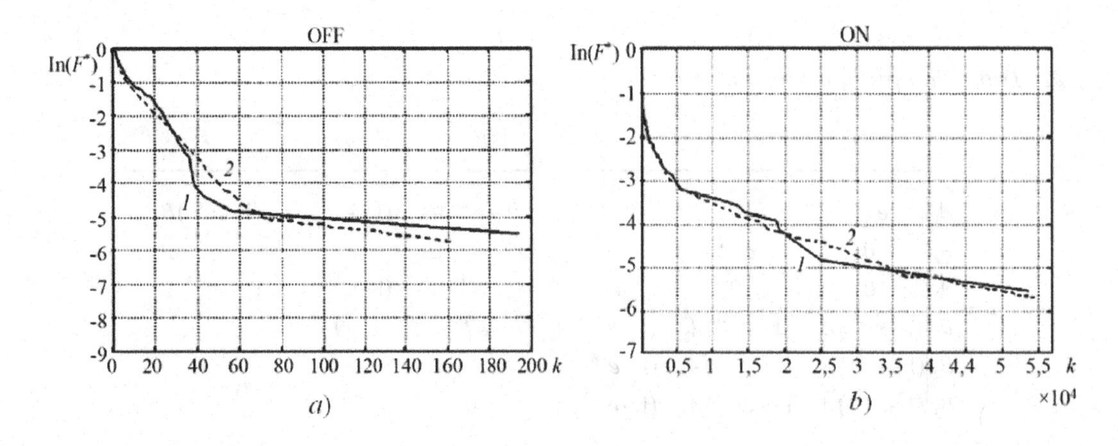

Step 18: At this step of the algorithm, the system just transited to the next state, so turn to the next iteration of the parameter *i*.

Step 19: End program.

As a result, the amount of packets falling either in the received state or the lost state in a row is accumulated

$$(summa\_ON = summa\_ON + 1).$$

4. SIMULATION RESULTS

DF of ON- and OFF-processes for both the simulated and experimental sequences obtained using the described Markov model, shown in Figure 24.

The numerical experiments have shown that increasing the number of states of the Markov model describing the packetization of errors, allows to obtain a satisfactory correspondence between the results of the experimental data and the data obtained by simulation.

Figure 25. Distribution of error-free and erroneous values for arrays N°1 and N°2

Figure 26. Distribution of errors in a group of errors for arrays N°1 and N°2

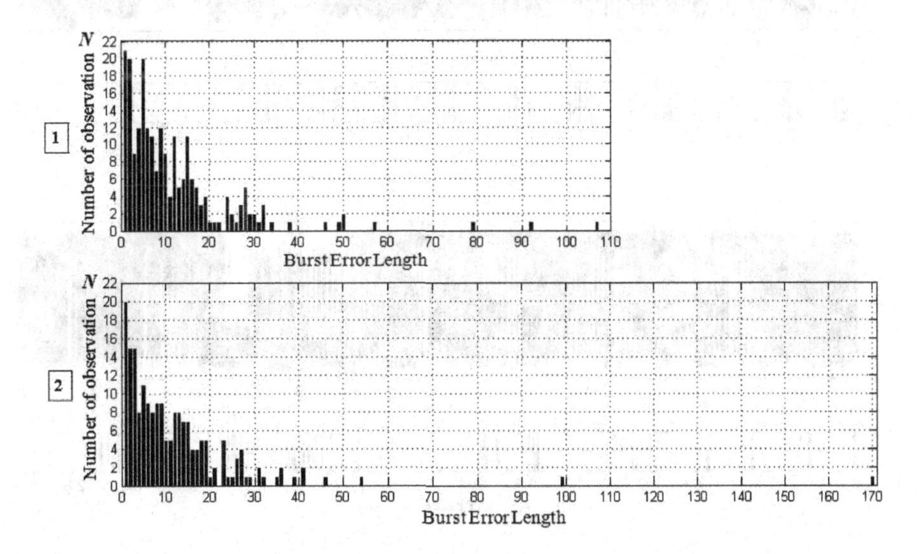

5. MARKOV MODEL OF PACKETIZATION OF ERRORS: SIMULATION RESULTS

Two independent data sets, each containing 300,000 values were generated with the aid of the developed Markov model. This amount of data will allow for compariing the number of RTP packets, according to results of the experiment conducted on the transmission of a 30-minute streaming video on a real WiMAX network, with the results of the experiment conducted using the HSC. Each value

Figure 27. Block diagram of the experiments N°1 and N°2

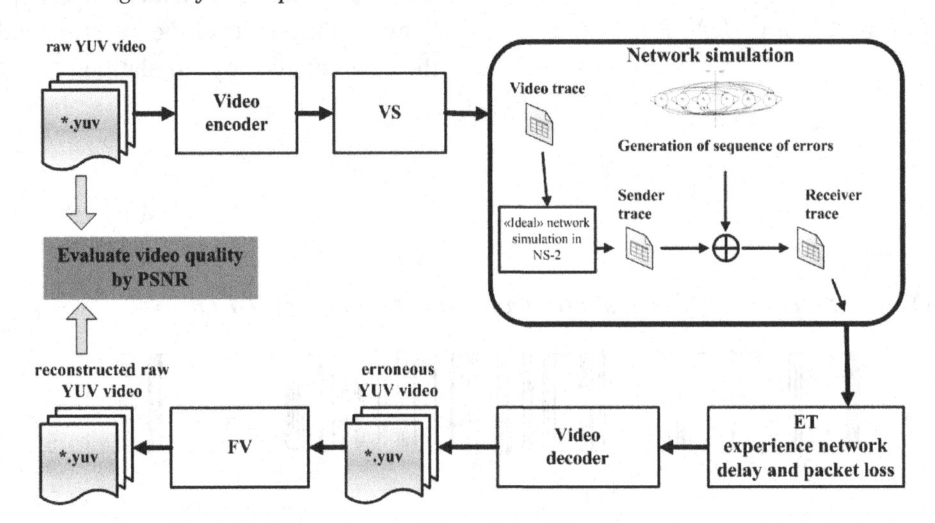

Figure 28. Change in PSNR indicator from experiments N°1 and N°2

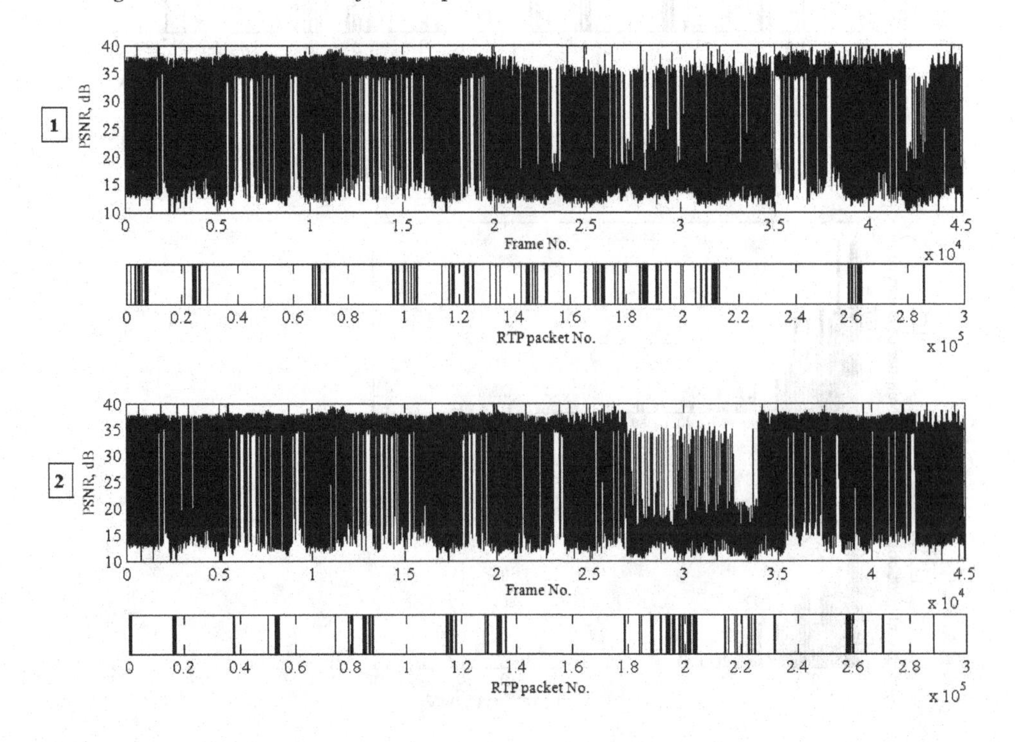

in the array is represented by the numbers 0 or 1, where 0 means error-free value, and 1 – erroneous value. Figure 25 shows the distribution of data set values, where the white areas correspond to error-free values (0), and black - erroneous values (1).

The first array contained 2,743 (0.91%), and the second had 2,430 (0.81%) error values. The distribution of the number of errors in the same group of errors is presented in the form of histograms in Figure 26.

It is shown that the distribution of errors can not be approximated by an exponential function, which confirms the validity of the Markov model. Furthermore, in order to study the influence of Markov model of packetization of errors on the quality of video streaming, simulation of the transmission of a 30-minute video in the structure of the HSC was conducted. Simulation of a network with Markov model for packetization of errors entailed the following: transmission and

Figure 29. Histogram and distribution function of the PSNR indicator in experiments N°1 and N°2

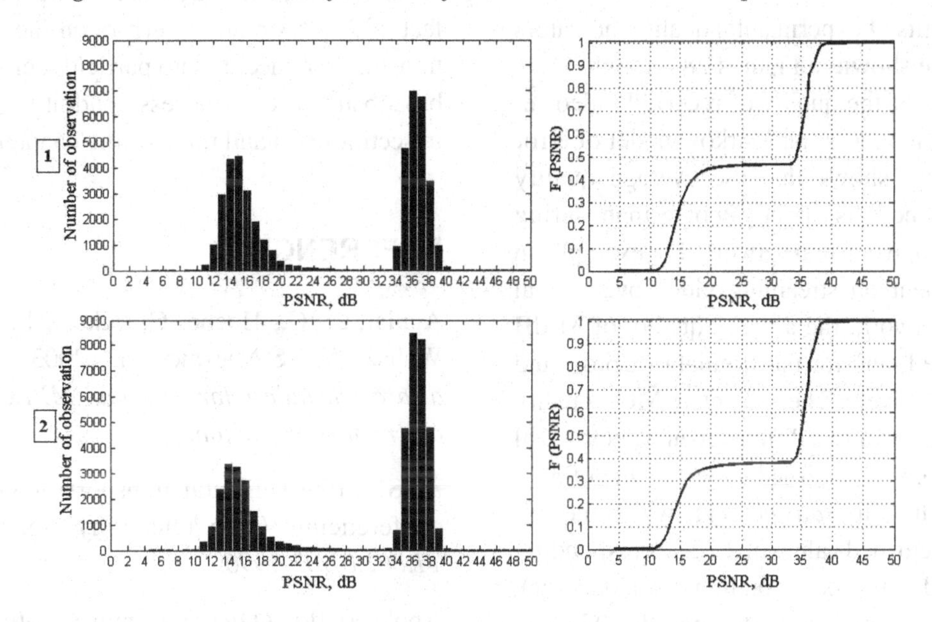

Figure 30. Quality Gradation in MOS value for video broadcast in experiments N°1 and N°2

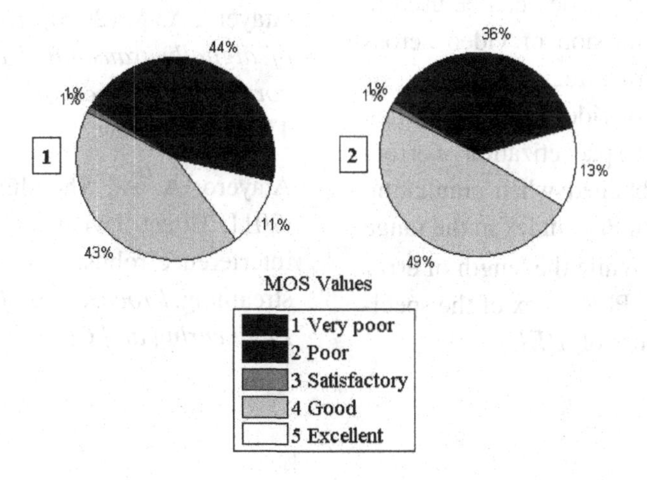

reception traces were obtained in the transmission over an "ideal" channel with unlimited bandwidth and no delay in the NS-2 environment. Then each packet of the receive trace was matched with a corresponding value from the data set array (packet id = serial value of the data set array). All packages corresponding to 1 (erroneous) were deleted. This allowed for simulating sequence of errors that occur in the network and to effect corrective decoding of the video stream. Thus, two experiments were carried out: with arrays N°1 and N°2. Figure 27 shows a block diagram of the experiments.

The results of experimental quality indicators obtained are shown in Figures 28 through 30.

Analysis of the quality of received video sequence when simulating Markov model of error packetization shows that the average quality video sequences is slightly worse than during transmission over a real network. For example, in an experiment on streaming video over a real WiMAX network, the average quality of 31 dB was obtained, and for the simulation 26 dB and 28 dB respectively. The subjective MOS quality indicator also shows a difference in values: a real WiMAX network returned a mean value of 3.59 (corresponding to *satisfactory*), while the experiments returned values of 2.72 (corresponding to *poor*) and 3.01 (corresponding to *satisfactory*), respectively. This suggests that the Markov model of packetization of error obtained from a real network for streaming video can be used in the simulaton of transmission of video across networks in the HSC structure.

The average quality of video sequences when simulating Markov model packetization of errors are similar to those obtained when simulating single packet errors with PER index in the range of $3 \times 10^{-3}\, to 1 \times 10^{-2}$. While the length of error group depending on the PER index of the specified range be attain values of $BEL \leq 10$.

CONCLUSION

We have presented in this chapter a detailed discussion of the fundamental concepts of video streaming. Characteristics of streaming traffic were enumerated and discussed and relevant parameters that characterize service continuity were mentioned. The peculiarities of transmitting H.264/AVC standard video over wireless access networks were highlited. The broadband wireless access network error models were explained, serving as background information for the report on the research findings of investigating the effect of video streaming errors on the quality of transmission media, with particular emphasis on broadband wireless access conduit as presented in sections two and three of the chapter.

REFERENCES

Aguiar, A. C., Hoene, C., Klaue, J., Karl, H., Wolisz, A., & Miesmer, H. (2003). *Channel-aware schedulers for voip and MPEG-4 based on channel prediction.*

ANSI. (1996). Digital transport of video teleconferencing/Video telephony signals. *ANSI T1.801.01/02-1996.*

Apple. (n.d.). *QuickTime player software.* Retrieved from http://www.apple.com

Atayero, A. A. (2000). *Estimation of the quality of digitally transmitted analogue signals over corporate VSAT networks.* (Unpublished Doctoral Thesis). Moscow.

Atayero, A. A., Sheluhin, O. I., & Ivanov, I. (2011). Effect of wideband wireless access systems interference robustness on the quality of video streaming. *Proceedings of the World Congress on Engineering and Computer Science, 2,* 848-854.

Atayero, A. A., Sheluhin, O. I., & Ivanov, Y. A. (2012). Modeling, simulation, and analysis of video streaming errors in wireless wideband access networks. *IAENG Transactions on Engineering Technologies*, *170*, 15–28. doi:10.1007/978-94-007-4786-9_2.

Atayero, A. A., Sheluhin, O. I., Ivanov, Y. A., & Alatishe, A. S. (2011). Estimation of the visual quality of video streaming under desynchronization conditions. *International Journal of Advanced Computer Science and Applications*, *2*(12), 1–11.

Baguda, Y., Fisal, N., Syed, S., Yusof, S., Mohd, S. A., Mohd, A., & Zulkarmawan, A. (2008). Mobile streaming of H.264 video over Gilbert-Elliotts channel. *PWASET, 36*.

Berts, J., & Persson, A. (1998). *Objective and subjective quality assessment of compressed digital video sequences*. (Master's thesis). Chalmers University of Technology, Göteborg, Sweden.

Channel Models for Fixed Wireless Applications. (n.d.). IEEE 802.16 broadband wireless access. *Working Group IEEE 802.16.3c-01/29r4*.

Cornaglia, B., & Spini, M. (1996). New statistical model for burst error distribution. In *European Transactions on Telecommunications*. Torino, Italy: John Wiley & Sons. doi:10.1002/ett.4460070308.

Dai, M., & Loguinov, D. (2005). Analysis and modeling of MPEG-4 and H.264 multi-layer video traffic. In *Proceedings of IEEE INFOCOM*. Miami, FL: IEEE.

Deb, S., Jaiswal, S., & Nagaraj, K. (2008). Real-time video multicast in WiMAX networks. In *Proceedings of IEEE INFOCOM*. IEEE.

Dvorkovich, A. V. (2005). Efficient encoding video in the new standard H.264/AVC. In *Proceedings of NIIR*. NIIR.

Ebert, J.-P., Willig, A. A., & Gilbert-Elliot. (1999). Bit error model and the efficient use in packet level simulation. In *Proceedings of TKN Technical Reports*. Berlin: TKN.

Elliot, E. O. (1963). Estimates of error rates for codes on burst-noise channels. *The Bell System Technical Journal*, *42*, 1977–1997.

ETSI TR 102 493. (n.d.). *Guidelines for the use of video quality algorithms for mobile applications*. ETSI.

Fantacci, R., & Scardi, M. (n.d.). Perfomance evaluation of preemptive polling schemes and ARQ techniques for indoor wireless networks. *IEEE Transaction on Vehicular technology, 45*(2), 248-257.

Feng, W.-C. (1997). *Buffering techniques for delivery of compressed video in video-on-demand systems*. Norwell, MA: Kluwer Academic Publisher.

Gilbert, E. N. (1960). Capacity of a burst-noise channel. *The Bell System Technical Journal*, *39*, 1253–1265.

Hertrich, D. (2002). *MPEG4 video transmission in wireless LANs-Basic QoS support on the data link layer of 802.11b*. (Minor Thesis).

Hohlfeld, O. (2008). Markovian packet loss generators and video QoE. *T Systems*. *Tcpdump.org*. (n.d.). Retrieved from http://www.tcpdump.org

IEEE. (2006). Layered video coding offset distortion traces for tracebased evaluation of video quality after network transport. In *Proceedings of IEEE Consumer Communications and Networking Conference CCNC*. Las Vegas, NV: IEEE.

Information and Communication Technologies. (n.d.). ADAMANTIUM. *D4.4 - PQoS Models and Adaptation Mechanisms*. Retrieved from www.ict-adamantium.eu

ISO-IEC. (1994). *International standard 13 818. Generic coding of moving pictures and associated audio information*. ISO-IEC.

ISO-IEC/JTC1/SC29/WG11. (1996). *Evaluation methods and procedures for July mpeg-4 tests*. ISO-IEC.

ITU. (n.d.). *P.800: Methods for subjective determination of transmission quality*. Retrieved from http://www.itu.int/rec/T-REC-P.800-199608-I/en

ITU-R BT. (n.d.). Methodology for the subjective assessment of the quality of television pictures. *ITU-R BT.*.

ITU-T. (1996). *Subjective video quality assessment methods for multimedia applications, interactive test methods for audiovisual communications, principles of a reference impairment system for video. Recommendations* (p. 910). ITU-T.

ITU-T. (1999). *Narrow-band visual telephone systems and terminal equipment. Recommendation H.320*. ITU-T.

Klaue, J., Rathke, B., & Wolish, A. (2003). EvalVid-A framework for video transmission and quality evaluation. In *Proceedings of the 13th International Conference on Modelling Techniques and Tools for Computer Performance Evaluation*. Urbana, IL: IEEE.

Kolkeri, V. (2008). *Error concealment techniques in H.264/AVC for video transmission over wireless network*. Arlington, TX: The University of Texas at Arlington.

Koutsakis, P., & Paterakis, M. (2004). Call-admission-control and traffic-policing mechanisms for the transmission of videoconference traffic from MPEG-4 and H.263 video coders in wireless ATM networks. *IEEE Transactions on Vehicular Technology*, *53*(5), 1525–1530. doi:10.1109/TVT.2004.833639.

Krunz, M., Sass, R., & Hughes, H. (1995). Statistical characteristics and multiplexing of MPEG streams. In *Proceedings of IEEE INFOCOM*. Boston: IEEE.

Krunz, M., & Tripathi, S. (1997). Exploiting the temporal structure of MPEG video for the reduction of bandwidth requirements. *Proceedings - IEEE INFOCOM*, *1*(1), 67–74. doi:10.1109/INFCOM.1997.635115.

Lakshman, T., Ortega, A., & Reibman, A. (1998). VBR video: Tradeoffs and potentials. *Proceedings of the IEEE*, *86*(5), 952–973. doi:10.1109/5.664282.

Lee, J. B., & Kalva, H. (2008). *The VC-1 and H.264 video compression standards for broadband video services*. Berlin: Springer. doi:10.1007/978-0-387-71043-3.

Lemmon, J. (2002). Wireless link statistical bit error model. NTIA Report. 02-394. Washington, DC: US Department of Commerce.

Marpe, D., Wiegand, T., & Sullivan, G. J. (2006). The H.264/MPEG4 advanced video coding standard and its applications. *IEEE Communications Magazine*, *44*(8), 134–143. doi:10.1109/MCOM.2006.1678121.

NS-2 Documentation. (n.d.). Retrieved from http://www.isi.edu/nsnam/ns/ns-documentation.html

Postel, J. (1980). User datagram protocol. *RFC 768*.

Postel, J. (1981a). Internet protocol. *RFC 791*.

Postel, J. (1981b). Transmission control protocol. *RFC 793*.

Project P905-PF EURESCOM. (2000). *Aquavit-Assessment of quality for audio-visual signals over internet and UMTS*. EURESCOM.

Qi, Q., Pei, Y., Modestino, J. W., & Tian, X. (2004). Source-adaptive FEC/UEP coding for video transport over bursty packet loss 3G UMTS networks: A cross-layer approach. In *Proceedings of 60th IEEE Vehicular Technology Conference (VTC'04),* (vol. 5, pp. 150-3154). IEEE.

Richardson. (2003). IH264 and MPEG-4 video compression: Video coding for next-generation. In *Multimedia*. Hoboken, NJ: John Wiley & Sons.

Rodriguez, E. (2008). *Robust error detection methods for H.264/AVC videos*. (Master's thesis). Universitat Politecnica de Catalunya, Vienna, Austria.

Romer, M. (2004). *MPEG-4 video quality analysis*. Ft. Lauderdale, FL: Florida Atlantic University.

Sanneck, H., Mohr, W., Le, L., & Hoene, C. (2002). *Quality of service support for voice over IP over wireless*. Wireless IP and Building the Mobile Internet.

Sarnoff Corporation. (2002). *Jndmetrix-iq software and JND: A human vision system model for objective picture quality measurements*. Sarnoff Corporation.

Schulzrinne, H., Casner, S., Frederick, R., & Jacobson, V. (1996). RTP: A transport protocol for real-time applications. *RFC 1889.*

Schulzrinne, H., Rao, A., & Lanphier, R. (1998). Real time streaming protocol (RTSP). *RFC 2326.*

Stuhlmuller, K., Farber, N., Link, M., & Girod, B. (2000). Analysis of video transmission over lossy channels. *IEEE Journal on Selected Areas in Communications*, *18*(6), 1012–1032. doi:10.1109/49.848253.

Telatar, I. (1999). *Capacity of multi-antenna gaussian channels, 10*(6), 585-595.

VCDemo Software. (n.d.). Retrieved from http://www.ict.ewi.tudelft.nl/vcdemo

VirtualDub Software. (n.d.). Retrieved from http://www.virtualdub.org

Wang, H., & Moayeri, N. (1995). Finite state Markov channel-A useful model for radio communication channels. *IEEE Transactions on Vehicular Technology*, *44*(2), 163–171. doi:10.1109/25.350282.

Wang, Y., Ostermann, J., & Zhang, Y.-Q. (2001). *Video processing and communications*. Upper Saddle River, NJ: Prentice Hall.

Wenger, S. (2003). H264/AVC Over IP. *IEEE Transactions on Circuits and Systems for Video Technology*, *13*(7), 645–656. doi:10.1109/TCSVT.2003.814966.

Wenger, S., Stockhammer, T., & Hannuksela, M. M. (2003). *RTP payload format for H.264 video*. Internet Draft.

Wiegand, T., Sullivan, G. J., Bjntegaard, G., & Luthra, A. (2003). Overview of the H.264/AVC video coding standard. *IEEE Transactions on Circuits and Systems for Video Technology*, *13*(1), 560–576. doi:10.1109/TCSVT.2003.815165.

Windump.polito.it. (n.d.). Retrieved from http://www.windump.polito.it

WireShark Software. (n.d.). Retrieved from http://www.wireshark.org

Wolf, S., & Pinson, M. (1999). Spatial-temporal distortion metrics for in-service quality monitoring of any digital video system. In *Proceedings of SPIE International Symposium on Voice, Video, and Data Communications.* Boston: SPIE.

Wolf, S., & Pinson, M. (2002). Video quality measurement techniques. *Technical Report 02 392.* Washington, DC: US Department of Commerce, NTIA.

Wu, D., Hou, Y. T., Zhu, W., Lee, H.-J., Chiang, T., Zhang, Y.-Q., & Chao, H. J. (2000). On end-to-end architecture for transporting MPEG-4 video over the internet. *IEEE Transactions on Circuits and Systems for Video Technology*, *10*(6), 923–941. doi:10.1109/76.867930.

KEY TERMS AND DEFINITIONS

Bit Error Rate (BER): Error probability of binary message elements, calculated before the channel decoder.

Markov Model: A stochastic model with a finite number of states and probabilities of transition from state to state used for modeling real-life events.

Model/Modeling: A model is a representation of an object, system or concept in a form different from that in which it exists naturally. A model is thus essentially an instrument for forecasting the effect of input signals on a given object, while modeling is a method of improving the reasoning efficiency and intuitive capacity of specialists.

Signal-to-Noise Ratio (SNR): A quantitative measure of signal quality calculated as a ratio of transmitted signal power to the power of Nyquist noise in the transmission medium.

Chapter 10
Mathematical Models of Video-Sequences of Digital Half-Tone Images

E.P. Petrov
Vyatka State University, Russia

E.V. Medvedeva
Vyatka State University, Russia

I.S. Trubin
Vyatka State University, Russia

S.M. Smolskiy
Moscow Power Engineering Institute, Russia

ABSTRACT

This chapter is devoted to Mathematical Models (MM) of Digital Half-Tone Images (DHTI) and their video-sequences presented as causal multi-dimensional Markov Processes (MP) on discrete meshes. The difficulties of MM development for DHTI video-sequences of Markov type are shown. These difficulties are related to the enormous volume of computational operations required for their realization. The method of MM-DHTI construction and their statistically correlated video-sequences on the basis of the causal multi-dimensional multi-value MM is described in detail. Realization of such operations is not computationally intensive; Markov models from the second to fourth order demonstrate this. The proposed method is especially effective when DHTI is represented by low-bit (4-8 bits) binary numbers.

INTRODUCTION

As at this writing, the intensification of scientific research and increased complexity of solving scientific and technological problems require the investigation of not only one-dimensional random processes, but also the investigation of the multi-dimensional ones, for example, different types of fields presented in the form of images or video-sequences. Image processing is of great interest to researchers and engineers in various fields of practice for example: engineers in the area of flaw inspection and the non-destructive testing, developers of industrial robots and systems for the visual inspection of technological processes, experts in automation of scientific research, in TV technologies, in security systems, in remote sensing of natural resources, in space investiga-

DOI: 10.4018/978-1-4666-2208-1.ch010

tions, biologists, medical experts, specialists in forensic crime detection, physicists, astronomers, meteorologists, geologists, cartographers, and so forth (Bykov, 1971; Pisarevsky & Chernyavsky, 1988; Vasiliev, 1995; Ablameiko & Lagunovskiy, 2000; Berchtold, 1999; Vasiliev, 2002; Elfeki, 2001; Shalizi, 2003; Bondur, 2003). It is difficult to find a scientific or technological area, in which applied problems of image processing is not present in one form or the other.

The transition to digital image processing using small-bit numbers (4-8 bits) has sharply extended the possibilities of image application as the most capacious carrier of various types of information. In this connection, digital image processing, because of its importance, has been distinguished as an independent scientific and communication area, involving a great number of highly qualified experts. There is every reason to believe that in the nearest future, there will be a great extension of the practical implementation of image processing methods from Medicare to other various types of technological processes.

The development and investigation of image processing algorithms are based on mathematical models (MM), which adequately represent real images. To date, a variety of MM for two-dimensional images are already developed, on the basis of which whole series of effective processing algorithms offered has been reported in the literature by Jine (1981) as well as Derin and Kelly (1989). Most of these algorithms however require enormous computational resources. Approximation of digital half-tone images (DHTI) by random Markov processes (MP) allows for the achievement of significant progress in the area of MM development and algorithms of image processing. Important contributions in the development of Markov type MM have been introduced by Russian researchers like Berchtold (1999), Bondur (2003), Krasheninnikov (2003), Vasiliev (1995), Vasiukov (2002), Furman (2003), Soifer (2003) as well as other experts such as Jine (1981), Abend (1965), Woods (1972), Besag (1974), Kashyap (1981), Vinkler (2002), Modestino (1993), Politis (1994), Chellapa (1982, 1985). The most interest for practical application is generated by multi-dimensional mathematical models of DHTI video-sequences. The number of publications devoted to such MM are few. Notable among them are Bykov (1971), Vasiliev (1995, 2002), Jine (1981), Derin and Kelly (1989), Spector (1985), Dagion and Mercero (1988), Politis (1994), Petrov (2003), Trubin (2004a, 2004b), Trubin and Butorin (2005).

The MM of DHTI video-sequences based on the multi-dimensional discrete-time and continuous-values Markov process are the most studied by researchers like Vasiliev (1995), Spector (1985), Dagion and Mercero (1988). Two-dimensional MM of DHTI presented by Jine in Jine (1981) and constructed on the basis two-dimensional Gaussian Markov process was developed by Krasheninnikov, Vasiliev, and Spector in Krasheninnikov (2003), Vasiliev (1995), Spector (1985) up to multi-dimensional image MM based on the multi-dimensional Gaussian MP. The structure of the algorithm for generating these processes is rather simple and clear, however, the MM proposed in Jine (1981) based on the causal two-dimensional Gaussian MP has found the widest application (see Box 1).

To realize the MM of equation (1) it is necessary to use four multiplications and three additions, which is fully acceptable for medium sized images.

Krasheninnikov (2003), Vasiliev (1995), Spector (1985), suggested on the analogy of equation (1), MMs of processes of larger dimensions. Thus, for the description of the image frame sequence with two spatial coordinates defining the location of the image element in the frame and the third coordinate: the number of the frame or the discrete time in the frame sequence, the MM will be of the form shown in Box 2.

The computational effectiveness defined by the required computer memory usage and the number of computational operations is one of the most important features of MM. We should con-

Box 1.

$$\mu_{i,j} = r_1\mu_{i-1,j} + r_2\mu_{i,j-1} + r_1 r_2\mu_{i-1,j-1} - \sigma_\xi^2\sqrt{\left(1-r_1^2\right)\left(1-r_2^2\right)}\,\xi\left(i,j\right), \quad (1)$$

where μ_{ij} is the image element with spatial coordinates $\left(i \in m,\ j \in n\right)$;

r_1, r_2 are horizontal and vertical correlation coefficients respectively;

$\xi\left(i,j\right)$ is sample of white Gaussian noise with zero mean and the unit variance σ_ξ^2.

sider as most effective the MMs, in which the necessary number of required calculation operations per the image element does not depend on the image size. Most of the known MMs require a number of computational operations proportional to $\log N$, N^2 and even larger powers for realization of the image with sizes $N \times N$. For example, in spite of the simple MM structure for the multi-dimensional Gaussian processes offered in Spector (1985), the number of calculation operations at its realization quickly increases with the growth of the dimension of the generating process. For instance, to generate one element of the three-dimensional Gaussian MP (equation 2), which is adequate for the video-sequence of Gaussian Markov images, it is necessary to have seven multiplications and six additions, which makes application of the method of MM construction for processes with large number of measurements and elements for each measurement offered in Spector (1985) problematic.

It is envisaged that difficulties in MM development will significantly increase when required to develop and examine algorithms for the DHTI processing and statistically couple video-sequences, which represent random processes with more than two dimensions. Random processes become not only multi-dimensional but multi-valued as well, taking $Q = 2^g$ discrete values where g is the number of bits of DHTI elements presentation. Therefore, we devote the main attention to the MM of DHTI construction and their video-sequences required for realizing minimal computation resources.

The problem of MM construction for DHTI video-sequences on the basis of multi-dimensional and multi-valued random processes require non-traditional approach to its solution because of the great computational complexity. In Petrov and Chasikov (2001) and Petrov, Trubin and Butorin (2005a), the validity of multi-dimensional discrete-value MP selection as the MM of the

Box 2.

$$\begin{aligned}\mu_{i,j,k} = {} & r_1\mu_{i-1,j,k} + r_2\mu_{i,j-1,k} + r_3\mu_{i,j,k-1} - r_1 r_2\mu_{i-1,j-1,k} - r_1 r_3\mu_{i-1,j,k-1} - \\ & -r_2 r_3\mu_{i,j-1,k-1} + \sigma_\xi^2\sqrt{\prod_{l=1}^{3}\left(1-r_l^2\right)}\,\xi\left(i,j\right),\end{aligned} \quad (2)$$

where $r_i\left(i \in 3\right)$ are correlation coefficients between the image elements in horizontal, vertical and in time, accordingly; $\mu_{i,j,k}$ $\left(i \in m,\ j \in n, k = 1,2,...\right)$ is the image element with sizes $m \times n$ in the *k*-th frame. On the analogy of Equation (2) we can construct MM of higher orders as shown in Vasiliev (1995).

DHTI video-sequences is based on the analysis of DHTI statistical features and the experience of application of two-dimensional and three-dimensional multi-valued MP as the DHTI MM at the synthesis of nonlinear filtering algorithms of DHTI video-sequences distorted by the additive white noise. Results of filtering of artificial and real DHTI presented in Petrov and Chasikov (2001) and Petrov, Trubin and Butorin (2005a) showed good adequacy of the mentioned MM to the real processes.

Many methods of processing one-dimensional random processes are based on the assumption that the data observed are the output of the causal system. In two-dimensional processes (e.g. an image) the data coordinates are spatial and any causal property (causality) related to an image is completely defined by the scanning method. In the causal model an image is presented in the form of the output of a linear scanning system, therefore the algorithm caused by it is recurrent by its nature. Methods of the causal representation are applicable during the development of recursive filters intended for noise smoothing and recovering of degraded (fuzzy) images, especially in cases when the degrading process is also causal (for instance, caused by the motion). Therefore, we take the causal multi-dimensional multi-valued random MP (i.e. the multi-dimensional Markov chain with several states) as the DHTI and their video-sequences MM.

The model of two statistically correlated video-sequences of DHTI representing the multi-dimensional (e.g. four-dimensional) multi-valued MP was studied by Petrov and Trubin in Petrov (2003) and Trubin (2004a, 2004b), where the multi-dimensional, multi-valued MP is represented by the set of the two-dimensional MP simple in realization with the computing resources, which do not depend upon the image size as demonstrated in Petrov (2003) and Trubin (2004a, 2004b). It was supposed that the statistical correlation between two-dimensional processes, which are the components of the three-dimensional and four-dimensional processes, is not essential. Investigations conducted in Petrov et al. (2006a, 2006b) showed that for modeling processes with more than three dimensions, this representation of the multi-dimensional process leads to a disturbance of the MM's correspondence to the real process and the greater the number of modeling process dimensions, the more the level of correspondence. The method of multi-dimensional causal MM construction of statistically correlated video-sequences of DHTI offered in Petrov et al. (2006a, 2006b) is free of shortcomings peculiar to MM in Trubin (2004a), which allows for the successful use of the developed MM for synthesis of DHTI filtering algorithms in various statistically correlated combinations. Petrov (2003), Trubin (2004a, 2004b), Trubin and Butorin (2005) and Petrov et al., (2006a, 2006b) present the division of DHTI into bit binary images (BBI), each of which represents the binary multi-dimensional MP, which uses the entropy approach to calculate the probability matrix of the Markov process.

TWO-DIMENSIONAL CAUSAL DISCRETE-VALUED MARKOV PROCESS

In order to solve the problem of constructing mathematical models of DHTI adequate for two-dimensional random field, it is necessary, to define *ab initio* the main requirements for the algorithm for processing it. It becomes evident that defining such requirements lead to high effectiveness of processing, minimal resources on implementation and the possibility of operation in real-time scale. In the case when the DHTI filtering against the distorting noise is taken as the processing, the recursive nonlinear filtering proposed by Derin and Kelly (1989) can adequately match such requirements. Assuming that the DHTI filtering is fulfilled in real-time scale from the left upper corner (from left-to the right-downward), i.e. the image element is processed just after receiving it from the communication channel, only earlier received image elements can fall in the aperture of this filter. Filtering can be executed repelling from the causally located element's variety only. The DHTI MM should therefore be in this case the causal random field as well. Based on the above-mentioned considerations, the unilateral Markov random field (UMRF) discussed in Jine (1981), Derin and Kelly (1989) were chosen as the digital half-tone image mathematical model.

We adopt the definition of the unilateral Markov field also called the two-dimensional Markov chain on the non-symmetric half-plane (NSHP) given in Derin and Kelly (1989):

Let $\mu = \left\{\mu_{i,j}\right\}$ be the random field specified on the rectangular mesh $L = \left\{(i,j) : 1 \le i \le m, 1 \le j \le n\right\}$ with sizes $m \times n$ elements. Let us assume that:

$$\Phi_{i,j} = \left\{(q,l); 1 \le q \le i, 1 \le l \le j\right\}, (i,j) \in L,$$

$$\Psi_{i,j} = \left\{(q,l)\right\} \in L;\ q \le i\ \ or\ \ (q = i, l < j) \qquad (3)$$

$$\Lambda_{i,j} \subset \Psi_{i,j}.$$

These subsets are shown in Figure 1.

In order for μ to be the unilateral Markov random field (a.k.a. the Markov chain on the non-symmetric half-plane) it is necessary to fulfill the condition shown in Box 3.

The main property of the UMRF is that, if the conditional dependence is defined starting from the upper left fragment, then $\mu_{i,j}$ depends on the random variables only from some subset $\Lambda_{i,j}$ of this fragment; this subset is called a neighborhood.

The key UMRF property consists in the fact that if the conditional function is defined from the left upper segment, value of $\mu_{i,j}$ depends upon the random variables from some subset $\Lambda_{i,j}$ of this segment called the vicinity. The vicinity $\Lambda_{i,j}$ may be any subset $\Psi_{i,j}$, but it usually has a fixed configuration with respect to $\mu_{i,j}$. The following vicinity configuration offered in Derin and Kelly (1989) best satisfies the causality condition:

$$\Lambda_{i,j} = \left\{\mu_{i,j-1}, \mu_{i-1,j}, \mu_{i-1,j-1}\right\}. \qquad (5)$$

Figure 1. OSMRF areas with the vicinity of three elements

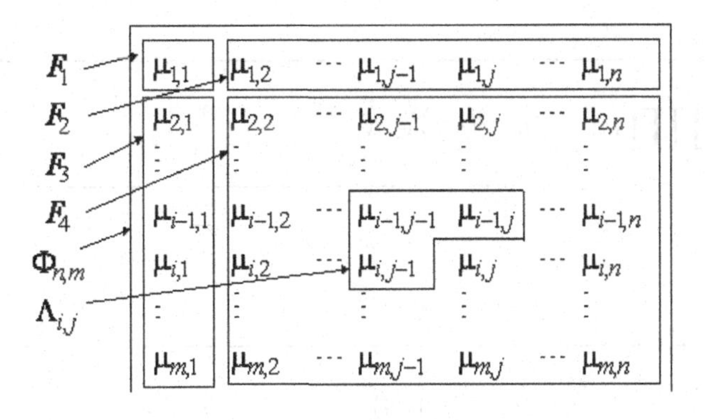

Box 3.

$$w\left(\mu_{i,j} \middle| \mu_{q,l}; (q,l) \in \Psi_{i,j}\right) = w\left(\mu_{i,j} \middle| \mu_{q,l}; (q,l) \in \Lambda_{i,j}\right). \qquad (4)$$

The most useful property of the causal field is the opportunity to express the mutual distribution $\left\{\mu_{ql},(q,l)\in\Phi_{mn}\right\}$ in the form if the product of the causal conditional distributions as described in Derin and Kelly (1989) (see Box 4).

The property is similar to those of the one-dimensional Markov chains and allows for the construction of processing algorithm for two-dimensional signals on the analogy of the one-dimensional signals.

It should be noted that on the field boundary, i.e. for $i = 1$ or $j = 1$ the vicinity $\Lambda_{i,j}$ has a configuration different from that of the internal points. Since the values of elements lying over an upper line of more left of the initial column are unknown (or not defined), the vicinity for the boundary elements is taken in the form of the intersection of the general carrier with the existing mesh. Thus, for these elements, only '*abbreviated*' vicinities are obtained. In other words, in the field boundary elements the conditional probability $w\left(\mu_{i,j}\left|\mu_{q,l};\left(q,l\in\Lambda_{i,j}\right)\right.\right)$ is given as depending upon only those parts of $\Lambda_{i,j}$, that fall in $\Psi_{i,j}$.

Thus, and in line with Derin and Kelly (1989), all UMRF area with the vicinity of type (5) can be conditionally divided into four parts, each of which has its own view of $\Lambda_{i,j}$ (Figure 1) (see Box 5).

This circumstance will be further considered investigated for obtaining the algorithm of UMRF element formation.

It has been shown by Petrov (2003), Trubin (2004a, 2004b), Trubin and Butorin (2005) and Petrov et al. (2006a, 2006b) that DHTI representation by the set of g bit binary images reduces the problem of constructing mathematical models for DHTI to one of the creation of mathematical models of BBI. This represents the stationary two-dimensional Markov chain with two equiprobable values of M_1 and M_2.

MATHEMATICAL MODEL OF THE TWO-DIMENSIONAL BINARY MARKOV IMAGE

Let us specify the vicinity $\Lambda_{i,j}$ of the element ν_4 in the form given in expression (5) and let us assume that BBI represents the stationary field of the Markov type with the autocorrelation function:

Box 4.

$$p\left(\mu_{q,l};\left(q,l\right)\in\Phi_{m,n}\right)=\prod_{i=1}^{m}\prod_{j=1}^{n}w\left(\mu_{i,j}\left|\mu_{q,l};\left(q,l\right)\in\Lambda_{i,j}\right.\right) \quad (6)$$

Box 5.

$$\Lambda_{i,j}=\begin{cases}\varnothing, & if\ \ (i,j)\in F_1\\ \{(i-1,j)\}, & if\ \ (i,j)\in F_2\\ \{(i,j-1)\}, & if\ \ (i,j)\in F_3\\ \{(i,j-1),(i-1,j),(i-1,j-1)\}, & if\ \ (i,j)\in F_4\end{cases} \quad (7)$$

$$\rho(k,l) = \mathrm{E}\left[\mu_{i,j}, \mu_{i+k,j+l}\right] = \sigma^2 \exp\left\{-\alpha_1 |l| - \alpha_2 |k|\right\}, \tag{8}$$

where $\mathrm{E}[\cdot]$ is the expected value; σ_μ^2 is the image signal variance; α_1, α_2 are multipliers depending upon the width of the power spectral density of the random processes on horizontal and on vertical. The fragment of the two-dimensional BBI corresponding to area F_4 of NSHP (Figure 1) is shown in Figure 2, where the following designation are taken:

$$\mathrm{v}_1 = \mu_{i,j-1};\ \mathrm{v}_2 = \mu_{i-1,j};\ \mathrm{v}_3 = \mu_{i-1,j-1};\ \mathrm{v}_4 = \mu_{i,j}. \tag{9}$$

Dotted lines in Figure 2 indicate the presence of the statistical correlation between image elements.

We consider the two-dimensional Markov chain on the NSHP with two equiprobable $(p_1 = p_2)$ values of M_1, M_2 and probability matrices of the transition from the value M_i to the adjacent value M_j on image horizontal and vertical, accordingly, as the MM of Markov BBI:

$${}^2\Pi = \begin{Vmatrix} {}^2\pi_{11} & {}^2\pi_{12} \\ {}^2\pi_{21} & {}^2\pi_{22} \end{Vmatrix}, \tag{10}$$

$${}^2\Pi = \begin{Vmatrix} {}^2\pi_{11} & {}^2\pi_{12} \\ {}^2\pi_{21} & {}^2\pi_{22} \end{Vmatrix}. \tag{11}$$

If we know the correlation coefficients between BBI elements in lines r_{hor} and in columns r_{ver}, the matrix elements of the transition probability (10) can be obtained so:

$${}^1\pi_{ii} = \frac{1 + r_{hor}}{2},$$

$${}^2\pi_{ii} = \frac{1 + r_{ver}}{2} \quad \pi_{ii} = 1 - \pi_{ij};\ i \neq j;\ (i,j). \tag{12}$$

The probability of appearance of the BBI element ν_4 (Figure 2) with the value M_1 or M_2 completely defines by the mutual information quantity between ν_4 and its vicinity $\Lambda_{ij} = \{\nu_1, \nu_2, \nu_3\}$.

According to Dech (1971), let us present the information quantity containing BBI elements ν_1, ν_2, ν_3 with regards to the element ν_4 in the form.

$$I(\nu_1,\nu_2,\nu_3,\nu_4) = \log \frac{p(\nu_1,\nu_2,\nu_3,\nu_4)}{p(\nu_1)p(\nu_2)p(\nu_3)p(\nu_4)}, \tag{13}$$

where $p(\nu_i)$, $i = \overline{1,4}$ are *a priori* probability densities values of BBI element; $p(\nu_1,\nu_2,\nu_3,\nu_4)$ is the mutual probability density of values of image element.

The quantity of mutual information between elements falling in the vicinity $\Lambda_{ij} = \{\nu_1, \nu_2, \nu_3\}$ can be written in the form on the analogy of (13):

$$I(\nu_1,\nu_2,\nu_3) = \log \frac{p(\nu_1,\nu_2,\nu_3)}{p(\nu_1)p(\nu_2)p(\nu_3)}. \tag{14}$$

In the complicated Markov chain, as BBI is, all elements falling in the vicinity $\Lambda_{i,j}$ must be independent. For this, we shall find the mutual information between the element ν_3 with elements

Figure 2. The image fragment with the vicinity of three elements

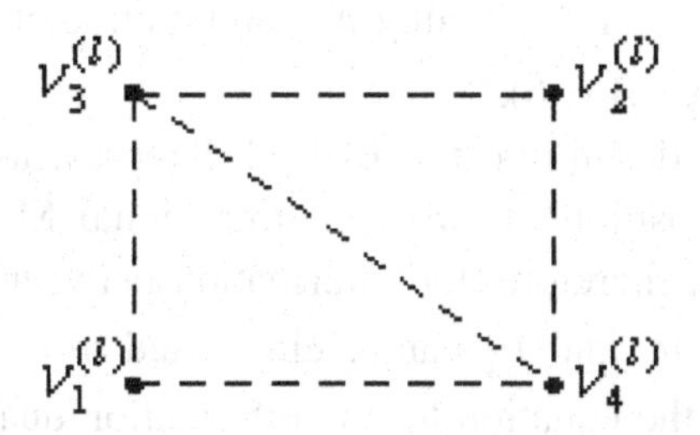

Box 6.

$$I(\nu_1,\nu_2,\nu_3,\nu_4) - I(\nu_1,\nu_2,\nu_3) = \log\frac{p(\nu_1,\nu_2,\nu_3)w(\nu_4 \mid \nu_1,\nu_2,\nu_3)}{p(\nu_1,\nu_2,\nu_3)p(\nu_4)} = \log\frac{w(\nu_4 \mid \nu_1,\nu_2,\nu_3)}{p(\nu_4)}, \quad (15)$$

where $w(\nu_4 \mid \nu_1,\nu_2,\nu_3)$ is the transition probability density in the three-dimensional Markov chain.

Box 7.

$$I(\nu_1,\nu_2,\nu_4) = \log\frac{w(\nu_4 \mid \nu_1,\nu_2,\nu_3)p(\nu_3)p(\nu_4)}{p(\nu_3)p(\nu_4)w(\nu_4 \mid \nu_3)} = \log\frac{w(\nu_4 \mid \nu_1,\nu_2,\nu_3)}{w(\nu_4 \mid \nu_3)} = \log\frac{w(\nu_4 \mid \nu_1)w(\nu_4 \mid \nu_2)}{w(\nu_4 \mid \nu_3)}. \quad (16)$$

Box 8.

$$w(\nu_4 \mid \Lambda_{ij}) = \sum_{j,q,r=1}^{2} \pi(\nu_4 = M_i \mid \nu_1 = M_j; \nu_2 = M_q; \nu_3 = M_r) \times \delta(\nu_1 - M_j)\delta(\nu_2 - M_q)\delta(\nu_3 - M_r), \quad (17)$$

where $\delta(\cdot)$ is the delta-function., $i = \overline{1,2}$.

Box 9.

$$\Pi = \begin{Vmatrix} \pi_{iiii} & \pi_{jiii} \\ \pi_{iiji} & \pi_{jiji} \\ \pi_{ijii} & \pi_{jjii} \\ \pi_{ijjj} & \pi_{jjjj} \end{Vmatrix} = \begin{Vmatrix} \alpha_1 & \alpha_1' \\ \alpha_2 & \alpha_2' \\ \alpha_3 & \alpha_3 \\ \alpha_4 & \alpha_4' \end{Vmatrix}, \quad i,j = \overline{1,2}; \quad i \neq j. \quad (18)$$

ν_1 and ν_2 i the vicinity $\Lambda_{i,j}$ and subtract it from (13) (see Box 6).

By definition, the BBI MM represents the superposition of two one-dimensional Markov chains, therefore, the information between elements ν_4 and ν_3 can be eliminated from (15). Then, the equation for the information quantity between the element ν_4 and elements ν_1, ν_2 takes the form (see Box 7).

The transition probability density in the complicated Markov chain $w(\nu_4 \mid \nu_1,\nu_2,\nu_3)$ can be expressed in the form (13) (see Box 8).

Using the entropy between mutually independent elements of the vicinity $\Lambda_{i,j}$ and the element

Box 10.

$$\alpha_1 = \pi_{iiii} = \pi(\nu_4 = M_1 \mid \nu_1 = M_1; \nu_2 = M_1; \nu_3 = M_1) = 1 - \frac{{}^1\pi_{ij}\,{}^2\pi_{ij}}{{}^3\pi_{ii}},$$

$$\alpha_2 = \pi_{iiji} = \pi(\nu_4 = M_1 \mid \nu_1 = M_1; \nu_2 = M_2; \nu_3 = M_1) = 1 - \frac{{}^1\pi_{ij}\,{}^2\pi_{ii}}{{}^3\pi_{ij}},$$

$$\alpha_3 = \pi_{ijii} = \pi(\nu_4 = M_1 \mid \nu_1 = M_2; \nu_2 = M_1; \nu_3 = M_1) = 1 - \frac{{}^1\pi_{ii}\,{}^2\pi_{ij}}{{}^3\pi_{ij}},\qquad (19)$$

$$\alpha_4 = \pi_{ijjj} = \pi(\nu_4 = M_2 \mid \nu_1 = M_2; \nu_2 = M_2; \nu_3 = M_2) = 1 - \frac{{}^1\pi_{ii}\,{}^2\pi_{ii}}{{}^3\pi_{ii}},$$

where ${}^3\pi_{ij}$ $(i, j = \overline{1,2};\ i \neq j)$ is the element of the matrix

$${}^3\Pi = {}^1\Pi \cdot {}^2\Pi = \begin{Vmatrix} {}^3\pi_{11} & {}^3\pi_{12} \\ {}^3\pi_{21} & {}^3\pi_{22} \end{Vmatrix}. \qquad (20)$$

ν_4, we can write the transition probability matrix for the complicated Markov chain as shown in Box 9.

Elements of the matrix Π are connected with the elements of matrices (10), (11) by the equations shown in Box 10.

Elements of the matrix (18) satisfy the normalization requirement, i.e.

$$\alpha_l + \alpha_l' = 1, \quad l = \overline{1,4}. \qquad (21)$$

For instance, elements α_1 and α_1' of the matrix, where

$$\alpha_1' = 1 - \alpha_1 = \frac{{}^1\pi_{ij}\,{}^2\pi_{ij}}{{}^3\pi_{ii}}, \qquad (22)$$

are equal in sum by 1, i.e. $\alpha_1 + \alpha_1' = 1$.

Let us consider the most important issues of the MM operation for the random Markov type BBI confirming its adequacy to real images.

Let the transition probability matrices in horizontal and on vertical be specified and equal, i.e. ${}^1\pi_{ij} = {}^2\pi_{ij}$ $(i, j = \overline{1,2};\ i \neq j)$.

We assume ${}^1\pi_{ii} = {}^2\pi_{ii} = 0,9$. Then, in accordance with (19) we obtain that shown in Box 11.

Values of matrix Π elements $\alpha_3 = \alpha_4 = 0,5$ are the specific checking point for correctness of the MM operation. Really, at equal transition probabilities ${}^1\pi_{ii} = {}^2\pi_{ii}$ (in horizontal and in vertical) and for opposite values of elements ν_1 and ν_2 the appearance of the value M_1 or M_2 in the element ν_4 is equiprobable.

Let us calculate the matrix Π elements using formula (19) for the limit cases of matrices ${}^1\Pi$ and ${}^2\Pi$.

Let

$${}^1\Pi = \begin{Vmatrix} 1 & 0 \\ 0 & 1 \end{Vmatrix}, \quad {}^2\Pi = \begin{Vmatrix} {}^2\pi_{ii} & {}^2\pi_{ij} \\ {}^2\pi_{ji} & {}^2\pi_{jj} \end{Vmatrix}.$$

Box 11.

$$\alpha_1 = \pi(\nu_4 = M_1 \mid \nu_1 = M_1; \nu_2 = M_1; \nu_3 = M_1) = 1 - \frac{{}^1\pi_{ij}\ {}^2\pi_{ij}}{{}^3\pi_{ii}} = 1 - \frac{0,1 \cdot 0,1}{0,82} = 0,9878$$

$$\alpha_2 = \pi(\nu_4 = M_1 \mid \nu_1 = M_1; \nu_2 = M_2; \nu_3 = M_1) = 1 - \frac{{}^1\pi_{ij}\ {}^2\pi_{ii}}{{}^3\pi_{ij}} = 1 - \frac{0,1 \cdot 0,9}{0,18} = 0,5$$

$$\alpha_3 = \pi(\nu_4 = M_1 \mid \nu_1 = M_2; \nu_2 = M_1; \nu_3 = M_1) = 1 - \frac{{}^1\pi_{ii}\ {}^2\pi_{ij}}{{}^3\pi_{ij}} = 1 - \frac{0,9 \cdot 0,1}{0,18} = 0,5$$

$$\alpha_4 = \pi(\nu_4 = M_2 \mid \nu_1 = M_2; \nu_2 = M_2; \nu_3 = M_2) = 1 - \frac{{}^1\pi_{ij}\ {}^2\pi_{ij}}{{}^3\pi_{ii}} = 1 - \frac{0,1 \cdot 0,1}{0,82} = 0,9878.$$

Then

$$\pi_{iiii} = 1 - \frac{{}^1\pi_{ij} \cdot {}^2\pi_{ij}}{{}^3\pi_{ii}} = 1 - 0 = 1, \quad i \neq j.$$

If

$${}^1\Pi = \begin{Vmatrix} 0,5 & 0,5 \\ 0,5 & 0,5 \end{Vmatrix}, \quad {}^2\Pi = \begin{Vmatrix} {}^2\pi_{ii} & {}^2\pi_{ij} \\ {}^2\pi_{ji} & {}^2\pi_{jj} \end{Vmatrix},$$

then

$$\pi_{iiii} = 1 - \frac{{}^1\pi_{ij} \cdot {}^2\pi_{ij}}{{}^3\pi_{ii}} = 1 - \frac{0,5 \cdot {}^2\pi_{ij}}{0,5} = {}^2\pi_{ii}, i \neq j.$$

Let us check the normalization requirement for the matrix Π on the example of the first line. For this we calculate the element located in the matrix right column (see Box 12).

Let us sum the values of the first line elements

$$\pi_{iiii} + \pi_{jiii} = 0,9878 + 0,0122 = 1, \quad i \neq j.$$

As we see, the normalization requirements are fulfilled and for other lines as well.

BBI MATHEMATICAL MODELS WITH VICINITY OF FOUR ELEMENTS

Let the vicinity of element ν_4 consist of four BBI elements (Figure 3) located at the upper-left, according to Krasheninnikov (2003). At that, the condition of the strict causality peculiar to the vicinity of (5) type is something disturbed but this disturbance is not critical as to define the causal properties or UMRF it is not required any addi-

Box 12.

$$\alpha_1' = \pi(\nu_4 = M_2 \mid \nu_1 = M_1; \nu_2 = M_1; \nu_3 = M_1) = \frac{{}^1\pi_{ij}\ {}^2\pi_{ij}}{{}^3\pi_{ii}} = \frac{0,1 \cdot 0,1}{0,82} = 0,0122.$$

tional element sets besides the left segment Φ_{ij} or accordingly NSHP Ψ_{ij} (Figure 1).

The probability of appearance of the BBI element ν_4 with the value M_1 or M_2 is completely defined by the mutual information quantity between elements of the vicinity

$$\Lambda'_{i,j} = \{v_1, v_2, v_3, v_5\}, \quad (23)$$

and the image element ν_4 (Figure 3).

The information quantity between Λ'_{ij} and the element ν_4 can be determined as shown in Box 13.

At mutual independence of elements of the vicinity $\Lambda'_{i,j}$ the information quantity between the element ν_4 and $\Lambda'_{i,j}$ can be determined on the analogy of (15) (see Box 14).

Because of v_4 is the element of the two-dimensional Markov chain, the information between

Figure 3. The image fragment with the vicinity of four elements

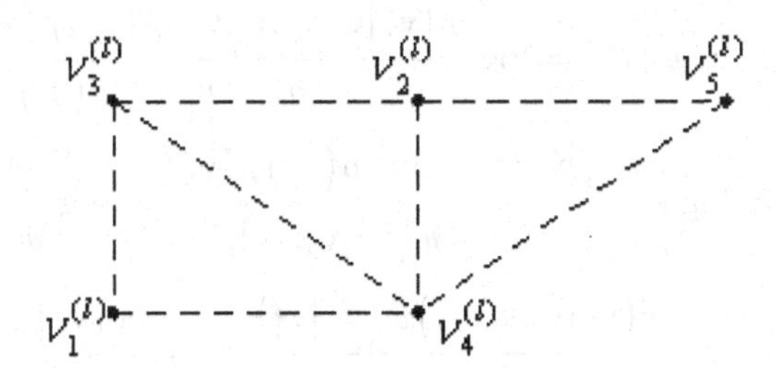

elements v_3, v_4 and v_5, v_4 is redundant disturbing the information balance between elements v_1, v_2 and the element v_4.

Let us subtract the redundant information caused by elements ν_3 and ν_5 from equation (25) (see Box 15).

Having compared (26) and (16), we can conclude that the use of the vicinity (5) or (23) does not change the probability of the element ν_4 value.

Box 13.

$$I(v_1,v_2,v_3,v_4,v_5) = \log \frac{p(v_1,v_2,v_3,v_4,v_5)}{p(v_1)p(v_2)p(v_3)p(v_4)p(v_5)}, \quad (24)$$

where $p(v_i),\ i=\overline{1,5}$ are *a priori* probability densities of values of image elements; $p(v_1,v_2,v_3,v_4,v_5)$ is the mutual probability density.

Box 14.

$$I'(v_1,v_2,v_3,v_4,v_5) = I(v_1,v_2,v_3,v_4,v_5) - I(v_1,v_2,v_3,v_5)$$
$$= \log \frac{p(v_1,v_2,v_3,v_5)\, w(v_4 | v_1,v_2,v_3,v_5)}{p(v_1,v_2,v_3,v_5)\, p(v_4)} = \log \frac{w(v_4 | v_1,v_2,v_3,v_5)}{p(v_4)}, \quad (25)$$

where $w(v_4 | v_1,v_2,v_3,v_5)$ is the transition probability density in the complicated Markov chain.

Box 15.

$$
\begin{aligned}
I\left(v_1, v_2, v_4\right) &= \log \frac{w\left(\mathrm{v}_4 \left| \mathrm{v}_1, \mathrm{v}_2, \mathrm{v}_3, \mathrm{v}_5\right.\right) p\left(\mathrm{v}_3\right) p\left(\mathrm{v}_4\right) p\left(\mathrm{v}_5\right)}{p\left(v_3, v_4, v_5\right) p\left(v_4\right)} \\
&= \log \frac{w\left(\mathrm{v}_4 \left| \mathrm{v}_1, \mathrm{v}_2, \mathrm{v}_3, \mathrm{v}_5\right.\right) p\left(\mathrm{v}_3\right) p\left(\mathrm{v}_5\right)}{p\left(\mathrm{v}_3, \mathrm{v}_5\right) w\left(\mathrm{v}_4 \left| \mathrm{v}_3, \mathrm{v}_5\right.\right)} = \log \frac{w\left(\mathrm{v}_4 \left| \mathrm{v}_1, \mathrm{v}_2, \mathrm{v}_3, \mathrm{v}_5\right.\right)}{w\left(\mathrm{v}_4 \left| \mathrm{v}_3\right.\right) w\left(\mathrm{v}_4 \left| \mathrm{v}_5\right.\right)} \\
&= \log \frac{w\left(\mathrm{v}_4 \left| \mathrm{v}_1, \mathrm{v}_2, \mathrm{v}_3\right.\right) w\left(\mathrm{v}_4 \left| \mathrm{v}_5\right.\right)}{w\left(\mathrm{v}_4 \left| \mathrm{v}_3\right.\right) w\left(\mathrm{v}_4 \left| \mathrm{v}_5\right.\right)} = \log \frac{w\left(\mathrm{v}_4 \left| \mathrm{v}_1, \mathrm{v}_2, \mathrm{v}_3\right.\right)}{w\left(\mathrm{v}_4 \left| \mathrm{v}_3\right.\right)}.
\end{aligned}
\qquad (26)
$$

THE ALGORITHM OF MARKOV BBI FORMATION

To construct the artificial BBI representing the two-dimensional Markov chain with two equiprobable values it is necessary to have the *a priori* known matrices of one-step transition probabilities (13) and the vector of initial probabilities of values $\mathbf{P} = \left[p_1, p_2\right]; \left(p_1 = p_2\right)$.

The BBI modeling includes several stages. The first line of BBI is modeling (areas F_1, F_2 in Figure 1) as thew one-dimensional stationary Markov chain with two equiprobable values and the given matrix $^1\Pi$. The length of state's sequences of Markov chain is equal to the length of the line m. The modeling of BBI elements of the area F_3 (Figure 1) is similar to those for elements of the first line.

The modeling of the area F_4 (Figure 1) is the most complicated and it consists in the following.

1. Matrices $^3\Pi$ and Π are calculated in the basis of known matrices $^1\Pi$ and $^2\Pi$;
2. We take an arbitrary number $\xi_l (l \leq m \cdot n)$, which is equally distributed on the interval $\left[0, 1\right]$;
3. From the first column of the matrix Π we select the element $\alpha_s (s = \overline{1, 4})$ corresponding to element values of the vicinity Λ_{ij};
4. The number ξ_l is compared to the selected element $\alpha_s (s = \overline{1, 4})$. If $\alpha_s (s = \overline{1, 4})$ and $\xi_l \leq \alpha_s$, the image element ν_4 takes the value $M_1 = 0$, otherwise $M_2 = 1$;
5. If $l \leq m \cdot n$, we transit to p. 2, otherwise – to point 6;
6. Stop.

To check the correctness of the model operation let us consider the process of the image formation for the extreme cases of the Markov chain along one of coordinates, when matrices $^1\Pi$ or $^2\Pi$ become either the unitary matrices or all elements in matrices are equal to 0.5.

Let the BBI probability matrix of transitions in horizontal be an unitary matrix:

$$
^1\Pi = \begin{Vmatrix} 1 & 0 \\ 0 & 1 \end{Vmatrix}. \qquad (27)
$$

For the probability matrix of transition in vertical $^2\Pi$ the following condition acts:

$$
^2\Pi \neq {}^1\Pi. \qquad (28)
$$

The BBI with sizes 256×256 obtained in accordance of the above-described algorithm and the matrix (27) is presented in Figure 4a. The BBI with the unitary matrix $^2\Pi$ is shown in Figure

Box 16.

$$r_{l,q,s} = \mathrm{E}\left[\mu_{i,j,t}, \mu_{i+l,j+q,t+s}\right] = \sigma_\mu^2 \exp\left\{-\alpha_1 |l| - \alpha_2 |q| - \alpha_3 |s|\right\}, \quad (29)$$

where $\mathrm{E}\left[\cdot\right]$ has the sense of the mathematical expectation; σ_μ^2 is the image signal variance; $\alpha_1, \alpha_2, \alpha_3$ are coefficients similar to (8). In accordance with (29), the image sequence can be presented as the superposition of three one-dimensional discrete-valued MP with two equiprobable $\left(p_1 = p_2\right)$ values M_1, M_2 and transition probability matrices from one value to another inside the image frame (10) and between adjacent frames ${}^4\Pi$

$${}^1\Pi = \begin{Vmatrix} {}^1\pi_{11} & {}^1\pi_{12} \\ {}^1\pi_{21} & {}^1\pi_{22} \end{Vmatrix}, \; {}^2\Pi = \begin{Vmatrix} {}^2\pi_{11} & {}^2\pi_{12} \\ {}^2\pi_{21} & {}^2\pi_{22} \end{Vmatrix}, \; {}^4\Pi = \begin{Vmatrix} {}^4\pi_{11} & {}^4\pi_{12} \\ {}^4\pi_{21} & {}^4\pi_{22} \end{Vmatrix} \quad (30)$$

accordingly.

Box 17.

$$\Lambda_{i,j,k} = \begin{cases} \varnothing, & if \ (i,j) \in F_{1k} \\ \left\{(i-1,j,k)\right\}, & if \ (i,j) \in F_{2k} \\ \left\{(i,j-1),k\right\}, & if \ (i,j) \in F_{3k} \\ \left\{(i,j-1,k),(i-1,j,k),(i-1,j-1,k)\right\}, & if \ (i,j) \in F_{4k} \end{cases} \quad (32)$$

4b. Figures 5a,b show the binary artificial images with sizes 256x256 obtained for ${}^1\pi_{ii} = {}^2\pi_{ii} = 0,5$; ${}^1\pi_{ii} = {}^2\pi_{ii} = 0,9$ with estimates of the transition probabilities ${}^1\hat{\pi}_{ii}$ и ${}^2\hat{\pi}_{ii}$, $i = \overline{1,2}$ calculated on the basis of artificial images and the two-dimensional auto-correlation function.

Estimates ${}^r\hat{\pi}_{ii}\left(r = \overline{1,2}\right)$ of elements of the transfer probabilities if artificial images coincide with the high accuracy (less than 0.2%) with the given values ${}^r\hat{\pi}_{ii} = 0,9$ on the statistic with sizes 512×512.

Figure 4. The artificial BBI with unitary matrices ${}^1\Pi$ and ${}^2\Pi$ a) ${}^1\pi_{ii} = 1$, ${}^2\pi_{ii} = 0,5$; b) ${}^1\pi_{ii} = 0,5$, ${}^2\pi_{ii} = 1$

THE MATHEMATICAL MODEL OF THE DHTI

The mathematical model of DHTI represented by g-bit binary numbers is formed by the simple bitwise "summation" of g binary images in the register of the binary number. The factual summation is absent as the own bit position in the register with the appropriate weight corresponds to each BBI. It should be noted that proper transi-

Figure 5. The binary artificial images with sizes 256x256 and the two-dimensional auto-correlation function a) ${}^1\pi_{ii} = {}^2\pi_{ii} = 0,5$; *b)* ${}^1\pi_{ii} = {}^2\pi_{ii} = 0,9$

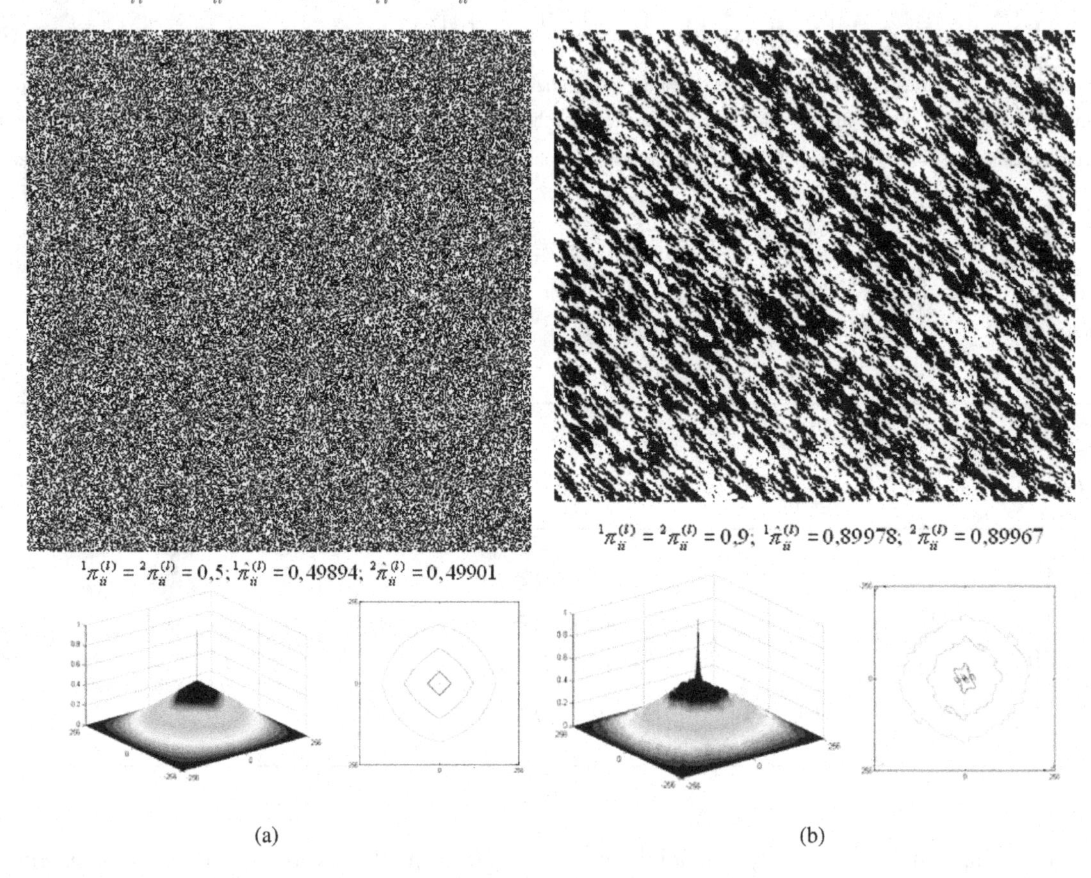

Figure 6. Graphs of a value variation of the transition matrices' (10), (11) elements of DHTI averaged over a great number of the real DHTI

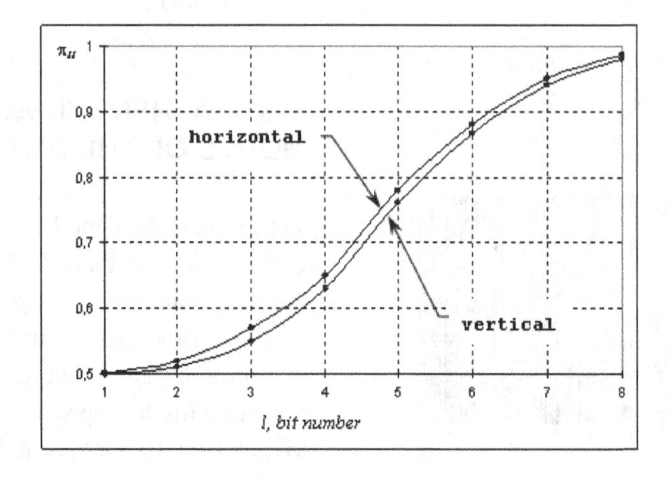

Figure 7. The real DHTI "Lena"

Figure 8. The artificial DHTI obtained with the help of MM at statistical characteristics of the real DHTI "Lena"

tion matrices (10), (11) satisfying the condition (16) correspond to the each l-th $(l \in g)$ binary image. At constructing the DHTI MM adequate to the real situation, it is necessary to know values of transition matrix elements for each BBI. The graphs of value variation of transition matrix (10), (11) elements of DHTI averaged over the great number of the real DHTI, are presented in Figure 6. These graphs concern to presentation in the form of g-bit (g=8) binary numbers and it follows from them that the correlation connection between DHTI elements bitwise is nonlinear in general case and it should be taken into consideration at modeling the BBI adequate to the real situation.

Figures 7 and 8 shows the real DHTI "Lena" and the artificial DHTI obtained with the help of MM at equal statistical characteristics. The BBI of 8,6,1 bits of the real and artificial DHTI "Lena" are presented in Figures 9,a,b,c.

The developed mathematical model of the artificial BBI was used to design nonlinear filtering algorithms for the real DHTI represented by 8-bit binary numbers and it showed high degree of correspondence with the real images which corroborates the findings of Petrov and Chasikov (2001) and Petrov, Trubin and Butorin (2005a).

MATHEMATICAL MODELS OF BBI VIDEO-SEQUENCES

The DHTI representation by the set of g binary sections reduces the problem of MM construction of the DHTI sequence to the construction of MM of the BBI sequence.

We shall assume that the sequence of BBI frames is the three-dimensional discrete-valued Markov process $\mu_k = \mu(i, j, k)$ with two spatial coordinates $(i, j; i \in m, j \in n)$ and time as the third coordinate k = 1,2..., related to the frame number in the image sequence.

We suppose that the correlation function of the BBI frame sequence has the form shown in Box 16.

Let us choose UMRF on NSHP with the vicinity of the form shown in Figure 1 as the mathematical model of BBI (see Box 17).

We consider the case when the BBI random binary element ν_4 in the k-th frame (Figure 10) belonging to the area $F_{4,k}$ should be modeled. The modeling of BBI elements belonging to areas $F_{1,k}$, $F_{2,k}$ and $F_{3,k}$ is simpler than the area $F_{4,k}$ and it can be reduced to modeling of one-dimensional and two-dimensional stationary Markov chains.

Figure 9. The BBI of the real and artificial DHTI "Lena": a) 8-bit; b) 6-bit; c) 1-bit

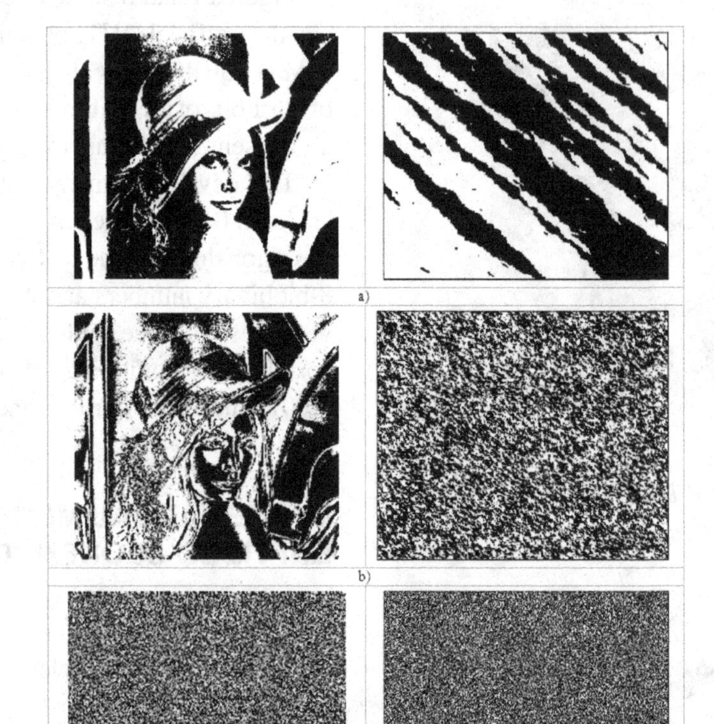

The vicinity of the image element ν_4 at modeling of the video-sequence will be increased up to seven adjacent elements

$\Lambda_{i,j,k} = \left\{ \nu_1; \nu_2; \nu_3; \nu'_1; \nu'_2; \nu'_3, \nu'_4 \right\}$ (Figure 10).

The following designations are used in Figure 11:

$$\nu_1 = \mu\left(i, j-1, k\right),$$
$$\nu_2 = \mu\left(i-1, j, k\right),$$
$$\nu_3 = \mu\left(i-1, j-1, k\right),$$
$$\nu_4 = \mu\left(i, j, k\right),$$
$$\nu'_1 = \mu\left(i, j-1, k-1\right),$$
$$\nu'_2 = \mu\left(i-1, j, k-1\right),$$
$$\nu'_3 = \mu\left(i-1, j-1, k-1\right),$$
$$\nu'_4 = \mu\left(i, j, k-1\right).$$

The statistical connections between BBI elements including inside the vicinity $\Lambda_{i,j,k}$ of the element ν_4 are shown by the firm and dotted lines in Figure 11.

The information quantity containing in elements of the vicinity

$$\Lambda_{ijk} = \left\{\nu_1, \nu_2, \nu_3, \nu_4, \nu'_1, \nu'_2, \nu'_3, \nu'_4\right\}$$

with regards to the element ν_4, can be determine from equation of the view shown in Box 18.

Figure 10. The OSMRF area with the vicinity of seven elements

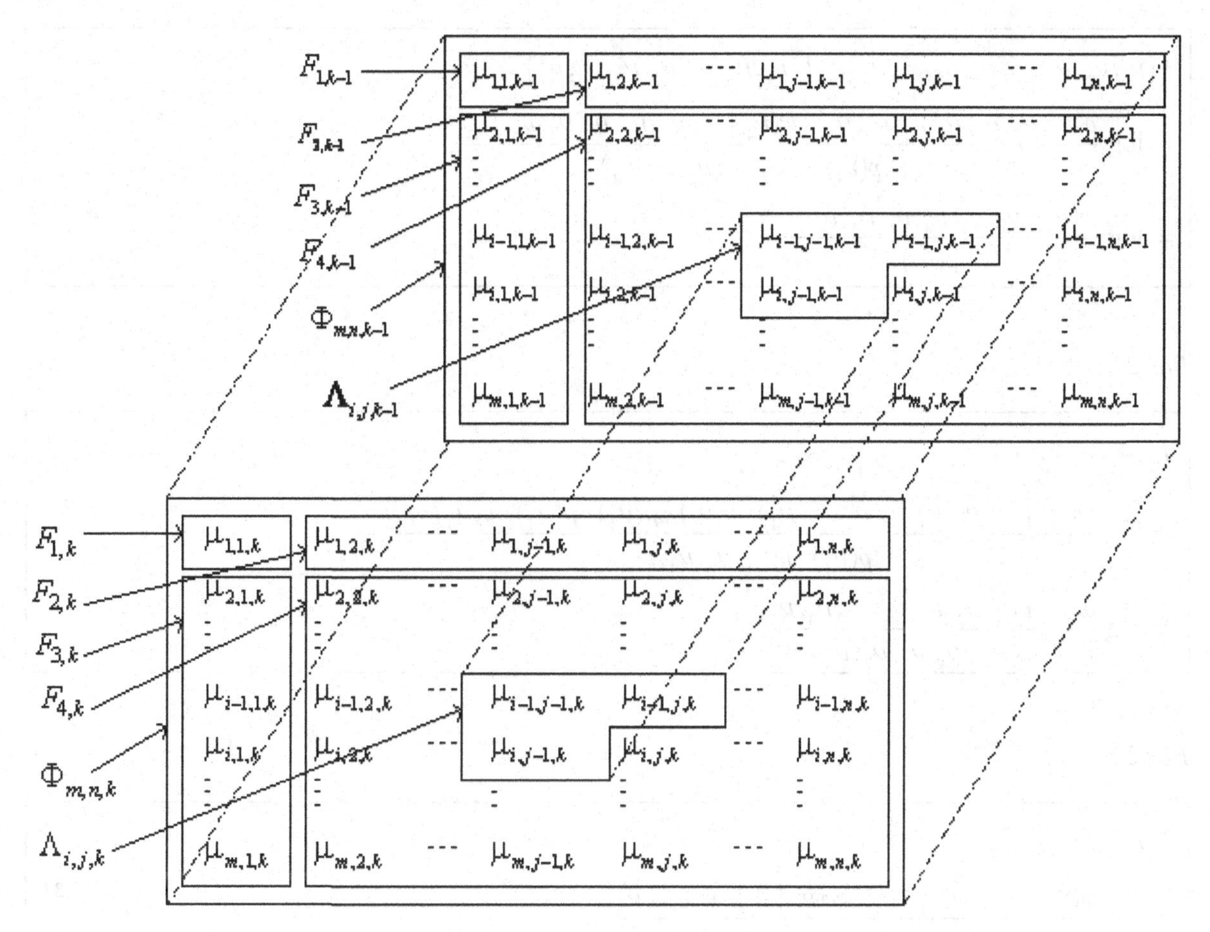

Box 18.

$$I\left(\nu_1,\nu_2,\nu_3,\nu_4,\nu_1',\nu_2',\nu_3',\nu_4'\right) = \log\frac{p(\nu_1,\nu_2,\nu_3,\nu_4,\nu_1',\nu_2',\nu_3',\nu_4')}{\prod_{i=1}^{4} p(\nu_i)\cdot\prod_{i=1}^{4} p(\nu_i')}. \tag{33}$$

Box 19.

$$I\left(\nu_1,\nu_2,\nu_3,\nu_1',\nu_2',\nu_3',\nu_4'\right) = \log\frac{p(\nu_1,\nu_2,\nu_3,\nu_1',\nu_2',\nu_3',\nu_4')}{\prod_{i=1}^{3} p\left(\nu_i\right)\prod_{i=1}^{4} p\left(\nu_i'\right)}. \tag{34}$$

Box 20.

$$I\left(\nu_1,\nu_2,\nu_3,\nu_4,\nu_1^{'},\nu_2^{'},\nu_3^{'},\nu_4^{'}\right)-I\left(\nu_1,\nu_2,\nu_3,\nu_1^{'},\nu_2^{'},\nu_3^{'},\nu_4^{'}\right)$$
$$=\log\frac{p(\nu_1,\nu_2,\nu_3,\nu_1^{'},\nu_2^{'},\nu_3^{'},\nu_4^{'})\cdot w(\nu_4\mid\nu_1,\nu_2,\nu_3,\nu_1^{'},\nu_2^{'},\nu_3^{'},\nu_4^{'})}{p(\nu_4)\cdot p(\nu_1,\nu_2,\nu_3,\nu_1^{'},\nu_2^{'},\nu_3^{'},\nu_4^{'})} \quad (35)$$
$$=\log\frac{w(\nu_4\mid\nu_1,\nu_2,\nu_3,\nu_1^{'},\nu_2^{'},\nu_3^{'},\nu_4^{'})}{p(\nu_4)}.$$

Box 21.

$$I\left(\nu_1,\nu_2,\nu_4^{'},\nu_4\right)$$
$$=\log\frac{w(\nu_4\mid\nu_1,\nu_2,\nu_3,\nu_1^{'},\nu_2^{'},\nu_3^{'},\nu_4^{'})\cdot p(\nu_1^{'})\cdot p(\nu_2^{'})\cdot p(\nu_3^{'})\cdot p(\nu_3)\cdot p(\nu_4)}{p(\nu_4)\cdot p(\nu_1^{'},\nu_2^{'},\nu_3^{'},\nu_3,\nu_4)} \quad (36)$$
$$=\log\frac{w(\nu_4\mid\nu_1,\nu_2,\nu_3,\nu_1^{'},\nu_2^{'},\nu_3^{'},\nu_4^{'})}{w(\nu_4\mid\nu_1^{'},\nu_2^{'},\nu_3^{'},\nu_3)}.$$

Box 22.

$$I\left(\nu_1,\nu_2,\nu_4^{'},\nu_4\right)$$
$$=\log\frac{w(\nu_4\mid\nu_1)\cdot w(\nu_4\mid\nu_4^{'})\cdot w(\nu_4\mid v_2)\cdot w(\nu_4\mid\nu_3^{'})}{w(\nu_4\mid\nu_3)\cdot w(\nu_4\mid\nu_1^{'})\cdot w(\nu_4\mid\nu_2^{'})}. \quad (37)$$

Box 23.

$$\pi_{ijklmnqr}=\pi(\nu_4=M_i\mid\nu_1=M_j,\nu_2=M_k;\nu_3=M_l;\nu_1^{'}=M_m;$$
$$\nu_2^{'}=M_n;\nu_3^{'}=M_q;\nu_4^{'}=M_r),i,j,k,l,m,n,q,r=\overline{1,2}. \quad (38)$$

The information containing between BBI elements falling inside the vicinity $\Lambda_{i,j,k}$ can be calculated similar to (33) (see Box 19).

In the complicated Markov chain representing the video-sequence the image elements inside the vicinity Λ_{ijk} should be independent. To fulfill this condition we shall obtain the difference of expressions (33) and (34) (see Box 20).

By the data, the BBI sequence represents three-dimensional discrete-valued Markov chain formed by the superposition of three one-dimensional independent Markov chains. Therefore, the information containing in BBI elements $\nu_3, \nu_1', \nu_2', \nu_3'$ with regard to the element ν_4 is redundant and we must eliminate it. In this case the equation for information between BBI elements ν_4 and ν_1, ν_2, ν_4' will take the form shown in Box 21.

Having eliminated information about the element ν_3 in elements ν_3, ν_1', ν_2' in the conditional probability density $w\left(\nu_4 \left| \nu_1', \nu_2', \nu_3, \nu_3' \right.\right)$, equation (36) can be presented as shown in Box 22.

The transition probability density for the complicated Markov chain, which can be approximated the BBI sequence is completely defined by the transition probability matrix Π, which elements have the form shown in Box 23.

For known matrices ${}^1\Pi$, ${}^2\Pi$, ${}^4\Pi$, in order to calculate the matrix Π elements, it is necessary to calculate preliminarily matrices

$$\begin{aligned} {}^3\Pi &= {}^1\Pi \cdot {}^2\Pi; \\ {}^5\Pi &= {}^1\Pi \cdot {}^4\Pi; \\ {}^6\Pi &= {}^2\Pi \cdot {}^4\Pi; \\ {}^7\Pi &= {}^3\Pi \cdot {}^4\Pi = {}^1\Pi \cdot {}^2\Pi \cdot {}^4\Pi. \end{aligned} \tag{39}$$

Using the entropy approach to statistically connected in-pairs the elements of the BBI video-sequence, we can rewrite the transition probability matrix for the complicated Markov chain in the form shown in Box 24.

Matrix Π element values (36) can be calculated in accordance with (35). For example, expressions for calculation of elements of the first line of the matrix Π have the form:

$$\begin{aligned} \pi_{iiiiiii} &= 1 - \frac{{}^1\pi_{ij} \cdot {}^2\pi_{ij} \cdot {}^4\pi_{ij} \cdot {}^7\pi_{ij}}{{}^3\pi_{ii} \cdot {}^5\pi_{ii} \cdot {}^6\pi_{ii}}, \\ \pi_{jiiiiii} &= \frac{{}^1\pi_{ij} \cdot {}^2\pi_{ij} \cdot {}^4\pi_{ij} \cdot {}^7\pi_{ij}}{{}^3\pi_{ii} \cdot {}^5\pi_{ii} \cdot {}^6\pi_{ii}}, i \neq j. \end{aligned} \tag{41}$$

The determination of other elements of the matrix Π is executed in accordance with the vicinity $\Lambda_{i,j,k}$ element values. For instance, elements of the second line can be calculated as:

$$\begin{aligned} \pi_{iiijiii} &= 1 - \frac{{}^1\pi_{ij} \cdot {}^2\pi_{ij} \cdot {}^4\pi_{ii} \cdot {}^7\pi_{ii}}{{}^3\pi_{ii} \cdot {}^5\pi_{ij} \cdot {}^6\pi_{ij}}, \\ \pi_{jiijiii} &= \frac{{}^1\pi_{ij} \cdot {}^2\pi_{ij} \cdot {}^4\pi_{ii} \cdot {}^7\pi_{ii}}{{}^3\pi_{ii} \cdot {}^5\pi_{ij} \cdot {}^6\pi_{ij}}, i \neq j. \end{aligned} \tag{42}$$

Box 24.

$$\Pi = \begin{Vmatrix} \pi_{iiiiiii} & \pi_{jiiiiii} \\ \pi_{iiijiii} & \pi_{jiijiii} \\ \pi_{iijiiii} & \pi_{jijiiii} \\ \pi_{iijjiii} & \pi_{jijjiii} \\ \pi_{ijiiiii} & \pi_{jjiiiii} \\ \pi_{ijijiii} & \pi_{jjijiii} \\ \pi_{ijjiiii} & \pi_{jjjiiii} \\ \pi_{ijjjiii} & \pi_{jjjjiii} \end{Vmatrix} = \begin{Vmatrix} \alpha_1 & \alpha_1' \\ \alpha_2 & \alpha_2' \\ \alpha_3 & \alpha_3' \\ \alpha_4 & \alpha_4' \\ \alpha_5 & \alpha_5' \\ \alpha_6 & \alpha_6' \\ \alpha_7 & \alpha_7' \\ \alpha_8 & \alpha_8' \end{Vmatrix}, \quad i, j = \overline{1, 2}; \quad i \neq j. \tag{40}$$

Figure 11. Seven elements of vicinity of the image element ν_4

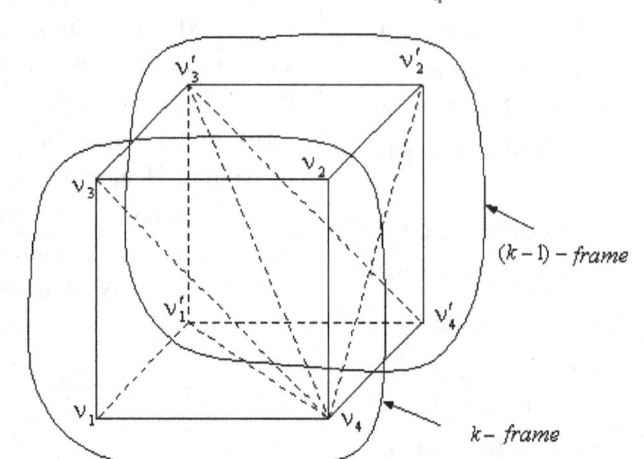

Similarly, we can write formulas for calculating the matrix Π elements for various combinations of values of the vicinity $\Lambda_{i,j,k}$ elements.

If one of the initial matrices ${}^1\Pi$, ${}^2\Pi$ or ${}^4\Pi$ is the unitary matrix, elements of the matrix Π will contain 1 and 0 only. The element ν_4 value will coincide with the value of the vicinity $\Lambda_{i,j,k}$ element, whose transition probability is defined by the unitary matrix. In the case when one of matrices ${}^1\Pi$, ${}^2\Pi$ or ${}^4\Pi$ consists of elements with value equaled 0.5 (equiprobable independent transitions), the product of this matrix with the others gives a similar matrix. Computation of the matrix Π element becomes simpler. For instance, if elements of the matrix ${}^1\Pi$ are equal to 0.5, elements of matrices ${}^3\Pi$, ${}^5\Pi$, ${}^7\Pi$ also equal to 0.5. The value of the BBI element will be defined by matrices' ${}^2\Pi$ and ${}^4\Pi$ elements only. If elements of matrices ${}^1\Pi$ and ${}^2\Pi$ are equal to 0.5, the appearance of this or that value of the BBI element ν_4 will depend upon values of the matrix ${}^4\Pi$ elements only. For the same and equal to 0.5 elements of ${}^1\Pi$, ${}^2\Pi$, ${}^4\Pi$ the appearance of this or that value of the BBI element ν_4 is equiprobable. Matrix Π elements will be equal to 0.5.

Let us consider the case when matrices ${}^1\Pi$, ${}^2\Pi$ and ${}^4\Pi$ are equal, i.e.

$$ {}^1\Pi = {}^2\Pi = {}^4\Pi = \begin{Vmatrix} 0,9 & 0,1 \\ 0,1 & 0,9 \end{Vmatrix}. \quad (43) $$

Let all elements of the vicinity have the equal values $M_1 = 0$ or $M_2 = 1$. We calculate by formulas (38) probability of appearance and absence the element value $\nu_4 = M_1 = 0$.

$$ \pi_{iiiiiiii} = 1 - \frac{0,1 \cdot 0,1 \cdot 0,1 \cdot 0,756}{0,82 \cdot 0,82 \cdot 0,82} = 0,99863, $$

$$ \pi_{ijjjjjjj} = \frac{0,1 \cdot 0,1 \cdot 0,1 \cdot 0,756}{0,82 \cdot 0,82 \cdot 0,82} = 0,00137. $$

THE ALGORITHM OF FORMATION OF THE MARKOV BBI SEQUENCE

The basis for the mathematical model construction for Markov BBI sequence is the equation (37). The modeling of the Markov BBI sequence includes several stages.

1. Specify the transition matrices ${}^1\Pi$, ${}^2\Pi$, ${}^4\Pi$ and calculate matrices ${}^3\Pi$, ${}^5\Pi$, ${}^6\Pi$, ${}^7\Pi$ and the matrix Π;
2. Take the random number $\xi_l (l \le m \cdot n)$ equally distributed over the interval $[0,1]$.

3. Select the element $\alpha_s(s=\overline{1,8})$ corresponding to values of the vicinity $\Lambda_{i,j,k}$ elements from the first column of the matrix Π;
4. The number ξ_l is compared with the chosen element $\alpha_s(s=\overline{1,8})$ and if $\alpha_s=\overline{1,8}$ and $\xi_l \le \alpha_s$, the image elements ν_4 takes the value $\nu_4 = M_1 = 0$, otherwise $\nu_4 = M_2 = 1$;
5. If $i < n; j < m; k < K$, where K is the sequence length we pass to point 3, otherwise to point 6;
6. Stop.

Investigations of mathematical models of the BBI sequence for various statistical correlation between adjacent BBI elements in the space (frame) and time (between frames) was carried out.

MATHEMATICAL MODELS OF VIDEO-SEQUENCE OF MARKOV DHTI

The mathematical model of the DHTI video-sequence represents the three-dimensional Markov chain with $q=2^g$ values and consists of g MM sequences of Markov BBI ordered by bits of binary numbers of the DHTI representation. Combination of BBI - DHTI in the each video-sequence frame is fulfilled on the g-bits register and does not require calculation operations. At that, the memory volume does not exceed one frame of DHTI. At DHTI modeling we need to take into account that each BBI has its own individual matrices of the transition probabilities of type (30).

Figure 11 shows 1st, 5th, 10th, 20th frames of the video-sequence of the artificial BBI at matrix values

$${}^{1}\pi_{ii}^{(1)} = {}^{2}\pi_{ii}^{(1)} = 0,6,$$

$${}^{1}\pi_{ii}^{(2)} = {}^{2}\pi_{ii}^{(2)} = 0,65,$$

$${}^{1}\pi_{ii}^{(3)} = {}^{2}\pi_{ii}^{(3)} = 0,7,$$

$${}^{1}\pi_{ii}^{(4)} = {}^{2}\pi_{ii}^{(4)} = 0,75$$

$${}^{1}\pi_{ii}^{(5)} = {}^{2}\pi_{ii}^{(5)} = 0,8,$$

$${}^{1}\pi_{ii}^{(6)} = {}^{2}\pi_{ii}^{(6)} = 0,85,$$

$${}^{1}\pi_{ii}^{(7)} = {}^{2}\pi_{ii}^{(7)} = 0,9$$

$${}^{1}\pi_{ii}^{(8)} = {}^{2}\pi_{ii}^{(8)} = 0,95$$

and

$${}^{4}\pi_{ii} = 0,9.$$

The auto-correlation function analysis of video-sequences of artificial and real DHTI shows that the MM is adequate to the real process.

Results obtained from the construction of two- and three-dimensional mathematical models allow for assuming that the approximation of the statistically correlated video-sequences of DHTI by the multi-dimensional and multi-valued Markov process is the reasonable approach to solving the problem of construction of multi-dimensional mathematical models realized by means of minimal computation resources.

Let $\mu(\Theta_1,\Theta_2,...,\Theta_h)$ (where Θ_i are discrete coordinates) be the multi-dimensional multi-level multi-valued Markov process, this corresponds to statistically correlated video-sequences of DHTI. Let us construct the mathematical models of several statistically correlated video-se-

Box 25.

$$r_{i,\, j,\, l, \ldots, h} = \sigma_\mu^2 \exp\{-\alpha_1 |i| - \alpha_2 |j| - \alpha_3 |l| - \ldots - \alpha_h |h|\}, \quad (43)$$

where $\alpha_1, \ldots \alpha_h$ are coefficients similar to those in expression (9).

quences of DHTI, whose realization requires the minimal computing resources. In constructing the mathematical models, we shall assume that $\mu(\Theta_1, \Theta_2, \ldots, \Theta_h)$ represents the superposition of h one-dimensional, multi-valued Markov process.

The correlation function of this process has a form shown in Box 25.

For better understanding of the method of multi-dimensional mathematical model construction we will be limited by four-dimensional, multi-valued Markov process, which is adequate for the spread of statistically correlated DHTI video-sequences in the space.

MATHEMATICAL MODELS OF TWO STATISTICALLY CORRELATED BBI SEQUENCES

Let us represent Markov DHTI with sizes $m \times n$ elements as a sum of g BBI. Similar to the previous mathematical model, we first construct the mathematical model of two statistically correlated BBI sequences.

The more the dimensions of the random processes, the more complicated it is to select an example of its physical implementation. We assume that the three-dimensional random binary Markov process described earlier moves discretely in the space with equal intervals, sensing the image of the same object from the different locations. We shall suppose that the sequence of BBI elements from one position to another is the four-dimensional, multi-level, discrete-valued Markov process with the correlation function of the following form:

$$\begin{aligned} r_{f,\, q,\, s,\, p}^{(l)} &= E[\mu_{i,j,t,v}^{(l)}\, \mu_{i+f,j+q,t+s,v+p}^{(l)}] \\ &= \sigma_\mu^2 \exp\{-\alpha_1^{(l)} |f| - \alpha_2^{(l)} |q| - \alpha_3^{(l)} |s| - \alpha_4^{(l)} |p|\}, \end{aligned} \quad (44)$$

where $E[\mu_{i,j,t,v}^{(l)}\, \mu_{i+f,j+q,t+s,v+p}^{(l)}]$ is the mathematical expectation; σ_μ^2 is a variance of the random process; $\alpha_i^{(l)} (i = \overline{1, 4})$ are the scale multipliers related to the process' spectrum on each coordinate.

Box 26.

$$\Lambda_{i,j,k} = \{\mu_{i,j-1,k,d}, \mu_{i-1,j,k,d} \mu_{i-1,j-1,k,d}\}, \quad (46)$$

$$\Lambda_{i,j,k,d} = \begin{cases} \varnothing, & if \ (i,j) \in F_{1kd} \\ \{(i-1, j, k, d)\}, & if \ (i,j) \in F_{2kd} \\ \{(i, j-1), k, d\}, & if \ (i,j) \in F_{3kd} \\ \{(i, j-1, k, d), (i-1, j, k, d), (i-1, j-1, k, d)\}, & if \ (i,j) \in F_{4kd} \end{cases} \quad (47)$$

The random Markov process represents a superposition of four one-dimensional Markov chains with two states.

Let us construct the mathematical model for the l-th bit $\left(p_1^{(l)} = p_2^{(l)}\right)$ of DHTI based on the four-dimensional stationary Markov chain with two equiprobable states M_1, M_2 and the matrices of one-step transition probabilities from one value to another inside the frame ${}^1\Pi^{(l)}$, ${}^2\Pi^{(l)}$, from frame to frame ${}^4\Pi^{(l)}$ and from position to position ${}^8\Pi^{(l)}$, accordingly:

$$\begin{gathered} {}^1\Pi = \begin{Vmatrix} {}^1\pi_{11} & {}^1\pi_{12} \\ {}^1\pi_{21} & {}^1\pi_{22} \end{Vmatrix}, \quad {}^2\Pi = \begin{Vmatrix} {}^2\pi_{11} & {}^2\pi_{12} \\ {}^2\pi_{21} & {}^2\pi_{22} \end{Vmatrix}, \\ {}^4\Pi = \begin{Vmatrix} {}^4\pi_{11} & {}^4\pi_{12} \\ {}^4\pi_{21} & {}^4\pi_{22} \end{Vmatrix}, \quad {}^8\Pi = \begin{Vmatrix} {}^8\pi_{11} & {}^8\pi_{12} \\ {}^8\pi_{21} & {}^8\pi_{22} \end{Vmatrix}. \end{gathered} \tag{45}$$

Let the random Markov process $\mu_{ijkd}^{(l)}$ being the process of l-th $\left(l \in g\right)$ binary bit of DHTI in k-th frame and in position d represent a superposition of four one-dimensional binary Markov processes. We take as the BBI mathematical model in k-th frame in position d, the UMRF in NSHP with the vicinity of type Figure 12 (see Box 26).

Consider the case when the BBI element ν_4 in $k-$th frame in position d belonging to $F_{4,k,d}$ area^w (Figure 12) is the subject for modeling. Modeling of the BBI elements belonging to areas $F_{1,k,d}$, $F_{2,k,d}$ and $F_{3,k,d}$ is simpler than the area $F_{4,k,d}$ and reduces to modeling of one-dimensional, two-dimensional and three-dimensional stationary Markov chains.

Fragments of mathematical model of two statistically correlated sequences (Figure 13) for two adjacent frames and two adjacent positions in the space are presented in Figure 14.

BBI elements in position d (Figure 14) will be designated as: $\nu_1 = \mu_{i,j-1,k,d}$, $\nu_2 = \mu_{i-1,j,k,d}$, $\nu_3 = \mu_{i-1,j-1,k,d}$, $\nu_4 = \mu_{i,j,k,d}$, $\nu_1' = \mu_{i,j-1,k-1,d}$, $\nu_2' = \mu_{i-1,j,k-1,d}$, $\nu_3' = \mu_{i-1,j-1,k-1,d}$, $\nu_4' = \mu_{i,j,k-1,d}$, an as $\varepsilon_1 = \mu_{i,j-1,k,d-1}$, $\varepsilon_2 = \mu_{i-1,j,k,d-1}$, $\varepsilon_3 = \mu_{i-1,j-1,k,d-1}$, $\varepsilon_4 = \mu_{i,j,k,d-1}$, $\varepsilon_1' = \mu_{i,j-1,k-1,d-1}$, $\varepsilon_2' = \mu_{i-1,j,k-1,d-1}$, $\varepsilon_3' = \mu_{i-1,j-1,k-1,d-1}$, $\varepsilon_4' = \mu_{i,j,k-1,d-1}$ are the image elements in position $d-1$.

The vicinity of BBI element ν_4 in position d has 15 adjacent image elements (see Box 27).

The quantity of information contained in elements of the vicinity (48) with regard to element ν_4 without taking into account the statistical correlation between elements of the Λ_{ijkd} vicinity can be represented similar to expression (35) in the form shown in Box 28.

The modeling process is the four-dimensional Markov chain, therefore, the information quantity defining the appearance of this or that value

Figure 12. Frames of the video-sequence of the artificial BBI

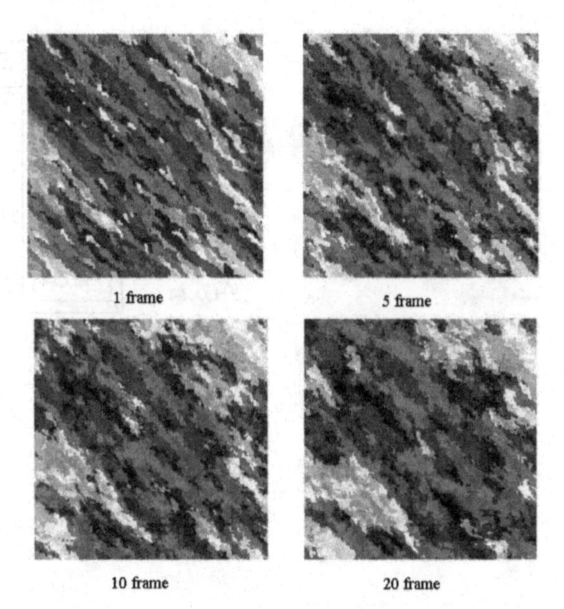

Figure 13. The mathematical model of two statistically correlated BBI sequences

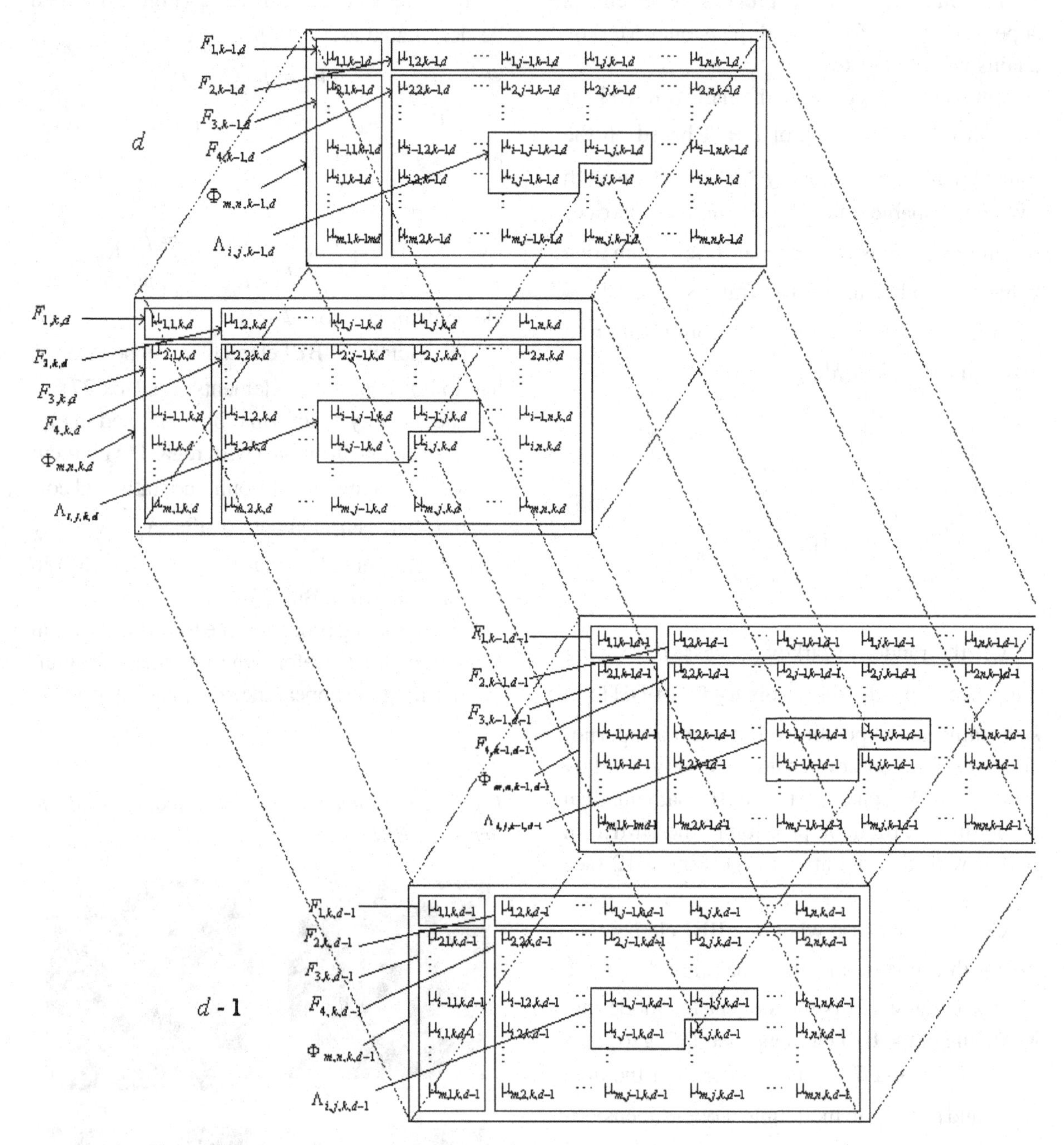

Figure 14. The MM fragment of two statistically correlated video-sequences

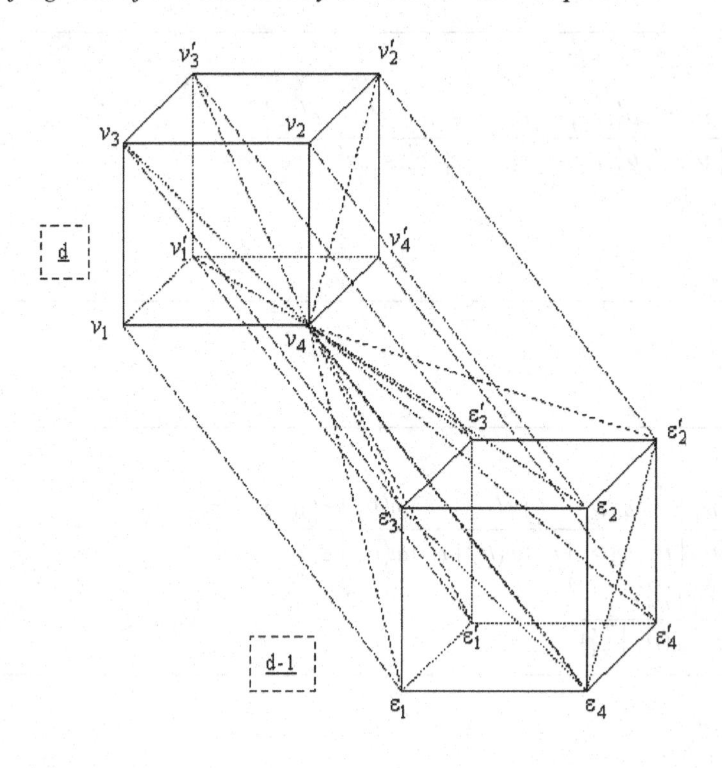

Box 27.

$$\Lambda_{i,j,k,v} = \left(\nu_1,\nu_2,\nu_3,\nu_1',\nu_2',\nu_3',\nu_4',\varepsilon_1,\varepsilon_2,\varepsilon_3,\varepsilon_4,\varepsilon_1',\varepsilon_2',\varepsilon_3',\varepsilon_4'\right). \quad (48)$$

Box 28.

$$I(\nu_1,\nu_2,\nu_4',\nu_4,\ \varepsilon_4) = \log\frac{w(\nu_4 \mid \nu_1,\nu_2,\nu_3,\nu_4,\nu_1',\nu_2',\nu_3',\varepsilon_1,\varepsilon_2,\varepsilon_3,\varepsilon_4,\varepsilon_1',\varepsilon_2',\varepsilon_3',\varepsilon_4')}{p(\nu_4)}, \quad (49)$$

where $w(\cdot)$ is the multi-dimensional probability density in the complicated Markov chain.

Box 29.

$$I(\nu_1,\nu_2,\nu_4',\nu_4,\varepsilon_4) = \log\frac{w(\nu_4\mid\nu_1,\nu_2,\nu_3,\nu_1',\nu_2',\nu_3',\nu_4',\varepsilon_1,\varepsilon_2,\varepsilon_3,\varepsilon_4,\varepsilon_1',\varepsilon_2',\varepsilon_3',\varepsilon_4')}{w(\nu_4\mid\nu_3,\nu_1',\nu_2',\nu_3',\varepsilon_1,\varepsilon_2,\varepsilon_3,\varepsilon_1',\varepsilon_2',\varepsilon_3',\varepsilon_4')} \times\frac{w\left(v_4\left|v_3',\varepsilon_1',\varepsilon_2',\varepsilon_3,\varepsilon_3'\right.\right)}{w\left(v_4\left|\varepsilon_3'\right.\right)}. \tag{50}$$

Box 30.

$$I(\nu_1,\nu_2,\nu_4',\varepsilon_4) = \log\frac{w(\nu_4\mid\nu_1)w(\nu_4\mid\nu_2)w(\nu_4\mid\nu_4')w(\nu_4\mid\varepsilon_4)w(\nu_4\mid\varepsilon_1')w(\nu_4\mid\varepsilon_2')}{w(\nu_4\mid\nu_3)w(\nu_4\mid\nu_1')w(\nu_4\mid\nu_2')w(\nu_4\mid\varepsilon_1)} \times\frac{w(\nu_4\mid\varepsilon_3)w(\nu_4\mid\nu_3')}{w(\nu_4\mid\varepsilon_2)w(\nu_4\mid\varepsilon_4')w(\nu_4\mid\varepsilon_3')} \tag{51}$$

Box 31.

$$\pi_{ijklmnqrtsfhuvpw} = \pi(\nu_4\mid\nu_1 = M_j;\nu_2 = M_k;\nu_3 = M_l;\nu_4' = M_n;\nu_3' = M_r; \varepsilon_1 = M_t;\varepsilon_2 = M_s;\varepsilon_3 = M_f;\varepsilon_4 = M_h;\varepsilon_1' = M_u;\varepsilon_2' = M_v;\varepsilon_3' = M_p;\varepsilon_4' = M_w), \quad i,j,k,l,m,n,\ q,r,t,s,f,h,u,v,p,w = 1,2. \tag{52}$$

of the BBI element ν_4, should depend upon the statistical correlation only between the element ν_4 and elements $\nu_1,\nu_2,\nu_4',\varepsilon_4$ of the vicinity (48) (see Box 29).

Taking into consideration that conditions of mutual independence of the vicinity Λ_{ijkd} elements are fulfilled, equation (50) can be transformed to the form shown in Box 30.

Equation (51) is the basis of the model construction of the four-dimensional discrete-valued Markov process with two values.

Transition probabilities for the discrete-valued four-dimensional MP are defined by the matrix of transition probabilities Π, with elements of the form shown in Box 31.

Let matrices of the single-step transition probabilities on the four coordinates (dimensions) be specified. For the three-dimensional MP these are ${}^1\Pi$, ${}^2\Pi$, ${}^4\Pi$ in position d and similar matrices of transition probabilities are ${}^1\Pi'$, ${}^2\Pi'$, ${}^4\Pi'$ for three-dimensional MP in position $d-1$. The statistical correlation between the three-dimensional processes in positions d and $d-1$ is characterized by the matrix of transition probabilities ${}^8\Pi$. We shall assume that the multi-dimensional random

MP is stationary on all coordinates. Evidently, in this case there are 15 transition matrices:

$$
\begin{aligned}
&{}^{1}\Pi,\ {}^{1}\Pi',\ {}^{2}\Pi,\ {}^{2}\Pi',\ {}^{4}\Pi,\ {}^{4}\Pi',\\
&{}^{3}\Pi = {}^{1}\Pi' \times {}^{2}\Pi',\\
&{}^{3}\Pi' = {}^{1}\Pi' \times {}^{2}\Pi',\\
&{}^{5}\Pi,\ {}^{5}\Pi' = {}^{1}\Pi' \times {}^{4}\Pi';\\
&{}^{6}\Pi,\ {}^{6}\Pi' = {}^{2}\Pi' \times {}^{4}\Pi',\\
&{}^{7}\Pi,\ {}^{7}\Pi' = {}^{3}\Pi' \times {}^{4}\Pi',\\
&{}^{9}\Pi = {}^{3}\Pi' \times {}^{8}\Pi;\\
&{}^{10}\Pi = {}^{5}\Pi' \times {}^{8}\Pi,\\
&{}^{11}\Pi = {}^{6}\Pi' \times {}^{8}\Pi,\\
&{}^{12}\Pi = {}^{7}\Pi' \times {}^{8}\Pi,\\
&{}^{13}\Pi = {}^{1}\Pi' \times {}^{8}\Pi;\\
&{}^{14}\Pi = {}^{2}\Pi' \times {}^{8}\Pi;\\
&{}^{15}\Pi = {}^{4}\Pi' \times {}^{8}\Pi.
\end{aligned}
\tag{53}
$$

Probabilities of appearance of the BBI element ν_4 with the value $\nu_4 = M_1$ or $\nu_4 = M_2$ depend upon combinations of values of BBI elements

Box 32.

$$
\Pi = \begin{Vmatrix}
\pi_{iiii\underbrace{ii\cdots ii}_{11}} & \pi_{jiii\underbrace{ii\cdots ii}_{11}} \\
\pi_{iiij\underbrace{ii\cdots ii}_{11}} & \pi_{jiij\underbrace{ii\cdots ii}_{11}} \\
\vdots & \vdots \\
\pi_{ijjji\underbrace{jj\cdots jj}_{11}} & \pi_{jjjji\underbrace{jj\cdots jj}_{11}} \\
\pi_{ijjjj\underbrace{jj\cdots jj}_{11}} & \pi_{jjjjj\underbrace{jj\cdots jj}_{11}}
\end{Vmatrix}
= \begin{Vmatrix}
\alpha_1 & \alpha_1' \\
\alpha_2 & \alpha_2' \\
\vdots & \vdots \\
\alpha_{15} & \alpha_{15}' \\
\alpha_{16} & \alpha_{16}'
\end{Vmatrix}, \quad i,j = \overline{1,2}; \quad i \neq j. \tag{54}
$$

Box 33.

$$
\begin{aligned}
\pi_{iiii\underbrace{ii\cdots ii}_{11}} &= 1 - \frac{{}^{1}\pi_{ij}\,{}^{2}\pi_{ij}\,{}^{4}\pi_{ij}\,{}^{8}\pi_{ij}\,{}^{7}\pi_{ij}\,{}^{9}\pi_{ij}\,{}^{10}\pi_{ij}\,{}^{11}\pi_{ij}}{{}^{3}\pi_{ii}\,{}^{5}\pi_{ii}\,{}^{6}\pi_{ii}\,{}^{13}\pi_{ii}\,{}^{14}\pi_{ii}\,{}^{15}\pi_{ii}\,{}^{12}\pi_{ii}};\\
\pi_{jiii\underbrace{ii\cdots ii}_{11}} &= \frac{{}^{1}\pi_{ij}\,{}^{2}\pi_{ij}\,{}^{4}\pi_{ij}\,{}^{8}\pi_{ij}\,{}^{7}\pi_{ij}\,{}^{9}\pi_{ij}\,{}^{10}\pi_{ij}\,{}^{11}\pi_{ij}}{{}^{3}\pi_{ii}\,{}^{5}\pi_{ii}\,{}^{6}\pi_{ii}\,{}^{13}\pi_{ii}\,{}^{14}\pi_{ii}\,{}^{15}\pi_{ii}\,{}^{12}\pi_{ii}}; i \neq j.\\
\pi_{iiij\underbrace{ii\cdots ii}_{11}} &= 1 - \frac{{}^{1}\pi_{ij}\,{}^{2}\pi_{ij}\,{}^{4}\pi_{ij}\,{}^{8}\pi_{ii}\,{}^{7}\pi_{ii}\,{}^{9}\pi_{ij}\,{}^{10}\pi_{ij}\,{}^{11}\pi_{ij}}{{}^{3}\pi_{ij}\,{}^{5}\pi_{ij}\,{}^{6}\pi_{ii}\,{}^{13}\pi_{ij}\,{}^{14}\pi_{ij}\,{}^{15}\pi_{ij}\,{}^{12}\pi_{ij}};\\
\pi_{jiij\underbrace{ii\cdots ii}_{11}} &= \frac{{}^{1}\pi_{ij}\,{}^{2}\pi_{ij}\,{}^{4}\pi_{ij}\,{}^{8}\pi_{ii}\,{}^{7}\pi_{ii}\,{}^{9}\pi_{ij}\,{}^{10}\pi_{ij}\,{}^{11}\pi_{ij}}{{}^{3}\pi_{ij}\,{}^{5}\pi_{ij}\,{}^{6}\pi_{ii}\,{}^{13}\pi_{ij}\,{}^{14}\pi_{ij}\,{}^{15}\pi_{ij}\,{}^{12}\pi_{ij}}.
\end{aligned}
\tag{55}
$$

falling in the vicinity (48) and form the matrix shown in Box 32.

Values of the element of matrix Π may be calculated in accordance with the argument of the logarithm (51) using the entropy between the generating element ν_4 in position d and mutually independent elements of the vicinity $\Lambda_{i,j,k,d}$. For example, at known values of the matrices in (53), expressions for element calculation of the first two lines of the matrix Π have the form shown in Box 33.

We calculate the probability $\pi_{ii...i}$ under the condition that

$$^{1}\Pi = {}^{2}\Pi = {}^{4}\Pi = {}^{1}\Pi' = {}^{2}\Pi' = {}^{4}\Pi' = {}^{8}\Pi = \begin{Vmatrix} 0,9 & 0,1 \\ 0,1 & 0,9 \end{Vmatrix}.$$

$$\pi_{j\underbrace{iiii\,ii\cdots ii}_{11}} = 0,0001522.$$

Other elements are calculated in the similar way depending on combinations of element values in the vicinity Λ_{ijkd}.

From (55) one can easily obtain the matrix Π for the model of the discrete-valued Markov process of the smaller dimension. For example, excepting the element of the transition probability matrix $^{8}\Pi$ and associated elements of transition probability matrices $^{9}\Pi \ldots {}^{15}\Pi$, we obtain the matrix Π for the model of the three-dimensional discrete-valued Markov process. If matrices associated with matrices $^{4}\Pi$ and $^{8}\Pi$ are excluded, we obtain the matrix Π for two-dimensional discrete-valued Markov process. Using the similarity with the approach of the four-dimensional mathematical model constructions, we can construct mathematical model of several statistically correlated DHTI corresponding to the multi-dimensional multi-valued Markov process of higher order.

THE ALGORITHM OF FORMATION OF STATISTICALLY CORRELATED SEQUENCES OF MARKOV BBI

The matrix Π (54) and equation (51) are the basis for constructing the mathematical model for statistically correlated DHTI video-sequences representing the four-dimensional discrete Markov process. The algorithm of mathematical model operation consists of the following stages:

Step 1: The size of the random two-dimensional field (image) of $m \times n$ elements, the video-sequence length K and the number of positions D, matrices of transitions $^{1}\Pi$, $^{2}\Pi$, $^{4}\Pi$, $^{8}\Pi$ are specified and matrices $^{3}\Pi, {}^{5}\Pi, {}^{6}\Pi, {}^{7}\Pi, {}^{9}\Pi, \ldots, {}^{15}\Pi$ and Π are calculated;

Step 2: We take the random number $\xi_l (l \le m \cdot n \cdot K \cdot D)$ uniformly distributed over interval $\left[0,1\right]$;

Step 3: From the first column of the matrix Π we choose the element $\alpha_s (s = \overline{1,16})$ corresponding to element values of the vicinity Λ_{ijkd};

Step 4: The number ξ_l is compared with the chosen element $\alpha_s (s = \overline{1,16})$ and if $\alpha_s \left(s = \overline{1,16}\right)$ and $\xi_l \le \alpha_s$, then the image element ν_4 takes the value $\nu_4 = M_1 = 0$, otherwise $\nu_4 = M_2 = 1$;

Step 5: If $i < n; j < m; k < K; d < D$, where K is the video-sequence length, D if the number of positions, then we pass to p. 3, otherwise to p. 6;

Step 6: Stop.

Figure 15. Frames of the statistically correlated video-sequences of the artificial DHTI

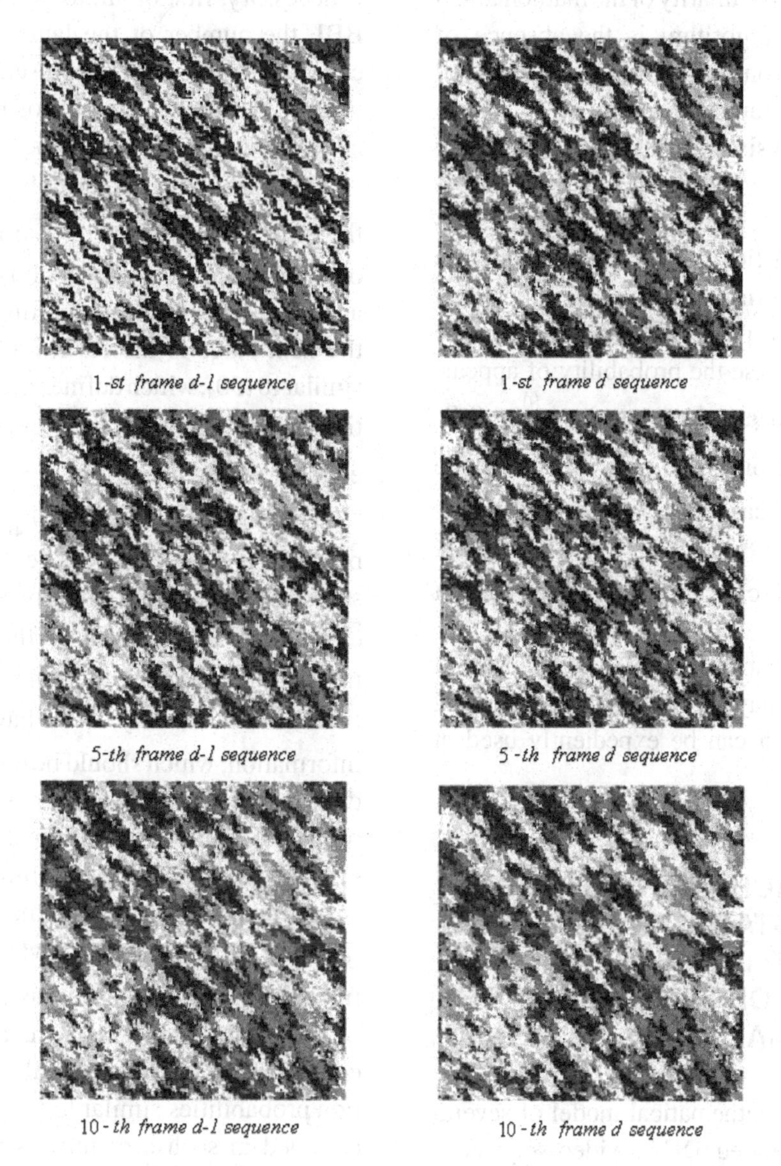

MATHEMATICAL MODEL OF TWO STATISTICALLY CORRELATED DHTI VIDEO-SEQUENCES

Mathematical model of statistically correlated DHTI video-sequences represented by g-bit binary numbers are formed by the simple bitwise presentation of g values of binary images into the g-bit register of the binary number representing the sample of the four-dimensional multi-valued Markov process.

Figure 15 shows 1st, 5th, and 10th frames of two statistically correlated video-sequences of the artificial DHTI obtained with the help of the developed mathematical model for ${}^1\pi_{ii}^{(1)} = {}^2\pi_{ii}^{(1)} = 0,6$, ${}^1\pi_{ii}^{(2)} = {}^2\pi_{ii}^{(2)} = 0,65$, ${}^1\pi_{ii}^{(3)} = {}^2\pi_{ii}^{(3)} = 0,7$, ${}^1\pi_{ii}^{(4)} = {}^2\pi_{ii}^{(4)} = 0,75$ ${}^1\pi_{ii}^{(5)} = {}^2\pi_{ii}^{(5)} = 0,8$, ${}^1\pi_{ii}^{(6)} = {}^2\pi_{ii}^{(6)} = 0,85$, ${}^1\pi_{ii}^{(7)} = {}^2\pi_{ii}^{(7)} = 0,9$ и ${}^4\pi_{ii} = {}^8\pi_{ii} = 0,9$.

The important peculiarity of the mathematical model operation algorithm is the absence of computing operations at creation of the artificial DHTI in the k-th frame in position d.

From the analysis of results obtained for the three-dimensional and four-dimensional mathematical models, it follows that for the same statistical characteristics of the random process components its statistical redundancy increases with growth of the process dimension. If in the one-dimensional case the probability of appearance of the same image value is equal to $\pi_{ii}^{(l)} = 0,9$, in the two-dimensional case $\pi_{ii}^{(l)} = 0,987$, in the three-dimensional case $\pi'_{\underbrace{ii...i}_{7}} = 0,998629$, in the four-dimensional case $\pi^{(l)}_{\underbrace{ii...i}_{15}} = 0,9998478$. It follows from this that statistically correlated DHTI video-sequences may have a very large statistical redundancy, which can be expediently used at DHTI processing.

THE APPROACH TO CONSTRUCT THE MM OF STATISTICALLY CORRELATED DHTI VIDEO-SEQUENCES OF THE BASIS OF THE H-DIMENSIONAL MULTI-VALUED MP

To construct the mathematical model of several statistically correlated DHTI video-sequences based on the h-dimensional Markov process, it is necessary, first of all, to divide the DHTI into BBI, the number of the latter is equal to digit capacity of the DHTI representation. Then we need to define the vicinity of the BBI element generating in the given moment.

If we succeeded to form the vicinity $\Lambda_{ij...h}$ of the generating element ν_{41} (similar to the developed mathematical model) on the basis of the analysis of the h-dimensional discrete-valued MP, the next stage is the rewriting of the equation similar to (50), which defines the mutual information quantity between the vicinity $\Lambda_{ij...h}$ and the element ν_{41} (see Box 34).

The value of the element ν_{41} in mathematical model of h-th order should be determined by the statistical correlation only between the generating element ν_{41} and elements of the vicinity belonging to h independent coordinates. All other elements of the vicinity $\Lambda_{ij...h}$ have the redundant information, which should be eliminated. We can do it by means of the successive transformation of the multi-dimensional transition probabilities in (56) with the purpose to eliminate the statistical correlation between elements of any group falling in the vicinity $\Lambda_{ij...h}$, which allows transfer from multi-dimensional transition probabilities of the complicated Markov chain to the simple equation for one-dimensional single-step transition probabilities similar to (51). The expression obtained in such a manner is the basis for the structure of construction of elements of the tran-

Box 34.

$$I\left(\nu_{11},...,\nu_{41},\nu'_{11},...,\nu'_{41},...,\gamma_{1k},...,\gamma_{4k},\gamma'_{1k},...,\gamma'_{4k},...,\lambda_{1h},...,\lambda_{4h},\lambda'_{1h},...,\lambda'_{4h}\right)$$
$$= \ln \frac{w\left(\nu_{41}\left|\nu_{11},...,\nu_{31},\nu'_{11},...,\nu'_{41},...,\gamma_{1k},...,\gamma_{4k},\gamma'_{1k},...,\gamma'_{4k},...,\lambda_{1h},...,\lambda_{4h},\lambda'_{1h},...,\lambda'_{4h}\right.\right)}{w\left(\nu_{41}\left|\nu_{31},\nu'_{11},...,\nu'_{31},...,\gamma_{1k},...,\gamma_{3k},\gamma'_{1k},...,\gamma'_{4k},...,\lambda_{1h},...,\lambda_{3h},\lambda'_{1h},...,\lambda'_{4h}\right.\right)}, \quad (56)$$

where $\nu_{11},\nu_{21},\nu'_{41},...,\gamma_{4k},...,\lambda_{4h}$ are elements of the vicinity $\Lambda_{ij...h}$ belonging to h independent coordinates of the h-dimensional discrete-valued MP. The second index of variables in (56) indicates the number of the DHTI sequence.

Box 35.

$$\Pi = \begin{Vmatrix} \pi_{i\underbrace{ii\cdots ii}_{2^h-1}} & \pi_{j\underbrace{ii\cdots ii}_{2^h-1}} \\ \vdots & \vdots \\ \pi_{i\underbrace{jj\cdots jj}_{2^h-1}} & \pi_{i\underbrace{jj\cdots jj}_{2^h-1}} \end{Vmatrix} = \begin{Vmatrix} \alpha_1 & \alpha'_1 \\ \vdots & \vdots \\ \alpha_{2^h} & \alpha'_{2^h} \end{Vmatrix}, \quad i,j = \overline{1,2}; \quad i \neq j, \tag{57}$$

and the number of the transition matrices of type (53) will be $2^h - 1$.

sition matrix Π in h-dimensional Markov chain. The matrix Π in this case will have the form (see Box 35).

The algorithm of set formation of statistically correlated DHTI video-sequences consists of the following steps:

1. The initial probabilities of the multi-dimensional binary Markov process p_1 and p_2 and matrices of one-dimensional single-step transition probabilities ${}^1\Pi, {}^2\Pi, \ldots, {}^h\Pi$ are specified and matrices of transition probabilities and the matrix Π (associated with the former) are calculated;
2. We take the random number $\xi_l (l \leq m \cdot n \cdot K \cdot D \cdot T)$ uniformly distributed over the interval $\left[0,1\right]$;
3. From the first column of the matrix Π we choose the element $\alpha_s (s = \overline{1, 2^h})$ corresponding to values of the vicinity $\Lambda_{ij\ldots h}$ elements;
4. The number ξ_l is compared with the chosen element $\alpha_s (s = \overline{1, 2^h})$ and if $\xi_l \leq \alpha_s$, then the image element ν_4 takes the value $\nu_4 = M_1 = 0$, otherwise $\nu_4 = M_2 = 1$;
5. If $i < n; j < m; k < K; d < D; t < T$, where K is the video-sequence length, D is the number of positions, T is the number of sets, we pass to p. 3, otherwise to p. 6;
6. Stop.

The mathematical model of the set of statistically correlated DHTI sequences represented by g-bit binary numbers is formed by the simple bitwise presentation of g values of the BBI elements in the g-bit register of the binary number representing the sample of the h-dimensional multi-valued process similar to p. 6.

Realization of the developed mathematical model does not require computation operations, and the memory volume at modeling of the h-dimensional process does not exceed BBI size of $\left(h-2\right) \cdot g$.

CONCLUSION

The main conclusions are the following:

1. The theory of conditional Markov processes is expanded to the static and dynamic DHTI representing the multi-dimensional discrete-valued random processes with several states.
2. The method of DHTI division is offered presented by g-bit binary numbers per g BBI (binary sections) each of which represents the causal binary Markov field or the binary Markov chain on the non-symmetrical half-plane.
3. On the basis of the Markov type DHTI division method onto bit binary sections and using the entropy approach to probability calculation of each BBI element values, the DHTI mathematical models have been synthesized.

4. The model adequacy to real image is confirmed by element estimations of the transition probability matrices calculated for the artificial and real images.
5. The spatial-time MM of the DHTI video-sequence is synthesized, which is the three-dimensional multi-valued Markov process with the dividable exponential correlation function allowing the presentation of the three-dimensional multi-valued Markov process as a superposition of three one-dimensional multi-valued Markov processes.
6. The approach for MM construction of several statistically correlated DHTI video-sequences is offered, which can be presented by *h-dimensional* multi-valued Markov processes. This approach can be reduced to formal procedures of the sequential elimination of the statistical redundancy between vicinity elements of the simulating image element belonging to h independent coordinates and all others.

DIRECTIONS OF FURTHER RESEARCHES AND DEVELOPMENTS

Developed methods for construction of DHTI and video-sequence mathematical models are the effective tool for development of simple, reliable and affective algorithms of multi-dimensional signals allowing approximation by the discrete-valued Markov random processes.

We suppose to apply the DHTI MM and video-sequences synthesized at development of new algorithms on the basis of Markov chains with several states.

Investigation of multi-dimensional non-stationary mathematical models is interesting as well, which have been created of the basis of Markov chains with several states.

The authors in the of this chapter have done extensive research and are widely published in the area of development of DHTI mathematical models and the synthesis on its basis of algorithms of recovering images distorted by the noise.

REFERENCES

Abend, K., Harley, T. J., & Kanal, L. N. (1965). Classification of binary random patterns. *IEEE Transactions on Information Theory*, *11*, 538–544. doi:10.1109/TIT.1965.1053827.

Ablameiko, S. V., & Lagunovskiy, D. M. (2000). *Image processing: Technology, methods, application*. Amalphea Publishing.

Berchtold. (1999). *The double chain Markov model* (Technical Report N° 348). Seattle, WA: University of Washington, Department of Statistics.

Besag, J. E. (1974). Spatial interaction and statistical analysis of lattice systems. *Journal of the Royal Statistical Society. Series B. Methodological*, *36*, 192–236.

Bondur, V. G. (2003). Modeling of multi-spectral airspace images of the dynamic fields of brightness (in Russian). *Investigation of Earth from Space*, (2), 3-17.

Bykov, V. V. (1971). *Digital modeling in the statistical radio engineering*. Moscow: Sovetskoe Radio Publishing.

Chellappa, R. (1985). Two-dimensional discrete Gaussian Markov random fields for image processing. In *Progress in Pattern Recognition 2*. Amsterdam: Elsevier Science Publishers BV.

Chellappa, R., & Kashyap, R. L. (1982). Digital image restoration using spatial interaction models. *IEEE Transactions on Acoustics, Speech, and Signal Processing*, *30*, 461–472. doi:10.1109/TASSP.1982.1163911.

Dagion, D., & Mercero, R. (1988). *Digital processing of multi-dimensional signals*. Moscow: MIR Publishing.

Dech, G. (1971). *Manual to the practical application of the Laplace transformation and z-transformation*. Moscow: Nauka Publishing.

Derin, H., & Kelly, P. (1989). Random processes of Markov type with discrete arguments. *TIEEE, 77*(10), 42–71.

Dragan, Y. P. (1993). *Status and development prospects of probabilistic models of random signals and fields*. Kharkiv, Ukraine: HIRE Publishing.

Elfeki, A. A., & Dekking, M. (2001). Markov chain model for subsurface characterization: Theory and applications. *Mathematical Geology, 33*, 569–589. doi:10.1023/A:1011044812133.

Fano, R. (1965). Statistical theory of communication. In *Transmission of Information*. Moscow: MIR Publishing.

Furman, Y. A. (2003). *Introduction to contour analysis and its application to signal and image processing*. Moscow: FIZMATLIT Publishing.

Jain, A. K. (1974). Noncausal representation for finite discrete signals. In *Proceedings of IEEE Conference on Decision and Control*. IEEE Publishing.

Jain, A. K., & Jain, J. R. (1978). Partial differential equations and finite difference methods in image processing, part II: Image restoration. *IEEE Transactions on Automatic Control, 23*, 817–834. doi:10.1109/TAC.1978.1101881.

Jain, A. K., & Rangansth, S. (1980). Image coding by autoregressive synthesis. In *Proceedings of ICASSP'80*. IEEE.

Jain, A. K., & Wang, S. H. (1977). *Stochastic image models and hybrid coding*. NOSC.

Jine, A. K. (1981). Achievements in the field of mathematical models for image processing. *TIEEE, 69*(5), 9–39.

Kashyap, R. L. (n.d.). Analysis and synthesis of image patterns by spatial interaction models. In *Progress in Pattern Recognition*. New York: Elsevier North-Holland.

Krasheninnikov, B. P. (2003). *Fundamentals of the image processing theory*. Ulyaniovsk, Russia: UlGTU Publ.

McGill, W. J. (1954). Multivariate information transmission, transactions PGIT. In *Proceedings of Symposium on Information Theory*. PGIT.

Modestino, J. W., & Zhang, J. (1993). A Markov random field model-based approach to image interpretation. In *Markov Random Fields: Theory and Applications*. Boston: Academic Press, Inc..

Nahi, N. E., & Franco, C. A. (1972). Application of Kalman filtering to image enhancement. In *Proceedings of IEEE Conference on Decision and Control*. IEEE Publishing.

Petrov, E. P. (2006). The spatial-time mathematical model of the sequence of digital half-tone image of Markov type. *Problems of Information Processing, 1*(6), 46–52.

Petrov, E. P., & Chastikov, A. V. (2001). Method of adaptive filtering of binary pulse correlated signals. *Radio Engineering and Electronics, 46*(10), 1155–1158.

Petrov, E. P., & Prozorov, D. E. (n.d.). Filtering of Markov processes with several states. *Radar, Navigation, and Communications.*.

Petrov, E. P., Smolskliy, S. M., & Kharina, N. L. (2007). Synthesis of models of multi-dimensional multi-valued Markov processes. *Vestnik of MPEI,* (1), 147-152.

Petrov, E. P., Trubin, I. C., & Butorin, E. L. (2002). The spatial-time model of digital Markov images. In *Proceedings of VIII Conference: Radar Technology, Navigation, and Communications,* (vol. 1, pp. 371-380). Voronezh, Russia: RTNC.

Petrov, E. P., Trubin, I. C., & Butorin, E. L. (2003). The spatial-time model of digital Markov images. In *Proceedings of IX Conference of Radar Technology, Navigation, and Communications,* (vol. 1, pp. 330-337). Voronezh, Russia: RTNC.

Petrov, E. P., Trubin, I. S., & Butorin, E. L. (2005). Nonlinear filtering of the sequence of digital half-tone images. *Radio Engineering and Electronics, 10*(10), 1265–1272.

Petrov, E. P., Trubin, I. S., & Harina, N. L. (2006). *Modeling of multi-dimensional multi-valued Markov processes*. Radio Engineering.

Petrov, E. P., Trubin, I. S., & Harina, N. L. (2006). Problems of information processing. *Vestnik, 1*(6), 41–46.

Pisarevsky, A. N., & Chernyavsky, A. F. (1988). *Systems of technical vision (principal fundamentals, hardware and software support)*. Leningrad, Russia: Mashinostroenie Publishing.

Politis, D. N. (1994). Markov chains in many dimensions. *Advances in Applied Probability*. doi:10.2307/1427819.

Shalizi, C. R. (2003). Optimal nonlinear prediction of random fields on networks. In *Proceedings of Center for the Study of Complex Systems*. University of Michigan.

Soifer, V. A. (2003). *Methods of computer image processing*. Moscow: FIZMATLIT Publishing.

Spector, A. A. (1985). Multi-dimensional discrete Markov fields and its filtering at the presence of the non-correlated noise. *Radio Engineering and Electronics*, (5): 512–523.

Spector, A. A. (1987). Two-stage filtering of random fields at interference presence. In *Methods of Processing of Digital Signals and Fields under Condition of Interference*. Novosibirsk, Russia: IEEE Publishing.

Tikhonov, V. I., & Mironov, M. A. (1977). *Markov processes*. Moscow: Sovetskoe Radio Publishing.

Trubin, I. S. (2004). Mathematical model of two statistically correlated video-sequences. []. St. Petersburg, Russia: SP Technical University Publishing.]. *Proceedings of Universities in Communications, 171*, 90–97.

Trubin, I. S., & Butorin, E. L. (2004). Mathematical model of the digital image sequence. In *Proceedings of Russian NTO Popov Society: Digital Processing of Signals and its Application* (*Vol. 2*, pp. 166–169). Moscow: NTO.

Trubin, I. S., & Butorin, E. L. (2005). Spatial-time Markov model of digital half-tone images. *Radio Engineering,* (10), 10-13.

Vasiliev, K. K. (1995). Digital processing of image sequences in global monitoring problems of the Earth surface, the medicine, the air motion control, radar systems and hydro-location. In *Conversion of Military Complex, Double-Application Technologies*. Moscow: RIA Publishing.

Vasiliev, K. K. (1995). *Applied theory of random processes and fields*. Ulyanovsk, Russia: UIGTU Publishing.

Vasiliev, K. K. (2002). Representation and fast processing of multi-dimensional images. *New Scientific Technologies,* (3), 4-24.

Vasiukov, V.N. (2002). New approaches to solution of the image recognition and processing. *New Scientific Technologies*, (3), 44-51.

Vinkler, G. (2002). Image analysis, random fields, and dynamic methods of Monte-Carlo. In *Mathematical Fundamentals*. Novosibirsk, Russia: Siberian Division of RAS Publishing.

Vishnevsky, V. M. (2003). *Theoretical bases of computer network design*. Moscow: Technosphere Publishing.

Wong, E. (1978). Recursive causal linear filtering for two-dimensional random fields. *IEEE Transactions on Information Theory, 24*, 50–59. doi:10.1109/TIT.1978.1055818.

Woods, J. W. (1972). Two-dimensional discrete Markov fields. *Information Theory, 22*, 232–240. doi:10.1109/TIT.1972.1054786.

APPENDIX

List of Abbreviations

- **BBI:** Bit binary image
- **DHTI:** Digital half-tone image
- **MAP:** Maximal *a posteriori* probability
- **MC:** Markov chain
- **MM:** Mathematical model
- **MP:** Markov process
- **MTP:** Matrix of transition probability
- **NF:** Nonlinear filter
- **NSHP:** Non-symmetric half-plain
- **OSMRF:** One-sided Markov random field
- **RRD:** Radio receiving device
- **VS:** Video-sequence
- **WGN:** White Gaussian noise

Chapter 11
Performance Analysis of Multi-Antenna Relay Networks over Nakagami-m Fading Channel

E. Soleimani-Nasab
K. N. Toosi University of Technology, Iran

A. Kalantari
K. N. Toosi University of Technology, Iran

M. Ardebilipour
K. N. Toosi University of Technology, Iran

ABSTRACT

In this chapter, the authors present the performance of multi-antenna selective combining decode-and-forward (SC-DF) relay networks over independent and identically distributed (i.i.d) Nakagami-m fading channels. The outage probability, moment generation function, symbol error probability and average channel capacity are derived in closed-form using the Signal-to-Noise-Ratio (SNR) statistical characteristics. After that, the authors formulate the outage probability problem, optimize it with an approximated problem, and then solve it analytically. Finally, for comparison with analytical formulas, the authors perform some Monte-Carlo simulations.

1. INTRODUCTION

Cooperative communication has been an interesting topic for researchers in recent years. Cooperative communications refer to systems or techniques that allow users to help transmit each other's messages to the destination. Most cooperative transmission schemes involve two phases of transmission: a coordination phase, where users exchange their own source data and control messages with each other and/or the destination, and a cooperation phase, where the users cooperatively retransmit their messages to the destination.

To enable cooperation among users, different relay technology can be employed depending on the relative user location, channel condition and

DOI: 10.4018/978-1-4666-2208-1.ch011

transceiver complexity. There are some of the basic cooperative relaying techniques such as Decode-and-Forward (DF) in which the relay decodes the received signals and forwards it either as is or re-encoded to the destination regardless whether the relay can decode correctly or not.

The relay could also only forward the correctly decoded messages, which is referred to as the Selective DF (S-DF) protocol, Amplify-and Forward (AF) in which the signal received by the relay is amplified, frequency translated and retransmitted, Coded Cooperation (CC) that can be viewed as a generalization of DF relaying schemes where more powerful channel codes (other than simple repetition codes used in the DF schemes) are utilized in both phases of the cooperative transmission. When using repetition codes, the same codeword is transmitted twice (either by the source or the relay) and, thus, bandwidth efficiency is decreased by one half and Compress and Forward (CF) schemes, which refer to cases where the relay forwards quantized, estimated, or compressed versions of its observation to the destination. In contrast to DF or CC schemes, the relay in CF schemes need not decode perfectly the source message, but need only to extract, from its observation, the information that is most relevant to the decoding at the destination. The amount of information extracted and forwarded to the destination depends on the capacity of the rely-destination link Dohler and Li (2010).

LITERATURE REVIEW

Because the relay selection schemes make an efficient use of time and frequency resources, several selective combining schemes have been introduced in recent years. In Blatses et al. (2006), the authors introduced an opportunistic relaying method, which a single relay based on the best end-to-end instantaneous SNR criterion is selected and then forwards the message to the destination. They derived analytical results at high SNRs and the outage probability wasn't derived in closed-form. The authors in Beaulieu and Hu (2006) and Hu and Beaulieu (2007) analyzed an adaptive DF relay method, which only a number of relays were selected to send the messages to the destination. They proved that increasing the number of relays could not always decrease the outage probability.

A selection combiner at the destination with AF relays have been studied in Sagias et al. (2008) on Nakagami-m fading channels where, a closed-form formula for the outage probability was derived. Different relaying schemes are investigated in Jing et al. (2009), the authors have calculated the diversity of some existing single-relay selection schemes. They have managed to develop the relay selection idea to the case in which more than one relay is taking part in cooperation. They have researched the complexity of these schemes, too. In Duong et al. (2009), the authors presented closed-form formulas for the performance of selective DF relaying in Nakagami-m fading channels without considering the direct link between source and destination. The authors in Ikki and Ahmed (2010) introduced a closed-form expression for the outage probability and average channel capacity using the best relay selection scheme over independent and non-identical Rayleigh fading channels. In Amarasuriya et al. (2010) the authors have developed a Multiple Relay Selection (MRS) scheme. In this method the relays are selected so that the output SNR satisfies a predefined SNR. The authors in Kalantari et al. (2011) have derived closed form expressions for the outage probability in opportunistic AF and DF relaying over Log-normal fading channels. In their method, the weakest channel of each relay is defined, and then the relay that its weakest channel is stronger than others is selected. The Log-normal distribution not only models the moving objects, but also the reflection of the bodies. Moreover, it models the action of communicating with robots in a closed environment like a factory. In indoor radio propagation environments, terminals with low mobility have to rely on macroscopic diversity to overcome the shadowing from indoor obstacles and moving human bodies. However, to the best of our knowledge, no one derived exact closed-form expressions for the outage probability, symbol error probability and average channel capacity for multi-antenna SC-DF relay networks over *Nakagami*-m fading channels.

In this chapter, we present our derived closed-form formulas for outage probability, moment generation function, symbol error probability and average channel capacity. In addition, we minimized the outage probability with optimal and adaptive power allocation. The reminder of this paper is organized as follows. Section II introduces the system model under consideration. Section III gives an analytical approach to evaluating the outage probability, MGF, symbol error probability and average channel capacity of the system. In Section IV, we formulate outage probability problem to optimize the approximate version of our problem which leads to a closed from analytical solution. Finally, Section V presents Monte-Carlo simulation to verify the analytical results.

2. SYSTEM MODEL

Consider a cooperative relay system that consists of $K+1$ users, one acting as the source and K serving as the relays (see Figure 1 for the system model). Each relay has two receive antennas. Let us denote the source by s, the destination by d, and label the relays from 1 to K. P_s is the source transmission power, $h_{s,k,1}$ and $h_{s,k,2}$ are the channel coefficients between source and first receiver antenna of relay k (i.e., the $s-k-1$ link), and between source and the second receiver antenna of relay k (i.e., the $s-k-2$ link), respectively. $h_{k,d}$ is the channel coefficient between relay k and the destination (i.e., the $k-d$ link. σ_k^2 and σ_d^2 are noise variances at relay k and destination, respectively. Moreover, the instantaneous SNR for $s-k-1$, $s-k-2$ and $k-d$ links are given by $\gamma_{s,k,1} = P_s\left|h_{s,k,1}\right|^2 / \sigma_k^2$, $\gamma_{s,k,2} = P_s\left|h_{s,k,2}\right|^2 / \sigma_k^2$ and $\gamma_{k,d} = P_r\left|h_{k,d}\right|^2 / \sigma_d^2$.

In DF selection relaying, all relays attempt to decode the source's message in phase I and act as candidate relays for selection in phase II only if it has successfully decoded the message. For simplicity, we assume the case where no diversity combining is employed at the destination. Hence, the system reduces to a dual-hop transmission where the maximum achievable rate is limited by the minimum capacity among $s-k$ and $k-d$ links. Given that relay k was selected, the end-to-end SNR can be computed as

$$\gamma_{SC} = \max_{k=1,\ldots,K} \min(\gamma_{s,k}, \gamma_{k,d}) \tag{1}$$

where $\gamma_{s,k} = \max\left(\gamma_{s,k,1}, \gamma_{s,k,2}\right)$

3. PERFORMANCE ANALYSIS

The SNR per symbol of the channel, γ, is distributed according to a gamma distribution given by Simon & Alouini (2005), where m is Nakagami-m fading parameters and $\bar{\gamma}$ is average SNR per symbol. The Cumulative Distribution Function (CDF) of this channel are given by Ikki & Ahmed (2007), where $\Gamma(b,x)$ is the upper incomplete gamma function which is defined as $\Gamma(b,x) = \int_x^\infty e^{-t} t^{b-1} dt$ and $\alpha = \frac{m}{\bar{\gamma}}$. Where $\alpha_k = \frac{m1_k}{\Omega 1_k}$, $\eta_k = \frac{m2_k}{\Omega 2_k}$ and $\beta_k = \frac{m3_k}{\Omega 3_k}$ are the

Figure 1. System model of a selective combining cooperation

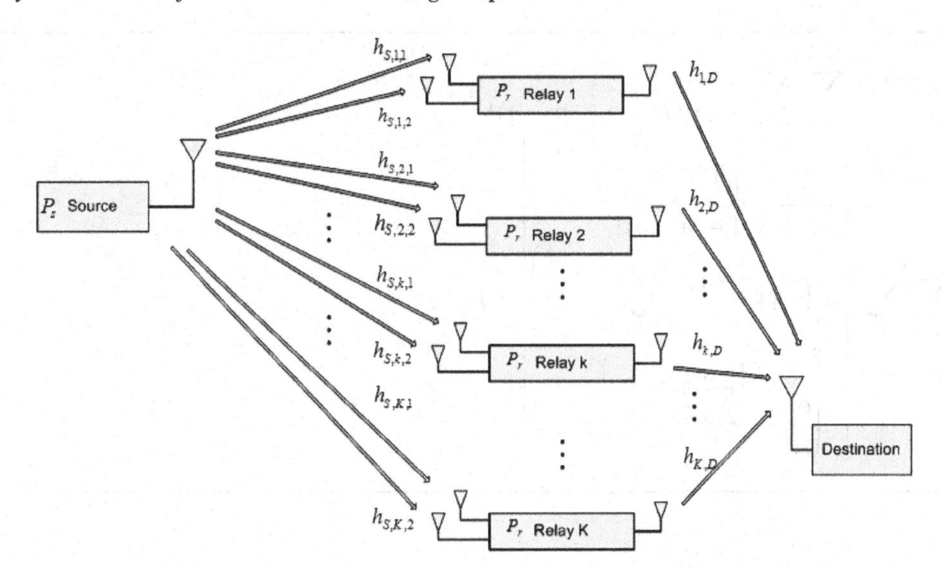

channel parameters for $s-k-1$, $s-k-2$ and $k-d$ links, respectively.

Since $\gamma_{s,k}$ and $\gamma_{k,d}$ are independent gamma random variables and assuming that m is integer and then by using $\Gamma(n,x)=(n-1)!e^{-x}\sum_{i=0}^{n-1}\frac{x^i}{i!}$ Spiegel et al. (2009), the CDF of k-th branch can be written as (see appendix)

$$P_{\gamma_k}(\gamma)=1-\left[1-\left\{1-e^{-\alpha\gamma}\sum_{i=0}^{m-1}\frac{\alpha^i\gamma^i}{i!}\right\}^2\right]\left[e^{-\alpha\gamma}\sum_{l=0}^{m-1}\frac{\alpha^l\gamma^l}{l!}\right]$$
$$=1-2e^{-2\alpha\gamma}\sum_{i=0}^{m-1}\sum_{l=0}^{m-1}\frac{\alpha^{i+l}\gamma^{i+l}}{i!l!}+e^{-3\alpha\gamma}\sum_{i=0}^{m-1}\sum_{j=0}^{m-1}\sum_{l=0}^{m-1}\frac{\alpha^{i+j+l}\gamma^{i+j+l}}{i!j!l!} \quad (2)$$

The Probability Density Function (PDF) of γ_k can be computed by differentiating (1) with respect to γ and after some simple manipulations as follows:

$$p_{\gamma_k}(\gamma)=\frac{4e^{-2\alpha\gamma}}{(m-1)!}\sum_{u=0}^{m-1}\frac{\alpha^{m+u}\gamma^{m-1+u}}{u!}-\frac{3e^{-3\alpha\gamma}}{(m-1)!}\sum_{v=0}^{m-1}\sum_{w=0}^{m-1}\frac{\alpha^{m+v+w}\gamma^{m-1+v+w}}{v!w!} \quad (3)$$

The PDF of selective combining SNR can be written as

$$p_{\gamma_{sc}}=K\,P_{\gamma_k}^{K-1}\,p_{\gamma_k}(\gamma) \quad (4)$$

Using multinomial coefficient as (5) and after some manipulations, (4) can be simplified as (6) (see Box 1).

Using multinomial coefficients and some simple manipulations, following relation is always held.

$$\left[\sum_{i=0}^{m-1}\frac{\alpha^i\gamma^i}{i!}\right]^{2p}=\sum_{i_1=0}^{m-1}\cdots\sum_{i_{2p}=0}^{m-1}\frac{(\alpha\gamma)^{\sum_{t=1}^{2p}(i_t)}}{\prod_{t=1}^{2p}i_t!} \quad (7)$$

Substituting (7) and (3) in (6) and after some simple manipulation the $p_{\gamma_{sc}}(\gamma)$ can be derived by that shown in Box 2.

After taking the Laplace transform of the PDF and some simple algebraic manipulations, the MGF can be determined by that shown in Box 3.

Box 1.

$$(a+b+c)^{K-1} = \sum_{p=0}^{K-1}\sum_{q=0}^{K-1-p} \frac{K!}{p!q!(K-1-p-q)!} \mathrm{a}^p \mathrm{b}^q \mathrm{c}^{K-1-p-q} \tag{5}$$

$$p_{\gamma_{sc}} = \sum_{p=0}^{\text{K-1}}\sum_{q=0}^{\text{K-1}-p} \left\{ \begin{array}{l} \dfrac{\text{K}!}{p!q!(\text{K-1}-p-q)!} \\ \times\left((-2)^p e^{-2p\alpha\gamma}\left[\sum_{i=0}^{m-1}\dfrac{\alpha^i\gamma^i}{i!}\right]^{2p}\right) \\ \times\left(e^{-3q\alpha\gamma}\left[\sum_{j=0}^{m-1}\dfrac{\alpha^j\gamma^j}{j!}\right]^{3q}\right) \end{array} \right\} \times p_{\gamma_k}(\gamma) \tag{6}$$

Box 2.

$$p_{\gamma_{SC}} = \widetilde{\sum}\sum_{u=0}^{m-1}\zeta e^{-\tau\gamma}\gamma^{\varphi} - \widetilde{\sum}\sum_{v=0}^{m-1}\sum_{w=0}^{m-1}\psi\gamma^{\phi}e^{-\lambda\gamma} \tag{8}$$

where

$$\zeta_{p,q,u} = \frac{4}{u!(m-1)!}\frac{\alpha^{\sum_{t=1}^{3q} j_t + \sum_{t=1}^{2p} i_t + m + u}}{\prod_{t=1}^{3q} j_t! \prod_{t=1}^{2p} i_t!}\frac{\text{K}!(-2)^p}{p!q!(\text{K-1}-p-q)!}$$

$$\tau_{p,q} = (2(p+1)+3q)\alpha$$

$$\varphi_{p,q,u} = \sum_{t=1}^{3q} j_t + \sum_{t=1}^{2p} i_t + m - 1 + u$$

$$\psi_{p,q,v,w} = \frac{3}{v!w!(m-1)!}\frac{\alpha^{\sum_{t=1}^{3q} j_t + \sum_{t=1}^{2p} i_t + m + v + w}}{\prod_{t=1}^{3q} j_t! \prod_{t=1}^{2p} i_t!}\frac{\text{K}!(-2)^p}{p!q!(\text{K-1}-p-q)!}$$

$$\lambda_{p,q} = (2p+3(q+1))\alpha$$

$$\phi_{p,q,v} = \sum_{t=1}^{3q} j_t + \sum_{t=1}^{2p} i_t + m - 1 + v + w$$

$$\widetilde{\sum} = \sum_{p=0}^{\text{K-1}}\sum_{q=0}^{\text{K-1}-p}\sum_{i_1=0}^{m-1}\cdots\sum_{i_{2p}=0}^{m-1}\sum_{j_1=0}^{m-1}\cdots\sum_{j_{3q}=0}^{m-1}$$

Box 3.

$$M_{\gamma_{sc}}(s) = \widetilde{\sum}\sum_{u=0}^{m-1} \frac{\zeta_u \varphi_u !}{(\tau + s)^{\varphi_u + 1}} - \widetilde{\sum}\sum_{v=0}^{m-1}\sum_{w=0}^{m-1} \frac{\psi_{v,w} \phi_{v,w} !}{(\lambda + s)^{\phi_{v,w}+1}} \tag{9}$$

The Symbol Error Probability (SEP) can be derived in closed-form using the MGF in (9). For M-PSK modulation, the SER is given by Simon & Alouini (2005) and approximation is given by Elkashlany et al. (2010).

The channel capacity can be computed as refer to Ikki & Ahmed (2010)

$$\overline{C} = \frac{BW}{2} \int_0^{\infty} \log_2(1+\gamma) p_{\gamma}(\gamma) d\gamma \tag{10}$$

where BW is the transmitted signal bandwidth. By substituting (8) in (10) and using Prudnikov et al. (1992), the averaged channel capacity can be obtained in closed-form in (11)

$$\overline{C} = \frac{BW}{2\ln 2} \left[\begin{array}{l} \widetilde{\sum}\sum_{u=0}^{m-1} \zeta_u \tau^{-\varphi_u - 1} G_{3,2}^{1,3}\left(\frac{1}{\tau} \middle|_{1,0}^{-\varphi_u,1,1} \right) - \\ \widetilde{\sum}\sum_{v=0}^{m-1}\sum_{w=0}^{m-1} \psi_{v,w} \eta^{-\phi_{v,w}-1} G_{3,2}^{1,3}\left(\frac{1}{\eta} \middle|_{1,0}^{-\phi_{v,w},1,1} \right) \end{array} \right] \tag{11}$$

where $G_{p,q}^{m,n}\left(\cdot \middle|_{(b_p)}^{(a_p)} \right)$ is the Meijer-G function referring to Prudnikov et al. (1992).

4. OPTIMIZATION PROBLEM

To minimize the outage probability, we define optimization problem as follows:

$$\begin{aligned} &\min_{P_s,P_r} P_{out} \\ &s.t.\ \mathrm{P}_s + P_r = P_{tot} \\ &P_s > 0,\ \mathrm{P}_r > 0 \end{aligned} \tag{12}$$

where P_{tot} is the total power of the system. Because of non-convexity of the above problem refer to Boyd & Vandenberghe (2004), we solved this problem numerically for Nakagami-m fading channels. We have compared the optimal power allocation with adaptive and equal power allocation. In adaptive power allocation, source and relay powers are allocated as follows:

$$P_s = \left(\frac{1}{Ant+1} + \frac{\Omega 3_k}{\Omega_k + \Omega 3_k} + \frac{m_k}{m_k + m3_k} \right) \frac{P_{tot}}{3},$$

$$P_r = \left(\frac{Ant}{Ant+1} + \frac{\Omega_k}{\Omega_k + \Omega 3_k} + \frac{m3_k}{m_k + m3_k} \right) \frac{P_{tot}}{3} \tag{13}$$

where Ant is the number of antennas, $m_k = m1_k = m2_k$ and $\Omega 1_k = \Omega 2_k = \Omega_k$.

For the Rayleigh case, The problem can be formulated as follows:

$$\begin{aligned} &\min_{P_s,P_r} \prod_{k=1}^{K} P_{\gamma_k} \equiv \min_{P_s,P_r} \sum_{k=1}^{K} \log(P_{\gamma_k}) \\ &s.t.\ \mathrm{P}_s + P_r = P_{tot}, P_s > 0,\ \mathrm{P}_r > 0 \end{aligned} \tag{14}$$

By approximating the CDF of k-th branch, then we have refer to The Wolfram Functions Site (2011),

$$P_{out} = \prod_{k=1}^{K}\left(\beta_k\gamma + \alpha_k\eta_k\gamma^2 - \alpha_k\eta_k\beta_k\gamma^3\right) \quad (15)$$

We can rewrite problem as follow:

$$\begin{aligned}&\min_{P_s,P_r}\sum_{k=1}^{K}\log\left(\frac{a_k}{P_r}+\frac{b_k}{P_s^2}-\frac{c_k}{P_s^2P_r}\right)\\ &s.t.\ \mathrm{P}_s + P_r = P_{tot}\\ &P_s > 0,\ \mathrm{P}_r > 0\end{aligned} \quad (16)$$

where

$a_k = \sigma_d^2\gamma_{th} / \mu_{k,d}^2$, $b_k = \sigma_k^4\gamma_{th}^2 / \mu_{s,k,1}^2\mu_{s,k,2}^2$ and $c_k = \sigma_k^4\sigma_d^2\gamma_{th}^3 / \mu_{s,k,1}^2\mu_{s,k,2}^2\mu_{k,d}^2$.

$\gamma_{s,k,1}$, $\gamma_{s,k,2}$ and $\gamma_{k,d}$ are exponentially distributed with means $\Omega 1_k = P_s\mu_{s,k,1}^2 / \sigma_k^2$, $\Omega 2_k = P_s\mu_{s,k,2}^2 / \sigma_k^2$ and $\Omega 3_k = P_r\mu_{k,d}^2 / \sigma_d^2$, respectively.

By introducing the Lagrange multiplier and by applying the KKT conditions *Boyd & Vandenberghe* (2004), after some simple manipulations, the power allocation equation can be obtained as

$$P_s^3 + h_1P_s^2 + h_2P_s + h_3 = 0 \quad (17)$$

where

$$h_1 = -\frac{2b_k}{a_k}, h_2 = \frac{4b_kP_{tot} - 3c_k}{a_k}, h_3 = \frac{2c_kP_{tot} - 2b_kP_{tot}^2}{a_k}$$

Using Speigel et al. (2009) and after some simple manipulation, the optimal power allocation can be obtained as that shown in Box 4.

5. SIMULATION RESULTS

To verify our analytical results, we show statistical simulation results and compare them with our analytical for the outage probability, symbol error probability and average channel capacity.

In all simulation and analytical results we consider the system with 16PSK modulation and $\gamma_{th} = 3$ for two topologies:

1. Symmetric case e.g.,

$\Omega 1_k = \Omega 2_k = \Omega 3_k = 3,\ \mathrm{m}1_k = \mathrm{m}2_k = \mathrm{m}3_k = 2,$ and

2. Asymmetric case e.g.,

$\Omega 1_1 = \Omega 2_1 = \mathrm{m}1_1 = \mathrm{m}2_1 = 1,\ \Omega 1_2 = \Omega 2_2 = \mathrm{m}1_2 = \mathrm{m}2_2 = 2,\ \Omega 1_3 = \Omega 2_3 = \mathrm{m}1_3 = \mathrm{m}2_3 = 3,$

$\Omega 3_1 = \mathrm{m}3_1 = 3,\ \Omega 3_2 = \mathrm{m}3_2 = 2,\ \Omega 3_3 = \mathrm{m}3_3 = 1.$

Box 4.

$$P_s = \begin{cases} S + T - \dfrac{h_1}{3} & \mathrm{D} \geq 0 \\ 2\sqrt{-Q}\cos(\dfrac{\theta + 4\pi}{3}) - \dfrac{h_1}{3} & \mathrm{D} < 0 \end{cases} \quad (18)$$

$$\mathrm{P}_r = P_{tot} - P_s$$

where

$$Q = \frac{3h_2 - h_1^2}{9}, R = \frac{9h_1h_2 - 27h_3 - 2h_1^3}{54}; S = \sqrt[3]{R + \sqrt{D}}\ ; T = \sqrt[3]{R - \sqrt{D}}, D = Q^3 + R^2\ \cos(\theta) = \frac{R}{\sqrt{-Q^3}}$$

In Figures 2 and 3, the outage and symbol error probability for DF relay selection scheme versus SNR for Nakagami-m fading channels are shown. As we can see, our proposed approach has more than 1 dB performance in comparison with Duong et al. (2009).

In Figure 4, the outage probability versus SNR in different number of relays and different number of relay antennas are shown. As we can see, as the number of relays increase, the double antennas case has more advantage versus single antenna case. Also, using 4 relays with two antennas has more advantage than using 5 relays with single antenna in considerable range of SNR.

It was shown that the average SNR gain increases with the number of the diversity combining antennas, but not linearly. The largest gain increment is achieved by going from one receiver antenna (no diversity) to two antennas. Increasing the number of receiving antenna from

Figure 2. Outage probability of the selective combining DF relay system

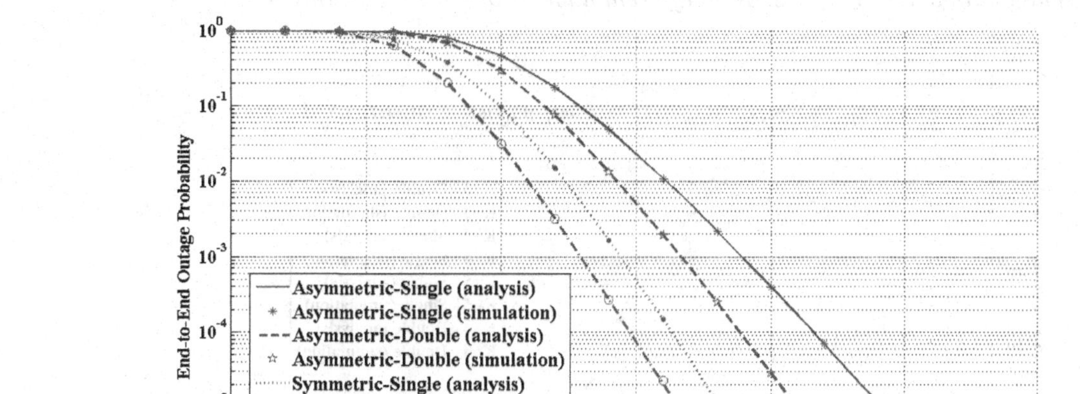

Figure 3. Symbol error probability of the selective combining DF relay system

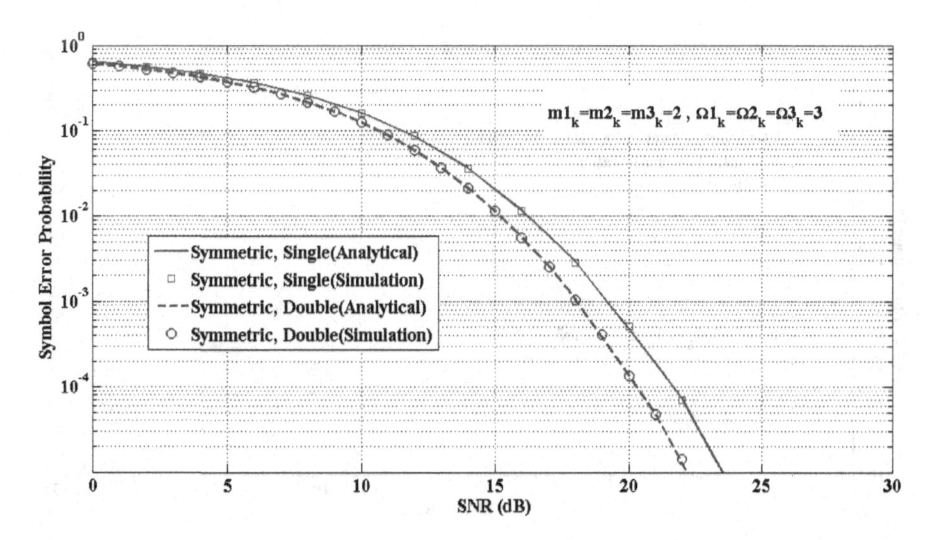

two to three will give much less gain than going from one to two refer to Adinoyi & Yanikomeroglu (2007). Therefore, in this paper we studied a relay system with two receiving antennas in order to have the largest gain increment and the least complexity increment.

In Figures 5 and 6, we have shown the outage probability of the SC-DF relay for Nakagami-m and Rayleigh fading channels, respectively. As we can see, the optimal power allocation has more than 1dB performance in comparison with equal power allocation. Also, approximate optimal power allocation is very close to optimal numerical optimization.

In Figure 7, the average channel capacity in analytical and simulation for Nakagami-m fading channels has been shown. Where K is the number of relays. As we can see, the average channel capacity increases as K increases. Moreover, SC scheme can outperform the direct transmission at higher SNR if the total number of relays (K) can be increased.

Figure 4. Outage probability versus SNR in different number of relays relay antennas

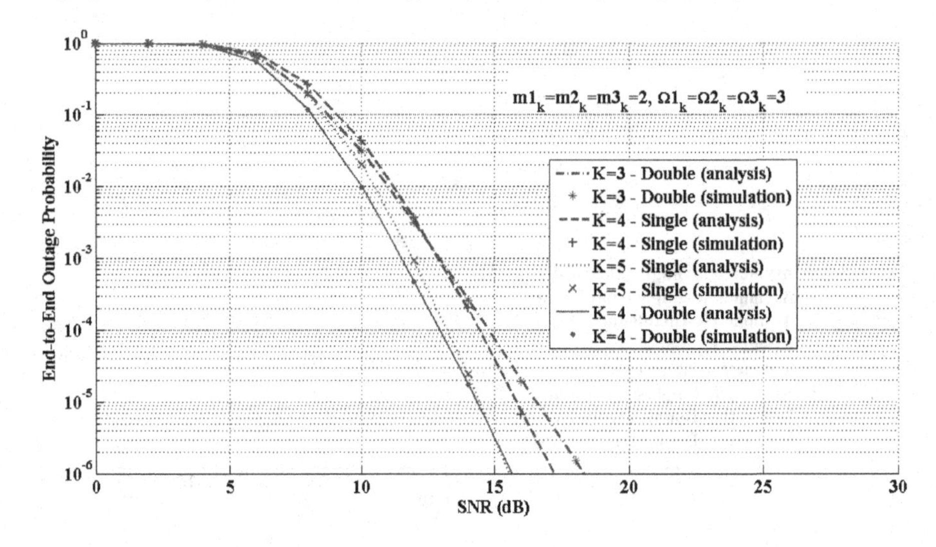

Figure 5. Outage probability of the SC-DF relay system (optimal and equal power allocation)

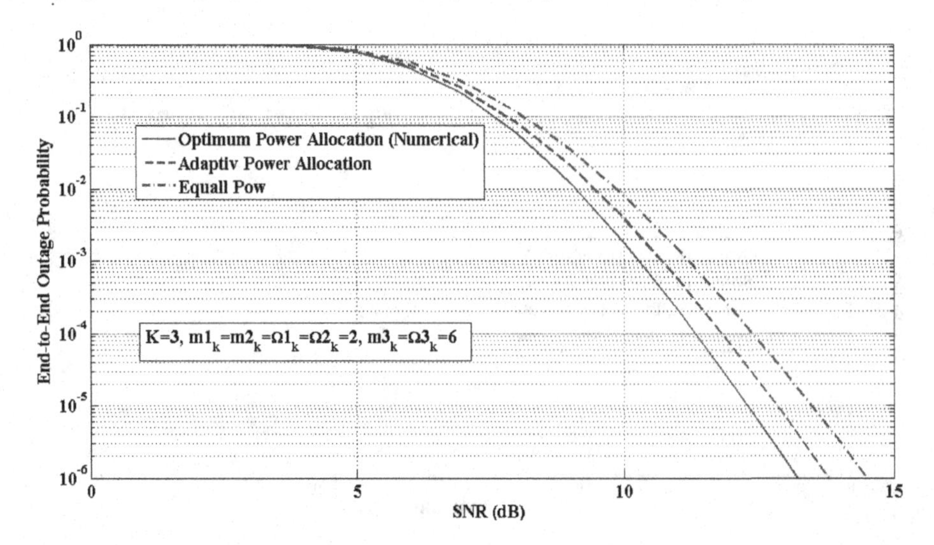

Figure 6. Outage probability of the SC-DF relay system (Rayleigh fading)

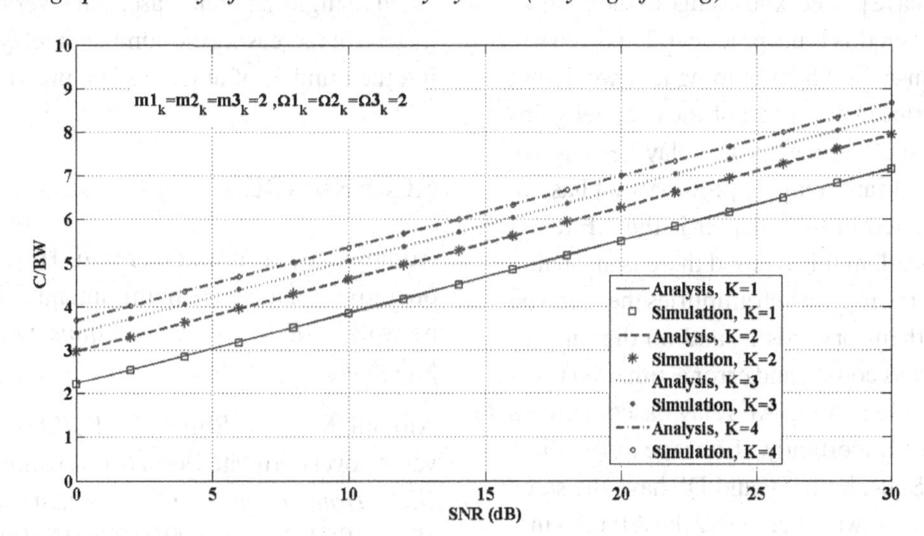

Figure 7. Average channel capacity for the SC-DF relay system (with and without direct link)

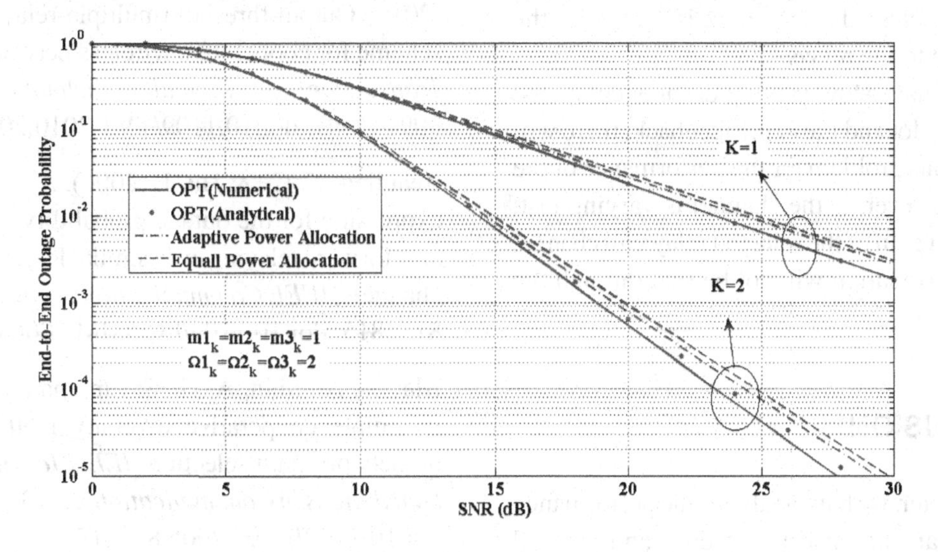

FUTURE RESEARCH DIRECTIONS

There are other channels that can be analyzed under this strategy such as Log-normal, Rican (Nakagami-n) and Hoyt (Nakagami-q) fading channels. From the practical point of view, Log-normal distribution is encountered in many communication scenarios. For instance, when indoor communication is used at which users are moving, Log-normal distribution not only models the moving objects, but also the reflection of the bodies. Moreover, it models the action of communicating with robots in a closed environment like a factory.

In indoor radio propagation environments, terminals with low mobility have to rely on macroscopic diversity to overcome the shadowing from indoor obstacles and moving human bodies. Indeed, in such slowly varying channels, the small-scale and large-scale effects tend to get mixed. In this case, Log-normal statistics accurately describe the distribution of the channel path gain. In most of the scenarios, we assume that the relay and the destination have perfect knowledge of the channel gains; however, this is not practical. This scenario can be reconsidered by assuming that we do not have the perfect knowledge of the channel gains between the source-relay and the relay-destination. Another important relaying protocol that has not been considered in this chapter is the AF relaying. As we said, in this method there is an analog amplifier in the relay witch amplifies the received signal and then forwards it, and no digital processing such as coding and error estimation takes effect, so implementing AF relay based network is easy. Most importantly, if our area of work is in the high SNR, both AF and DF have the same performance, so we'd better use the AF relaying. One of other important drawbacks of the wireless communication systems is the delay feedback in which the selected relay index is sent from the destination to the relays.

Till we have slow varying channel compared to the time slot and the delay feedback, there will be no serious problem for the performance of the system; however, if the channel is varying fast, the channel gain of the selected relay will change, and the information will not be sent through the best channel.

CONCLUSION

In this chapter, we have analyzed the performance of a multi-antenna selective decode-and-forward relaying system over Nakagami-m fading channels without and with the direct link between source and destination. We have derived the outage probability, moment generation function, symbol error probability and average channel capacity in closed-form. Also, we derived an approximation problem to minimize outage probability and then we solved the problem. Simulation results verified the accuracy and the correctness of the proposed analysis. The complexity of double antenna case versus single antenna case, isn't very high and instead of increasing the number of relays, increasing the number of antennas is a practical option.

REFERENCES

Adinoyi, A., & Yanikomeroglu, H. (2007). Cooperative relaying in multi-antenna fixed relay networks. *IEEE Communications Letters*, *6*(2), 533–544.

Alouini, M.-S., & Simon, M. K. (2002). Dual diversity over correlated log-normal fading channels. *IEEE Transactions on Communications*, *50*(12), 1946–1959. doi:10.1109/TCOMM.2002.806552.

Amarasuriya, G., Ardakani, M., & Tellambura, C. (2010). Output-threshold multiple-relay-selection scheme for cooperative wireless networks. *IEEE Transactions on Vehicular Technology*, *59*(6), 3091–3097. doi:10.1109/TVT.2010.2048767.

Beaulieu, N. C., & Hu, J. (2006). A closed-form expression for the outage probability of decode-and-forward relaying in dissimilar Rayleigh fading channels. *IEEE Communications Letters*, *10*(12), 813–815. doi:10.1109/LCOMM.2006.061048.

Blatses, A., Shin, A. H., & Lippman, A. (2006). A simple cooperative diversity method based on network path selection. *IEEE Journal on Selected Areas in Communications*, *24*(3), 659–672. doi:10.1109/JSAC.2005.862417.

Boyd, H. S., & Vandenberghe, L. (2004). *Convex optimization*. New York: Cambridge University Press.

Di, R. M., Graziosi, F., & Santucci, F. (2008). Performance of cooperative multi-hop wireless systems over log-normal fading channels. In *Proceedings of IEEE Global Telecommunications Conference (GLOBECOM 08)*. IEEE.

Dohler, M., & Li, Y. (2010). *Cooperative communication: Hardware, channel and PHY*. New York: John Wiley & Sons. doi:10.1002/9780470740071.

Duong, T. Q., Bao, V. N. Q., & Zepernick, H. J. (2009). On the performance of selective decode-and-forward relay networks over Nakagami-m fading channels. *IEEE Communications Letters*, *13*(3), 172–174. doi:10.1109/LCOMM.2009.081858.

Elkashlany, M., Yeohyz, P. L., Sungy, C. K., & Collings, I. B. (2010). Distributed multi-antenna relaying in nonregenerative cooperative networks. In *Proceedings of IEEE 21st International Symposium on Personal Indoor and Mobile Radio Communications*. IEEE Press.

Hasna, M. O., & Alouini, M. S. (2003). End-to-end performance of transmission systems with relays over Rayleigh-fading channels. *IEEE Transactions on Wireless Communications*, *2*(6), 1126–1131. doi:10.1109/TWC.2003.819030.

Hu, J., & Beaulieu, N. C. (2007). Performance analysis of decode-and forward relaying with selection combining. *IEEE Communications Letters*, *11*(6), 489–491. doi:10.1109/LCOMM.2007.070065.

Ikki, S. S., & Ahmed, M. H. (2007). Performance analysis of cooperative diversity wireless networks over Nakagami-m fading channels. *IEEE Communications Letters*, *11*(4), 334–336. doi:10.1109/LCOM.2007.348292.

Ikki, S. S., & Ahmed, M. H. (2010). Performance analysis of adaptive decode-and-forward cooperative diversity networks with best-relay selection. *IEEE Transactions on Communications*, *58*(1), 68–72. doi:10.1109/TCOMM.2010.01.080080.

Kalantari, A., Mohammadi, M., & Ardebilipour, M. (2011). Performance analysis of opportunistic relaying over imperfect non-identical lognormal fading channels. In *Proceedings of 22nd IEEE Personal Indoor Mobile Radio Communications (PIMRC11 - WACC)*. Toronto, Canada: IEEE Press.

Prudnikov, A. P., Brychkov, Y. A., & Marichev, O. I. (1992). Integrals and series: *Vol. 4. Direct laplace transforms*. Boca Raton, FL: CRC Press.

Sagias, N. C., Lazarakis, F. I., Tombras, G. S., & Datsikas, C. K. (2008). Outage analysis of decode and forward relaying over Nakagami-m fading channels. *IEEE Signal Processing Letters*, *15*, 41–44. doi:10.1109/LSP.2007.910317.

Simon, M. K., & Alouini, M. S. (2005). *Digital communication over fading channels*. New York: John Wiley & Sons.

Speigel, M. R., Lipschutz, S., & Liu, J. (2009). *Mathematical handbook of formulas and tables*. New York: McGraw Hill.

Wolfram Functions Site. (2011). Retrieved from http://functions.wolfram.com/GammaBetaErf/Gamma2

Yindi, J., & Jafarkhani, H. (2009). Single and multiple relay selection schemes and their achievable diversity orders. *IEEE Transactions on Wireless Communications*, *8*(3), 1414–1423. doi:10.1109/TWC.2008.080109.

ADDITIONAL READING

Aalo, V. A., & Chayawan, C. (2000). Outage probability of cellular radio systems using maximal ratio combining in Rayleigh fading channel with multiple interferers. *IEEE Electronics Letters*, *36*(15), 1314–1315. doi:10.1049/el:20000910.

Amarasuriya, G., Ardakani, M., & Tellambura, C. (2010). Output-threshold multiple-relay-selection for cooperative wireless networks. *IEEE Transactions on Vehicular Technology*, *59*(6), 3091–3094. doi:10.1109/TVT.2010.2048767.

Chen, F., Su, W., Batalama, S., & Matyjas, J. D. (2011). Joint power optimization for multi-source multi-destination relay networks. *IEEE Transactions on Signal Processing*, *59*(5), 2370–2381. doi:10.1109/TSP.2011.2109958.

Chen, X., Siu, T. W., Zhou, Q. F., & Lau, F. C. M. (2010). High-SNR analysis of opportuinistic relaying based on the maximum harmonic mean selection criterion. *IEEE Signal Processing Letters*, *17*(8), 719–722. doi:10.1109/LSP.2010.2051946.

Di Renzo, M., Graziosi, F., & Santucci, F. (2009). On the performance of cooperative systems with blind relays over Nakagami-m and Weibull fading. In Proceedings of *Wireless Communications and Networking Conference*. IEEE Press.

Gedik, B., & Uysal, M. (2009). Impact of imperfect channel estimation on the performance of amplify-and-forward relaying. *IEEE Transactions on Wireless Communications*, *8*, 1468–1479. doi:10.1109/TWC.2008.080252.

Hadzi-Velkov, Z., Zlatanov, N., & Karagiannidis, G. K. (2009). On the second order statistics of the multi-hop rayleigh fading channel. *IEEE Transactions on Communications*, *57*, 1815–1823. doi:10.1109/TCOMM.2009.06.070460.

Hasna, M. O., & Alouini, M. S. (2003). End-to-end performance of transmission systems with relays over Rayleigh-fading channels. *IEEE Transactions on Wireless Communications*, *2*(6), 1126–1131. doi:10.1109/TWC.2003.819030.

Hasna, M. O., & Alouini, M. S. (2004). A performance study of dual-hop transmissions with fixed gain relays. *IEEE Transactions on Wireless Communications*, *3*(6), 1963–1968. doi:10.1109/TWC.2004.837470.

Hong, Y.-W., Huang, W.-J., Chiu, F.-H., & Kuo, C.-C. J. (2007). Cooperative communications in resource-constrained wireless networks. *IEEE Signal Processing Magazine*, *24*(3), 47–57. doi:10.1109/MSP.2007.361601.

Hunter, T., & Nosratinia, A. (2002). Cooperative diversity through coding. In *Proceedings of the IEEE International Symposium on Information Theory (ISIT)*. IEEE Press.

Hunter, T. E., Sanayei, S., & Nosratinia, A. (2006). Outage analysis of coded cooperation. *IEEE Transactions on Information Theory*, *52*(2), 375–391. doi:10.1109/TIT.2005.862084.

Ikki, S. S., & Ahmed, M. H. (2009). On the performance of amplify-and-forward cooperative diversity with the Nth best-relay selection scheme. In *Proceedings of IEEE International Conference on Communications*. IEEE Press.

Ikki, S. S., & Ahmed, M. H. (2009). Performance of cooperative diversity using equal gain combining (EGC) over Nakagami-m fading channels. *IEEE Transactions on Wireless Communications*, *8*, 557–562. doi:10.1109/TWC.2009.070966.

Kalantari, A., Soleimani-Nasab, E., & Ardebilipour, M. (2011). Performance analysis of best selection DF relay networks over Nakagami-n fading channels, In Proceeding of IEEE 19th Iranian Conference on Electrical Engineering (ICEE). Tehran, Iran: IEEE Press.

Soleimani-Nasab, E., Matthaiou, M., Ardebilipour, M., & Karagiannidi, G. K. (2013). Twoway AF relaying in the presence of co-channel interference. IEEE Transactions on Communications, 61. doi: 10.1109/TCOMM.2013.053013.120840.

Soleimani-Nasab, E., Matthaiou, M., & Ardebilipour, M. (2013). Multi-relay MIMO system with OSTBC over Nakagami-m fading channels. IEEE Transactions on Vehicular Technology, doi: 10.1109/TVT.2013.2262009.

Soleimani-Nasab, E., & Ardebilipour, M. (2013). Two-way multi-antenna AF relaying over Nakagami-m fading channels, Springer Wireless Personal Communications. doi: 10.1007/s11277-013-1212-y.

Soleimani-Nasab, E., Ardebilipour, M. & Kalantari, A. (2013). Performance analysis of selective DF relay networks over Nakagami-n and Nakagami-q fading channels, Wiley Wireless Communications and Mobile Computing. doi: 10.1002/wcm.2301.

Soleimani-Nasab, E., Ardebilipour, M., Kalantari, A., & Mahboobi, B. (2013). Performance analysis of multi-antenna relay networks with imperfect channel estimation, Elsevier Journal on Electronics and Communications. 67(1), 45-57. doi: 10.1016/j.aeue.2012.06.007.

Soleimani-Nasab, E., Matthaiou, M., Karagiannidi, G. K., & Ardebilipour, M. (2013). Twoway interference limited relaying over Nakagami-m fading channels, In Proceeding of IEEE Global-Communications Conference (GLOBECOM). Atlanta, USA: IEEE Press.

Soleimani-Nasab, E., Matthaiou, M., & Karagiannidi, G. K. (2013). Two-way interference limited AF relaying with selection combining, In Proceeding of International Conference on Acoustics, Speech, and Signal Processing (ICASSP). Vancouver, Canada: IEEE Press.

Soleimani-Nasab, E., Matthaiou, M., & Ardebilipour, M. (2013). On the performance of multi-antenna AF relaying systems over Nakagami-m fading channels, In Proceeding of IEEE International Conference on Communications (ICC). Budapest, Hungary: IEEE Press.

Soleimani-Nasab, E., & Ardebilipour, M. (2012). On the performance of multi-antenna AF two-way relay networks over Nakagami-m fading channels, In Proceeding of International Symposium onTelecommunication (IST). Tehran, Iran: IEEE Press.

Soleimani-Nasab, E., Kalantari, A., & Ardebilipour, M. (2011). On the performance of selective DF relay networks over Rician fading channels, In Proceeding of 16thIEEE Symposium on Computers and Communications (ISCC). Corfu, Greece: IEEE Press.

KEY TERMS AND DEFINITIONS

Convex Optimization: A convex optimization problem is one in which the objective and constraint functions are convex.

Cooperative Communication: Cooperation is referred to as any architecture that deviates from this traditional approach that is where a user's communication link is enhanced in a supportive way by relays or in a cooperative way by other users.

Decode-and-Forward: DF detects the signal, decodes it and re-encodes it prior to retransmission.

Multi-Antenna: The case that each relay has more than one antenna called multi-antenna.

Outage Probability: The outage probability is defined as the instantaneous error probability exceeds a specified value, or equivalently the case in which probability that the output SNR falls below a certain threshold.

Selection Combining: In selection combining, best relay among all of relays will be selected.

Symbol Error Probability: The probability that a transmitted symbol receives with error is SEP.

Chapter 12
A Generic Method for the Reliable Calculation of Large-Scale Fading in an Obstacle-Dense Propagation Environment

Theofilos Chrysikos
University of Patras, Greece

Stavros Kotsopoulos
University of Patras, Greece

Eduard Babulak
EU CORDIS, Belgium

ABSTRACT

The aim of this chapter is to summarize and present recent findings in the field of wireless channel modeling that provide a new method for the reliable calculation of the statistical parameters of large-scale variations of the average received signal (shadow fading). This algorithm is theoretically based on a path loss estimation model that incorporates losses due to walls and floors. This has been confirmed to be the most precise mathematical tool for average signal strength prediction for various frequencies of interest and propagation environments. The total path loss is estimated as a sum of two independent attenuation processes: free space loss and losses due to obstacles. This solution allows for a direct and reliable calculation of the deviation of the fluctuations of the average received signal in an obstacle-dense environment.

BACKGROUND

Information propagated over a wireless channel as an electromagnetic wave is subject to large-scale attenuation (path loss) due to free space loss and losses caused by interfering objects of various size, type and number. Large-scale attenuation can be calculated with path loss models (mostly logarithmic) which have been developed either theoretically (deterministic models) or based on experimental measurements (empirical models). In order to provide reliable predictions of the aver-

DOI: 10.4018/978-1-4666-2208-1.ch012

age received power. The accuracy of the path loss models is of critical importance with regard to the design and implementation of wireless systems (Goldsmith, 2005).

When physical obstacles, whose dimensions are significantly larger than the wavelength of the transmitted signal, obstruct radio propagation, then the attenuation effect is known as shadowing (Rappaport, 1999). In such cases, the fluctuation of the average received signal strength can be approximated via statistical models (distributions). Shadowing occurs over a time period of minutes or hours, depending on the mobility of the obstacle and the transmitting and receiving antennas. Experimental work has confirmed that the fluctuations of the local mean strength of the received signal follow the *log-normal* distribution (Jakes, 1973).

Moreover, the transmitted Radio Frequency (RF) signal suffers small-scale attenuation (fading) over a period of milliseconds (ms) due to multipath propagation and, conditionally, Doppler spread (Parsons, 2000). Additional statistical models have been developed to describe fading phenomena (i.e. Rayleigh, Rice, Nakagami-m).

The adequate description and mathematical expression of all large-scale and small-scale variations of the received signal for a given propagation topology formulate the field of Wireless Channel Characterization.

WIRELESS CHANNEL CHARACTERIZATION: OPEN ISSUES

Many published works have raised the issue of path loss modeling in an outdoor propagation environment for the GSM/UMTS frequencies (Lee & Miller, 1998; Seybold, 2005). Various empirical and semi-empirical (deterministic) path loss models have been developed and validated in terms of mean error (%) in their predictions of average received power at any given distance from the transmitter throughout a propagation environment (Parsons, 2000; Rappaport, 1999). Intrinsic topology characteristics have been incorporated in the mathematical expressions of these models and various extensions of these models have been provided in terms of distance coverage and carrier frequency shifting (Iskander, Yun, & Zhang, 2001).

Over the years, many published works have dealt with finding the appropriate small-scale fading distribution to describe an indoor propagation topology (Cheung, Sau, & Murch, 1998; Henderson, Durkin, & Durkin, 2008; MacLeod, Loadman, & Chen, 2005; Walker, Zepernick, & Wysocki, 1998). However, there was not, until recently, a comparative validation of indoor path loss models for the estimation of the large-scale attenuation of an RF signal propagated in an indoor environment. Even more so, there had been no validation of path loss modeling for the 2.4 GHz frequency, which holds a dominant role in indoor wireless networks (802.11b/g/n) and will continue to be of importance as next-generation networks come into the forefront.

In addition, the log-normal shadowing distribution has been examined in terms of obtaining a closed-form expression for the statistical expression of the instantaneous received amplitude. The impact of shadow losses on the prediction reliability of path loss modeling, however, was not investigated any further. As a rule, the calculation of the shadowing deviation (in dB) requires an extensive set of on-site RF measurements that provide a pool of (logarithmic) local mean values out of which the mean value and the shadowing deviation (dB) are derived. In this chapter, however, a novel empirical method will be presented, allowing for the direct calculation of shadowing deviation and therefore the precise characterization of large-scale variations of the received signal strength for three different indoor propagation topologies.

INDOOR PROPAGATION TOPOLOGIES

Whereas all path loss and fading phenomena occur in both outdoor and indoor environments, the indoor propagation environment presents even more challenges for researchers and engineers alike, given the increased number of obstacles of various dimensions and material. Obstacles whose dimensions are comparable to the signal wavelength cause signal scattering, which adds to the complexity of the wireless channel characterization. Further attenuation is caused by signal penetration of walls and floors, which are also responsible for reflection phenomena.

It is more than evident that the indoor propagation channel demands a lot more than just a deterministic formula that calculates the average signal strength as a function of distance and frequency. In order to provide an accurate model that incorporates all propagation and attenuation mechanisms in its formula, it is imperative to take into consideration all obstacles and the attenuation of the propagated signal caused by these obstacles, be it walls, floors, other objects or even losses due to human bodies, labeled as human body shadowing (Mathur, Klepal, McGibney, & Pesch, 2004).

In order to examine the impact of the obstacles and overall intrinsic channel characteristics on radio propagation and signal attenuation, three different propagation topologies were chosen for extensive on-site RF measurements and validation of path loss models: an office topology (Chrysikos, Georgopoulos, Birkos, & Kotsopoulos, 2009), a commercial topology (Chrysikos, Georgopoulos, & Kotsopoulos, 2010) and a residential (home) topology (Chrysikos, Georgopoulos, & Kotsopoulos, 2011). In compliance with the indoor topologies classification of ITU (International Telecommunication Union Radio-communication Sector [ITU-R], 1999). In each case, an already operating 802.11g network providing wireless internet access (Wi-Fi, WLAN) was used for RF measurements. The Access Point (AP) served as the transmitter, and the receiver was a laptop equipped with the NetStumbler 0.40 software for recording and storing the local mean values of the received signal power in each measurement location.

The indoor propagation topologies and the corresponding measurement locations are depicted in the following figures.

Figure 1 demonstrates the office propagation topology, at the premises of the Wireless Telecommunications Laboratory, located at the second floor of a building belonging to the Department of Electrical and Computer Engineering, at the University of Patras. As it can be observed, the topology in question goes beyond the typical notion of an office scenario, with an increased degree of complexity: a large room where the AP is located (on the external wall). A total of 22 measurements were taken for the single floor measurements, 10 measurements for the one-floor difference (fixed transmitter on the second floor, moving receiver on the third floor of the building) and 7 measurements in the auditoriums and public hall of the ground floor marking a two-floor difference between the transmitter and the moving receiver (T-R separation). Overall, a total of 39 measurement locations were selected for the office propagation topology.

Figure 2 depicts the commercial topology, which is the main hall of the Public Library located at the campus of the University of Patras. The transmitting AP is located above the information desk (reception). Desks, furniture and other obstacles are also in abundance. A total of 32 measurements were performed throughout the

Figure 1. Office topology

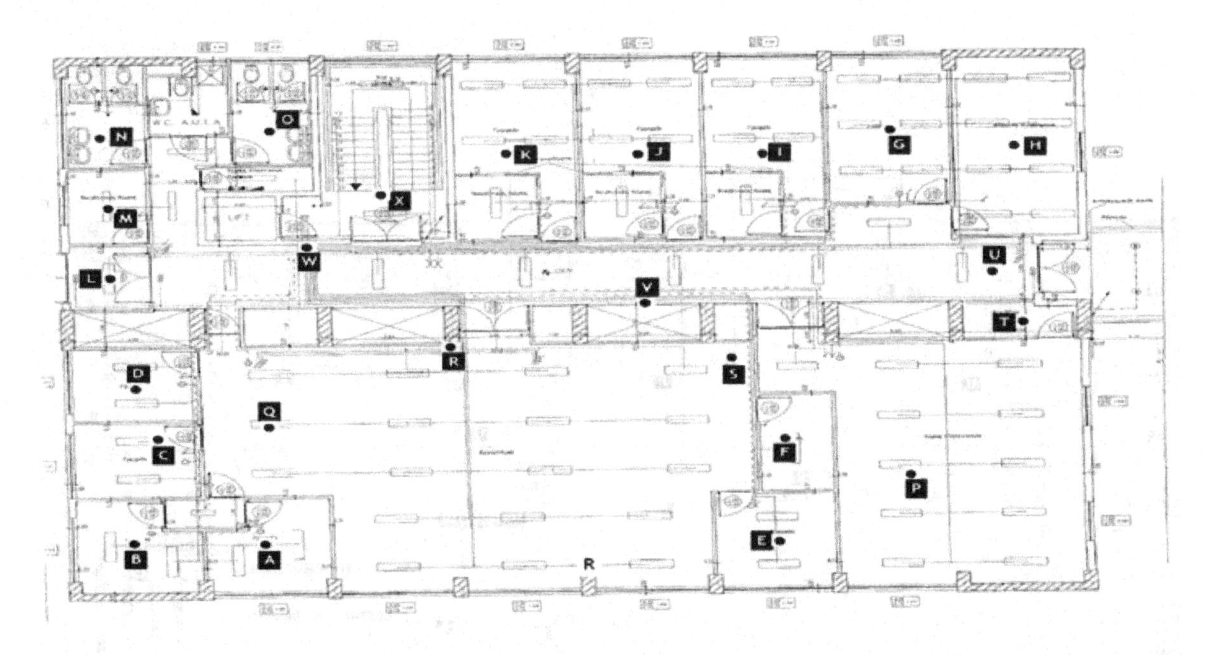

main hall (single floor measurements), providing empirical data for wireless channel characterization and validation of path loss models. Even though the Library is not a *de jure* commercial topology, it is qualified as such *de facto* by its characteristics according to ITU classification. In fact, part of the overall work in the context of Wireless Channel Characterization has been to confirm or re-evaluate, if needed, the correctness of the original ITU classification of indoor propagation topologies.

Figure 3 depicts the measurement locations for the home indoor propagation topology. The majority of measurement locations are scattered in the surrounding rooms of the flat containing the router. A measurement location marked as 'R' was chosen in the reference T-R distance (1 m). In relation to the Access Point (AP). Measurement location Q is in the entrance of the residence. Four more locations were chosen in the public area outside all apartments of the given floor (V,W,X,Y) where the maximum T-R distance is being observed. Finally, locations Z, A2 and A3 were chosen in the neighboring flat. Overall, a total of 28 measurements were performed on the same floor, 15 measurements were also performed on the ground floor of the building, establishing a one-floor separation between transmitting AP and receiving laptop.

SITE-SPECIFIC VALIDATION OF INDOOR PATH LOSS MODELS

The received power in each measurement location of the aforementioned indoor propagation topologies has been measured and recorded in order to provide the necessary experimental data for the validation of path loss models. An interesting example that points out the different impact of topology characteristics on signal attenuation concerns the distance break point where the average received power drops below the threshold of $-70dBm$. For the residential (home) topology, the distance break point is approximately 10 meters (Chrysikos et al, 2011), for the office to-

Figure 2. Library (commercial) topology

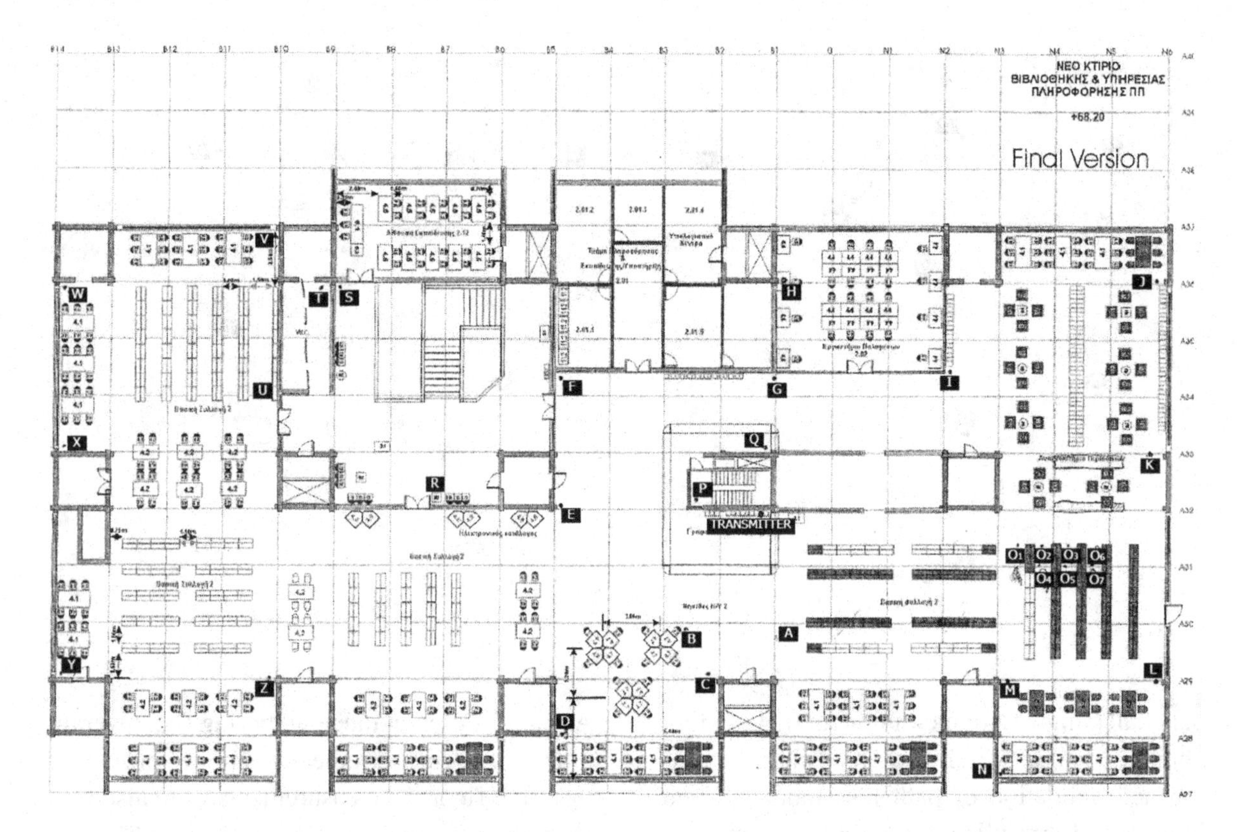

pology the respective distance break point is approximately 20 meters (Chrysikos et al, 2009), where as for the library (commercial) topology the respective value is approximately 30 meters (Chrysikos et al, 2010).

The fundamental reference path loss model is the Free Space model, which is a logarithmic expression of the Friis formula, assuming an ideal propagation scenario with no obstacles, or terrain geographic characteristics, and no antenna heights (Goldsmith, 2005). According to path loss modeling theory, the average received power at a given measurement location is provided by (Jakes, 1973),

$$P_r(dBm) = P_t(dBm) + K(dB) - 10n\log_{10}\left(\frac{d}{d_0} \right) \quad (1)$$

where d is expressed in meters (T-R separation), do is the reference distance which in indoor propagation schemes equals 1 meter, n is the path loss exponent (set to 2 for the Free Space model) and K is the reference path loss at 1 m, which equals $-40dB$ for $2.4GHz$ (802.11g protocol). Average path loss according to the Free Space model is given by (Seybold, 2005),

$$P_L = 32.45 + 20\log_{10}\left(f(MHz)\right) + 20\log_{10}\left(d(km)\right) \quad (2)$$

where *f* is the carrier frequency of the transmitted signal (MHz), and d is the T-R separation (in km). Equation 2 is an equivalent expression of the Free Space model. In both equations, the T-R separation distance has been calculated in order to incorporate the transmitter and receiver antenna heights.

The idealistic propagation assumptions of the Free Space model render it reliable only for Line-of-Sight (LOS) cases. Indeed. In the published

Figure 3. Home topology

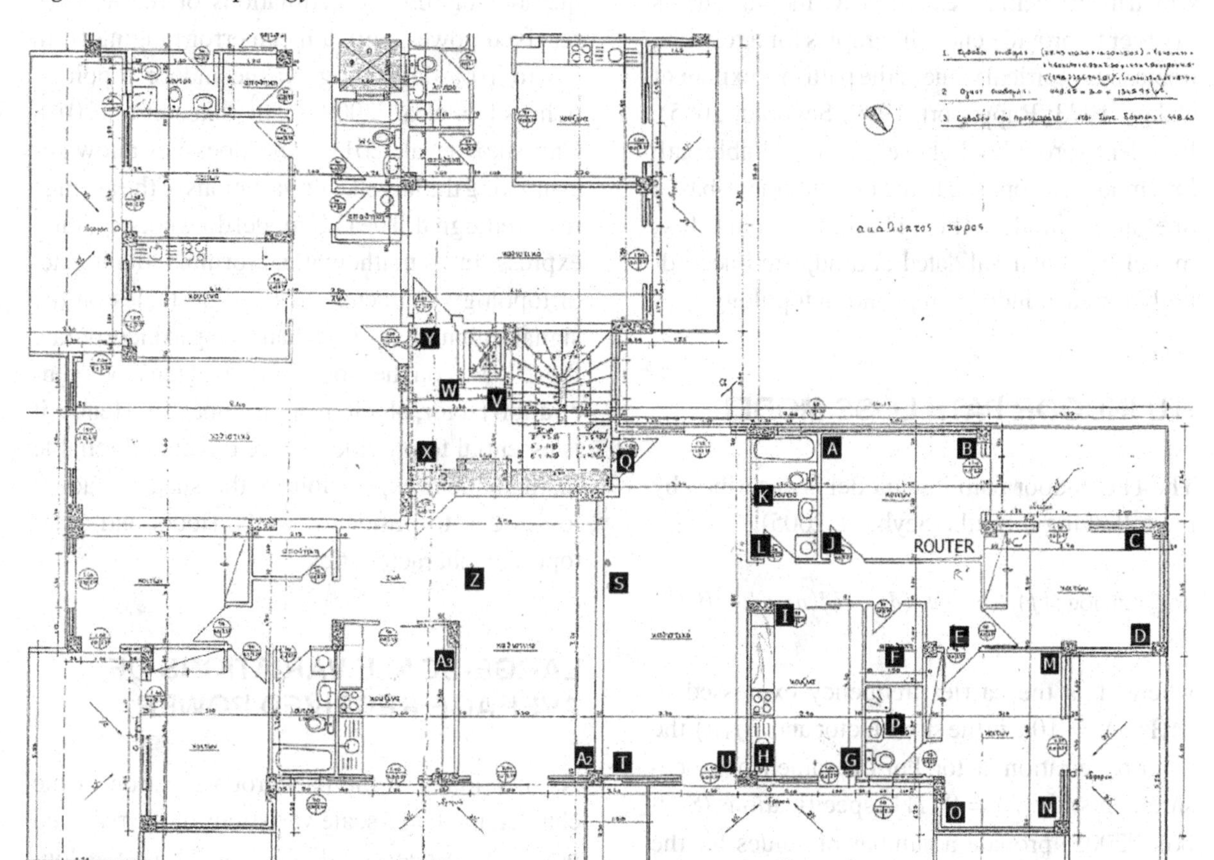

results the Free Space model is highly erroneous and unreliable with the exception of measurement locations where there is LOS propagation between transmitter and receiver. In the original Free Space formula, the path loss exponent is set to $n = 2$, which is in accordance with the inverse-square law, derived out of the Friis equation (ideal propagation of electromagnetic wave into free space).

Our measurements however have confirmed that in all three indoor propagation topologies, the path loss exponent for the Free Space model needs to be set to 1.8 in order for the model to be reliable in its estimations for LOS cases (Chrysikos et al, 2009, Chrysikos et al, 2010, Chrysikos et al, 2011).

It should be noted that especially for the office propagation topology (same floor measurements) where three specific locations comply with the LOS scenario, the path loss exponent is set to a value of 1.73. This has been validated via mean square error techniques (Chrysikos et al, 2009).

Expanding the mean square error technique for the total of the available measurement locations, an empirical path loss exponent can be derived for all cases: Line-of-Sight (LOS), Obstructed-Line-of-Sight (OLOS) and Non-Line-of-Sight (NLOS), providing a universal adjustment of the free space model that complies with all propagation scenarios. This has been described as the one-slope empirical model (Seybold, 2005).

Mean error values for the one-slope model for all three indoor propagation topologies demonstrate a much more reliable behavior than the original Free Space model and the Free Space model with $n = 1.8$. The main setback, however, of this model is that it requires experimental data (local mean values of average received power) which in turn demand extensive RF measurements in order to provide enough samples for a reliable, unbiased empirical value of the path loss exponent (Jakes, 1973; Rappaport, 1999; Seybold, 2005). In order to provide a lightweight and reliable path loss model as opposed to the measurement-based one-slope model, the ITU indoor path loss model has been validated and adjusted accordingly for each indoor propagation topology.

ITU INDOOR PATH LOSS MODEL

The ITU indoor path loss model is described by the following formula (Seybold, 2005),

$$P_L = 20\log_{10}(f) + N\log_{10}(d) + Lf(n) - 28dB \quad (3)$$

where: f is the carrier frequency expressed in MHz, $N = 10n$ is the slope factor and $Lf(n)$ the floor penetration factor. For the same floor measurements, $Lf(n) = 0$. ITU specifications (Seybold, 2005) provide a number of values for the slope factor (path loss exponent), for different carrier frequencies.

However, these original specifications have been proven to be inaccurate for the 2.4 GHz frequency band for all indoor propagation topologies (office, library, home). Numerical adjustments have been provided for the slope factor values for each topology, and for the multiple floors measurements in the office topology, the floor penetration factor has also been corrected, with empirically derived values (Chrysikos, Georgopoulos, & Kotsopoulos, 2009a).

The aforementioned numerical corrections to the original ITU formula have increased the reliability of the model predictions, providing better results than the Free Space and the One-Slope model, without the latter's need for a substantial pool of measured values of local mean strength of the received signal. However, this site-specific method is suitable as a lightweight, on-the-fly method for reliable estimations of the average received power, with a mean error ranging from 5% to 10% depending on the indoor topology (Chrysikos et al, 2009a; Chrysikos et al, 2010; Chrysikos et al, 2011), and does not allow for estimating the large-scale variations of the average received signal. The ITU model does not explicitly express. In its mathematical formula, the impact of topology characteristics and obstacles on the signal attenuation, other than trying to incorporate those losses on the slope factor and the floor penetration factor, albeit in approximation. Hence, it is essential to provide a more direct and reliable mathematical expression of the shadow fading losses due to obstacles, walls, floors and other topology characteristics.

LARGE-SCALE VARIATIONS OF AVERAGE RECEIVED POWER

As mentioned in the background section of the chapter, the large-scale variations of the received power have been confirmed to follow the log-normal distribution. Hence, the logarithmic values of the local mean power (dBw or dBm) comply with the Gaussian distribution. The Probability Density Function (PDF) of the Gaussian distribution for the logarithmic values of the received power values is derived by (Jakes; 1973),

$$p(x) = \frac{1}{\sigma\sqrt{2\pi}} e^{-\frac{(x-\overline{x})^2}{2\sigma^2}} \quad (4)$$

where x is the received power (logarithmic value) in each measurement location (local mean strength), $\overline{x}$ is the average received power (logarithmic value) for all measurement locations (median value of the received power overall the topology in question), and σ is the standard deviation of the shadowing losses (in dB).

Given a pool of experimentally obtained i received power values corresponding to respective measurement locations in a propagation topology, the mean value and standard deviation of the distribution of these values can be calculated by (Parsons, 2000; Seybold, 2005),

$$\overline{x} = \frac{1}{n}\sum_{i=1}^{n} x_i \tag{5}$$

$$\sigma^2 = \frac{1}{n}\sum_{i=1}^{n} (x_i - \overline{x})^2 \tag{6}$$

On the grounds of these empirical calculations, it is possible to compare the distribution of the i received power values (in dBm) with the Gaussian distribution in order to confirm the logarithmic nature of the large-scale fluctuations of the propagated radio signal due to shadowing. In order to provide unbiased results, a significantly large number of i samples are required (Rappaport, 1999).

For the home topology, such a comparison has been accomplished (Chrysikos et al, 2011) and the results are demonstrated in the Figures 4 and 5.

Figures 4 and 5 confirm that the fluctuations of the received power for the total of the measurement locations of the home propagation topology are indeed of log-normal nature (Gaussian distribution of the logarithmic values).

Being able to describe the shadow fading phenomena and their impact on signal propagation is critical in order to predict in reliable manner the outage probability, i.e. the probability that the received power will drop below a defined threshold, the Outage Probability is mathematically linked to the Cumulative Distribution Function (CDF) of the fading distribution that describes signal propagation in the said topology (Rappaport, 1999).

Figure 6 and Figure 7 depict the CDF of the Log-normal distribution (with mean value and shadowing deviation provided by Equations 5 and 6) for the same floor and multiple floor measurements of the home topology respectively, versus a CDF derived empirically from the measured received power values.

The results confirm that the log-normal distribution with a shadowing deviation calculated from the measured received power values is indeed in compliance with the empirical data (CDF de-

Figure 4. Log-normal distribution of average received power for home topology (same floor)

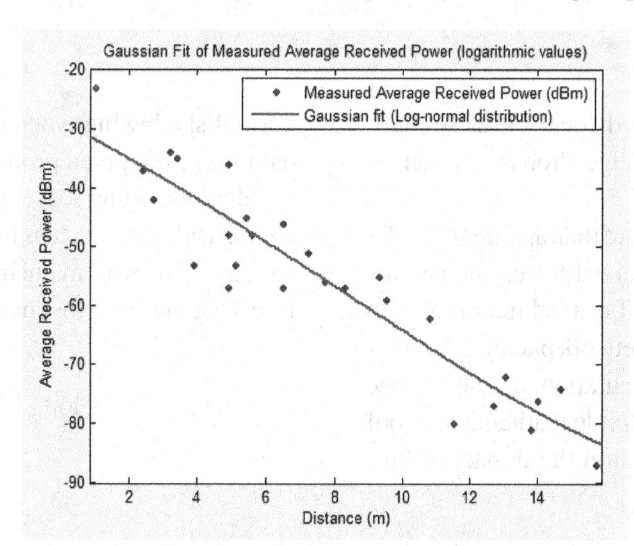

Figure 5. Log-normal distribution of average received power for home topology (multiple floors)

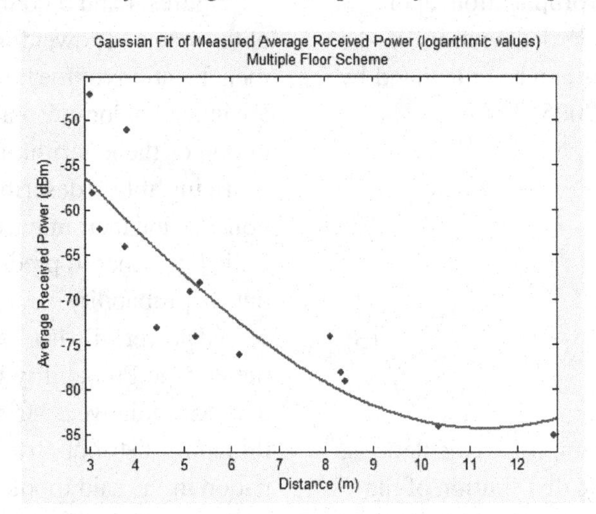

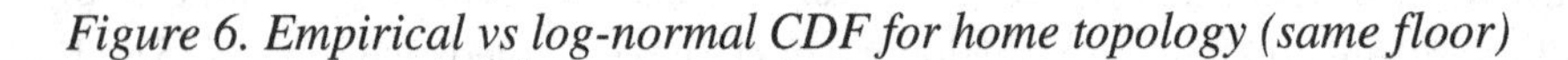
Figure 6. Empirical vs log-normal CDF for home topology (same floor)

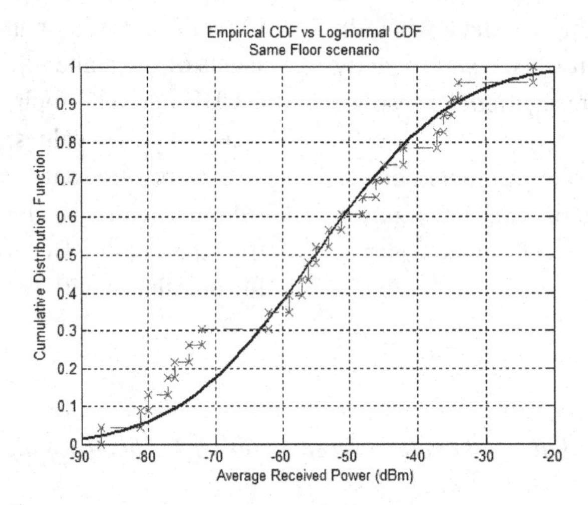

rived out of the measured local mean strength values) therefore the Outage Probability can be reliably calculated.

From the above it is more than apparent that the accurate prediction of received power fluctuations around a mean value is of critical importance in order to achieve a robust network planning in terms of Outage Probability calculation. It is necessary, therefore, to develop a reliable mathematical tool for taking into consideration the impact of log-normal shadowing when estimating the average path loss for a given propagation scenario.

Shadow fading losses can be incorporated in the logarithmic path loss formula with a Gaussian variable. This is the mathematical expression of the Log-Distance path loss model (Rappaport, 1999),

$$P_L = PL(d_0) + N\log_{10}\left(d / d_0 \right) + X_\sigma \tag{7}$$

Figure 7. Empirical vs log-normal CDF for home topology (multiple floors)

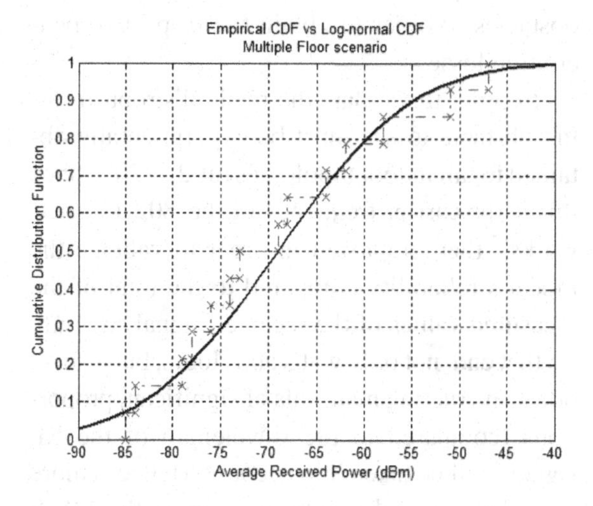

$$X_{\sigma} = z \times \sigma(dB) = 1.645 \times \sigma(dB) \quad (8)$$

Whereas: P(do) is the reference path loss at 1 m from the transmitter, N is the slope factor and X_{σ} is a zero-mean Gaussian variable (dB) that expresses the losses due to (log-normal) shadowing. The parameter z stands for the percentage of coverage probability (Rappaport, 1999). For best case scenarios with a coverage probability of 98%, z equals 2. In sub-optimal, realistic schemes, as the one considered in this work, z equals 1.645 for a coverage probability of 95% (Seybold, 2005).

The Log-Distance model, however, requires a precise value assignment for both the path loss exponent and the log-normal shadowing variable in order to provide reliable estimations. Though such experimentally derived data exist in literature (Rappaport, 1999), the model's complexity does not allow for reliable predictions (Chrysikos et al, 2009).

If the path loss exponent were to be set as 1.8. In accordance with the free space model for indoor environments, then an unbiased experimental derivation of the shadowing deviation would require a large number of measured values of received signal strength throughout the propagation topology. This would require extensive on-site RF measurements, which would be time-consuming and unpractical in terms of path loss prediction.

On the other hand, the Multi-Wall-Floor (MWF) model, extended to include all major obstacles in addition to walls and floors, has been validated to be the most reliable model for path loss prediction.

MULTI-WALL-FLOOR MODEL

The Multi-Wall-Floor model is a path loss model whose formula is provided by (Lott & Forkel, 2001),

$$L = L_0 + 10n\log_{10}(d) + \sum_{i=1}^{I}\sum_{k=1}^{K_{wi}} L_{wik} + \sum_{j=1}^{J}\sum_{k=1}^{K_{fj}} L_{fjk} \quad (9)$$

where:

I, J is the number of types of walls and floors

L_{wik} is the attenuation due to kth traversed wall type i

L_{fjk} is the attenuation due to kth traversed floor type j K_{wi}

K_{wi} is the number of walls type i

K_{fj} is the number of floors type j.

The mathematical expression assumes two categories of losses: losses due to free space propagation and losses caused by all the various types of walls and floor that may come into the path of the propagated signal. Moreover, the Multi-Wall-Floor model considers different losses for different types of materials, at a given frequency of transmission.

The Multi-Wall-Floor (MWF) model takes also into account the decreasing penetration loss of walls and floors of the same material as their number increases (Lott & Forkel, 2001). This marks a significant departure from other schemes, most notably the Motley-Keenan model (Lima & Menezes, 2005) that eventually becomes unreliable because it fails to incorporate this decrease in its mathematical formula (Chrysikos et al, 2009).

The fundamental concept of the Multi-Wall-Floor model can be extended and applied to estimate reliably the large-scale variations of received signal strength in a given propagation topology.

A NOVEL EMPIRICAL METHOD FOR THE CALCULATION OF SHADOWING DEVIATION

The excess path loss is defined by Jakes (1973) as the difference (in decibels) between the computed value of the received signal strength in free space and the actual measured value of the local mean received signal (pp. 120). If the large-scale variations of the average received power are log-normal, the excess path loss is also log-normal (Jakes, 1973).

Therefore, the losses (in decibels) caused by walls and floors and expressed by $\sum_{i=1}^{I}\sum_{k=1}^{K_{wi}} L_{wik} + \sum_{j=1}^{J}\sum_{k=1}^{K_{fj}} L_{fjk}$ in the MWF model formula, are Gaussian. This serves as the basis of a novel empirical method for the calculation of shadowing deviation (Chrysikos, Georgopoulos, & Kotsopoulos, 2009b),

$$\sigma(dB) = \frac{\sum_{i=1}^{I}\sum_{k=1}^{K_{wi}} L_{wik} + \sum_{j=1}^{J}\sum_{k=1}^{K_{fj}} L_{fjk}}{z} \quad (10)$$

Thus, the shadowing deviation (in dB) is calculated directly from the losses caused by obstacles along the signal propagation path. This method does not require extensive RF measurements. It only requires limited measurements near the obstacles in order to obtain the respective penetration losses.

In order to validate the method's robustness, the obstacle losses must be experimentally obtained for all indoor topologies (at $2.4GHz$ since this is the carrier frequency of the $802.11g$ networks), then employed in order to validate the model's reliability compared to the total of the measured values of the received signal strength. To that end, not only walls and floors, but also all other obstructing materials of significant proportions (compared to the wavelength of the RF signal) will be taken into account. Hence, a more extended, generalized application of the MWF model will be employed.

By performing limited measurements near and around the obstacles in each propagation environment, Tables 1 through 3 are derived (Chrysikos et al, 2009b; Chrysikos et al, 2010; Chrysikos et al, 2011),

Table 1. Measured obstacle losses for office topology

No.	Internal Walls	Pillar	Wide Wall	Elevator
1	7-8 dB	10 dB	7-8 dB	10 dB
2	5-6 dB			
3	3-4 dB			
4	1-2 dB			

Table 2. Measured obstacle losses for library topology

No.	Walls	Internal Walls	Bookcase
1	15 dB	7 dB	3 dB
2	8 dB	5 dB	
3	3 dB		

Table 3. Measured obstacle losses for home topology

No.	Internal Walls (in Flat)	Walls Separating Flats	Floor Penetration	Elevator
1	8 dB	15 dB	15 dB	13 dB
2	6 dB	12 dB	12 dB	
3	4 dB			
4	2 dB			
5	1 dB			

From the results presented in the tables, it is apparent that the penetration losses of same type obstacles decreases as their number increases. This is a fundamental concept of the MWF model which is confirmed by our experimental measurements near and around the obstacles, not only for walls and floors as in the original model (Lott & Forkel, 2001) but also for all other significant obstructing materials. Taking into account all these aforementioned losses and incorporating them into the path loss formula, the results shown in Figures 8 through 12 are obtained, which are compared to the measured values of the received signal strength for each topology.

It is obvious that the predictions of the MWF model (including obstacles) are very close to the measured values. The mean error for each case study has been calculated and is depicted in Table 4 (Chrysikos et al, 2009b; Chrysikos et al, 2010; Chrysikos et al, 2011),

The mean error (%) of the MWF model ranges from 1.88% to 3.44% for all case studies except the library topology, where the mean error increases up to 6.36%. Still, it is significantly

Figure 8. MWF performance for office topology (same floor)

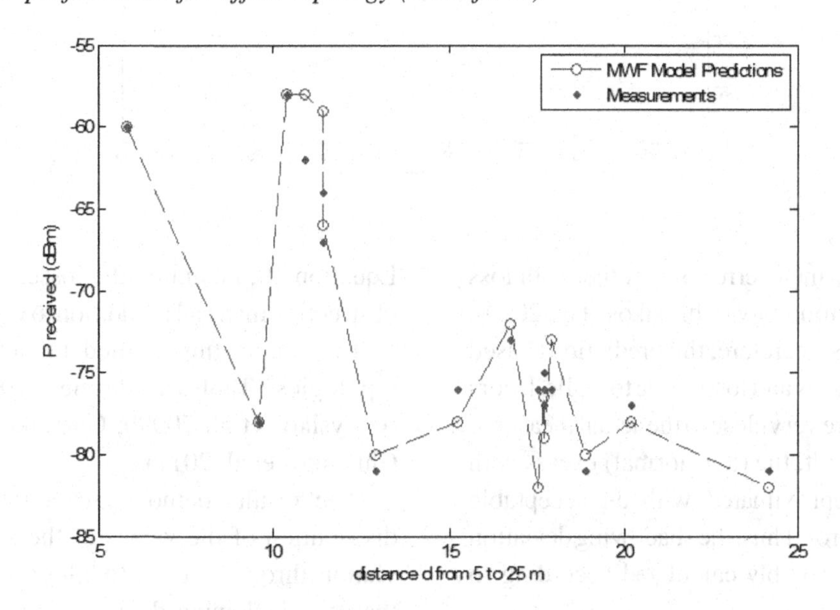

Figure 9. MWF performance for office topology (multiple floors)

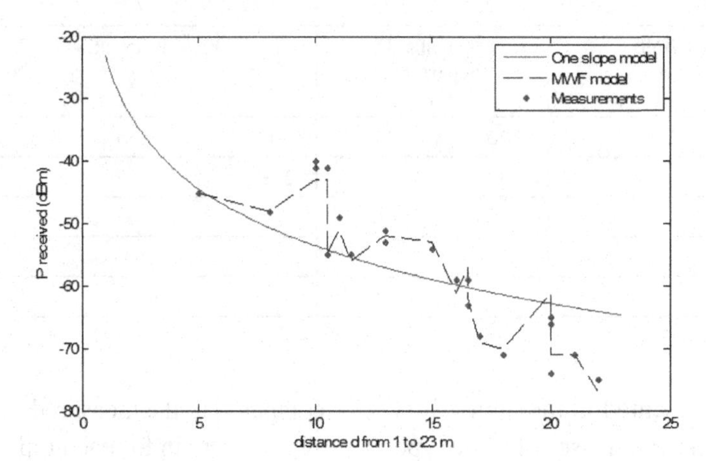

Figure 10. MWF performance for library topology

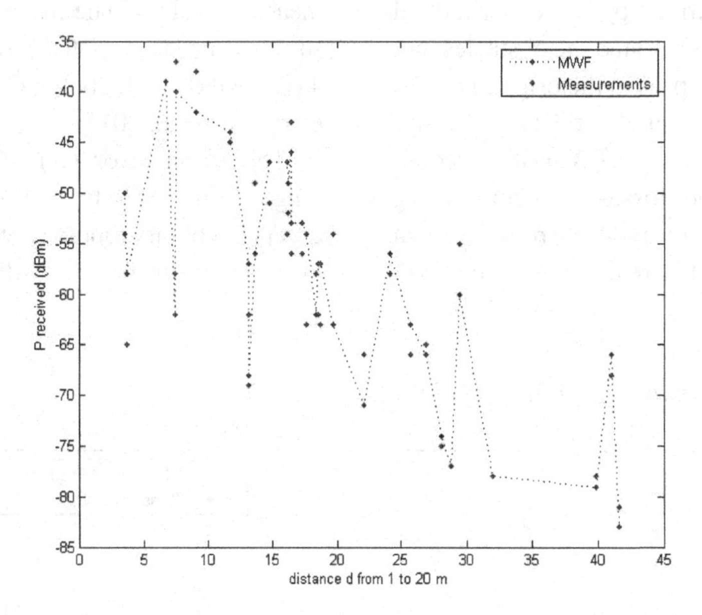

smaller than the mean error of all other path loss models for that topology (Chrysikos et al, 2010). In all topologies, therefore, the predictions based on free space losses and losses due to walls, floors and obstacles, are very close to the actual measured values. As a result, the (log-normal) excess path loss can be approximated with an acceptable percentage of error. Thus, the shadowing deviation (in dB) can be reliably calculated according to Equation 10, including the losses from all other obstructing material in addition to walls and floors.

Employing this method for all propagation topologies, Tables 5 through 10 are derived (Chrysikos et al, 2009b; Chrysikos et al, 2010; Chrysikos et al, 2011),

The results demonstrate a rather dynamic distribution of the values of the shadowing deviation throughout the topologies. It is evident that the shadowing deviation does not increase

Figure 11. MWF performance for home topology (same floor)

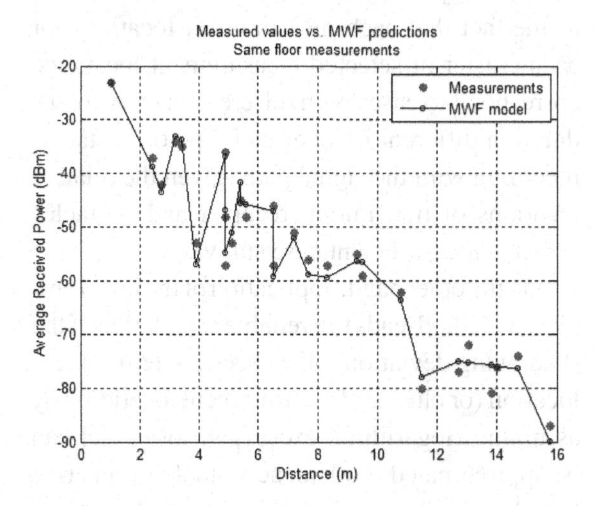

Table 4. Mean error of multi-wall-floor model

Topology	MWF Mean Error
Office (same floor)	2.41%
Office (multiple floors, 1 floor T-R separation)	1.88%
Office (multiple floors, 2 floors T-R separation)	2.22%
Library	6.36%
Home (same floor)	3.44%
Home (multiple floors)	2.14%

with distance, confirming similar outdoor experimental findings (Jakes, 1973; Seybold, 2005). The shadowing deviation depends on the topology intrinsic characteristics and expresses the penetration losses caused by all obstructing materials (walls, floors and other obstacles). This marks a departure from the conventional log-normal concept, where the shadowing deviation is a statistical metric of the fluctuations of the received power values (Jakes, 1973).

Table 11 depicts the shadowing deviation (in dB) for the home propagation topology (same floor and multiple floor measurements) for both methods (Chrysikos et al, 2011). The second column shows the values of shadowing deviation (in dB) as a product of Equation 6, that is in the context of the classic log-normal scenario, where the shadowing deviation (in dB) is calculated on the basis of an experimental data set of measured values of the received signal strength. The third column features the dB values of the shadowing deviation as a product of the novel empirical method, where the shadowing deviation is calculated on the basis of penetration losses of obstructing materials (walls, floors and other obstacles).

The classic log-normal concept can actually be employed in order to calculate the distribution

Table 5. Shadowing deviation (in dB) for office topology (same floor)

Location	σ (dB)
A	6.04
B	8.38
C	6.52
D	6.37
E	6.7
F	5.3
G	12.15
H	14.93
I	15.74
J	9.07
M	11.54
N	17.11
O	17.01
P	8.86
Q	0.35
R	0
S	0
T	11.34
U	14.22
V	4.97
W	6.37
X	8.91

Figure 12. MWF performance for home topology (multiple floors)

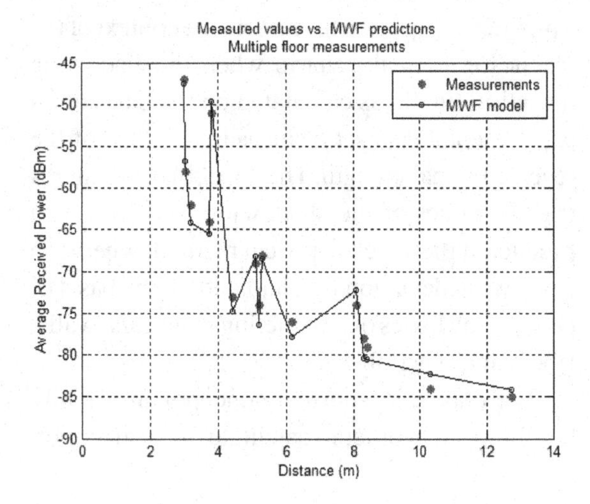

Table 6. Shadowing deviation (in dB) for office topology (one floor T-R separation)

Location	σ (dB)
A'	15.03
B'	15.72
C'	12.92
D'	10.74
E'	15.72
F'	18.78
G'	19.48
H'	18.26
I'	17.35
J'	18.87

CDF and therefore the Outage Probability for a given signal strength threshold. This, however, as mentioned earlier, requires an extensive number of on-site RF measurements – a grid of measurements throughout each given propagation topology – which is time consuming and more prone to error.

In addition, the shadowing deviation in this case cannot be applied to the Log-Distance path loss model in order to predict the local mean strength at any given distance from the transmitter throughout the topology (Chrysikos et al, 2009). This is due to the fact that each measurement locations, or each cluster of selected measurement locations, correspond to cases with different shadow losses due to a different number and type of obstacles meddling with the signal path (given the relative locations of transmitter, receiver and obstacles for each measurement case study).

On the other hand, application of the novel empirical method leads to a reliable calculation of the shadowing deviation for each such measurement location (or cluster of measurement locations) by assuming a logarithmic excess path loss which can be approximated (with an acceptable mean error less than 3.5% with the exception of the library commercial topology, where it is still significantly smaller than the mean error of all other path loss models) by the sum of losses of all walls, floors and obstacles meddling with the propagation path of the transmitted signal.

This method does not require but a limited number of on-site measurements near and around each obstacle. If there is already an available data set of measured obstacle losses such as in Tables 1 through 3, then no additional measurements are required and the link budget can be immediately calculated on the basis of these known penetration losses. The shadowing deviation (in dB) is confirmed to be independent of distance as with previous experimental findings and is dependent solely on the number of type of obstacles for each measurement location (or cluster of measurement locations). These directly calculated values of shadowing deviation can be employed for path loss prediction throughout the topology.

Moreover, this method confirms the notion that shadow fading should not be considered as merely the quantitative residue that is left over when implementing path loss prediction for a set of measured received power values, at a given distance and frequency, as proven already for

Table 7. Shadowing deviation (in dB) for office topology (two floors T-R separation)

Location	σ (dB)
A''	23.32
B''	19.67
C''	18.81
D''	21.56
E''	20.26
F''	20.54
G''	21.97

outdoor propagation case studies (Salo, Vuokko, El-Sallabi, & Vainikainen, 2007).

Overall, this method can be employed for any given propagation topology and any given frequency of interest, as long as the respective losses for all significant obstructing materials are measured. At different frequencies of interest (i.e. 2.1 GHz, 3.5 GHz, 5.2 GHz), the same type of materials may cause different penetration losses, so that should be taken into consideration. Previous experimental works have demonstrated that the shadowing deviation (in dB) is frequency-dependent (Jakes, 1973; Seybold, 2005). Confirming that notion is one of the future research directions in relation to this empirical method.

FUTURE RESEARCH DIRECTIONS

Immediate future work consists of expanding the findings of this empirical method in the field of Wireless Information-Theoretic Security (WITS). WITS has been suggested (Bloch, Barros, Rodrigues, & McLaughlin, 2008) as an information-theoretic solution against eavesdropping that can be implemented as complementary to cryptography schemes or independently, especially in an infrastructure-less scenario (ad hoc networks) or in the case of an emergency scenario (emergency services, physical disasters). Instead of the classic Gaussian eavesdropping scenario, Rayleigh fading is assumed for the main channel (channel established between transmitter and legitimate receiver) and the wiretap channel (channel established between transmitter and eavesdropper). It

Table 8. Shadowing deviation (in dB) for library topology

Location	σ (dB)
A	0
B	0
C	0
D	0
E	0.48
F	2.19
G	10.49
H	14.52
I	10.26
J	9.49
K	10.22
L	4.93
M	5.53
N	3.47
O1	3.03
O2	4.41
O3	5.30
O4	3.18
O5	9.47
O6	8.62
O7	9.18
P	11.65
Q	18.10
R	6.22
S	8.67
T	14.56
U	15.64
V	15.75
W	16.33
X	14.71
Y	8.50
Z	2.16

Table 9. Shadowing deviation (in dB) for home topology (same floor)

Location	σ (dB)
R	0
E	4.35
F	6.83
B	1.16
J	1.48
M	11.77
A	0.35
C	7.65
P	13.12
I	10.49
D	5.36
L	5.36
K	7.01
O	5.09
G	11.77
N	7.64
H	10.36
U	10.61
S	8.86
Q	11.19
T	12.40
A2	23.04
V	20.75
Z	17.58
A3	22.79
W	19.68
X	18.23
Y	25.80

has been proven that in this case, perfect secrecy is available even when the average Signal-to-Noise ratio (SNR) of the main channel is less than the average SNR of the wiretap channel, albeit with a probability less than 0.5 (Barros & Rodrigues, 2006).

Recent work has demonstrated that the WITS scheme is actually very dependent on the intrinsic channel characteristics and that its performance is radically influenced by different propagation scenarios (Chrysikos & Kotsopoulos, 2009). It is therefore imperative to investigate the specific impact of shadowing, as a product of the intrinsic channel and topology characteristics, on Wireless Information-Theoretic Security, and confirm theoretical deductions with experimental findings from on-going measurements.

In addition, the novel empirical method must be put to test for outdoor propagation topologies where different channel scenarios apply and compare the results with those presented in this

Table 10. Shadowing deviation (in dB) for home topology (one floor T-R separation)

Location	σ (dB)
R'	9.37
I	15.98
L	18.18
C	18.64
N	10.66
M	23.32
J	20.20
H	23.15
K	19.42
G	23.57
B	21.07
A	23.38
F	23.93
E	25.98
D	25.60

Table 11. Shadowing deviation (in dB) for home topology

Home Propagation Topology	Shadowing Deviation (dB) [Equation 6]	Shadowing Deviation (dB) [Equation 10]
Same Floor	16	10.74
Multiple Floor	11	20.16

chapter. Moreover, as already mentioned, the impact of different frequency employment on the obstacle losses, and therefore on the (dB) values of the shadowing deviation, needs to be further investigated for both outdoor and indoor propagation topologies.

CONCLUSION

In this book chapter, a novel empirical method was presented that allows the direct calculation of the shadowing deviation (in dB) as a product of the penetration losses of walls, floors and obstacles at a given propagation topology. The reliability of the method in terms of excess path loss estimation was confirmed to be within acceptable mean error values, and significantly more precise in comparison to all other existing path loss models. The direct calculation of the shadowing deviation allows for the characterization of the large-scale variations of the local mean strength of the received signal throughout the propagation topology. The nature of these variations was confirmed to be log-normal. The Gaussian distribution was employed for approximation of the logarithmic values of the received signal acquired over extensive on-site measurements.

This method, however, does not require but a limited number of on-site measurements near and around each obstacle and it can be employed for any given propagation topology and any given frequency of interest, as long as the respective losses for all significant obstructing materials are measured. Immediate and on-going research work will address more open issues in the ever-important field of wireless channel characterization.

REFERENCES

Akl, R., Tummala, D., & Li, X. (2006). *Indoor propagation modeling at 2.4 GHz for IEEE 802.11networks.* Paper presented at the 6th IASTED International Multi-Conference on Wireless and Optical Communications. Banff, Canada.

Barros, J., & Rodrigues, M. R. D. (2006). *Secrecy capacity of wireless channels.* Paper presented at the IEEE International Symposium on Information Theory (ISIT 2006). Seattle, WA.

Bloch, M., Barros, J., Rodrigues, M. R. D., & McLaughlin, S. W. (2008). Wireless information-theoretic security. *IEEE Transactions on Information Theory, 54*(6), 2515–2534. doi:10.1109/TIT.2008.921908.

Cheung, K. W., Sau, J. H. M., & Murch, R. D. (1998). A new empirical model for indoor propagation prediction. *IEEE Transactions on Vehicular Technology, 47*(3), 996–1001. doi:10.1109/25.704854.

Chrysikos, T., Georgopoulos, G., Birkos, K., & Kotsopoulos, S. (2009). *Wireless channel characterization: On the validation issues of indoor RF models at 2.4 GHz.* Paper presented at the Panhellenic Conference on Electronics and Telecommunications (PACET). Patras, Greece.

Chrysikos, T., Georgopoulos, G., & Kotsopoulos, S. (2009a). *Site-specific validation of ITU indoor path loss model at 2.4 GHz.* Paper presented at the IEEE Workshop on Advanced Experimental Activities on Wireless Networks and Systems. Kos Island, Greece.

Chrysikos, T., Georgopoulos, G., & Kotsopoulos, S. (2009b). *Empirical calculation of shadowing deviation for complex indoor propagation topologies at 2.4 GHz.* Paper presented at the International Conference on Ultra Modern Telecommunications (ICUMT 2009). St. Petersburg, Russia.

Chrysikos, T., Georgopoulos, G., & Kotsopoulos, S. (2010). *Impact of shadowing on wireless channel characterization for a public indoor commercial topology at 2.4 GHz*. Paper presented at the International Congress on Ultra Modern Telecommunications (ICUMT 2010). Moscow, Russia.

Chrysikos, T., Georgopoulos, G., & Kotsopoulos, S. (2011). *Wireless channel characterization for a home indoor propagation topology at 2.4 GHz*. Paper presented at the Wireless Telecommunications Symposium (WTS 2011). New York, NY.

Chrysikos, T., & Kotsopoulos, S. (2009). *Impact of channel-dependent variation of path loss exponent on wireless information-theoretic security*. Paper presented at the Wireless Telecommunications Symposium (WTS 2009). Prague, Czech Republic.

Goldsmith, A. (2005). *Wireless communications*. Cambridge, UK: Cambridge University Press. doi:10.1017/CBO9780511841224.

Henderson, A. H., Durkin, C. J., & Durkin, G. D. (2008). *Finding the right small-scale distribution for a measured indoor 2.4 GHz channel*. Paper presented at the IEEE Antennas and Propagation Society International Symposium (APSURSI 2008). San Diego, CA.

International Telecommunication Union Radiocommunication Sector (ITU-R). (1999). *Prediction methods for the terrestrial land mobile service in the VHF and UHF bands*. ITU-R.

Iskander, M., Yun, Z., & Zhang, Z. (2001). *Outdoor/indoor propagation modeling for wireless communications systems*. Paper presented at the IEEE Antennas and Propagation Society International Symposium (APSURSI 2001). Boston, MA.

Jakes, W. C. (Ed.). (1974). *Microwave mobile communications*. New York: Wiley Interscience.

Lee, J. S., & Miller, L. E. (1998). *CDMA systems engineering handbook*. Norwood, MA: Artech House.

Lima, A., & Menezes, L. (2005). *Motley-Keenan model adjusted to the thickness of the wall*. Paper presented at the SBMO/IEEE MTT-S International Microwave and Optoelectronics Conference. Brasilia.

Lott, M., & Forkel, I. (2001). *A multi wall and floor model for indoor radio propagation*. Paper presented at the IEEE Vehicular Technology Conference (VTC 2001-Spring). Rhodes Island, Greece.

MacLeod, H., Loadman, C., & Chen, Z. (2005). *Experimental studies of the 2.4-GHz ISM wireless indoor channel*. Paper presented at the Annual Communication Networks and Services Research Conference (CNSR 2005). Halifax, Canada.

Mathur, R., Klepal, M., McGibney, A., & Pesch, D. (2004). *Influence of people shadowing on bit error rate of IEEE 802.11 2.4 GHz channel*. Paper presented at the International Symposium on Wireless Communication Systems (ISWCS 2004). Port-Louis, Mauritius.

Parsons, J. D. (2000). *The mobile radio propagation channel*. Hoboken, NJ: Wiley Interscience. doi:10.1002/0470841524.

Rappaport, T. (1999). *Wireless communications: Principles & practice*. Upper Saddle River, NJ: Prentice Hall.

Salo, J., Vuokko, L., El-Sallabi, H. M., & Vainikainen, P. (2007). An additive model as a physical basis for shadow fading. *IEEE Transactions on Vehicular Technology*, *56*(1), 13–26. doi:10.1109/TVT.2006.883797.

Seybold, J. (2005). *Introduction to RF propagation*. Hoboken, NJ: Wiley Interscience. doi:10.1002/0471743690.

Walker, E., Zepernick, H. J., & Wysocki, T. (1998). *Fading measurements at 2.4 GHz for the indoor radio propagation channel.* Paper presented at the International Zurich Seminar on Broadband Communications. Zurich, Switzerland.

ADDITIONAL READING

Abdi, A., & Kaveh, M. (2011). A comparative study of two shadow fading models in ultrawideband and other wireless systems. *IEEE Transactions on Wireless Communications*, *10*(5), 1428–1434. doi:10.1109/TWC.2011.031611.100309.

Abramowitz, M., & Stegun, I. (1970). *Handbook of mathematical functions with formulas, graphs, and mathematical tables*. New York, NY: Dover Publications.

Ahmed, I., Orfali, S., Khattab, T., & Mohamed, A. (2011). *Characterization of the indoor-outdoor radio propagation channel at 2.4 GHz.* Paper presented at the IEEE GCC Conference & Exhibition. Dubai, UAE.

Al-Nuaimi, M. O., & Siamarou, A. G. (2001). *Effects of human shadowing, traffic, and antenna movements on 62.4GHz indoor RLAN's channels.* Paper presented at the IEEE Vehicular Technology Conference (VTC 2001-Spring). Rhodes Island, Greece.

Butterworth, K. S., Sowerby, K. W., Williamson, A. G., & Neve, M. J. (1998). *Influence of correlated shadowing and base station configuration on in-building system capacity.* Paper presented at the IEEE Vehicular Technology Conference (VTC 1998-Spring). Ottawa, Canada.

Chia-Chin, C., Youngeil, K., & Seong-Soo, L. (2005). *Statistical characterization of the UWB propagation channel in various types of high-rise apartments.* Paper presented at the IEEE Wireless Communications and Networking Conference (WCNC 2005). New Orleans, LA.

Chrysikos, T., Georgopoulos, G., Kotsopoulos, S., & Zevgolis, D. (2010). *Site-specific validation of indoor RF models for commercial propagation topologies at 2.4 GHz.* Paper presented at the International Symposium on Wireless Communication Systems (ISWCS 2010). York, UK.

Claussen, H. (2005). *Efficient modeling of channel maps with correlated shadow fading in mobile radio systems.* Paper presented at the IEEE International Symposium on Personal, Indoor and Mobile Radio Communications (PIMRC 2005). Berlin, Germany.

Devasirvatham, D. M. J., Banerjee, C., Murray, R. R., & Rappaport, D. A. (1991). *Four-frequency radiowave propagation measurements of the indoor environment in a large metropolitan commercial building.* Paper presented at the IEEE Global Telecommunications Conference (GLOBECOM 1991). Phoenix, AZ.

Ezzine, R., Al-Fuqaha, A., Braham, R., & Belghith, A. (2008). *A new generic model for signal propagation in Wi-Fi and WiMAX environments.* Paper presented at the IFIP Wireless Days (WD 2008). Dubai, UAE.

Ghassemzadeh, S. S., & Tarokh, V. (2003). *UWB path loss characterization in residential environments.* Paper presented at the IEEE MTT-S International Microwave Symposium Digest. Philadelphia, PA.

Graziosi, F., & Santucci, F. (2002). A general correlation model for shadow fading in mobile radio systems. *IEEE Communications Letters*, *6*(3), 102–104. doi:10.1109/4234.991146.

Heliot, F., Ghavami, M., & Nakhai, M. R. (2008). An accurate closed-form approximation of the average probability of error over a log-normal fading channel. *IEEE Transactions on Wireless Communications*, *7*(5), 1495–1500. doi:10.1109/TWC.2008.061019.

Heliot, F., Xiaoli, C., Hoshyar, R., & Tafazolli, R. (2009). A tight closed-form approximation of the log-normal fading channel capacity. *IEEE Transactions on Wireless Communications, 8*(6), 2842–2847. doi:10.1109/TWC.2009.080972.

Hongchuan, Y., & Alouini, M. S. (2002). *A hierarchical Markov model for wireless shadowed fading channels.* Paper presented at the IEEE Vehicular Technology Conference. Birmingham, AL.

JaeWoo. L., Sewoong, K., YoungJoong, Y., & JongGwan, Y. (2006). *A path loss and shadow fading modeling in various radio environment of Seoul City based on measurement data at 5.3GHz and 2.1GHz bands.* Paper presented at the European Conference on Wireless Technology. Manchester, UK.

Janaswamy, R. (2005). *A new shadow model for indoor wireless channels at 60 GHz.* Paper presented at the IEEE Antennas and Propagation Society International Symposium. Washington, DC.

Jia-Liang, L., & Valois, F. (2006). *Performance evaluation of 802.11 WLAN in a real indoor environment.* Paper presented at the IEEE International Conference on Wireless and Mobile Computing, Networking and Communications (WiMob 2006). Montreal, Canada.

Karedal, J., Johansson, A. J., Tufvesson, F., & Molisch, A. F. (2008). A measurement-based fading model for wireless personal area networks. *IEEE Transactions on Wireless Communications, 7*(11), 4575–4585. doi:10.1109/TWC.2008.070500.

Lähteenmäki, J. (1992). *Radiowave propagation in office buildings and underground halls.* Paper presented at the European Microwave Conference (EurMC 1992). Espoo, Finland.

Motamedi, Z., & Soleymani, M. R. (2007). *For better or worse: The impact of shadow fading on the capacity of large MIMO networks.* Paper presented at the IEEE Global Telecommunications Conference (GLOBECOM 2007). Washington, DC.

Nam-Ryul, J., Kyung-Hoe, K., Jung-Hwan, C., & Seong-Cheol, K. (2010, September). *A spatial correlation model for shadow fading in indoor multipath propagation.* Paper presented at the IEEE Vehicular Technology Conference (VTC 2010-Fall). Ottawa, Canada.

Oestges, C., Czink, N., Bandemer, B., Castiglione, P., Kaltenberger, F., & Paulraj, A. (2009). *Experimental characterization of indoor multi-link channels.* Paper presented at the IEEE International Symposium on Personal, Indoor and Mobile Radio Communications (PIMRC 2009). Tokyo, Japan.

Patzold, M., Avazov, N., & Nguyen, V. D. (2010). *Design of measurement-based correlation models for shadow fading.* Paper presented at the International Conference on Advanced Technologies for Communications (ATC 2010). Ho Chi Minh City, Vietnam.

Patzold, M., & Nguyen, V. D. (2004). *A spatial simulation model for shadow fading processes in mobile radio channels.* Paper presented at the IEEE International Symposium on Personal, Indoor and Mobile Radio Communications (PIMRC 2004). Barcelona, Spain.

Poutanen, J., Haneda, K., Kolmonen, V. M., Salmi, J., & Vainikainen, P. (2009). Analysis of correlated shadow fading in dual-link indoor radio wave propagation. *IEEE Antennas and Wireless Propagation Letters, 8*, 1190–1193. doi:10.1109/LAWP.2009.2034989.

Poutanen, J., Salmi, J., Haneda, K., Kolmonen, V., & Vainikainen, P. (2011). Angular and shadowing characteristics of dense multipath components in indoor radio channels. *IEEE Transactions on Antennas and Propagation*, *59*(1), 245–253. doi:10.1109/TAP.2010.2090474.

Roberts, B., & Pahlavan, K. (2009). *Site-specific RSS signature modeling for WiFi localization.* Paper presented at the IEEE Global Telecommunications Conference (GLOBECOM 2009). Honololulu, HI.

Salo, J., Vuokko, L., El-Sallabi, H. M., & Vainikainen, P. (2006). *Shadow fading revisited.* Paper presented at the IEEE Vehicular Technology Conference (VTC 2006-Spring). Melbourne, Australia.

Shankar, P. M., & Gentile, C. (2010). *Statistical analysis of short term fading and shadowing in ultra wideband systems.* Paper presented at the IEEE International Conference on Communications (ICC 2010). Cape Town, South Africa.

Shannon, C. E. (1949). Communication theory of secrecy systems. *Bell Technical Journal*, *29*, 656–715.

Sharma, R. K., & Wallace, J. W. (2009). *Experimental characterization of indoor multiuser shadowing for collaborative cognitive radio.* Paper presented at the European Conference on Antennas and Propagation (EuCAP 2009). Berlin, Germany.

Szyszkowicz, S. S., Yanikomeroglu, H., & Thompson, J. S. (2010). On the feasibility of wireless shadowing correlation models. *IEEE Transactions on Vehicular Technology*, *59*(9), 4222–4236. doi:10.1109/TVT.2010.2082006.

Valenzuela, R. A., Chizhik, D., & Ling, J. (1998). *Measured and predicted correlation between local average power and small scale fading in indoor wireless communication channels.* Paper presented at the IEEE Vehicular Technology Conference (VTC 1998-Spring). Ottawa, Canada.

Wyner, A. D. (1975). The wire-tap channel. *Bell Technical Journal*, *54*, 1355–1387.

KEY TERMS AND DEFINITIONS

Channel Characterization: The field and methodology of qualitative and quantitative expression of the mechanisms and effects that alter in any way the transmitted signal in any given propagation topology.

Fading: The small-scale variations of the received signal strength, mostly due to multipath.

Multipath: The amplitude and phase distortion of the received signal due to the arrival of many different wave components at the receiver with different amplitude and time delay.

Path Loss: The ratio of attenuated signal due to free space propagation, obstruction and other mechanisms.

Shadowing: The large-scale variations of the received signal strength due to obstacles of significantly larger dimensions than the signal wavelength.

Shadowing Deviation: The deviation (usually in dB) of the large-scale fluctuations of the received signal strength values.

Chapter 13
Development of Nonlinear Filtering Algorithms of Digital Half-Tone Images

E. P. Petrov
Vyatka State University, Russia

E. V. Medvedeva
Vyatka State University, Russia

I. S. Trubin
Vyatka State University, Russia

S. M. Smolskiy
Moscow Power Engineering Institute, Russia

ABSTRACT

This chapter is devoted to solving the problem of algorithms and structures investigations for Radio Receiver Devices (RRD) with the aim of the nonlinear filtering of Digital Half-Tone Images (DHTI) representing the discrete-time and discrete-value random Markovian process with a number of states greater than two. At that, it is assumed that each value of the DHTI element is represented by the binary g-bit number, whose bits are transmitted via digital communication links in the presence of Additive White Gaussian Noise (AWGN). The authors present the qualitative analysis of the optimal DHTI filtering algorithm. The noise immunity of the optimal radio receiver device for the DHTI filtering with varying quantization and dimension levels is investigated.

INTRODUCTION

The assumption in synthesis of algorithms and devices for the one-dimension (per line) optimal and quasi-optimal digital half-tone image filtering that the filtering process represents the discrete valued Markovian Process (MP) with several states, has no a practical significance. It however permits better understanding of the synthesis approach of more complicated algorithms and structures of static and dynamic digital half-tone image filtering. That notwithstanding, we shall assume that the sample volume of the discrete multi-level MP is limited (for example, by the image line length) and each sample can be represented by the binary g-bit number, whose bits are transmitted through digital communication links in the presence White Gaussian Noise (WGN). The realization of a line (a column) of the digital half-tone image can be an example of such processes.

DOI: 10.4018/978-1-4666-2208-1.ch013

First solutions of the continuous prototype of this type of problems for binary signals were obtained by Stratoniovich, Kulman, Tikhonov, Yarlykov, Sosulin, and others (Kulman, 1961; Stratonovich, 1959, 1960; Tihanov, 1970; Yarlykov, 1980). The filtering equations in (Kulman, 1961; Stratonovich 1959, 1960; Tihanov 1970; Yarlykov 1980) represented in the continuous form are rather complicated in realization and are not suitable for the investigation of the characteristics of pulse signal processing devices. Moreover, the absence of qualitative and quantitative features does not permit the evaluation of its effectiveness. Another interpretation of the sequence of multi-level correlated pulse signals is offered in the literature (Trubin et al, 2004; Petrov, Trubin, & Butorin, 2005; Petrov, Trubin, & Chastikov, 2007; Petrov, Trubin, & Tikhonov, 2003). The discrete signal parameter can be approximated in them via the Markov chain (MC) with several states. Equations of nonlinear filtering for the uniform MC with two equiprobable states obtained in (Petrov, Trubin, Butorin; 2005; Petrov, Trubin, & Chastikov; 2007), and devices for binary correlated signal filtering synthesized on its basis had demonstrated a high efficiency, have the simple structure, are suitable in implementation and research. The significant peculiarity of the filtering devices synthesized in (Petrov & Trubin; 2007; Petrov, Trubin, & Butorin; 2005; Petrov, Trubin, & Chastikov; 2007) is the presence the nonlinear function unit, which contains all *a priori* data about statistics of the filtered process. This creates the favorable conditions for investigation of the filtering efficiency, its stability to variation of *a priori* data and to construction of the adaptive filtering algorithms. The structure of filtering devices in (Petrov, Trubin, & Butorin, 2005; Petrov, Trubin, & Chastikov, 2007) is such that it can serve as a basis for construction of filtering devices of multi-dimension DHTI.

EQUATIONS OF ONE-DIMENSION NONLINEAR FILTERING OF THE DISCRETE-VALUE MARKOVIAN PROCESSES

Now we suppose that a discrete parameter of pulse correlated signals, which are adequate to elements of static and dynamic DHTI, represents the uniform Markovian chain with the finite state number and the finite dimension. It is necessary to obtain the filtering equations of such signals and to synthesize the filtering device structures for DHTI recovering, which are distorted by the additive WGN $n(t)$ with zero mean value and the variance σ_n^2.

Let us consider the per line (one-dimension) DHTI filtering. Let the discrete parameter μ_k of the pulse signal $s(\mu_k, t_k)$ of $k-$th image element of the independent line takes in the each time step $k = 1 \ldots m-1$ (m is the number of elements in the image line) of operation one of several values $M_1, \ldots, M_N$ with probabilities $p_1, \ldots, p_N$, accordingly. We assume that the process μ_k is the uniform Markovian chain with the given matrix of transition probability (MTP) from the state M_i in $k-$th sample into the value M_j in $(k+1)-$th sample of the following type:

$$\Pi = \begin{pmatrix} \pi_{11} & \pi_{12} & \ldots & \pi_{1N} \\ \ldots & & & \\ \pi_{N1} & \pi_{N2} & \ldots & \pi_{NN} \end{pmatrix}. \quad (1)$$

Signals applied to the RRD input increase the knowledge about the process $\mu_1, \mu_2 \ldots \mu_{k+1}$ compared with *a priori* information. Now this knowledge is defined in the $(k+1)-$th time step of system operation by the multi-dimension *a posteriori* probability density, which can be calculated in accordance with the inverse probability formula (Stratonovich, 1959, 1960; Tihanov, 1970; Yarlykov, 1980).

$$p^{as}\left(\mu_1,...,\mu_{k+1}\right) = cL\left(\mu_1,...,\mu_{k+1}\right)p^{ap}\left(\mu_1,...,\mu_{k+1}\right), \tag{2}$$

where $L\left(\mu_1,...,\mu_{k+1}\right)$ is a multi-dimension likelihood function; $p^{ap}\left(\mu_1,...,\mu_{k+1}\right)$ is the multi-dimension *a posteriori* probability density; c is factor of normalization.

In order to construct the estimation of the filtered MP μ_{k+1} in $(k+1)$ – th time step of system operation on the basis of data entered in RRD input, it is necessary to form the final *a posteriori* probability density

$$p^{as}\left(\mu_{k+1}\right) = \int_{-\infty}^{\infty}...\int_{-\infty}^{\infty} p^{as}\left(\mu_1,...,\mu_{k+1}\right)d\mu_1...d\mu_k. \tag{3}$$

We assume that on the basis of *a priori* signal knowledge, which are used for transmission of the digital half-tone image elements, and on the basis of RRD properties we can calculate the likelihood function o the parameter μ_{k+1} in $(k+1)$ – th time step

$$L\left(\mu_{k+1}\right) = \exp\left\{f\left(\mu_{k+1}\right)\right\}, \tag{4}$$

where $f\left(\mu_{k+1}\right)$ is the logarithm of the likelihood function.

Thus, if noises from one time step to another are independent, then

$$L\left(\mu_1,...,\mu_{k+1}\right) = \exp\left\{\sum_{m=1}^{k+1} f\left(\mu_m\right)\right\}, \tag{5}$$

and the equation for the final a posteriori probability density for parameter μ in $(k+1)$ – th time step with account of the recurrence property of the Markovian chain has the following form (Kulman, 1961; Petrov, Trubin, & Tikhonov, 2003).

$$p^{as}\left(\mu_{k+1}\right) = \exp\left\{f\left(\mu_{k+1}\right)\right\}\int p^{as}\left(\mu_k\right)w\left(\mu_{k+1}\left|\mu_k\right.\right)d\mu_k, \tag{6}$$

where the one-step probability density for transition $w\left(\mu_{k+1}\left|\mu_k\right.\right)$ from value of process μ_k to the adjacent μ_{k+1} can be presented in the form (Kulman, 1961) (see Box 1).

Let us write the final *a posteriori* probability density of parameter μ_k in the k – th time step

$$p^{as}\left(\mu_k\right) = \sum_{j=1}^{N} p_{jk}\delta\left(\mu_k - M_j\right) \tag{8}$$

and substituting Equations (7) and (8), into Equation (6) we obtain

Box 1.

$$w\left(\mu_{k+1}\left|\mu_k\right.\right) = \sum_{j=1}^{N}\pi\left(M_i\left|M_j\right.\right)\ \delta\left(\mu_{k+1} - M_i\right);\ \ i = \overline{1,N}, \tag{7}$$

where $\delta\left(\cdot\right)$ is delta-function.

$$\sum_{i=1}^{N} p_{i(k+1)}\delta\left(\mu_{k+1}-M_{i}\right)=c\cdot\exp f\left(\mu_{k+1}\right)\int\sum_{j=1}^{N} p_{jk}$$
$$\times\,\delta\left(\mu_{k}-M_{j}\right)\sum^{N}\pi\left(M_{i}\middle|M_{j}\right)\delta\left(\mu_{k+1}-M_{j}\right)d\mu_{k}. \qquad (9)$$

Equating coefficients at similar δ – functions in the right and the left parts of Equation (9) and using the filtering property of δ-function, we obtain the equation for the final *a posteriori* probability of i-th value of parameter μ_{k+1} (see Box 2).

Equation (10) is the basis for synthesis of devices for pulse correlated signal filtering, which are approximated by the stationary discrete-value Markovian chain with $N = 2^g$ values.

Dividing Equation (10) for $i = 1,\dots N-1$ by equations for $i = N$, we come to the equation system shown in Box 3.

Having taken the logarithm of Equation (11) and introducing a designation $u_{ik} = \ln\dfrac{p_{ik}}{p_{Nk}}$, we obtain the system of nonlinear recurrent equations (see Box 4).

Equation (12) defines those optimal operations, which can be performed by RRD under the received signal of the discrete MP element with the purpose of its best recovering.

If MP samples $\mu_1,\mu_2,\dots,\mu_k$ are presented by g-bit binary numbers $y_1,y_2,\dots,y_k$, the number of discrete values of the process will be equal to $N = 2^g$. For example, for $g = 8$ the number of values $N = 256$. Realization of Equation (12) for such number of discrete values requires considerable computation resources. Another approach to realize Equation (12) using a theorem given in (Petrov, Trubin; 2007) is more productive. In accordance with this theorem, the multi-level discrete-value MP presented by 2^g binary numbers y_k may be changed to g binary MP with MTP for l – th bit as

$$\Pi^{(l)}=\begin{pmatrix}\pi_{11}^{(l)} & \pi_{12}^{(l)}\\ \pi_{21}^{(l)} & \pi_{22}^{(l)}\end{pmatrix},\quad l=\overline{1,g}. \qquad (14)$$

Elements of bit MTP satisfy the conditions of normalization and coordination

Box 2.

$$p_{i(k+1)}=c\cdot\exp\left\{f_{k+1}\left(M_{i}\right)\right\}\sum_{j=1}^{g} p_{jk}\pi\left(M_{i}\middle|M_{j}\right),\ i,j=\overline{1,g}. \qquad (10)$$

Box 3.

$$\frac{p_{i(k+1)}}{p_{N(k+1)}}=\exp\left\{f_{k+1}\left(M_{i}\right)-f_{k+1}\left(M_{N}\right)\right\}\frac{p_{ik}}{p_{Nk}}\frac{1+\sum_{j=1}^{N}\left[\dfrac{p_{jk}}{p_{Nk}}\Big/\dfrac{p_{ik}}{p_{Nk}}\right]\pi_{ji}}{1+\sum_{j=1}^{N}\dfrac{p_{jk}}{p_{Nk}}\pi_{jN}}, \qquad (11)$$

where $i,j=\overline{1,N},\ \ i\neq j.$

Box 4.

$$u_{i(k+1)} = f_{k+1}\left(M_i\right) - f_{k+1}\left(M_N\right) + u_{ik} + z\left(u_{ik}, \pi_{ii}\right),\ i = \overline{1,N}, \tag{12}$$

where

$$z\left(u_{ik}, \pi_{ii}\right) = \ln \frac{1 + \sum_{j=1}^{N} \exp\left(u_{jk} - u_{ik}\right) \cdot \pi_{ji}}{1 + \sum_{j=1}^{N} \exp\left(u_{jk}\right) \cdot \pi_{jN}}. \tag{13}$$

$$\sum_{j=1}^{2} \pi_{ij}^{(l)} = 1,\ i = 1,2;\ l = \overline{1,g} \tag{15}$$

$$p_i^{(l)} = \sum_{j=1}^{2} p_j^{(l)} \pi_{ji}^{(l)},\ i = 1,2;\ l = \overline{1,g}. \tag{16}$$

For binary MP the following condition holds

$$\pi_{ii}^{(1)} \leq \pi_{ii}^{(2)} \leq \ldots \leq \pi_{ii}^{(g)}. \tag{17}$$

Having considered that the symbol sequence of l – th bit of binary numbers $y_1^{(l)}, \ldots, y_{k+1}^{(l)}$ forms the discrete-value MP with two equiprobable $\left(p_1^{(l)} = p_2^{(l)}\right)$ values M_1 and M_2 and MTP (14) and assuming (although it is not principal) that all bits are transmitted simultaneously through binary communication links, we obtain the system of g nonlinear recurrent equations for binary MP filtering similar to (12) (see Box 5).

$f_{k+1}^{(l)}\left(M_1^{(l)}\right) - f_{k+1}^{(l)}\left(M_2^{(l)}\right)$ is the logarithm difference of likelihood functions of the binary signal parameter values of l-th bit of number y_{k+1};

$u_{ik}^{(l)} = \ln \frac{p_{ik}^{(l)}}{p_{nk}^{(l)}}$ is the logarithm of *a posteriori* probabilities ratio in k – th time step of l – th bit of number y_k.

SYNTHESIS OF A DEVICE FOR ONE-DIMENSION NONLINEAR FILTERING OF BIT BINARY IMAGES

On the basis of the filtering equations obtained in the previous section, we synthesize an optimal device of nonlinear Bit Binary Images (BBI)

Box 5.

$$u_{1(k+1)}^{(l)} = f_{k+1}^{(l)}\left(M_1^{(l)}\right) - f_{k+1}^{(l)}\left(M_2^{(l)}\right) + u_{1k}^{(l)} + z_1^{(l)}\left(u_{1k}^{(l)}, \pi_{ij}^{(l)}\right), \tag{18}$$

where

$$z^{(l)}\left(u_{1k}^{(l)}, \pi_{ij}^{(l)}\right) = \ln \frac{\pi_{11}^{(l)} + \pi_{21}^{(l)} \exp\left\{-u_{1k}^{(l)}\right\}}{\pi_{22}^{(l)} + \pi_{12}^{(l)} \exp\left\{u_{1k}^{(l)}\right\}};\ i,j = 1,2;\ l = \overline{1,g}; \tag{19}$$

filtering approximated by the discrete MP with two equiprobable values.

The estimate value of the BBI line element calculated in accordance with Equation (18) can be determined by comparison of $u_{1(k+1)}^{(l)}$ with the threshold chosen in accordance with some criterion of binary signal distinguish. For the considered problem of discrete element filtering of binary correlated signals of BBI element the ideal observer criterion (Stratonovich, 1959, 1960; Tihanov, 1970; Yarlykov 1980) is the most acceptable. In accordance with this criterion the distinguishing of signals with parameter $M_1^{(l)}$ or $M_2^{(l)}$ is performed in RRD on the basis of comparison of $u_{1(k+1)}^{(l)}$ with the threshold $H^{(l)}$, i.e.

$$u_{1(k+1)}^{(l)} \geq H^{(l)}. \tag{20}$$

For pulse signals the condition (20) means that the value $M_1^{(l)}$ is fixed in the cases when $u_{1(k+1)}^{(l)} \geq H^{(l)}$ and the value $M_2^{(l)}$ – when $u_{1(k+1)}^{(l)} < H^{(l)}$. At that, two types of errors may occur (Stratonovich, 1959, 1960; Tihanov, 1970; Yarlykov, 1980): errors of the first kind when the decision is made about the presence of the parameter value M_1 in the received signal, while the signal was transmitted with the parameter value M_2. Errors of the second kind occur at presence of the opposite situation.

Let us designate the probability of the first kind of errors as $p'^{(l)}$ and the second kind as $p''^{(l)}$. In accordance with the ideal observer criterion, the threshold $H^{(l)}$ is set so that to minimize the average error probability $p^{(l)}$ (Stratonovich, 1959, 1960; Tihanov, 1970; Yarlykov, 1980)

$$p^{(l)} = \frac{1}{2}\left[p'^{(l)} + p''^{(l)}\right] = \min. \tag{21}$$

In the specific case of the binary pulse signal reception in the symmetric communication system $H^{(l)} = 0$ for all $l = \overline{1, g}$.

In accordance with the Equation (18), at forming the logarithm of the *a posteriori* probabilities in the $(k+1)$-th time step $u_{1(k+1)}^{(l)}$, the input data defined by the first term are added in the summer with the value of the logarithm of the *a posteriori* probabilities ratio for the previous time step $u_{1k}^{(l)}$ and with calculated value $z^{(l)}\left(u_{1k}^{(l)}, \pi_{ij}^{(l)}\right)$, which contains the *a priori* data about the filtering process. At that, our knowledge about the true value of parameter $\mu_{k+1}^{(l)}$ in the received signal increases due to *a priori* data and the average probability of the erroneous decisions $p^{(l)}$ at RDD output decreases. The reduction of the average error probability characterizes this method's benefit at pulse correlated signal processing compared with the uncorrelated case.

ONE-DIMENSION NONLINEAR DHTI FILTERING

To transmit of DHTI represented by $g-$bit binary numbers with the minimal error, it is necessary that binary symbols (0 and 1) of each $l-$th bit $(l \in g)$ were transmitted through communication link with the minimal error. The structure of optimal $g-$channel RRD performing the reception of the $g-$bit DHTI is shown in Figure 1. Each of g channel of the RRD contains a discriminator calculating the logarithm difference of the likelihood functions of discrete parameter values of binary RDD signals

$$\left[f_{k+1}^{(l)}\left(M_1\right) - f_{k+1}^{(l)}\left(M_2\right)\right],$$

a nonlinear filter $\left(\mathrm{NF}\right)^{(l)}$, a threshold device $\Pi^{(l)}\left(l \in g\right)$, which output is connected to a register of estimation formation of the binary number symbols $\hat{Y}_{k+1} = \left\{\hat{Y}^{(1)}_{k+1}\nu_1, ..., \hat{Y}^{(g)}_{k+1}\nu_g\right\}$. Nonlinear filters in each channel has the structure similar to $\left(\mathrm{NF}\right)^{(l)}$ of the l – th channel.

The typical peculiarity of the system of equations of type (18) consists in the fact that all *a priori* information about the extracting symbol $M_i^{(l)}\left(i = 1,2\right)$ of the l – th bit is included in the last term. The family of curves of conversion $z^{(l)}\left(u_{1k}^{(l)}, \pi_{ij}^{(l)}\right)$ for various values of $\pi_{ij}^{(l)}\left(i = j\right)$ is shown in Figure 2.

It follows from the analysis of curve family $z^{(l)}\left(u_{1k}^{(l)}, \pi_{ij}^{(l)}\right)$ that for the large signal/noise ratio $\rho_e^2 >> 1$ and for probabilities $\pi_{ii}^{(l)}$, which are not close to 1, the curves of the function $z^{(l)}\left(u_{1k}^{(l)}, \pi_{ij}^{(l)}\right)$ can be approximated by the line segments. At that, calculation of function $z^{(l)}\left(u_{1k}^{(l)}, \pi_{ij}^{(l)}\right)$ is simplified, which allows the transfer from the optimal RRD to quasi-optimal.

The DHTI representation by the one-dimension Markovian chains is suitable by the possibility of specifying of *a priori* data for the separate line (column) of ê for the line (column) groups of the digital half-tone images, which allows the most complete consideration of the static data non-uniformity in the field of digital half-tone images.

The filtering result of the real DHTI for signal/noise ratio ρ_e^2 is presented in Figure 3. The initial DHTI "The aircraft" is shown in Figure 3a, the noisy DHTI for $\rho_e^2 = -\ 6$ dB at RRD input is shown in Figure 3b, filtered DHTI – in Figure 3c.

Figure 1. The structure of the optimal g – channel RRD

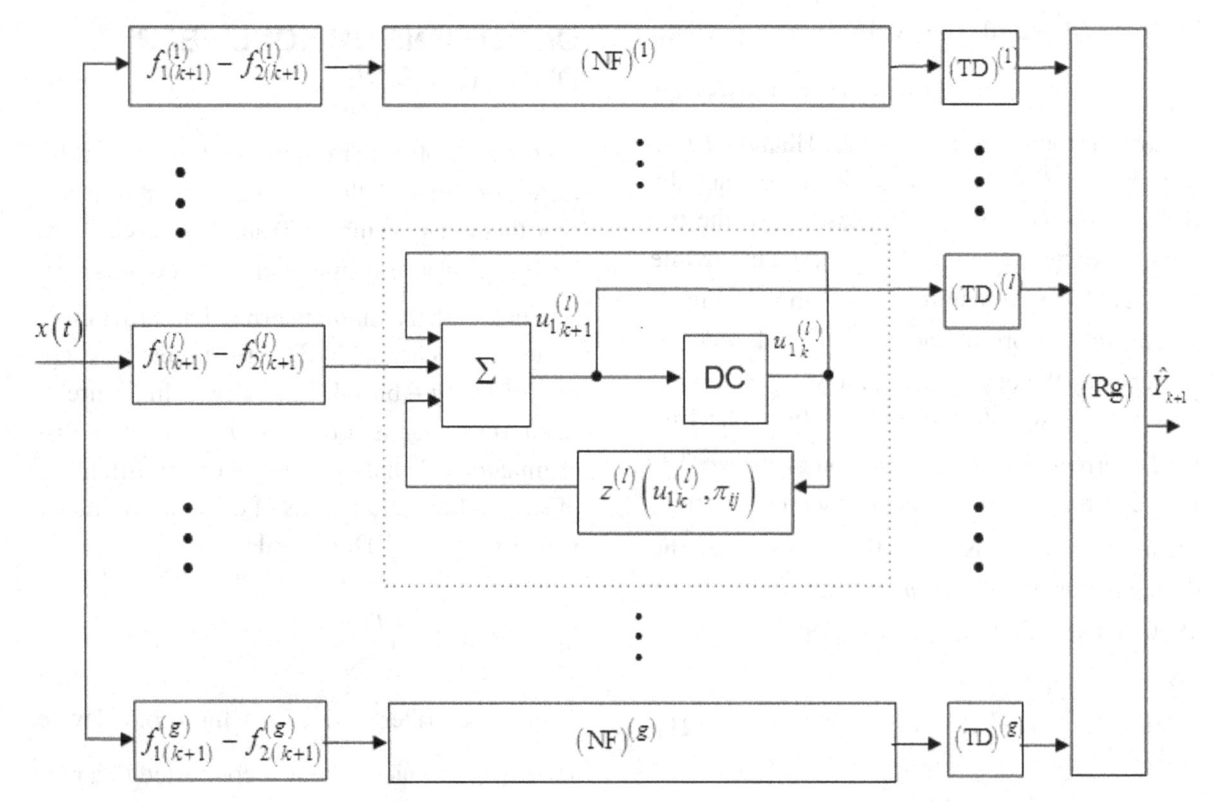

Figure 2. The family of $z\left(u_{1k}, \pi_{ij}\right)$ *– functions*

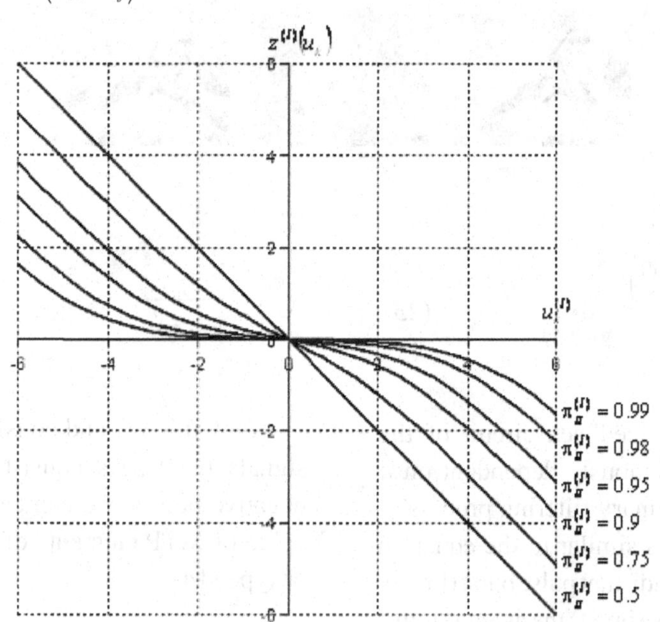

ANALYSIS OF NOISE-IMMUNITY OF THE ONE-DIMENSION DHTI FILTERING ALGORITHM

Synthesized devices of nonlinear filtering allow realization of the BBI statistical redundancy owing to the most probable value prediction of each following image element on the basis of previous element and *a priori* knowledge about the correlation degree of the received signals of image elements.

The more correlation between binary signals, the more exact the prediction of the received signal, and the higher accuracy of the transmitted information, i.e. the higher the noise immunity of the synthesized filtering device. Investigations (Petrov, Trubin, Butorin; 2005; Petrov, Trubin, Chastikov; 2007) showed that application of the BBI statistical redundancy in l-th RRD channel (Figure 1) allows obtaining the essential benefit in signal power $\eta^{(l)}\left(\pi_{ii}^{(l)}, \rho_e^2\right)$ especially at small signal/noise ratio ρ_e^2 at RRD input. The largest benefit in accordance with (17) can be achieved in the BBI transmission channel of high-order bit (l=g) of the binary number, which is the most correlated. The total benefit in all g channels is the impartial estimation of filtering effectiveness of DHTI, represented by the multi-level discrete-value MP.

One of the quantitative estimations of noise immunity of the BBI filtering device is the average error probability $p^{(l)}$ defined by Equation (21). It is necessary to establish connection between the error probability $p^{(l)}$ and MTP ${}^{1}\Pi^{(l)}$ of one-dimension filtering process.

Let us present the Equation (18) in the standard form of a recursive filter

$$u_{1(k+1)}^{(l)} = a_{k+1}^{(l)}[f_{k+1}^{(l)}(M_1^{(l)}) - f_{k+1}^{(l)}(M_2^{(l)})] + b_{k+1}^{(l)} u_{1k}^{(l)}, \quad (22)$$

where $a_{k+1}^{(l)}$ is a coefficient ensuring the maximal receiving of *a posteriori* data about an image element signal in l-th bit, i.e. we can assume that $a_{k+1}^{(l)} = a_0^{(l)} = 1$;

Figure 3. An example of one-dimension nonlinear filtering of the artificial DHTI

$$b_{k+1}^{(l)} = \frac{u_{1k}^{(l)} + z^{(l)}\left(u_{1k}^{(l)}, \pi_{ij}^{(l)}\right)}{u_{1k}^{(l)}} \tag{23}$$

is a coefficient in the feedback circuit of the recursive filter unambiguously dependent on *a priori* statistics of the binary filtering process.

The Equation (22) is similar to the equation of recirculator of the equidistant pulse burst (Lezin, 1969) if we use (as a pulse burst) the average pulse burst equaled to an average length of pulse series containing the discrete values $M_1^{(l)}$ or $M_2^{(l)}$ and the coefficient in the feedback circuit $b_{k+1}^{(l)}$ can be averaged during the action time of such pulse burst.

Since the sequence $\left\{\mu_{k+1}^{(l)}\right\}$ is by the data the Markovian chain, the probability density of events consisting in the fact that series of *n* time steps contain only values $M_1^{(l)}$ or $M_2^{(l)}$, is equal

$$w^{(l)}\left(n\right) = p_i^{(l)} \cdot \left(w^{(l)}\right)^{n-1}; \; i = 1,2, \tag{24}$$

where $w^{(l)} = \pi_{ii}^{(l)}\delta\left(w^{(l)} - \pi_{ii}^{(l)}\right)$ is a probability density of transition absence from one value $\mu_k^{(l)}$ ti adjacent $\mu_{k+1}^{(l)}$ in the line of $l-$th BBI, $p_i^{(l)}$ is the initial probability of *i*-th state of the Markovian chain.

The average length of the sequence (the burst) $\chi^{(l)} = \left\langle n^{(l)}\right\rangle$ consisting of values $M_1^{(l)}$ or $M_2^{(l)}$ only, we can obtain from the equation

$$\chi^{(l)} = \frac{p_i^{(l)}}{1-\pi_{ii}^{(l)}}. \tag{25}$$

Knowing $\chi^{(l)}$ and considering that at bipolar signals the bursts consist of the positive and negative pulses, we can calculate from (25) the value of MTP elements of the Markovian chain of type (14):

$$\pi_{ii}^{(l)} = 1 - \frac{2p_i^{(l)}}{\chi^{(l)}}, \; \pi_{ij}^{(l)} = 1 - \pi_{ii}^{(l)}, \; i = 1,2, \; i \neq j. \tag{26}$$

Having averaged the coefficient $b_{k+1}^{(l)}$ for the action time of the pulse burst wit length $\chi^{(l)}$, we obtain

$$\left\langle b_{k+1}^{(l)}\right\rangle_{\chi^{(l)}} = b^{(l)}. \tag{27}$$

Taking into consideration that burst consist of pulses of the same sign, the effect of accumulation of pulse bursts with the opposite signs in RRD with nonlinear filtering decreases two times compared with the recirculator accumulating the burst of single-sign pulses. Therefore, the signal/noise ratio in signal power at the output of the *l*-th channel of RRD (Figure 1) $\rho_{e\ out}^2$ can be determined similar to (Lezin, 1969).

$$\left(\rho_{e\ out}^2\right)^{(l)} = \rho_e^2 \frac{1+b^{(l)}}{2\left(1-b^{l}\right)}\left[1-\left(b^{(l)}\right)^{\chi^{(l)}}\right]^2, \tag{28}$$

where ρ_e^2 is signal/noise ratio at RRD input.

From Equation (28) we can find the benefits in signal power at output of the l – th channel of RRD with

For binary phase-modulated (PM) for $\left(\pi_{ii}^{(l)} = 0,95\right)$ the average pulse burst length $\chi^{(l)}$ is equal

$$\chi^{(l)} = 2 \cdot 0,5/\left(1 - 0,95\right) = 20. \qquad (0.1)$$

An estimation of average value of the coefficient $\hat{b}^{(l)}$ in the feedback circuit of nonlinear filter of the l – th RRD channel obtained by calculation way on PC for signal/noise ratio at RRD input $\rho_e^2 = -3$ dB is equal to $\hat{b}^{(l)} = \left\langle b_{k+1}^{(l)} \right\rangle_{\chi^{(l)}=20} = 0,62$. Substituting $\hat{b}^{(l)}$ in Equation (0.1), we find benefits in signal power at RRD output

$$\eta_e^{(l)} = \frac{1+0,62}{2\left(1-0,62\right)}\left(1 - 0,62^{20}\right)^2 \cong \frac{1,62}{0,76} = 3,3 \text{ dB} \qquad (0.2)$$

Simulation of the optimal RRD (Figure 1) on PC gives benefits in power $\eta_e^{(l)} = 3,3$ dB confirming correctness of this approach to analysis of RRD noise immunity for binary correlated signals of the DDI elements representing the uniform Markovian chain with two equiprobable values.

Using the formula for error probability at distinguishing of two determined signals (Stratonovich 1959, 1960; Tihanov, 1970; Yarlykov, 1980) we find the error probability $p^{(l)}$

$$p^{(l)} = 1 - \Phi\left[\sqrt{\eta_e^{(l)}\left(\rho_e^{(l)}\right)^2\left(1 - r_s\right)}\right], \qquad (0.3)$$

where r_s is the normalized auto-correlation function of the binary signal; $\Phi\left(\cdot\right)$ is the integral of error probability (Stratonovich 1959, 1960; Tihanov, 1970; Yarlykov, 1980).

STABILITY OF ALGORITHMS OF THE ONE-DIMENSION NONLINEAR DHTI FILTERING TO INACCURACY OF A PRIORI DATA

After development of the device for nonlinear DHTI filtering it is necessary to investigate its stability to inaccuracy of specifying or calculation of *a priori* statistical data about the filtering process. The importance of these investigations is caused by the fact that we understand *a priori* data as the averaged statistical characteristics obtained by averaging over the large image ensemble, however, in the real life these data may not coincide (with different degree) with the specific realization data – the specific real image or even its separate fragments. Thus, it is necessary to investigate at which degree this lack of coincidence may influence on the RRD noise immunity.

For l – th channel of the optimal RRD (Figure 1) we conducted the check on stability of its effectiveness for $\pi_{ii}'^{(l)} \neq \pi_{ii}^{(l)}$, $(i = \overline{1,2})$, which is well known in RRD theory. The check was fulfilled for those values of $\pi_{ii}^{(l)}$, which deviation from the true values of transition probability can lead to essential error increase at RRD output.

Investigation was conducted using the artificial images obtained on the model described in the Chapter 10 of this book (sections 1.2 and 1.4). In the nonlinear filtering device $\left(\text{NF}\right)^{(l)}$ (Figure 1) we specified the statistical data different from values used at image generation.

The obtained results showed that the lower the signal/noise ratio ρ_e^2 at RRD input the higher the sensitivity to mismatching. At fixed ρ_e^2, the higher the true value of the transition probability $\pi_{ii}^{(l)}$ in $l-$th BBI of half-tine image, the higher the sensitivity of $\left(\mathrm{NF}\right)^{(l)}$ to mismatching.

So, if for ${}^{1}\pi_{ii}^{(8)}=0,90$ the mismatching of $\pm 3\%$ does not influence practically on the filtering effectiveness, then for ${}^{1}\pi_{ii}^{(8)}=0,95$ the similar error may lead to the loss more than 1 dB in the case of overestimation of the transition probability. Taking this into account, the requirements to the presentation accuracy of *a priori* data in the high-order bit (the most correlated) should be higher.

Since the bit binary images of the digital half-tone images are processed independently, stability of the nonlinear filtering algorithm of the digital half-tone images directly depends on stability of the $(NL)^{(l)}$ $l-$th bit binary images.

EQUATIONS OF TWO-DIMENSION NONLINEAR DHTI FILTERING

Let in $t_{k+1}-$th time step of system operation in the interval $T=t_{k+1}-t_{k}$ one BBI element is transmitted with the help of the signal $s^{(l)}\left(\mu_{i,j}^{(l)}\right)$, $\left(i=\overline{1,m};\ j=\overline{1,n};\ l=\overline{1,g}\right)$, which discrete parameter $\mu_{i,j}^{(l)}$ (a frequency, a phase etc.) takes one of the two possible values $M_{1}^{(l)}$, $M_{2}^{(l)}$.

We chose the one-way Markovian random field (Chapter 10) as the DHTI model. In accordance with the mathematical model (MM) of the two-dimension DHTI we assume that the element sequence $\left\{\mu_{i,j}^{(l)}\right\}$ of $l-$th BBI forms the two-dimension stationary Markovian chain on the non-symmetrical half-plane (NSHP) (Chapter 10, Figure 1.1) with equiprobable values $p_{1}^{(l)}=p_{2}^{(l)}$ and with the conditional transition probabilities (see Box 6).

For complicated Markovian chain *a priori* distribution $p_{ap}^{(l)}$ of parameter values in $l-$th bit can be presented in the form (Petrov, Trubin, 2007; Petrov, Kharina; 2006) with account of the given MM of two-dimension DHTI (see Box 7).

Since by the data the distorting noise is white, the likelihood function for the signal sequence of elements of $l-$th BBI can be written in the following form (Stratonovich 1959, 1960; Tihanov, 1970; Yarlykov, 1980):

Box 6.

$$\pi_{khqr}^{(l)}=w\left(\mu_{i,j}^{(l)}=M_{k}^{(l)}\middle|\mu_{i-1,j}^{(l)}=M_{r}^{(l)};\ \mu_{i,j-1}^{(l)}=M_{h}^{(l)};\ \mu_{i-1,j-1}^{(l)}=M_{q}^{(l)}\right), \tag{33}$$

where $i=\overline{1,m}$; $j=\overline{1,n}$; $l=\overline{1,g};$ $n\times m$ - is the size of image field; $k,h,q,r=1,2.$

Box 7.

$$\begin{aligned}
&p_{ap}^{(l)}\left(\mu_{1,1}^{(l)},\mu_{1,2}^{(l)},\ldots,\mu_{i-1,j}^{(l)},\mu_{i-1,j-1}^{(l)},\mu_{i,j-1}^{(l)}\right)\\
&=p_{ap}^{(l)}\left(\mu_{1,1}^{(l)},\mu_{1,2}^{(l)},\mu_{2,1}^{(l)}\right)w\left(\mu_{2,2}^{(l)}\middle|\mu_{1,1}^{(l)},\mu_{1,1}^{(l)},\mu_{2,1}^{(l)}\right)\\
&\times\ldots\times w^{(l)}\left(\mu^{(l)}\middle|\mu^{(l)},\ldots\mu^{(l)},\ldots\mu^{(l)},\ldots\right).
\end{aligned} \tag{34}$$

$$L^{(l)}\left(\mu_{1,1}^{(l)};\mu_{1,2}^{(l)};\ldots;\mu_{2,1}^{(l)};\mu_{2,2}^{(l)};\ldots;\mu_{i-1,j}^{(l)};\mu_{i,j}^{(l)}\right)$$
$$=\exp\left[\sum_{q=1}^{i}\sum_{r=1}^{j}f^{(l)}\left(\mu_{q,r}^{(l)}\right)\right], \tag{35}$$

where $f^{(l)}\left(\mu_{q,r}^{(l)}\right)$ is the logarithm of the likelihood function of the parameter of the element of $l-$th BBI with coordinates $\left(q,r\right)$; $q=\overline{1,m}$; $r=\overline{1,n}$.

With account of (33), (34) and (35), *a posteriori* distribution of the discrete parameter of the two-dimension field of l-th BBI will be that shown in Box 8.

Having integrated (36) over all values of elements $\left\{\mu_{q,r}^{(l)}\right\}$ with account of (34), we obtain the equation of the final *a posteriori* probability density of the element $\nu_4^{(l)}$ value (see Box 9).

The direct realization of the Equation (37) is difficult due to multi-dimension character of the *a posteriori* probability density and the transition probability density in the right part. All *a priori* in formation about the value of the element of l-th BBI $\mu_{i,j}^{(l)}$ with coordinates $\left(i,j\right)$ is contained in the integrand (37).

1. Taking into account properties of the complicated Markovian chain and assumptions made at construction of the spatial model of two-dimension Markovian process with discrete arguments in the Chapter 10, we present (with account of Figure 1.2 of Chapter 10) the integrand in (37) in the form:

$$p_{as}^{(l)}\left(\nu_1^{(l)},\nu_2^{(l)},\nu_3^{(l)}\right)w^{(l)}\left(\nu_4^{(l)}\middle|\nu_1^{(l)},\nu_2^{(l)},\nu_3^{(l)}\right)$$
$$=\frac{p_{as}^{(l)}\left(\nu_1^{(l)}\right)w^{(l)}\left(\nu_1^{(l)}\middle|\nu_4^{(l)}\right)p_{as}^{(l)}\left(\nu_2^{(l)}\right)w^{(l)}\left(\nu_2^{(l)}\middle|\nu_4^{(l)}\right)}{p_{as}^{(l)}\left(\nu_3^{(l)}\right)w^{(l)}\left(\nu_3^{(l)}\middle|\nu_4^{(l)}\right)}. \tag{38}$$

Having changed in (37) the integrand to (38), we obtain an equation for the final *a posteriori* probability density of the filtering element $\nu_4^{(l)}$

Box 8.

$$p_{as}^{(l)}\left(\mu_{1,1}^{(l)},\mu_{1,2}^{(l)},\ldots,\mu_{2,1}^{(l)},\mu_{2,2}^{(l)},\ldots,\mu_{i-1,j}^{(l)},\mu_{i,j}^{(l)}\right)$$
$$=c\cdot\exp\left\{\sum_{q=1}^{i}\sum_{r=1}^{j}f^{(l)}\left(\mu_{q,r}^{(l)}\right)\right\}p_{ap}^{(l)}\left(\mu_{1,1}^{(l)},\mu_{1,2}^{(l)},\mu_{2,1}^{(l)}\right) \tag{36}$$
$$\times w^{(l)}\left(\mu_{2,2}^{(l)}\left(\mu_{1,1}^{(l)},\mu_{1,2}^{(l)},\mu_{2,1}^{(l)}\right)\times\ldots\times w^{(l)}\left(\mu_{i,j}^{(l)}\left(\mu_{i-1,j}^{(l)},\mu_{i,j-1}^{(l)},\mu_{i-1,j-1}^{(l)}\right),\right.\right.$$

where c is the normalizing coefficient.

Box 9.

$$p_{as}^{(l)}\left(\nu_4^{(l)}\right)=c\cdot\exp\left\{f^{(l)}\left(\nu_4^{(l)}\right)\right\}\iiint p_{ac}^{(l)}\left(\nu_1^{(l)},\nu_2^{(l)},\nu_3^{(l)}\right)$$
$$\times w^{(l)}\left(\nu_4^{(l)}\middle|\nu_1^{(l)},\nu_2^{(l)},\nu_3^{(l)}\right)d\nu_1^{(l)}d\nu_2^{(l)}d\nu_3^{(l)}, \tag{37}$$

where $\nu_1^{(l)}=\mu_{i-1,j}^{(l)};\nu_2^{(l)}=\mu_{i,j-1}^{(l)};\nu_3^{(l)}=\mu_{i-1,j-1}^{(l)};\nu_4^{(l)}=\mu_{i,j}^{(l)}.$

Box 10.

$$p_{as}^{(l)}\left(\nu_4^{(l)}\right)=c\cdot\exp\left\{f^{(l)}\left(\nu_1^{(l)}\right)\right\}$$
$$\times\iiint\frac{p_{as}^{(l)}\left(\nu_1^{(l)}\right)w^{(l)}\left(\nu_4^{(l)}\middle|\nu_1^{(l)}\right)p_{as}^{(l)}\left(\nu_2^{(l)}\right)w^{(l)}\left(\nu_4^{(l)}\middle|\nu_2^{(l)}\right)}{p_{as}^{(l)}\left(\nu_3^{(l)}\right)w^{(l)}\left(\nu_4^{(l)}\middle|\nu_3^{(l)}\right)}d\nu_1^{(l)}d\nu_2^{(l)}d\nu_3^{(l)}. \qquad (39)$$

Box 11.

$$p_{as}^{(l)}\left(\nu_k^{(l)}\right)=\sum_{\alpha=1}^{2}p_{\alpha}^{(l)}\left(\nu_k^{(l)}\right)\delta\left(\nu_k^{(l)}-M_{\alpha}^{(l)}\right),\ \left(k=\overline{1,4}\right); \qquad (40)$$

$$w^{(l)}\left(\nu_i^{(l)}\middle|\nu_j^{(l)}\right)=\sum_{\beta=1}^{2}{}^{r}\pi_{\alpha\beta}^{(l)}\delta\left(\nu_i^{(l)}-M_{\beta}^{(l)}\right),$$
$$\left(i=3,4;\ j=\overline{1,3};\ r=\overline{1,3};\ \alpha=1,2\right), \qquad (41)$$

where $p_{\alpha}^{(l)}\left(\nu_k^{(l)}\right)$ is *a posteriori* probability of value $M_{\alpha}^{(l)}$ in $\left(\nu_k^{(l)}\right)$ – th element of l – th binary section; ${}^{r}\pi_{\alpha\beta}^{(l)}$ is the transition probability from value $M_{\alpha}^{(l)}$ to $M_{\beta}^{(l)}$ in field elements in horizontal $\left(r=1\right)$, vertical $\left(r=2\right)$ and diagonal $\left(r=3\right)$ lines; $\delta\left(\cdot\right)$ is the delta-function.

Box 12.

$$p_{\beta}^{(l)}\left(\nu_4^{(l)}\right)=c'\exp\left\{f\left(M_{\beta}^{(l)}\left(\nu_4^{(l)}\right)\right)\right\}$$
$$\times\frac{\sum_{\alpha=1}^{2}p_{\alpha}^{(l)}\left(\nu_1^{(l)}\right)\cdot{}^{1}\pi_{\alpha\beta}^{(l)}\sum_{\theta=1}^{2}p_{\theta}^{(l)}\left(\nu_2^{(l)}\right)\cdot{}^{2}\pi_{\theta\beta}^{(l)}}{\sum_{\phi=1}^{2}p_{\phi}^{(l)}\left(\nu_3^{(l)}\right)\cdot{}^{3}\pi_{\phi\beta}^{(l)}};\ \beta=\overline{1,2};\ 1=\overline{1,g}. \qquad (42)$$

expressed through *a posteriori* probability densities of the elements adjacent to $\nu_4^{(l)}$ (Figure 1.2) and one-dimension probability densities of their transitions from one value to another in horizontal or vertical line of l – th BBI (see Box 10).

Let us present *a posteriori* probability densities of the field element values and the transition probability densities for the values of image elements in (39) in the form shown in Box 11.

Substituting (40) and (41) into (39) and integrating with delta-functions, we obtain an equation

Box 13.

$$u^{(l)}\left(\nu_4^{(l)}\right)=f\left(M_1^{(l)}\left(\nu_4^{(l)}\right)\right)-f\left(M_2^{(l)}\left(\nu_4^{(l)}\right)\right)$$
$$+u^{(l)}\left(\nu_1^{(l)}\right)+z_1^{(l)}\left(u^{(l)}\left(\nu_1^{(l)}\right),{}^1\pi_{\alpha\beta}^{(l)}\right)$$
$$+u^{(l)}\left(\nu_2^{(l)}\right)+z_2^{(l)}\left(u^{(l)}\left(\nu_2^{(l)}\right),{}^2\pi_{\alpha\beta}^{(l)}\right)$$
$$-u^{(l)}\left(\nu_3^{(l)}\right)-z_3^{(l)}\left(u^{(l)}\left(\nu_3^{(l)}\right),{}^3\pi_{\alpha\beta}^{(l)}\right), \quad (43)$$

where

$$z_r^{(l)}\left(u^{(l)}\left(\nu_r^{(l)}\right),{}^r\pi_{\alpha\beta}^{(l)}\right)=\ln\frac{{}^r\pi_{\alpha\alpha}^{(l)}+{}^r\pi_{\beta\alpha}^{(l)}\exp\left\{-u^{(l)}\left(\nu_r^{(l)}\right)\right\}}{{}^r\pi_{\beta\beta}^{(l)}+{}^r\pi_{\alpha\beta}^{(l)}\exp\left\{u^{(l)}\left(\nu_r^{(l)}\right)\right\}}; \quad (44)$$
$$\left(l=\overline{1,g};\ r=\overline{1,3};\ \alpha,\beta=\overline{1,2}\right).$$

for the final *a posteriori* probability of the signal discrete parameter in $\left(i,j\right)$ – th element of l – th BBI of the digital half-tone image (see Box 12).

Dividing Equation (42) at $\beta=1$ by equation at $\beta=2$ and using results obtained in (Kulman, 1961), we come to an equation for nonlinear filtering of elements of l – th BBI of the digital half-tone image (see Box 13).

The nonlinear recurrent Equation (43) defines optimal operations, which should be fulfilled under given elements of l-th BBI, for the purpose of the best its recovering under influence of the white Gaussian noise. Taking into account that DHTI is presented in the form of g BBI, the DHTI filtering equation we represent as a system from g equations of type (43) (Petrov, Trubin and Butorin, 2003; Petrov, Trubin; 2007).

All *a priori* information about statistical dependence of elements of l-th binary image is concentrated in term of type (14), where ${}^r\pi_{\alpha\beta}^{(l)}\left(\alpha,\beta=\overline{1,2}\right)$ are elements of the transition probability matrices of elements of l-th bit of the digital half-tone image in horizontal ${}^1\Pi_{\alpha\beta}^{(l)}$, vertical ${}^2\Pi_{\alpha\beta}^{(l)}$ and diagonal ${}^3\Pi_{\alpha\beta}^{(l)}$ lines, interconnected by the equation

$${}^3\Pi_{\alpha\beta}^{(l)}={}^1\Pi_{\alpha\beta}^{(l)}\,{}^2\Pi_{\alpha\beta}^{(l)}=\begin{pmatrix}{}^1\pi_{11}^{(l)} & {}^1\pi_{12}^{(l)}\\ {}^1\pi_{21}^{(l)} & {}^1\pi_{22}^{(l)}\end{pmatrix}\cdot\begin{pmatrix}{}^2\pi_{11}^{(l)} & {}^2\pi_{12}^{(l)}\\ {}^2\pi_{21}^{(l)} & {}^2\pi_{22}^{(l)}\end{pmatrix}. \quad (45)$$

THE STRUCTURE OF THE DEVICE FOR TWO-DIMENSION NONLINEAR DHTI FILTERING

Since *a priori* data about the filtering process is assumed known (similar to algorithms of the one-dimension DHTI filtering), we take as a criterion of distinguishing the BBI element values the criterion of the ideal observer. In accordance with this criterion, the decision about the presence in the received realization of the signal $s^{(l)}\left(\mu_{i,j}^{(l)}\right)$ with BBI element values $M_1^{(l)}$ or $M_2^{(l)}$ is performed on the basis of comparison of the logarithm *a posteriori* probability ratio with some threshold $H^{(l)}$

$$u^{(l)}\left(\nu_4^{(l)}\right) \geq H^{(l)}. \quad (46)$$

The RRD structure for two-dimension filtering of g – bit DHTI, which simulates the system of g Equation (43) and the decision rule (46) is presented in Figure 4.

This structure contains discriminators of binary signals $\left(\mathrm{D}^{(1)},...,\mathrm{D}^{(g)}\right)$ realizing operations of calculation the logarithm difference of the likelihood functions of l-th channel $\left[f\left(M_1^{(l)}(\nu_4)\right) - f\left(M_2^{(l)}(\nu_4)\right)\right]$, $\left(l=\overline{1,g}\right)$; nonlinear bit filters $\left(\mathrm{NF}^{(1)},...,\mathrm{NF}^{(g)}\right)$, memory units $\left(\mathrm{SD}_1^{(l)}\right)$ for delay of image elements in horizontal, vertical and diagonal lines and $\left(\mathrm{SD}_2^{(l)}\right)$ for storage of MTP element values $\left({}^1\Pi^{(l)}, {}^2\Pi^{(l)}, {}^3\Pi^{(l)}, l=\overline{1,g}\right)$, summers, computational units for nonlinear function (44) and the same threshold devices $\left[(\mathrm{TD})^{(1)},...,(\mathrm{TD})^{(g)}\right]$.

A nonlinear filter smoothes the single samples arriving from a detector in discrete time moments

Figure 4. The device of two-dimension nonlinear DHTI filtering

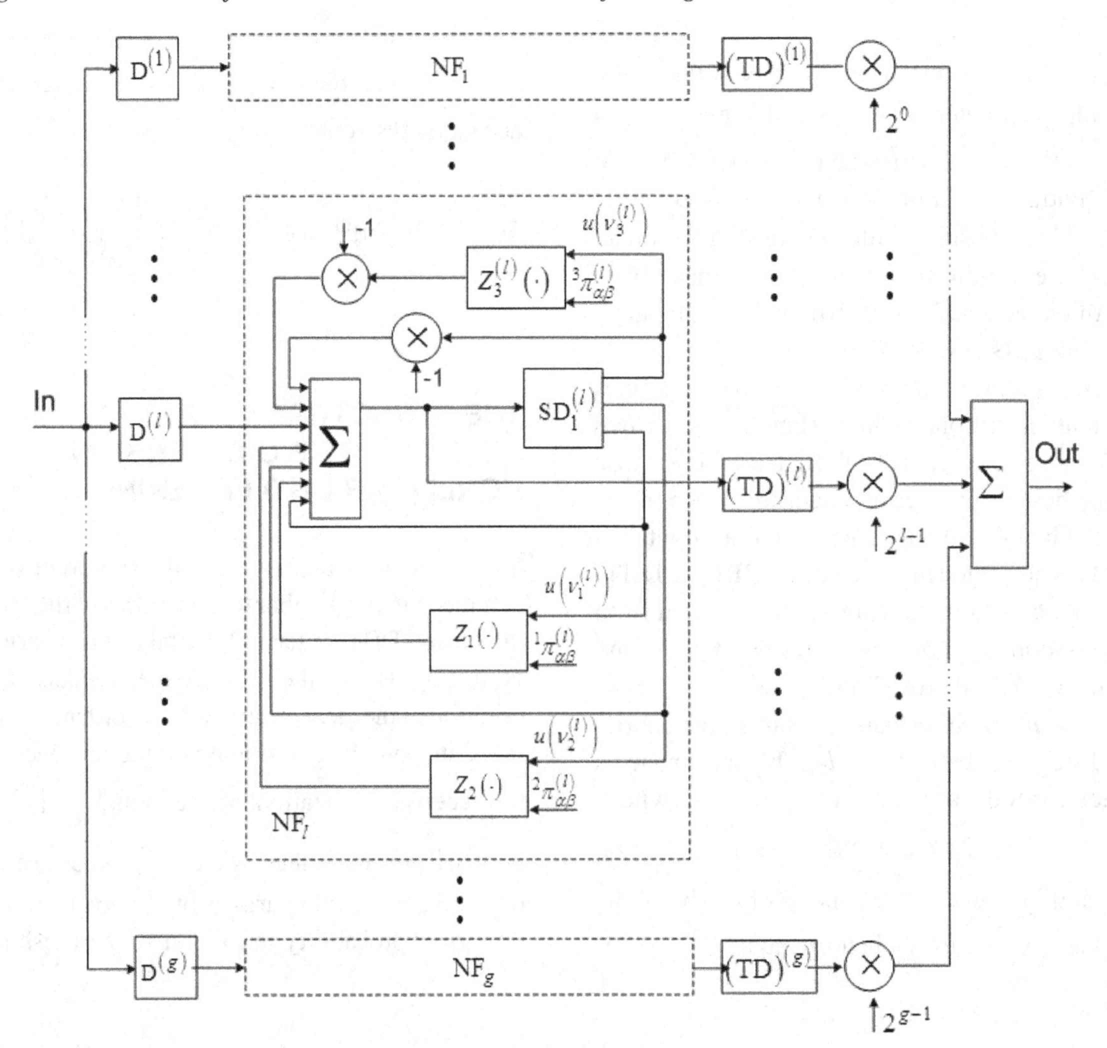

and includes the summer $\left(\Sigma^{(l)}\right)$, the memory unit $\left(\mathrm{SD}_1^{(l)}\right)$ for storing m DHTI elements equaled to the element number on the single line (i elements of the current line and m-i elements of the previous line), and three loops of feedback each containing the unit realizing the nonlinear function $z_r^{(l)}(\cdot),\ \left(r=\overline{1,3}\right)$.

As it is seen from Figure 4, in formation of $u^{(l)}\left(\nu_4^{(l)}\right)$ the following data participate: input data, data about values of adjacent (to $\nu_4^{(l)}$) elements of $l-$th BBI belonging to the vicinity $\Lambda_{i,j}^{(l)}=\left\{\nu_1^{(l)},\nu_2^{(l)},\nu_3^{(l)}\right\}$ and calculated values of nonlinear functions $z_r^{(l)}(\cdot),\ \left(r=\overline{1,3}\right)$, in which there is *a priori* information about the filtering process.

Because of the fact that nonlinear functions $z_r^{(l)}(\cdot),\ \left(r=\overline{1,3}\right)$ depend on *a priori* statistics, they have the special significance for formation of $u^{(l)}\left(\nu_4^{(l)}\right)$.

In the case of statistical independence of field elements $\left({}^{r}\pi_{ii}^{(l)}=0,5\right)$ functions $z_r^{(l)}(\cdot),\ \left(r=\overline{1,3}\right)$ take the values

$$z_1^{(l)}\left(u^{(l)}\left(\nu_1^{(l)}\right),\ {}^{1}\pi_{\alpha\beta}^{(l)}\right)=-u^{(l)}\left(\nu_1^{(l)}\right);$$
$$z_2^{(l)}\left(u^{(l)}\left(\nu_2^{(l)}\right),\ {}^{2}\pi_{\alpha\beta}^{(l)}\right)=-u^{(l)}\left(\nu_2^{(l)}\right);$$
$$z_3^{(l)}\left(u^{(l)}\left(\nu_3^{(l)}\right),\ {}^{3}\pi_{\alpha\beta}^{(l)}\right)=-u^{(l)}\left(\nu_3^{(l)}\right),$$

and $u^{(l)}\left(\nu_4^{(l)}\right)$ is forming only on the basis of input data, i.e. on the basis of logarithm difference of the likelihood functions

$$u^{(l)}\left(\nu_4^{(l)}\right)=\left[f\left(M_1^{(l)}\left(\nu_4^{(l)}\right)\right)-f\left(M_2^{(l)}\left(\nu_4^{(l)}\right)\right)\right]. \quad (47)$$

At that, loops of feedback (Figure 4) are breaking and a decision about the presence in the received signal of the image element with the value $M_k^{(l)},\left(k=1,2\right)$ is made on the basis of a single sample.

After filtering, the BBI elements are collected in the $g-$bit register $\left(\mathrm{Rg}\right)$ for estimation of the binary number with the appropriate weighting coefficients:

$$\overline{y}_{i,j}=\sum_{l=1}^{g} y_{i,j}^{(l)}\cdot 2^{l-1} \quad (48)$$

Factual summing is absent because each BBI corresponds to own bit position in the register with the appropriate weight.

THE NOISE IMMUNITY ANALYSIS OF ALGORITHMS FOR TWO-DIMENSION NONLINEAR DHTI FILTERING

2. Radio receiving device (Figure 4) was modeled on PC. The artificial binary and half-tone images with the number of elements 1024x1024 constructed on the basis of the model described in Chapter 10 and the real images represented in the digital view, which have 2^8=256 brightness levels and is enough for description of the half-tone images, were taken as the initial images. At that, we assumed that the image elements are transmitted in bit-by-bit manner at different signal/noise ratio in power ρ_e^2 at RRD input. The following ratio (Petrov, Trubin; 2007) was taken as the quantitative estimation of recovering of $l-$th BBI:

$$\eta_e^{(l)} = 10\lg\left(\left(\rho_{\text{out}}^2\right)^{(l)} / \rho_e^2\right) \text{ dB}, \tag{49}$$

where $\left(\rho_{\text{out}}^2\right)^{(l)}$ is the signal/noise ratio in power at the nonlinear filter output of $l-$th BBI ($\rho_e^{2(1)}, \rho_e^{2(2)}, ..., \rho_e^{2(g)} = \rho_e^2$).

The power benefit η is shown in Figure 5 for one-dimension (curve 1) and two-dimension (curve 2) filtering of the same real DHTI. The analysis of curves presented in Figure 5, demonstrates the higher effectiveness of two-dimension filtering of digital half-tone images compared to one-dimension case.

Figure 6 shows the example of two-dimension filtering of the artificial DHTI with ${}^1\pi_{\alpha\alpha} = {}^2\pi_{\alpha\alpha} = 0{,}9$ distorted by WGN for $\rho_e^2 = -6$ dB and recovered with the help of the optimal algorithm. ${}^1\pi_{\alpha\alpha} = {}^2\pi_{\alpha\alpha} = 0{,}9$ $\rho_e^2 = -6$ dB. The benefit in signal power $\eta^{(l)}$ is 8.8 dB.

In Figure 7 the example of the real binary image filtering with transition probability matrix elements ${}^1\Pi^{(l)}$ and ${}^2\Pi^{(l)}$ in horizontal and vertical lines accordingly ${}^1\pi_{ii}^{(l)} = 0{,}946$, ${}^2\pi_{ii}^{(l)} = 0{,}947$ distorted by WGN $\left(\rho_e^2 = -9 \text{ dB}\right)$ is shown. The benefit $\eta^{(l)}$ is 9.8 dB.

At investigation of filtering effectiveness of artificial digital half-tone images, the MTP was specified in accordance with averaged values obtained on the basis of analysis of large number of real image samples presented in the digital form (Lezin, 1969; Trubin et al, 2004). The analysis of distribution of MTP element values on bits of the digital half-tone images shows that transition probability in horizontal and vertical lines have the similar character: MTP element values in vertical line is usually less than in horizontal line by 3…5%.

Figure 8 shows the function of benefit in signal power η for developed optimal (curve 1) and known (Butorin, 2004) filtering methods of half-tone images such as the method of the two-dimension maximal *a posteriori* estimation (MAP estimation) based on the matrix equation solution for different values of a convergence criterion

Figure 5. Benefit in power η for filtering of the same real DHTI (1- one-dimension-; 2- two-dimension-; 3-three-dimension filtering)

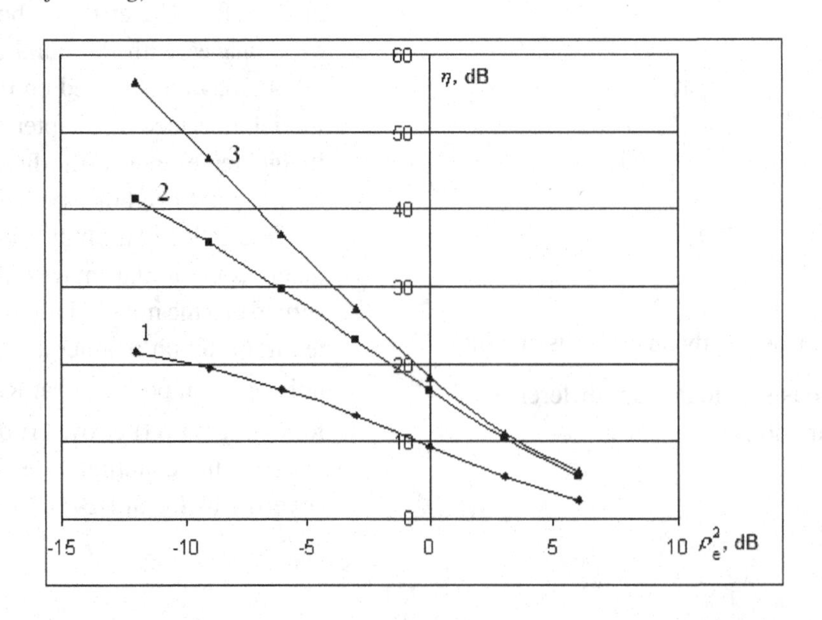

Figure 6. Example of two-dimension filtering of the artificial BBI: a) initial; b) noisy; c) filtered

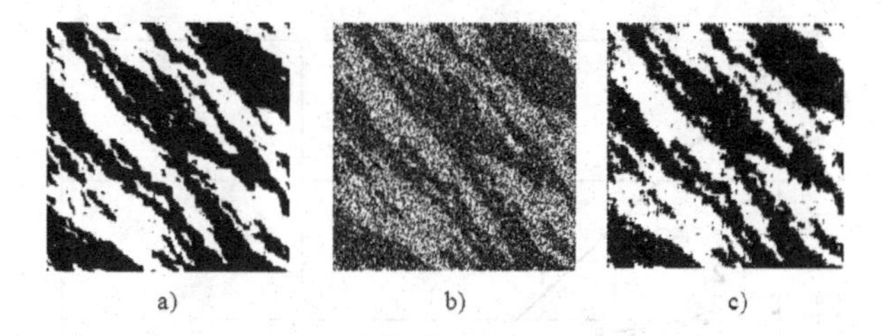

(curves 2, 3); the method of consecutive smoothing (curve 4); the method of an one-dimension filter (curve 5) and the two-dimension method of filter loop (curve 6). From analysis of curves of Figure 8 it follows that in the coincident range of signal/noise ratios $\rho_e^2 = 0 \ldots 5$ dB the offered method of two-dimension nonlinear DHTI filtering gives the best results essentially exceeding in computation resource saving.

From analysis of the curves presented in Figures 5 and 8 we see that the offered filtering algorithm is essentially effective in the case when the signal power is equal or less than the noise power. It is evident that more correlated high-order bits make the most contribution to the total filtering benefit. Moreover, distortions in low-order bits are practically indistinguishable by the human eye due to their less contribution to the total brightness level of the image. Therefore, the calculation volume can be essentially reduced if to refuse from low-order bit processing passing to 4-bit representation of digital half-tone images (Kulman, 1961).

So, if in the simulated image it is possible not to process four low-order bits, the loss is not more than 2 dB compared to the complete processing (~37 dB) for signal/noise ratio at device input up to -12 dB, and at that, the computational complexity will reduce exactly twice. Figure 9 shows an example of image "Church" processing distorted by the white noise at $\rho_e^2 = 0$ dB. The benefit in signal power η is 19 dB.

The analysis of two-dimension filtering results of the static DHTI shows that representation of the digital half-tone image by the set of g BBI permits to obtain filtering algorithms providing the image reception noise immunity, which does not yield the known algorithms, and to keep the high uniformity of RRD structure and essentially reduce the number of computation operations and a memory volume, which size in RRD with nonlinear filtering is equal to the number of image elements of an one line.

NONLINEAR FILTERING OF THE DHTI VIDEO-SEQUENCE

We carry out the synthesis and investigation of the filtering algorithm on the basis of the math-

Figure 7. Example of filtering of the real binary image: a) initial; b) noisy; c) filtered

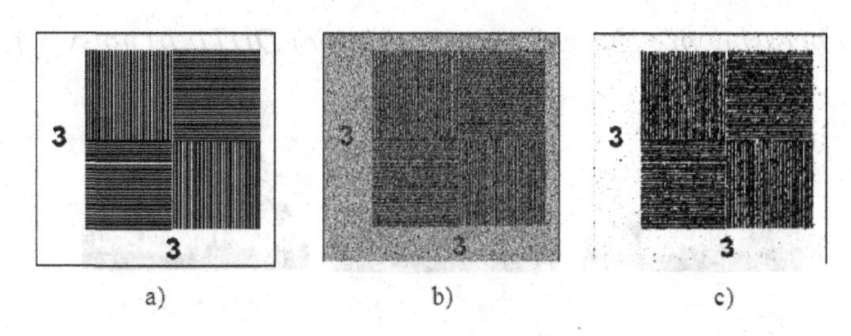

Figure 8. Benefit in signal power η for the most known filtering methods for half-tone images

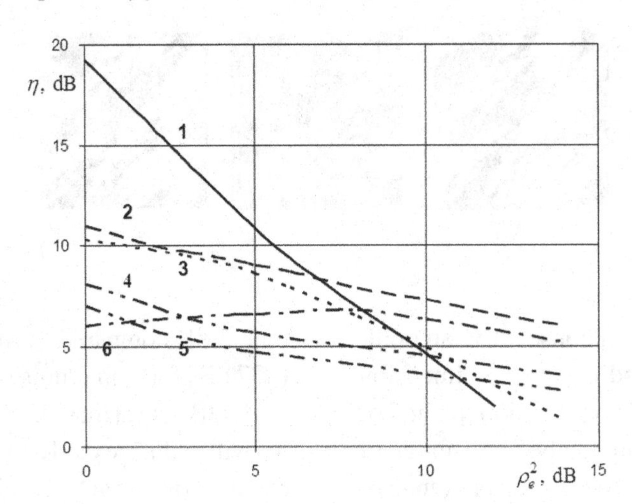

ematical model of three-dimension discrete-value Markovian process considered in Chapter 10.

At digital representation of half-tone images by the set of g BBI (g is a digit capacity of a binary number) the problem of DHTI video-sequence filtering can be reduced to the problem of BBI video-sequence filtering.

Let in $k-$th frame in the interval $T = t_h - t_{h-1}$ $\left(h = \overline{1, m \times n}\right)$ we transmit the one BBI element by the signal $s\left(\mu_{i,j,k}^{(l)}\right)$, $\left(l = \overline{1, g}\right)$, which discrete parameter $\mu_{i,j,k}^{(l)}$ takes one from two possible values $M_1^{(l)}$ or $M_2^{(l)}$.

We assume that the sequence of BBI element values $\left\{\mu_{i,j,k}^{(l)}\right\}$ forms the complicated stationaty Markovian chain with equiprobable $p_1^{(l)} = p_2^{(l)}$, $\left(l = \overline{1, g}\right)$ states $M_1^{(l)}$, $M_2^{(l)}$, and with conditional transition probabilities from one value to another (see Box 14).

Let $\nu_4^{(l)} = \mu_{i,j,k}^{(l)}$ be the $\left(i, j, k\right)-$th element of l-th BBI in the k-th sequence frame of quantized half-tone images of the Markovian type. Than for the multi-dimension *a priori* probability density we can write the expression of type shown in Box 15.

At presence of the additive WGN distorting the image, the likelihood function for the sequence of element values of $l-$th BBI can be written in the form shown in Box 16.

Taking into consideration (50), (51) and (52), *a posteriori* value distribution of the three-dimension l-th binary Markovian process will have the form shown in Box 17.

The direct realization o Equation (54) is difficult due to the multi-dimension character of probability densities in the right part of and the

Figure 9. Example of processing of "church" image: a) initial DHTI; b) noisy; c) filtered

presence of the statistical correlation between arguments. All *a priori* information concerning the possible element value of $l-$th BBI $\nu_4^{(l)}$ is defined by the multipliers under integral designations in (54).

Let us change an integrand in (54) by some equivalent obtained on the basis calculation of mutual information between elements of $l-$th BBI belonging to the vicinity $\Lambda_{i,j,k}^{(l)} = \left\{\nu_1^{(l)}, \nu_2^{(l)}, \nu_3^{(l)}, \nu_1'^{(l)}, \nu_2'^{(l)}, \nu_3'^{(l)}, \nu_4'^{(l)}\right\}$ andthe image element $\nu_4^{(l)}$ (Trubin et al, 2004; Petrov, Trubin; 2007) (see Box 18).

Substituting (55) into (54), we obtain the equation for *a posteriori* probability density of the image element value $\nu_4^{(l)}$ expressed through one-dimension *a posteriori* probability densities of elements of $l-$th BBI entering in $\Lambda_{i,j,k}^{(l)} = \left\{\nu_1^{(l)}, \nu_2^{(l)}, \nu_3^{(l)}, \nu_1'^{(l)}, \nu_2'^{(l)}, \nu_3'^{(l)}, \nu_4'^{(l)}\right\}$ andthe probability density of its possible transitions into values of the signal parameter of the image element $\nu_4^{(l)}$ (see Box 19).

Let us represent *a posteriori* probability densities and the transition probability densities in (56) as shown in Box 20.

Substituting (57), (58) into (56), having integrated with delta-functions and equating coefficients at the same delta-functions, we obtain the equation for the final *a posteriori* probability of the element value of $l-$th BBI $\nu_4^{(l)}$ (see Box 21).

Having divided Equation (59) at $\beta = 1$ by the equation at $\beta = 2$ and taking the logarithm in left and right parts, we obtain a system from g recurrent equation of nonlinear filtering of $l-$th

Box 14.

$$\pi_{lqrstfgh}^{(l)} = \pi^{(l)}\left\{\mu_{i,j,k}^{(l)} = M_l^{(l)} \middle| \mu_{i,j-1,k}^{(l)} = M_q^{(l)}; \mu_{i-1,j,k}^{(l)} = M_r^{(l)}; \mu_{i-1,j-1,k}^{(l)} = M_t^{(l)}; \mu_{i,j,k-1}^{(l)} = M_t^{(l)}; \mu_{i,j-1,k-1}^{(l)} = M_f^{(l)}; \mu_{i-1,j,k-1}^{(l)} = M_g^{(l)}; \mu_{i-1,j-1,k-1}^{(l)} = M_h^{(l)}\right\} \quad (50)$$

where $l, q, r, s, t, f, g, h = 1, 2.$

Box 15.

$$P^{(l)}\left\{\mu_{i,j,q}^{(l)}; i = \overline{1,m}; j = \overline{1,n}; q = \overline{1,k}\right\} = \prod_{q=1}^{k}\prod_{i=1}^{m}\prod_{j=1}^{n} P^{(l)}\left\{\mu_{i,j,q}^{(l)}\right\} \times w^{(l)}\left\{\mu_{i,j,k}^{(l)} \middle| \mu_{i,j-1,k}^{(l)}, \mu_{i-1,j-1,k}^{(l)}, \mu_{i-1,j,k}^{(l)}, \mu_{i,j-1,k-1}^{(l)}, \ldots \mu_{i-1,j-1,k-1}^{(l)}, \mu_{i-1,j,k-1}^{(l)}, \mu_{i,j,k-1}^{(l)}\right\}, \; l = \overline{1,g}. \quad (51)$$

If $i = j = q = 1$, than $P^{(l)}\left\{\mu_{i,j,q}^{(l)}\right\} = 0,5;$

If $i = 1, j > 1, q = 1$, then $P^{(l)}\left\{\mu_{1,j,1}^{(l)}\right\} = P^{(l)}\left\{\mu_{1,1,1}^{(l)}\right\}\prod_{j=2}^{n} w^{(l)}\left\{\mu_{1,j,1}^{(l)} \middle| \mu_{1,j-1,1}^{(l)}\right\};$

If $i > 1, j > 1, q = 1$, then $P^{(l)}\left\{\mu_{i,j,1}^{(l)}\right\} = P^{(l)}\left\{\mu_{1,1,1}^{(l)}\right\}\prod_{j=2}^{m}\prod_{i=2}^{n} w^{(l)}\left\{\mu_{i,j,1}^{(l)} \middle| \mu_{i-1,j-1,1}^{(l)}\right\}.$

Box 16.

$$F\left\{\mu_{i,j,q}^{(l)};i=\overline{1,m};j=\overline{1,n};q=\overline{1,k}\right\}=\exp\left\{\sum_{q=1}^{m}\sum_{j=1}^{n}\sum_{q=1}^{k}f\left(\mu_{i,j,q}^{(l)}\right)\right\}, \quad (52)$$

where $f\left(\mu_{i,j,q}^{(l)}\right)$ is a logarithm of the likelihood function of the element value $\left(i,j,q\right)$ in q – th frame and l – th BBI.

Box 17.

$$p_{as}^{(l)}\left\{\mu_{i,j,q}^{(l)};i=\overline{1,m};j=\overline{1,n};q=\overline{1,k}\right\}$$
$$=c\exp\left\{\sum_{i=1}^{m}\sum_{j=1}^{n}\sum_{q=1}^{k}f\left[\mu_{i,j,q}^{(l)}\right]\right\}\prod_{q=1}^{k}\prod_{i=1}^{m}\prod_{j=1}^{n}P\left\{\mu_{1,1,1}^{(l)}\right\} \quad (53)$$
$$\times w^{(l)}\left\{\mu_{i,j,q}^{(l)}\left|\mu_{i,j-1,q}^{(l)},\mu_{i-1,j-1,q}^{(l)},\mu_{i-1,j,q}^{(l)},\mu_{i,j-1,q-1}^{(l)},\mu_{i-1,j-1,q-1}^{(l)},\mu_{i-1,j,q}^{(l)},\mu_{i,j,q-1}^{(l)}\right.\right\},$$

where c is the normalizing coefficient, $\alpha=1,2;\ l=\overline{1,g}$. Having integrated (53) over all values of $\left\{\mu_{i,j,k}^{(l)}\right\}$, we obtain the equation of final *a posteriori* probability of the value $\left\{\mu_{i,j,k}^{(l)}\right\}$ in element $\nu_4^{(l)}$ of l-th BBI with account of designations taken in Chapter 10 (Figure 1.2):

$$p_{as}^{(l)}\left(\nu_4^{(l)}\right)=c\exp\left\{f\left(\nu_4^{(l)}\right)\right\}$$
$$\times\int\cdots\int p_{as}^{(l)}\left(\nu_1^{(l)},\nu_2^{(l)},\nu_3^{(l)},\nu_1'^{(l)},\nu_2'^{(l)},\nu_3'^{(l)},\nu_4'^{(l)}\right) \quad (54)$$
$$\times w^{(l)}\left(\nu_4^{(l)}\left|\nu_1^{(l)},\nu_2^{(l)},\nu_3^{(l)},\nu_1'^{(l)},\nu_2'^{(l)},\nu_3'^{(l)},\nu_4'^{(l)}\right.\right)d\nu_1^{(l)}d\nu_2^{(l)}d\nu_3^{(l)}d\nu_1'^{(l)}d\nu_2'^{(l)}d\nu_3'^{(l)}d\nu_4'^{(l)}.$$

Box 18.

$$p_{as}^{(l)}\left(\nu_1^{(l)},\nu_2^{(l)},\nu_3^{(l)},\nu_1'^{(l)},\nu_2'^{(l)},\nu_3'^{(l)},\nu_4'^{(l)}\right)\times$$
$$\times w^{(l)}\left(\nu_4^{(l)}\left|\nu_1^{(l)},\nu_2^{(l)},\nu_3^{(l)},\nu_1'^{(l)},\nu_2'^{(l)},\nu_3'^{(l)},\nu_4'^{(l)}\right.\right)=$$
$$=\frac{p^{(l)}\left(\nu_1^{(l)}\right)w^{(l)}\left(\nu_4^{(l)}\left|\nu_1^{(l)}\right.\right)p^{(l)}\left(\nu_2^{(l)}\right)w^{(l)}\left(\nu_4^{(l)}\left|\nu_2^{(l)}\right.\right)}{p^{(l)}\left(\nu_3^{(l)}\right)w^{(l)}\left(\nu_4^{(l)}\left|\nu_3^{(l)}\right.\right)}\times \quad (55)$$
$$\times\frac{p^{(l)}\left(\nu_4'^{(l)}\right)w^{(l)}\left(\nu_4^{(l)}\left|\nu_4'^{(l)}\right.\right)p^{(l)}\left(\nu_3'^{(l)}\right)w^{(l)}\left(\nu_4^{(l)}\left|\nu_3'^{(l)}\right.\right)}{p^{(l)}\left(\nu_1'^{(l)}\right)w^{(l)}\left(\nu_4^{(l)}\left|\nu_1'^{(l)}\right.\right)p^{(l)}\left(\nu_2'^{(l)}\right)w^{(l)}\left(\nu_4^{(l)}\left|\nu_2'^{(l)}\right.\right)}.$$

Box 19.

$$p_{as}^{(l)}\left(\nu_1^{(l)},\nu_2^{(l)},\nu_3^{(l)},\nu_1'^{(l)},\nu_2'^{(l)},\nu_3'^{(l)},\nu_4'^{(l)}\right)$$
$$\times w^{(l)}\left(\nu_4^{(l)}\left|\nu_1^{(l)},\nu_2^{(l)},\nu_3^{(l)},\nu_1'^{(l)},\nu_2'^{(l)},\nu_3'^{(l)},\nu_4'^{(l)}\right.\right)$$
$$=\frac{p^{(l)}\left(\nu_1^{(l)}\right)w^{(l)}\left(\nu_4^{(l)}\left|\nu_1^{(l)}\right.\right)p^{(l)}\left(\nu_2^{(l)}\right)w^{(l)}\left(\nu_4^{(l)}\left|\nu_2^{(l)}\right.\right)}{p^{(l)}\left(\nu_3^{(l)}\right)w^{(l)}\left(\nu_4^{(l)}\left|\nu_3^{(l)}\right.\right)} \tag{56}$$
$$\times\frac{p^{(l)}\left(\nu_4'^{(l)}\right)w^{(l)}\left(\nu_4^{(l)}\left|\nu_4'^{(l)}\right.\right)p^{(l)}\left(\nu_3'^{(l)}\right)w^{(l)}\left(\nu_4^{(l)}\left|\nu_3'^{(l)}\right.\right)}{p^{(l)}\left(\nu_1'^{(l)}\right)w^{(l)}\left(\nu_4^{(l)}\left|\nu_1'^{(l)}\right.\right)p^{(l)}\left(\nu_2'^{(l)}\right)w^{(l)}\left(\nu_4^{(l)}\left|\nu_2'^{(l)}\right.\right)}.$$

Box 20.

$$p_{as}^{(l)}\left(\nu_q^{(l)}\right)=\sum_{\alpha=1}^{2}p_\alpha^{(l)}\left(\nu_q^{(l)}\right)\delta\left(\nu_q^{(l)}-M_\alpha^{(l)}\right);$$
$$p_{as}^{(l)}\left(\nu_q'^{(l)}\right)=\sum_{\gamma=1}^{2}p_\gamma^{(l)}\left(\nu_q'^{(l)}\right)\delta\left(\nu_q'^{(l)}-M_\gamma^{(l)}\right);\quad q=\overline{1,4};\ l=\overline{1,g}, \tag{57}$$

$$w^{(l)}\left(\nu_4^{(l)}\left|\nu_j^{(l)}\right.\right)=\sum_{\beta=1}^{2}{}^r\pi_{\alpha\beta}^{(l)}\delta\left(\nu_4^{(l)}-M_\beta^{(l)}\right);j=\overline{1,3};r=\overline{1,3};\alpha,\beta=1,2;\ l=\overline{1,g};$$
$$w^{(l)}\left(\nu_4^{(l)}\left|\nu_h'^{(l)}\right.\right)=\sum_{\vartheta=1}^{2}{}^r\pi_{\alpha\vartheta}^{(l)}\delta\left(\nu_4^{(l)}-M_\vartheta^{(l)}\right);h=\overline{1,4};r=\overline{4,7};\alpha,\vartheta=1,2;\ l=\overline{1,g}, \tag{58}$$

where $p_\alpha^{(l)}\left(\nu_q^{(l)}\right)$ is *a posteriori* probability of value $M_\alpha^{(l)}$ in the element $\nu_q^{(l)}$ of $l-$th BBI in k-th frame; $p_\alpha^{(l)}\left(\nu_q'^{(l)}\right)$ is *a posteriori* probability of value $M_\alpha^{(l)}$ in the element $\nu_q'^{(l)}$ of $l-$th BBI in $\left(k-1\right)-$th frame; ${}^r\pi_{\alpha\beta}^{(l)}$, $r=\overline{1,7}$ are elements of $r-$th MTP ${}^1\Pi^{(l)}$, ${}^2\Pi^{(l)}$, ${}^3\Pi^{(l)}$, ${}^4\Pi^{(l)}$, ${}^5\Pi^{(l)}$, ${}^6\Pi^{(l)}$, ${}^7\Pi^{(l)}$ of type (1.32, 1.33, 1.42, 1.48, 1.59); $\delta\left(\cdot\right)$ is the delta-function.

Box 21.

$$p_\beta^{(l)}\left(\nu_4^{(l)}\right)=c'\exp\left\{f\left(M_{\beta,\nu_4^{(l)}}^{(l)}\right)\right\}\frac{p_\alpha^{(l)}\left(\nu_1^{(l)}\right)\cdot\left({}^1\pi_{\alpha\beta}^{(l)}\right)\cdot p_\theta^{(l)}\left(\nu_2^{(l)}\right)\cdot\left({}^2\pi_{\theta\beta}^{(l)}\right)}{p_\phi^{(l)}\left(\nu_3^{(l)}\right)\cdot\left({}^3\pi_{\phi\beta}^{(l)}\right)}$$
$$\times\frac{p_\gamma^{(l)}\left(\nu_4'^{(l)}\right)\cdot\left({}^4\pi_{\gamma\beta}^{(l)}\right)\cdot p_\omega^{(l)}\left(\nu_3'^{(l)}\right)\cdot\left({}^7\pi_{\omega\beta}^{(l)}\right)}{p_\psi^{(l)}\left(\nu_1'^{(l)}\right)\cdot\left({}^5\pi_{\psi\beta}^{(l)}\right)\cdot p_\nu^{(l)}\left(\nu_2'^{(l)}\right)\cdot\left({}^6\pi_{\nu\beta}^{(l)}\right)};\quad\alpha,\beta,\theta,\phi,\gamma,\omega,\psi,\nu=1,2;\ l=\overline{1,g}. \tag{59}$$

Box 22.

$$
\begin{aligned}
u^{(l)}(v_4) = {} & \left[f\left(M_1^{(l)}\left(\nu_4^{(l)}\right)\right) - f\left(M_2^{(l)}\left(\nu_4^{(l)}\right)\right)\right] \\
& + u^{(l)}\left(v_1^{(l)}\right) + z_1^{(l)}\left[u^{(l)}\left(v_1\right), {}^{1}\pi_{ij}^{(l)}\right] + u^{(l)}\left(v_2^{(l)}\right) + z_2^{(l)}\left[u^{(l)}\left(v_2^{(l)}\right), {}^{2}\pi_{ij}^{(l)}\right] \\
& + u^{(l)}\left(v_4'^{(l)}\right) + z_4^{(l)}\left[u^{(l)}\left(v_4'^{(l)}\right), {}^{4}\pi_{ij}^{(l)}\right] + u^{(l)}\left(v_3'^{(l)}\right) + z_7^{(l)}\left[u^{(l)}\left(v_3'^{(l)}\right), {}^{7}\pi_{ij}^{(l)}\right] \\
& - u^{(l)}\left(v_3^{(l)}\right) - z_3^{(l)}\left[u^{(l)}\left(v_3^{(l)}\right), {}^{3}\pi_{ij}^{(l)}\right] - u^{(l)}\left(v_1'^{(l)}\right) - z_5^{(l)}\left[u^{(l)}\left(v_1'^{(l)}\right), {}^{5}\pi_{ij}^{(l)}\right] \\
& - u^{(l)}\left(v_2'^{(l)}\right) - z_6^{(l)}\left[u^{(l)}\left(v_2'^{(l)}\right), {}^{6}\pi_{ij}^{(l)}\right],
\end{aligned} \tag{60}
$$

where $u^{(l)}\left(\nu_4^{(l)}\right) = \ln \dfrac{p_1^{(l)}\left(\nu_4^{(l)}\right)}{p_2^{(l)}\left(\nu_4^{(l)}\right)}, \ l = \overline{1, g};$

$$
z_p^{(l)}(\cdot) = \ln \frac{{}^{p}\pi_{\alpha\alpha} + {}^{p}\pi_{\beta\alpha} \exp\left\{-u^{(l)}\left(\nu_q^{(l)}\right)\right\}}{{}^{p}\pi_{\beta\beta} + {}^{p}\pi_{\alpha\beta} \exp\left\{u^{(l)}\left(\nu_q^{(l)}\right)\right\}}; p = \overline{1,3};\ j = \overline{1,3}; \tag{61}
$$

$$
z_p^{(l)}(\cdot) = \ln \frac{{}^{p}\pi_{\alpha\alpha} + {}^{p}\pi_{\beta\alpha} \exp\left\{-u^{(l)}\left(\nu_q'^{(l)}\right)\right\}}{{}^{p}\pi_{\beta\beta} + {}^{p}\pi_{\alpha\beta} \exp\left\{u^{(l)}\left(\nu_q'^{(l)}\right)\right\}}; q = \overline{1,4};\ p = \overline{4,7}. \tag{62}
$$

BBI in k-th frame (Petrov, Trubin and Butorin, 2003; Petrov, Trubin; 2007) (see Box 22).

Equations (60) are the basis for synthesis of the device for nonlinear spatial-time filtering of the binary Markovian image belonging to l-th section in k-th frame of the DHTI video-sequence.

SYNTHESIS OF THE DEVICE FOR NONLINEAR FILTERING OF THE DHTI VIDEO-SEQUENCE

The structure of Equation (60) has the high uniformity and it permits to synthesize filtering algorithms being rather simple in implementation.

We chose (as at synthesis of two-dimension filtering algorithms) as a criterion of distinguishing of discrete values $M_1^{(l)}$, $M_2^{(l)}$ of l-th BBI the ideal observer criterion (Stratonovich 1959, 1960; Tihanov, 1970; Yarlykov, 1980), in accordance with which the decision about the presence in the received signal realization $s\left(\mu_{i,j,k}^{(l)}\right)$ of the image element $\mu_{i,j,k}^{(l)}$, having the value $M_1^{(l)}$ *or* $M_2^{(l)}$ is made on the basis of comparison of logarithm of *a posteriori* probability ratio with some threshold H:

$$
u_{i,j,k}^{(l)}\left(\nu_4^{(l)}\right) \geq H \tag{63}
$$

In the symmetrical system, when $p_1^{(l)} = p_2^{(l)}$, the threshold H=0.

From Equation (60) we see that the following data contribute in forming of $u_{i,j,k}^{(l)}$: the input data, the data about values of image elements belonging to the vicinity

$$\Lambda_{i,j,k}^{(l)} = \left\{\nu_1^{(l)}, \nu_2^{(l)}, \nu_3^{(l)}, \nu_1'^{(l)}, \nu_2'^{(l)}, \nu_3'^{(l)}, \nu_4'^{(l)}\right\},$$

and calculated values of nonlinear functions $z_i^{(l)}(\cdot)$, $i = \overline{1,7}$, in which *a priori* information about the filtering process is contained.

The optimal RRD for filtering the video-sequence of binary images, which realizes Equations (60) – (62) and the decision rule (63) is presented in Figure 10. It contains of the discriminator $\left(\mathrm{D}^{(l)}\right)$ calculating the difference of logarithms of likelihood functions of the discrete parameter values of binary signals $\left[f_{k+1}^{(l)}\left(M_1\right) - f_{k+1}^{(l)}\left(M_2\right)\right]$; the nonlinear filter including the summer $\left(\Sigma^{(l)}\right)$, the memory cells to store values of the image elements in the vicinity

$$\Lambda_{i,j,k}^{(l)} = \left\{\nu_1^{(l)}, \nu_2^{(l)}, \nu_3^{(l)}, \nu_1'^{(l)}, \nu_2'^{(l)}, \nu_3'^{(l)}, \nu_4'^{(l)}\right\} -$$

$\left(\left(\mathrm{SD}_1^{(l)}\right)\right)$ and values of elements of the matrices of transition probabilities ${}^{r}\pi_{\alpha\beta}^{(l)}$, $r = \overline{1,7}$ – $\left(\left(\mathrm{SD}_2^{(l)}\right)\right)$, the seven loops of feedback, each of

Figure 10. Optimal RRD for filtering the video-sequence of binary images

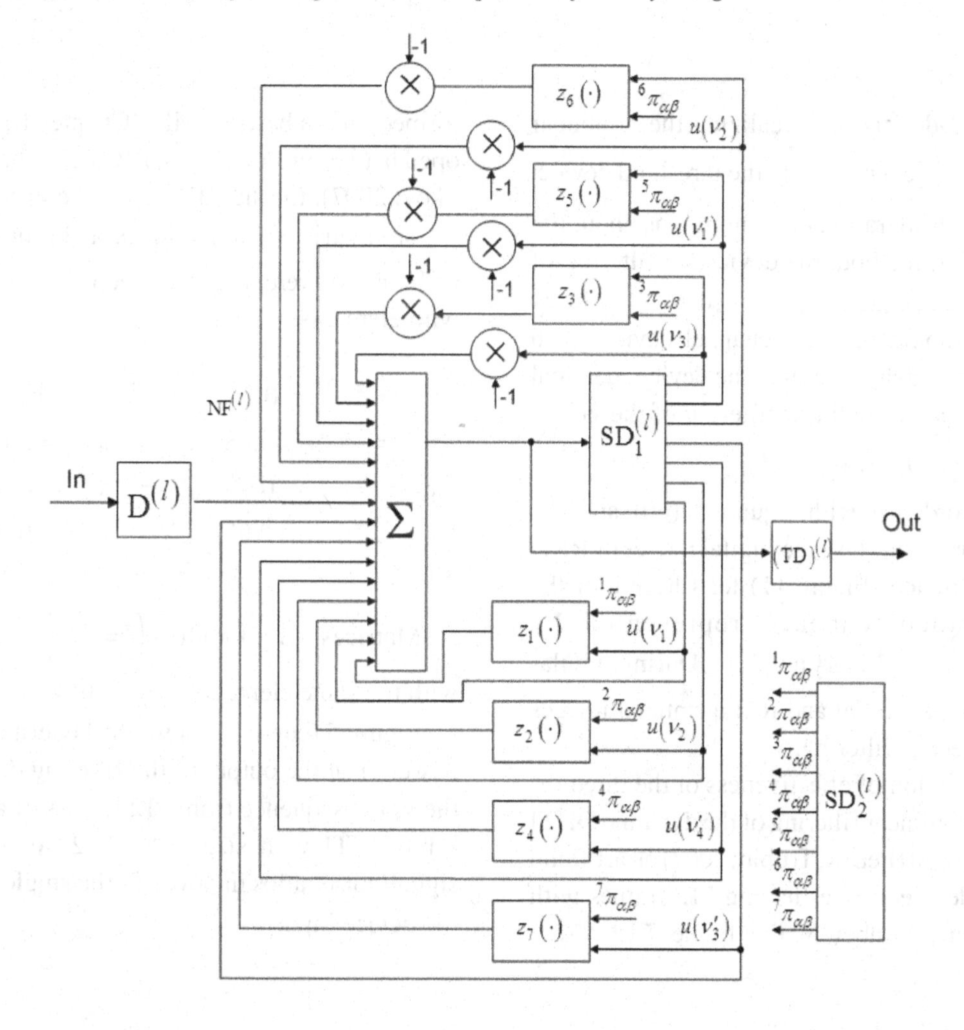

Figure 11. The g-channel device for filtering of the DHTI video-sequence

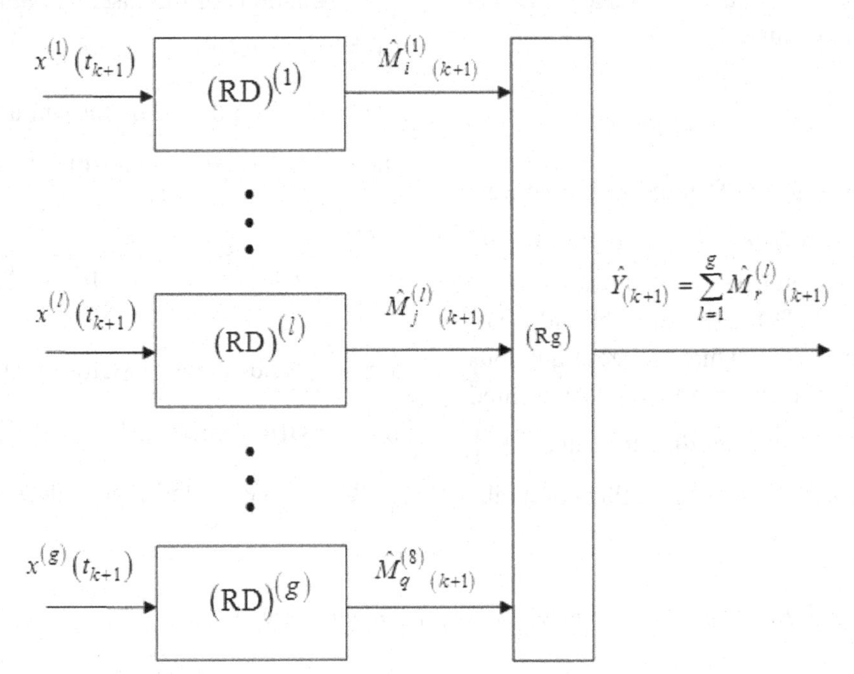

which includes the unit realizing the nonlinear function $z_r(\cdot)$, $\left(r=\overline{1,7}\right)$; the threshold device.

With consideration of assumptions about the transmission method, the device for filtering of DHTI video-sequence presented by 2^g binary numbers should be the g-channel device, each channel of which represents the device identical to the device of nonlinear filtering of the video-sequence $\left(\mathrm{RD}\right)^{(l)}$ (Figure 11).

In accordance with Equation (60) and the optimal criterion (63), the digital model of RRD was constructed (Figure 11) for filtering of the DHTI video-sequence represented by $q=2^8$ $\left(g=8\right)$ binary numbers. During simulation on PC, artificial and real quantized images were subject of filtering.

Investigation of effectiveness of the three-dimension nonlinear filtering of the dynamic DHTI was conducted (Petrov, Trubin; 2007) on artificial DHTI video-sequences having 512 frames with the element number in the frame 512×512, formed on the basis of MM (Chapter 10), developed in (Trubin et al, 2004; Petrov, Trubin, Chastikov; 2007), for the BBI number $g=8$.

The matrices of transition probabilities in lines and columns were specified as equal: ${}^1\Pi^{(l)} = {}^2\Pi^{(l)}$ with elements:

$$\begin{aligned} {}^1\pi_{ii}^{(1)} &= {}^2\pi_{ii}^{(1)} = 0.5;\ {}^1\pi_{ii}^{(2)} = {}^2\pi_{ii}^{(2)} = 0.53; \\ {}^1\pi_{ii}^{(3)} &= {}^2\pi_{ii}^{(3)} = 0.58;\ {}^1\pi_{ii}^{(4)} = {}^2\pi_{ii}^{(4)} = 0.65; \\ {}^1\pi_{ii}^{(5)} &= {}^2\pi_{ii}^{(5)} = 0.78;\ {}^1\pi_{ii}^{(6)} = {}^2\pi_{ii}^{(6)} = 0.88; \\ {}^1\pi_{ii}^{(7)} &= {}^2\pi_{ii}^{(7)} = 0.95;\ {}^1\pi_{ii}^{(8)} = {}^2\pi_{ii}^{(8)} = 0.98. \end{aligned} \tag{64}$$

Matrices ${}^4\Pi^{(l)}$ for all l $\left(l=\overline{1,g}\right)$ were taken with the same elements ${}^4\pi_{ii}^{(l)} = 0.9$.

Figure 5 (curve 3) shows the benefit in signal power η at the output of the filtering device for the video-sequence from 512 frames of artificial 8-bit DHTI with size 512×512 for different signal/noise ratios in power in the single pulse at the device input ρ_e^2.

Obtained results confirm the high effectiveness of the synthesized algorithm the dynamic DHTI filtering especially for slowly-varied scenes of video-sequences of the large-structured DHTI.

From analysis of the curves presented in Figure 5 we may conclude that at small signal/noise ratios $\rho_e^2 < 0$ dB the three-dimension filtering ensures the considerable benefit compared to one-dimension and two-dimension ones.

CONCLUSION

The main conclusions are the following:

1. The area of application of theory of Markov process is widened vis-à-vis the solution of problems of synthesis of mathematical models and the nonlinear filtering algorithm synthesis for digital half-tone images and video-sequences representing the multi-dimension, multi-valued random processes.
2. On the basis of the mathematical models developed and the filtering theory of conditional Markov processes, the algorithms and structures of the optimal radio receivers for nonlinear filtering of static and dynamic digital half-tone images are derived. The developed radio receiver device has a rather simple structure and high uniformity, which allows for ease of combination of radio receiver devices for increased dimension and number of discrete values of filtering process.
3. Qualitative and quantitative analysis of developed algorithms for nonlinear filtering of static and dynamic DHTI shows that filtering effectiveness increases with reduction of the signal/noise ratio and with growth of dimension of filtering process. At varying the signal/noise ratio at radio receiver device input ρ_e^2 from 0 dB to –9 dB, the benefit in signal power η increases from 9 to 19 dB for one-dimension filtering, from 17 to 38 dB for two-dimension one and from 18 dB to 46 dB for three-dimension filtering of the video-sequence of 8-bit DHTI.

DIRECTIONS OF FURTHER RESEARCHES AND DEVELOPMENTS

Starting from the obtained results of qualitative and quantitative investigations of the synthesized MM and filtering algorithms of static and dynamic DHTI, we can predict the behavior of mathematical models and filtering algorithms for higher order. For this, it is necessary in each specific case to investigate the problems of MM construction and development of nonlinear filtering algorithms differing by more complicated statistical peculiarities with the help of methods, which utility has been approved and generalized for several types of real processes. The solution of such problems may probably lead to obtaining new unknown results.

REFERENCES

Akasi, A. (1981). Recovering of Gaussian images with the help of two-dimension maximal a posteriori estimation. *Journal Densi Tsusin Gakkai Rombusini, A-64*(11), 908–915.

Amiantov, I. N. (1971). *Selected issues of the statistical communication theory*. Moscow, Russia: Sovetskoe Radio Publishing.

Butorin, E. L. (2004). *Nonlinear filtering devices for digital half-tone images of Markovian type*. (Unpublished Doctoral Thesis). Moscow Power Engineering Institute, Moscow, Russia.

Kulman, N. K. (1961). Nonlinear filter for telegraph signal filtering. *Radio Engineering and Electronics, 1*(9), 67–79.

Lezin, Y. S. (1969). *Optimal filters with pulse signal accumulation*. Moscow, Russia: Sovetskoe Radio Publishing.

Petrov, E. P., & Kharina, N. L. (2006). *Simulation of digital half-tone images of Markovian type with discrete arguments*. Vyatka, Russia: Vyatka State University Publishing.

Petrov, E. P., & Trubin, I. S. (2007). Mathematical models of video-sequences of digital half-tone images. *Achievements of Modern Radio Electronic,* (6), 3-31.

Petrov, E. P., Trubin, I. S., & Butorin, E. L. (2003). Spatial-time model of digital Markovian images. In *Proceedings of IX International Conference of Radar Technology, Navigation, and Communication,* (vol. 1, pp. 330-337). IEEE.

Petrov, E. P., Trubin, I. S., & Butorin, E. L. (2005). Nonlinear filtering of the sequence of digital half-tone images. *Radio Engineering and Electronics, 50*(10), 1265–1270.

Petrov, E. P., Trubin, I. S., & Chastikov, I. A. (2007). Nonlinear filtering of video-sequences of digital half-tone images of Markovian type. *Achievements of Modern Radio Electronic,* (3), 54-88.

Petrov, E.P., Trubin, I.S., & Tikhonov, E.P. (2003). Nonlinear digital filtering of half-tone images. *Radio Engineering,* (5), 7-10.

Stratonovich, R. L. (1959). Optimal nonlinear systems providing the extraction of the signal with constant parameters from noise. *Radiophysics, 11*(6), 892–901.

Stratonovich, R. L. (1960). Application of the Markovian process theory for signal optimal filtering. *Radio Engineering and Electronics, 11*, 1751–1763.

Tikhonov, V. I. (1966). *Statistic radio engineering*. Moscow: Sovetskoe Radio Publishing.

Tikhonov, V. I. (1970). Nonlinear optimal filtering and the quasi-coherent signal reception. *Radio-electronics, 13*(2), 152–169.

Trubin, I. S. (2004). *Methods of digital signal processing*. Vyatka, Russia: Vyatka State University Publishing.

Yarlykov. (1980). *Application of Markovian theory of nonlinear filtering in radio engineering*. Moscow: Sovetskoe Radio Publishing.

Chapter 14
Performance Analysis of Traffic and Mobility Models on Mobile and Vehicular Ad Hoc Wireless Networks

Lawal Bello
University of Greenwich, UK

Panos Bakalis
University of Greenwich, UK

ABSTRACT

Advances in wireless communication technology and the proliferation of mobile devices enable the capabilities of communicating with each other even in areas with no pre-existing communication infrastructure. Traffic and mobility models play an important role in evaluating the performance of these communication networks. Despite criticism and assumption from various researches on Transmission Control Protocols (TCP), weaknesses on Mobile Ad Hoc Network (MANET), and Vehicular Ad Hoc Network (VANET). A simulation was carried out to evaluate the performance of Constant Bit Rate, Variable Bit Rate and Transmission Control Protocol on MANET and VANET using DSR routing protocol. CBR, VBR, and TCP have different manufacturer operation mechanisms and these differences lead to significant performance of CBR and VBR over TCP with better throughput and less average maximal end-to-end delay. DSR was able to respond to link failure at low mobility which led to TCP's performance in packets delivery.

INTRODUCTION

Mobile Ad Hoc and vehicular ad hoc networks plays a vital role within the field of network communication. The recent developments in wireless technologies have made Vehicle-to-Vehicle communication (V2V) and Roadside Unit (RSU) achievable in mobile ad hoc networks. This has given birth and brought a new concept of Mobile Ad Hoc Wireless Network known as the vehicular ad hoc network. Vehicular Ad hoc Networks are self-organizing communities of wheeled mobile units consisting of large number of vehicles and a small number of fixed infrastructure nodes

DOI: 10.4018/978-1-4666-2208-1.ch014

such as roadside access units within radio communication range to each other. The initiative behind VANET is to facilitate road safety, traffic management and infotainment dissemination for drivers and passengers. In a domain which lacks communication infrastructure or where the existing infrastructure is inconvenient to use, mobile users can communicate through the formation of a temporary wireless Mobile Ad hoc Network. The nodes are mobile and free to move propagating packets freely and randomly without the need for any infrastructure. The application of these networks are highly needed in areas like battlefields, emergency rescue services, lecture theatres conference halls and other places where deployment of network infrastructures becomes difficult.

Due to the fact that their topology/location changes rapidly and unpredictably, these networks need network routing protocol as well as traffic model that can withstand these unpredicted topological changes immediately. These protocols are categorised into pro-active, reactive and hybrid routing protocols (Qasim *et al.,* 2009) and the identification of the most appropriate routing protocol to be used depends on different factors, namely: a) traffic and mobility models b) scalability and c) quality of service.

Despite the fact that considerable simulation work has been done, still more investigation is needed to evaluate the performance of the traffic and mobility models on MANET, VANET and comparison between them. Most of the researches such as (Rajagopalan *et al.,* 2006) evaluate only the performance of TCP traffic model using AODV routing protocol without considering the DSR protocol with CBR, TCP or VBR traffic models. Our work focused on the performance analysis of CBR, VBR and TCP traffic models on MANET and VANET networks using DSR protocol.

DYNAMIC SOURCE ROUTING PROTOCOL

Dynamic Source Routing (DSR) is a simple and efficient routing protocol designed specifically for use in multi-hop wireless ad hoc networks of mobile nodes which operate entirely on demand, and works on two mechanisms i.e. route discovery and route maintenance. The route discovery is initiated if and only if the routes to destinations are not known, for which it initiates a route discovery by sending a route request (RREQ) to all its neighbouring nodes containing the IP address of both sender and receiver in the packet header allowing the routing packet overhead of DSR to scale automatically to only what is needed to react to changes in the routes currently in use (Broach *et al.,* 1998). Performance evaluation conducted on both proactive and on demand protocols by Qasim *et al.* (2009), Kumar *et al.* (2008), and Raju and Mungara (2010) showed that DSR performed better than AODV and other proactive protocols in terms of throughput, less end-to-end delay, as well as less packets drop. The DSR performance was attributed to its characteristics of having multiple routes to other destination. In case of link failure, it does not require a new route discovery processes. Because of this, end-to-end delay is reduced as well as less packet dropping. Hence, the DSR protocol was chosen as genial candidate for carrying out further research

BACKGROUND OF THE STUDY

Various on demand, proactive and hybrid ad hoc routing protocols have been studied analytically and simulation method using TCP (Transmission Control Protocol), CBR (Constant Bit Rate) and VBR (Variable Bit Rate) traffic models (Rajagopalan & Shen, 2006; Triantafyllidou *et al.,*2007; Bakalis & Lawal, 2010). Analysis revealed that TCP traffic models performed poorly by misinterpretation of packet losses, link failure, and late acknowledgement as a sign of network congestion (TCP was designed for static wired networks). Explanations of what causes the packet losses in MANET have not fully been given and which routing protocol from all categories is the best to respond to the link failure and packet loss before the TCP's algorithm response is also unknown. According to (John Wiley, 2009), mobility, high bit error rate, unpredictability of the mobile node movement, variability and congestion are the main factors that affect the performance of TCP traffic model in MANET and VANET. Most researches (Abdullah *et al.,* 2008; Sesay *et al.,* 2004; Anisur *et al.,* 2009) used CBR traffic model due to the assumption and criticism of the TCP's weaknesses in these networks.

VANET networks are identical to MANET network in that they rapidly and dynamically change network topologies due to the fast motion of vehicles but differ because of the regular change in vehicular density, relative high speed of vehicular nodes, congestion on roads, traffic control mechanism and the mobility of vehicles are constrained by predefined roads. In (Garoui, 2005) presented an analysis of network traffic in ad hoc networks based on the Destination Sequenced Distance Vector (DSDV) protocol with an emphasis on mobility and communication patterns of the mobile nodes. The goal of the author's simulations was to measure the ability of (DSDV) routing protocol to react to multi-hop ad-hoc network topology changes in terms of scene size, mobile nodes movement, number of connections among mobile nodes, and also the amount of data each mobile node transmits. To measure this, the basic methodology was defined to a set of traffic and mobility communication patterns and applied to an ad hoc network. Different simulations were examined by changing the parameters for mobile nodes movement scenarios and their connection patterns. Increasing the number of connections among fixed number of nodes enhanced the routing overhead and the packet delivery rate. Increasing the transmission rate in an ad hoc network with fixed size and number of mobile node increased the number of transmitted packets in different groups (Sent, Received, Dropped and Forwarded). (Kumar *et al.,2008*), (Chan and Leung, 1988), revealed that despite the popularity of the most common routing protocols such as AODV, DSDV, DSR and OLSR, research efforts had not focussed much in evaluating their performance when applied to variable bit rate (VBR).

One of the major worries of Mobile ad hoc and Vehicular ad hoc networks is about their traffic and mobility models. Traffic and mobility models designed for Mobile Ad Hoc Networks (MANET) needs to be experimented on VANET to evaluate its performance in vehicular scenarios. However, conducting real experiments on roads for VANET network are dangerous and expensive. A real experiment might require the need to rent many vehicles (cars, Lorries, trucks, vans and so on), purchase communication gadgets and employ experimenters. At times, vehicles need to move on a high speed scenario which poses a possible danger such as collisions with other vehicles and even pedestrians. For this reason simulation model is used to carry out the research.

SIMULATION PARAMETERS

We start out by giving the detailed about the simulation model and environment which are presented in the rest of this section. In order to evaluate the performance of different traffic models (CBR, VBR and TCP on MANET and VANET networks, simulations were carried out using Ns-2 simulator [Online]. The topology consists of 1000 X 1000 meters with 50 mobiles nodes and 50 vehicles moving around using the random way point mobility model. Constant bit rate, Variable bit rate as well as Transmission Control Protocol agents were used for generating traffic in the network. Each simulation scenario was repeated six (6) times for over a period of 500 seconds real time, which enabled the simulations to converge for accurate result. The basic parameters used for the simulations are summarized in Table 1.

SIMULATION RESULTS

In this section, we present simulation results for the performance analysis of (CBR, VBR and TCP) on MANET and VANET networks. Figures 1 and 2 shows the end to end delay against throughput of receiving information bits in a vehicular network. This illustrates what happens to vehicle's delay in motion as the throughput of receiving information is being received. At the beginning of the route discovery, the network with VBR traffic model experienced an average delay of 0.11 seconds as compared to 5.0×10^{-3} seconds delay with CBR traffic model. When the route is discovered, the throughput broadcasted increases to 2.5×10^5 bits for VBR (see Figure 1) and 1.0×10^4 bits for CBR traffic model (see Figure 2) and the delay fell drastically to 0.01 and 0.001 seconds respectively. When VBR generated data traffic of 5.0×10^5 bits was received, there was a broken link and an alternative route needs to be taken. Instead of starting all the process afresh, the route had to re-initiate another route discovery process in which a delay was triggered to about 0.1 second. This shows that, as throughput of receiving bits of CBR generated traffic increases, the vehicles nodes stabilises and the delay tends to drop at interval.

Figures 3 and 4 shows CBR and TCP's traffic models performance on MANET network. From the figures it has been observed that at low mobility, CBR performed better than TCP with high throughputs of receiving packets and less end-to-end delay of 0.19 seconds compared to 0.41 seconds of TCP. The rise in the delay is due to the initial routing discovery process of the DSR routing protocol.

Due to the fact that, the network topology/location changes rapidly and unpredictably,TCP traffic model was unable to withstand the stress, which leads to route failure and consequently packets drop. It therefore, considers the failure to be a sign of network congestion and immediately applies congestion control mechanism, which increases the end–to-end delay exponentially and decreasing the throughput of receiveing bits as compared to CBR traffic model performance in the network (See Figures 3 and 4).

Table 1. Simulation parameters

Simulation Parameters	
Parameters	**Values**
Network Simulator	NS2-2.29.2
Ad Hoc Routing Protocol	DSR
Simulation Area	1000 x 1000 metres
Simulation Time	500 seconds
Number of vehicles	50
Number of Mobile nodes	50
Number of trials	6
Speed (VANET)	70 miles per hour
Speed (MANET)	0-20 meter per second
Node Placement	Random way point
Traffic Model	CBR,VBR, TCP
Mac Protocol	IEEE 802.11
Propagation Model	Two-ray Ground reflection model
Packet Size	532 bytes
Channel Type	Wireless Channel
Antenna Model	Omni directional

Figure 1. (VBR) end to end delay vs. throughput of receiving bits

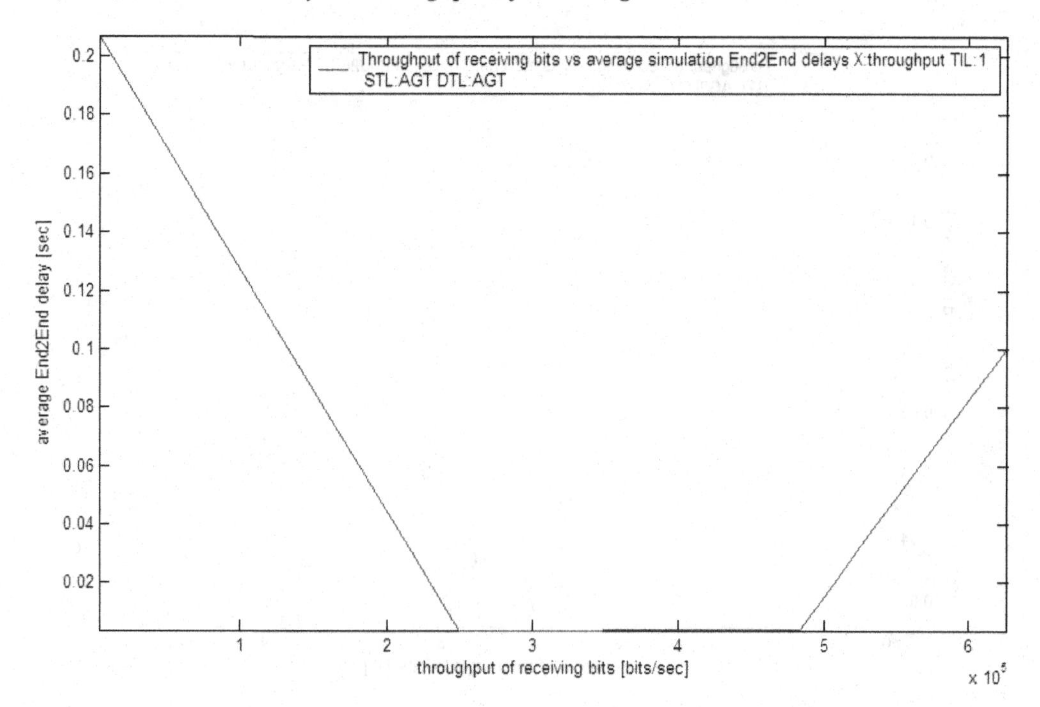

Figure 2. (CBR) end to end delay vs. throughput of receiving bits

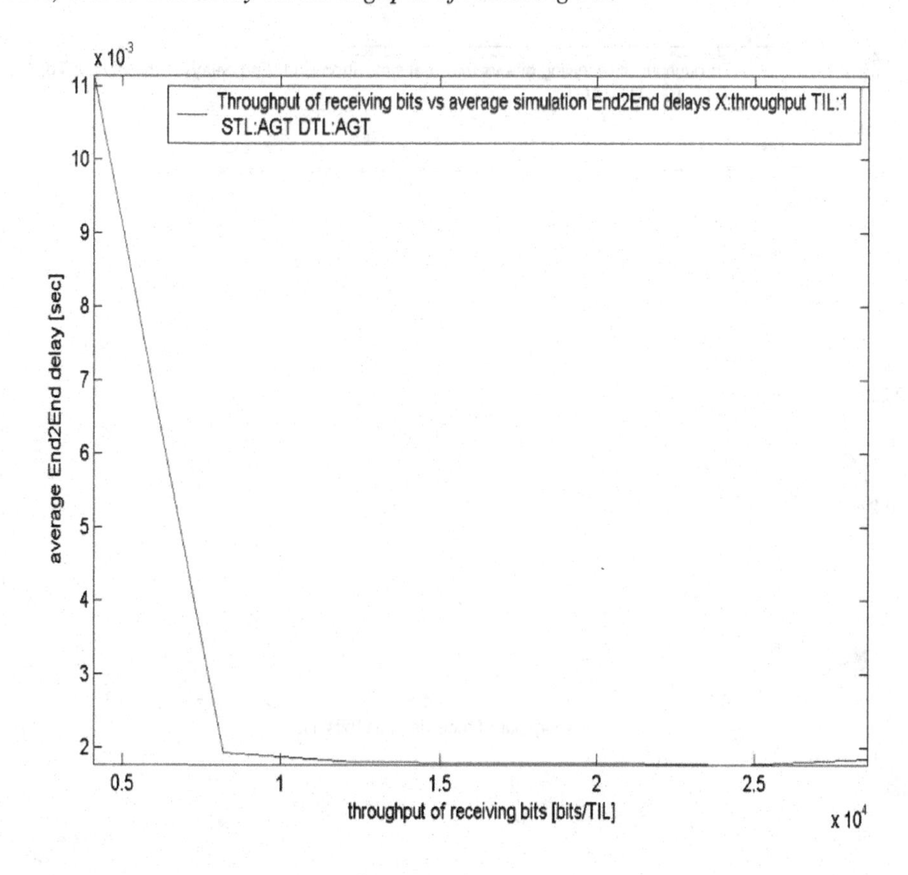

Figure 3. (CBR) end to end delay vs. throughput of receiving bits

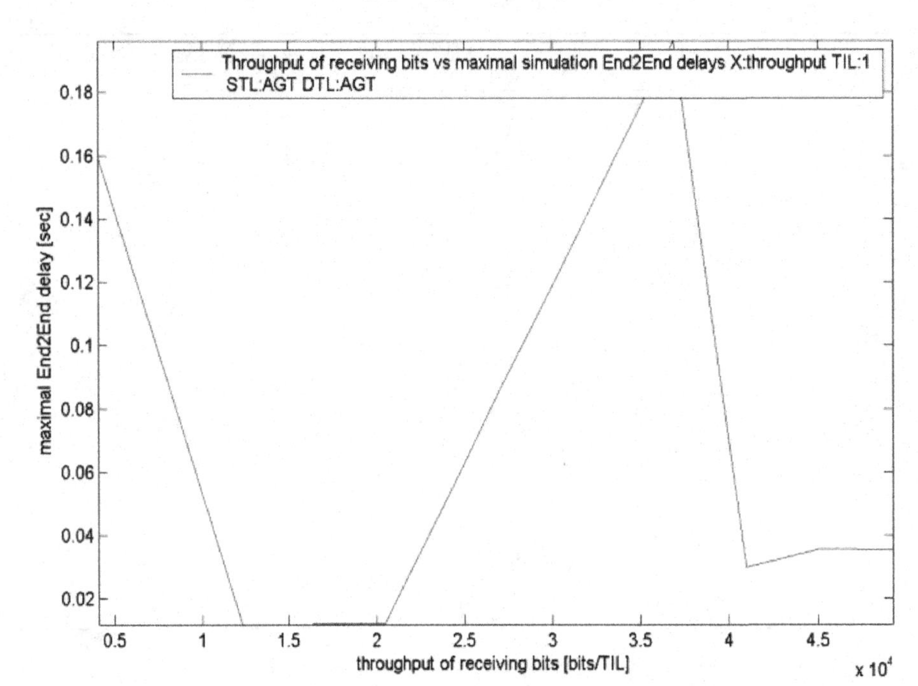

Figure 4. (TCP) end to end delay vs. throughput of receiving bits

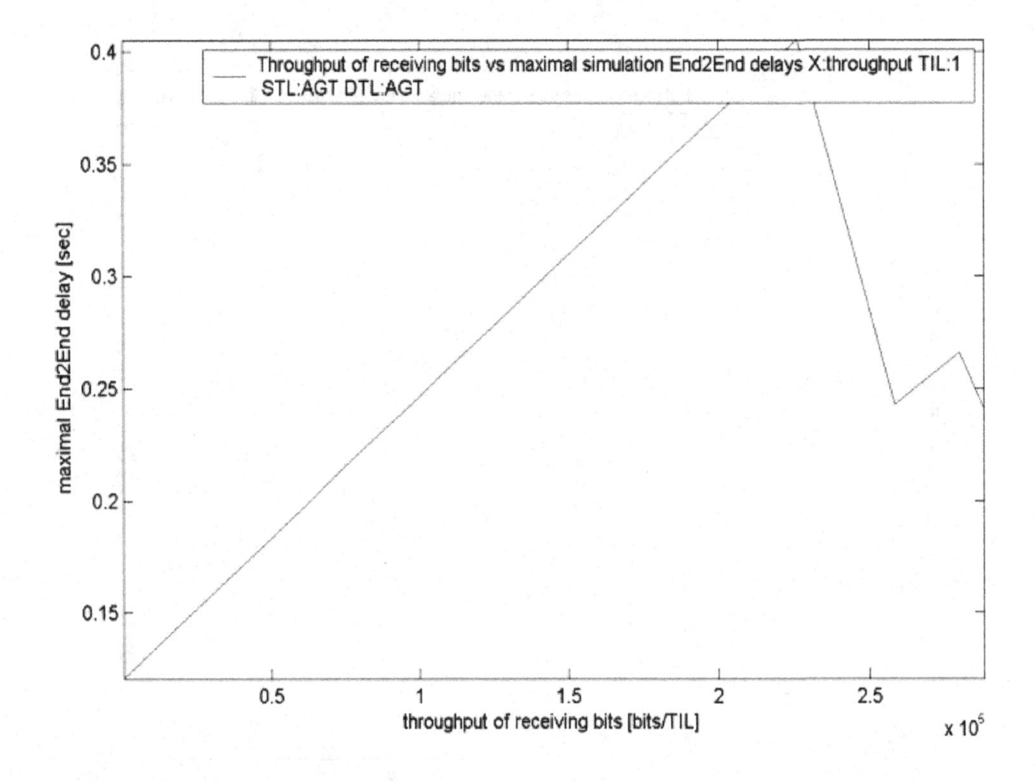

But there is considerable good response of DSR routing protocol to link failure at both low mobility before the TCP's congestion mechanism responds, and packets were successfully delivered while packets lost is due to increased in end-to-end delay, time-to- live (TTL) of routing protocol expiration and end of simulation time. Also, the simulation results revealed that, TCP traffic model can perform better in smaller networks, where unpredicted topology/location changes are less.

CONCLUSION

Based on the traffic and mobility models used, simulation results revealed that CBR, VBR performed better than TCP at low and high mobility with high throughput of receiving bits, less end-to-end delay and less packets dropped. DSR routing protocol was able to respond quickly to link failure which avoids TCP's congestion control algorithm response at low mobility. It is believed that most packets dropped are due to high end-to-end delay, Time-To-Live (TTL) expiration of the routing protocol and end of simulation time.

FUTURE RESEARCH

Future work should compare other ad hoc on demand routing protocols such as AODV and TORA, in order to analyse how effective and efficient these protocols are in response to TCP's weaknesses on MANET and VANET networks.

REFERENCES

Abdullah, A., Ramly, M., & Derhman. (2008). Performance comparison study of routing protocols for mobile grid environment. *IJCSNS International Journal of Computer science and Network security, 8*(2).

Anisur, R. Islam, & Talevski. (2009). Performance measurement of various routing protocols in ad hoc network. In *Proceeding of the International Multi-Conference of Engineers and Computer Scientists.* Hong Kong: MECS.

Arun-Kumar B. R., Lokanatha, C., Reddy, Prakash, S., & Hiremath. (2008). Performance comparison of wireless mobile ad hoc network routing protocols. *IJCSNS International Journal of Computer Science and Network Security, 8*(6).

Bakalis & Bello. (2010). Performance evaluation of CBR and TCP traffic models on MANET using DSR routing protocol. In *Proceedings of IEEE 2010 International Conference on Communications and Mobile Computing*. Shenzhen, China: IEEE.

Broch, Maltz, Johnson, Hu, & Jetcheva. (1998). *A performance comparison of multi-hop wireless ad hoc network routing protocols.* Pittsburgh, PA: Computer Science Department, Carnegie Mellon University.

Chan, H. C. B., & Leung, V. C. M. (1998). *A dynamic reservation protocol for integrating CBR/VBR/ABR traffic over IEEE 802.14 HFC networks*. Vancouver, Canada: The University of British Columbia. doi:10.1109/GLOCOM.1998.776644.

Garoui, V. (2005). *Analysis of network traffic in ad-hoc networks based on DSDV protocol with emphasis on mobility and communication patterns.* Paper presented at the first IEEE and IFIP International Conference in Central Asia. New Delhi, India.

John Wiley and Sons, Inc. (2009). *Algorithms and protocols for wireless and mobile ad hoc networks*. New York: John Wiley & Sons, Inc..

Kumar, A. B. R., Reddy, L. C., & Hiremth, P. S. (2008). Performance comparison of wireless mobile ad-hoc network routing protocols. *International Journal of Computer Science and Network Security, 8*(6), 337–343.

Qasim, Said, & Aghvami. (2009). Mobile ad hoc networking protocols evaluation through simulation for quality of service. *IAENG International Journal of Computer Science, 36*(1), 10.

Rajagopalan & Shen. (2006). What does using TCP as an evaluation tool reveal about MANET routing protocols. In *Proceeding of the 2006 International Conference on Wireless Communications and Mobile Computing*. Newark, DE: University of Delaware.

Raju, Jitendranath, & Mungara. (2010). Performance evaluation of ZRP over AODV and DSR in mobile ad hoc networks using qualnet. *European Journal of Scientific Research, 45*, 658–674.

Sesay, Yang, Qi, & He. (2004). Simulation comparison of four wireless ad hoc routing protocols. *Information Technology Journal,* 219-226.

The Network Simulator. (n.d.). *NS-2*. Retrieved from http://www.isi.edu/nsnam/ns/ns-build.html#allinone

Triantafyllidou & Al Agha. (2007). *Evaluation of TCP performance in MANETs using an optimized scalable simulation model.* Paper presented at International Conference of Modeling, Analysis, and Simulation of Computer and Telecommunication Systems. Istanbul, Turkey.

ADDITIONAL READING

Boukerche. (2004). Performance evaluation of routing protocols for ad hoc wireless networks. *Mobile Networks and Applications, 9*, 333–342.

Boukerche. (Ed.). (2009). *Algorithm and protocols for wireless and mobile ad hoc networks.* New York: John Wiley & Sons, Inc.

Chisalita & Shahmehri. (2004). Vehicular communication- A candidate technology for traffic safety. *Proceeding of IEEE International Conference on Systems, Man and, Cybernetics, 4*, 3903-3908.

Holland & Vaidya. (1999). Analysis of TCP performance over mobile ad hoc networks. In *Proceedings of ACM/IEEE MobiCom,* (pp. 219-230). ACM/IEEE.

Kopparty, K. Faloutsos, & Tripathi. (2002). Split TCP for mobile ad hoc networks. In *Proceedings of IEEE GLOBECOM,* (pp. 138-142). IEEE.

Lochert, H., & Tian, F. Hermann, & Mauve. (2003). A routing strategy for vehicular ad hoc networks in city environments. In *Proceedings of IEEE Intelligent Vehicles Symposium.* IEEE Press.

Pucha, Das, & Hu. (2004). The performance impact of traffic pattern on routing protocols in mobile ad hoc networks. In *Proceedings of MSWiM.* Venezia, Italy: MSWiM.

Usop, Abdullah, Faisal, & Abididn. (2009). Performance evaluation of aodv, dsdv, and dsr routing protocol in grid environment. *International Journal of Computer Science and Network Security, 19*(7).

Walton. (1991). The heavy vehicle electronic license plate program and crescent demonstration project. *IEEE Transactions on Vehicular Technology,* 147-151

Wang. (2005). The effect of wireless transmission range on path lifetime in vehicle formed mobile ad hoc networks on highways. In *Proceedings of the IEEE International Conference on Communications,* (pp. 3177-3181). IEEE.

Wenkelmann. (2003). Fleetnet-applications for inter-vehicle communication. In *Proceedings of the IEEE intelligent Vehicles Symposium,* (pp. 162-167). IEEE.

Xu & Sadawi. (2002). Performance evaluation of TCP algorithm in multi-hop wireless packet networks. *Wireless Communications and Mobile Computing*, 85-100.

KEY TERMS AND DEFINITIONS

CBR, VBR, and TCP: These are traffic mobility models used for the purpose of measuring the rate at which the encoding of the data takes place.

DSR: This is an ad hoc routing protocol used for routing data/packets from one node to another.

End-to-End Delay: The time (in seconds) taken for packets in bits to be transmitted across the network from one end-to-another.

MANET: A short term communication between mobile devices without using network infrastructure such as router or access point.

Throughput: This represents the total number of successful packets in (bits/sec) received at destination from all nodes in the network over a period of network simulation time.

VANET: Self-organizing communities of wheeled mobile units consisting of large number of vehicles and a small number of fixed infrastructure nodes such as roadside access units within radio communication range to each other.

Chapter 15
Modeling of Quantum Key Distribution System for Secure Information Transfer

K. E. Rumyantsev
Taganrog Institute of Technology, Russia

D. M. Golubchikov
Southern Federal University, Russia

ABSTRACT

This chapter is an analysis of commercial quantum key distribution systems. Upon analysis, the generalized structure of QKDS with phase coding of a photon state is presented. The structure includes modules that immediately participate in the task of distribution and processing of quantum states. Phases of key sequence productions are studied. Expressions that allow the estimation of physical characteristics of optoelectronic components, as well as information processing algorithms impact to rate of key sequence production, are formed. Information security infrastructure can be utilized, for instance, to formulate requirements to maximize tolerable error level in quantum channel with a given rate of key sequence production.

1. QUANTUM KEY DISTRIBUTION

Quantum Cryptography (QC) is a part of quantum computing that examines the methods of information security by using a quantum carrier (Kilin, Nizovtsev, & Horoshko, 2007; Scarani, 2006; Bouwmeester, Ekert, & Zeilinger, 2000; Gisin, Ribordy, Tittel, & Zbinden, 2002; Rumyantsev, 2010). QC proposes a new method of generating random private keys for quantum communication line users. Its privacy and eavesdropping protection is based upon quantum principles instead of Classical Cryptography (CC) methods (Kotenko, & Rumiantsev, 2009; Mao, 2003; Smart, 2004; Singh, 2000; Brassard, 2007) used now and based upon mathematical law, which can be cracked.

Quantum key distribution (QKD) is a technology based upon quantum principles for generation random bit strings, which could be used as privacy keys, between two remote users.

The hardware is the realization of the process of sending and receiving data, for example, a single photon used in a fiber link. An eavesdropping changes the influential parameters of the physical objects, which used as data carrier.

DOI: 10.4018/978-1-4666-2208-1.ch015

QC is permitted to generate random keys for two users, which has no shared confidential data initially, and that key will be unknown for eavesdroppers.

The quantum physics law starts influence when data transmission uses signals containing average photon number less than 0.1 instead of the signals containing many thousands of photon. The nature of QC privacy is based on this law in conjunction with CC procedures. One of these laws is Heisenberg's uncertainty principle, and in accordance with it, a trial measurement of a quantum state changes to an initial state

The main gain of QC is that eavesdropping will be known to legal users, besides of absolute privacy.

Indivisible quantum and entanglement are very specific features of quantum physics (Kilin, Nizovtsev, & Horoshko, 2007; Scarani, 2006; Bouwmeester, Ekert, & Zeilinger, 2000; Gisin, Ribordy, Tittel, & Zbinden, 2002). QC uses both of these features.

The necessity in symmetric encryption systems arises in process of data transmission for reducing economic and social risks.

1.1. Symmetric Ciphers Require a Single Key to Encrypt and Decrypt

The quantum channel and open data link for checking of eavesdropping are the main components of QKD. The quantum channel and open data link connect legal users. The term of quantum channel mean that data carrier is a quantum in it.

QKD starts from transmission quantum between legal users. A matching of keys is realized through open data link. The eavesdropper has access to open data link, but it could not change information in it.

The sender encode the message into bit string (a_m is binary number) by using a random key a_k in symmetric encryption systems. Each bit of message add to same bit of key to make ciphertext as $a_t = a_m \oplus a_k$. Here $\oplus$ is congruence addition by 2 without carry (XOR). A receiver decode ciphertext by subtract key from it as $a_t - a_k = a_m \oplus a_k - a_k = a_m$. The bits of the ciphertext are random as the bits of the keys, so they are not contain any information. That cryptosystems are secure in accordance with information theory.

The system is secure absolutely on condition that the sender Alice and receiver Bob have shared private key, which has the same length as the message, and the key is used only once for encode.

The eavesdropper Eva can record all ciphertexts in order to create an image of plaintexts and the key if the key is used more than once.

If Eva has two ciphertexts a_{t1} and a_{t2} which encoded by single key a_k then she could add both ciphertexts and get a sum of plaintexts:

$$a_{t1} \oplus a_{t2} = a_{m1} \oplus a_k \oplus a_{m2} \oplus a_k$$
$$= a_{m1} \oplus a_{m2} \oplus a_k \oplus a_k = a_{m1} \oplus a_{m2}.$$

The symmetric encryption systems *require for all users shared private key which* has the same length as the message and can be used only once.

The main idea of QC is trusted key distribution between users never met each other.

QC proposes a perspective way based on physical principles to solve the key distribution problem.

Statement 1: An unknown quantum state could not be cloned.

Statement 2: Information from the nonorthogonal quantum states could not be obtained without distortion it.

Statement 3: Any measurement performed by an eavesdropper leads to changes quantum state of data carrier.

Hardware-software solution for confidential data transmission with QKD system and synchronizing system is shown of Figure 1.

Figure 1. The structure of hardware-software complex for confidential data transmission

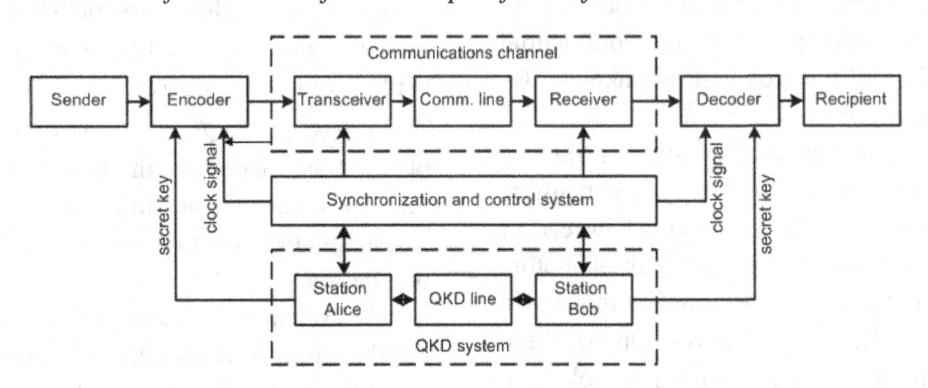

On Figure 1 data source generate digital signals correspond to specified type of telecommunication data. The encoder realizes the signal characteristics encode process for protection against eavesdropping. The communications channel consists of transceiver, receiver and communication link, which used for transmission encrypted data. The communications channel creates the route of data transfer from sender to recipient (Kotenko, & Rumiantsev, 2009).

In a symmetric cryptosystem sender and recipient of data using the same secret key, which requires periodic updating. The complex (Figure 1) uses the QKD system, which consists of two stations, called Alice and Bob, to perform the function of key updating.

Stations have control inputs and outputs for synchronizing its operation, monitoring QKD system parameters and control the communication channel.

Generation of secret keys is implemented through the communication line, where the single photons transmitted. QKD systems use three types of coding of quantum states: the polarization encoding, phase encoding, and encoding by time shifts. QKD line can be a free space or an Optical Fiber (OF). Commercial QKD systems using fiber-optic communication lines (FOL).

Each station generates shared secret keys and distributes it between the legitimate users. These keys use for encryption data of sender and decryption data for the recipient.

Synchronization system provides synchronization of spatially separated transmitter and receiver in the communication channel, Alice and Bob stations in the QKD (Quantum Key Distribution). system, as well as the encoder and decoder. The accuracy of the arrival of the synchronization signals is lie within the range of tens of picoseconds, and strongly influences the overall system performance. The control system and synchronization software generates control commands.

2. COMMERCIAL QKD SYSTEMS WITH THE PHASE CODING OF STATES OF PHOTONS

The first commercial system of quantum cryptography was presented at the CeBIT-2002 exhibition, where engineers of GAP-Optique from the University of Geneva presented a system of QKD Scientists create a compact and reliable system, which was located in two cases, and could work without any setup immediately after connecting to a PC. It was used for key distribution through atmospheric and fiber-optic link between the cities of Geneva and Lausanne, the distance between which is 67 km (Stucki, Gisin, Guinnard, Ribordy, & Zbinden, 2002). The infrared laser with a wavelength of 1550 nm was source photons in it. Data transfer rate was low, because the high speed is not required for transmission keys with length from 27.9 up to 117.6 kilobits.

There are only three companies that enter the market with commercial QKD systems.

One of the earliest systems named id 500 Clavis (later version named id 3000 Clavis) began offering Swiss company id Quantique (Id Quantique SA, 2005). The system consists of two stations, operated by one or two external computer. The id 3000 Clavis software ensures quantum key distribution in automatic mode. The system supports two quantum cryptographic protocols BB84 and SARG04. The system generates the secret keys through the quantum line extending some 100 km. The system uses a built-in protocol sifting key and encryption protocol and file transfer. Generation rate of keys is up to 1500 bps.

Later, the id Quantique company released improved system id 3100 Clavis2 (Id Quantique SA, 2008) and the id 5000 Vectis (Id Quantique SA, 2005).

Manufacturers seek to develop integrated systems. For example, the system Vectis (2005) from the id Quantique company encrypts the data on the link layer using a cipher AES (Advanced Encryption Standard, 2001). The key can have a length of 128, 196 or 256 bits, and change with frequency up to 100 Hz. The maximum range of key transmission is 100 km (Id Quantique SA, 2005).

Company MagiQ Technologies (USA) offers a system QPN 5505 (2003), QPN 7505 (2005), and the QPN 8505 (2009).

The Quintessence Labs Pty Ltd (Australia) company enters the market in 2009 and joins to two other companies. It also offers QKD systems for fiber-optic lines (Pauli, 2009). This system is housed in a rack-mounted case which is generally used in the network infrastructure.

Now government organizations and corporations with high security requirements use the commercial QKD system. Id Quantique reports of the implementation of QKD system into the banking sector (Id Quantique, 2011). Reducing the price of QKD systems can make quantum cryptography accessible to a large number of organizations. It is expected that quantum cryptography could become the de facto standard for inter-bank communications in a few years.

Commercial QKD systems transmit data through fiber-optic communication lines and encode information about the key bits in the phase states of photons. This is due to the fact that the instability of the polarization state greatly complicates the use of a polarization coding of states of the photon.

The idea of phase coding of states of photons was first mentioned C. Bennett (1992). Figure 2 illustrates the principle of phase coding of states of a photon using the interferometer.

Figure 2. Implementation of BB84 protocol with phase coding of states of a photon

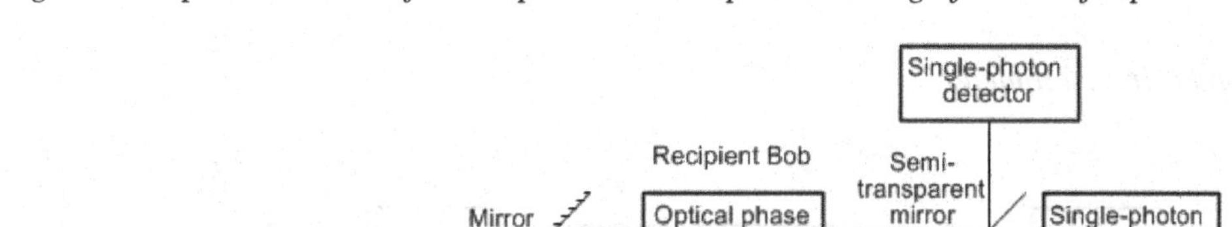

Transmitter and receiver create a system based on Mach-Zehnder interferometer to realize the BB84 protocol. The sender sets the angles of phase shift corresponding to the logical zero ($\Phi_A = 0$ or $\Phi_A = \pi/2$) and to the logical one ($\Phi_A = \pi$ or $\Phi_A = 3\pi/2$). The receiver sets its phase shifts for the equivalent vertical basis ($\Phi_B = 0$) and equivalent to the diagonal basis ($\Phi_B = \pi/2$).

In this context, *the phase shift of 2π using an optical phase modulator corresponds to the change in path length for one step of wavelength.*

The photons behave as particles in to photo-detection process, but they propagate as waves. The probability that a photon sent by the sender will be detection by the recipient, is

$$P_D = \cos^2\left(\frac{\Phi_A - \Phi_Б}{2}\right)$$

and determined by the interference of waves propagating along the two arms of Mach-Zehnder interferometer.

Detection probability will vary from 1 (for zero phase difference) to zero. Here it is assumed that the optical phase modulators sender Alice and receiver Bob use the phase shifts (Φ_A, Φ_B) = (0, $3\pi/2$) for zero bits and (Φ_A, Φ_B) = ($\pi/2$, π) for a single bit.

Preparing the quantum states and their analysis is realized in the interferometer, which can be implemented on single-mode fiber optic elements. Figure 3 shows a fiber-optic implementation of the Mach-Zehnder interferometer.

The interferometer consists of a fiber coupler (FC) Y-type, two fiber-optic phase modulators (PM) and FC X-type. In each arm of the interferometer includes one PM. Single-photon optical radiation can introduced into the interferometer and it will registered at the outputs of 3 and 4 FC X-type.

If the coherence length of single-photon source (SS) is greater than the difference between the lengths of the interferometer arms, then you can get an interference pattern.

In FC Y-type and FC X-type phase shift is *π/2 in each.* Because of the PM actions (Φ_A and Φ_B) and the difference between the lengths of arms in *ΔL*, the average number of photons during the observation period τ_{observ} at the input of the first single-photon avalanche detector (SPAD) is defined by

$$\overline{N}_{SPAD} = \overline{N}_{LS} \cdot \cos^2\left(\frac{\Phi_A - \Phi_B + k\Delta L}{2}\right)$$

where k is a wave number, and $\overline{N}_{LS}$ is the average number of photons SS during the observation period. Note that the first SPAD detects photons corresponding to the zero bits.

If the phase difference is $2n\pi$ (n is an integer), then destructive interference is on the input of the first SPAD which registering zero bits. Therefore, the number of photons detected by the first SPAD reaches a minimum value. Ideally, the second SPAD register all photons.

Figure 3. Mach-Zehnder interferometer

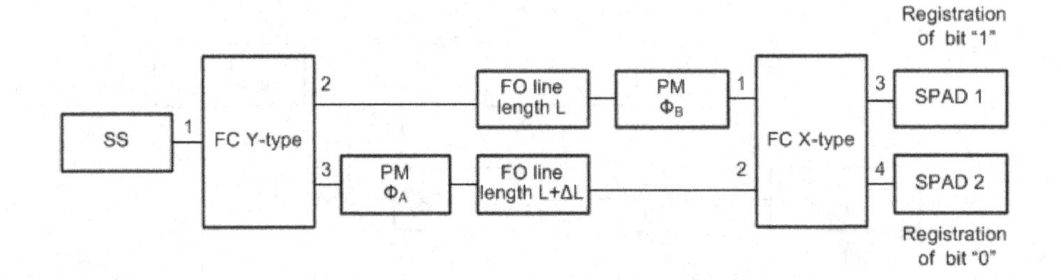

When the phase difference is $\pi + 2n\pi$, the situation is opposite. The destructive interference is at the input of the second SPAD, while the average number of photons at the input of the first SPAD reaches a maximum. The optical radiation can be detected at the inputs of both SPAD in case of errors of SPAD.

Mach-Zehnder interferometer with single-photon source and the two SPAD can be used in quantum cryptography (see Figure 4). Station Alice in this case should consist the optical transmitting module (OTM) based on laser diode, fiber optic attenuator (VOA), FC Y-type and the first PM. Optical pulse of OTM through the VOA send to the port 1 FC Y-type as an single photons (Golubchikov, & Rumiantsev, 2008).

It should be noted that it is extremely important is to maintain a constant and small difference between the lengths of the interferometer arms to get a stable interference.

Bob station consists of the second PM, FC X-type and two photon counters based on SPAD.

We consider the using BB84 protocol with four states in such scheme. Station Alice through the first PM implement one of the four phase shifts (0, $\pi/2$, π, $3\pi/2$). The bit value 0 corresponds to the phase shift of 0 and $\pi/2$, the bit value 1 corresponds shift of π and $3\pi/2$. The Bob station through the second PM makes the choice of basis in random order, by shifting the phase by 0 or $\pi/2$. The photon which came to the first photon counter is assigned the 0 value of bit., & the photon which came to the second counter corresponds to 1 value of bit

When the phase difference equal to 0 or π, then the stations Alice and Bob use compatible bases and obtain definite results. In such cases, the station Alice can determine which of the SPAD of the Bob stations gets a photon, and hence, it can determine the value of the bit. For its part, the Bob station can determine which phase shift is selected by Alice station. In the case where the phase difference takes values $\pi/2$ or $3\pi/2$, the stations use incompatible bases, so the photon will be detected on random SPAD of Bob station.

All possible combinations of phase shifts in BB84 protocol with four states listed in Table 1.

Note that the system is extremely important to maintain a stable difference in the lengths of the interferometer arms pending the all key distribution session. This difference shouldn`t change more than a fraction of the emission wavelength. Changes in the one arm length may lead to a phase drift and to the errors in the key in the result. This scheme works well in laboratory conditions, but

Figure 4. Quantum system with a Mach-Zehnder interferometer

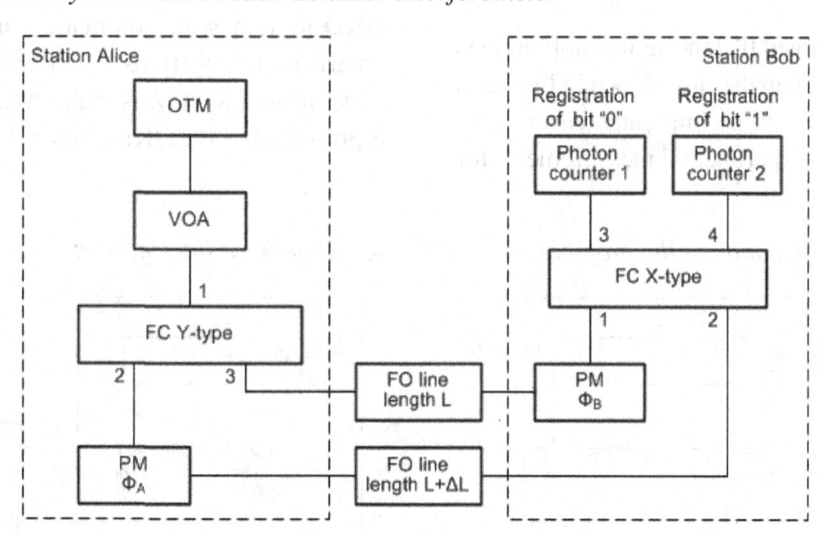

Table 1. BB84 protocol with phase coding of states of photons

Alice Station		Bob Station		
Bit Value	Phase Shift Φ_A	Phase Shift Φ_B	Phase Difference $\Phi_A - \Phi_B$	Bit Value
0	0	0	0	0
0	0	$\pi/2$	$3\pi/2$	underdeterminable
1	π	0	π	1
1	π	$\pi/2$	$\pi/2$	underdeterminable
0	$\pi/2$	0	$\pi/2$	underdeterminable
0	$\pi/2$	$\pi/2$	0	0
1	$3\pi/2$	0	$3\pi/2$	underdeterminable
1	$3\pi/2$	$\pi/2$	π	1

in practice not possible to maintain the lengths of the arms when users are separated from each other by more than a few meters.

In (Bennett, 1992) showed how to solve this problem by using two unbalanced Mach-Zehnder interferometer connecting by FOL (Figure 5).

In this scenario, the sender and recipient have identical unbalanced Mach-Zehnder interferometers. The phase difference between long and short arms should be much longer than the coherence length of the light source. For this reason, the interference in unbalanced interferometer does not occur. But it occurs at the interferometer output of receiver. The probability that the amplitude of the photonic pulses will interfere is equal $P_D = 0,25 \times \left[1 + \cos\left(\Phi_A - \Phi_Б\right)\right]$

It should be noted that the signal amplitude is two times less than in the case shown in Figure 2.

Signal splitter can be implemented in fiber-optic link as FC. Experimental measurements for 14 km FOL shown the effectiveness of the key bits generation at the level of 0,22% with bit error probability (BER) of about 1.2%.

The commercial QKD systems use more complicated coding scheme of the phase states of photons, which includes distributed interferometer with passive mode automatic compensation of polarization distortions (Ribordy, Gautier, Gisin, Guinnard, & Zbinden, 2000). Distortion compensation is required to observe a clear interference pattern of single photons on the SPAD input.

3. STRUCTURE OF COMMERCIAL QKD SYSTEMS

QKD system with automatic compensation of polarization distortions, which works on the principle of plug & play, is the only technology that is presented on the QKD market (Golubchikov, &

Figure 5. Implementation of the protocol on the B92 two unbalanced interferometers

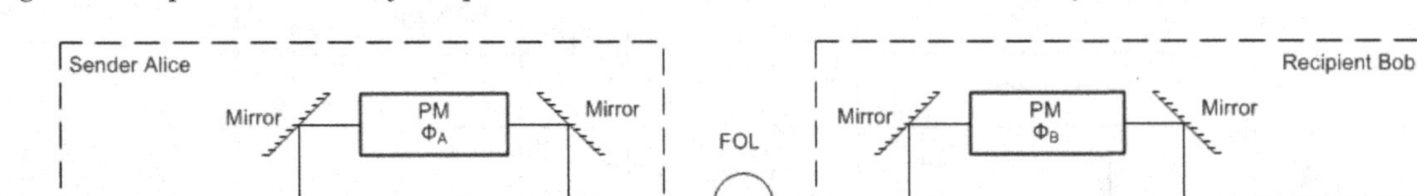

Rumiantsev, 2008). Key bits are encoded using the phase states of photons of two pulses that propagate from one station to another and backward.

The first system based on this principle, called id 500 Clavis, has been produced by id Quantique since 2003. The system consists of two stations located in two cases and a software package for their control (Id Quantique SA, 2005). The first station is a transceiver, codenamed QKDS-B or Bob. The second station QKDS-A, or Alice, is the coding and does not contain transceiver equipment.

Let the Bob station to Alice station propagate optical pulses, and from Alice station to Bob station propagate photonic pulses. The term of optical pulse means a laser pulse with the average number of photons $\mu >> 1$. The term of photonic pulse is a pulse containing a countable number of photons (in the QKD systems, as a rule, $\mu < 1$).

Let's perform an analysis of the structure of QKD system (Golubchikov, 2008) on a commercial system id 3000 Clavis manufactured by id Quantique company (Switzerland).

A Diagram of transceiving station Bob of id 3000 Clavis system is shown on Figure 6. It is purposed to generate optical pulses, receiving and processing the encoded quantum state of photons.

The station includes OTM, fiber optic circulator (FOC), two receiving optical module (ROM), FC X-type, FOL, PM and fiber-optic polarization coupler (FPC). Polarization-maintaining optical fiber (PMOF) connects these functional elements.

Station Alice of id 3000 Clavis system is shown in Figure 7. It is purposed to encode the phase states of photons. The coding station includes FC Y-type with a division factor of 1:9 from the port 1 to ports 2 and 3, respectively, two variable fiber-optic attenuators (VOA), FODL, PM, Faraday mirror and OF connecting all these elements.

A laser pulse with a wavelength of 1550 nm is emitted at the Bob station. It goes through FOC to FC X-type with a 50/50 division factor from port 1 to ports 2 and 3, respectively (see Figure 6). Thus. In the FC X-type laser pulse is split into two pulses.

The polarization of the optical pulse from port 3 FC X-type (first pulse) in the OF change its state to the orthogonal on the way to port 1 FPC.

Figure 6. Diagram of the transceiving station of id 3000 Clavis system

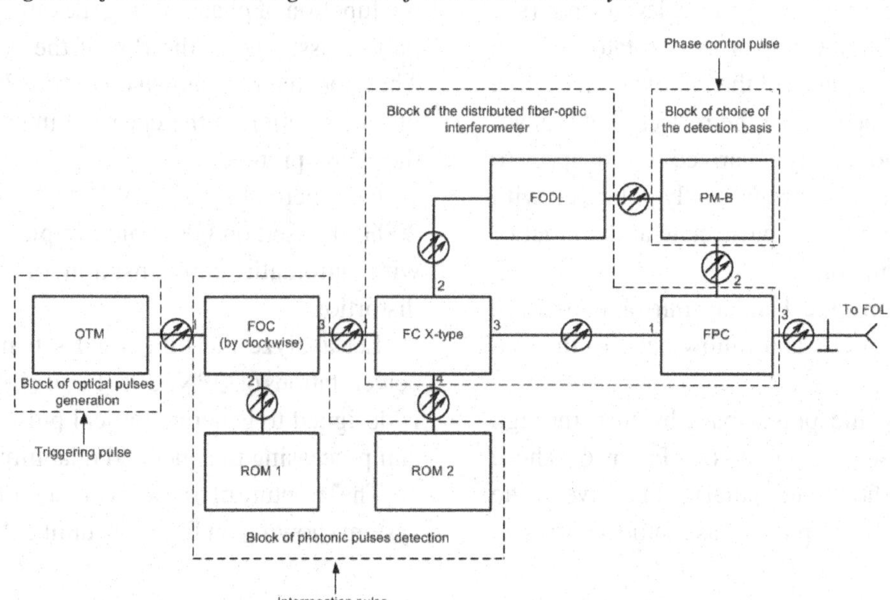

Figure 7. Diagram of the coding station of id 3000 Clavis system

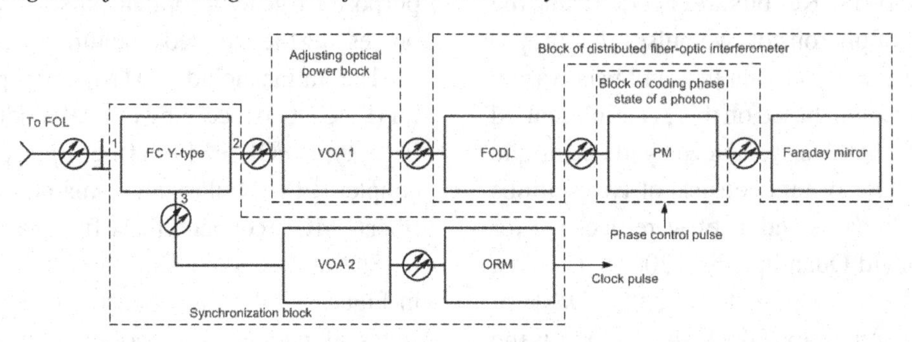

A laser pulse from port 2 FC X-type (second pulse) goes through FODL and PM to port 2 FPC. The second pulse is delayed on 50 ns relative to the first as a result of the propagation through two different optical paths.

Note that signals propagated in different arms of the interferometer are orthogonally polarized, which is due to the fact that the fast axis of PMOF in two arms are rotated by an angle of 90° to each other.

Fiber-optic polarization coupler is a passive element. Since the orthogonally polarized pulses from ports 1 and 2 FPC out to the port 3, then FPC represents the polarization multiplexer, which output is the output of transceiving station Bob.

Impulses are going to the station Alice via FOL and are reflected by Faraday mirror (see Figure 7). Faraday mirror is a rotator with a fixed angle of rotation of the polarization by 90°. The consequence is that the reflected pulses are not only orthogonally polarized with respect to each other, but also orthogonally polarized with respect to the primary pulse state at the input of the Faraday mirror.

Reflected by the Faraday mirror pulses are weakened by VOA and follow back to the station Bob.

Both photonic pulses pass by turn through FPC into transceiver stations (see Figure 6). These pulses are orthogonally polarized relative to the primary state. The pulses pass into the arms in which there are no the direct propagation. Here FPC works as a polarization demultiplexer.

Photonic pulses pass to FC X-type at the same time and interfere. Then the interference is detected on the first or second ROM.

Since both pulses pass the same optical path, such an interferometer automatically compensate of the polarization distortion.

To implement the BB84 protocol at the Alice station the second pulse is phase shifted by one of the randomly selected values of the series 0, $\pi/2$, π, $3\pi/2$. At the Bob station chooses a basis of measurement by the phase shift of the first pulse at 0 or $\pi/2$ at the backward pulse propagation.

Note that in the station Bob combines the functions of the transmitter and receiver. However, the function of phase coding the quantum state of photon assigned to the PM of the Alice station. Thus, the diagram shown on Figure 7 is a scheme of Alice station in the classical interpretation of the BB84 protocol.

Commercial system QPN 5505 presented in 2003. It based on QKD plug & play technology with automatic compensation of polarization distortion.

Let analyze the functional scheme of transceiver stations of QPN 5505 (Figure 8). The station is designed to generate optical pulses, receiving and processing the encoded quantum states.

The structure of transceiving station QPN 5505 system showing on Figure 8, unlike the system id

Figure 8. Diagram of optical transmitter-receiver station system QPN 5505

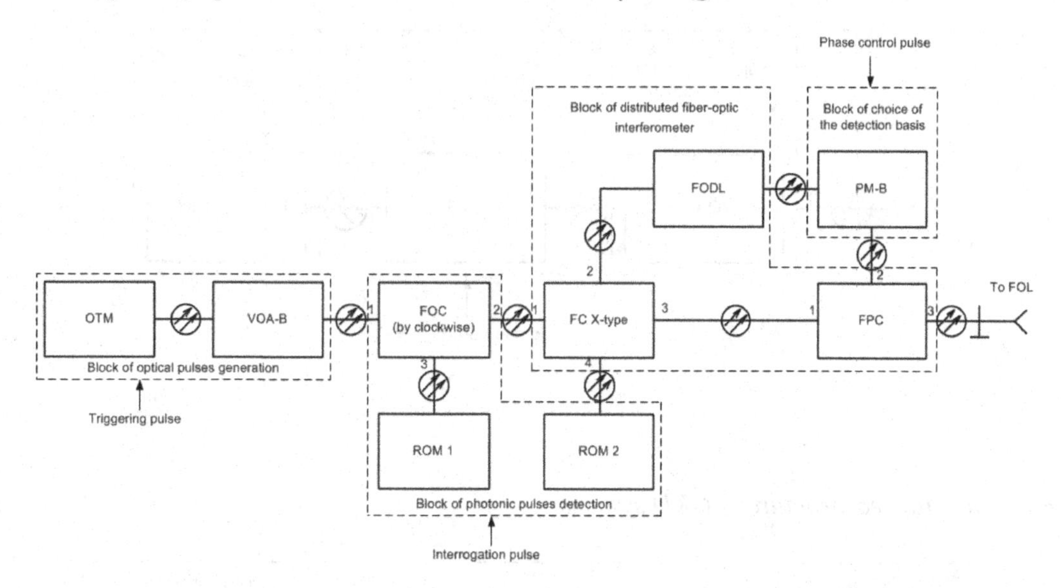

3000 Clavis, has VOA through which the OTM is connected to port 1 on FC. All blocks, as in the system id 3000 Clavis, connected by PMOF.

There are significant differences in the structure of the coding station of the QPN 5505 system (Figure 9) from the id 3100 Clavis system (Figure 7).

The coding station consists of an adjusting optical power block, block of coding phase state of a photon, and a block of distributed fiber-optic interferometer. All the blocks are interconnected by OF.

Due to the presence of features implemented in the coding station QPN 5505 system has not synchronization block. The system id 3100 Clavis used to synchronize optical pulses passing through FOL from Bob station to Alice station. In the QPN 5505 synchronization is ensured by an additional communication line and an additional transceiver module.

For the system id 3100 Clavis is necessary and sufficient one FOL, since clock line and the QKD link combined, but for the system QPN 5505 requires additional FOL for synchronization and data transfer.

4. GENERALIZED STRUCTURE OF QUANTUM KEY DISTRIBUTION SYSTEM WITH PHASE CODING OF PHOTONS STATES

The analysis of commercial systems id 3100 Clavis and QPN 5505 allowed to identify common structural similarity solutions: the block of optical pulses generation, the block of the distributed fiber-optic interferometer, the block of choice of the detection basis, the block of photonic pulses detection, the block of power control, the block of coding states of the photon, and synchronization block.

We propose a generalized structure of the QKD system with phase coding of photons, which shown on Figure 10 and based on the analysis above.

Transceiving Bob station is designed to generate optical pulses, receiving and processing the encoded quantum states of photons.

The structure of transceiving stations consist OTM, VOA (VOA-B), FOC, two ROM (ROM-B1 and ROM-B2), FC X-type, FODL (FODL-B), the polarization rotator by 90°, PM (PM-B), fiber-optic polarizing multiplexer/demultiplexer (FPC). All blocks are interconnected by PMOF.

Figure 9. Diagram of the coding station of the QPN 5505 system

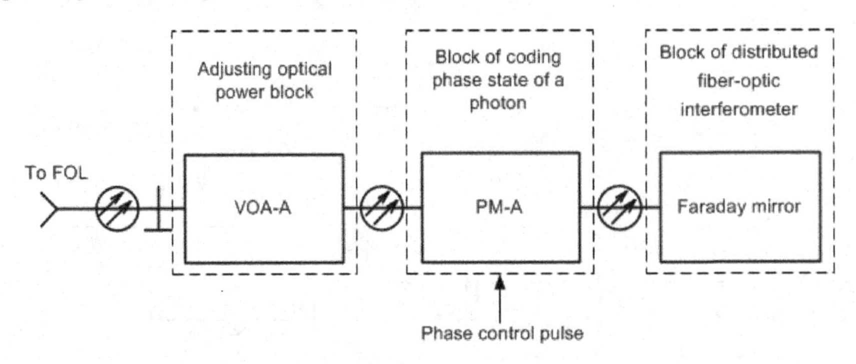

Figure 10. Generalized structure of QKD systems

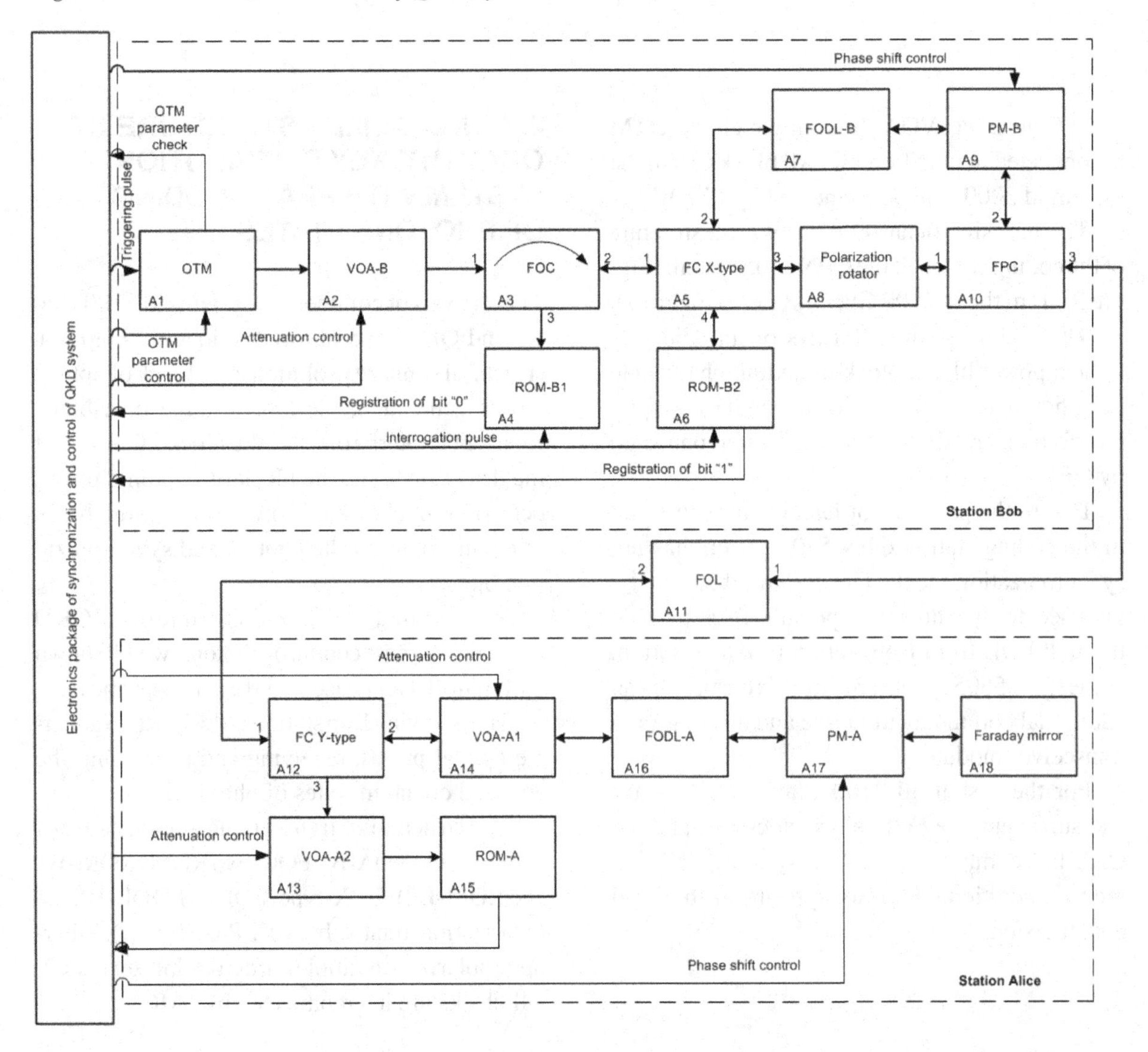

OTM includes a laser and is designed to generate coherent optical radiation with a wavelength of 1550 nm and a spectral width not exceeding 0.6 nm (optical output 2). The light source based on the principle of distributed feedback due to which it is possible to achieve a narrow spectral width. The small width of the spectrum permits to emit a signal with high temporal coherence, which can increase the transmission distance and reduce the effects of dispersion distortions. In the OTM can also be integrated photodiode for direct measurement of the laser power (output 1). Electronic control module can adjust the power of the source and the duration of the emitted laser pulses.

Electronically controlled VOA-B has a wide range of attenuation from 1.5 to 50 dB. Change the voltage onto the control input 2 of VOA-B may prevent interception of optical pulses and reduce the reflected from the Faraday mirror emission to the level of the photonic pulse.

FOC has three ports, each of which can be input and output. The principle of operation is based on the transfer of energy from port 1, which is in the circuit is connected to the OTM, to the nearest clockwise port 2 connected to the FC X-type. Transmission in the opposite direction from port 2 to port 1 is excluded due to the large attenuation of the radiation. However, the energy is transferred from port 2 to port 3. Fiber-optic circulator is a passive optical element and has no electrical control inputs.

ROM-B1 and ROM-B2 are designed to detect photonic pulses. The structure of the modules is complex and has many control inputs, which used for adjustment of the bias, dead time period, wait time period and others. The module includes SPAD, cooling device, gain controller and control device.

When working SPAD possibly causing an avalanche of electrons in the absence of a photon at the input. Such a process is defined as the dark current SPAD. The frequency of a dark count is characterized by the number of false count SPAD per time unit and has the dimension of hertz.

One of the important factors that influence the dark count rate is temperature of SPAD. In ROM photodiode temperature set by the user and continuously monitored using a thermistor. Peltier cooler is used for cooling SPAD. The drift of the temperature does not exceed 0.1°C. The temperature difference of 1°C has a significant impact on the frequency of dark count.

Gain controller designed to amplify the response of the detection of single-photon pulse by SPAD.

The control device is designed for analyzing the signals from the SPAD, temperature control, regulating the amplitude, duration and the filing of bias. In most schemes, the method of bias booster is used. This method keeps up the permanent bias voltage on the control input of SPAD, but at a level not enough to generate an avalanche. This scheme allows to reducing the time of transients at the moment of applying bias voltage required for the registration of single-photon pulse.

FC X-type is a passive element with 4 ports. With direct distribution of an optical pulse generated by OTM only pass to port 1 of FC X-type, where the energy is distributed equally on the two ports 2 and 3.

With the passage of the photonic signal from the Alice station was in the FC X-type came two waves and interfere with each other. Then the result of interference sent to one of two ports 1 and 4, respectively, leading to ROM-B1 or ROM-B2.

FODL-B is the segment PMIF and is intended to introduce a time delay between the signals coming from different optical interferometer arms.

PM-B is based on electro-optical crystal of lithium niobate. The principle of operation based on the Kerr effect. Modulator allows you to make a phase shift in the signal passing through the long arm in the reverse signal propagation. The range of phase shifts is from 0 to 2π.

Photonic signal from the Alice station at port 3 FPC, will be redirected to the opposite interferometer arm. This is because after the passage of

FOL the pulse changes its polarization orthogonal in the Faraday mirror of Alice station.

Signals that propagate in different arms of the interferometer are polarized orthogonally because the polarization rotator by 90° is used.

Optical pulses arriving at the two ports 1 and 2 of FPC are sent to port 3, which is the output of transceiving Bob station.

Alice encoding station in Figure 10 is designed to encode the phase states of photons. It consists of FC Y-type, two VOA (VOA-A1 and VOA-A2), FODL (FODL-A), PM (PM-A), ROM (ROM-A), Faraday mirror and OF linking all of the elements.

FC Y-type is intended to separate the energy of the optical signal. Pulse passing FOL, get to port 1 of FC Y-type, which is divided into two pulses with the energy ratio of 1:9.Two ports 2 and 3, respectively, pulses are sent to VOA-A1 and VOA-A2.

To ROM-A is sent 90% of the energy of the optical pulse receiving by the Alice station. The remaining 10% of the energy of input pulses is sent to the FODL-A input through the VOA-A1.

Electronically controlled VOA-A1 and VOA-A2 have attenuation band up to 50 dB. Changing the level of voltage onto the control input of VOA helps to prevent damage an optical components in case of trying to introduce high-power optical pulses (wide pulse attack), or in case if the attenuation of the pulse energy is too small because the FOL is too short, and as well as to reduce the reflected emission from the Faraday mirror to the level of the photonic signal.

At the Alice station ROM-A has two functions:

1. Synchronize the stations clock and mark the moment of arrival of the pulse for the subsequent issuance of electronic control signal to PM-A,
2. Monitoring of incoming signals level to detect an attacker in the channel.

FODL-A is OF line segment with length about 10...12 km and is intended to prevent false alarms of SPAD in ROM in consideration of Rayleigh backscattered radiation from the elements of encoding station established between port 2 FC Y-type and Faraday mirror.

PM-A apply a phase shift only for photons of the second pulse, which delayed to the first in the reverse signal propagation. Structurally PM-A is identical to the modulator used in the station Bob.

To implement the BB84 protocol the PM-A uses the following values of the phase shift:

1. Zero bit 0 is encoded in a linear basis, zero phase shift,
2. Single bit 1 in the linear basis is encoded by a phase shift of π,
3. Zero bit 0 is encoded in the diagonal basis of a phase shift of $\pi/2$,
4. Single bit 1 in diagonal basis is encoded phase shift of $3\pi/2$.

Faraday mirror is a rotator of polarization angle by 90°. Thus, the photon pulses in backward propagation will have orthogonal polarization relative to the pulses at the input Faraday mirror.

After reflection from the Faraday mirror the photon pulses via port 2 of FC Y-type coming in the opposite direction to the station Bob through the FOL.

Synchronization in a QPN 5505 is provided with an additional synchronization and monitoring block. That block in comparison with the QKD system is external, while mounted on a same case. In id 3000 Clavis id used to synchronize the optical pulses by direct spread from station to station, Bob Alice.

Designed the generalized structure of the QKD system with phase coding of photons includes all the blocks that have a direct influence on the propagation and processing of quantum states and are available in 4 commercial systems.

Excluding of the generalized structure QKD systems the FC Y-type, FODL-A, VOA-A2 and ROM-A, we get the structure of MagiQ QPN 5505. To obtain the structure of the system id 3100 Clavis enough to exclude from the generalized structure VOA-B.

Generalized structure used to estimate the influence of component parameters on the process of signal propagation in commercial QKD.

5. MODEL OF INFORMATION SECURITY INFRASTRUCTURE WITH QUANTUM KEY DISTRIBUTION

The pulses of the transmitter can be multi-photon. In addition, single-photon detectors have a spontaneous emission noise. Therefore, the data Alice and Bob share will be different even in the absence of eavesdropping. Consequently, the generation of the secret key is preceded a number of intermediate processing steps to correct the difference in key sequences of Alice and Bob.

Step 1: Generation of raw key sequence (Figure 11). At the first stage the OTM generates a train of optical pulses. The next operations are performed sequentially: transmission the train of pulses through FOL from Bob to Alice, the PM encode a phase state inside the Alice station, the shaping of photonic pulse for transmission through FOL from Alice to Bob and, finally, the measurement of quantum states of photons in receiver modules ROM-B1 and ROM-B2 (Figure 10). After that Alice and Bob have the *raw key sequence*.

In this sequence of N_0 elements (number of ROMs gating) contains the results of measurements, where the two receiver modules ROM-B1 and ROM-B2 at the Bob station don`t detected

Figure 11. Block-diagram of the raw key sequence generaion

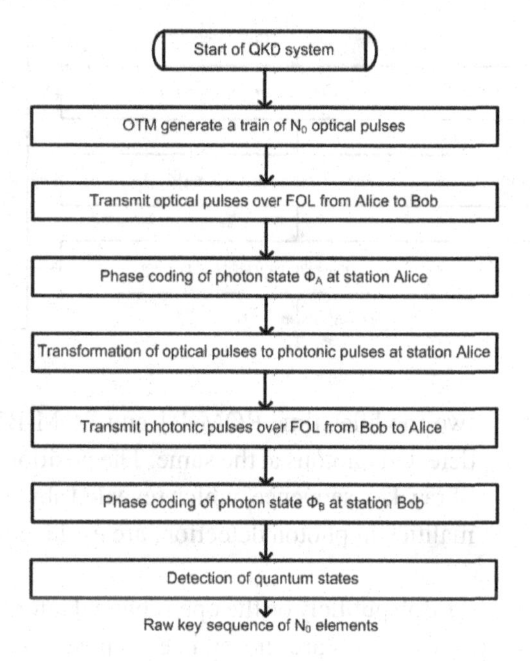

any single photon. In addition, this sequence has the results of measurements in which the two modules ROM-B1 and ROM-B2 detected photons at the same time. Finally. In the sequence are the results of measurements in which users are using different bases.

During subsequent refinement through the exchange of data by open channel Alice and Bob can get a version of a key sequence, suitable for the shaping and sharing of the secret key, or discard the raw key sequence and repeat the process of generation and transmission of quantum state. Refinement may include the following four steps (Center for KvanteInformatik).

Step 2: Generation of the sifted key sequence (Figure 12). Users Alice and Bob reveal the strobe pulse intervals in which the receiving module ROM-B1 and ROM-B2 don`t detect any photons. In addition, Bob show the positions of strobe pulse intervals in which the

Figure 12. Block-diagram of the sifted key sequence generaion

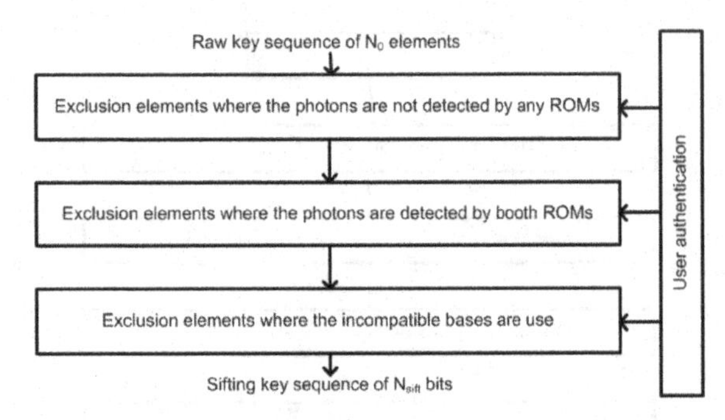

two modules time ROM-B1 and ROM-B2 detected photons at the same. The positions of raw key sequence, which revealed abnormalities in photon detection, are excluded.

User Bob publicly on the open channel inform Alice which bases are chosen in each position of the remaining sequence. Alice confirms or not confirms chosen bases. Any communication channel in which is implemented a standard protocol RSA with public key or the Internet may use as open channel.

From raw key sequence excludes also the results of measurements in which users are using different bases.

As a result of these three operations generated *sifted key sequence* which contains only the bits corresponding to the same basis. Note that the length N_{sift} of the sifted key sequence of bits does not exceed the size of the train of optical pulses.

Step 3: Generation of approved key sequence (Figure 13). As the ideal communication channels do not exist then sifted key sequence may contain errors. Therefore, the formation of identical user key sequence is necessary to estimate the probability of bit errors in the sifted key sequence of bits.

To estimate the error probability Alice announces by open channel the subset of N_{control} positions in the sifted key sequence N_{sift} length

Figure 13. Block-diagram of the approved key sequence generaion

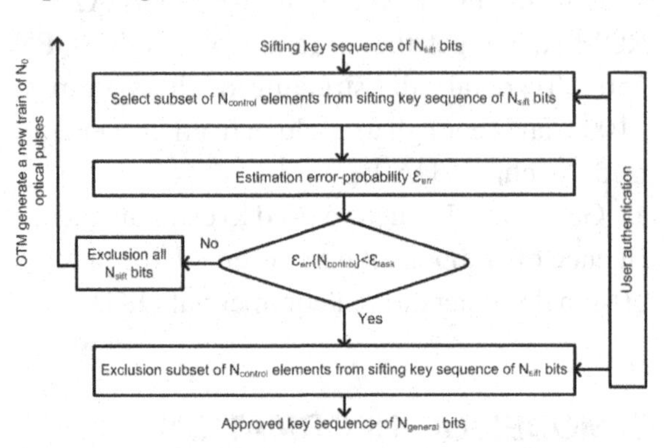

and the corresponding values of the bits. Recipient Bob also sends to Alice the value of bits detected in the same positions. Alice and Bob compute the error probability of his observations $\varepsilon_{err}\left\{N_{control}\right\}$ on the N_{control} length of the subset. The result of the transfer of key sequences is considered positive if the measured error probability is $\varepsilon_{err}\left\{N_{control}\right\}$ less than the permissible level ε_{task}, i.e. $\varepsilon_{err}\left\{N_{control}\right\} < \varepsilon_{task}$. In this case announced subset of bits N_{control} is removed from the sifted key sequences. The *approved key sequence* length is $N_{\text{general}} = N_{\text{sift}} - N_{\text{control}}$. In the case of $\varepsilon_{err}\left\{N_{control}\right\} \geq \varepsilon_{task}$ the generation of the train of optical pulses N_0 is repeated.

Note that in a perfect quantum channel without a noise reveal the mismatch in the one open position is enough for the detection of an eavesdropper. In a real situation it is impossible to recognize errors that occurred due to noise and errors that occurred the attacker.

In (Shor, & Preskill, 2000) showed that if the error rate $\varepsilon_{\text{err}}\left\{N_{\text{control}}\right\}$ does not exceed 11% then the legitimate users can extract the secret key from approved key sequence after the stages of errors correction and privacy amplification. In addition, the key will not be known to the attacker.

Step 4: Generation consistent key sequence (error correction). The minimum number of *m* bits that Alice and Bob must share openly to correct errors in its bit sequences is determined by the Shannon's coding theorem. In our case, when the error probability of any bit sequence is constant and equal to p_{bit}, Shannon's theorem states that

$$m = N_{\text{general}}\left[-p_{\text{bit}}\log\left(p_{\text{bit}}\right) - \left(1 - p_{\text{bit}}\right)\log\left(1 - p_{\text{bit}}\right)\right]$$

Shannon's theorem suggests the possibility of error correction at the opening of m bits of the key sequence of N_{general} elements. However, the theorem does not give explicit error correction procedure. Conventional linear error-correcting codes in this respect rather inefficient.

In QKD systems Alice and Bob perform the matching procedure on approved key sequence using an iterative error correction algorithm based on the parity check (Brassard, & Salvail, 1993).

In the first step, users Alice and Bob group their bits in the N_{block1} blocks of a certain size (Figure 14). They share information about the parity of each j-th block of N_{block1} by open channel.

If the parity of the j-th block is equal then Alice and Bob proceed to the next $(j + 1)$-th block. If the parity of the j-th block is not equal then Alice and Bob conclude that within the bock imply odd number of errors. In this case users are search for an error in the j-th block recursively. To do this they divide the j-th block into two sub-blocks and compare the parity of the sub-blocks. If the parity in the first sub-block is the same of Alice and Bob, then the second sub-block must contain an odd number of errors. If the parity of the first sub-blocks is different so the odd number of errors is disposed in the first sub-block. Error correction procedure recursively continues in the sub-block with an odd number of errors.

After a first step each block contains either an even number of errors or none. Therefore, the second step (j = 2) Alice and Bob change the position of their bits and repeat the same procedure with N_{block2} blocksoflargersize ($N_{\text{block1}} > N_{\text{block2}}$). However, if the error is corrected then Alice and Bob can conclude that in some previously examined blocks now contain an odd number of errors.

Figure 14. Block-diagram of the consistent key sequence generation

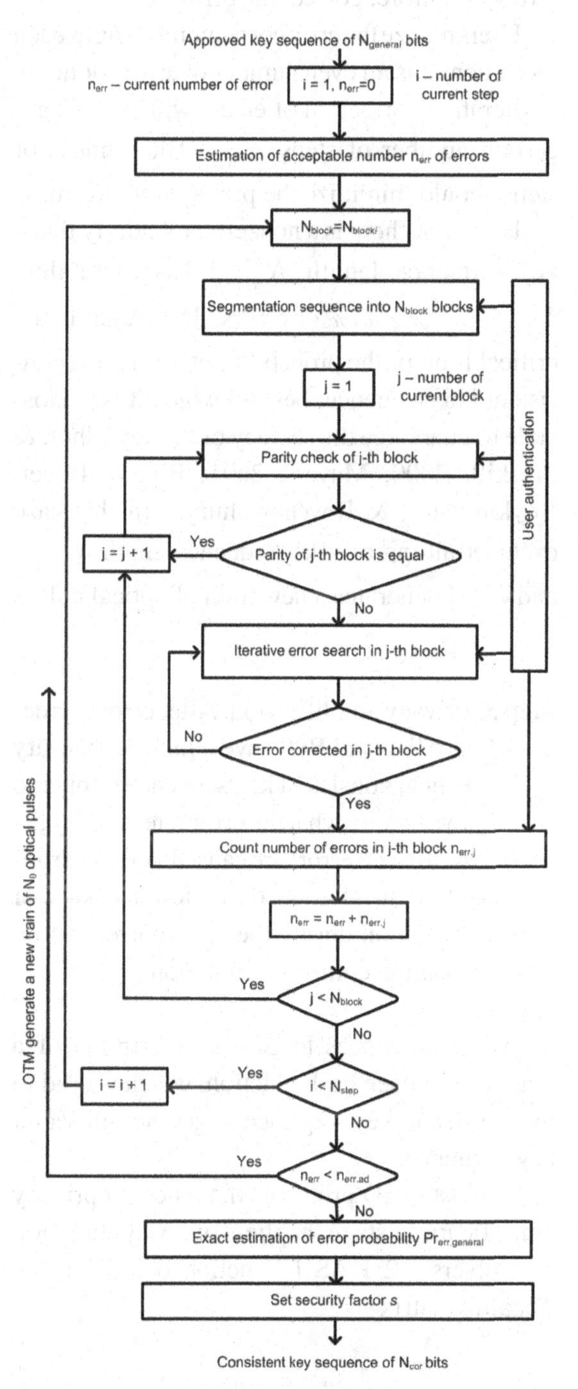

They choose the least of these blocks and recursively, as before, correct the error.

Users realize the error correction as long as each block contains an even number of errors or none.

Iterative correction of errors will stop after a certain number of steps N_{step}. The number of steps should minimize the probability of errors.

However, there is a nonzero probability that a key sequence length $N_{general}$ has more than $\Pr_{err.general.ad} = 11\%$ of errors. This value is the critical limit of the probability of errors in a consistent key sequence, beyond which it is impossible to guarantee the secrecy of the key (Shor, & Preskill, 2000; Mayers, 2001; Biham, Boyer, Boykin, Mor, & Roychowdhury,). In this case excluded all approved key sequence length $N_{general}$ and OTM generates a new train of optical pulses N_0.

Step 5: Privacy amplification. After error correction Alice and Bob have a high probability identical consistent key sequence of bit and know exactly what the error rate is. They assume that all errors are caused by eavesdropper Eve. In addition, they allow a leakage of information during the error correction by setting the compression options s.

Alice announces to Bob a description of a randomly chosen hash function, which is used to the consistent key sequence to get the full secret key sequence.

In most QKD protocols the Alice on privacy amplification stage applies one-way function or Universal 2 HASH Function based on any Toeplitz matrix

$$\left\| rnd_{ij} \right\|_{(N_{\text{hash}} \times N_{\text{cor}})} = \left\| \begin{matrix} rnd_{11} & rnd_{12} & \dots & rnd_{1N_{\text{cor}}} \\ rnd_{21} & rnd_{11} & \dots & \dots \\ \dots & \dots & rnd_{11} & rnd_{12} \\ rnd_{N_{\text{hash}}1} & \dots & rnd_{21} & rnd_{11} \end{matrix} \right\|$$

Matrix size is $N_{\text{hash}} \times N_{cor}$, where $N_{\text{hash}} = N_{\text{cor}} - s$, rnd_{ij} are random numbers takes the value 0 or 1. This matrix Alice sends to Bob by open channel (Figure 15).

Let the values of bits of the consistent key sequence given as elements of the column matrix X_i with $N_{cor} \times 1$ size. Transformed key sequence Y_j will be determined by the elements of the row matrix $1 \times N_{\text{hash}}$ size. So (Bouwmeester, Ekert, & Zeilinger, 2000)

$$\left(Y_1 \;\; Y_2 \;\; \dots \;\; Y_{N_{\text{hash}}} \right) = \left\| Y_{ij} \right\|_{(1 \times N_{\text{hash}})}$$
$$\left\| rnd_{ij} \right\|_{(N_{\text{hash}} \times N_{\text{cor}})} \times \left\| X_{ij} \right\|_{(N_{\text{cor}} \times 1)}$$
$$\begin{pmatrix} rnd_{11} & rnd_{12} & \dots & rnd_{1N_{corr}} \\ rnd_{21} & rnd_{11} & \dots & \dots \\ \dots & \dots & rnd_{11} & rnd_{12} \\ rnd_{N_{\text{hash}}1} & \dots & rnd_{21} & rnd_{11} \end{pmatrix} \times \begin{pmatrix} X_1 \\ X_2 \\ \dots \\ X_{N_{cor}} \end{pmatrix} \pmod 2. \tag{1}$$

Alice and Bob randomly selected N_{priv} control bits of the transformed sequence N_{hash} length.

Figure 15. Block-diagram of the secret key sequence generation

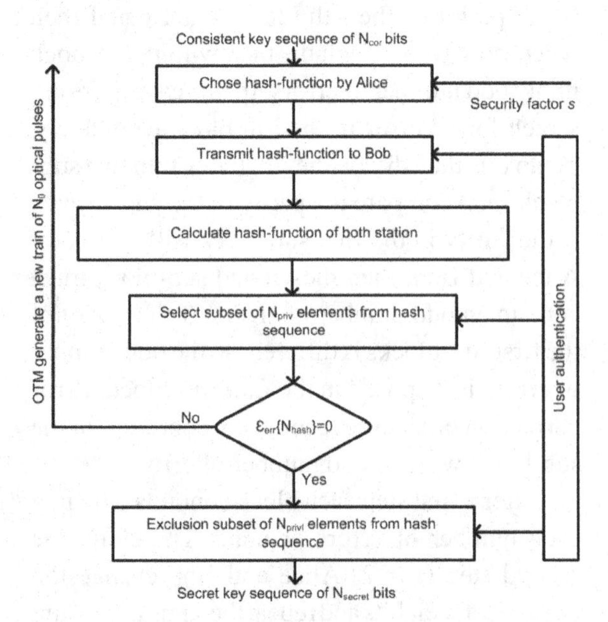

No errors $\varepsilon_{err}\{N_{\text{priv}}\}$ in the selected bits ensure that the sequence N_{hash} of the users Alice and Bob are identical with probability close to 1. The remaining bits $N_{\sec ret} = N_{hash} - N_{\text{priv}}$ form the secret key sequence.

In the case of $\varepsilon_{err}\{N_{\text{priv}}\} \neq 0$ all consistent key sequence is excluded, OTM generates a new stack of N_0 optical pulses.

As the result of these actions, illustrated in Figures 11-15, the legitimate users Alice and Bob have the identical sequence of bits. These bits are the secret key sequence. The secret key of a required length is taken from the secret key sequence. Users with the secret key are able to encode and decode private information and transmit information over the insecure data line.

The authentication should use in the stages of key generation to prevent an attack the man in the middle. The authentication allows users to make sure that message comes from a legitimate user. Only after approval and authentication key can be used for encryption or other cryptographic purposes.

The combination of public key cryptography for authentication and quantum key distribution leads to high levels of long-term security.

6. ESTIMATION OF THE REDUCING OF KEY RATE GENERATION AT THE PHYSICAL LEVEL

Efforts of developer of quantum cryptography systems are concentrated on increase the key rate, increase the communication range, exclusion the probability of hack the system through quantum channel.

One of the main limitations of commercial systems produced by id Quantque, MagiQ Technologies and Quintessence Labs companies are a low rate of the secret key generation (Golubchikov, & Rumiantsev, 2008). So for the system id 3100 Clavis2 rate of raw key sequence is 500 bps at the length of the quantum channel 25 km (Dixon, Yuan, Dynes, Sharpe, & Shields, 2010).

Using the generalized structure of QKD systems (Figure 10) and the model of information security infrastructure (Figures 11-15) we estimate the influence of each stage on a rate of key generation.

Infrastructure of information security for quantum key distribution provides the physical and logical levels of the key generation. The physical layer includes the optical pulse generation by OTM, optical pulse transmission from Alice station to station Bob, the weakening of the power of optical pulse to the level of the photonic pulse, the phase coding of states of photons, the photonic pulse transmission from station Alice to station Bob, the choice of measurement basis of the photon states, the detection of photons in the receiver modules ROM-B1 and PROM-B2 in Bob stations (Figure 10).

Let the OTM in the generalized structure of QKD systems in Figure 10 generates optical pulses with energy E_{OTM}, repetition rate of f_{OTM} and duration of τ_{OTM}. This is equivalent to generating an average duration of an optical pulse of photons:

$$\mu_{OTM} = \frac{\text{E}_{OTM}}{\text{E}_{ph}} = \frac{\text{E}_{OTM}}{hc_{opt}/\lambda_{opt}}. \tag{2}$$

The photon energy $\text{E}_{ph} = hc_{opt}/\lambda_{opt}$ is determined by Planck constant $h = 6,628 \times 10^{-34} J \cdot s$, wavelength λ_{opt} and the velocity of propagation c_{opt} of optical radiation.

The optical pulse is attenuated while pass through component of QKD system. The average number of photons per pulse absorbed at the photocathode of one of the two-SPAD

$$\mu_{APD} = K_{\text{B}} \cdot K_{\text{A}} \cdot K_{\text{link}} \cdot \mu_{OTM} \tag{3}$$

In accordance to Figure 10 μ_{APD} is determined by the losses of FOL K_{link}, the attenuation K_{B} of the fiber-optical structures of Bob station (VOA-B, FOC, FC X-type, FODL-B, PM-B, the polarization rotator, PFC) and K_{A} of Alice station (FC Y-type, VOA-1, FODL-A, PM-A, Faraday mirror). When the FOL uses optical fiber with length of L_{FOL} and linear attenuation of the radiation, so losses can be calculated by

$$K_{\text{link}} = \exp\left(-\alpha_{\text{OF}} \cdot L_{\text{link}}\right). \quad (4)$$

The security condition of the QKD system is re-emission in the direction of the Bob station photonic pulse. Quantum key distribution system is configured so that each photonic pulse consists on average no more than one photon. In such conditions, the probability of receiving n_{ph} photons per pulse while strobe duration $\tau_{strobe} > \tau_{\text{OTM}}$ in receiving optical modules ROM-B1 and ROM-B2 of Bob station and the average of number of photon μ_{ROM} has the Poisson distribution (Bychkov, & Rumiantsev, 2000)

$$\Pr\left\{n_{ph} \middle| \mu_{\text{ROM}}\right\} = \frac{\mu_{\text{ROM}}^{n_{ph}}}{n_{ph}!} \exp\left(-\mu_{\text{ROM}}\right). \quad (5)$$

In quantum cryptography photonic pulse mean that $\mu_{\text{ROM}} = 0.1..\ 0.2$. Then, for $\mu_{\text{ROM}} = 0.1$ the proportion of pulses at the input of ROM with two photons is 0.45%, and three photons is 0.015%. Almost 9 out of 10 gated intervals will not contain any photons.

The average number of click of SPAD is

$$\mu_{APD} = \eta_{APD} \cdot \mu_{\Pi POM} + \nu_{\text{dark}} \cdot \tau_{strobe} \quad (6)$$

determined by the quantum efficiency of SPAD η_{APD}. The second summand in (6) is associated with the pulses of the dark current and afterpulsing effect. We assume that it frequency is ν_{dark}.

It is known that the quantum efficiency of existing SPAD at 1550 nm does not exceed 10% (Gisin, Ribordy, Tittel, & Zbinden, 2002; Dusek, Lutkenhaus, & Hendrych, 2006). Consequently, the average number of detected photons will not exceed $\mu_{\text{APD}} = 0.01..\ 0.02$. In this case, using the formula

$$\Pr\left\{n \middle| \mu_{\text{APD}}\right\} = \frac{\mu_{\text{APD}}^{n}}{n!} \exp\left(-\mu_{\text{APD}}\right), \quad (7)$$

we find that the proportion of gated intervals in which received two or more photons do not exceed 0.005%. The proportion of pulses where there will be no photons increases to 99%.One photon is detected in 0.99% pulses.

Due to sifting stage will be excluded gated intervals in which the photons are not detected. Due to this, the rate of key sequence generation decrease to values

$$V_1 = \left[1 - \exp\left(-\mu_{\text{APD}}\right)\right] \cdot f_{\text{OTM}}. \quad (8)$$

Since the value $V_0 = f_{\text{OTM}}$ can be interpreted as the maximum rate of key distribution, so

$$K_1 = \left[1 - \exp\left(-\mu_{\text{APD}}\right)\right] \quad (9)$$

is the factor of slowing the rate of key sequence generation because the photon is not detected.

At the sifting stage can occur simultaneously click of two ROM. Moreover, click one of the two ROM is associated with the pulses of the dark current and afterpulsing effect.

Because this response are not correlated the probability of such event according to (6) and (7) will be

$$\begin{gathered}\Pr\left\{n \geq 1 \middle| \mu_{\text{APD}}\right\} \Pr\left\{n \geq 1 \middle| \nu_{\text{dark}} \tau_{strobe}\right\} = \\ \left[1 - \Pr\left\{n = 0 \middle| \mu_{\text{APD}}\right\}\right] \cdot \left[1 - \Pr\left\{n = 0 \middle| \nu_{\text{dark}} \tau_{strobe}\right\}\right] = \\ = \left[1 - \exp\left(-\mu_{\text{APD}}\right)\right] \cdot \left[1 - \exp\left(-\nu_{\text{dark}} \tau_{strobe}\right)\right].\end{gathered}$$

After exclusion the positions in the key sequence in which the double click of ROM is occur, the rate of key generation decrease by

$$V_2 = \left[1 - \exp\left(-\mu_{\text{APD}}\right)\right] \cdot \left[1 - \exp\left(-\nu_{\text{dark}} \tau_{strobe}\right)\right] \cdot V_1. \tag{10}$$

According to (10) the factor of slowing the rate of key sequence generation from double click of ROM is

$$K_2 = \left[1 - \exp\left(-\mu_{\text{APD}}\right)\right] \cdot \left[1 - \exp\left(-\nu_{\text{dark}} \tau_{strobe}\right)\right]. \tag{11}$$

Commercial QKD systems (Golubchikov, & Rumiantsev, 2008) using the protocols BB84 and SARG04. To implement the protocol BB84 (Gisin, Ribordy, Tittel, & Zbinden, 2002) at the station Alice delayed optical pulse is modulated in phase by one of four randomly selected values Φ_A the series 0, π/2, π, 3π/2. At the Bob station randomly selected measuring basis Φ_B of the phase shift of the first photon pulse by 0 or π/2.

The probability of a correct choice of the basis is defined as the Equations shown in Box 1.

In a perfectly tuned QKD system that probability is that shown in Box 2.

Consequently, due to the mismatch bases of Alice and Bob in the implementation of the BB84 protocol every second bit of the key sequence will be rejected. The rate of the key sequence generation reduce by the value

$$V_3 = \Pr_{bc} V_2. \tag{12}$$

The expression shows that the probability of a correct choice of basis $\Pr_{cb}$ can be interpreted as a factor of reducing the length of the key sequence of bits by $\Pr_{cb} = K_3 = 0.5$ at the sifting stage as the result of the mismatch measuring bases on stations Alice and Bob.

Note that the coefficient in (12) $\Pr_{cb} = K_3$ is 0.25 when the B92 protocol is use.

In a real QKD system factor of slowing of key sequence generation as the result of the mismatch bases in Alice and Bob is that shown in Box 3.

An analysis of Formulas (2)-(7) and (14) shows that the rate of reduction $K_{\text{ph.level}} = K_1 \cdot \text{K}_2 \cdot \text{K}_3$ of length of key sequence of bits on sifting stage is defined by:

- The energy E_{OTM}, repetition rate f_{OTM} and duration of optical pulses τ_{OTM},

Box 1.

$$\Pr_{bc} = \Pr\{\Phi_{\text{A}} = 0,\ \Phi_{\text{B}} = 0\} + \Pr\{\Phi_{\text{A}} = \pi/2,\ \Phi_{\text{B}} = \pi / 2\} + \Pr\{\Phi_{\text{A}} = \pi,\ \Phi_{\text{B}} = 0\} + \Pr\{\Phi_{\text{A}} = 3\pi/2,\ \Phi_{\text{B}} = \pi/2\}.$$

where $\Pr\{\Phi_{\text{A}},\ \Phi_{\text{B}}\} = \Pr\{\Phi_{\text{A}}\} \cdot \Pr\{\Phi_{\text{B}}\}$

Box 2.

$$\Pr\{\Phi_{\text{A}} = 0\} = \Pr\{\Phi_{\text{A}} = \pi/2\} = \Pr\{\Phi_{\text{A}} = \pi\} = \Pr\{\Phi_{\text{A}} = 3\pi/2\} = 0{,}25$$

$$\Pr\{\Phi_{\text{B}} = 0\} = \Pr\{\Phi_{\text{B}} = \pi/2\} = 0{,}5$$

whence $\Pr_{bc} = 0{,}5$.

Box 3.

$$K_3 = \Pr_{bc} = \left(\Pr\{\Phi_A = 0\} + \Pr\{\Phi_A = \pi\}\right) \cdot \Pr\{\Phi_B = 0\} + \left(\Pr\{\Phi_A = \pi/2\} + \Pr\{\Phi_A = 3\pi/2\}\right) \cdot \Pr\{\Phi_B = \pi / 2\}. \quad (13)$$

The expression (8)-(13) allow us to calculate general expression for the rate of the sifted key sequence generation after the second stage(13)

$$V_{\text{ph.level}} = K_1 \cdot K_2 \cdot K_3 \cdot f_{\Pi OM}. \quad (14)$$

- The length L_{link} of FOL and linear attenuation α_{OF} of the optical fiber,
- The duration gating pulses τ_{strobe} in optical receiver modules ROM-B1 and ROM-B2,
- The SPAD parameters such as quantum efficiency η_{APD}, frequency of dark current pulses and afterpulsing effects ν_{dark},
- The precise of phase shifts in PM-A and PM-B,
- The protocol of quantum key distribution.

7. ESTIMATION OF THE REDUCING OF KEY RATE GENERATION AT THE LOGICAL LEVEL

Logic level carry out the generation of approved, consistent and the secret key sequences of bit (Figures 13-15).

Approved the key sequence generation: Let the error estimates for the selected subset of N_{control} bits in the sifted key sequence length N_{sift}. If the measured error in a subset of $\varepsilon_{err}\left\{N_{control}\right\}$ does not exceed a target level ε_{task}, i.e. $\varepsilon_{err}\left\{N_{control}\right\} < \varepsilon_{task}$, then a key sequence is approved. Let the probability of this event is $P_{\text{task}} = \Pr\left\{\varepsilon_{err}\left\{N_{control}\right\} < \varepsilon_{task}\right\}$.

Approved sequence is formed by elimination of subsets N_{control} from sifted sequences of bits. In the event of $\varepsilon_{err}\left\{N_{control}\right\} \geq \varepsilon_{task}$ then excluded all the N_{sift} bits.

Therefore, an evaluation of the probability of error rate of a key sequence generation is reduced in K_4 time, where

$$K_4 = \sum_{z_1 \geq 1} \left(\begin{array}{l} \left(z_1 - 1\right) N_0 + \\ \dfrac{N_{\text{sift.z1}} - N_{control}}{N_{\text{sift.z1}}} P_{\text{task}} \left(1 - P_{\text{task}}\right)^{z_1 - 1} \end{array} \right). \quad (15)$$

Here z_1 is the number of the current cycle of generation of OTM train of N_0 optical pulses.

Error correction: At the 4-th stage as the result of error correction in approved key sequences are searched and corrected wrong values of the bits.

In (Brassard, & Salvail, 1993) proposed a cascade algorithm for errors correction in the approved key sequence. This method allows to correcting errors in the sequences with the percentage of errors up to 15%. The cascade algorithm for error correction based on the calculation of the parity of individual blocks. The approved key sequence is divided into that blocks.

In the process of error correction of the approved key sequence length N_{general} Alice and Bob stations exchange the information about the parity data blocks over open channel. Bit corrects the value if an error is detected. The error bit is removed from the key sequence after the end of correction process. So the key sequence in the process of error correction reduces its length.

The process of iterative error correction has the following operations: the division into blocks, parity check, error correction, permutation of sequence. Permutation operation is performed for uniform distribution errors per blocks.

Let the approved key sequence length is N_{general} and quantity of errors is k_{err}. The probability of this event is defined by

$$\Pr\left\{k_{err}\right\} = C_{N_{general}}^{k_{err}} p_{bit}^{\ k_{err}} \left(1 - p_{bit}\right)^{N_{general} - k_{err}} \quad (16)$$

At the first step of cascade algorithm the sequence is divided into the blocks $N_{block1} = N_{block}$ of $n_{block1} = n_{block}$ bits in each, and

$$n_{block} \geq \frac{\alpha}{p_{bit}},$$

where the constant α = 0,73 is determined empirically(Brassard, & Salvail, 1993).

Note that in practice for implementation of the algorithm the length of the block n_{block} is selected multiple of two, i.e. $n_{block} = 2^k$. Consequently, the parameter of block length must satisfy the condition

$$k = \left\lceil \log\left(\frac{\alpha}{p_{bit}}\right) \right\rceil. \quad (17)$$

The sign $\lceil x \rceil$ in (17) means the smallest integer no less than a real x.

The error will be distributed in blocks uniformly after the permutation if the condition (17) is performed.

Error bits are statistically independent. Therefore, the appearance of error in any of the blocks of length n_{block} is uniformly.

Consequently, single-errors should be detected and corrected at the first step as the most probable errors.

Therefore. In each block of N_{block} check the parity, which detects a single-error by bisectional search method.

Let an odd number of errors detected in m_1 blocks on the first step.

In the process of correcting the quantity of disclosed bits in the key sequence is calculated as

$$k_1 = m_1 \cdot (1 + \log(n_{block1})) = m_1 \cdot (1 + \log(n_{block})).$$

After the first step will be $k_{err} - m_1$ errors. With increasing a priori probability of single errors increases the number of detected and corrected errors at the first step.

The block size is doubled $n_{block2} = 2n_{block1}$ after permutation at the second step. The operation of permutation is performed and single errors is correcting in double sized blocks.

Consequently, if the number of blocks with a single error at the second step is equal to m_2, then the number of bits disclosed in a key sequence is

$$k_2 = m_2\left(1 + \log\left(n_{block2}\right)\right) = m_2\left(2 + \log\left(n_{block}\right)\right).$$

In the second step corrects double errors, which at the first step was in one block.

The number of errors after the second step further reduced to m_2 and becomes equal to $k_{err} - m_1 - m_2$ errors.

Double errors of the second step will correct at the third step, with an increase of the cost of error correction at 1 bit.

Consequently, the number of bits disclosed in all $N_{block.i} = N_{block} \cdot 2^{1-i}$ blocks size of $n_{block.i} = n_{block} \cdot 2^{i-1}$ during *i*-th step is equal to

$$k_i = m_i \left(1 + \log\left(n_{blocki}\right)\right) = m_i \left(i + \log\left(n_{block}\right)\right). \quad (18)$$

The error probability at each next step is reduced (Brassard, & Salvail, 1993).

Iterative procedure includes N_{step} steps of searching and correcting single errors. The $k_i, i = \overline{1, N_{step}}$ is the value of the cost of error correction in the key sequence at the *i*-th step. Note that according to (18) the cost of correction of one error in a block at each next step increases by 1 bit.

Iterative procedure ensures reduction of errors at each next step, i.e. $\lim_{i \to \infty} m_i = 0$. In this case the best solution is to remembering the location of bit positions in the blocks where single errors detected in the previous steps. This minimizes the number of disclosed bits.

The resulting number of disclosed $N_{err.cor}$ bits in the approved key sequence after the parity check is that shown in Box 4.

If the key sequence has no errors, then only one bit will be disclosed in each block. Number of blocks at the *i*-th step. In which no single errors detected is equal

$$k_{0i} = N_{block.i} - m_i = N_{block} \cdot 2^{1-i} - m_i.$$

Consequently, after the parity check will be dropped an additional bits (see Box 5).

The length of the consistent key sequence after the error correction will be that shown in Box 6.

Box 4.

$$N_{err.cor} = \sum_{i=1}^{N_{step}} k_i = \sum_{i=1}^{N_{step}} m_i \left(i + \log n_{block}\right) = \sum_{i=1}^{N_{step}} i \cdot m_i + \log n_{block} \sum_{i=1}^{N_{step}} m_i. \quad (19)$$

Box 5.

$$N_{cor0} = \sum_{i=1}^{N_{step}} k_{0i} = \sum_{i=1}^{N_{step}} \left(N_{block} \cdot 2^{1-i} - m_i\right) = N_{block} \sum_{i=1}^{N_{step}} 2^{1-i} - \sum_{i=1}^{N_{step}} m_i = N_{block} \left(2 - 2^{1-N_{step}}\right) - \sum_{i=1}^{N_{step}} m_i. \quad (20)$$

Box 6.

$$N_{cor1} = N_{general} - N_{err.cor} - N_{cor0} = N_{general} - \sum_{i=1}^{N_{step}} \left(i - 1\right) \cdot m_i - \log n_{block} \sum_{i=1}^{N_{step}} m_i - N_{block} \left(2 - 2^{1-N_{step}}\right). \quad (21)$$

Therefore, as a result of the error correction the rate of the key sequence generation is reduced in K_{cor1} times, where

$$K_{\text{cor1}} = \frac{N_{general} - N_{\text{cor1}}}{N_{general}} = \frac{N_{err.cor} + N_{\text{cor0}}}{N_{general}}. \quad (22)$$

With (19)-(21) we find the average length of the consistent key sequence after error correction stage

$$\overline{N_{cor1}} = \sum_{N_{cor1}} N_{cor1} \Pr\{N_{cor1}\}$$

where $\Pr\{N_{cor1}\}$ is the probability of consistent key sequence of length N_{cor1} after error correction stage.

Since the cascade algorithm of error correction is not deterministic, the number of disclosed bits N_{cor1} depends on the amount of mutual information $I\{A, B \mid E\}$ of Alice and Bob taking into account the Eve actions. The amount of information available to Eve is determined after the error correction and estimated as error rate in the approved key sequence.

There is a nonzero probability that number of errors found in key sequence of length $N_{general}$ exceeds a critical limit $\Pr_{err.general.ad} = 11\%$. Thus, it is necessary to take into account the probability of exception of all approved key sequence $N_{general}$ if a probability of error $\Pr_{err.general} = N_{err.cor} / N_{general}$ is more than the maximum threshold $\Pr_{err.general.ad}$.

Let $N_{cr} = \lfloor N_{general} \cdot \Pr_{err.general.ad} \rfloor$ is a critical quantity of errors in the key sequence of length $N_{general}$ bit. The sign $\lfloor x \rfloor$ means the greatest integer not exceeding this real x. Then

$$\Pr_{err.general} = \Pr\{N_{err.cor} \geq N_{cr}\} = \sum_{N_{err.cor}=N_{cr}}^{N_{general}} \Pr\{N_{err.cor}\}.$$

In this case all approved key sequence of $N_{general}$ length is excluded. OTM generates a new train of N_0 optical pulses. Naturally, the length of the new approved key sequence and critical errors in it will be different.

Let z_2 is the number of the current generation cycle of train of optical pulses. Then the error

Box 7.

$$\Pr_{err.general.z2} = \Pr\{N_{err.cor.z2} \geq N_{cr.z2}\} = \sum_{N_{err.cor}=N_{cr.z2}}^{N_{general.z2}} \Pr\{N_{err.cor.z2}\}. \quad (23)$$

Box 8.

$$K_{\text{rej}} = \sum_{z_2 \geq 1} \left(1 + \frac{(z_2 - 1) N_0}{N_{\text{cor1}.z2}}\right) \Pr_{err.general.z2} \left(1 - \Pr_{err.general.z2}\right)^{z_2 - 1}. \quad (24)$$

Box 9.

$$K_6 = \sum_{z_3 \geq 1} \frac{\left(z_3 - 1\right) N_0 + N_{hash.z3} - N_{priv}}{N_{cor.z3}} p_0 \left(1 - p_0\right)^{z_3 - 1}. \quad (26)$$

probability in z_2 generation cycle is that shown in Box 7.

The rate of key sequence generation is reduced in the K_{rej} time, where Equation (24) in Box 8.

Taking into accountant (22)–(24) the resulting factor reducing the length of key sequence during the error correction is

$$K_5 = K_{cor1} \cdot K_{rej}. \quad (25)$$

After the error correction in the approved key sequence formed a consistent key sequence of bits $N_{\text{cor}} = N_{\text{cor1}} - N_{\text{cr}}$ length.

It should be remembered that the cascade algorithm for correcting errors has finite and non-zero probability of resulting error because it has the finite number of steps.

Privacy amplification: The transformation (1) building on the matrix Toeplitz is use in quantum cryptography systems at the step of privacy amplification. The dimension of the matrix and the length of the converted sequence is $N_{\text{hash}} < N_{\text{cor}}$.

Alice and Bob check for errors in N_{priv} control bits in the converted sequence. If the selected bits have no errors then the secret key sequence is $N_{secret} = N_{hash} - N_{\text{priv}}$ bits. In the case of $\varepsilon_{err}\left\{N_{\text{priv}}\right\} \neq 0$ all consistent key sequence is excluded and OTM generates a new train of N_0 optical pulses.

Consequently, after the privacy amplification reducing the length of the sequence is given by that shown in Box 9.

Here z_3 is the number of the current cycle of generation of train of N_0 optical pulses. The value $p_0 = \Pr\left\{\varepsilon_{err}\left\{N_{\text{priv}}\right\} = 0\right\}$ is the probability of no errors in the selected N_{priv} bits.

Parameters in (26) are the length N_{cor} of the consistent key sequence, the size N_{hash} of the hash function, the compression option *s*, the amount of Eve known information and the number N_{priv} of control bits.

8. THE RATE OF A SECRET KEY SEQUENCE GENERATION

The resulting reduction of the length of key sequences estimated with accountant to (9), (11), (13), (15), (25) and (26) as coefficient

$$K_{QKD} = K_1 \cdot K_2 \cdot K_3 \cdot K_4 \cdot K_5 \cdot K_6. \quad (27)$$

Importantly, the decrease of the rate of key sequences generation on all stages is a random process. Where the coefficient $K_1 - K_3$ are the mathematical expectation of random variables. As for the coefficient $K_4 - K_6$ they require averaging over a number of generating cycles of optical pulses trains, the number of blocks with an odd number of errors and some other parameters.

In these circumstances, the union of block-diagrams in Figures 11-15 provides an algorithm for simulating the process of secret key sequence generation. The model allows to estimating the influence of various parameters of physical elements of the QKD system and the error correction and privacy amplification stages on the key distribution process.

As an example of the developed model, we estimate the length of the sifted key sequence required to generate secret keys with lengths of 128, 192 and 256 bits. These lengths are typical for the algorithm AES used in commercial quantum cryptography.

The length N_{sift} of sifted key sequence is estimated with expression (27) with no account taken of stage of generation of approved key sequence ($\varepsilon_{task} = 0$).

The curves on Figure 16 show that more than 158 bit sifted key N_{sift} is needed to generate $N_{\text{secret}} = 128$ bit private key with safety factor $s = 30$ and bit-error probability $P_{bit} = 0$ conditions, but the sifted key N_{sift} should be more than 610 bits if safety factor $s = 30$ and bit-error probability $P_{bit} = 0.11$. The 256 bit private key generation demands 1104 bits of sifted key length with bit-error probability $P_{bit} = 0.11$. The 610 and 1104 bits values define the least upper limit of sifted key length used for estimation of sifted key rejection coefficient K_{rej}.

The further quantitative analysis uses length of sifted key that is divisible by 8 bits. This assumption is needed in order to use the computational modeling.

Let's estimate the coefficient of rejection of sifted key if it has eavesdropper known bits quantity of more than the critical limit.

The curves on Figure 17 show that if the bit-error probability P_{bit} is high the coefficient of rejection is high too and may reach value of 0.5. This fact means that every second key will be rejected completely.

The curves on Figure 18 show the dependence of the probability of generation of one private key bit from one sifted key bit to the bit-error probability. The figure also shows the influence of rejection coefficient K_{rej}.

From the dependences in Figures 16–18 found that for the range of parameters appropriate to Id3100 Clavis2 commercial system we can state that the error correction stage decreases the rate of key generation average on 3.9% per one percent

Figure 16. The dependence of sifted key length to the error probability

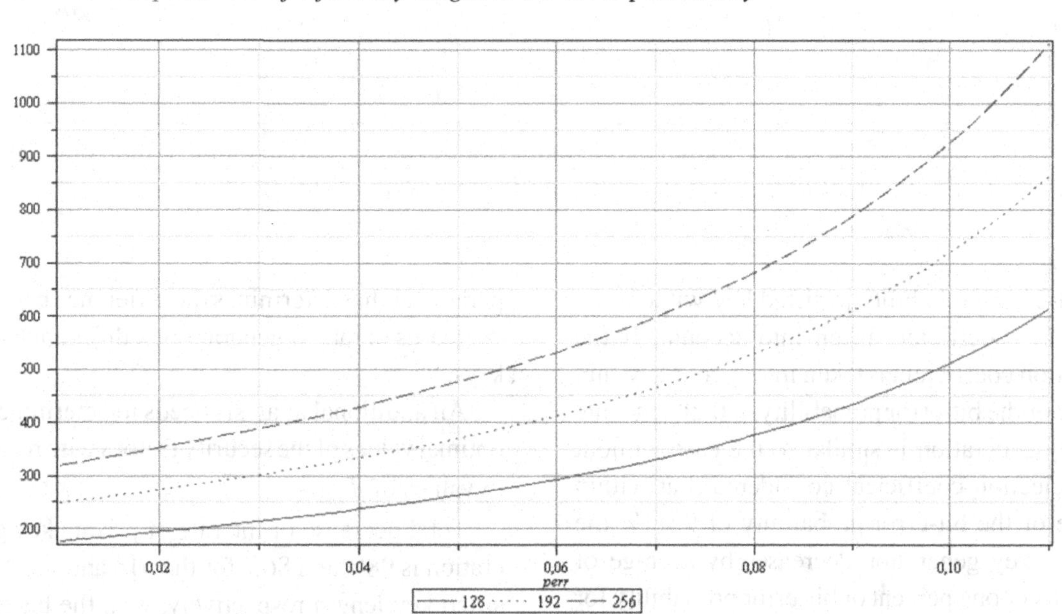

Figure 17. The dependence of the rejection coefficient to the bit-error probability

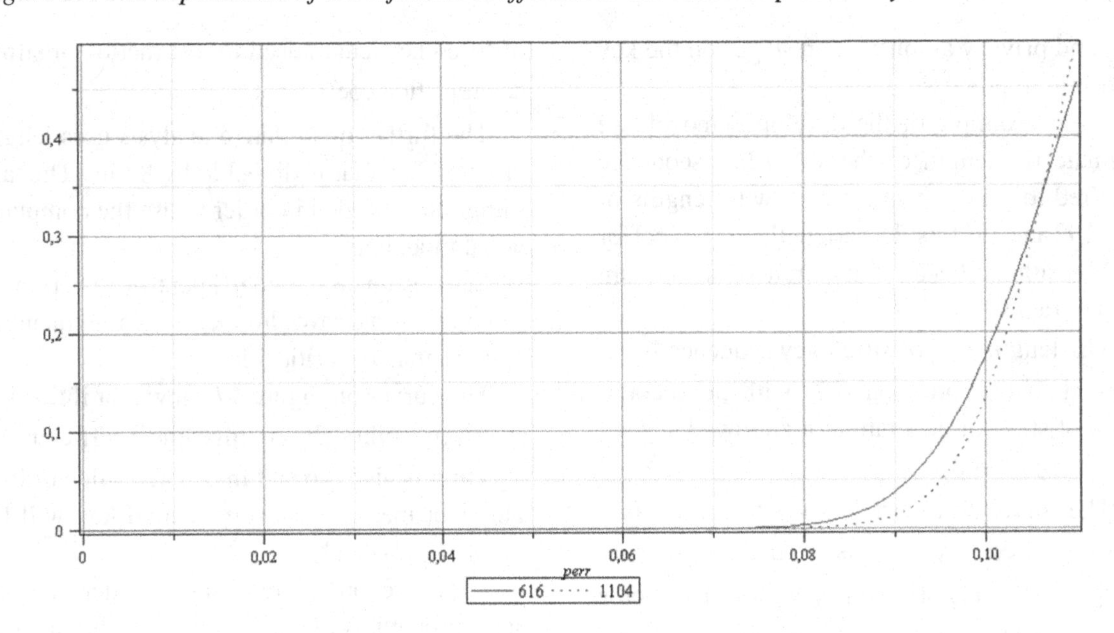

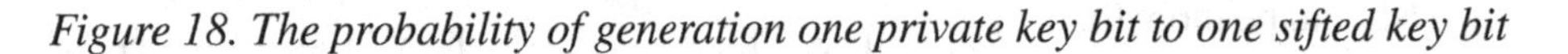

Figure 18. The probability of generation one private key bit to one sifted key bit

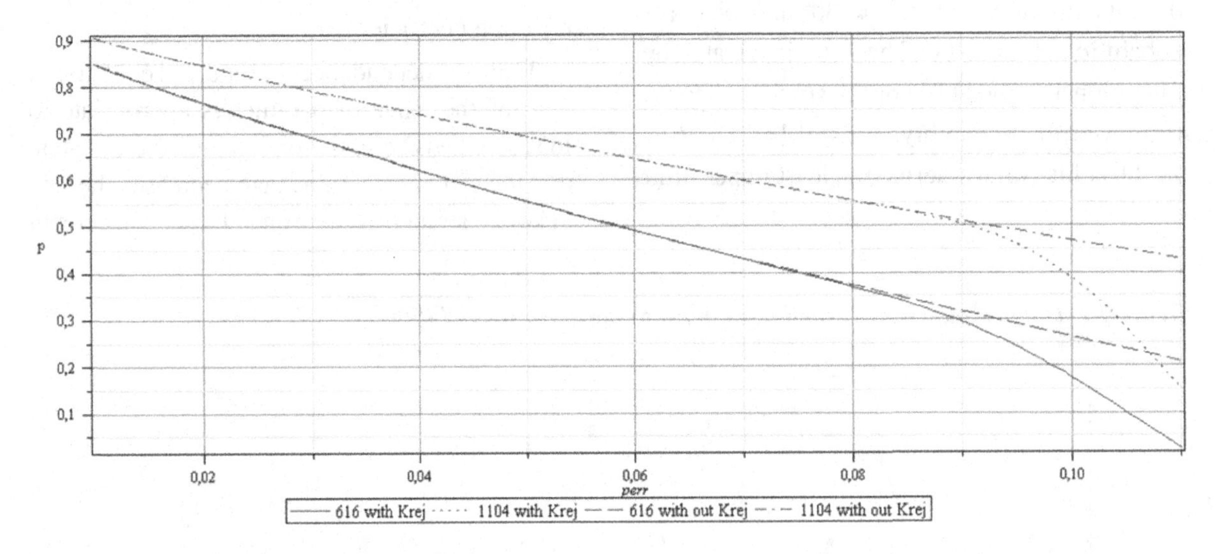

of bit-error probability in sifted key without the rejection coefficient taken into account. If the rejection coefficient is taken into account, within range of the bit-error probability of 0..9% the rate of key generation is similar to the case without the rejection coefficient considered, but within range of the bit-error probability of 9..11% the rate of key generation decreases by average of 17.5% per one percent of bit-error probability for 1104 bits sifted key. The safety factor *s* is the main parameter that determines the difference between decreases of rate of generation of different length keys.

An additional analysis needs to determine the optimal values of the security factor *s* with relation to values of P_{bit}

Total decrease of the rate of private key generation is 98% and 86% for the 616 and 1104 bits sifted key length respectively, with the bit-error probability value close to 11%.

CONCLUSION

Based on the analysis of existing commercial systems produced by id Quantique (Switzerland), MagiQ Technologies (USA) and Quintessenc Labs Pty Ltd (Australia) proposed the generalized structure of the QKD systems with phase coding of photon states. The structure includes all the modules that have a direct influence on the propagation and processing of quantum states.

The stages of the raw, sifted, approved, consistent and secret key sequences are analyzed. Combining the block-diagrams of five stages of key sequences generation provides the Model of information security infrastructure with quantum key distribution.

The expressions (1)-(27) establish the dependence of length of secret key sequence to the parameters of the transmitter and receiver modules, optical fiber, the duration of gate pulses, the precision of the phase shifts, protocol of key distribution, the allowable level of bit-error probability, the iterative algorithm of error correction and size of the hash function on the stage privacy amplification.

As an example shows that the use of QKD model allows to estimate the reduction rate of key sequence generation at the stages of error correction and privacy amplification.

REFERENCES

Advanced Encryption Standard (AES). (2001). *National institute for standards and technology*. Gaithersburg, MD: AES.

Bennett, C. (1992). Quantum cryptography using any two non-orthogonal states. *Physical Review Letters*, *68*, 3121–3124. doi:10.1103/PhysRevLett.68.3121 PMID:10045619.

Biham, E., Boyer, M., Boykin, P. O., Mor, T., & Roychowdhury, V. A. (n.d.). *Proof of the seurity of quantum key distribution*. Retrieved from http://arxiv.org/abs/quant-ph/9912053v1

Bouwmeester, D., Ekert, A. K., & Zeilinger, A. (2000). *The physics of quantum information: Quantum cryptography, quantum teleportation, and quantum computation*. Berlin: Springer.

Brassard, G. (2007). *Modern cryptology: A tutorial*. New York: Springer-Verlag.

Brassard, G., & Salvail, L. (1993). Secret-key reconciliation by public discussion: Advances in cryptology. In *Proceedings of Eurocrypt '93*. Lofthus, Norway: IEEE Press.

Bychkov, S. I., & Rumiantsev, K. E. (2000). *Search and detection of optical signals*. Moscow, Russia: Radio and Connection Publisher.

Center for KvanteInformatik. (n.d.). *Implementation of the B92 QKD protocol*. Retrieved from www.cki.au.dk/experiment/qrypto/doc/QuCrypt/b92prot.html

Dixon, A. R., Yuan, Z. L., Dynes, J. F., Sharpe, A. W., & Shields, A. J. (2010). Continuous operation of high bit rate quantum key distribution. *Applied Physics Letters*. doi:10.1063/1.3385293.

Dusek, M., Lutkenhaus, N., & Hendrych, M. (2006). Quantum cryptography. *Progress in Optics*, *49*, 381–454. doi:10.1016/S0079-6638(06)49005-3.

Gisin, N., Ribordy, G., Tittel, W., & Zbinden, H. (2002). Quantum cryptography. *Reviews of Modern Physics*, *74*, 145–195. doi:10.1103/RevModPhys.74.145.

Golubchikov, D. M. (2008). Structure and operation principles of Id 3000 Clavis system. *Proceedings of the South Federal University Technical Sciences*, *3*(80), 149–157.

Golubchikov, D. M., & Rumiantsev, K. E. (2008). Quantum cryptography: Principle, protocol, system. *All-Russian competitive selection analytical survey in priority guidelines of information and telecommunication systems*. Retrieved from http://www.ict.edu.ru/ft/005712/68358e2-st14.pdf

Hammond, A. (2006). *MagiQ and Verizon smash distance and cost barriers with world's longest cascaded network for practical quantum cryptography. New Technology Enables Ultra Secure Communications*. Business Wire.

Id Quantique. (2011). *Swiss bank encrypts critical low-latency backbone links with the Id Quantique centauris encryptors*. Retrieved from http://www.idquantique.com/news/swissquote.html

Id Quantique, S. A. (2005). Id 3000 Clavis: Plug & play quantum cryptography. *Specifications, 2.1*. Retrieved from http://www.idquantique.com/images/stories/PDF/clavis2-quantum-key-distribution/clavis2-specs.pdf

Id Quantique, S. A. (2005). Id 5000 Vectis. *Specifications, 1.2*. Retrieved from http://www.idquantique.com/images/stories/PDF/clavis2-quantum-key-distribution/clavis2-specs.pdf

Id Quantique, S. A. (2008). Quantum cryptography. *The Key to Future-Proof Confidentiality, 3.1*. Retrieved from http://www.idquantique.com/images/stories/PDF/clavis2-quantum-key-distribution/clavis2-specs.pdf

Id Quantique, S. A. (2010). *Practical quantum cryptography*. Paper presented at the Session of Second Winter School. New York, NY.

Kilin, S. Y., Nizovtsev, A. P., & Horoshko, D. B. (2007). *Quantum cryptography: Ideas and practice*. Minsk, Belarus: Belaruskaya Nauka.

Kotenko, V. V., & Rumiantsev, K. E. (2009). *Information theory and telecommunication security*. Rostov-on-Don, Russia: SFedU publishers.

MagiQ Technologies, Inc. (2004). QPN 5505. *Reference Manual*.

Mao, W. (2003). *Modern cryptography: Theory and practice*. Upper Saddle River, NJ: Prentice Hall.

Mayers, D. (2001). Unconditional security in quantum cryptography. *Journal of the ACM*, *48*, 351–406. doi:10.1145/382780.382781.

News. (n.d.). Retrieved from http://www.gap-optique.unige.ch

Pauli, D. (2009). Aussie govt considers quantum leap in secure comms. *Computer World*. Retrieved from http://www.computerworld.com.au/article/278658/aussie_govt_considers_quantum_leap_secure_comms/

Ribordy, G., Gautier, J.-D., Gisin, N., Guinnard, O., & Zbinden, H. (2000). Fast and user-friendly quantum key distribution. *Journal of Modern Optics*, *47*, 517–531.

Rumyantsev, K. E. (2010). Quantum communication: Theory, experiments, applications. *Info-Telecommunication and Computer Technology, Equipment, and Systems in South Federal University*. Rostov-on-Don, Russia: SFedU Publishers.

Scarani, V. (2006). *Quantum physics: A first encounter: Interference, entanglement, and reality*. Oxford, UK: Oxford University Press.

Shor, P. W., & Preskill, J. (2000). Simple proof of security of the BB84 quantum key distribution protocol. *Physical Review Letters*, *85*, 441–444. doi:10.1103/PhysRevLett.85.441 PMID:10991303.

Singh, S. (2000). *The code book: The secret history of codes and code breaking*. London, UK: Forth Estate.

Smart, N. (2004). *Cryptography: An introduction*. New York: McGraw-Hill College.

Stucki, D., Gisin, N., Guinnard, O., Ribordy, G., & Zbinden, H. (2002). Quantum key distribution over 67 km with a plug&play system. *New Journal of Physics*, *4*, 41.1– 41.8.

Chapter 16
ANFIS Modeling of Dynamic Load Balancing in LTE

Matthew K. Luka
Modibbo Adama University of Technology, Nigeria

Aderemi A. Atayero
Covenant University, Nigeria

ABSTRACT

Modelling of ill-defined or unpredictable systems can be very challenging. Most models have relied on conventional mathematical models which does not adequately track some of the multifaceted challenges of such a system. Load balancing, which is a self-optimization operation of Self-Organizing Networks (SON), aims at ensuring an equitable distribution of users in the network. This translates into better user satisfaction and a more efficient use of network resources. Several methods for load balancing have been proposed. While some of them have a very buoyant theoretical basis, they are not practical. Furthermore, most of the techniques proposed the use of an iterative algorithm, which in itself is not computationally efficient as it does not take the unpredictable fluctuation of network load into consideration. This chapter proposes the use of soft computing, precisely Adaptive Neuro-Fuzzy Inference System (ANFIS) model, for dynamic QoS aware load balancing in 3GPP LTE. The use of ANFIS offers learning capability of neural network and knowledge representation of fuzzy logic for a load balancing solution that is cost effective and closer to human intuition. Three key load parameters (number of satisfied user in the network, virtual load of the serving eNodeB, and the overall state of the target eNodeB) are used to adjust the hysteresis value for load balancing.

INTRODUCTION

Mobile communication systems are unpredictable and stochastic in nature due to a number of factors such as constantly changing propagation channels, random mobility of users and sudden changes in network load. This renders conventional mathematical tools less effective for system modelling of communication systems. Thus communication systems can be best modelled by adopting soft computing which exploits the tolerance for imprecision, partial truth and uncertainty to achieve robustness, low solution cost and tractability. One of such soft computing platforms is the Adaptive Neuro-Fuzzy Inference System (ANFIS). ANFIS is an architecture which can serve as a basis for constructing a set of fuzzy if-then rules with appropriate membership functions to give the

DOI: 10.4018/978-1-4666-2208-1.ch016

specified input/output pairs model (Jang, 1993). ANFIS modelling have been utilized in a number of applications such modelling of Microarray Cancer Gene Expression Data (Wang, 2005), Speed Control of Induction Motor (Kusagur, Kodad, & Ram, 2010), and for Optimization of Multiple Response Systems (Cheng, Cheng, & Lee, 2002). This chapter proposes the use of ANFIS modelling for dynamic load balancing for the Third Generation Partnership Project (3GPP) Long Term Evolution (LTE).

The 3GPP LTE is Self-Organizing Network (SON). Self-Organizing Network operation was introduced to enhance system performance by improving network operations and maintenance. SON operations are also promising in reducing both CAPital EXpenditure (CAPEX) and OPerational EXpenditure (OPEX). Load balancing is a SON operation which aims at ensuring an equitable distribution of cell load among eNodeBs in order to improve the overall system capacity of the network (ETSI TS 136 300, 2011), (M. of WINNER, 2005). To this end, several algorithms have been proposed. In (Lobinger, Stefanski, Jansen, & Balan, 2010), a load balancing algorithm aimed at finding the Optimum Handover (OH) offset value between the overloaded cell and a possible target cell was proposed. Another approach, which is based on a network formulation of heterogeneous services with different quality of service requirements was proposed in (Wang et al, 2010). A utility-based load-balancing framework was used to develop an algorithm called Heaviest-First Load Balancing (HFLB) in (Wang et al, 2010). However, these methods and algorithms are not computationally efficient because they involve the use of iterative processes. Moreover, the need to minimize load overhead due to excessive handover and Ping-Pong effect needs to be taken into consideration. Also, to make a more informed and informed load balancing decision, there is a need to consider not only the load of the serving cell, but other indicators such as the overall state of the serving cell and the number of satisfied users in the entire network must be taken into account. These challenges points to the need for a robust and cost effective approach.

OVERVIEW OF 3GPP LTE

The Long Term Evolution (LTE) started in 3GPP (Third Generation Partnership Project) release 8 and continued in release 10 with the objective of meeting the increasing performance requirements of mobile broadband (Dahlman, Parkvall, & Skold, 2011). LTE is a new radio-access technology geared towards higher data rates, high spectral efficiency, very low latency, support of variable bandwidth, simple protocol architecture, and support for Self-Organizing Networks (SON) operation. Release 10, otherwise known as LTE advanced is a fourth generation (4G) specification that provides enhanced peak data rates to support advanced services and applications (100 Mb/s for high mobility and 1 Gb/s for low mobility). LTE is the radio access network for Evolved Packet System (EPS), which has a core network known as Evolved Packet Core (EPC). The overall architecture of the EPS is shown in Figure 1.

The LTE radio access network consists of evolved Node Bs (eNodeBs) and no centralized controller (for normal user traffic). Due to the absence of a network controller, it is said to have a flat architecture. This structure reduces system complexity and cost and allows better performance over the radio interface. The eNBs are interconnected by the X2 interface. The S1-MME interface connects the eNBs to the key control plane of the core network-the MME, while the S1-U interface connects the eNBs and the S-GW. Intra-LTE load balancing is usually accomplished over the X2 interface.

Figure 1. EPS network elements

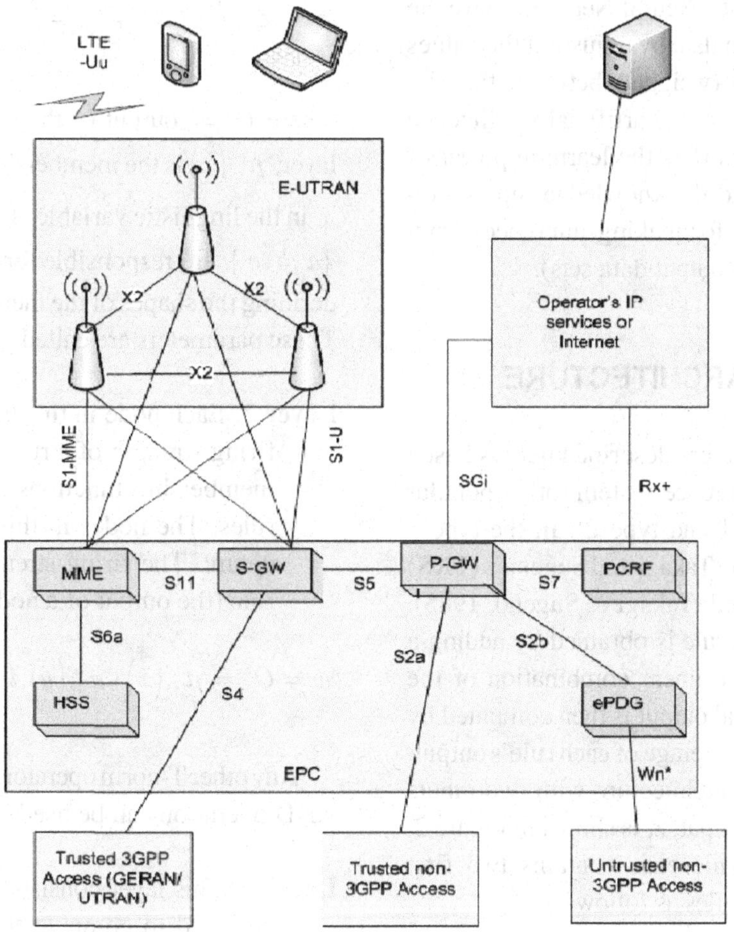

REVIEW OF ANFIS MODELLING

Adaptive Neuro-Fuzzy Inference System (ANFIS) otherwise referred to as Adaptive Network-based Fuzzy inference System was originally proposed in (Jang, 1993). ANFIS is a blend of Fuzzy Logic (FL) and Artificial Neural Network (ANN) that captures the strengths and offsets the limitations of both techniques for building Inference Systems with improved results and enhanced intelligence. Fuzzy logic is associated with the theory of fuzzy set, which relates to classes of objects with rough boundaries in which membership is a matter of degree. It is an extensive of multivalued logical system that departs in concept and substance from the traditional multivalued logical systems. Much of fuzzy logic may be viewed as a platform for computing with words rather than numbers. The use of words for computing is closer to human intuition and exploits the tolerance for imprecision, thereby lowering the cost of the solution (Mathwork Inc., 2011). However, there are no known appropriate or well-established methods of defining rules and membership functions based on human knowledge and experience for fuzzy inference systems. ANFIS uses ANN for adapting these membership functions by adjusting the adaptive parameters associated with the membership functions. Artificial Neural Networks are made up of simple processing elements operating concurrently. These elements model the biological nervous system, with the network functions predominantly determined by the connections between the elements. Neural Networks have the ability to learn from data by adjusting the values of the connections (weights) between the elements. Merging these two artificial intelligence paradigms together offers the learning power of neural networks and the knowledge representation of fuzzy logic for making inferences from observations (input/output data sets).

BASIC ANFIS ARCHITECTURE

The ANFIS architecture described here is based on type 3 fuzzy inference system (other popular types are the type 1 and type 2). In the type 3 inference system, the Takagi and Sugeno's (TKS) if-then rules are used (Takagi & Sugeno, 1985). The output of each rule is obtained by adding a constant term to the linear combination of the input variables. Final output is then computed by taking the weighted average of each rule's output. The type 3 ANFIS architecture with two inputs (x and y) and one output, z, is shown in Figure 2.

Assuming the rule base contains two first order TKS if-then rules as follows:

$$Rule1: if\ x\ is\ A_1\ and\ y\ is\ B_1, then\ z_1 = p_1x + q_1y + r_1$$

$$Rule2: if\ x\ is\ A_2\ and\ y\ is\ B_2, then\ z_2 = p_2x + q_2y + r_2$$

The ANFIS structure is functionally equivalent to a supervised, feed-forward neural network with one (1) input layer, three (3) hidden layers and one output layer, whose functionality are:

Layer 1: Every node in this layer is an adaptive layer that generates the membership grades of the input vectors. A bell-shaped (Gaussian) function with maximum equal to 1 and minimum equal to 0 is often used for implementing the node function:

$$O_i^1 = \mu_{A_i}(x) = \frac{1}{1 + \left|(x - c_i) / a_i\right|^{2b_i}} \quad (1)$$

where O_i^1 = output of the ith node in the first layer, $\mu_{A_i}(x)$ is the membership function of input x in the linguistic variable A_i. The parameter set $\{a_i, b_i, c_i\}$ are responsible for are responsible for defining the shapes of the membership functions. These parameters are called premise parameters.

Layer 2: Each node in this layer determines the firing strength of a rule by multiplying the membership functions associated with the rules. The nodes in this layer are fixed in nature. The firing strength of a particular rule (the output of a node) is given by:

$$w = O_i^2 = \mu_{A_i}(x) \cdot \mu_{B_i}(y), i = 1,2,\ldots \quad (2)$$

Any other T-norm operator that performs fuzzy AND operation can be used in this layer.

Layer 3: This layer consists of fixed nodes that are used to compute the ratio of the ith rule's firing strength to the total of all firing strengths:

$$\bar{w} = O_i^3 = \frac{w_i}{w_1 + w_2}, i = 1,2,\ldots \quad (3)$$

The outputs of this layer are otherwise known as *normalized firing strength* for convenience.

Layer 4: This is an adaptive layer with node function given by:

$$\bar{w}_i z_i = O_i^4 = \bar{w}_i(p_ix + q_iy + r_i) \quad (4)$$

Figure 2. Type 3 ANFIS architecture

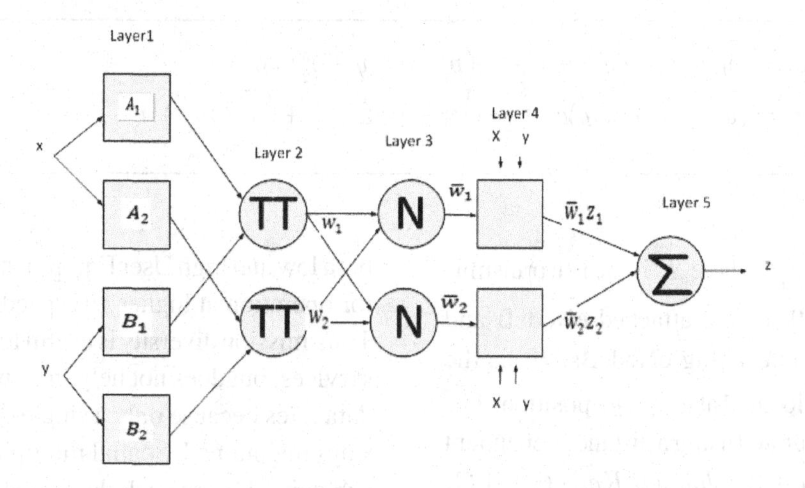

This layer essentially computes the contribution of each rule to the overall output. It is the defuzzification layer and provides output values resulting from the inference of rules. The parameters in this layer $\{p_i, q_i, r_i\}$ are known as consequent parameters.

Layer 5: There is only one fixed node in this layer. It computes the overall output as the summation of contribution from each rule:

$$\sum_i \bar{w}_i z_i = O_i^5 = \sum_i \frac{w_i z_i}{\sum_i z_i} \tag{5}$$

HYBRID LEARNING ALGORITHM

The objective of learning is to tune all the adjustable parameters to make the ANFIS output match the desired data. In order to improve the training efficiency, a combination of learning algorithms is adopted to adjust the parameters of the input and output membership functions. The consequent parameters are optimized using the least square method with the antecedent parameters fixed. After updating the consequent parameters, the gradient descent method using back-propagation training algorithm is used to fine-tune the premise parameters (Jang, 1993). Assuming the premise parameters are held fixed, then the overall output of the ANFIS will be a linear combination of the consequent outputs given by that show in Box 1.

LOAD BALANCING SYSTEM MODEL AND METRIC

The system model is based on a 3GPP downlink multi-cell network serving multiple users with a homogenous QoS requirement. Specifically, constant bit error rate (CBR) users are taken into account. The Signal to Interference Noise Ratio (SINR) is used as a metric measuring the link quality of the link model (M. of WINNER, 2005). Performance analysis is hinged on two factors, namely: fairness distribution of load and the number of unsatisfied users in the network.

Link Model

The post-equalization symbol SINR was determined from three parts of the link measurement model: (1) shadow fading, (2) macroscopic pathloss and (3) small scale fading (for Multiple-Input-Multiple Output). The propagation pathloss due to distance and antenna gain can be modelled by the macroscopic pathloss between an eNodeB sector and a User Equipment. The pathloss can

Box 1.

$$z = \overline{w_1} z_1 + \overline{w_2} z_2 = \overline{w_1}(p_1 x + q_1 y + r_1) + \overline{w_2}(p_2 x + q_2 y + r_2) \quad (6)$$

$$z = \overline{w_1} z_1 + \overline{w_2} z_2 = (\overline{w_1} x) p_1 + (\overline{w_1} y) q_1 + (\overline{w_1}) r_1 + (\overline{w_2} x) p_2 + (\overline{w_2} y) q_2 + r_2 \quad (7)$$

be noted as $L_{mp,\ T_i,U_j}$ where T_i is the i-th transmitter (denoted as 0 for the attached eNodeB and $1,\ldots,N$ for the interfering eNodeBs. U_j is the j-th UE which is located at an (x,y) position. The pathloss was generated using a distance dependent pathloss of $128.1 + 37.6 log_{10}(R[Km])$ (ETSI TR 136 942, 2009) and a $\theta_{3dB} = 65^{\circ} / 15$dBi antenna (3GPP TR 25.814, 2006). Shadow fading occurs due to obstacles in the propagation path between the eNodeB and UE. Shadow fading can be seen as the changes in the geographical properties of the terrain associated with the mean pathloss derived from the macroscopic pathloss model. It is often approximated by a log-normal distribution of standard deviation 10 dB and mean 0 dB. A UE moving in the Region of Interest (ROI) will experience a slowly changing pathloss due to the shadow fading of the attached eNodeB being correlated with the shadow fading of the interfering eNodeBs. Shadow fading can be denoted by $L_{sf,\ T_i,U_j}$. The large scales fading (shadow fading and pathloss) are position dependent and time-invariant. Small scale fading results primarily due to the presence of reflectors and scatterers that cause multiple versions of the transmitted signal to arrive at receiver. The small scale fading is modelled as a time dependent process for different transmission modes.

LTE supports both Single-Input Single-Output (SISO) and Multiple-Input Multiple-Output (MIMO) transmission techniques. The MIMO transmission modes supported are Transmit Diversity and Spatial Multiplexing. Transmit diversity provides a source of diversity for averaging out the channel variation either for delay sensitive services (Such as voice over internet protocol) at both low and high User Equipment (UE) speeds or for operation at higher UE speeds (Khan, 2009). Transmission diversity is useful for delay sensitive services, but does not help in improving the peak data rates because only a single data stream is always maintained. Spatial multiplexing facilitates achieving higher peak data rates by utilizing the multiple transmission antennas at the eNodeB in combination with multiple receive antennas at the UE. The MIMO OSLM channel can be modelled to obtain the per-layer SINR. This transmission mode consists of a precoding for Spatial Multiplexing (SM) with large-delay Cyclic Delay Diversity (CDD) (ETSI TS 136 211 (2011)). The OLSM MIMO precoding is defined by:

$$\begin{bmatrix} y_{(0)}(i) \\ \vdots \\ y_{(N_t-1)}(i) \end{bmatrix} = W(i) D(i) U \begin{bmatrix} x_{(0)}(i) \\ \vdots \\ x_{(v-1)}(i) \end{bmatrix} \quad (8)$$

where:

$N_t =$ Number of transmit antennas
$v =$ Number of layers (a layer is a mapping of symbols to the transmit antenna)
$W(i) = N_t \times v$ Is the precoding matrix
D and U are $v \times v$ diagonal matrixes introducing the CDD.

For the MIMO OLSM, the SINR for the UE can be expressed as Equation (9) in Box 2.

A given MCS (Modulation Coding Scheme) requires a certain SINR (measured at the receiver of the UE) to operate with an acceptably low BER (Bit Error Rate) in the output data. An

Box 2.

$$SINR_{c,\ u} = \frac{\alpha_i L_{sf,\ 0,U} L_{pl,\ 0,U} P_1}{\beta_i P_1 + \gamma_i \sigma^2 + \sum_1^{N_{int}} \theta_{i,1} L_{sf,\ T_i,U_j} L_{pl,\ T_i,U_j} P_1} \quad (9)$$

Where

α_i and β_i models the channel estimation errors, $P_1 = P_{tx} / v$ represents the homogenously distributed transmit power, γ_i models a simple Zero Forcing (ZF) receiver noise enhancement, σ^2 is the uncorrelated receiver noise and θ models the interference. $L_{sf,\ T_i,U_j}$ and $L_{pl,\ T_i,U_j} P_1$ stand for the shadow fading and pathloss between the UE, u and its attached eNodeB c (for $T_i = 0$) and its interferers (for $T_i = 1,\ldots,N_t$) respectively.

MCS with a higher throughput needs a higher SINR to operate [7]. We assume that the best modulation coding scheme (MCS) is used for a given SINR and the highest data rate $R(SINR)$ is achievable, this can be represented by Shannon formula as shown below:

$$R\left(SINR_u\right) = \log_2(1 + SINR_u) \quad (10)$$

For better approximation to realistic MCS, the mapping function is scaled by attenuation factor (say 0.75) and is bounded by the minimum required SINR (-6.5 dB) and a maximum bitrate (4.8 bps/Hz).

LOAD METRIC

The specific number of subcarriers allocated to users for a predetermined amount of time is referred to as the Physical Resource Blocks (PRBs) (Zyren & McCoy, 2007). PRBs possess both frequency and time dimension. The eNodeB is responsible for the allocation of PRBs using a scheduling function. The amount of Physical Resource Blocks (PRBs) required by user u can be expressed as:

$$N_u = \frac{D_u}{R\left(SINR\right)_u \cdot BW} \quad (11)$$

where $D_u =$ required data rate and BW is the transmission bandwidth of one resource blocks (180 kHz for LTE). The load of cell c can be expressed as the sum of required resources of all users connected to cell c to the total number of resources N_t:

$$\rho_c = \min\left(\frac{\sum_{u:X(u)=c} N_u}{N_t}, 1\right) \quad (12)$$

The total number of available resources (subcarriers) depends on the chosen transmission bandwidth of the system as shown in Table 1 (Holma & Toskala, 2009).

If we chose the number of unsatisfied users as an assessment and simulation metric, then we can focus on the CBR traffic rather than the network throughput. In this case, the UEs either get exactly the CBR or they totally unsatisfied. Equation (12) implies that the cell load parameter should not exceed 1 for all users to be satisfied. This can be extended to give a general indication of how overloaded (or otherwise) a cell is, by defining a virtual load given by:

Table 1. PRBs of different downlink bandwidths

Bandwidth (MHz)	Physical Resource Blocks (N_t)
1.4	6
3.0	15
5.0	25
10	50
20	100

$$\hat{\rho}_C = \frac{\sum_{u:X(u)=c} N_u}{N_t} \tag{13}$$

where $\hat{\rho}_C \leq 1$ means all users in the cell are satisfied, $\hat{\rho}_C = U$ means $1/U$ of the users are satisfied

The total number of unsatisfied users in the whole network (With a total number of M_c users in cell c) is given by:

$$z = \sum_c \max(0, M_c \cdot (1 - 1/\hat{\rho}_C)) \tag{14}$$

For performance analysis, the use of a fairness distribution index proposed in (Jain, Chiu, & Hawe, 1984) is employed. Thus, the load distribution index measuring the degree of load balancing of the entire network is given as:

$$\mu(t) = \frac{\left(\sum_c \rho_c(t)\right)^2}{|N| \sum_c (\rho_c(t))^2} \tag{15}$$

where $|N|$ is the number of cells in the network (used for simulation) and t is the simulation time. The load balance index $\mu(t)$ takes the value in the interval $\left[\frac{1}{|N|}, 1\right]$. A larger μ indicates a more balanced load distribution among the cells. Thus, the load distribution index is 1 when the load is completely balanced. The aim of load balancing (for CBR users) is to maximize is to maximize $\mu(t)$ at each time t.

In order to improve the load balancing performance among adjacent cells, it is necessary to find the optimum target cell. This can be achieved by adopting a two-layer inquiry scheme proposed in (Zhang et al, 2011). The source eNodeB (the cell requiring load balancing) requests both the load state and environment state from all neighbouring eNBs (first layer cells). The load state is the load of the first layer cell, while the environment state is the average load of the first layer cell's adjacent cells excluding the one to be adjusted (denoted as the second layer cells). The Overall State of the first layer cell i is obtained by a weighted combination of the load state (LS_i) and environment state (ES_i) in one figure as follows:

$$OS_i = \alpha LS_i + (1 - \alpha) ES_i \tag{16}$$

where the environmental state is given by:

$$ES_i = (\rho_{1i} + \rho_{2i} + \ldots + \rho_{ni}) / n = \frac{\sum_{j=1}^{n} \rho_j}{n} \tag{17}$$

$LS_i = \rho_i$, the load of first layer cell i, and α is a parameter that indicates the relative contribution of LS_i and ES_i to OS_i.

OS_i gives a comprehensive load information of the first layer cell, thereby indicating whether the eNodeB can be a target cell. Taking the value of $\alpha = 0.2$ Equation (17) can be expressed as:

$$OS_i = \left(0.2 \times \rho_i\right) + 0.8 \times \left(\frac{\sum_{j=1}^{n} \rho_j}{n}\right) \quad (18)$$

DESIGN OF LOAD BALANCING INFERENCE SCHEME

In the first stage, that is, the fuzzification process, the crisp variables (the virtual load of the source cell, the overall state of the target cell and number of unsatisfied users) are converted into fuzzy (linguistic) variables. The fuzzification maps the three (3) input variables to fuzzy labels of the fuzzy sets. Each linguistic variable has a corresponding membership function. A triangular-shaped membership function was determined to be the most suitable for this scenario. There are three 3 inputs and 3 fuzzified variables; thus the inference system has a set of 27 rules (Figure 5). The 27 rules included in the inference system are given in Figure 3 in the form of a flowchart:

The neural network training helps select the appropriate rule to be fired. Next, the rules are de-fuzzified to produce quantifiable results. De-fuzzification can be achieved using several techniques such as maximum methods, centre of gravity method, centre of singleton method etc. The centre of gravity method is adopted for this work. The de-fuzzified output is then used for making dynamic load balancing decisions. The structure of the ANFIS Model used is depicted in Figure 4. The model consists of 78 nodes, 27 fuzzy rules, 27 linear parameters and 27 nonlinear parameters. The total number of parameter is very important in deciding the number of training data pairs required. In order to realize a good generalization capability, it is recommended to have the number of training data points to be many times larger than the number of parameters being evaluated (Mathwork Inc., 2011). 1500 input/output pairs of training data was used for training. Thus, the ratio between the data points and parameters is about twenty seven times (1500/54).

For parameter optimization, hybrid training (which combines least square errors and back-propagation) was used. To ascertain how well the training data models the load balancing system, model validation using checking and testing data sets was adopted. Model validation involves presenting input/output data sets on which the inference system was not trained to check the degree to which the inference system model predicts the corresponding data set outputs values. This is achieved using the *testing data set*. The second type of data set for model validation is the *checking data set*. The checking data helps prevent the potential of model overfitting of the data, by selecting model parameters that corresponds to the minimum checking data model error. The training, testing and checking data sets used for modelling were obtained from simulation result using a tweaked version of an open source LTE system level simulator (Ikuno, Wrulich, & Rupp, 2010). A sample of training, testing and is given in Table 2.

SIMULATION RESULTS AND DISCUSSION

The Neuro-fuzzy model was developed using the ANFIS Editor GUI (Graphical User Interface). In the initial stage of the simulation, the UEs in the network are scheduled using the best channel quality indicators (CQIs) scheduling function of the eNodeB. The 27 rules written using the rule editor of the ANFIS Editor GUI is saved as a .fis file. The .fis file is then imported into the simulator using Matlab command line function *readfis*. After running the simulator, the three (3) inputs and one (1) output training parameters are stored in a variable in the command window. The ANFIS is properly trained using the *anfis* Matlab command function which takes the fuzzy rule base, training

Figure 3. Fuzzy inference system flowchart

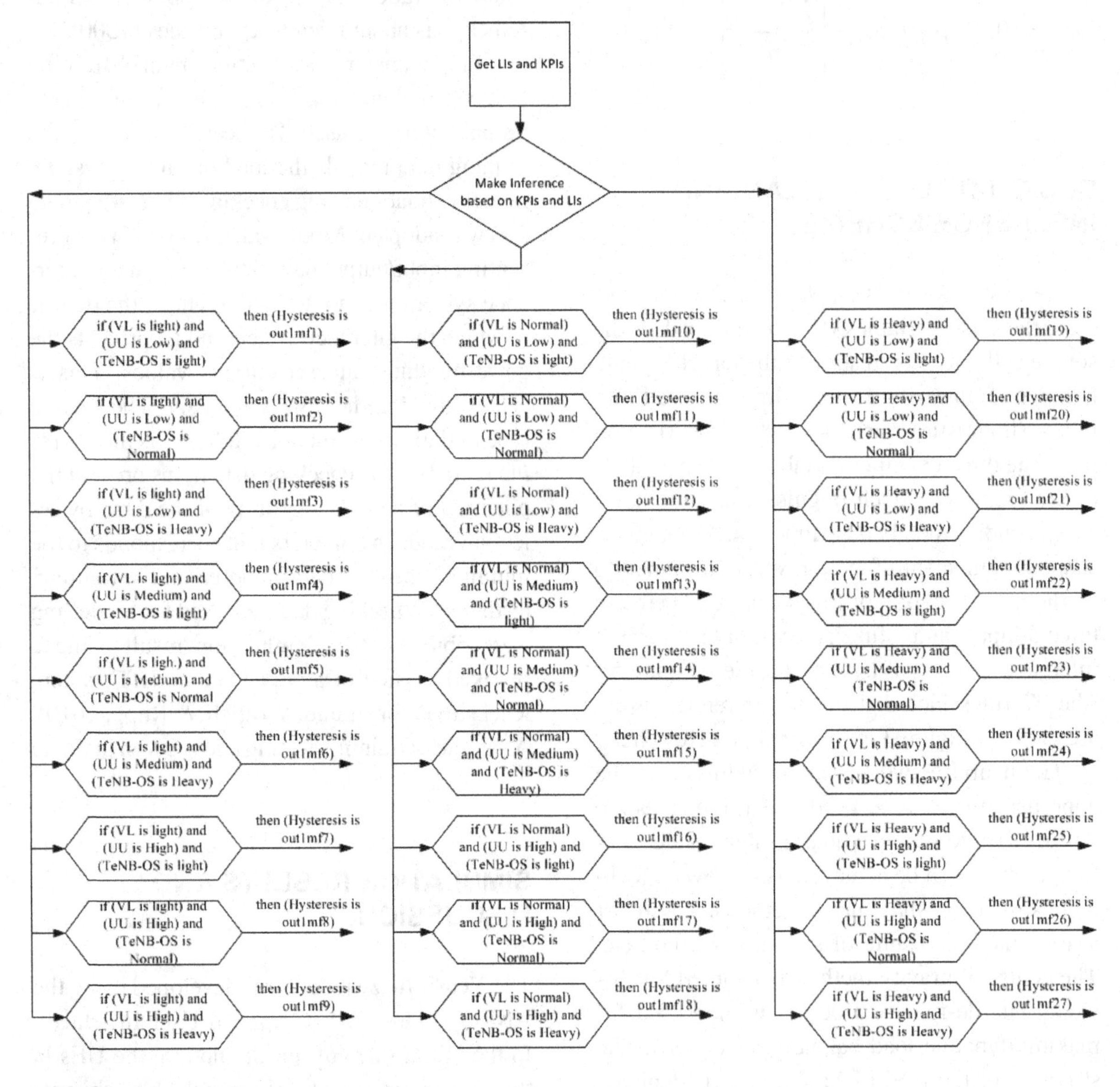

VL=Virtual Load, UU = Unsatisfied Users and TeNB-OS = Overall state of target eNodeB

data and the optional checking data as input arguments. The *checking data set* was used to control the potential of overfitting the data. The checking data and the training data are presented to the ANFIS so that the fuzzy inference model selects parameters associated with the minimum checking data model error. An average checking error of 0.087521 was realized using 1500 input/output checking data set (Figure 6). The ANFIS model was validated using *testing data sets.* The testing data sets were presented to the trained ANFIS to see how well the ANFIS model predicts output values. An average testing error of 0.086525 was achieved for an average training error of 0.0067812 using 20 training epochs.

Having trained and validated the model, it is now ready use in making inferences for load balancing. The simulation is now run with the

Figure 4. Rule viewer for the inference system

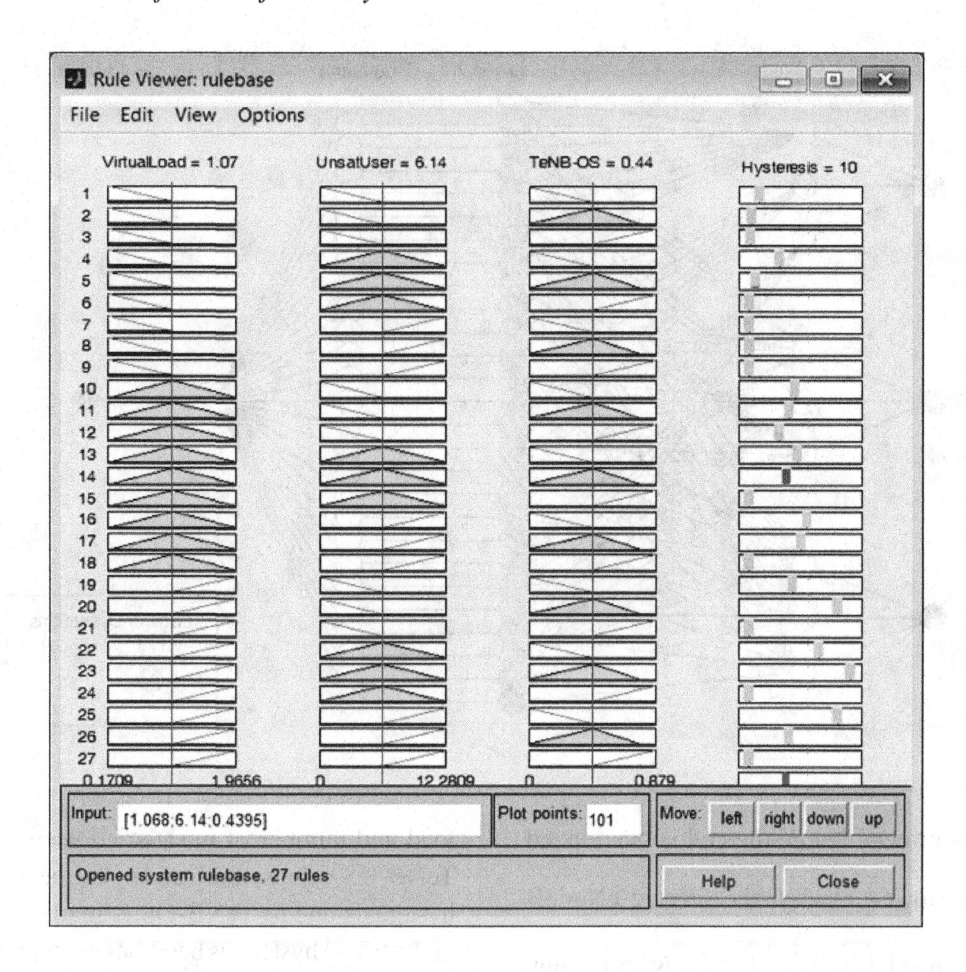

functionality for load balancing activated and the ANFIS model incorporated. As the simulation runs, the ANFIS model evaluates the hysteresis using the Matlab function *evalfis*. The output is used to decide the number of UEs to be transferred from the overloaded cell in order to improve users' satisfaction and load distribution fairness index which indicates equitable distribution of UEs in the network. The steps needed for the simulation purposes can be summed up in the following steps:

1. Write the rules using the ANFIS rule editor and save the rules as a .fis file in the same directory with the LTE system level simulator.
2. Import the .fis file into the Matlab Work Space (WS).
3. Run the simulator to schedule users and get training parameters for the ANFIS, omitting the evaluation (usage) stage of the ANFIS model.
4. Train the ANFIS using hybrid training algorithm and a suitable number of epochs.
5. Run the simulator again; this time skip the training stage and include the evaluation stage of the ANFIS Model.

The ANFIS model uses the hysteresis value for load balancing. The hysteresis increases as the virtual load of the serving eNodeB increases. This

Figure 5. ANFIS model structure

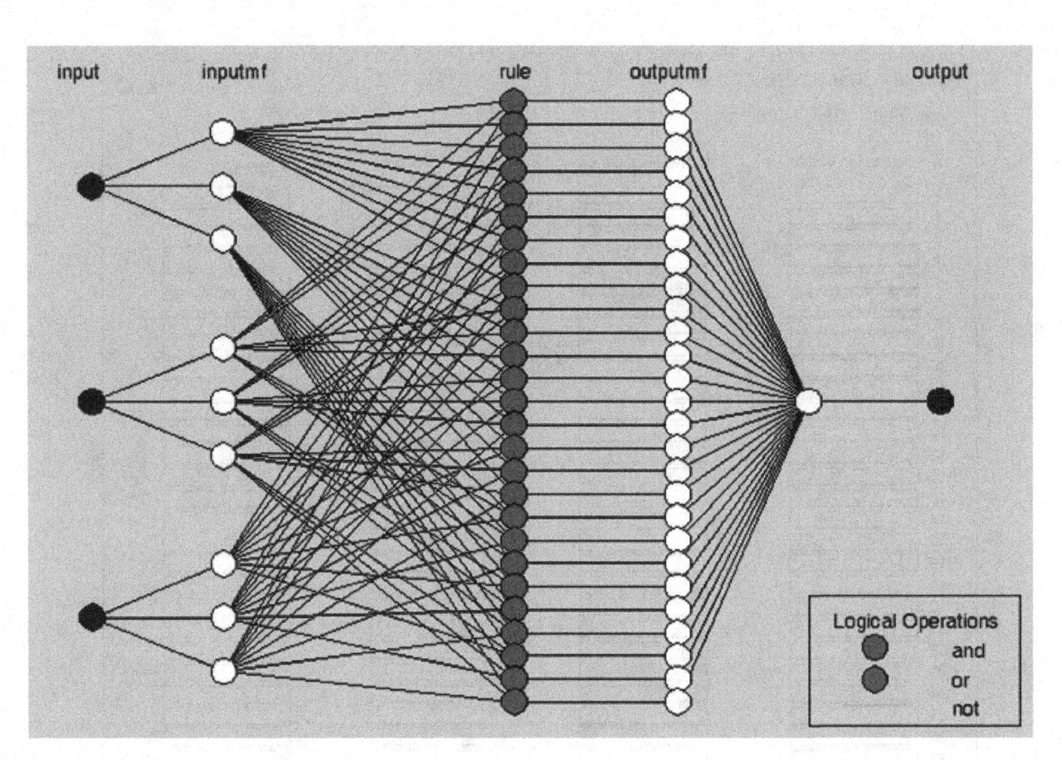

increase is gradual before the cell is overloaded $(\hat{\rho}_C \leq 1)$. However, when the serving eNodeB gets overloaded $(\hat{\rho}_C > 1)$, the hysteresis value increases rapidly Figure 7. Before the number of unsatisfied users reaches a certain threshold (in this particular case, 6), the hysteresis tend to decrease. This is due to overriding influence of other parameters (especially the overall state of the target eNodeB). However, the trend changes spontaneously when the number of unsatisfied users becomes significant (or reaches a certain threshold). The slope of increase in hysteresis when the threshold is attained is much higher than the rate of decrease experienced earlier: see Figure 8. The change in hysteresis due to the overall state of the target eNodeB (TeNB-OS) depicts a completely different trend from that of the other two indicators. Generally, the TeNB-OS sets a check on the value of the hysteresis due virtual load and number of unsatisfied users. Between TeNB-OS values of 0.0 and 0.45, the decrease in hysteresis due to TeNB-OS is gradual. The rate of decline in hysteresis becomes more pronounced between TeNB-OS values of 0.45 and 0.75. When the TeNB-OS approaches the value of 1.0, it forces the hysteresis to zero, indicating that the target eNodeB cannot accept more loads even if the source eNodeB is still overloaded, see Figure 9. When this happens, the serving eNodeB is forced to choose another target eNodeB.

When the virtual load of the serving eNodeB is benchmarked against the TeNB-OS of the selected target eNodeB, their respective effects is depicted in Figure 10. If the decrease in hysteresis value due TeNB-OS does not offset the increase in hysteresis value due to virtual load, another target eNodeB will be selected (when TeNB-OS for the currently selected target eNodeB reaches 0.8). This is necessary in order to avoid

Table 2. Training and testing data sets for the ANFIS modelling

S/N	Training Data				Testing Data			
	Inputs			Output	Inputs			Output
	$\hat{\rho}_C$	z	OS_i	Hysteresis	$\hat{\rho}_C$	z	OS_i	Hysteresis
1	1.361042	3.390306	0.180923	12.72999	0.353646	0	0.749619	1.766065
2	0.986637	0.187466	0.286651	10.57362	0.330942	0	0.765693	1.517912
3	1.156888	1.838407	0.235804	11.60829	0.313339	0	0.778156	1.332797
4	1.007555	0	0.394951	8.38957	0.303509	0	0.785115	1.232539
5	1.079373	0	0.48721	6.560096	0.290151	0	0.794573	1.100192
6	0.854589	0	0.52705	5.783147	0.282019	0	0.80033	1.022009
7	0.72428	1.68249	0.240914	11.5041	0.288542	0	0.795712	1.084577
8	0.668008	0	0.427388	7.74233	0.296069	0	0.790383	1.158243
9	1.072156	0	0.470869	6.881359	0.285589	0	0.797803	1.056098
10	0.808774	0	0.481104	6.679979	0.769553	0	0.455156	7.191513
11	0.74736	0	0.422182	7.845935	0.296266	0	0.790243	1.1602
12	0.732904	0	0.482266	6.657147	0.274937	0	0.805344	0.95548
13	0.816126	0	0.430747	7.675532	0.330087	0	0.766298	1.508767
14	0.731263	0	0.51925	5.9345	0.308539	0	0.781554	1.283552
15	0.80403	8.511785	0	17.97495	0.365803	0	0.741012	1.902821
16	0.679026	7.971445	0	17.26954	0.350186	0	0.752068	1.727625
17	1.516234	3.992071	0.157461	13.21086	0.473118	0	0.665032	3.197888
18	1.468122	8.975134	0	18.61837	0.711819	0	0.496032	6.387242
19	1.190027	3.390306	0.180923	12.72999	0.446675	0	0.683754	2.866685
20	1.560075	0.187466	0.286651	10.57362	0.438088	0	0.689834	2.760585

overloading the target eNodeB. Wedging the number of unsatisfied users against TeNB-OS yields a similar result. As the number of unsatisfied users increase from 0 to 10, the hysteresis value increases correspondingly. However, a corresponding increase in the TeNB-OS tends to reduce the hysteresis value in order to force the serving eNodeB to choose another target cell as the current target cell's overall load state approaches (0.8 see Figure 11). The interplay between virtual load and the number of unsatisfied users is illustrated in Figure 12. The impact virtual load on determining load balancing (hysteresis) is more pronounced than that of the number

Figure 6. Model validation using checking data sets

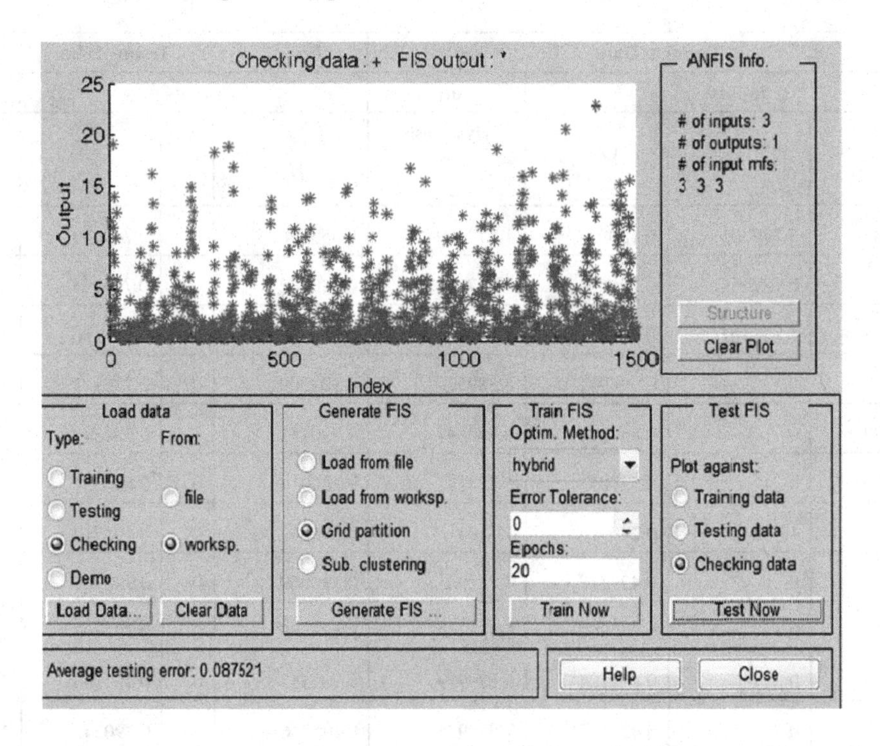

Figure 7. Relative contribution of virtual load to hysteresis value

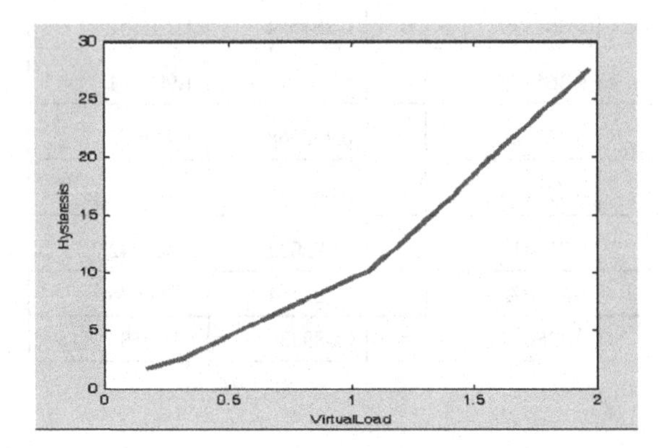

Figure 8. Relative contribution of unsatisfied users to hysteresis value

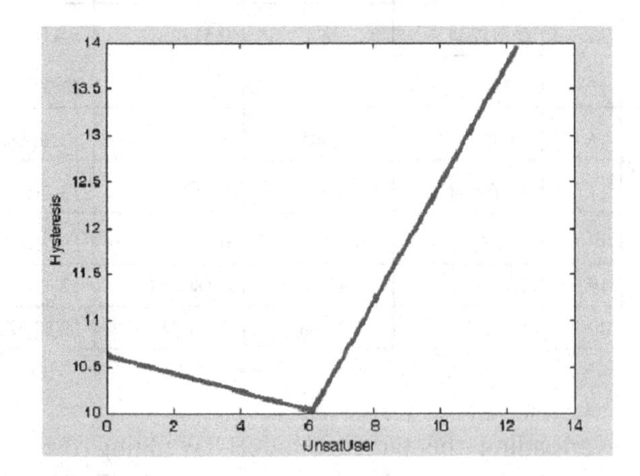

of unsatisfied users. This is because the virtual load is more specific to the source eNodeB, which is directly involved in the load balancing, whereas the number of unsatisfied users is a network wide performance indicator.

CONCLUSION

A systematic method of equitably distributing the loads among cells in an LTE network by means of

Figure 9. Relative contribution of target eNodeB overall state users to hysteresis value

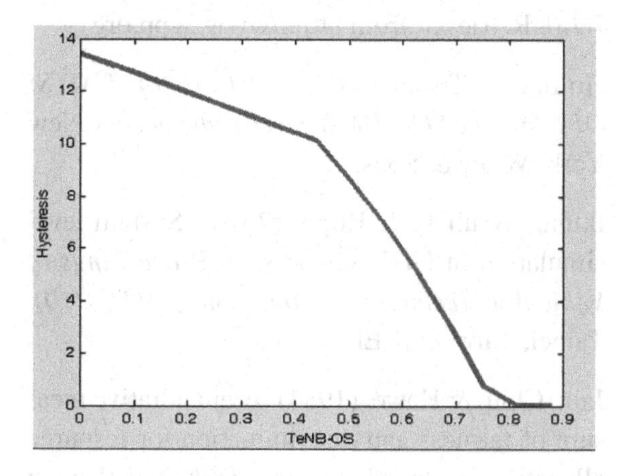

Figure 10. Combined effect of virtual load and overall state on load balancing hysteresis

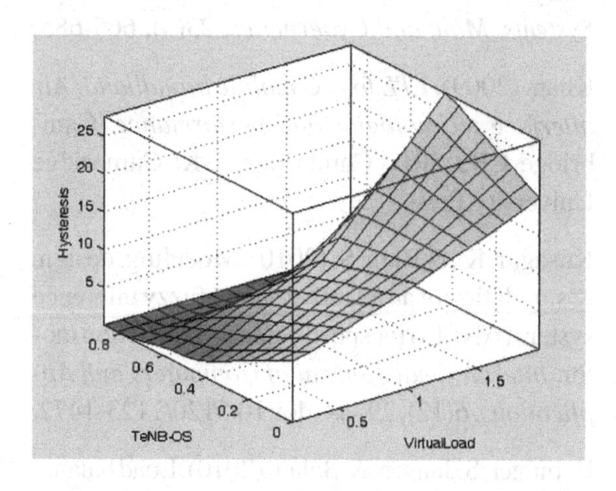

Figure 11. Combined effect of unsatisfied user and overall state on load balancing hysteresis

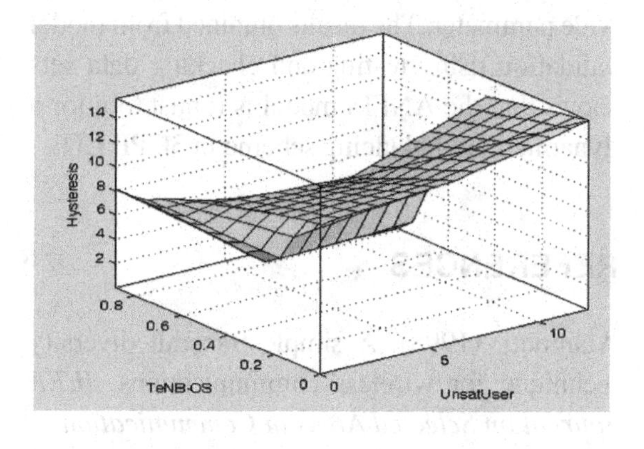

Figure 12. Combined effect of unsatisfied user and virtual load on load balancing hysteresis

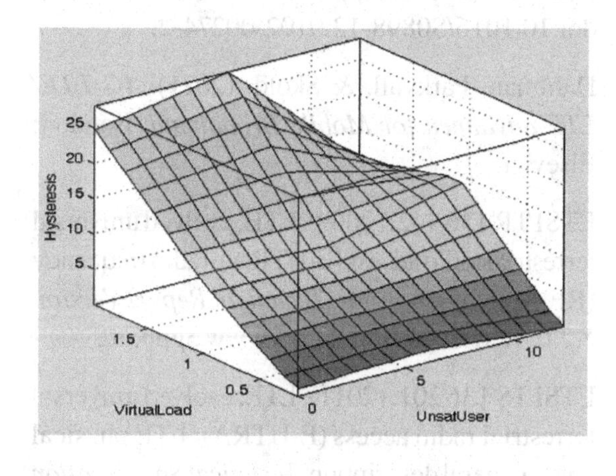

Adaptive Neuro-Fuzzy Inference System has been investigated in this chapter. The ANFIS Model was developed using Matlab and incorporated into an LTE system level simulator. The Inference system of the ANFIS is hinged on 27 fuzzy rules. The main advantage of using the ANFIS model in load balancing is to exploit the tolerance for imprecision and uncertainty associated with wireless network to achieve a cost effective load balancing strategy.

The virtual load of the source eNodeB plays a more vital load in determining the output value of the ANFIS model associated with load balancing. The overall load state of the target eNodeB ensures that the target eNodeB is not overload by the source eNodeB by forcing the hysteresis to zero when it is getting overloaded. The number of unsatisfied users in the entire tends to decrease the load balancing hysteresis when the source eNodeB is not overloaded and increase the hysteresis when the source cell is overloaded because it is a network wide parameter. The results obtained from model validation using testing and checking data sets shows that the ANFIS model is robust tool for a dynamic load-balancing scheme in 3GPP LTE.

REFERENCES

Alamouti. (1998). A simple transmit diversity technique for wireless communications. *IEEE Journal on Selected Areas in Communications.*

Cheng, Cheng, & Lee. (2002). Neuro-fuzzy and genetic algorithm in multiple response optimization. *International Journal of Computers & Mathematics with Applications*, *44*, 1503–1514. doi:10.1016/S0898-1221(02)00274-2.

Dahlman, Parkvall, & Skold. (2011). *4G LTE/LTE-advanced for Mobile Broadband.* London: Elsevier.

ETSI TR 136 942. (2009). LTE; evolved universal terrestrial radio access (E-UTRA); radio frequency (RF) system scenarios. *Technical Report Version 8.2.0.* Retrieved from http://www.3gpp.org

ETSI TS 136 201. (2011). LTE; evolved universal terrestrial radio access (E-UTRA); LTE physical layer; general description. *Technical Specification Version 10.0.0.* Retrieved from http://www.3gpp.org

ETSI TS 136 211. (2011). LTE; evolved universal terrestrial radio access (E-UTRA); physical channels and modulation. *Technical Specification Version 10.2.0.* Retrieved from http://www.3gpp.org

ETSI TS 136 300. (2011). LTE; evolved universal terrestrial radio access (E-UTRA) and evolved universal terrestrial radio access network (E-UTRAN); overall description; stage 2. *Technical Specification Version 10.4.0.* Retrieved from http://www.3gpp.org

3. GPP TR 25.814. (2006). Physical layer aspects for E-UTRA. *Technical Specification Version 7.1.0.* Retrieved from http://www.3gpp.org

Holma & Toskala. (2009). *LTE for UMTS: OFDMA and SC-FDMA based radio access*. New York: Wiley & Sons.

Ikuno, Wrulich, & Rupp. (2010). System level simulation of LTE networks. In *Proceedings of Vehicular Technology Conference (VTC '10).* Taipei, Taiwan: IEEE Press.

Jain, Chiu, & Hawe. (1984). A quantitative measure of fairness and discrimination for resource allocation in shared systems. *Technical Report: Digital Equipment Corporation, DEC-TR-301.*

Jang. (1993). ANFIS: Adaptive network-based fuzzy inference system. *IEEE Transactions on Systems, Man, and Cybernetics, 23*(3), 665-685.

Khan. (2009). *LTE for 4G mobile broadband: Air interface technologies and performance.* Cambridge CB2 8RU. Cambridge, UK: Cambridge University Press.

Kusagur, K., & Ram, S. (2010). Modeling, design, & simulation of an adaptive neuro-fuzzy inference system (ANFIS) for speed control of induction motor. *International Journal of Computers and Applications*, *6*(12), 29–44. doi:10.5120/1123-1472.

Lobinger, S. Jansen, & Balan. (2010). Load balancing in downlink LTE self-optimizing networks. In *Proceedings of IEEE 71st Vehicular Technology Conference 2010.* Taipei, Taiwan: IEEE Press.

M. of WINNER. (2005). Assessment of advanced beamforming and MIMO technologies. *WINNER, IST-2003-507581.*

Mathwork Inc. (2011). *Fuzzy logic toolbox user guide version 2.2.14.* Retrieved from www.mathworks.com

Sesia, Toufik, & Baker. (2009). *LTE-The UMTS long term evolution: From theory to practice.* New York: Wiley & Sons, Ltd.

Takagi & Sugeno. (1985). Fuzzy identification of systems and its application to modelling and control. *IEEE Transactions on Systems, Man, and Cybernetics, 15*, 116–132.

Wang. (2005). Neuro-fuzzy modeling for microarray cancer gene expression data. *First Year Transfer Report*. Oxford, UK: Linacre College, Oxford University, Computing Laboratory.

Wang. (2010a). Dynamic load balancing in 3GPP LTE multi-cell networks with heterogeneous services. In *Proceedings of ICST Conference*. Beijing, China: LNCIST.

Wang. (2010b). *Dynamic load balancing and throughput optimization in 3GPP LTE networks (IWCMC 2010)*. Caen, France: IWCMC.

Zhang, Liu, Zhang, Jia, & Duan. (2011). A two-layer mobility load balancing in LTE self-organization networks. In *Proceedings of IEEE Internal Conference on Communication Technology*. Beijing: IEEE Press.

Zyren & McCoy. (2007). Overview of the 3GPP long term evolution physical layer. (White Paper) *Document number:3GPPEVOLUTIONWP Rev. 0: Freescale semiconductor.*

ADDITIONAL READING

Ali-Yahiya. (2011). *Understanding LTE and its performance*. Berlin: Springer.

Atayero, A. A., & Luka, M. K. (2012). Adaptive neuro-fuzzy Inference System for load balancing in 3GPP LTE. *International Journal of Advanced Research in Artificial Intelligence, 1*(1), 11–16.

Atayero, A. A., & Luka, M. K. (2012). A soft computing approach to dynamic load balancing in 3GPP LTE. *International Journal of Computers and Applications, 43*(19), 35–41. doi:10.5120/6213-8895.

Atayero, A. A., Luka, M. K., Orya, M. K., & Iruemi, J. O. (2001). 3GPP long term evolution: Architecture, protocols, and interfaces. *IJICT Journal, 1*(7), 307–310.

Corporation, N. E. C. (2009). *Self-organizing network: NEC's proposal for next-generation radio network management* (White Paper). NEC Corporation.

Dahlman, P. Sköld, & Beming. (2007). 3G evolution HSPA and LTE for mobile broadband. New York: Elsevier.

Ergen. (2009). *Mobile broadband including WiMAX and LTE*. Berlin: Springer.

Ericsson. (2009). Radio network measurement guidelines. Ericsson WCDMA Radio Access Network: Ericsson Internal Document, 1(64).

Fakhreddine, O. Karray, & de Silva. (2004). Soft computing and intelligent systems design. Upper Saddle River, NJ: Pearson, Education, Ltd.

Jang, Sun, & Mizutani. (1997). *Neuro-fuzzy and soft computing: A computational approach to learning and machine intelligence*. Englewood Cliffs, NJ: Prentice Hall.

Konar, A. (1999). *Artificial intelligence and soft computing: Behavioural and cognitive modelling of the human brain*. Boca Raton, FL: CRC Press. doi:10.1201/9781420049138.

Luka & Atayero. (2012). *Adaptive neuro-fuzzy inference system models for dynamic load balancing in 3GPP LTE*. Berlin: Lambert Academic Publishing. Retrieved from http://qr.net/anfis2

Mehlführer, C. (2011). The Vienna LTE simulators – Enabling reproducibility in wireless communications research. *EURASIP Journal on Advances in Signal Processing*. doi:10.1186/1687-6180-2011-29.

Ofcom Consultants. (2011). *LTE technical modelling: Revised methodology. 800 MHz & 2.6 GHz Combined Award–Technical Modelling for Competition Assessment*. Canada: Annex Business Media.

Piro. (2010). Simulating LTE cellular systems: An open source framework. *IEEE Transaction on Vehicular Technology.*

Proakis & Salehi. (1998). *Contemporary communication systems using Mathlab*. Boston: PWS Publishers.

Chapter 17
Neural Network Control of a Laboratory Magnetic Levitator

J. Katende
Botswana International University of Science and Technology, Botswana

M. Mustapha
Bayero University, Nigeria

ABSTRACT

Magnetic levitation (maglev) systems are nowadays employed in applications ranging from non-contact bearings and vibration isolation of sensitive machinery to high-speed passenger trains. In this chapter a mathematical model of a laboratory maglev system was derived using the Lagrangian approach. A linear pole-placement controller was designed on the basis of specifications on peak overshoot and settling time. A 3-layer feed-forward Artificial Neural Network (ANN) controller comprising 3-input nodes, a 5-neuron hidden layer, and 1-neuron output layer was trained using the linear state feedback controller with a random reference signal. Simulations to investigate the robustness of the ANN control scheme with respect to parameter variations, reference step input magnitude variations, and sinusoidal input tracking were carried out using SIMULINK. The obtained simulation results show that the ANN controller is robust with respect to good positioning accuracy.

1. INTRODUCTION

Essentially magnetic levitation (maglev) is the use of controlled magnetic fields (or magnetic forces) to cause a magnetic object to float in air in defiance of gravity (Richard, 2004). Maglev systems are widely used in various fields, such as magnetic (non-contact) bearings (Hassan & Mohamed, 2001), high-speed maglev passenger trains (Murai & Tanaka, 2000) and vibration isolation of sensitive machinery (Shen, 2002). Most of the current maglev systems are of the electromagnetic suspension (EMS) type, whereby electric current variations control the attractive force of an electromagnet. The mathematical models of such systems are highly nonlinear and open-loop unstable (Yang, Miyazaki, Kanae & Wada, 2005). Hence it is not a trivial task to construct a high performance controller to accurately position the levitated object.

In recent years, many techniques have been reported in the technical literature for controlling maglev systems. Barrie and Chiasson (1996) as well as Joo and Seo (1997) employed feedback

DOI: 10.4018/978-1-4666-2208-1.ch017

linearization techniques to design control laws for maglev systems. Al-Muthairi and Zbiri (2004) and Phuah, Lu and Yahagi (2005) applied the nonlinear sliding mode control technique to improve the positioning accuracy of maglev systems. Other types of controllers for maglev systems reported in the technical literature include: phase-lead compensation (Wong, 1986; Sani, 2004); fuzzy logic controllers (Golob, 2000; Tzes, Chen, & Peng, 1994) and artificial neural network controllers (Kemal, 2003).

Artificial neural networks (ANNs) have shown a great promise in identification and control of nonlinear systems. ANNs constitute a powerful data-modelling tool that is able to capture and represent complex input/output relationships. The motivation for the development of ANN technology stemmed from the desire to develop an artificial system that could perform "intelligent" tasks similar to those performed by the human brain (Hagan, M., Demuth, H., & De Jesus, 2002). ANNs are composed of simple elements operating in parallel. These elements were inspired by biological nervous systems. One can train a neural network to perform a particular function by adjusting the values of the connections (weights) between elements. ANNs have been trained to perform complex functions in various fields of application including pattern recognition, identification, classification, vision and automatic control.

This work considers a laboratory maglev system that was implemented by Sani (2004) and controlled using a lead compensator. An artificial neural network controller for the system is proposed and simulated in the MATLAB/SIMULINK environment. The proposed controller is trained based on the performance of a linear state feedback controller, which was designed to satisfy a pair of dominant poles in the state-space. The rest of the chapter is organized as follows. Section 2 deals with the mathematical modelling of the maglev system. In Section 3 a linear state feedback controller for the maglev system is designed based on well-known engineering specifications of peak overshoot and settling time. Section 4 contains the design and training of an ANN controller for the maglev system. Section 5 presents and discusses simulation results of the proposed ANN controller. Conclusions drawn from the study are given in the last section.

2. MATHEMATICAL MODEL OF THE MAGLEV SYSTEM

The maglev system considered in this paper consists of ferromagnetic ball suspended in a magnetic field. Only the vertical motion is considered. The objective is to keep the ball at a prescribed reference level. The dynamical equations of the maglev system are derived using the Lagrange method.

Figure 1 shows a photograph of the maglev system while Figure 2 shows the corresponding schematic diagram, where: M is the levitated ball mass (kg); g is acceleration due to gravity (m/s^2); V is the voltage (V) applied to the electromagnet

Figure 1. Photograph of a laboratory magnetic levitation system

Figure 2. Schematic diagram of a magnetic levitation system

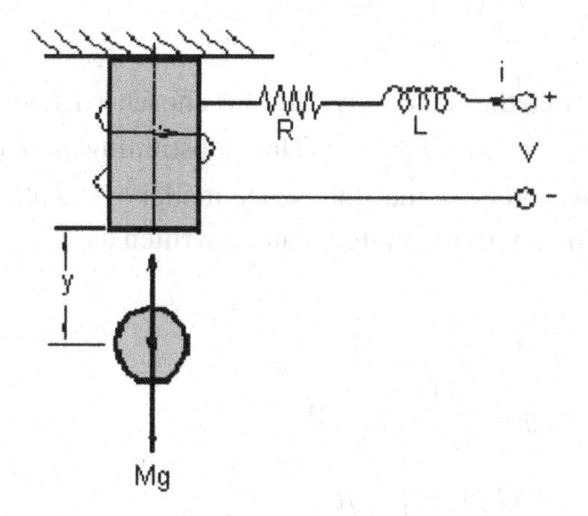

coil; i is current (A) through the coil; R is the coil resistance (Ω); L is the coil inductance (H).

The Lagrange formulation uses the kinetic and potential energies in the system to determine the dynamical equations of motion (Boldia & Nasar, 1986). The kinetic energy of the system (T) is the sum of the kinetic energy of the levitated ball and that of the inductance of the coil and is given by:

$$T = \frac{1}{2}M\dot{y}^2 + \frac{1}{2}L(y)i^2 \quad (1)$$

The potential energy (P) of the system is given by:

$$P = -Mgy \quad (2)$$

The Rayleigh dissipation function is given by:

$$F = \frac{1}{2}Ri^2 \quad (3)$$

The Lagrange function (Γ) is the difference between the kinetic and the potential energies of the system:

$$\Gamma = T - P = \frac{1}{2}M\dot{y}^2 + \frac{1}{2}L(y)i^2 + Mgy \quad (4)$$

The inductance $L(y)$ is a nonlinear function of the ball's position, y, that is [8]:

$$L(y) = L_1 + \frac{L_0 y_0}{y} = L_1 + \frac{2C}{y} \quad (5)$$

where y_0 is an arbitrary reference position for the inductance, L_1 is the coil inductance in the absence of the ball, L_0 is additional inductance due to the levitated ball and C is the force constant.

Substituting (5) in (4) yields

$$\Gamma = \frac{1}{2}M\dot{y}^2 + \frac{1}{2}\left(L_1 + \frac{2C}{y}\right)i^2 + Mgy \quad (6)$$

The Lagrangian equations are given by

$$\frac{d}{dt}\left(\frac{\partial \Gamma}{\partial \dot{y}}\right) - \frac{\partial \Gamma}{\partial y} = 0 \quad (7)$$

$$\frac{d}{dt}\left(\frac{\partial \Gamma}{\partial i}\right) + \frac{\partial F}{\partial i} = V \quad (8)$$

The partial derivatives from (6) are,

$$\frac{\partial \Gamma}{\partial \dot{y}} = M\dot{y} \quad (9)$$

$$\frac{\partial \Gamma}{\partial y} = Mg - \frac{C}{y^2}i^2 \quad (10)$$

$$\frac{\partial \Gamma}{\partial i} = \left(L_1 + \frac{2C}{y^2}\right)i \quad (11)$$

$$\frac{\partial F}{\partial i} = Ri \tag{12}$$

Substituting (9) and (10) in (7) yields

$$M\ddot{y} - Mg + \frac{C}{y^2} i^2 = 0 \tag{13}$$

$$\ddot{y} = g - \frac{C}{M}\left(\frac{i^2}{y^2}\right) = 0 \tag{14}$$

Substituting (11) and (12) in (8) yields

$$\frac{d}{dt}\left(L_1 i + \frac{2C}{y} i\right) + Ri = V \tag{15}$$

$$L_1 \frac{di}{dt} + \frac{2Cy\frac{di}{dt} - 2Ci\dot{y}}{y^2} + Ri = V \tag{16}$$

$$L_1 \frac{di}{dt} + \frac{2C\frac{di}{dt}}{y} - \frac{2Ci\dot{y}}{y^2} + Ri = V \tag{17}$$

$$\left(L_1 + \frac{2C}{y}\right)\frac{di}{dt} - \frac{2Ci\dot{y}}{y^2} + Ri = V \tag{18}$$

It was experimentally found that L_1 is more than 25 times greater than $\frac{L_0 y_0}{y} = \frac{2C}{y}$ [8]. Therefore, by neglecting the term $\frac{2C}{y}$, Equation (18) becomes

$$L_1 \frac{di}{dt} - \frac{2Ci\dot{y}}{y^2} + Ri = V \tag{19}$$

$$\frac{di}{dt} = \frac{2C}{L_1}\left(\frac{i\dot{y}}{y^2}\right) - \frac{R}{L_1} i + \frac{V}{L_1} \tag{20}$$

Let the state variables be chosen such that $x_1 = y, x_2 = \dot{y}, x_3 = i$. Thus substituting these in (14) and (20), the state space model of the magnetic levitation system can be written as

$$\begin{aligned} \dot{x}_1 &= x_2 \\ \dot{x}_2 &= g - \frac{C}{M}\left(\frac{x_3}{x_1}\right)^2 = 0 \\ \dot{x}_3 &= \frac{2C}{L_1}\left(\frac{x_2 x_3}{x_1^{\,2}}\right) - \frac{R}{L_1} x_3 + \frac{V}{L_1} \end{aligned} \tag{21}$$

3. LINEAR STATE FEEDBACK CONTROLLER DESIGN

The objective is to design a state feedback controller such that the system works according to the following specifications:

- Peak overshoot of approximately 5%.
- Settling time of less than 1 second.

Equations (21) were used to model the open loop maglev system. However, for the design of the linear state feedback controller, the linearized model is required. Using the Jacobian linearization (Katende, 2004), the linear approximation to Equation (21) about the equilibrium point $x_0 = [x_{10}, x_{20}, x_{30}] = [y_0, 0, i_0]$, $u_0 = [0, 0, V]$ is given by

$$\delta\dot{x} = A\delta x + B\delta u \tag{22}$$

$$y = C\delta x. \tag{23}$$

where

$$A = \begin{bmatrix} 0 & 1 & 0 \\ \dfrac{2Cx_{30}^2}{Mx_{10}^3} & 0 & -\dfrac{2Cx_{30}}{Mx_{10}^2} \\ 0 & \dfrac{2Cx_{30}}{L_1 x_{10}^2} & -\dfrac{R}{L_1} \end{bmatrix}$$

$$B = \begin{bmatrix} 0 \\ 0 \\ \dfrac{1}{L_1} \end{bmatrix}, C = \begin{bmatrix} 1 & 0 & 0 \end{bmatrix} \quad (24)$$

From (24) the linear state space model of the maglev system is

$$\begin{aligned} \dot{x}_1 &= x_2, \\ \dot{x}_2 &= \frac{2Cx_{30}^2}{Mx_{10}^3} x_1 - \frac{2Cx_{30}}{Mx_{10}^2} x_3, \\ \dot{x}_3 &= \frac{2Cx_{30}}{L_1 x_{10}^2} x_2 - \frac{R}{L_1} x_3 + \frac{V}{L_1}. \end{aligned} \quad (25)$$

Figure 3 shows the SIMULINK model of the maglev system represented by the state space model in Equation (25). Figure 4 shows an encapsulation of the SIMULINK model into a single block that is set up using a mask. The mask makes it possible to change the values of M, R, L_1, x_{10}, x_{30} and C for different simulations.

Figure 3. SIMULINK model of the magnetic levitation system

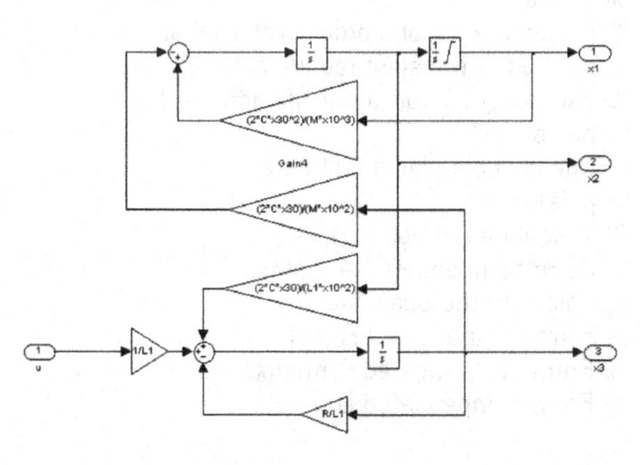

Figure 4. SIMULINK block of the magnetic levitation system

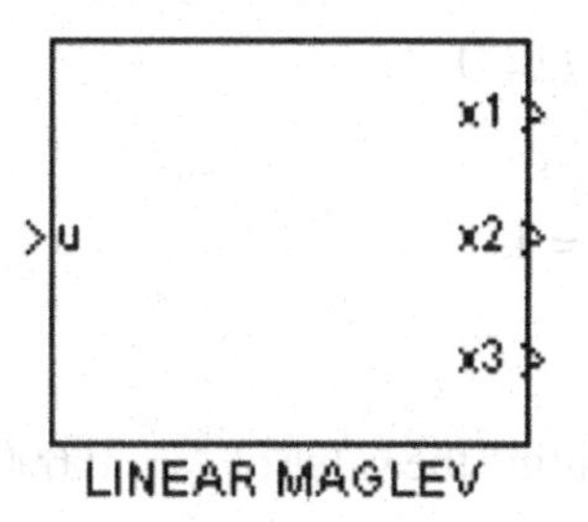

The desired system performance is prescribed by the poles of the general second order system transfer function given in parametric form as (Ogata, 2002)

$$G(s) = \frac{\omega_n^2}{s^2 + 2\zeta\omega_n s + \omega_n^2} \quad (26)$$

The maglev system's closed loop poles are to be placed at $s = p_i (i = 1, 2, 3)$, where p_1 and p_2 are the dominant poles which are determined based on the given specifications in terms of the parameters of Equation (26).

From the specification on peak overshoot, the damping ratio ζ may be computed using (Ogata, 2002):

Peak overshoot

$$M = e^{-\zeta\pi/\sqrt{1-\zeta^2}} x100\% = 5\% \quad (27)$$

$$\Rightarrow \frac{5}{100} = e^{-\zeta\pi/\sqrt{1-\zeta^2}} = 0.05$$

From which the value of ζ can be calculated as $\zeta = \sqrt{\dfrac{8.9744}{\pi^2 + 8.9744}} = \sqrt{0.4762} = 0.6901$

From the specification on settling time, the un-damped natural frequency ω_n may be computed using (23)

$$t_s = \frac{4}{\zeta\omega_n} = 1 \tag{28}$$

Substituting the value of $\zeta = 0.6901$ in Equation (28) and solving for ω_n gives

$$\omega_n = \frac{4}{0.6901*1} = 5.7963$$

Substituting $\omega_n = 5.7963$ and $\zeta = 0.6901$ in (26) gives

$$G(s) = \frac{33.60}{s^2 + 8s + 33.60} \tag{29}$$

Thus the required dominant poles are $p_1 = -4.0000 + j4.1952$, and $p_2 = -4.0000 - j4.1952$. The remaining pole is to be located far to the left of the dominant pole-pair and is given as $p_3 = -40$. The state feedback control law is:

$$u = \boldsymbol{K}x + \boldsymbol{N}r \tag{30}$$

where r is the reference command signal. State feedback controller matrix K assigns the closed loop poles while N is a scalar to eliminate off-set between the actual output and the desired output.

Based on the prescribed set of poles the MATLAB pole placement function acker is used to

Box 1.

```
% Matlab code for determining the controller matrix K and scale factor N
I=0.5; L=0.0425; R=3; m= 0.02312; Y=0.01; C=9.07*10^-5;
A=[0 1 0;(2*C*I^2)/(m*Y^3) 0 -(2*C*I)/(m*Y^2);0 (2*C*I)/(L*Y^2) -R/L];
B=[0;0;1/L];
C=[1 0 0];
D=[0];
M=5;                                    % Input desired percent overshoot.
Ts=1;                                   % Input desired settling time.
zeta=(-log(M/100))/(sqrt(pi^2+log(M/100)^2));
                                        % Calculate required damping ratio.
wn=4/(zeta*Ts);                         % Calculate required natural
                                        % frequency.
[num,den]=ord2(wn,zeta);                % Produce a second-order system that
                                        % meets the transient requirements.
r=roots(den);                           % Use denominator to specify dominant
                                        % poles.
poles=[r(1) r(2) -40];                  % Specify pole placement for all
                                        % poles.
K=acker(A,B,poles)                      % Calculate controller gains.
Anew=A-B*K;                             % Form compensated A matrix.
N=-inv(C*inv(Anew)*B)                   % Calculate the scale factor
Bnew=B*N;                               % Form compensated B matrix.
Cnew=C;                                 % Form compensated C matrix.
Dnew=D;                                 % Form compensated D matrix.
```

compute the controller matrix K. The MATLAB code in Box 1 determines the controller matrix K and the scale factor N.

Running this MATLAB code gives the state feedback controller matrix K and input scale factor N as

$$K = [-103.4559\ -1.6011\ -0.9600] \tag{31}$$

$$N = -1.4559 \tag{32}$$

A SIMULINK model of state feedback controller is developed as shown in Figure 5. The model is encapsulated in a subsystem as shown in Figure 6.

4. NEURAL NETWORK CONTROLLER DESIGN

The ANN structure used in this paper is a 3-layer feed forward network with an input layer, one hidden layer and one output layer as shown in Figure 7.

The input layer, which is not neural, has 3 nodes, the hidden layer has 5 neurons and the output layer has 1 neuron. The activation functions used in the hidden layer and output layer are tansigmoid and pure linear respectively. The network is trained by supervised learning using the pole-assignment state feedback controller as a teacher. The training function uses the Levenberg-Marquardt back-propagation algorithm implemented by the MATLAB function *trainlm*, which updates the ANN weight and bias values (Mathworks, 1998).

For generating the training data a random input, which consists of a series of pulses of random amplitude and duration, is used. Figure 8 shows the SIMULINK model of the maglev system with the pole-assignment state feedback controller for generating the training data. The three controller input signals (x_1, x_2 and x_3) are stored in MATLAB. The target for the neural network is the control signal u generated by the state feedback controller. The three state variables and the control signal are exported to the MATLAB workspace for training the ANN controller.

The MATLAB code in Box 2 trains the neural network.

When the training is finished, the SIMULINK model of the ANN controller is generated using the MATLAB gensim command. The state feedback controller is replaced with the neural network controller as shown in Figure 9.

Figure 5. SIMULINK model of a state feedback controller

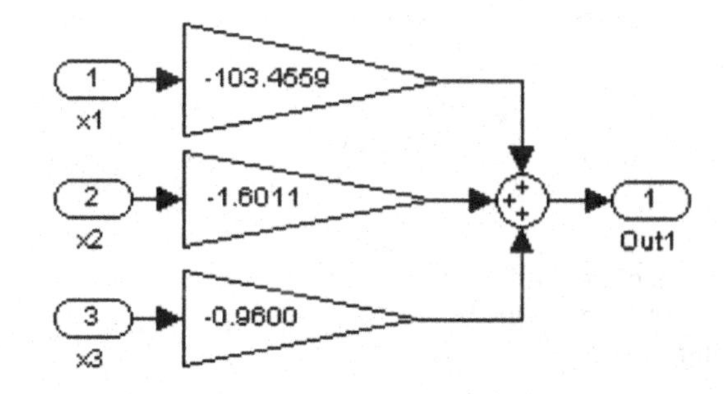

Figure 6. State feedback controller subsystem mask

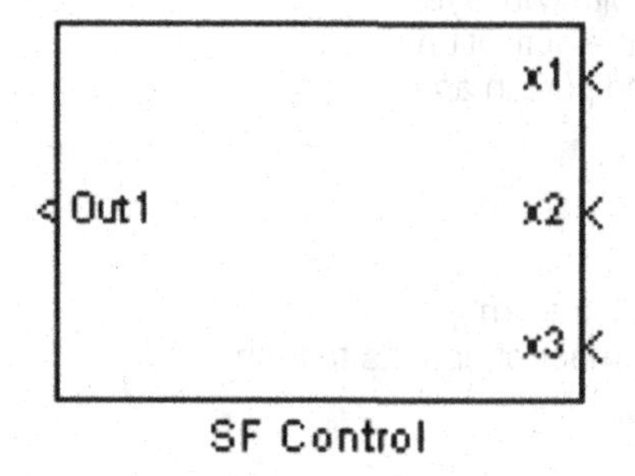

5. SIMULATION RESULTS

Simulation runs were carried out to investigate a number of scenarios. These include:

- Effect of ball mass variations.
- Effect of magnitude of step input command.
- Tracking of sinusoidal reference input.

Figure 7. 3-layer feed forward network

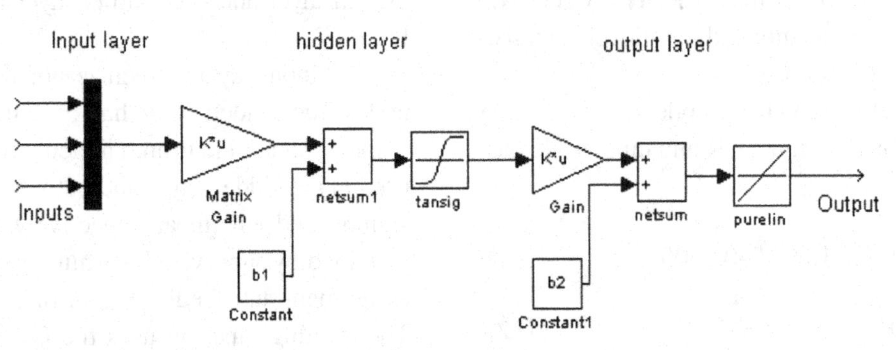

Figure 8. Maglev system for generating the training data

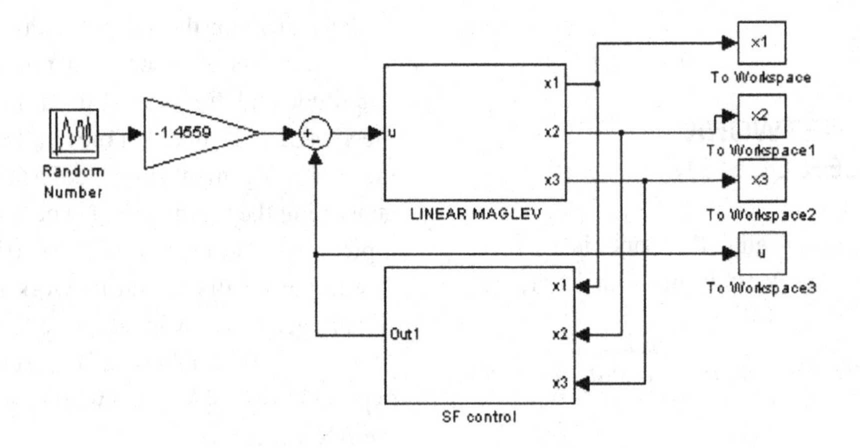

Box 2.

```
% DEFINING THE MODEL PROBLEM
% We would like to train a network to model state feedback
% controller with three inputs and one target output, which
% are exported to matlab workspace after running the
% simulink model of figure 4.

% P is a vector of three input signals.
% newff creates a new feed-forward network with two layers
% (hidden layer with 5 neurons and tansig as the activation
% function, and outpout layer with 1 neuron and purelin as
% the activation function).
% trainlm is the training function

P=[[x1'];[x2'];[x3']];
net=newff([-2 2;-2 2;-2 2],[5,1],{'tansig' 'purelin'},'trainlm');
net.trainParam.epochs=5000; % maximum number of epochs to train
net=train(net,P,u');
```

Figure 9. Maglev system with ANN controller

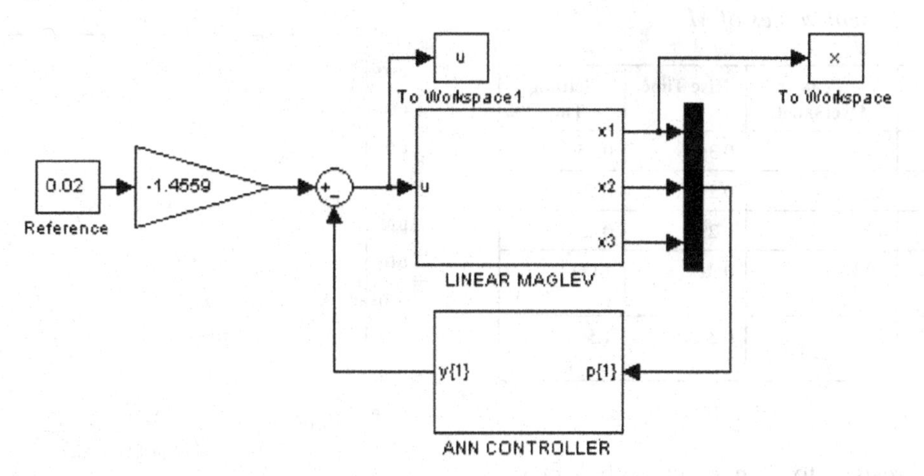

The parameters of the maglev system are as follows [10].

Mass of the ball, M = 0.02312kg,
Coil resistance, R = 3Ω, t
Coil inductance, L_1 = 0.0425H,
Magnetic force constant, C = 9.07x10^{-5}Nm^{2}A^{-2},
Nominal state variables: x_{10} = 0.01m, and x_{30} = 0.5A.

5.1. Ball Mass Variation

To investigate the robustness of the ANN control scheme with respect to parameter variations, simulations were performed with different values of the mass M of the levitated ball commanded to move from the nominal position $y_0 = 0.01m$ to a new position $y = 0.02m$. Thus simulations were performed with the nominal mass M = 0.02312kg, M±25%, and M±50%. Figures 10 and 11 show the plots of ball position versus time. Table 1 summarize the results with respect to peak overshoot, rise time and settling time for the ball position.

From the simulation results, it can be seen that the ball position converges to the commanded value even when the mass of the levitated object varies by ± 50%. Hence, the control system is

Figure 10. Response for M, M+ 25% and M+ 50%

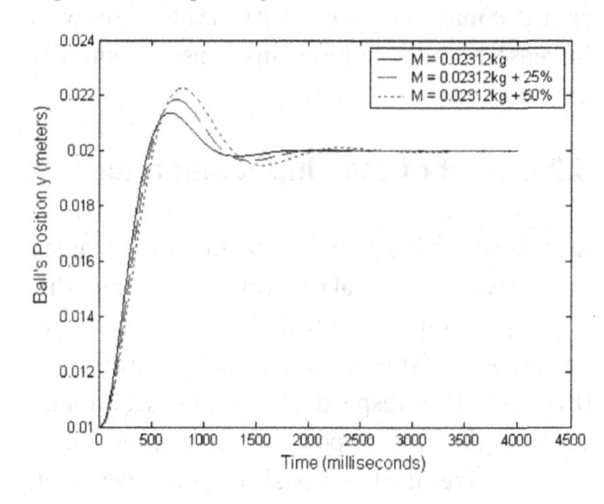

Figure 11. Response for M, M - 25% and M - 50%

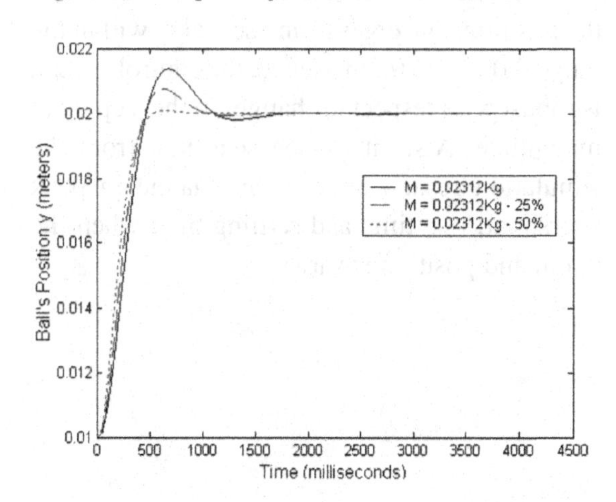

Table 1. Summary of ANN controller simulation results for different values of M

Ball Mass	Peak Overshoot	Rise Time	Settling Time
0.02312kg	14%	0.3s	0.95s
0.02312 - 25%	8%	0.29s	0.76s
0.02312 - 50%	1%	0.29s	0.42s
0.02312 + 25%	19%	0.31s	1.06s
0.02312 + 50%	23%	0.34s	1.5s

robust with respect to changes in the ball mass. Also, it can be seen that from the simulation results the percent overshoot and settling time decrease with decrease in mass and increase with the increase in mass. While the rise time increases with increase in mass and remains constant with decrease in mass.

5.2. Effect of Step Input Magnitude

Simulations were also performed for the maglev system with the neural network controller for different positions of the ball. The simulations are performed with the position set to 0.002m, 0.02m, 0.1m and 0.3m respectively. Figures 12 through 15 show the plots of position versus time. Table 2 summarizes the ball's position peak overshoot, rise time and settling time.

From the simulation results, it can be seen that the position converges to any set value within the range 0.002m to 0.3m. Hence, the control system is robust with respect to changes in the step input magnitude. Also, it can be seen that from the simulation results there is no change in peak overshoot, rise time and settling time when the command position is varied.

Figure 12. Step response for 0.002m

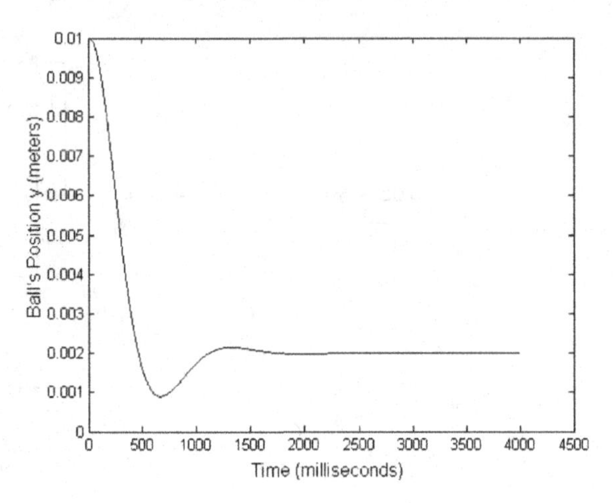

Figure 13. Step response for 0.02m

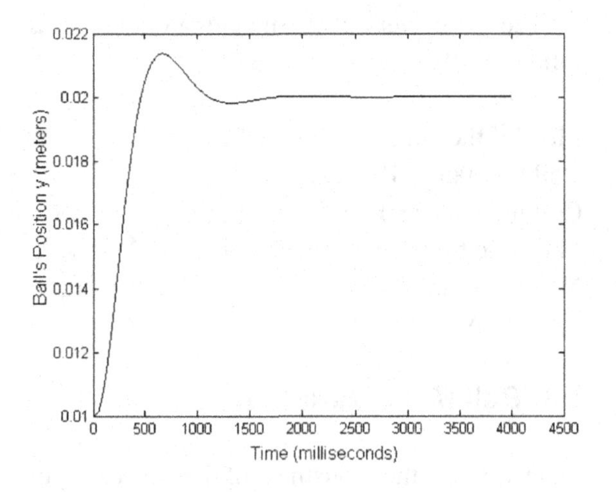

Figure 14. Step response for 0.1m

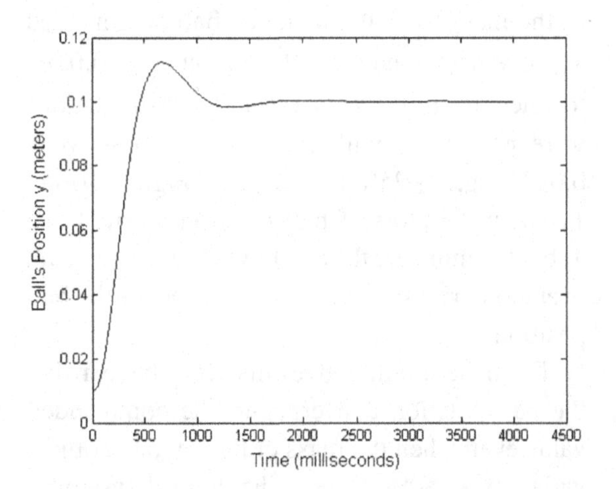

Figure 15. Step response for 0.3m

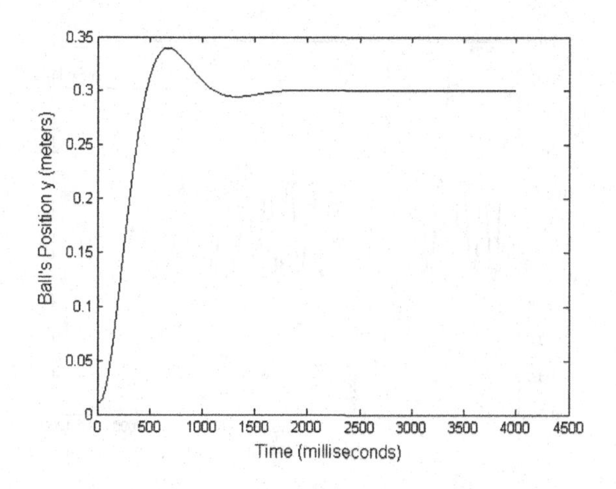

Table 2. Summary of ANN controller simulation results for different ball positions

Ball's Position	Percent Overshoot	Rise Time	Settling Time
0.002m	14%	0.3s	0.95s
0.02m	14%	0.3s	0.95s
0.1m	14%	0.3s	0.95s
0.3m	14%	0.3s	0.95s

5.3. Sinusoidal Input Tracking

Simulations were also performed for the maglev system with the neural network controller using sinusoidal reference input of amplitude 0.001m with different frequencies. The simulations were performed with the frequency of the reference signal set to 0.1Hz, 1Hz, 1.2Hz, 1.4Hz, 1.6Hz, 1.8Hz, and 2Hz, respectively. Figures 16 through 22 show the plots of position versus time. From the simulation results, it can be seen that as the frequency of the input signal increases, the amplitude of the response decreases. Table 3 summarizes the simulation results.

In order to find the bandwidth of the system a graph of gain versus frequency was plotted as shown in Figure 23, using the Matlab code in Box 3.

Box 3.

```
frequency =[0.1 1 1.2 1.4 1.6 1.8 2];
gain =[1 0.82 0.62 0.46 0.34 0.26 0.21];
plot(frequency,gain,'black')
```

Figure 16. Position for 0.1Hz

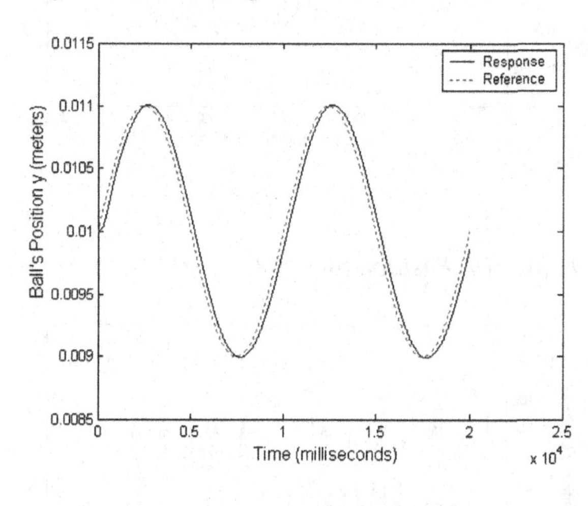

Figure 17. Position for 1Hz

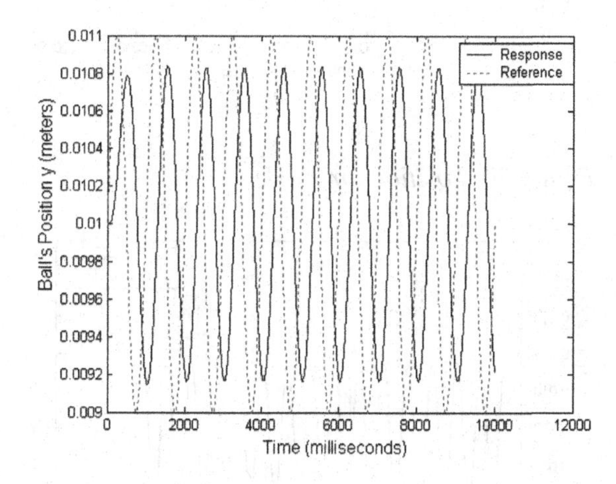

From Figure 23 it can be seen that the bandwidth of the system is 1.115Hz.

Figure 18. Position for 1.2Hz

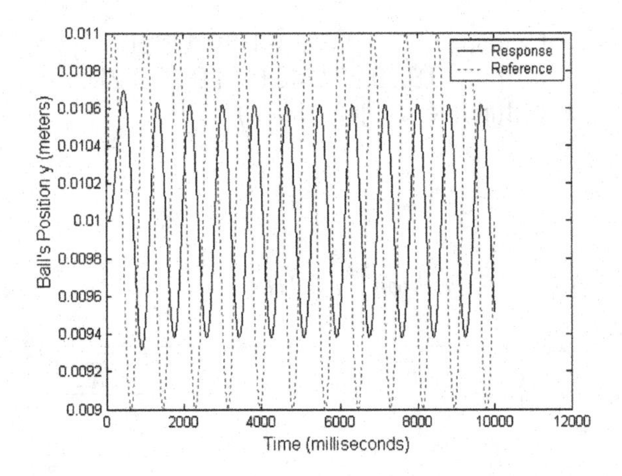

Figure 19. Position for 1.4Hz

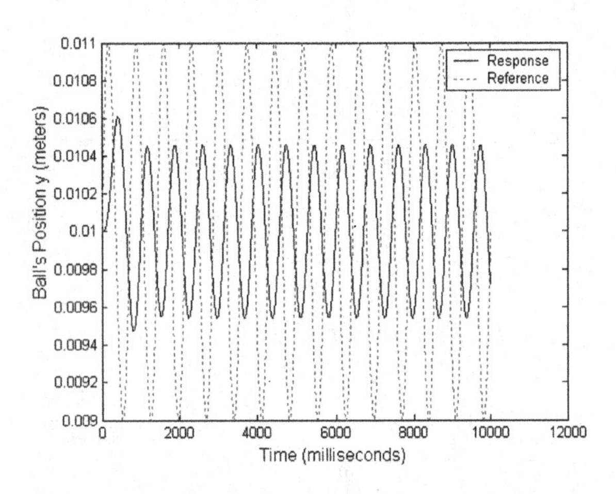

Figure 20. Position for 1.6Hz

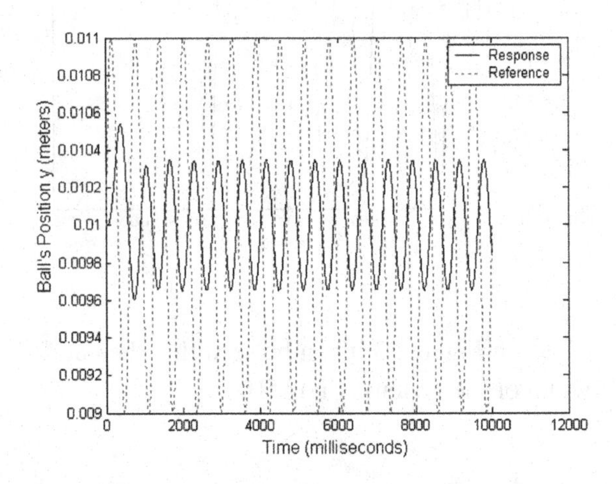

Figure 21. Position for 1.8Hz

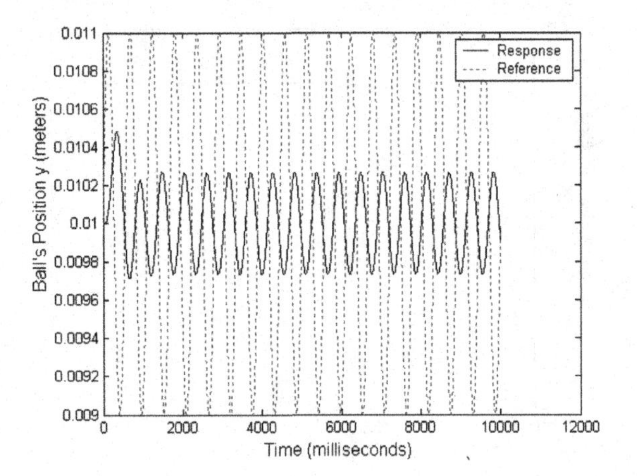

Figure 22. Position for 2Hz

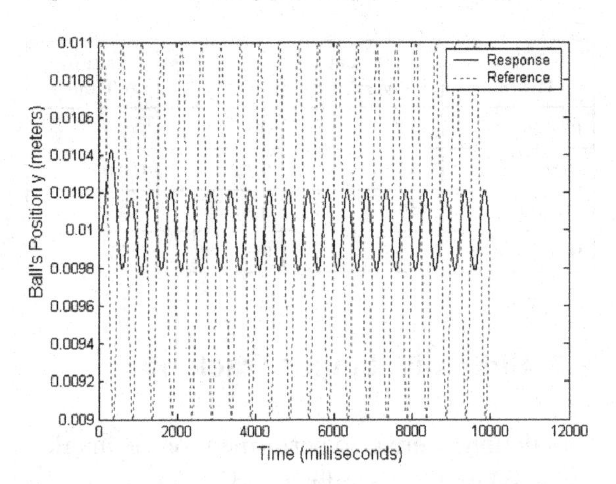

Table 3. Summary of ANN controller simulation results with sinusoidal input for different frequencies

Frequency (Hz)	Amplitude of Response Signal (m)	Gain
0.1	0.00100	1.00
1.0	0.00082	0.82
1.2	0.00062	0.62
1.4	0.00046	0.46
1.6	0.00034	0.34
1.8	0.00026	0.26
2.0	0.00021	0.21

Figure 23. Frequency response of ANN-controlled maglev system

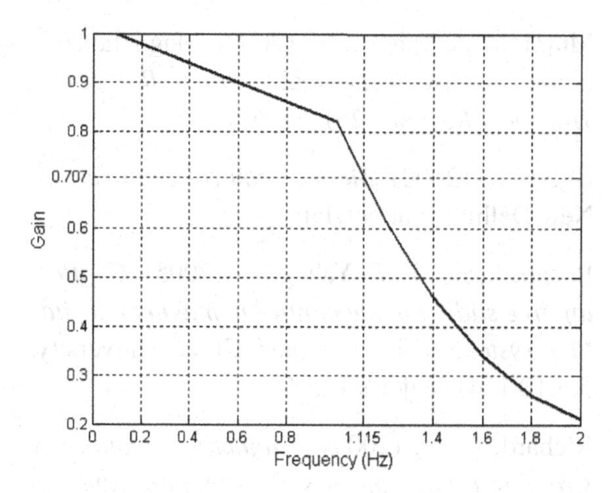

CONCLUSION

In this work, a neural network controller was designed for a laboratory maglev system. The neural network consisted of three layers; the input layer, one hidden layer, and the output layer, with 5 neurons in the hidden layer and 1 neuron in the output layer. The activation functions used in the hidden layer and output layer were *tansig* (hyperbolic tangent sigmoid transfer function) and *purelin* (linear transfer function) respectively. The network was trained by supervised learning using a pole-assignment state feedback controller as a teacher with a random signal as reference. After training a SIMULINK model of the ANN controller was generated.

To evaluate the performance of the ANN controller, simulations were carried using SIMULINK. The ball's mass was varied in the range ± 50% of the nominal value and the step response simulation results showed that, the ball position converges to the desired value even when the mass of the levitated ball varies by ± 50%. It was observed that the peak overshoot decreases if the ball mass is less than the nominal value and increases when the ball mass is greater the nominal value. Moreover, the ANN-controlled system's peak overshoot was higher than the specified 5% even though the desired position was achieved in all simulation scenarios. Thus in terms of positioning accuracy, the ANN is very robust but the dynamic accuracy was found to be inadequate.

The ball's command position was varied in the range 0.002m and 0.3m. The simulation results showed that in all cases the ball position converges to its desired value and there was no change in the peak overshoot, settling time and rise time (i.e. 14%, 0.95s, and 0.3s respectively). The maximum ball's position that the ANN controller can handle was 0.4m.

Simulations were also performed for the maglev system with the ANN controller using sinusoidal reference input of amplitude 0.001m with different frequencies. The simulation results showed that, the ANN controller tracks the sinusoidal reference input in the bandwidth of 1.115Hz. Further work is looking into how to effectively reduce the peak overshoot and practical implementation of the ANN controlled maglev system.

REFERENCES

Al-Muthairi, N. F., & Zbiri, M. (2004). Sliding mode control of a magnetic levitation system. *Mathematical Problems in Engineering*, *2*, 93–107. doi:10.1155/S1024123X04310033.

Barrie, W., & Chiasson, J. (1996). Linear and nonlinear state-space controllers for magnetic levitation. *International Journal of Systems Science*, *27*(11), 1153–1163. doi:10.1080/00207729608929322.

Boldia, I., & Nasar, S. A. (1986). *Electric machines dynamics*. New York: Macmillan.

Demuth & De Jesus, O. (2002). An introduction to the use of neural networks in control systems. *International Journal of Robust and Nonlinear Control*, *12*(11), 959–985. doi:10.1002/rnc.727.

Golob, M. (2000). *Decomposition of a fuzzy controller based on the inference break-up*. (Doctoral Thesis). University of Maribor, Maribor, Slovenia.

Hassan, I. M. M., & Mohamed, A. M. (2001). Variable structured control of a magnetic levitation system. In *Proceedings of the American Control Conference*. Arlington, VA: IEEE Press.

Joo, S., & Seo, J. H. (1997). Design and analysis of the nonlinear feedback linearizing control for an electromagnetic suspension system. *IEEE Transactions on Control Systems Technology*, *5*(1), 135–144. doi:10.1109/87.553672.

Katende, J. (2004). *Linear systems theory*. (Unpublished Master's Thesis). Bayero University, Kano, Nigeria.

Kemal, N. A. (2003). *Control of magnetic suspension system using state feedback, optimal, and neural network controllers*. (Unpublished Master's of Engineering Thesis). Bradley University, Maribor, Slovenia.

Mathworks. (1998). Retrieved from http://www.mathworks.com

Murai, M. & Tanaka, M. (2000). Magnetic levitation (maglev) technologies. *Japan Railway & Transport Review,* (25), 61–67.

Ogata, K. (2002). *Modern control engineering*. New Delhi: Prentice-Hall.

Phuah, J., Lu, J., & Yahagi, T. (2005). *Chattering free sliding mode control in magnetic levitation systems*. Chiba, Japan: Chiba University. doi:10.1541/ieejeiss.125.600.

Richard, C. D. (2004). *Magnetic levitation: A straightforward and fast information guide to magnetic levitation.* Retrieved from www.clearlyexplained.com

Sani, D. S. (2004). *Design and development of a magnetic levitation system.* (Unpublished Master's of Engineering Thesis). Bayero University, Kano, Nigeria.

Shen, J. (2002). H^{∞} control and sliding mode control of magnetic levitation system. *Asian Journal of Control*, *4*(3), 333–340. doi:10.1111/j.1934-6093.2002.tb00361.x.

Tzes, A., Chen, J. C., & Peng, P. Y. (1994). Supervisory fuzzy control design for a magnetic suspension system. In *Proceedings of the 30th IEEE Conference on Fuzzy Systems,* (vol. 1, pp. 138-143). IEEE Press.

Wong, T. (1986). Design of a magnetic levitation system. *IEEE Transactions on Education*, *29*, 196–200. doi:10.1109/TE.1986.5570565.

Yang, Z., Miyazaki, K., Kanae, S., & Wada, K. (2004). Robust position control of a magnetic levitation system via dynamic surface control technique. *IEEE Transactions on Industrial Electronics*, *51*(1), 26–34. doi:10.1109/TIE.2003.822095.

Chapter 18
Constitutive Modeling of Wind Energy Potential of Selected Sites in Nigeria:
A Pre-Assessment Model

O. O. Ajayi
Covenant University, Nigeria

R. O. Fagbenle
Obafemi Awolowo University, Nigeria

J. Katende
Botswana International University of Science and Technology, Botswana

ABSTRACT

In this chapter, the authors present the result of a study carried out to develop a pre-assessment model that can be used to carry out a preliminary study on the availability of wind energy resources of a site. 21 years' (1987 – 2007) monthly average wind speeds for 18 locations in Nigeria were used to create the simple constitutive model. The locations span across the six geopolitical zones of the nation with three stations from each zone. Various statistical procedures were employed in the development of the model. The outcome gave an empirical model, which if employed, will lead to determining the modest range of wind energy potential of a site. Further, the results from this model were compared with those from the well-established two-parameter Weibull statistical distribution function and found to be reasonably adequate. Thus with this model, decision on site selection for complete assessment can be made without much rigour.

INTRODUCTION

The impact of electricity to a nation cannot be overemphasized. The socio-economic growth of national economies has been proved to depend to a large extent on the balance between demand and supply of electrical energy. Moreover, the level of availability and utilization of energy in a country is reported to be responsible for the increase or decrease in the population of a community, it is also directly linked to the growth of national product (Hermann, 2001). Countries with low

DOI: 10.4018/978-1-4666-2208-1.ch018

energy availability and high-energy demand have been found to have correspondingly high proportion of poverty, illiteracy and migration. Also, the principles of the millennium development goals, access to information technology systems and improved telecommunication, literacy programmes and birth control policies will not do well if the current trend of energy shortages experienced by developing nations is not addressed globally (Hermann, 2001).

However, energy production has over the years been dependent to a large extent on fossil fuels in the form of coal, oil and natural gas. An estimate revealed that, 65% of the global sources of energy generation are from fossil fuels (Stiebler, 2008; Ajayi et al., 2010). It is reported. In Nigeria for instance, that major telecommunication systems and masts depend majorly on electricity produced from diesel generators on a daily basis. The emissions from this source have been found to include various gases, which have direct or indirect effects on the ozone layer. This creates a depleting effect of the layer and also in the process interferes with the self-cooling of the natural atmosphere (Ajayi et al., 2010).

Recently, concerns over the environment's quality have become subjects of global discussion, prompting various legislations, debates and declarations. Majority of the arguments have favoured the reduction of anthropogenic emissions that are deleterious to the environment and promotes the utilization of renewable energy resources for power generation (Ajayi et al., 2010). However, utilization of renewable energy resources, such as wind, for power generation in a given location requires the first step of resource assessment. This is in order to have adequate information on the intensity and viability of its prospects at the location (Fadare, 2009; Islam et al., 2009). The development of wind as a source of renewable electricity in developing countries, especially Africa, has been hindered by the absence of adequate measurements and/or assessment studies (Ajayi et al., 2013b). It is worthy of note that, before embarking on wind energy investments, the investors would first want to know the magnitude of likely wind energy output from a site's wind speed. A complete resource assessment therefore ranges from site selection and preparation, installation of wind speed measuring equipment, data gathering, analyses, and modelling to decision making. The analyses and modelling stage is critical to the study as it exposes the site's potential and degree of viability for a wind-to-power project. Various means exist for modelling wind energy potential of a site.

Based on the aforementioned, modelling can be explained to mean a process of creating suitable and qualified approximations which could be used to replace real life systems, repetitive or fluctuating data, or phenomena. However, without appropriate models, foretelling climatic variables, such as wind resources, will be a process that becomes expensive and could be frustrating. Several studies have been conducted and published on using statistical probability density functions to describe wind speed frequency distributions. Some of those that have been used in time past (pre-1970 analyses) range from using standard parametric distributions to distributions that relate to applying the principle of maximum entropy. Some authors have also suggested the use of univariate and bivariate distributions, unimodal, bimodal, bitangential and hybrid distributions (Justus, 1978; Auwera, 1980; Koeppl, 1982; Ozerdem, 2003; Shata & Hanitsh, 2006; Ramirez & Carta, 2006; Akpinar & Akpina, 2007; Tar, 2007; Chang & Tu, 2007; Shamilov et al., 2008; Carta et al., 2009).

In the post-1970 analyses, better statistical models surfaced. The use of the gamma distribution function of two parameters (scale and shape parameters), normal and lognormal, Rayleigh, Weibull and other statistical distributions were proposed (Ozerdem, 2003; Akpinar & Akpina, 2007; Ngala et al., 2007; Carta et al., 2009). According to Carta et al. (2009), the Rayleigh distribution function of one parameter corresponds to the chi-distribution for two degrees of freedom.

It also coincides with the 2-parameter Weibull distribution when the shape parameter (k) of the latter takes the value 2. The probability distribution has enjoyed wide application in wind speed analysis either exclusively or in combination with Weibull probability distribution. Moreover, of these two and other probability distribution methods, the Weibull distribution technique has enjoyed more emphasis. It has been employed in various regions of the world fundamentally for evaluating wind energy potential, carrying out the statistical analyses of wind characteristics, wind power density. In the estimation of the energy output and performance of wind energy systems, etc. (Burton et al., 2001; Kose et al., 2004; Akpinar & Akpinar, 2005a; Akpinar & Akpinar, 2005b; Fadare, 2008; Yang et al., 2008; Carta et al., 2009; Kamau et al., 2009; Soon-Duck, 2010).

However, the use of these models, especially the Rayleigh and Weibull distributions involve the utilization of a set of historical wind speed data covering some period of years for statistical significance. Based on this, some investors may be unwilling to commit resources to embark on this task since they are not sure of the outcome. This therefore creates a need for the development of an empirical model that can be used as a first stop before complete assessment study. Such model when available will serve as a pre-assessment model and aid in the selection of a site for complete resource assessment. The modelling procedure involved employing wind speed data set of some years to create a simple model that can be used for a site's pre-assessment study. The outcome from this empirical model will give rise to a modest estimation as well as the least magnitude of wind energy potential of the site.

MATERIALS AND METHODS

Data used for the study were 21 years' (1987-2007) monthly mean wind speeds at 10 m heights obtained from the Nigeria meteorological department, Oshodi. These data covered for 18 stations spread across the six geopolitical zones of Nigeria, with a station per state and three states per zone out of the 36 states of the federation. The data were then analyzed on annual basis. Figure 1 gives the annual average wind profile distribution for all the stations covering the period of analyses, while Figure 2 gives the range of annual average wind speeds for each station. Figure 3 presents the 21 years annual average wind speed per station. Table 1 gives the information relating to the station location.

MODELING TOOLS

Wind Power

The average power extractable from the wind by a wind turbine is estimated to vary with the cube of average wind speed as:

$$P = \frac{1}{2}\left(A\rho C_p \frac{1}{x}\sum_{i}^{x} v_i^{3} \right) \quad (1)$$

where:

P = Power Flux,
ρ = air density,
ν_i = wind speeds,
C_p = Coefficient of power,
x = number of data points,
A = wind turbine rotor area

Wind Energy Flux Density

The average wind energy per unit rotor area of a turbine, extractable from the wind by a wind turbine is obtained from the average power by:

$$E = P \times \eta \times T_i \quad (2)$$

Figure 1. 21 years' annual average wind speed for all distribution stations

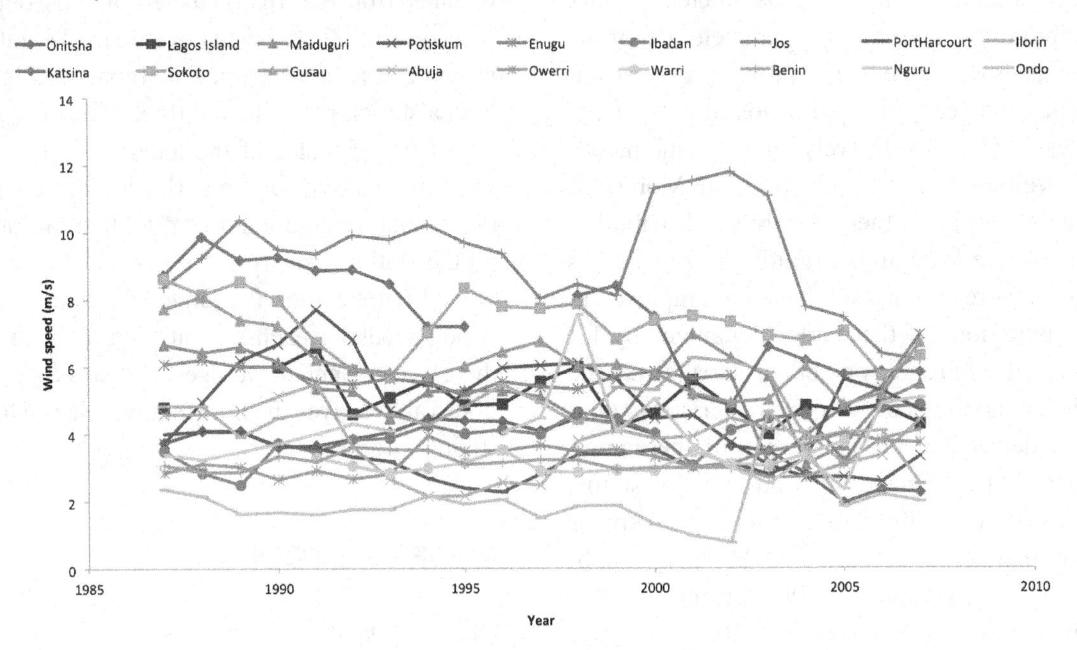

Figure 2. 21 years' annual range of wind speeds for each station

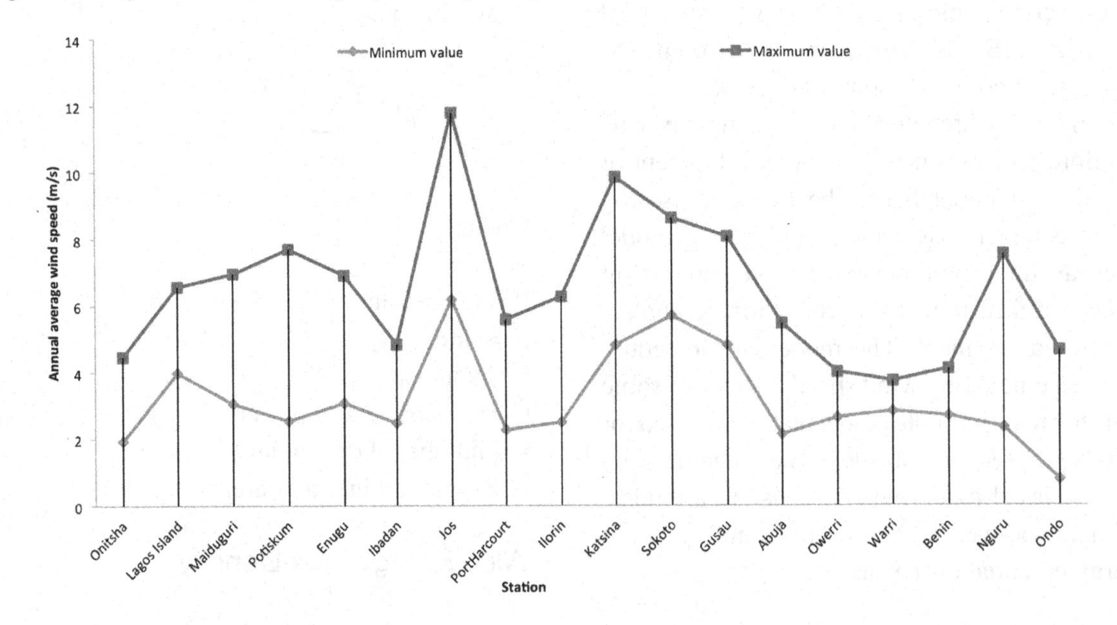

where:

η = turbine efficiency,
T_i = mean period

The mean period, T_i, is given by the Rayleigh probability distribution model as:

$$T_i = T_{\max} e^{-\frac{\pi}{4}\left(\frac{v_m - 1}{v_m}\right)^2} \quad (3)$$

Figure 3. 21 years' annual average wind speed for each station

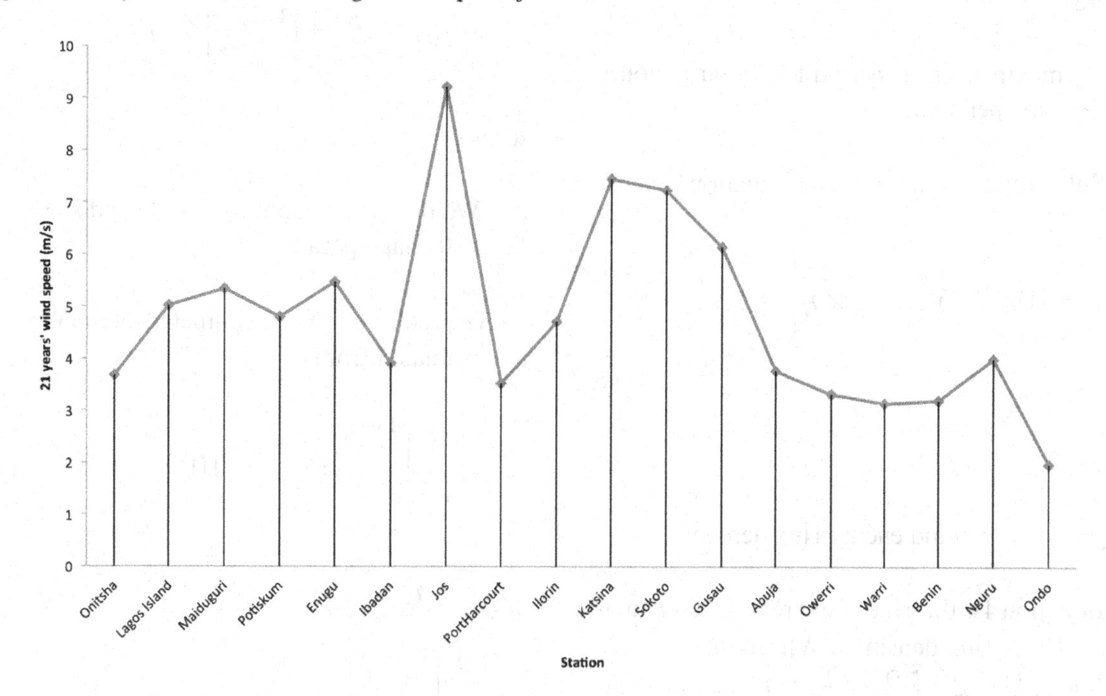

Table 1. Details of the meteorological stations

Station	Station No.	Latitude (N)	Longitude (E)	State	Elevation (m)	Density (kg/m³)
Onitsha	65245	06.09'	06.47'	Anambra	67.0	1.2173
Lagos Island	65205	06.26'	03.25'	Lagos	2.0	1.2248
Maiduguri	65082	11.51'	13.05'	Borno	353.8	1.1842
Potiskum	65073	11.42'	11.02'	Yobe	414.8	1.1771
Enugu	65257	06.28'	07.33'	Enugu	141.8	1.2086
Ibadan	65208	07.26'	03.54'	Oyo	227.2	1.1988
Jos	65134	09.52'	08.45'	Plateau	1217.0	1.085
Port-Harcourt	65250	04.51'	07.01'	Rivers	19.5	1.2228
Ilorin	65101	08.29'	04.35'	Kwara	307.4	1.1895
Katsina	65028	13.01'	07.41'	Katsina	517.6	1.1653
Sokoto	65010	13.01 '	05.15'	Sokoto	350.8	1.1845
Gusau	65015	12.10'	06.42'	Zamfara	463.9	1.1715
Abuja	65125	09.15'	07.00'	Fct	343.1	1.1854
Owerri	65252	05.29'	07.00'	Imo	91.0	1.2145
Warri	65236	05.31'	05.44'	Delta	6.1	1.2243
Benin	65229	06.19'	05.06'	Edo	77.8	1.216
Nguru	65064	12.53'	10.28'	Yobe	343.1	1.1854
Ondo	65222	07.06'	04.50'	Ondo	287.3	1.1919

where:

T_{max} = maximum time period for a year in hours = 8760 hrs. per year.

Substituting Equation 9 into Equation 8 gives:

$$E_{ave} = 10529.52 \times C_p \times \eta \left(v_m^3 \times e^{-\frac{\pi}{4}\left(\frac{v_m - 1}{v_m}\right)^2} \right) \quad (4)$$

where:

E_{ave} = Average wind energy flux density

Equation 4 is the general expression for annual wind energy flux density in Whr/m²yr.

Since $10529.52 \times C_p \times \eta$ is a constant, it therefore follows that:

$$E_{ave} = f\left(v_m\right) \quad (5)$$

Based on the relation of Equation 5, the exact relationship between v_m and E_{ave} can be determined through the procedure of regression statistics. This will lead to the determination of the constitutive relationship between v_m and E_{ave}.

The 2-Parameter Weibull Statistics

In order to determine the accuracy of the model generated, it became necessary to determine the degree of convergence of the results from the model with those from a well established statistics. The 2-parameter Weibull statistical distribution was therefore employed according to literature (Akpinar and Akpinar, 2005a; Keyhani et al., 2010; Fagbenle et al., 2011). The magnitude of the annual wind energy per unit area obtained from the Weibull statistics ($E_{Weibull}$) can be evaluated from (Keyhani et al., 2010),

$$E_{Weibull} = \frac{1}{2} \rho c^3 \Gamma \left(1 + \frac{3}{k} \right) \times T_i \quad (6)$$

where:

c = Weibull scale parameter (m/s) and k = Weibull shape parameter.

The scale and shape parameters of the Weibull are evaluated from:

$$k = \left(\frac{\sigma}{v_m} \right)^{-1.086} \quad \left(1 \le k \le 10 \right) \quad (7)$$

$$c = \frac{v_m}{\Gamma \left(1 + \frac{1}{k} \right)} \quad (8)$$

where Γ is the gamma function of () given by: $\Gamma\left(x\right) = \int_0^{\infty} e^{-u} u^{x-1} du$ (Keyhani et al., 2010), σ = standard deviation (m/s).

Performance Estimation of the Weibull Statistics

Before the Weibull results can be applied to this study, its predictive accuracy to the actual measured wind speed values ($v_{actual,}$) were evaluated using the some statistics. These are the coefficient of determination, R^2, the Root Mean Square Error (RMSE) and the Nash-Sutcliffe model Coefficient Of Efficiency (COE) (Ajayi *et al.*, 2011; Ajayi *et al.* 2011). Based on these, the Weibull result is judged accurate if the values of R^2 and COE are closer to 1 or the values of RMSE are closer to zero.

RESULTS AND DISCUSSION

Wind Profile Characteristics

Figure 1 shows the annual mean wind speed profiles across the stations. While some stations such as those of Enugu, Ondo, Benin, Ilorin, Abuja, Potiskum, Maiduguri, Nguru and Jos demonstrated stable monthly mean wind speeds' distribution across the period, others reveal fluctuations in their profiles. However, the annual fluctuations of wind speeds profiles across the period for all stations are not very pronounced except for Jos in Plateau state. Figure 2 shows the annual wind speed range across the 21 years period and reveals that Jos station had the best wind speed range, followed by Katsina, Sokoto and Gusau, while Onitsha and Ondo experienced the least. Moreover, on the 21 years average values, Jos has the best wind energy potential followed by stations in the North-West geopolitical zones of Nigeria.

Ranking the stations in each geopolitical zones according to their monthly and yearly wind profiles showed that the stations in the North-West zone have the greatest potential for wind energy harvest, followed by those of North-Central, North-East, South-East, South-West and South-South zones. Based on the data from the 18 locations of this study, it can be deduced that stations and sites in the northern Nigeria are capable of large wind-to-power projects, while those of the southern parts are capable of medium to small scale (or standalone) projects except for Enugu and Lagos Island.

Modelling Wind Energy Potential of the Sites, Zones, and Nation

Equation 4 was employed for the modelling. The equation reveals that the values of E_{ave} depend on v_m, C_p and η respectively. Thus with the different values of v_m and varying values of η and C_p, the magnitudes of E_{ave} can be evaluated for the different stations. However, carrying out a regression analysis of E_{ave} depend on v_m for different values of η while keeping C_p constant gives Figure 4 for Onitsha. The range of η used lay within $0.15 \leq \eta \leq 1$.

Figure 4 shows that:

$$E_{ave} = \beta v_m^{\ 2.657} \tag{9}$$

Further observing Figure 4 also reveal the relation:

$$\beta = f(\eta) \tag{10}$$

Based on Equations 9 and 10, it became necessary to establish the exact relationship between E_{ave} and v_m. This gives Figure 5 after a regression of β against η.

Thus combining Equations 9 and 10 from Figures 4 and 5 gives Equation 11 for Onitsha as:

$$E_{ave} = 10900 \times \eta \times v^{2.657} \tag{11}$$

Varying the values of C_p, as was done for η gave Equation 11 as:

$$E_{ave} = 10900 \times \eta \times C_p \times v_m^{\ 2.657} \tag{12}$$

Equation 12 is therefore the constitutive wind energy model which is suitable for analyzing wind energy situation of Onitsha station. Repeating the procedure for the other stations gave Equations 13 to 29.

Katsina: $E_{ave} = 8657 \times \eta \times C_p \times v_m^{2.805}$ (13)

Sokoto: $E_{ave} = 8617 \times \eta \times C_p \times v_m^{2.807}$ (14)

Gusau: $E_{ave} = 8966 \times \eta \times C_p \times v_m^{2.786}$ (15)

Figure 4. Regression plots of wind energy against annual wind speed for Onitsha

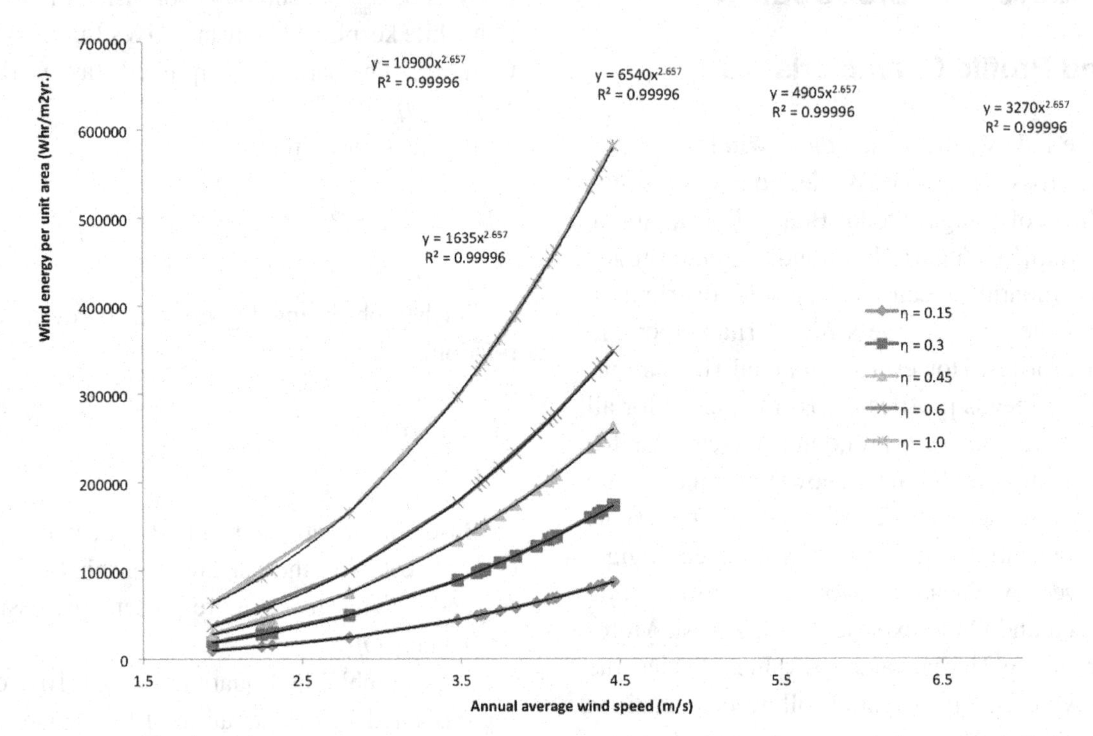

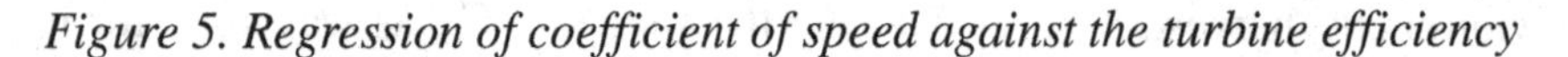

Figure 5. Regression of coefficient of speed against the turbine efficiency

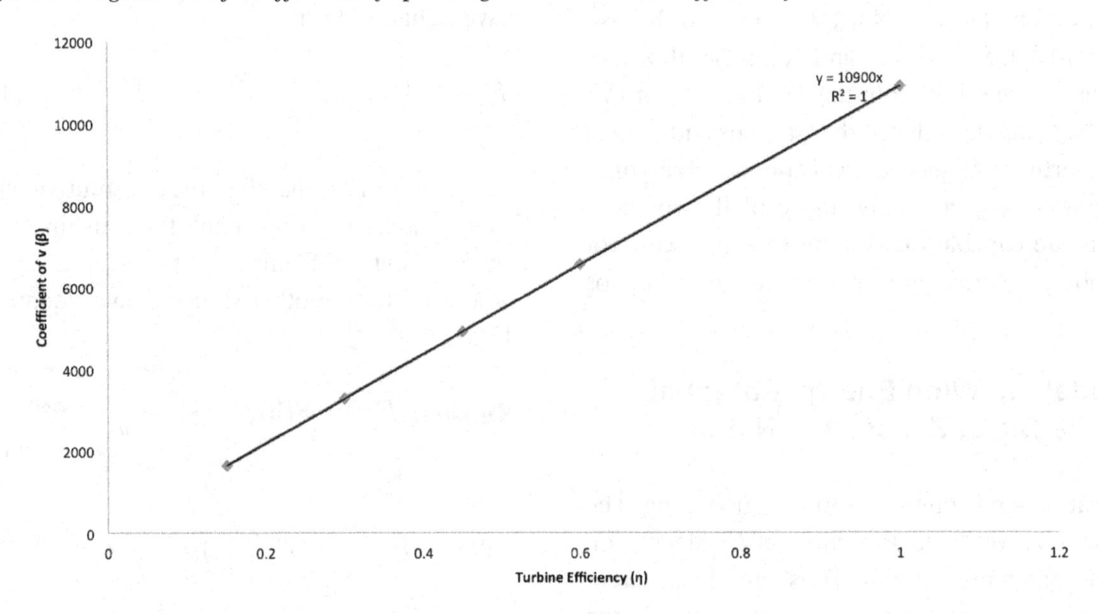

Maiduguri: $E_{ave} = 9732 \times \eta \times C_p \times v_m^{2.739}$ (16)

Potiskum: $E_{ave} = 10074 \times \eta \times C_p \times v_m^{2.720}$ (17)

Nguru: $E_{ave} = 10216 \times \eta \times C_p \times v_m^{2.707}$ (18)

Jos: $E_{ave} = 8100 \times \eta \times C_p \times v_m^{2.837}$ (19)

Ilorin: $E_{ave} = 10133 \times \eta \times C_p \times v_m^{2.712}$ (20)

Abuja: $E_{ave} = 10697 \times \eta \times C_p \times v_m^{2.673}$ (21)

Lagos Island:
$E_{ave} = 9502 \times \eta \times C_p \times v_m^{2.752}$ (22)

Ibadan: $E_{ave} = 10513 \times \eta \times C_p \times v_m^{2.684}$ (23)

Ondo: $E_{ave} = 10409 \times \eta \times C_p \times v_m^{2.726}$ (24)

Enugu: $E_{ave} = 9859 \times \eta \times C_p \times v_m^{2.731}$ (25)

Owerri: $E_{ave} = 10732 \times \eta \times C_p \times v_m^{2.665}$ (26)

Port-Harcourt:
$E_{ave} = 10530 \times \eta \times C_p \times v_m^{2.684}$ (27)

Warri: $E_{ave} = 10753 \times \eta \times C_p \times v_m^{2.663}$ (28)

Benin: $E_{ave} = 10697 \times \eta \times C_p \times v_m^{2.668}$ (29)

The R^2 values that relates to the models all lie within $0.998 \leq R^2 \leq 1.000$. This reveals that the models as they are, are adequate at explaining over 99% variations in the average wind energy per unit area of the locations.

Doing the same for the nation in order to obtain the national model gave Equation 30. This was obtained by taking the arithmetic mean of the annual wind speeds of all the stations.

National model:

$$E_{ave} = 9712 \times \eta \times C_p \times v_m^{2.738} \quad (30)$$

Range of Average Wind Energy Potential

Each of Equations 12 to 29 gives the magnitude of wind energy per unit area that can be harvested from the station. Moreover, for the purpose of simplicity and ease of application, it became necessary to develop a model which can be used to determine the maximum and minimum range of values of wind energy per unit area that can be harvested from any sites within the nation. This was achieved by employing the statistical tolerance limit method together with the set of Equations 12 to 29. The outcome gave Equation 31.

$$6793.28 \times \eta \times C_p \times v_m^{2.518} \leq E_{ave} \leq 13105 \times \eta \times C_p \times v_m^{2.928} \quad (31)$$

Thus with Equation 31, the range of average wind energy per unit area can be determined. This is given to lie within $E_{ave} = 6793.28 \times \eta \times C_p \times v_m^{2.518}$ and $E_{ave} = 13105 \times \eta \times C_p \times v_m^{2.928}$ (Whr/m²yr.).

Based on the aforementioned, Figures 6 presents the values of average wind energy per unit area of each stations corresponding to employing the individual models of Equations 12 to 29 and range of Equation 31

Figure 6 shows that the results from employing Equations 12 to 30 fall within that of Equation 31. This therefore means that Equation 31 is a better model representation for all the stations and in the geopolitical zones and anywhere in the country. Thus with this model, predictions can be made on the likely range of average wind energy flux density that can be generated from a site/station when the average wind speed of the site and station is known. Moreover, since investors are always interested in the optimum (E_{op}) value of the wind energy that can be harvested from a particular wind speed value, the maximum of Equation 31 is selected and called the optimum or maximum modest average wind energy harvestable from a site/station. This is given as:

$$E_{op} = 13105 \times \eta \times C_p \times v_m^{2.928} \quad (32)$$

Equation 32 can therefore be the useful model for estimating the most probable maximum likelihood magnitude of wind energy per unit area from any site in Nigeria.

Evaluation of the Performance of the Model Represented by Equation 32

Since Equation 32 can give the probable maximum value of wind energy flux density of any location in Nigeria, it became important to estimate its accuracy. In order to determine this, the 2-parameter Weibull statistical distribution was fitted to the wind speed data set employed for this study. Some of the Weibull results are presented in Table 2. The outcome of the Weibull analysis ($E_{Weibull}$) was then compared to the results of employing the minimum of Equation 31 and also the results of E_{op}. This is shown in Figure 7.

Table 2 shows that the model representation of Equation 32 predicted between 65 and above 100% of the value values of $E_{Weibull}$. However, at each point the percentage difference was negative, the value of E_{op} was more than $E_{Weibull}$. It is noted that for Enugu, Owerri, Warri, and Benin where

Figure 6. Magnitude of wind energy per unit area corresponding to Equations 12 to 30 and the model range of Equation 31

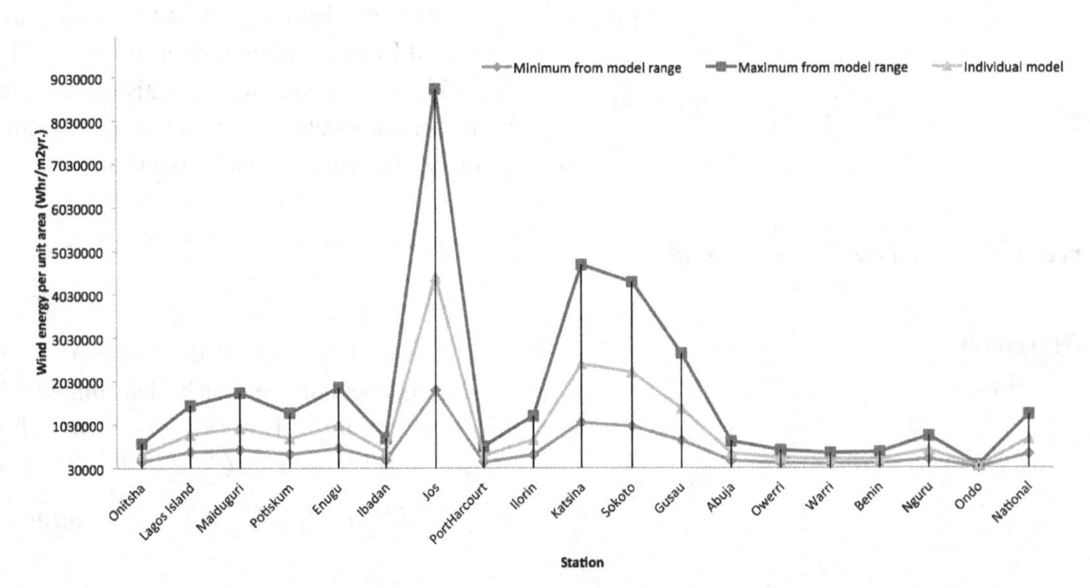

Table 2. Results obtained from Weibull analysis and those of Equations 31 and 32

Station	v_m (m/s)	k (-)	c (m/s)	Weibull analysis ($E_{weibull}$) (Whr/m²/yr)	Minimum from model range (Eq. 31) ((Whr/m²/yr)	E_{op} (Whr/m²/yr)	R^2	RMSE	COE	Percentage difference between $E_{weibull}$ & E_{op} (%)
Onitsha	3.68	4.00	4.10	632472.00	180051.82	592271.00	1.00	0.10	1.00	6.36
Lagos Island	5.03	3.70	5.60	1739736.00	396293.79	1482273.00	0.90	0.30	0.90	14.80
Maiduguri	5.35	4.00	5.90	1935960.00	462833.99	1775464.78	1.00	0.10	1.00	8.29
Potiskum	4.81	2.50	5.50	1903548.00	354276.08	1301149.08	1.00	0.20	1.00	31.65
Enugu	5.47	3.70	6.20	1072224.00	489669.58	1895726.19	0.80	2.30	0.30	-76.80
Ibadan	3.91	3.70	4.40	803292.00	210185.77	709037.56	0.90	0.20	1.00	11.73
Jos	9.22	3.30	10.50	12045000.00	1827333.46	8766249.18	0.80	1.20	0.70	27.22
PortHarcourt	3.52	3.80	3.90	560640.00	161473.53	521822.95	1.00	0.20	1.00	6.97
Ilorin	4.71	3.20	5.30	1525116.00	336728.91	1226516.56	1.00	0.20	1.00	19.58
Katsina	7.46	3.50	8.30	5626548.00	1070019.13	4704810.40	1.00	0.50	1.00	16.38
Sokoto	7.24	4.50	7.90	4430808.00	992917.61	4312959.98	1.00	0.20	1.00	2.66
Gusau	6.14	3.70	6.80	3050232.00	655801.31	2662579.44	1.00	0.30	1.00	12.71
Abuja	3.77	2.90	4.30	855852.00	192134.90	638737.48	0.90	0.30	0.90	25.37
Owerri	3.32	5.70	3.60	375804.00	139019.55	438439.59	0.90	0.20	0.90	-16.67
Warri	3.14	5.30	3.40	337260.00	121049.04	373256.11	0.80	0.20	0.90	-10.67
Benin	3.19	6.20	3.40	322368.00	126200.09	391788.94	1.00	0.10	1.00	-21.53
Nguru	4.00	2.30	4.50	1166832.00	223493.55	761503.97	1.00	0.20	1.00	34.74
Ondo	1.97	2.10	2.20	142788.00	37659.79	96018.81	1.00	0.20	1.00	32.75

Figure 7. Comparison of the values of results from Weibull analysis with those form Equation 31 and E_{op}

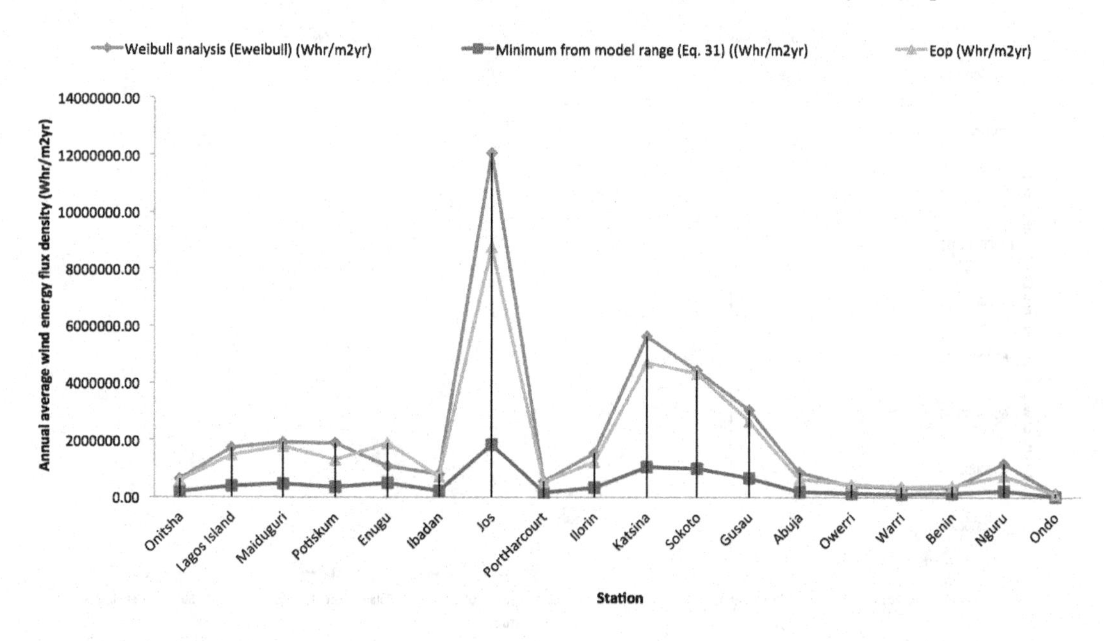

the values of E_{op} were more than $E_{Weibull}$, the excess prediction of E_{op} were between 11 and 77%. While those of Owerri, Warri and Benin were reasonably low, that of Enugu was high (see Figure 7). The reason for this is explained by the values of RMSE (2.30) and COE (0.3). The values of these estimation parameters contradicted the interpretation given earlier. The interpretation to this phenomenon is given in Ajayi et al. (2011). This is given as, the greater than the actual measured data is the value of the Weibull prediction, the closer to or greater than 1.0 is the value of RMSE and the closer to zero the value of COE. Thus it means that at this point there is an over prediction by the Weibull result. This invariably referred to the fact that the percentage difference is expected to be less than the 77%. Further to this, apart from the results for Potiskum, Nguru and Ondo stations, the values of E_{op} reasonably predicted the Weibull results ($E_{Weibull}$). The percentage differences for the other stations apart from the three aforementioned are above 72% of the Weibull results. Based on this, it can be concluded that the model representation of Equation 32 is adequate for a preassessment study of a site. It can reasonably predict good enough percentages of wind energy harvestable from a site and therefore could lead to accurate decision making on a site.

When the model was tested with other published results (Akpinar and Akpinar, 2005a; Kamau *et al.*, 2009; Keyhani *et al.*, 2010) it gave Figure 8. Sulaiman et al. (2002) carried out the study of the wind characteristics of four different locations in Oman out of which two (Salalaha and seeb) were employed. Akpinar and Akpinar (2005a) carried out the statistical analysis of the wind speed data of Keban-Elazig, Turkey. Kamau *et al.* (2009) on the other hand studied the 6 years wind data for Marsabit Kenya, while Keyhani *et al.* (2010) carried out the assessment of wind energy potential for power generation of Tehran, Iran. The studies employed the 2-parameter Weibull statistical distribution for the analyses. Figure 8 shows that apart from kamau et al. (2010), Equation 32 reasonably predicted the results of the other researches. Figure 8 therefore reveals that the model represented by Equation 32 can be used as a preliminary check to predict the likely

Figure 8. Comparison of the results from E_{op} with published Weibull results

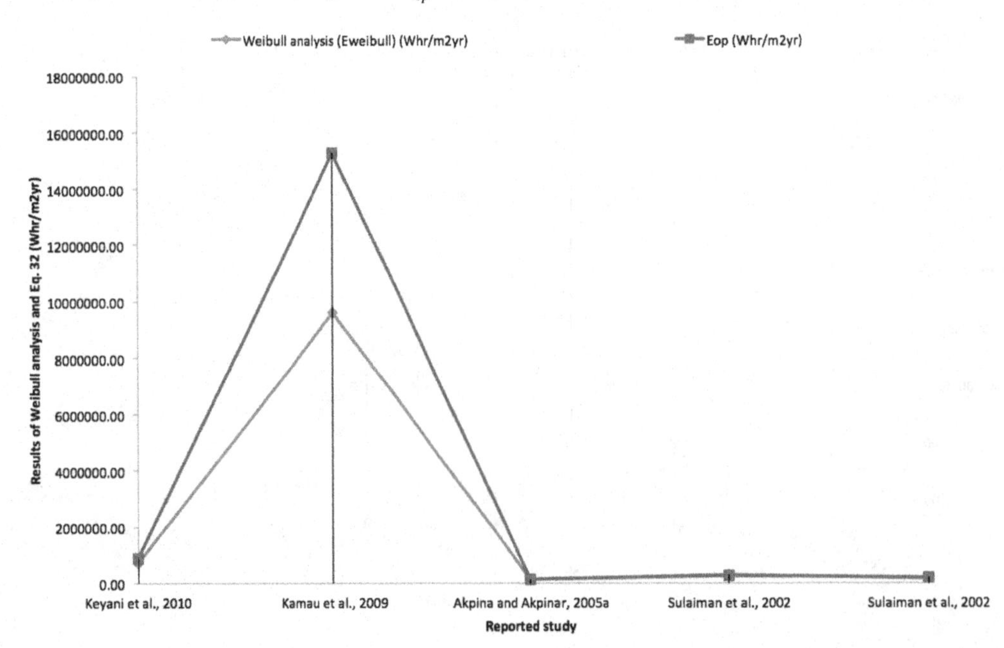

potential of wind energy harvestable from a site before embarking on detailed assessment study of such site.

CONCLUSION

The development of a model suitable for carrying out the pre-assessment study of a site has been developed. Although it is always necessary to embark on a thorough assessment study of a site proposed for a wind farm, investors would however want to know the viability of such site before hand. This is as to be able to arrive at a preliminary decision that a complete assessment study would depend on. Such questions as to how much on the least and what optimum or maximum modest value is likely to be the situation of the wind energy distribution of the location can be evaluated by simply knowing the magnitude of the average wind speeds of a location or a region. Most times such information is available at a national (meso-scale) level and at times site's specific local level. With the knowledge of such wind speeds and the use of models of Equations 31 and 32, it is possible to determine the minimum and optimum (or maximum modest) values of wind energy flux density of the local site or region.

REFERENCES

Ajayi, O. O., Fagbenle, R. O., & Katende, J. (2011). Wind profile characteristic and econometrics analysis of wind power generation of a site in Sokoto State, Nigeria. *Energy Science and Technology*, *1*(2), 54–66.

Ajayi, O. O., Fagbenle, R. O., Katende, J., & Okeniyi, J. O. (2011). Availability of wind energy resource potential for power generation at Jos, Nigeria. *Frontiers of Energy*.

Ajayi, O. O., Fagbenle, R. O., Katende, J., & Okeniyi, J. O. (2011). Availability of wind energy resource potential for power generation at Jos, Nigeria. *Frontier of Energy* 5(4), 376-385.

Ajayi, O. O., Fagbenle, R. O., Katende, J., Okeniyi, J. O., & Omotosho, O. A. (2010). Wind energy potential for power generation of a local site in Gusau, Nigeria. *International Journal of Energy for a Clean Environment* 11 (1-4), 99-116.

Akpinar, E. K., & Akpinar, S. (2005a). A statistical analysis of wind speed data used in installation of wind energy conversion systems. *Energy Conversion and Management*, *46*, 515–532. doi:10.1016/j.enconman.2004.05.002.

Akpinar, E. K., & Akpinar, S. (2005b). An assessment on seasonal analysis of wind energy characteristics and wind turbine characteristics. *Energy Conversion and Management*, *46*, 1848–1867. doi:10.1016/j.enconman.2004.08.012.

Akpinar, S., & Akpinar, E. K. (2007). Wind energy analysis based on maximum entropy principle (MEP)-type distribution function. *Energy Conversion and Management*, *48*, 1140–1149. doi:10.1016/j.enconman.2006.10.004.

Auwera, L. V., Meyer, F., & Malet, L. M. (1980). The use of the Weibull three-parameter model for estimating mean wind power densities. *Journal of Applied Meteorology*, *19*, 819–825. doi:10.1175/1520-0450(1980)019<0819:TUOTWT>2.0.CO;2.

Burton, T., Sharpe, D., Jenkins, N., & Bossanyi, E. (2001). *Wind energy handbook*. Hoboken, NJ: Wiley. doi:10.1002/0470846062.

Carta, J. A., Ramı'rez, P., & Velázquez, S. (2009). A review of wind speed probability distributions used in wind energy analysis: Case studies in the Canary Islands. *Renewable & Sustainable Energy Reviews*, *13*, 933–955. doi:10.1016/j.rser.2008.05.005.

Chang, T. J., & Tu, Y. L. (2007). Evaluation of monthly capacity factor of WECS using chronological and probabilistic wind speed data: A case study of Taiwan. *Renewable Energy*, *32*, 1999–2010. doi:10.1016/j.renene.2006.10.010.

Fadare, D. A. (2009). Modeling of solar energy potential in Nigeria using artificial neural network model. *Applied Energy*, *86*(9), 1410–1422. doi:10.1016/j.apenergy.2008.12.005.

Fadare, D. A. A. (2008). Statistical analysis of wind energy potential in Ibadan, Nigeria, based on Weibull distribution function. *The Pacific Journal of Science and Technology*, *9*(1), 110–119.

Fagbenle, R. O., Katenje, J., Ajayi, O. O., & Okeniyi, J. O. (2011). Assessment of wind energy potential of two sites in North-East, Nigeria. *Renewable Energy*, *36*, 1277–1283. doi:10.1016/j.renene.2010.10.003.

Islam, M. D., Kubo, I., Ohadi, M., & Alili, A. A. (2009). Measurement of solar energy radiation in Abu Dhabi, UAE. *Applied Energy*, *86*, 511–515. doi:10.1016/j.apenergy.2008.07.012.

Justus, C. G. (1978). *Winds and wind system performance*. Philadelphia, PA: Franklin Institute Press.

Kamau, J. N., Kinyua, R., & Gathua, J. K. (2010). 6 years of wind data for Marsabit, Kenya average over 14 m/s at 100 m hub height: An analysis of the wind energy potential. *Renewable Energy*, *36*(6), 1298–1302. doi:10.1016/j.renene.2009.10.008.

Koeppl, G. W. (1982). *Putnam's power from the wind*. New York: Van Nostrand Reinhold.

Ngala, G. M., Alkali, B., & Aji, M. A. (2007). Viability of wind energy as a power generation source in Maiduguri, Borno state, Nigeria. *Renewable Energy*, *32*(13), 2242–2246. doi:10.1016/j.renene.2006.12.016.

Ozerdem, B., & Turkeli, M. (2003). An investigation of wind characteristics on the campus of Izmir Institute of Technology, Turkey. *Renewable Energy*, *28*, 1013–1027. doi:10.1016/S0960-1481(02)00155-6.

Ramirez, P., & Carta, J. A. (2006). The use of wind probability distributions derived from the maximum entropy principle in the analysis of wind energy: A case study. *Energy Conversion and Management*, *47*, 2564–2577. doi:10.1016/j.enconman.2005.10.027.

Shata, A. S. A., & Hanitsch, R. (2006). Evaluation of wind energy potential and electricity generation on the coast of Mediterranean Sea in Egypt. *Renewable Energy*, *31*, 1183–1202. doi:10.1016/j.renene.2005.06.015.

Soon-Duck, K. (2010). Uncertainty analysis of wind energy potential assessment. *Journal of Applied Energy*, *87*, 856–865. doi:10.1016/j.apenergy.2009.08.038.

Sulaiman, M. Y., Akaak, A. M., Wahab, M., Zakaria, A., & Suradi, J. (2002). Wind characteristics of Oman. *Energy*, *27*, 35–46. doi:10.1016/S0360-5442(01)00055-X.

Tar, K. (2007). Some statistical characteristics of monthly average wind speed at various heights. *Renewable & Sustainable Energy Reviews*, *12*(6), 1712–1724. doi:10.1016/j.rser.2007.01.014.

Yang, G., Du, Y., & Chen, M. (2008). Computer aided investigation towards the wind power generation potentials of Guangzhou. *Computer and Information Science*, *1*(3), 13–19.

ADDITIONAL READING

Adekoya, L.O., & Adewale. (1992). Wind energy potential of Nigeria. *Renewable Energy*, *2*(1), 35–39. doi:10.1016/0960-1481(92)90057-A.

Çetin, N. S., Yurdusev, M. A., Ata, R., & Özdemir, A. (2005). Assessment of optimum tip speed ratio of wind turbines. *Mathematical and Computational Applications*, *10*(1), 147–154.

El Bassam, N., & Maegaard. (2004). *Integrated renewable energy for rural communities: Planning guidelines and technological application.* Amsterdam: Elsevier LTD.

Han, S. G., Yu, & Park. (2007). PSCAD/EMTDC-based simulation of wind power generation system. *Renewable Energy*, *32*(1), 105–117. doi:10.1016/j.renene.2005.12.008.

Ramirez, P., & Carta, J. A. (2006). The use of wind probability distributions derived from the maximum entropy principle in the analysis of wind energy: A case study. *Energy Conversion and Management*, *47*, 2564–2577. doi:10.1016/j.enconman.2005.10.027.

Sorensen, H. A. (1983). *Energy conversion systems*. New York: Wiley.

Stiebler, M. (2008). *Wind energy systems for electric power generation, green energy, and technology*. London: Springer.

Wood, D. (2011). *Small wind turbine: Analysis, design, and application*. London: Springer-Velag. doi:10.1007/978-1-84996-175-2.

Chapter 19
Cross-Layer Optimization in OFDM Wireless Communication Network

Babasanjo Oshin
Covenant University, Nigeria

Adeyemi Alatishe
Covenant University, Nigeria

ABSTRACT

The wide use of OFDM systems in multiuser environments to overcome problem of communication over the wireless channel has gained prominence in recent years. Cross-layer Optimization technique is aimed to further improve the efficiency of this network. This chapter demonstrates that significant improvements in data traffic parameters can be achieved by applying cross-layer optimization techniques to packet switched wireless networks. This work compares the system capacity, delay time and data throughput of QoS traffic in a multiuser OFDM system using two algorithms. The first algorithm, Maximum Weighted Capacity, uses a cross-layer design to share resources and schedule traffic to users on the network, while the other algorithm (Maximum Capacity) simply allocates resources based only on the users channel quality. The results of the research shows that the delay time and data throughput of the Maximum Weighted Capacity algorithm in cross layer OFDM system is much better than that of the Maximum Capacity in simply based users channel quality system. The cost incurred for this gain is the increased complexity of the Maximum Weighted Capacity scheme.

INTRODUCTION

Describe the general perspective of the chapter. Toward the end, specifically state the objectives of the chapter.

The current visible trend in the current communication market is the increase in the wireless technology. Current phone manufacturer such as Samsung and Nokia are daily increasing in the sales of smart phones and even PDAs. A number of these hand held devices come with one or more wireless technologies such as Bluetooth, WI-Fi or even connections to cellular mobile networks. Due to the continuous growth of the internet and its various applications, a lot of emphasis is the past years have being placed on satisfying the needs of mobile users.

DOI: 10.4018/978-1-4666-2208-1.ch019

In order to satisfy the ever growing wireless users, a new paradigm, called cross-layer optimization was proposed. Cross-layer optimization exploits layer dependencies and thus allows the propagation of ambient parameter changes quickly throughout the protocol stack. Hence, it is well-suited for mobile multimedia applications where the characteristics of the wireless medium and the application requirements vary over time.

Wireless Local Area Networks (WLAN) can successfully transmit at data rates of up to a hundred megabyte currently; but its low range which is typically a few tens of meters makes it unsuitably for large scale deployments. High speed wireless communication systems would require a Metropolitan Area Network (MAN) infrastructure to provide efficient and scalable services. Designing a wireless communication system supporting data and real-time traffic using a packet switched approach and having a high spectral efficiency is difficult.

Orthogonal Frequency Division Multiplexing (OFDM) increases the efficiency of limited spectral resources available when compared with other multiplexing schemes such as Frequency Division Multiplexing (FDM) and Time Division Multiplexing (TDM) (Nicopolitidis, 2003). OFDM has gained a lot of interest to combat wireless link impairments and simultaneously offering flexibility at the link layer (Herrman, 1999). OFDM promises higher user data rate and great resilience to severe signal fading effects of the wireless channel at a reasonable level of implementation complexity. It has been taken as the primary physical layer technology in high data rate Wireless LAN/MAN standards. Furthermore next generation wireless communication systems uses OFDM technology (Muhammad, 2004).

Current wireless networks are said to be all IP based and using the standard protocol stack for example TCP/IP stack to ensure interoperability (Jamalipour, 2001). The standard protocol stacks are architected and implemented in a layered manner and function inefficiently in mobile wireless environments (Xylomenos, 1999). This is due to the highly variable nature of wireless links and the resource-poor nature of mobile devices. Data communication over wireless connection can be improved by Cross-Layer Optimization or design (Shakkottai, 2003).

At the end of this work, we would have used cross-layer optimization techniques to:

- Improved Quality of Service (QoS) provisioning for multi-user wireless networks. Users of these networks want multimedia services with various QoS requirements. The cross-layer design used in this project is intended to balance delay, QoS and efficient resource utilization by exploiting the knowledge of channel and queuing states along with users' subjective performance metrics.
- Showed in this work that QoS delay for Real Time (RT), non-Real Time (nRT) and Best Effort (BE) traffic can be significantly reduced while ensuring a degree of fairness by using the Maximum Weighted Capacity (MWC) algorithm. This algorithm, using a joint physical and MAC layer optimization approach, addresses the requirements of the packet switched data sent from the base station to users. It uses information about the channel to allocate resource at the physical layer and schedule resources at the MAC layer to satisfy the data requirements.

A wholly physical layer system is compared to the MWC system in other to determine the amount of gains that has been achieved by it. The Maximum capacity (MC) algorithm is described by (Jurdak, 2007). This system uses an algorithm that allocates wireless resources to users that can maximize its use.

BACKGROUND

Traditionally, all data networks operate using the Open System Interconnect (OSI) protocol stack which is divided into seven layers for easier development and flexibility (i.e. Physical, Datalink, Network, Transport, Session, Presentation and Application layers) (Tanenbaum, 2003). Each layer is only able to communicate with adjacent layers as the message is transmitted from the source host to the destination host. Each is responsible for a subset of the system's operational functions. Messages are interchanged between entities of the same layer in both the transmitter and receiver side. Each layer is aware of its own messages and embeds its information into upper layer messages when they go down in the layer stack, while it's discarding the lower layers information when messages go up.

Cross-Layer Design takes into account the dependencies and the interactions among layers and allows optimization across their boundaries. A common misconception about CLD is that it consists of designing networks without layers. Layering is just a standard that allows for simplification of the network design and management tasks. Cross-Layer Design allows the joint optimization of the parameters of multiple layers. Therefore, Cross-Layer Design/Optimization should not be viewed as an alternative to the layering paradigm, but rather as a complement. Layering and cross-layer optimization are tools that can be used together to design highly adaptive wireless networks in the nearest future (Ravil, n.d.).

This traditional approach was successful with wired networks but this network architecture does not utilize resources effectively in wireless networks (Srivastava, 2005). Wireless networks have to cope with various elements such as congestion, scheduling, fading channels, limited bandwidth, competition for limited air resources between multiple users and an overwhelming increase in demands for high speed multi-media services (Srivastava, 2005). The busty nature of data communication means that packet switched network have to deal with channel states that change from good to bad within a few milliseconds (Haykin, 1994). Circuit switched wireless networks cope well with this variations because users monopolize their respective time-slots regardless of usage.

Cross-layer Design was defined by (Aune, 2004) as a process in which, " to fully optimize wireless broadband networks, both the challenges from the physical medium and the QoS-demands from the applications have to be taken into account. Rate, power and coding at the physical layer can be adapted to meet the requirements of the applications given the current channel and network conditions. Knowledge has to be shared between all layers to obtain the highest possible adaptivity".

OVERVIEW OF OFDM

OFDM is a multicarrier scheme which transmits data using several subcarriers which are orthogonal in the frequency domain. It is a concept that was proposed and implemented about 50 years ago (Saltzberg, 2000). A resurgence of OFDM in wideband digital communication, whether wireless or over copper wires is being experienced as a result of the availability of low cost all-digital implementation of the Fast-Fourier Transform (FFT) (Van, 2002). This has significantly lowered the cost of the signal processing that is needed to implement OFDM systems.

OFDM systems transmit data on parallel subcarriers which overlap in the frequency domain, unlike frequency division multiplexing systems which do not overlap. Orthogonality between the subcarriers ensures that they are spaced such that the center frequency of one subcarrier coincides with the spectral zeros of all other subcarrier (Langton, 2004). This is done by ensuring that the subcarrier periods are integer multiples for each subcarrier and the difference between adjacent subcarrier periods must be exactly one. This way, interferences that may occur between the subcarriers are prevented. See Figure 1 for the OFDM transceiver block diagram.

At the OFDM transmitter modem, a high rate data sequence is split into a number of lower rate sequences which are then transmitted simultaneously over a number of subcarriers. These streams of data experience flat fading because the bandwidth of each subcarrier is smaller than the coherent bandwidth of the channel. Thus, a highly frequency selective channel is converted into a large set of individual flat fading narrowband channels.

Orthogonal waveform modulation is carried out by using an inverse FFT and a parallel-to-serial converter. The inverse FFT block converts the inputs from the subcarriers (in the frequency domain) to an output several taps which is then converted from parallel to serial to form a symbol (in the time domain).

A Cyclic Prefix (CP) is appended to the symbol produced. A cyclic prefix, which is a repeat of the end of a symbol at the beginning of the symbol, is used to allow a multipath channel to settle before the start of the next symbol. The cyclic prefix allows OFDM to remain robust despite Inter-Block-Interference (Oppenheim, 1989). An OFDM symbol with CP is shown in Figure 2.

BENEFITS OF OFDM

There are various advantages of OFDM that aids its use in most wireless communication systems. They include:

- It is very useful in combating multipath fading of a signal.
- For high bit rate transmission over mobile wireless channels.
- It also alleviates the effect of impulse noise.
- It is good for power allocation.
- Higher transmission rates can be sent over the subcarrier so as to improve throughput and simultaneously to ensure an acceptable BER on each subcarrier.

Figure 1. OFDM transceiver block diagram

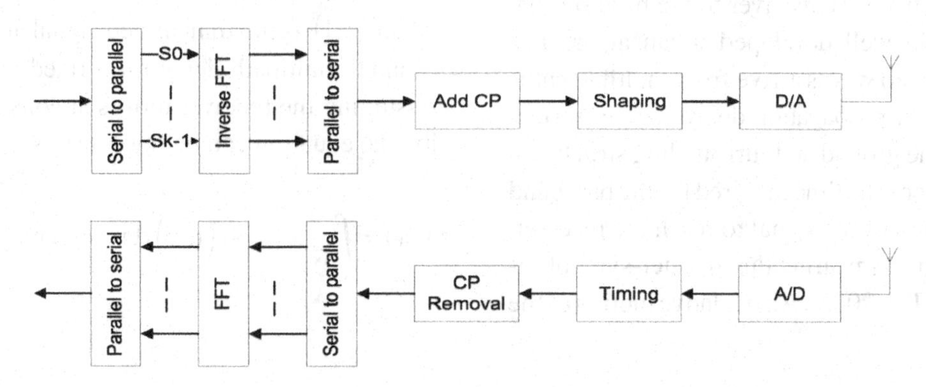

Figure 2. Cyclic prefix in an OFDM symbol (Emad, 2008)

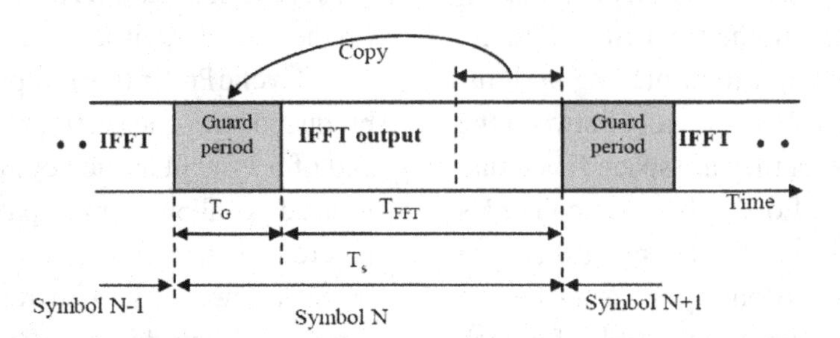

FADING CHANNEL

The mechanism behind electromagnetic wave propagation can generally be attributed to reflection, diffraction and scattering (Rappaport, 2002). Propagation models traditionally focus on predicting the average received signal strength at a given distance from the transmitter, as well as its variability in close spatial proximity to a particular location. Large scale propagation models characterize signal strength over large distance separation (hundreds to thousands of meters) between the transmitter and the receiver. This is useful for estimating the radio coverage area of a transmitter.

However, propagation models that characterize the rapid fluctuation of the received signal strength over very short distance or for short time durations are described as small scale fading models. Fading is caused by interference between two or more versions of the transmitted signal which arrive at the receiver at slightly different times.

Fading occurs when there are several line-of-sight paths from the receiver to the base station, especially in well developed urban areas. The incoming radio waves arrive from multiple paths with different propagation delays due to reflection from the ground and surrounding structures. This lengthens the time required for the baseband signal portion of the signal to reach the receiver, causing signal smearing due to inter-symbol interference (Tse, 2005). Also relative motion of the mobile device, surrounding objects and the base station can induce Doppler shift in the multipath components.

The signal received at the mobile at any point in space may consist of a large number of plane waves having randomly distributed amplitudes, phase and angles of arrival. This causes time dispersion of received signal, rapid changes in signal strength over a small travel distance or time interval and random frequency modulation due to varying Doppler shift of different multipath signals.

Due to the different multipath waves with propagation delays that vary over different spatial locations of the receiver, the impulse response of the linear time invariant channel should also be a function of position of the receiver. The received signal $y(d,t)$ at position d transmitted over a channel with impulse response $h(d,t)$ is given as

$$y(d,t) = x(t) \otimes h(d,t) = \int_{-\infty}^{\infty} x(\tau) h(d, t-\tau) d\tau \tag{1}$$

where $x(t)$ is the transmitted signal and A is the channel multipath delay for a fixed value of t. Assuming the receiver moves at constant velocity, the equation can be rewritten as

$$y(t) = \int_{-\infty}^{\infty} x(\tau) h(t,\tau) d\tau = x(t) \otimes h(t,\tau) \tag{2}$$

FLAT FADING

This is the type of fading in which the multipath structure of the channel is such that the spectral characteristics of the transmitted signal is preserved at the receiver. The reciprocal bandwidth of the transmitted signal is much larger than the multi-path time delay spread of the channel. Flat fading channels are sometimes called narrowband channels because the bandwidth of the applied signal is narrow compared to the channel bandwidth. The characteristics of the flat fading channel are illustrated in Figure 3.

A signal under goes flat fading if

$$B_s << B_c \text{ and } T_s >> \sigma\tau \quad (3)$$

where T_s is the symbol period and B_s is the bandwidth, respectively of the transmitted modulation; and $\sigma\tau$ and B_c are the rms delay spread and coherence bandwidth, respectively, of the channel.

FREQUENCY SELECTIVE FADING

If a channel possesses a constant gain and linear phase response over a bandwidth that is smaller than the bandwidth of the transmitted signal, then the channel creates frequency selective fading on the transmitted signal. The received signal contains multiple versions of the transmitted waveform which are attenuated and delayed in time. The received signal is distorted due to ISI induced by the channel. In essence, the gain of various frequency components vary with the receive signal spectrum.

Frequency selective fading channels are also known as wideband channels since the bandwidth of the signal $S(t)$ is wider than the bandwidth of the impulse response of the channel. The characteristics of the frequency selective fading channels are illustrated in Figure 4.

A signal under goes flat fading if

$$B_s > B_c \text{ and } T_s < \sigma\tau \quad (4)$$

FAST FADING

The channel impulse response changes rapidly within the symbol duration. That is, the coherence time of the channel is smaller than the symbol period of the transmitted signal. In the frequency domain, signal distortion due to fast fading increases with increasing Doppler spread relative to the bandwidth of the transmitted signal. Hence

$$B_s < B_d \text{ and } T_s > T_c \quad (5)$$

Figure 3. Flat fading channel characteristics

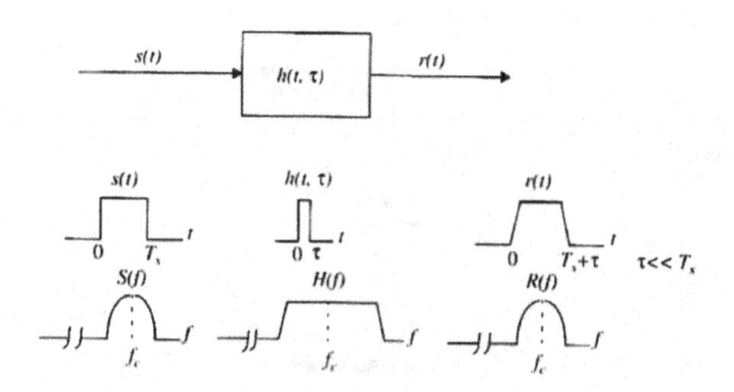

Figure 4. Frequency selective fading channel characteristics

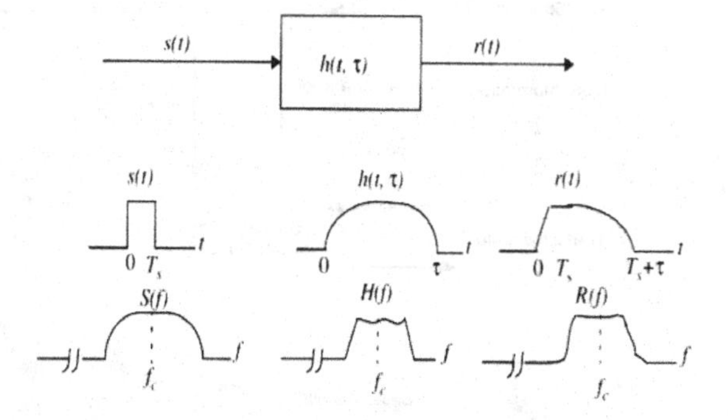

SLOW FADING

In a slow fading channel, the channel impulse response changes at a rate much slower than the transmitted baseband signal. The channel seems static over one or several reciprocal bandwidth intervals. The Doppler spread of the channel is much less than the bandwidth of the baseband signals in the frequency domain. So the signal undergoes slow fading if

$$B_s >> B_d \text{ and } T_s << T_c \quad (6)$$

CROSS-LAYER OPTIMIZATION FOR OFDM WIRELESS NETWORK

Downlink Model

We have been able to establish that there are significant challenges involved with data transmission over the wireless communication medium. The nature of the medium necessitates that instantaneous measurements of the medium is done and results of this is used to dynamically allocate the required channel resources to the user. OFDM is used to implement this process.

The Multiuser OFDM system model considered in this project is illustrated in Figure 5. This is a downlink model that is made up of two parts; the base station and the mobile user. Downstream data traffic destined for various users arrive at the base station. The base station module must ensure the data for each of the user is transmitted to it as efficiently as possible. The Subcarrier and Power Controller, at the Physical layer, perform subcarrier and power allocation while the Traffic Controller at the MAC layer performs data scheduling, respectively. The traffic controller transfers the QoS information of each user to the Subcarrier and Power Controller for the purpose of resource allocation, and the result of the resource allocation process is fed back to the traffic controller in the base station for the scheduling of the data to be sent out in each slot. The subcarrier and Power controller checks the wireless channel for the channel state information (CSI) of each user. It uses this information to efficiently allocate resources to users.

The OFDM transceiver at the transmitter delivers the OFDM symbols to the receiver. Figure 6 shows the transceivers at the base station and mobile station (Debbah, 2002).

Figure 5. Multiuser OFDM system model

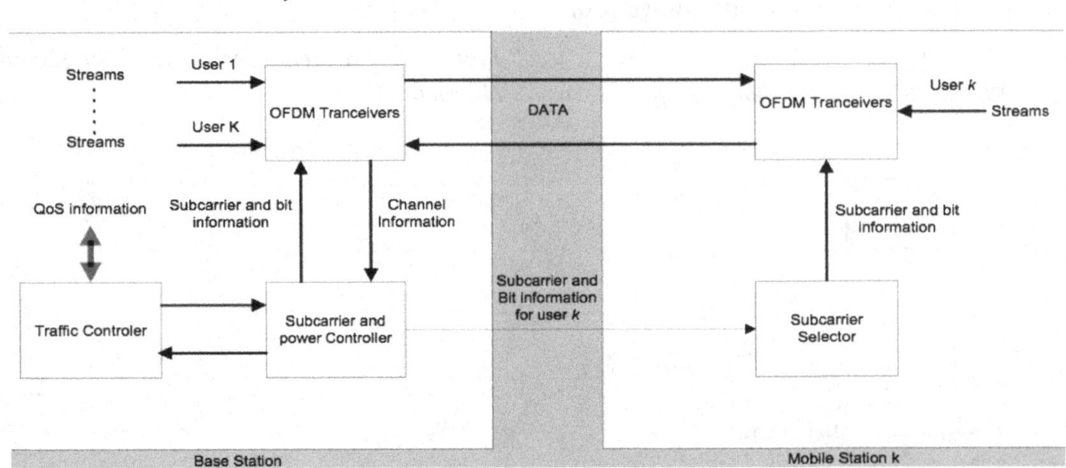

BENEFITS OF CROSS-LAYER OPTIMIZATION

Allocation and management of resources is crucial to the operation wireless networks, this is due to the scarce wireless spectral resources that are shared by multiple users. In the current layered network architecture, each layer is designed to operate independently in order to support transparency between the layers. Among these layers, the physical layer whose function is to transmit raw-bit, and the medium access control (MAC) layer as a function which involves controlling multiuser access to the shared wireless resources. However, wireless channels suffer from time-varying multipath fading; which is looked at in this project work. Also, the channel characteristics of different users are different. The sub-optimality and inflexibility of this architecture result in inefficient resource utilization in wireless networks. We need an integrated adaptive design across different layers. Therefore, cross layered design and optimization across the physical and MAC layers are desired for wireless resource allocation and packet scheduling (Shakkottai, 2003; Akyildiz, 2004).

For cross-layer optimization, channel-aware scheduling strategies are proposed to adaptively transmit data and dynamically assign wireless resources based on channel state information (CSI). The key idea of channel-aware scheduling is to choose a user with good channel conditions to transmit packets (Viterbi, 1995). Taking advantage of the independent channel variation across users, channel-aware scheduling can substantially improve the network performance through multiuser diversity, whose gain increases with the number of users (Viswanath, 2002; Knopp, 1995). To guarantee fairness for resource allocation and exploit multiuser diversity, utility-pricing structures in network economics are usually preferred for scheduling design (Liu, 2001).

- It overcomes limitations such as jitter, delay and fading experienced in wireless mediums.
- It allows coordination, interaction and joint optimization of protocols crossing different layers.
- It improves wireless system indices such as throughput, delay.

RESOURCE ALLOCATION

The current trend in wireless communication networks is the provisioning of multimedia services such as voice services, videophone services and animation services (Hendrik). There are different QoS requirements for each of these multimedia applications over the wireless channel (Jose). The high data rate needed by the applications make the use of one single channel for each user insufficient. The use of multicarrier systems is seen as the solution to the problem.

OFDM is the multicarrier system of choice because it divides an entire channel into many orthogonal narrowband subcarriers to deal with frequency-selective fading and to support an increased data rate. Furthermore, in an OFDM-based wireless network, different subcarriers can be allocated to different users to provide a flexible multiuser access scheme and exploit multiuser diversity. OFDM offers a high degree of flexibility of radio resources management which can significantly improve the performance of OFDM networks. Using data rate adaption, the transmitter can send higher transmission rate over the subcarriers with better conditions so as to improve throughput and simultaneously ensure an acceptable bit-error rate (BER) at each subcarrier (Nanda, 2000).

Dynamic resource allocation is used. This research work uses a rate adaptive multiuser optimization technique to maximize each user's error free capacity under given total power constraint. The resource allocation is done at the physical layer, while the MAC layer controller schedules data to be transmitted. The following algorithms are looked at:

1. Maximum Capacity Algorithm
2. Maximum Weighted Algorithm

MAXIMUM CAPACITY (MC) BASED RESOURCE ALLOCATION

The Maximum Capacity algorithm is the first resource allocation algorithm to be discussed. It is based on (Jang, 2003). A transmit power adaptation scheme was developed, which maximizes the total data rate of multiuser OFDM systems in downlink transmission. The transmit power adaptation method solves the maximization problem in two step; assigning subcarriers to users first, then allocating power to each of this subcarriers. Transmit power is distributed over the subcarriers using the water-filling policy.

SUBCARRIER ALLOCATION

In order to maximize the total data rate of the system, Jang and Lee set the BER to a fixed value, thereby imposing an upper limit to the system. The modulation constellation is modified by changing the number of bits in each transmitted symbol depending on the channel gain for each subcarrier. Setting the BER imposes an upper bound on the system, such that by continually adapting the constellation size, this BER would be the maximum for any channel condition.

For an OFDM system with a bandwidth B, total transmit power $\overline{S}$ and N subcarriers, the problem is formulated as:

$$R = \frac{B}{N}\sum_{n=1}^{N}\log_2\left(1 + s_{k_n^*}\left|\alpha_{k_n^*}\right|^2 \frac{N}{N_0 B\Gamma}\right)$$

$$k_n^* = \arg_k \max\left\{\left|\alpha_{1,n}\right|^2, \left|\alpha_{2,n}\right|^2, \ldots, \left|\alpha_{K,n}\right|^2\right\} \text{for } n = 1, 2, \ldots, N. \quad (7)$$

Figure 6. OFDM transceivers

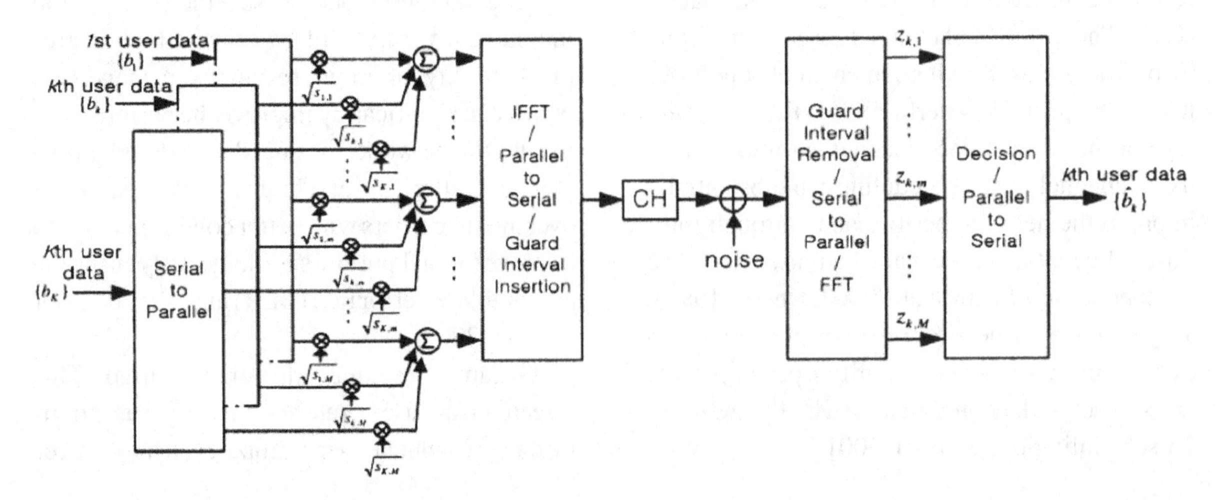

Subject to

$$\sum_{n=1}^{N} s_{k_n^*} = \bar{S} \quad (8)$$

where $\alpha_{k_n^*}$ and $s_{k_n^*}$ are the channel gain and power assigned to user k with the best channel gain for subcarrier. Γ is a function of the required BER and is defined as $\Gamma = -\ln(5BER)/1.5$ (Song, 2005).

The algorithm selects the user with the best channel gain for a subcarrier and assigns the subcarrier to the user in order to maximize the total data rate in Equation (7). Since there is no constraint on the user data rate, a user may not be assigned any subcarrier if the user has no best subcarrier.

POWER ALLOCATION

The transmit power adaptation method used for the maximum capacity algorithm is water-filling over the subcarriers with the best channel gains among multiple users. The method takes the inverse of the channel gains of all users as a container in which when power is poured in, it is distributed over all users so that the power levels of all users are uniform. In essence, more power is allocated to a user with a high channel gain and less or no power is allotted to a user with lower channel gain. The aim of the process is to maximize the sum of data rate for each sub-channel. From Equation (7), we can see that capacity is a logarithmic function of power, hence, so there is a significant difference in the increase in capacity when a given power value is assigned to a subcarrier with high gain vis-à-vis one with low gain.

Thus, the water-filling algorithm adapts power allocation for subcarriers to the channel condition for a given total power in order to achieve maximum data rates. The optimum water level changes when the channel condition changes, so it has to be updated accordingly each time these changes occur.

To maximize the total data rate of the multiuser OFDM system, the transmit power should be allocated as

$$\begin{cases} s_{k_n^*} = \dfrac{N_0 B\Gamma}{N}\left[\dfrac{1}{\lambda_0} - \dfrac{1}{\left|\alpha_{k_n^*}\right|^2}\right]^+ , \text{for } n = 1,2,\ldots,N \\ s_{k_n^*} = 0, \qquad \text{for } k \neq k_n^* \end{cases} \quad (9)$$

$[.]^+$ represents the outcome of the water-filling algorithm. λ_0 is a threshold to be determine from the total transit power constraint in Equation (8) and is given as

$$\lambda_0 = (\bar{S} + \sum_{n=1}^{N} \frac{1}{\alpha_{k_n^*}}) / N \quad (10)$$

MAXIMUM WEIGHTED CAPACITY (MWC) BASED RESOURCE ALLOCATION

The maximum weighted capacity (MWC) algorithm as proposed by Zhou in (Zhou, 2008) is a resource allocation algorithm which can improve the QoS at the physical layer for multimedia data while maintaining high capacity in a multiuser OFDM network. This resource allocation algorithm is optimized with information about the channel state that is shared between the physical layer and the MAC layer. It uses a batch dependent scheduling scheme for the downlink system. Traffic data is classified broadly into 3 types based on their QoS requirements (i.e. Real Time, non Real Time and Best Effort). There are multiple queues per user; one for each traffic type.

A downlink OFDM multiuser system with a total of K users is considered for MWC. For simplicity, each subcarrier is occupied by only one user. At the base station, QoS information is transferred from the traffic controller to the subcarrier and power controller for resource allocation and the resource allocationresults are fed back to the traffic controller for scheduling as shown in Figure 6.

OPTIMAL SUBCARRIER ALLOCATION

A total bandwidth of B is shared by N subcarriers and the OFDM signalling is time slotted where the duration of each slot is T_{slot}. QoS information from the traffic controller is received at the physical layer in as weights, W. The weight for each user is denoted as W_k. Assuming perfect CSI, the achievable instantaneous data rate of user k on subcarrier n is expressed as:

$$R_{k,n} = \frac{B}{N}\log_2\left(1 + s_{k,n}\left|\alpha_{k,n}\right|^2 \frac{N}{N_0 B\Gamma}\right) \quad (11)$$

Thus, the total instantaneous data rate of user k is given by:

$$R_k = \sum_{n\in\Omega_k} R_{k,n} \quad (12)$$

Ω_k is the set of all subcarriers allocated to user k.

So the MWC resource allocation strategy uses cross-layer optimization to maximize the sum of weighted capacities given as:

$$J = \sum_{k=1}^{K} W_k R_k \quad (13)$$

Subject to $s_{k,n} \geq 0, \sum_{k=1}^{K}\sum_{n\in\Omega_k} s_{k,n} \leq \bar{S}$, $\Omega_i \cap \Omega_j = \varnothing (i \neq j)$, $\Omega_1 \cup \Omega_2 \cup \ldots \Omega_k \subseteq \{1, 2, \ldots, N\}$ and $R_k T_{slot} \leq Q_k$

Q_k denotes the total amount of data awaiting transmission for user k. The constraint $R_k T_{slot} \leq Q_k$ guarantees that no more resource is allocated to user k if the user has already obtained sufficient resources, to allow as much data as possible to be transmitted in the current slot.

OPTIMAL POWER ALLOCATION

Power allocation in for MWC uses the water filling strategy to assign power to users on the system. However, the water filling algorithm has to be modified to put the weights calculated at the MAC layer for each user into consideration. The proportion of power allocated to a user is a function of the total weight for the user relative to the sum total of the weight of all users. The optimal power allocation solution is given as

$$s_{k,n} = \left[\frac{W_k}{\sum_{m=1}^{K}\left(W_m\left|\Omega_m\right|\right)}\left(\bar{S} + \sum_{m=1}^{K}\sum_{q\in\Omega_i}\frac{1}{\alpha_{m,q}}\right) - \frac{1}{\alpha_{k,n}}\right]^+ \quad (14)$$

where $[x]^+ = \begin{cases} x, & x > 0 \\ 0, & x \leq 0 \end{cases}$, and $\left|\Omega_m\right|$ denotes the number of subcarriers in set Ω_m.

SIMULATIONS, RESULTS AND DISCUSSIONS

The simulation result for the MWC and MC schemes are presented in this section. The results are used to compare the performance of the MC scheme, which is a wholly physical layer scheme, and the MWC scheme. The MWC uses cross-layer optimization between the physical layer and the MAC layer to improve the performance system-centric quantities of QoS traffic. In order for the comparison to be fair, a modified version of the DS based scheduling algorithm used for MWC is applied to MC. The first part of the simulation is to reproduce the results for MC reported in (Jang, 2003) to show that the scheduling algorithm does not affect the physical layer properties of MC.

Since MC only maximises the R (Equation (8)) for the system, the weight $W_{k,i,l} = 1$ is assigned to all slots. MC scheme is ignorant of the QoS requirement of data traffic transmitted. The QoS coefficient is the same for all traffic types, i.e. $\beta_i = 1, \forall i$.

For MWC, the QoS coefficient, β_i for Real Time, non Real Time and Best Effort traffic are 1024, 512 and 1, respectively (see Tables 1 and 2). For subcarrier allocation, uniform power allocation is assumed across all subcarriers. So each subcarrier is allocated power $\bar{S} / N$.

The total bandwidth of the downlink OFDM system is $B = 1$MHz, which is divided into $N = 256$ subcarriers for $K = 16$ users to share. The total power is $\bar{S} = 1$W. The targeted bit error rate is $BER = 1 \times 10^{-3}$. The channel has five independent Rayleigh fading paths with an exponential delay profile. The maximum delay tolerance for RT, nRT and BE traffic are set at 100msec, 400msec and 1sec, respectively (Zhou, 2008). Using voice traffic as a model for RT traffic, incoming data stream is fixed at 64Kbits. nRT traffic (using video traffic as a model), has an arrival rate that is Poisson distributed with a minimum data rate of 120Kbits and a maximum of 420Kbps. BE traffic has a Poisson distribution between 0 and 50 Kbit for each slot. It is assumed that perfect CSI of the downlink channel is available at the base station. SNR is defined as the average received signal power to noise power for each user. These values are standard values used in all simulation unless otherwise stated.

Figure 7 depicts the average system capacity versus the average SNR for each user. We can see here that MC has a maximum data rate that is higher than MWC with a constant difference of about 0.4 bit/sec/Hz. The AWGN curve shows the capacity of the AWGN channel and serves as a benchmark.

The MC scheme has a higher capacity because it assigns subcarriers to the user with the best channel gain for that subcarrier. However, the MWC scheme considers other parameters other than the channel gain to determine subcarrier allocation. Thus, there is more fairness in MWC, because a user stands a higher chance of having its data transmitted if it had poor channel gains.

Figure 8 shows the average delay of RT traffic. We can see that the delay experienced by traffic in this QoS class is significantly lower for MWC compared with MC. There is a difference of about 240msec to 200msec in the average packet delay at various SNR values. With the maximum delay tolerance expected for RT set at 100msec,

Table 1.

Quality of Service Coefficient		
Real Time Traffic	**Non-Real Time Traffic**	**Best Effort Traffic**
1024	512	1

Table 2.

Downlink OFDM System	
Bandwidth	1mhz
Number of subcarriers	256
Number of users	16
Total power	1w
Targeted BER	1×10^{-3}

Figure 7. System bandwidth efficiency versus average SNR

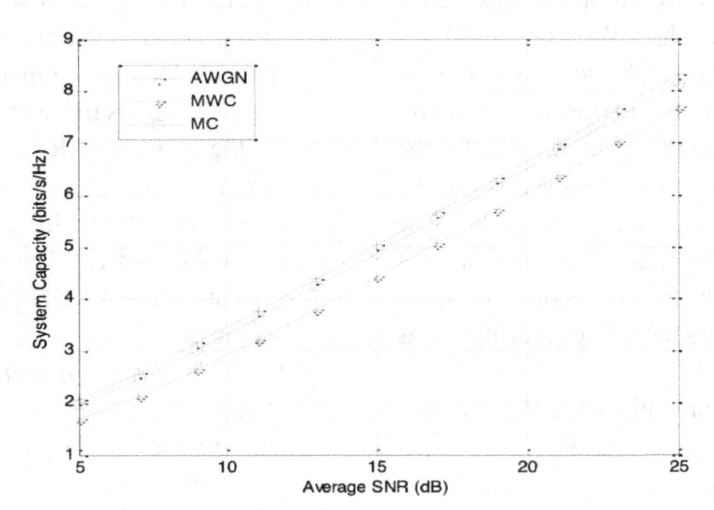

Figure 8. Average real time packet delay versus average SNR

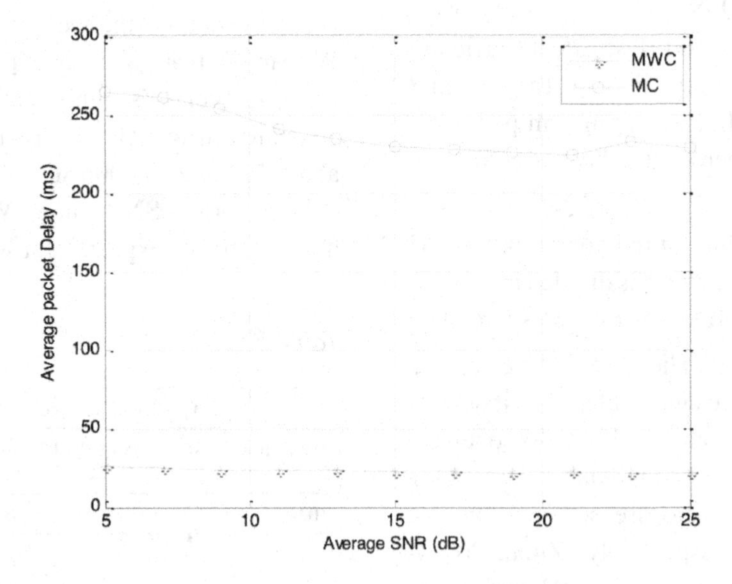

we can see that RT traffic would perform badly with MC scheme.

Figure 9 shows that nRT traffic performs well under the MWC scheme in terms of delay. Traffic in this QoS class transmitted using this scheme is able to meet the delay time requirements at all SNR values. However, for MC traffic in this class had to endure an average delay time of over 400msec at SNR values below 13dB. The differences in the delays experienced nRT traffic for MWC and MC varies between about 1sec at 5dB and 300msec at 25dB.

The scenario that is played out with BE traffic is different. Figure 10 shows that, in this case, the

Figure 9. Average non real time packet delay versus average SNR

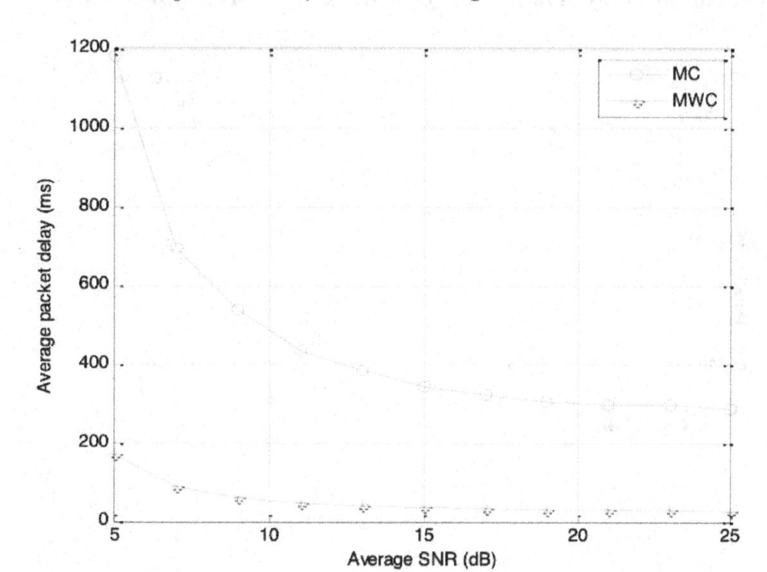

Figure 10. Average best effort packet delay versus average SNR

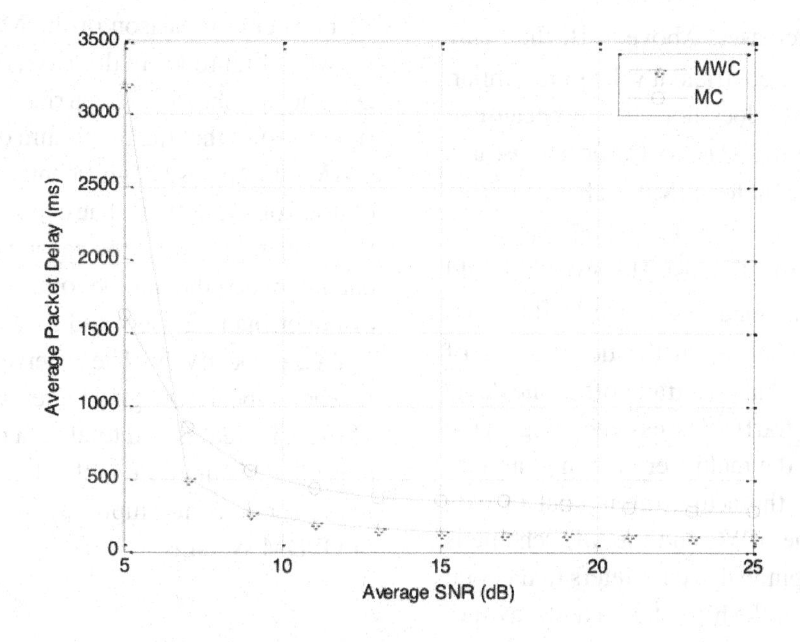

delay times experienced under MWC at low SNR value is quite large. This values falls rapidly so that at 7dB the delay time is 500msec, which is lower than the maximum tolerance of 1sec for BE traffic. The same is also true for MC. At higher SNR values, the delay experience by traffic in this class reduces slowly. At SNR values higher than 7dB, difference in the delay times for MWC and MC is about 200msec.

It is obvious that the delay time at SNR values below 7dB exceeds the maximum delay tolerance for MWC. Increasing the QoS coefficient β_i assigned to BE traffic would, however, reduce the the delay.

Figure 11. Best effort packet delay versus average SNR at $\beta_i = 1,2,5$ *for MWC*

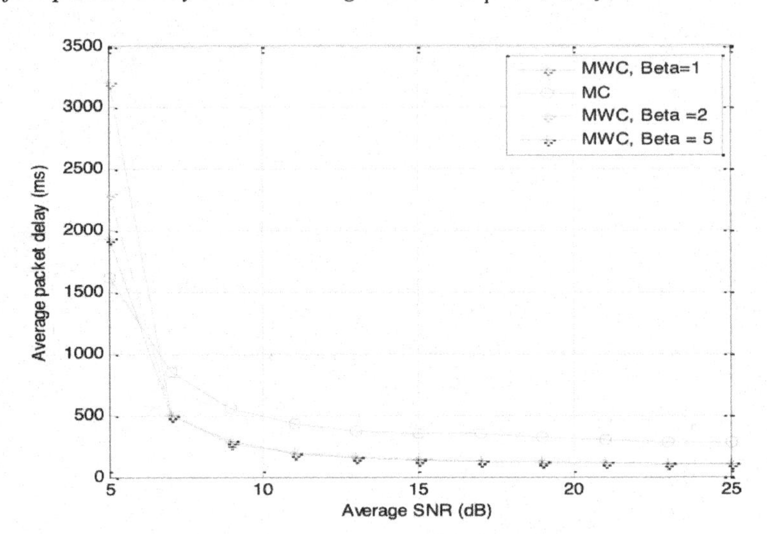

So in Figure 11, the plot for MWC curves at $\beta_i = 1, 2, 5$ is done. The delay time for BE traffic reduces as β_i increases. Above 7dB, the delay curves for the three coefficient values are similar. The curve for MC does not change because it ignores the QoS traffic class for traffic it transmits. Hence, β_i is constant for it (MC). Thus, it is possible to vary the delay time by changing the QoS coefficients of the traffic class. However, it should be noted that changing β_i for one traffic class would result in changes in the delay times of other QoS traffic. This is a trade-off of the delay time for different traffic classes depending on the specifications of the multiuser system required.

In Figure 12, the actual throughput of data transmitted by the MWC and the MC scheme is shown. Throughput in this case refers to the total data that arrived at the base station and was successfully transmitted to all users by the base station in the simulation. The data structure for RT, nRT and BE traffic was described earlier in this section. It can be seen that the increase in throughput by MWC relative to MC varies from about 30% (at SNR of 5dB) to about 50% (at SNR values greater than 9dB). This is despite the fact that the maximum system capacity for MC, shown in Figure 7, is constantly higher than MWC at all SNR values.

Further comparison of the MWC and MC is shown in Figure 13. In this case, the SNR = 10dB and the number of subcarriers $N = 256$. This figure shows that the maximum data rate for MC and MWC increases significantly with the number of users on the system. The capacity of the system becomes higher than the capacity of the AWGN channel when the number of users K is equal to or larger than 22 users and 57users, for MC and MWC, respectively. The received average SNR for each subcarrier signal increases as the number of users increases and total data rate increases as a result. This increase in the data rate shows that multiuser diversity improves the system capacity of OFDM systems.

SOLUTIONS AND RECOMENDATIONS

There is no doubt that the current OSI model/standard as had an overwhelming impact in the wired communication network. This is not the same in the area of wireless communication system due to the various environmental factors

Figure 12. Total data throughput versus the average SNR

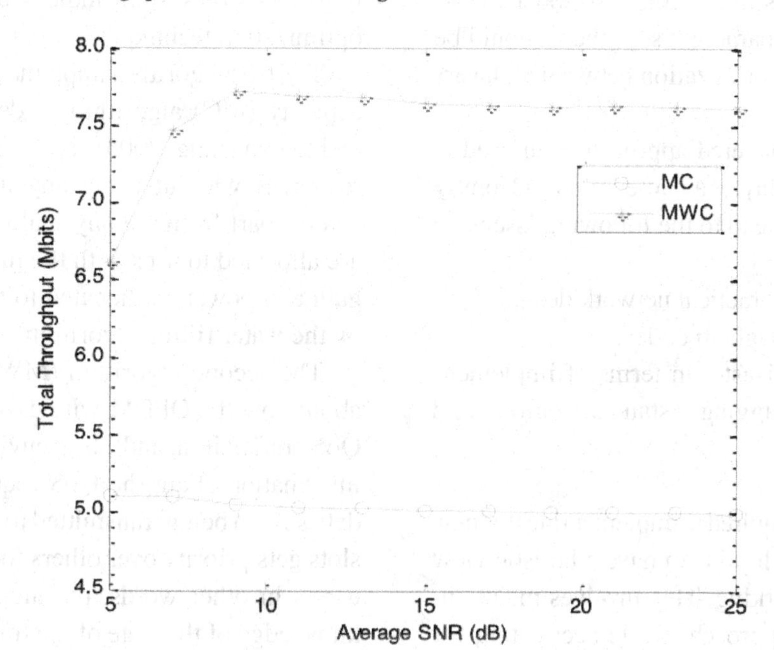

Figure 13. System capacity versus number of Users

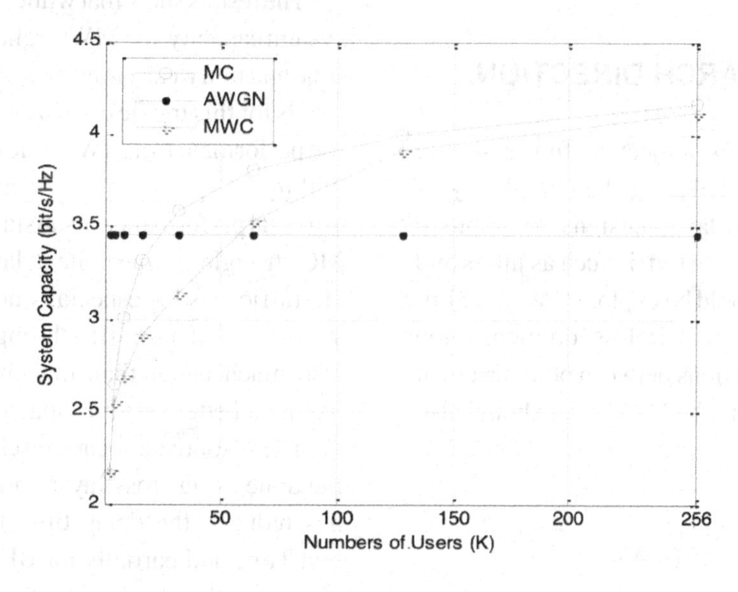

that mitigate wireless communications networks. Such environmental factors include jitter, delay and fading.

We have been able to establish in this work that OFDM as a transmission channel helps in addressing some of these impairments experienced by wireless communication system.

There are quite a number of misconceptions about cross-layer optimization. Cross-layering does not mean there will be a new OSI model or standard, it only says there should be interaction between the various layers in the OSI model. Cross-layering as a new paradigm says there should be joint sharing and optimization between all layers of the OSI stack.

If the current layered approach been used is eliminated and all layers are integrated and jointly optimized, it will lead to the following issues

- A clearly impractical network design.
- It leads to spaghetti codes.
- It leads to disaster in terms of implementation, debugging, standardization and upgrading.

The solution required in implementing this new technique or paradigm is to have a holistic view of wireless networking. This involves maintaining the layered approach, while accounting for interactions between various protocols at different layers, more like a loose coupling design.

FUTURE RESEARCH DIRECTION

Further work on this project in future should investigate ways of reducing the complexity of MWC. Other cross-layer designs to improve other parameters of data traffic such as jitters and dropped packets should be explored. Ways of improving the efficiency of wireless communication system using interactions between other layers of the system apart from the MAC layer should also be explored.

CONCLUSION

This work is a comparative framework of two algorithms for resource allocation in a wireless system with multiple users vying for wireless network resources. The wireless channel is shared by using OFDMA. The main aim of the project is to improve system indices using cross-layer optimization techniques.

The first algorithm implemented is maximum capacity (MC) algorithm as described by Jang and Lee in (Jang, 2003). The algorithm allocates resources without using any information from layers apart from the physical layer. Subcarriers are allocated to uses with the maximum channel gain and power is allocated to these subcarriers by the water filling algorithm.

The second algorithm (MWC) is concerned about how the OFDM wireless network handles QoS traffic in a multiuser environment. It uses information about the QoS requirements of the data stream being transmitted to determine which slots gets priority over others for transmission to users. In other words, the algorithm combines knowledge of the state of the traffic packet at the MAC layer to apportion resources and schedule traffic to users.

The results show that while the MC has a higher system capacity, the MWC reliable transmits Real time and non Real Time traffic within the requirements for this traffic class. For Best Effort traffic, the performance of MWC at low SNR value is not within the specification. At higher SNR (above 7dB), its performance is satisfactory. On the hand, MC struggles to meet the delay requirements for all traffic classes, especially at lower SNR value. The overall data traffic throughput for MWC is also much better than that of MC despite MC having a better system capacity.

The resource allocation scheme and scheduling done using cross-layer optimization in MWC has reduced the delay time for real time, non real Time and partially for BE traffic. It has also improved the throughput for the system when compared with MC, which is a purely physical layer resource allocation scheme. The trade-off here is the complexity of the two algorithms. The complexity required to implement the scheduling in MWC increases the computational costs of the system, compared to MC.

REFERENCES

Akyildiz, I., Altunbasak, Y., Fekri, F., & Sivakumar, R. (2004). AdaptNet: An adaptive protocol suite for the next generation wireless internet. *IEEE Communications Magazine*, *42*, 128–136. doi:10.1109/MCOM.2004.1273784.

Aune, F. (2004). *Cross-layer design tutorial*. Trondheim, Norway: Norwegian University of Science and Technology.

Debbah, M. (2002). *Short introduction to OFDM*. Washington, DC: IEEE Press.

Emad, A. (2008). *Basic principles of OFDM system*. Paper presented at the Electrical Engineering and Electronics Dept, University of Liverpool. Liverpool, UK.

Haykin, S. (1994). *Communication systems*. New York: John Wiley & Sons, Inc..

Jamalipour, A & Tekinay. (Eds.). (2001). Fourth generation wireless networks and interconnecting standards. *IEEE Personal Communications, 8*.

Jang, J., & Lee, K. (2003). (n.d.). Transmit power adaptation for OFDM systems. *IEEE Journal on Selected Areas in Communication.* [*Qos requirement for multimedia services.* IEEE Press.]. *Ignacio & Javier*.

Jurdak, R. (2007). *Wireless ad hoc and sensor networks: A cross-layer design perspective*. New York: Springer.

Knoche & McCarthy. (n.d.). Mobile users' needs and expectations of future multimedia services. *Wireless World Research Forum.*

Knopp, R., & Humblet, P. (1995). Information capacity and power control in single-cell multiuser communications. In *Proceedings of IEEE International Conference on Communication.* Seattle, WA: IEEE Press.

Langton, C. (2004). *Orthogonal frequency divisional multiplexing tutorial.* Retrieved from www.complextoreal.com

Liu, X., Chong, E., & Shroff, N. (2001). Opportunistic transmission scheduling with resource-sharing constraints in wireless networks. *IEEE Journal on Selected Areas in Communications, 19*, 2053–2064. doi:10.1109/49.957318.

Nanda, S. K., & Balachandran, S., & Kumar. (2000, January). Adaptation techniques in wireless packet data services. *IEEE Communications Magazine*. doi:10.1109/35.815453.

Nicopolitidis. (2003). *Wireless networks.* London: Wiley.

Oppenheim, A., & Schafer, R. (1989). *Discrete-time signal processing*. Upper Saddle River, NJ: Prentice-Hall.

Rahman, S. D. & Fitzek. (2004). OFDM based WLAN systems. *Technical Report R-04- 1002.* Denmark: Aalborg University.

Rappaport, T. (2002). *Wireless communication: Principles and practice*. Upper Saddle River, NJ: Prentice Hall.

Ravi, K., Hussain, & Tirupathi. (n.d.). A new paradigm for the next generation wireless optimization cross layer design. *International Journal Computer Technology Applications, 2*(3), 475-484.

Rohling, M. Bruninghaus, & Grunheid. (1999). Broad-band OFDM radio transmission for multimedia applications. *Proceedings of the IEEE, 87*(10), 1778–1789.

Saltzberg, B. (2000). Performance of an efficient parallel data transmission system. *IEEE Signal Processing Magazine*, 17.

Shakkottai, Rappaport, & Karlsson. (2003). Cross-layer design for wireless networks. *IEEE Communications Magazine*. doi:10.1109/MCOM.2003.1235598.

Song, G. (2005). *Cross-layer resource allocation and scheduling in wireless multicarrier networks*. Atlanta, GA: Georgia Institute of Technology.

Srivastava, V., & Motani, M. (2005, December). Cross-layer design: A survey and the road ahead. *IEEE Communications Magazine*. doi:10.1109/MCOM.2005.1561928.

Tanenbaum, A. (2003). *Computer networks*. Upper Saddle River, NJ: Prentice Hall.

Tse, D., & Viswanath, P. (2005). *Fundamentals of wireless communication*. Cambridge, UK: Cambridge University Press. doi:10.1017/CBO9780511807213.

Van Nee, R. (2002). New high-rate wireless LAN standards. *IEEE Communications Magazine*, 40.

Viswanath, P., Tse, D. N. C., & Laroia, R. L. (2002). Opportunistic beamforming using dumb antennas. *IEEE Transactions on Information Theory*, *48*, 1277–1294. doi:10.1109/TIT.2002.1003822.

Viterbi, A. (1995). *CDMA: Principles of spread spectrum communication*. Boston: Addison Wesley Longman, Inc..

Warrier, Le, & Rhee (n.d.). *Cross-layer optimization made practical*. Raleigh, NC: Department of Computer Science, North Carolina State University.

Xylomenos, G. C., & Polyzos. (n.d.). Internet protocol performance over networks with wireless links. *IEEE Network*, *13*(4), 55–63.

Zhou, N. (2008). *Novel batch dependant cross-layer scheduling for multiuser OFDM systems*. Washington, DC: IEEE Press. doi:10.1109/ICC.2008.728.

ADDITIONAL READING

Bingham, J. A. C. (1990, May). Multicarrier modulation for data transmission: An idea whose time has come. *IEEE Communications Magazine*. doi:10.1109/35.54342.

Chuang, J., & Sollenberger, N. (2000). Beyond 3G: Wideband wireless data access based on OFDM and dynamic packet assignment. *IEEE Communication Magazine*.

Chuang, J. C. (1987). The effect of time delay spread on portable radio communications channels with digital modulation. *IEEE Journal on Selected Areas in Communications*, *5*, 879–889. doi:10.1109/JSAC.1987.1146591.

Cimini, L. (1985). Analysis and simulation of a digital mobile channel using orthogonal frequency division multiplexing. *IEEE Transactions on Communications*, *33*, 665–675. doi:10.1109/TCOM.1985.1096357.

Debbah, M. (2002). *Short introduction to OFDM*. Washington, DC: IEEE Press.

Hui & Yeung. (2003). Challenges in the migration to 4G mobile systems. *IEEE Communications Magazine*, *41*, 54–59. doi:10.1109/MCOM.2003.1252799.

Johnsson, K. B., & Cox. (2005). An adaptive cross-layer scheduler for improved QoS support of multiclass data services and wireless systems. *IEEE Journal of Selected Areas of Communication*, *23*(2), 334–343.

Kawadia, V., & Kumar, P. R. (2005). A cautionary perspective on cross-layer design. *IEEE Wireless Communication*, *12*(1), 3–11. doi:10.1109/MWC.2005.1404568.

Keller, T., & Hanzo. (n.d.). Adaptive modulation techniques for duplex OFDM transmission. *IEEE Transactions on Vehicular Technology, 49*(5), 1893–1906.

Khan, S. Y., Peng, E., Steinbach, M., & Sgroi, W., Kellerer, & Docomo. (2006). Application-driven cross-layer optimization for video streaming over wireless networks. *IEEE Communications Magazine*, 123–130.

Kliazovich, D., & Graneill, F. (2004). A cross-layer scheme for TCP performance improvement in wireless LANs. In *Proceedings of IEEE Global TeleCommunications Conference,* (vol. 2, pp. 840–844). IEEE.

Kwon, K. Choi, & Lee. (2005). Lifetime maximization under reliability constraint via cross-layer strategy in wireless sensor networks. *Proceedings of IEEE Wireless Communications and Networking Conference, 3*, 1891–1896.

Laroia, R. S., & Uppala, J. L. (2004, September). Designing a mobile broadband wireless access network. *IEEE Signal Processing Magazine*. doi:10.1109/MSP.2004.1328085.

Lazos, L., & Poovendran. (2004). Cross-layer design for energy-efficient secure multicast communications in ad hoc networks. In *Proceedings of 2004 IEEE International Conference on Communications,* (vol. 6, pp. 3633–3639). IEEE Press.

Litwin & Pugel. (2001). *The principles of OFDM*. Washington, DC: IEEE Press.

Liu, H., & Li, G. (2005). *OFDM-based broadband wireless networks: Design and optimization*. Boston: John Wiley & Sons. doi:10.1002/0471757195.

Liu, Zhou, & Giannakis. (2004). Cross-layer modeling of adaptive wireless links for QoS support in multimedia networks. In *Proceedings of First International Conference of Quality of Service in Heterogeneous Wired/Wireless Networks*. Houston, TX: Springer.

Madueno, M., & Vidal, J. (2005). Joint physical–MAC layer design of the broadcast protocol in ad hoc networks. *IEEE Journal on Selected Areas in Communications, 23*(1), 65–75. doi:10.1109/JSAC.2004.837346.

Myung, H. (2007). Single carrier orthogonal multiple access techniques for broadband wireless communication. In *Electrical and Computer Engineering*. New York: Polytechnic University.

Pham, P. S., Perreau, & Jayasuriya. (2005). New cross-layer design approach to ad hoc networks under Rayleigh fading. *IEEE Journal on Selected Areas of Communication, 23*(1), 28–39.

Prasad, R., & Hara. (2003). *Multicarrier techniques for 4G mobile communications*. London: Artech House.

Proakis, J. (2005). *Digital communications*. Singapore: McGraw-Hill Book Co..

Rappaport, T. A., & Annamalai, R., & Buehrer. (2002). Wireless communication: Past events and a future perspective. *IEEE Communications Magazine*, 40.

Rhee & Cioffi. (2000). Increase in capacity of multiuser OFDM systems using dynamic. In *Proceedings of Subchannel Allocation*. Tokyo, Japan: VTC.

Scaglione, A., & van der Schaar. (2005). Cross-layer resource allocation for delay constrained wireless video transmission. In *Proceedings of IEEE International Conference of Acoustics, Speech, and Signal Processing,* (vol. 5, pp. 909–912). IEEE Press.

Schulze & Luders. (2005). *Theory and applications of OFDM and CDMA*. West Sussex, UK: John Wileys & Son, Inc..

Stallings, W. (2002). *Wireless communications and networking*. Upper Saddle River, NJ: Prentice Hall.

Tassiulas, L., & Ephremides, A. (1993). Dynamic server allocation to parallel queues with randomly varying connectivity. *IEEE Transactions on Information Theory*, *39*, 466–478. doi:10.1109/18.212277.

Tse, D. (1999). Forward link multiuser diversity through proportional fair scheduling. In *Proceedings of Presentation at Bell Labs*. Bell Labs.

Verikoulis, Alonso, & Giamalis. (2005). Cross-layer optimization for wireless systems: A European research key challenge. In *Global Communication Newsletter*. IEEE Press.

Weintein, S., & Ebert, P. (n.d.). Data transmission by frequency division multiplexing using the discrete Fourier transform. *IEEE Transactions on Communications*.

Wong, C. Y., Cheng, R. S., Letaief, K. B., & Murch, R. D. (1999). Multiuser OFDM with adaptive subcarrier, bit, and power allocation. *IEEE Journal on Selected Areas in Communications*, *17*, 1747–1758. doi:10.1109/49.793310.

Wu, Y., Chou, P.A., Zhang, J. K., Zhu, & Kung. (n.d.). Network planning in wireless ad hoc networks: A cross-Layer approach. *IEEE Journal on Selected Areas in Communication, 23*(1), 136–150.

Yao, Wong, & Chew. (2004). Cross-layer design on the reverse and forward links capacities balancing in cellular CDMA systems. *Proceedings of IEEE Wireless Communications and Networking Conference, 4*, 2004–2009.

KEY TERMS AND DEFINITIONS

Bit Error Rate: In digital transmission, the number of bit errors is the number of received bits of a data stream over a communication channel that has been altered due to noise, interference, distortion or bit synchronization errors. The bit error rate or Bit Error Ratio (BER) is the number of bit errors divided by the total number of transferred bits during a studied time interval. BER is a unit less performance measure, often expressed as a percentage.

Multiplexing: In telecommunications and computer networks, multiplexing is a method by which multiple analog message signals or digital data streams are combined into one signal over a shared medium. The aim is to share an expensive resource.

Quality of Service (QoS): Quality of service is the ability to provide different priority to different applications, users, or data flows, or to guarantee a certain level of performance to a data flow. For example, a required bit rate, delay, jitter, packet dropping probability and/or bit error rate may be guaranteed. Quality of service guarantees are important if the network capacity is insufficient, especially for real-time streaming multimedia applications such as voice over IP, online games and IP-TV, since these often require fixed bit rate and are delay sensitive, and in networks where the capacity is a limited resource, for example in cellular data communication.

Signal to Noise Ratio: (Often abbreviated SNR or S/N) Is a measure used in science and engineering that compares the level of a desired signal to the level of background noise. It is defined as the ratio of signal power to the noise power. A ratio higher than 1:1 indicates more signal than noise.

Throughput: Throughput or network throughput is the average rate of successful message delivery over a communication channel. This data may be delivered over a physical or logical link, or pass through a certain network node. The throughput is usually measured in bits per second (bit/s or bps), and sometimes in data packets per second or data packets per time slot.

Transmission Control Protocol /Internet Protocol (TCP/IP): Transmission Control Protocol /Internet Protocol is the communication protocol for the internet. TCP/IP defines the rule computers must follow to communicate with each other over the internet. TCP/IP provides end-to-end connectivity specifying how data should be formatted, addressed, transmitted, routed, and received at the destination.

Compilation of References

Abdel-Badeeh, M. S., & Rania, A. (2005). A case based expert system for supporting diagnosis of heart diseases, *AIML Journal, 5*(1).

Abdullah, A., Ramly, M., & Derhman. (2008). Performance comparison study of routing protocols for mobile grid environment. *IJCSNS International Journal of Computer science and Network security, 8*(2).

Abend, K., Harley, T. J., & Kanal, L. N. (1965). Classification of binary random patterns. *IEEE Transactions on Information Theory, 11*, 538–544. doi:10.1109/TIT.1965.1053827.

Ablameiko, S. V., & Lagunovskiy, D. M. (2000). *Image processing: Technology, methods, application.* Amalphea Publishing.

Adinoyi, A., & Yanikomeroglu, H. (2007). Cooperative relaying in multi-antenna fixed relay networks. *IEEE Communications Letters, 6*(2), 533–544.

Advanced Encryption Standard (AES). (2001). *National institute for standards and technology.* Gaithersburg, MD: AES.

Aguiar, A. C., Hoene, C., Klaue, J., Karl, H., Wolisz, A., & Miesmer, H. (2003). *Channel-aware schedulers for voip and MPEG-4 based on channel prediction.*

Ahn, S., & Abt, R. C. (2006). Productivity measurement with improved index numbers: Application to the sawmills and planning mills industry of the US: 1947–2000. *Forest Policy and Economics, 8*, 323–335. doi:10.1016/j.forpol.2005.02.006.

Ajayi, O. O., Fagbenle, R. O., Katende, J., & Okeniyi, J. O. (2011). Availability of wind energy resource potential for power generation at Jos, Nigeria. *Frontiers of Energy.*

Ajayi, O. O., Fagbenle, R. O., Katende, J., & Okeniyi, J. O. (2013b). Availability of wind energy resource potential for power generation at Jos, Nigeria. *Frontier of Energy.*

Ajayi, O. O., Fagbenle, R. O., Katende, J., Okeniyi, J. O., & Omotosho, O. A. (2013a). Wind energy potential for power generation of a local site in Gusau, Nigeria. *International Journal of Energy for a Clean Environment.*

Ajayi, O. O., Fagbenle, R. O., & Katende, J. (2011). Wind profile characteristic and econometrics analysis of wind power generation of a site in Sokoto State, Nigeria. *Energy Science and Technology, 1*(2), 54–66.

Akasi, A. (1981). Recovering of Gaussian images with the help of two-dimension maximal a posteriori estimation. *Journal Densi Tsusin Gakkai Rombusini, A-64*(11), 908–915.

Akl, R., Tummala, D., & Li, X. (2006). *Indoor propagation modeling at 2.4 GHz for IEEE 802.11networks.* Paper presented at the 6th IASTED International Multi-Conference on Wireless and Optical Communications. Banff, Canada.

Akpinar, E. K., & Akpinar, S. (2005a). A statistical analysis of wind speed data used in installation of wind energy conversion systems. *Energy Conversion and Management, 46*, 515–532. doi:10.1016/j.enconman.2004.05.002.

Akpinar, E. K., & Akpinar, S. (2005b). An assessment on seasonal analysis of wind energy characteristics and wind turbine characteristics. *Energy Conversion and Management, 46*, 1848–1867. doi:10.1016/j.enconman.2004.08.012.

Akpinar, S., & Akpinar, E. K. (2007). Wind energy analysis based on maximum entropy principle (MEP)-type distribution function. *Energy Conversion and Management*, *48*, 1140–1149. doi:10.1016/j.enconman.2006.10.004.

Akyildiz, I., Altunbasak, Y., Fekri, F., & Sivakumar, R. (2004). AdaptNet: An adaptive protocol suite for the next generation wireless internet. *IEEE Communications Magazine*, *42*, 128–136. doi:10.1109/MCOM.2004.1273784.

Alamouti. (1998). A simple transmit diversity technique for wireless communications. *IEEE Journal on Selected Areas in Communications.*

Alberto, L., & Widjaja, I. (2004). *Communications networks: Fundamental concepts and key architectures*. New York: McGraw Hill.

Alli, O. A., Ogunwolu, L., & Oke, O. (2009). Maintenance Productivity Measurement: Case Study of a Manufacturing Company, *Advanced Materials Research, 62-64, 565-570. doi:10.4028/*www.scientifi.net/AMR.62-64.565.

Al-Muthairi, N. F., & Zbiri, M. (2004). Sliding mode control of a magnetic levitation system. *Mathematical Problems in Engineering*, *2*, 93–107. doi:10.1155/S1024123X04310033.

Alouini, M.-S., & Simon, M. K. (2002). Dual diversity over correlated log-normal fading channels. *IEEE Transactions on Communications*, *50*(12), 1946–1959. doi:10.1109/TCOMM.2002.806552.

Alsyouf, I. (2007). The role of maintenance in improving companies' productivity and profitability. *International Journal of Production Economics*, *105*, 70–78. doi:10.1016/j.ijpe.2004.06.057.

Amarasuriya, G., Ardakani, M., & Tellambura, C. (2010). Output-threshold multiple-relay-selection scheme for cooperative wireless networks. *IEEE Transactions on Vehicular Technology*, *59*(6), 3091–3097. doi:10.1109/TVT.2010.2048767.

Amiantov, I. N. (1971). *Selected issues of the statistical communication theory*. Moscow, Russia: Sovetskoe Radio Publishing.

Anantharam, V. (1993). An approach to the design of high-speed networks for bursty traffic. In *Proceedings of the 32nd IEEE Conference on Decision and Control.* San Antonio, TX: IEEE.

Anisur, R. Islam, & Talevski. (2009). Performance measurement of various routing protocols in ad hoc network. In *Proceeding of the International Multi-Conference of Engineers and Computer Scientists.* Hong Kong: MECS.

ANSI. (1996). Digital transport of video teleconferencing/Video telephony signals. *ANSI T1.801.01/02-1996.*

Anurag, K., Manjunath, D., & Kuri, J. (2004). *Communication networking: An analytical approach.* San Francisco, CA: Morgan Kaufmann Publishers.

Apple. (n.d.). *QuickTime player software.* Retrieved from http://www.apple.com

Armstrong, H. (2009). Advanced IT education for the vision impaired via e-learning. *Journal of Information Technology Education*, *8*, 244–256.

Aroyo, L., & Dicheva, D. (2004). The new challenges for e-learning: The educational semantic web. *Journal of Educational Technology & Society*, *7*(4), 59–69.

Arpaci. (2001). *Congestion avoidance in TCP/IP networks.* Retrieved from http://www.csc.gatech.edu/~mutlu/arpaci_thesis.pdf

Arun-Kumar B. R., Lokanatha, C., Reddy, Prakash, S., & Hiremath. (2008). Performance comparison of wireless mobile ad hoc network routing protocols. *IJCSNS International Journal of Computer Science and Network Security, 8*(6).

Atayero, A. A. (2000). *Estimation of the quality of digitally transmitted analogue signals over corporate VSAT networks.* (Unpublished Doctoral Thesis). Moscow.

Atayero, A. A., Sheluhin, O. I., & Ivanov, I. (2011). Effect of wideband wireless access systems interference robustness on the quality of video streaming. *Proceedings of the World Congress on Engineering and Computer Science, 2,* 848-854.

Atayero, A. A., Sheluhin, O. I., & Ivanov, Y. A. (2013). Modeling, simulation and analysis of video streaming errors in wireless wideband access networks. In *Proceedings of IAENG Transactions on Engineering Technologies* (pp. 15-28). Springer.

Atayero, A. A., Sheluhin, O. I., & Ivanov, Y. A. (2012). Modeling, simulation, and analysis of video streaming errors in wireless wideband access networks. *IAENG Transactions on Engineering Technologies*, *170*, 15–28. doi:10.1007/978-94-007-4786-9_2.

Atayero, A. A., Sheluhin, O. I., Ivanov, Y. A., & Alatishe, A. S. (2011). Estimation of the visual quality of video streaming under desynchronization conditions. *International Journal of Advanced Computer Science and Applications*, *2*(12), 1–11.

Aune, F. (2004). *Cross-layer design tutorial*. Trondheim, Norway: Norwegian University of Science and Technology.

Auwera, L. V., Meyer, F., & Malet, L. M. (1980). The use of the Weibull three-parameter model for estimating mean wind power densities. *Journal of Applied Meteorology*, *19*, 819–825. doi:10.1175/1520-0450(1980)019<0819:TUOTWT>2.0.CO;2.

Azeta, A. A., Ayo, C. K., Atayero, A. A., & Ikhu-Omoregbe, N. A. (2008c). Development of a telephone-based e-learning portal. In *Proceedings of the 1st International Conference on Mobile Computing, Wireless Communication, E-Health, M-Health and TeleMedicine (FICMWiComTelHealth'08)*, (pp. 141-149). Ogbomosho, Nigeria: FICMWiComTelHealth.

Azeta, A. A., Ayo, C. K., Atayero, A. A., & Ikhu-Omoregbe, N. A. (2009c). A case-based reasoning approach for speech-enabled e-learning system. In *Proceedings of 2nd IEEE International Conference on Adaptive Science & Technology (ICAST)*. Accra, Ghana: IEEE. Retrieved from http://ieeexplore.ieee.org/xpl/mostRecentIssue.jsp?punumber=5375737

Azeta, A. A., Ayo, C. K., Atayero, A. A., & Ikhu-Omoregbe, N. A. (2009b). Application of voiceXML in e-learning systems. In *Cases on Successful E-Learning Practices in the Developed and Developing World: Methods for the Global Information Economy*. Hershey, PA: IGI Global. doi:10.4018/978-1-60566-942-7.ch007.

Bacry, E., Muzy, J. F., & Arneodo, A. (1993). Singularity spectrum of fractal signals: Exact results. *Journal of Statistical Physics*, *70*(3/4), 635–674. doi:10.1007/BF01053588.

Baguda, Y., Fisal, N., Syed, S., Yusof, S., Mohd, S. A., Mohd, A., & Zulkarmawan, A. (2008). Mobile streaming of H.264 video over Gilbert-Elliotts channel. *PWASET*, *36*.

Bakalis & Bello. (2010). Performance evaluation of CBR and TCP traffic models on MANET using DSR routing protocol. In *Proceedings of IEEE 2010 International Conference on Communications and Mobile Computing*. Shenzhen, China: IEEE.

Balci, O. (1997). Verification, validation and accreditation of simulation models. In *Proceedings of the 29th Conference Winter, Simulation*, (pp. 47–52). IEEE.

Barrie, W., & Chiasson, J. (1996). Linear and nonlinear state-space controllers for magnetic levitation. *International Journal of Systems Science*, *27*(11), 1153–1163. doi:10.1080/00207729608929322.

Barros, J., & Rodrigues, M. R. D. (2006). *Secrecy capacity of wireless channels*. Paper presented at the IEEE International Symposium on Information Theory (ISIT 2006). Seattle, WA.

Beaulieu, N. C., & Hu, J. (2006). A closed-form expression for the outage probability of decode-and-forward relaying in dissimilar Rayleigh fading channels. *IEEE Communications Letters*, *10*(12), 813–815. doi:10.1109/LCOMM.2006.061048.

Bejerano, Y., Breithart, Y., Garofalakis, M., & Rastogi, R. (2003). Physical topology discovery for large multi-subnet networks. *IEEE Transactions on Networking*, *3*(6), 342–352.

Bennett, C. (1992). Quantum cryptography using any two non-orthogonal states. *Physical Review Letters*, *68*, 3121–3124. doi:10.1103/PhysRevLett.68.3121 PMID:10045619.

Berchtold. (1999). *The double chain Markov model* (Technical Report N° 348). Seattle, WA: University of Washington, Department of Statistics.

Berts, J., & Persson, A. (1998). *Objective and subjective quality assessment of compressed digital video sequences*. (Master's thesis). Chalmers University of Technology, Göteborg, Sweden.

Bertsekas, D., & Gallager, R. (1992). *Data networks*. Englewood Cliffs, NJ: Prentice Hall.

Besag, J. E. (1974). Spatial interaction and statistical analysis of lattice systems. *Journal of the Royal Statistical Society. Series B. Methodological*, *36*, 192–236.

Biham, E., Boyer, M., Boykin, P. O., Mor, T., & Roychowdhury, V. A. (n.d.). *Proof of the seurity of quantum key distribution*. Retrieved from http://arxiv.org/abs/quant-ph/9912053v1

Blatses, A., Shin, A. H., & Lippman, A. (2006). A simple cooperative diversity method based on network path selection. *IEEE Journal on Selected Areas in Communications*, *24*(3), 659–672. doi:10.1109/JSAC.2005.862417.

Bloch, M., Barros, J., Rodrigues, M. R. D., & McLaughlin, S. W. (2008). Wireless information-theoretic security. *IEEE Transactions on Information Theory*, *54*(6), 2515–2534. doi:10.1109/TIT.2008.921908.

Bobbie, P. O., Fordjour, I., Aboagye, D. O., Dzidonu, C., Darkwa, O., & Nyantakyi, K. (2008). Technology enablers for collaborative virtual education. In *Proceedings of 3rd International Conference on ICT for Development, Education and Training AICC*. Accra, Ghana: AICC.

Boldia, I., & Nasar, S. A. (1986). *Electric machines dynamics*. New York: Macmillan.

Bolot, J. (1993). Characterizing end-to-end packet delay and loss in the internet. *Journal of High-Speed Networks*, *2*(3), 305–323.

Bolotov, V. N., & Tkach, Y. V. (2006). Generating of signals with a fractal spectra. *Journal of Technical Physics*, *76*(4), 91–98.

Bolu, C. A. (2011). Curve fitting breakdown distribution of a 4-high aluminium rolling mills, Ota, Nigeria using MATLAB. (Unpublished Report).Department of Mechanical Engineering, Covenant University, Lagos, Nigeria.

Bondur, V. G. (2003). Modeling of multi-spectral airspace images of the dynamic fields of brightness (in Russian). *Investigation of Earth from Space*, (2), 3-17.

Bouwmeester, D., Ekert, A. K., & Zeilinger, A. (2000). *The physics of quantum information: Quantum cryptography, quantum teleportation, and quantum computation*. Berlin: Springer.

Boyd, H. S., & Vandenberghe, L. (2004). *Convex optimization*. New York: Cambridge University Press.

Bozhokin, S. V., & Parshin, D. A. (2001). *Fractals and multifractals* [Regularnaya i haoticheskaya dinamika]. Izhevsk, Russia: NIC.

Braden. (1998). Recommendations on queue management and congestion avoidance in the internet. *RFC 2039*.

Brassard, G. (2007). *Modern cryptology: A tutorial*. New York: Springer-Verlag.

Brassard, G., & Salvail, L. (1993). Secret-key reconciliation by public discussion: Advances in cryptology. In *Proceedings of Eurocrypt '93*. Lofthus, Norway: IEEE Press.

Brichet, F., Roberts, J., Simonian, A., & Veitch, D. (1996). Heavy traffic analysis of a storage model with long range dependent on/off sources. *Queueing Systems*, *23*, 197–215. doi:10.1007/BF01206557.

Broch, Maltz, Johnson, Hu, & Jetcheva. (1998). *A performance comparison of multi-hop wireless ad hoc network routing protocols*. Pittsburgh, PA: Computer Science Department, Carnegie Mellon University.

Bures, I. M., & Jelinek, I. (2004). Description of the adaptive web system for e-learning. In *Proceedings of IADIS International Conference E-Society 2004*, (Vol. 2). IADIS. Retrieved from http://www.iadis.net/dl/final_uploads/200402C042.pdf

Burton, T., Sharpe, D., Jenkins, N., & Bossanyi, E. (2001). *Wind energy handbook*. Hoboken, NJ: Wiley. doi:10.1002/0470846062.

Butorin, E. L. (2004). *Nonlinear filtering devices for digital half-tone images of Markovian type*. (Unpublished Doctoral Thesis). Moscow Power Engineering Institute, Moscow, Russia.

Bychkov, S. I., & Rumiantsev, K. E. (2000). *Search and detection of optical signals*. Moscow, Russia: Radio and Connection Publisher.

Bykov, V. V. (1971). *Digital modeling in the statistical radio engineering*. Moscow: Sovetskoe Radio Publishing.

Camel, D. E. (2003). *Principles, protocols, and structure*. Networks TCP/IP.

Carta, J. A., Ramı'rez, P., & Velázquez, S. (2009). A review of wind speed probability distributions used in wind energy analysis: Case studies in the Canary Islands. *Renewable & Sustainable Energy Reviews*, *13*, 933–955. doi:10.1016/j.rser.2008.05.005.

Center for KvanteInformatik. (n.d.). *Implementation of the B92 QKD protocol*. Retrieved from www.cki.au.dk/experiment/qrypto/doc/QuCrypt/b92prot.html

Chan, F. T. S., Lau, H. C. W., Ip, R. W. L., Chan, H. K., & Kong, S. (2005). Implementation of total productive maintenance: A case study. *International Journal of Production Economics*, *95*, 71–94. doi:10.1016/j.ijpe.2003.10.021.

Chang, T. J., & Tu, Y. L. (2007). Evaluation of monthly capacity factor of WECS using chronological and probabilistic wind speed data: A case study of Taiwan. *Renewable Energy*, *32*, 1999–2010. doi:10.1016/j.renene.2006.10.010.

Chan, H. C. B., & Leung, V. C. M. (1998). *A dynamic reservation protocol for integrating CBR/VBR/ABR traffic over IEEE 802.14 HFC networks*. Vancouver, Canada: The University of British Columbia. doi:10.1109/GLOCOM.1998.776644.

Channel Models for Fixed Wireless Applications. (n.d.). IEEE 802.16 broadband wireless access. *Working Group IEEE 802.16.3c-01/29r4*.

Chellappa, R. (1985). Two-dimensional discrete Gaussian Markov random fields for image processing. In *Progress in Pattern Recognition 2*. Amsterdam: Elsevier Science Publishers BV.

Chellappa, R., & Kashyap, R. L. (1982). Digital image restoration using spatial interaction models. *IEEE Transactions on Acoustics, Speech, and Signal Processing*, *30*, 461–472. doi:10.1109/TASSP.1982.1163911.

Cheng, Cheng, & Lee. (2002). Neuro-fuzzy and genetic algorithm in multiple response optimization. *International Journal of Computers & Mathematics with Applications*, *44*, 1503–1514. doi:10.1016/S0898-1221(02)00274-2.

Cheung, K. W., Sau, J. H. M., & Murch, R. D. (1998). A new empirical model for indoor propagation prediction. *IEEE Transactions on Vehicular Technology*, *47*(3), 996–1001. doi:10.1109/25.704854.

Chin, C. C., Hock, G. T., & Veerappan, C. M. (2006). VoiceXML as solution for improving web accessibility and manipulation for e-education. In *Proceedings of School of Computing and IT, INTI College*. Malaysia: INTI. Retrieved from http://intisj.edu.my/INTISJ/InfoFor/StaffResearch/10.pdf

Christensen, K., Hass, L., Noel, F., & Stole, N. (1995). Local area networks: Evolving from shared to switched access. *IBM Systems Journal*, 347–374. doi:10.1147/sj.343.0347.

Chrysikos, T., & Kotsopoulos, S. (2009). *Impact of channel-dependent variation of path loss exponent on wireless information-theoretic security*. Paper presented at the Wireless Telecommunications Symposium (WTS 2009). Prague, Czech Republic.

Chrysikos, T., Georgopoulos, G., & Kotsopoulos, S. (2009a). *Site-specific validation of ITU indoor path loss model at 2.4 GHz*. Paper presented at the IEEE Workshop on Advanced Experimental Activities on Wireless Networks and Systems. Kos Island, Greece.

Chrysikos, T., Georgopoulos, G., & Kotsopoulos, S. (2009b). *Empirical calculation of shadowing deviation for complex indoor propagation topologies at 2.4 GHz*. Paper presented at the International Conference on Ultra Modern Telecommunications (ICUMT 2009). St. Petersburg, Russia.

Chrysikos, T., Georgopoulos, G., & Kotsopoulos, S. (2010). *Impact of shadowing on wireless channel characterization for a public indoor commercial topology at 2.4 GHz*. Paper presented at the International Congress on Ultra Modern Telecommunications (ICUMT 2010). Moscow, Russia.

Chrysikos, T., Georgopoulos, G., & Kotsopoulos, S. (2011). *Wireless channel characterization for a home indoor propagation topology at 2.4 GHz*. Paper presented at the Wireless Telecommunications Symposium (WTS 2011). New York, NY.

Chrysikos, T., Georgopoulos, G., Birkos, K., & Kotsopoulos, S. (2009). *Wireless channel characterization: On the validation issues of indoor RF models at 2.4 GHz.* Paper presented at the Panhellenic Conference on Electronics and Telecommunications (PACET). Patras, Greece.

Comer, D. (2004). *Computer networks and intranets with internet applications.* Englewood Cliffs, NJ: Pearson Prentice Hall.

Cornaglia, B., & Spini, M. (1996). New statistical model for burst error distribution. In *European Transactions on Telecommunications.* Torino, Italy: John Wiley & Sons. doi:10.1002/ett.4460070308.

Costa, P., Netto, J., & Pereira, C. (2004). Analysis of traffic differentiation on switched ethernet. In *Proceedings of the International Workshop on Real-Time Networks.* Retrieved August 20, 2009 from http://www.ieeta.pt/lse/rtn2004/preprints

Cranefield, S., Hart, L., Dutra, M., Baclawski, K., Kokar, M., & Smith, J. (2002). UML for ontology development. *The Knowledge Engineering Review*, (17): 61–64.

Cruz, R. (1991). A calculus for network delay, part 1: Network elements in isolation. *IEEE Transactions on Information Theory, 37*(1), 114–131. doi:10.1109/18.61109.

Cuomo, K. M., & Oppenheim, A. V. (1993). Circuit implementation of synchronized chaos with applications to communications. *Physical Review Letters, 71*(1), 65–68. doi:10.1103/PhysRevLett.71.65 PMID:10054374.

Dagion, D., & Mercero, R. (1988). *Digital processing of multi-dimensional signals.* Moscow: MIR Publishing.

Dahlman, Parkvall, & Skold. (2011). *4G LTE/LTE-advanced for Mobile Broadband.* London: Elsevier.

Dai, M., & Loguinov, D. (2005). Analysis and modeling of MPEG-4 and H.264 multi-layer video traffic. In *Proceedings of IEEE INFOCOM.* Miami, FL: IEEE.

Dang, T. D. (2002). *New results in multifractal traffic analysis and modeling.* (Ph.D. Dissertation). Budapest, Hungary.

Deb, S., Jaiswal, S., & Nagaraj, K. (2008). Real-time video multicast in WiMAX networks. In *Proceedings of IEEE INFOCOM.* IEEE.

Debbah, M. (2002). *Short introduction to OFDM.* Washington, DC: IEEE Press.

Dech, G. (1971). *Manual to the practical application of the Laplace transformation and z-transformation.* Moscow: Nauka Publishing.

DeCoste, D. (1991). Dynamic across-time measurement interpretation. *Artificial Intelligence, 51*, 273–341. doi:10.1016/0004-3702(91)90113-X.

Dedieu, H., Kennedy, M. P., & Hasler, M. (1993). Chaos shift keying: modulation and demodulation of a chaotic carrier using self-synchronizing Chua's circuits. *IEEE Transactions on Circuits and Systems II, 40*, 634–642. doi:10.1109/82.246164.

Demuth & De Jesus, O. (2002). An introduction to the use of neural networks in control systems. *International Journal of Robust and Nonlinear Control, 12*(11), 959–985. doi:10.1002/rnc.727.

Derin, H., & Kelly, P. (1989). Random processes of Markov type with discrete arguments. *TIEEE, 77*(10), 42–71.

Devedzic, V. (2004). Education and the semantic web. *International Journal of Artificial Intelligence in Education, 14*, 9–65.

Di, R. M., Graziosi, F., & Santucci, F. (2008). Performance of cooperative multi-hop wireless systems over log-normal fading channels. In *Proceedings of IEEE Global Telecommunications Conference (GLOBECOM 08).* IEEE.

Dicheva, D., Sosnovsky, S., Gavrilova, T., & Brusilovsky, P. (2005). Ontological web portal for educational ontologies. In *Proceedings of International Workshop on Applications of Semantic Web Technologies for E-Learning (SW-EL).* Amsterdam: SW-EL. Retrieved from http://www.win.tue.nl/SW-EL/2005/swel05-aied05/proceedings/4-Dicheva-final-full.pdf

Divitini, M., Haugalokken, O., & Morken, E. M. (2005). Blog to support learning in the field: Lessons learned from a fiasco. In *Proceedings of the Fifth IEEE International Conference on Advanced Learning Technologies (ICALT '05)*, (pp. 219- 221). IEEE.

Dixon, A. R., Yuan, Z. L., Dynes, J. F., Sharpe, A. W., & Shields, A. J. (2010). Continuous operation of high bit rate quantum key distribution. *Applied Physics Letters.* doi:10.1063/1.3385293.

Dmitriev, A. S., & Panas, A. I. (2002). *Dynamic chaos: New information carriers for communication systems.* Moscow, Russia: Fizmatlit.

Dohler, M., & Li, Y. (2010). *Cooperative communication: Hardware, channel and PHY*. New York: John Wiley & Sons. doi:10.1002/9780470740071.

Donegan, M. (2000). BECTA voice recognition project report. *In Proceedings of BECTA*. Retrieved from http://www.becta.org.uk/teachers/teachers.cfm?section=2&id=2142

Dragan, Y. P. (1993). *Status and development prospects of probabilistic models of random signals and fields*. Kharkiv, Ukraine: HIRE Publishing.

Du Bois, & Reymond, P. (1875). Verch einer classification der willrurlichen functionen reeler argumente nach ihren aenderungen inden beinsten intervallen. *Journal Furder Reine und Angewandte Mathematiques*, *79*, 21–37.

Duong, T. Q., Bao, V. N. Q., & Zepernick, H. J. (2009). On the performance of selective decode-and-forward relay networks over Nakagami-m fading channels. *IEEE Communications Letters*, *13*(3), 172–174. doi:10.1109/LCOMM.2009.081858.

Dusek, M., Lutkenhaus, N., & Hendrych, M. (2006). Quantum cryptography. *Progress in Optics*, *49*, 381–454. doi:10.1016/S0079-6638(06)49005-3.

Dvorkovich, A. V. (2005). Efficient encoding video in the new standard H.264/AVC. In *Proceedings of NIIR*. NIIR.

Ebert, J.-P., Willig, A. A., & Gilbert-Elliot. (1999). Bit error model and the efficient use in packet level simulation. In *Proceedings of TKN Technical Reports*. Berlin: TKN.

Elfeki, A. A., & Dekking, M. (2001). Markov chain model for subsurface characterization: Theory and applications. *Mathematical Geology*, *33*, 569–589. doi:10.1023/A:1011044812133.

Elkashlany, M., Yeohyz, P. L., Sungy, C. K., & Collings, I. B. (2010). Distributed multi-antenna relaying in nonregenerative cooperative networks. In *Proceedings of IEEE 21st International Symposium on Personal Indoor and Mobile Radio Communications*. IEEE Press.

Elliot, E. O. (1963). Estimates of error rates for codes on burst-noise channels. *The Bell System Technical Journal*, *42*, 1977–1997.

Emad, A. (2008). *Basic principles of OFDM system*. Paper presented at the Electrical Engineering and Electronics Dept, University of Liverpool. Liverpool, UK.

Ermalai, I. And one, D., & Vasiu, R. (2009). Study cases on e-learning technologies used by universities in romania and worldwide. *WSEAS Transactions on Communications*, *8*(8), 785–794. Retrieved from http://www.wseas.us/E-library/transactions/communications/2009/29-640.pdf

Ersoy, C., & Panwar, S. (1993). Topological design of interconnected LAN/MAN networks. *IEEE Journal on Selected Areas in Communications*, *11*(8), 1172–1182. doi:10.1109/49.245906.

Eti, M. C., Ogaji, S. O. T., & Probert, S. D. (2004). Implementing total productive maintenance in Nigerian manufacturing industries. *Applied Energy*, *79*, 385–401. doi:10.1016/j.apenergy.2004.01.007.

ETSI TR 102 493. (n.d.). *Guidelines for the use of video quality algorithms for mobile applications*. ETSI.

ETSI TR 136 942. (2009). LTE; evolved universal terrestrial radio access (E-UTRA); radio frequency (RF) system scenarios. *Technical Report Version 8.2.0*. Retrieved from http://www.3gpp.org

ETSI TS 136 201. (2011). LTE; evolved universal terrestrial radio access (E-UTRA); LTE physical layer; general description. *Technical Specification Version 10.0.0*. Retrieved from http://www.3gpp.org

ETSI TS 136 211. (2011). LTE; evolved universal terrestrial radio access (E-UTRA); physical channels and modulation. *Technical Specification Version 10.2.0*. Retrieved from http://www.3gpp.org

ETSI TS 136 300. (2011). LTE; evolved universal terrestrial radio access (E-UTRA) and evolved universal terrestrial radio access network (E-UTRAN); overall description; stage 2. *Technical Specification Version 10.4.0*. Retrieved from http://www.3gpp.org

Fadare, D. A. (2009). Modeling of solar energy potential in Nigeria using artificial neural network model. *Applied Energy*, *86*(9), 1410–1422. doi:10.1016/j.apenergy.2008.12.005.

Fadare, D. A. A. (2008). Statistical analysis of wind energy potential in Ibadan, Nigeria, based on Weibull distribution function. *The Pacific Journal of Science and Technology*, *9*(1), 110–119.

Fagbenle, R. O., Katenje, J., Ajayi, O. O., & Okeniyi, J. O. (2011). Assessment of wind energy potential of two sites in North-East, Nigeria. *Renewable Energy, 36*, 1277–1283. doi:10.1016/j.renene.2010.10.003.

Falaki, S., & Sorensen, S. (1992). Traffic measurements on a local area computer network. *Butterworth Heinemann Computer Communications Journal, 15*(3), 192–197. doi:10.1016/0140-3664(92)90080-X.

Falconer, K. J. (1997). *Techniques in fractal geometry*. New York: John Wiley & Sons.

Fano, R. (1965). Statistical theory of communication. In *Transmission of Information*. Moscow: MIR Publishing.

Fantacci, R., & Scardi, M. (n.d.). Perfomance evaluation of preemptive polling schemes and ARQ techniques for indoor wireless networks. *IEEE Transaction on Vehicular technology, 45*(2), 248-257.

Farinazzo, V., Salvador, M., & Luiz, A. S. Kawamoto, & de Oliveira Neto, J. S. (2010). An empirical approach for the evaluation of voice user interfaces. *User Interfaces*. Retrieved from www.intechopen.com/download/pdf/pdfs_id/10804

Fawcett, T. (2003). *ROC graphs: Notes and practical considerations for data mining researchers*. Palo Alto, CA: HP Labs.

Feldmann, A., Gilbert, A. C., & Willinger, W. (1998). Data networks as cascades: Investigating the multifractal nature of internet WAN traffic. *ACM SIGCOMM Computer Communication Review, 28*(4), 42–55. doi:10.1145/285243.285256.

Feng, W.-C. (1997). *Buffering techniques for delivery of compressed video in video-on-demand systems*. Norwell, MA: Kluwer Academic Publisher.

Floyd & Fall. (1999). Promoting the use of end-to-end congestion control in the internet. *ACM/IEEE Transactions on Networking, 7*(4), 458–473.

Floyd. (1991). Connections with multiple congested gateways in packet-switched networks part 1: One-way traffic. *ACM Computer Communication Review, 21*(5), 30–47.

Forouzan, B. (2008). *Data communications and networking*. New Delhi: Tata McGraw-Hill.

Fowler, H., & Leland, W. (1991). Local area network traffic characteristics, with implications for broadband network congestion management. *IEEE Journal on Selected Areas in Communications, 9*(7), 1139–1149. doi:10.1109/49.103559.

Freepatentonline.com. (n.d.). Physical layer switch system for ethernet local area communication system. *US Patent No. 5889776*. Retrieved November 10, 2008 from http://www.freepatentsonline.com/5889776

Frigg, R., & Hartmann, S. (2009). Models in science. In Zalta, E. N. (Ed.), *The Stanford Encyclopedia of Philosophy*. Palo Alto, CA: Metaphysics Research Lab, Center for the Study of Language and Information, Stanford University.

Furman, Y. A. (2003). *Introduction to contour analysis and its application to signal and image processing*. Moscow: FIZMATLIT Publishing.

Gallivan, P., Hong, Q., Jordan, L., Li, E., Mathew, G., & Mulyani, Y. ... Tappert, C. (2002). VoiceXML absentee system. In *Proceedings of MASPLAS'02: The Mid-Atlantic Student Workshop on Programming Languages and Systems*. Retrieved from http://csis.pace.edu/csis/masplas/p10.pdf

Gallo, A., & Wilder, R. (1981). Performance measurement of data communication systems with emphasis on open system interconnections. In *Proceedings 8th IEEE Annual Symposium on Computer Architecture,* (pp. 149-161). Minneapolis, MN: IEEE.

Garcıa, V. M. A., Ruiz, M. P. P., & Perez, J. R. P. (2010). Voice interactive classroom, a service-oriented software architecture for speech-enabled learning. *Journal of Network and Computer Applications, 33*, 603–610. doi:10.1016/j.jnca.2010.03.005.

Garoui, V. (2005). *Analysis of network traffic in ad-hoc networks based on DSDV protocol with emphasis on mobility and communication patterns*. Paper presented at the first IEEE and IFIP International Conference in Central Asia. New Delhi, India.

Georges, J., Divoux, T., & Rondeau, E. (2002). Evaluation of switched ethernet in an industrial context using the network calculus. In *Proceedings of the 4th IEEE International Workshop on Factory Communication Systems,* (pp. 19-26). Vasteras, Sweden: IEEE.

Georges, J., Divoux, T., & Rondeau, E. (2003). Comparison of switched ethernet architecture models. In *Proceedings IEEE Conference on Emerging Technologies and Factory Automation,* (pp. 375-382). Lisbon, Portugal: IEEE.

Georges, J., Divoux, T., & Rondeau, E. (2005). Confronting the performances of a switched ethernet network with industrial constraints by using network calculus. *International Journal of Communication Systems, 18*, 877–903. doi:10.1002/dac.740.

Gerber, E., & Kirchner, C. (2001). Who's surfing? Internet access and computer use by visually impaired youths and adults. *Journal of Vision Impairment and Blindness, 95*, 176–181.

Gerd, K. (1989). *Local area networks*. New York: McGraw-Hill.

Ghaleb, F. F. M., Daoud, S. S., Hasna, A. M., Jaam, J. M., & El-Sofany, H. F. (2006). A web-based e-learning system using semantic web framework. *Journal of Computer Science, 2*(8), 619–626. doi:10.3844/jcssp.2006.619.626.

Gil, A., & García-Penalvo, F. J. (2008). Learner course recommendation in e-learning based on swarm intelligence. *Journal of Universal Computer Science, 14*(16), 2737–2755.

Gilbert, E. N. (1960). Capacity of a burst-noise channel. *The Bell System Technical Journal, 39*, 1253–1265.

Gillett, B. E. (1979). *Operations research – A computer-oriented algorithmic approach*. New Delhi: Tata McGraw-Hill Publishing Company Ltd..

Giordano, S., O'Connell, N., Pagano, M., & Procissi, G. (1999). A variational approach to the queuing analysis with fractional brownian motion input traffic. In *Proceedings of the 7th IFIP Workshop on Performance Modelling and Evaluation of ATM Networks*. Antwerp, Belgium: IFIP.

Gisin, N., Ribordy, G., Tittel, W., & Zbinden, H. (2002). Quantum cryptography. *Reviews of Modern Physics, 74*, 145–195. doi:10.1103/RevModPhys.74.145.

Gloss. (2004). Retrieved from http://www.abc.net.au/pipeline/radio/programs/gloss2.htm

Gluzman, S., & Sornette, D. (2002). Log-periodic route to fractal functions. *Physical Review Letters E, 6503*(3), 418–436.

Goldsmith, A. (2005). *Wireless communications*. Cambridge, UK: Cambridge University Press. doi:10.1017/CBO9780511841224.

Golob, M. (2000). *Decomposition of a fuzzy controller based on the inference break-up*. (Doctoral Thesis). University of Maribor, Maribor, Slovenia.

Golubchikov, D. M., & Rumiantsev, K. E. (2008). Quantum cryptography: Principle, protocol, system. *All-Russian competitive selection analytical survey in priority guidelines of information and telecommunication systems*. Retrieved from http://www.ict.edu.ru/ft/005712/68358e2-st14.pdf

Golubchikov, D. M. (2008). Structure and operation principles of Id 3000 Clavis system. *Proceedings of the South Federal University Technical Sciences, 3*(80), 149–157.

GPP TR 25.814. (2006). Physical layer aspects for E-UTRA. *Technical Specification Version 7.1.0*. Retrieved from http://www.3gpp.org

Greenberger, M., Crenson, M., & Crissey, B. (1976). *Models in the policy process: Public decision making in the computer era*. New York: Russel Sage Foundation.

Grossglanster & Bolot. (1996). On the relevance of long range dependence in network traffic. In *Proceedings of ACM SIGCOMM '96*. San Francisco, CA: ACM.

Halsall, F. (1992). Data communications. In *Computer Networks and Open Systems*. Reading, MA: Addison-Wesley.

Hamlin, J. L. (1979).Productivity appraisal for maintenance centre, *Industrial Engineering, 11*(9), September, 1979.

Hammond, A. (2006). *MagiQ and Verizon smash distance and cost barriers with world's longest cascaded network for practical quantum cryptography. New Technology Enables Ultra Secure Communications*. Business Wire.

Hasna, M. O., & Alouini, M. S. (2003). End-to-end performance of transmission systems with relays over Rayleigh-fading channels. *IEEE Transactions on Wireless Communications, 2*(6), 1126–1131. doi:10.1109/TWC.2003.819030.

Hassan, I. M. M., & Mohamed, A. M. (2001). Variable structured control of a magnetic levitation system. In *Proceedings of the American Control Conference*. Arlington, VA: IEEE Press.

Hauge, J. W., & Paige, K. N. (2004). *Learning Simul8: The complete guide*. Billingham, UK: PlainVu Publishers.

Haykin, S. (1994). *Communication systems*. New York: John Wiley & Sons, Inc..

Heiyanthuduwage, S. R., & Karunaratne, D. D. (2006). A learner oriented ontology of metadata to improve effectiveness of learning management systems. In *Proceedings of the Third International Conference on E-Learning for Knowledge-Based Society*. Bangkok, Thailand: IEEE.

Henderson, A. H., Durkin, C. J., & Durkin, G. D. (2008). *Finding the right small-scale distribution for a measured indoor 2.4 GHz channel*. Paper presented at the IEEE Antennas and Propagation Society International Symposium (APSURSI 2008). San Diego, CA.

Hertrich, D. (2002). *MPEG4 video transmission in wireless LANs-Basic QoS support on the data link layer of 802.11b*. (Minor Thesis).

Hohlfeld, O. (2008). Markovian packet loss generators and video QoE. *T Systems. Tcpdump.org*. (n.d.). Retrieved from http://www.tcpdump.org

Holma & Toskala. (2009). *LTE for UMTS: OFDMA and SC-FDMA based radio access*. New York: Wiley & Sons.

Holohan, E., Melia, M., McMullen, D., & Pahl, C. (2005). Adaptive e-learning content generation based on semantic web technology. In *Proceedings of Workshop on Applications of Semantic Web Technologies for E-Learning (SW-EL)*. Amsterdam: SW-EL. Retrieved from http://www.win.tue.nl/SW-EL/2005/swel05-aied05/proceedings/5-Holohan-final-full.pdf

Holzinger, A., Smolle, J., & Reibnegger, G. (2006). Learning objects (LO): An object-oriented approach to manage e-learning content. In *Encyclopedia of Information in Healthcare & Biomedicine*. Hershey, PA: IGI Global.

Huang, P., & Heidemann, J. (2000). Capturing TCP burstiness for lightweight simulation. In *Proccedings of Engineering and Networks Laboratory*. Zurich, Switzerland: IEEE.

Hu, J., & Beaulieu, N. C. (2007). Performance analysis of decode-and forward relaying with selection combining. *IEEE Communications Letters*, *11*(6), 489–491. doi:10.1109/LCOMM.2007.070065.

Hwang, W. L., & Mallat, S. (1994). Characterization of self-similar multifractals with wavelet maxima. *Journal of Applied and Computational Harmonic Analysis*, *1*, 316–328. doi:10.1006/acha.1994.1018.

Id Quantique, S. A. (2005). Id 3000 Clavis: Plug & play quantum cryptography. *Specifications, 2.1.* Retrieved from http://www.idquantique.com/images/stories/PDF/clavis2-quantum-key-distribution/clavis2-specs.pdf

Id Quantique, S. A. (2005). Id 5000 Vectis. *Specifications, 1.2.* Retrieved from http://www.idquantique.com/images/stories/PDF/clavis2-quantum-key-distribution/clavis2-specs.pdf

Id Quantique, S. A. (2008). Quantum cryptography. *The Key to Future-Proof Confidentiality, 3.1.* Retrieved from http://www.idquantique.com/images/stories/PDF/clavis2-quantum-key-distribution/clavis2-specs.pdf

Id Quantique, S. A. (2010). *Practical quantum cryptography*. Paper presented at the Session of Second Winter School. New York, NY.

Id Quantique. (2011). *Swiss bank encrypts critical low-latency backbone links with the Id Quantique centauris encryptors*. Retrieved from http://www.idquantique.com/news/swissquote.html

IEEE. (2006). Layered video coding offset distortion traces for tracebased evaluation of video quality after network transport. In *Proceedings of IEEE Consumer Communications and Networking Conference CCNC*. Las Vegas, NV: IEEE.

Ietf.org. (n.d.a). *Request for comments 2544.* Retrieved August 20, 2009 from http://www.ietf.org/rfc/rfc2544

Ietf.org. (n.d.b). *Integrated services mappings on IEEE 802 networks.* Retrieved August 20, 2009 from http://tools.ietf.org/html/rfc2815

Iglin, S. P. (2006). *Probability theory and the mathematical statistics on the basis of MATLAB: The manual*. Kharkov, Ukraine: NTU.

Ikhu-Omoregbe, N. A. (2010). *Development of a formal framework for usable operations support in e-health-based systems*. (Doctoral dissertation). Covenant University, Ota, Nigeria.

Ikki, S. S., & Ahmed, M. H. (2007). Performance analysis of cooperative diversity wireless networks over Nakagami-m fading channels. *IEEE Communications Letters*, *11*(4), 334–336. doi:10.1109/LCOM.2007.348292.

Ikki, S. S., & Ahmed, M. H. (2010). Performance analysis of adaptive decode-and-forward cooperative diversity networks with best-relay selection. *IEEE Transactions on Communications*, *58*(1), 68–72. doi:10.1109/TCOMM.2010.01.080080.

Ikuno, Wrulich, & Rupp. (2010). System level simulation of LTE networks. In *Proceedings of Vehicular Technology Conference (VTC '10)*. Taipei, Taiwan: IEEE Press.

Information and Communication Technologies. (n.d.). ADAMANTIUM. *D4.4 - PQoS Models and Adaptation Mechanisms*. Retrieved from www.ict-adamantium.eu

International Telecommunication Union Radiocommunication Sector (ITU-R). (1999). *Prediction methods for the terrestrial land mobile service in the VHF and UHF bands*. ITU-R.

Ipatov, V. (2007). *Wideband systems and CDMA: Principles and applications*. Moscow, Russia: Technosphera.

Iskander, M., Yun, Z., & Zhang, Z. (2001). *Outdoor/indoor propagation modeling for wireless communications systems*. Paper presented at the IEEE Antennas and Propagation Society International Symposium (APSURSI 2001). Boston, MA.

Islam, M. D., Kubo, I., Ohadi, M., & Alili, A. A. (2009). Measurement of solar energy radiation in Abu Dhabi, UAE. *Applied Energy*, *86*, 511–515. doi:10.1016/j.apenergy.2008.07.012.

ISO 9241-11. (1998). *Ergonomic requirements for office work with visual display terminals (VDTs) - Part 11: Guidance on usability*. Geneva, Switzerland: ISO.

ISO-IEC. (1994). *International standard 13 818. Generic coding of moving pictures and associated audio information*. ISO-IEC.

ISO-IEC/JTC1/SC29/WG11. (1996). *Evaluation methods and procedures for July mpeg-4 tests*. ISO-IEC.

ITU. (n.d.). *P.800: Methods for subjective determination of transmission quality*. Retrieved from http://www.itu.int/rec/T-REC-P.800-199608-I/en

ITU-R BT. (n.d.). Methodology for the subjective assessment of the quality of television pictures. *ITU-R BT.*.

ITU-T. (1996). *Subjective video quality assessment methods for multimedia applications, interactive test methods for audiovisual communications, principles of a reference impairment system for video. Recommendations* (p. 910). ITU-T.

ITU-T. (1999). *Narrow-band visual telephone systems and terminal equipment. Recommendation H.320*. ITU-T.

Jaffard, S. (1997). Multifractal formalism for functions parts I and II. *SIAM Journal on Mathematical Analysis*, *28*(4), 944–998. doi:10.1137/S0036141095282991.

Jain, A. K. (1974). Noncausal representation for finite discrete signals. In *Proceedings of IEEE Conference on Decision and Control*. IEEE Publishing.

Jain, A. K., & Ranganstth, S. (1980). Image coding by autoregressive synthesis. In *Proceedings of ICASSP'80*. IEEE.

Jain, Chiu, & Hawe. (1984). A quantitative measure of fairness and discrimination for resource allocation in shared systems. *Technical Report: Digital Equipment Corporation, DEC-TR-301*.

Jain, A. K., & Jain, J. R. (1978). Partial differential equations and finite difference methods in image processing, part II: Image restoration. *IEEE Transactions on Automatic Control*, *23*, 817–834. doi:10.1109/TAC.1978.1101881.

Jain, A. K., & Wang, S. H. (1977). *Stochastic image models and hybrid coding*. NOSC.

Jain, L. C., & Martin, N. M. (1998). *Fusion of neural network, fuzzy systems, and genetic algorithms: Industrial applications*. Boca Raton, FL: CRC Press International.

Jakes, W. C. (Ed.). (1974). *Microwave mobile communications*. New York: Wiley Interscience.

Jamalipour, A & Tekinay. (Eds.). (2001). Fourth generation wireless networks and interconnecting standards. *IEEE Personal Communications, 8*.

Jang. (1993). ANFIS: Adaptive network-based fuzzy inference system. *IEEE Transactions on Systems, Man, and Cybernetics, 23*(3), 665-685.

Jang, J., & Lee, K. (2003). (n.d.). Transmit power adaptation for OFDM systems. *IEEE Journal on Selected Areas in Communication.[Qos requirement for multimedia services.* IEEE Press.]. *Ignacio & Javier.*

Jasperneite, J., & Ifak, N. (2001). Switched ethernet for factory communication. In *Proceedings 8th IEEE International Conference on Emerging Technologies and Factory Automation (ETFA 2001),* (pp. 205-212). Antibes, France: IEEE.

Jasperneite, J., Neumann, P., Theis, M., & Watson, K. (2002). Deterministic real-time communication with switched ethernet. In *Proceedings of the 4th IEEE International Workshop on Factory Communication Systems,* (pp. 11-18). Vasteras, Sweden: IEEE.

Jianhua, W., Long, Z., Jun, Z., & Xiping, D. (2009). A voiceXML-based mobile learning system and its caching strategy. In *Proceedings of MLearn 2009, 8th World Conference on Mobile and Contextual Learning.* Orlando, FL: IEEE.

Jine, A. K. (1981). Achievements in the field of mathematical models for image processing. *TIEEE, 69*(5), 9–39.

John Wiley and Sons, Inc. (2009). *Algorithms and protocols for wireless and mobile ad hoc networks.* New York: John Wiley & Sons, Inc..

John, S.N., Anoprienko, A.Y., & Niru, A. (n.d.). Multilevel simulation of networks on the base of TCP/IP protocols stack using Matlab/Simulink environment. *Cybernetic and Computing Texnika, 39,* 271–297.

John, S.N., Anoprienko, A.Y., Rishka, S.V. (n.d.). Simulating of university network infrastructure. *Kremeshuk State Technical University, 2*(11), 271–297.

John. (2005). Increasing the efficiency of data exchange in a computer network based on the protocol of TCP/IP suite. *Information, Cybernetics, and Computing Engineering, 93,* 256-264.

John, S. N., Anoprienko, A. A., & Okonigene, R. E. (2010). Developed algorithm for increasing the efficiency of data exchange in a computer network. *International Journal of Computers and Applications, 6*(9), 16–19. doi:10.5120/1103-1446.

Joo, S., & Seo, J. H. (1997). Design and analysis of the nonlinear feedback linearizing control for an electromagnetic suspension system. *IEEE Transactions on Control Systems Technology, 5*(1), 135–144. doi:10.1109/87.553672.

Jurdak, R. (2007). *Wireless ad hoc and sensor networks: A cross-layer design perspective.* New York: Springer.

Justus, C. G. (1978). *Winds and wind system performance.* Philadelphia, PA: Franklin Institute Press.

Kalantari, A., Mohammadi, M., & Ardebilipour, M. (2011). Performance analysis of opportunistic relaying over imperfect non-identical lognormal fading channels. In *Proceedings of 22nd IEEE Personal Indoor Mobile Radio Communications (PIMRC11 - WACC).* Toronto, Canada: IEEE Press.

Kamau, J. N., Kinyua, R., & Gathua, J. K. (2010). 6 years of wind data for Marsabit, Kenya average over 14 m/s at 100 m hub height: An analysis of the wind energy potential. *Renewable Energy, 36*(6), 1298–1302. doi:10.1016/j.renene.2009.10.008.

Kanem, E., Torab, P., Cooper, K., & Custodi, G. (1999). Design and analysis of packet switched networks for control systems. In *Proceedings1999 IEEE Conference on Decision and Control,* (pp. 4460-4465). Phoenix, AZ: IEEE.

Kapranov, M. V., & Khandurin, A. V. (2009). Information transmission with fractal masking (framask) in communication system[in Russian]. *Vestnik MPEI, 1,* 89–92.

Kapranov, M. V., & Khandurin, A. V. (2011). Signals with additive fractal structure for information transmission. *Journal of Electromagnetic Waves and Electronic Systems, 16*(2), 23–36.

Kapranov, M. V., & Morozov, A. G. (1998). Application of chaotic modulation for information transfer. *Radiotechnicheskie Tetrady, 14,* 66–71.

Kapranov, M. V., & Tomashevsky, A. I. (2003). System of secure communication with usage of correlative reception and the synchronous chaotic response. *Journal of Electromagnetic Waves and Electronic Systems, 8*(3), 35–48.

Kashyap, R. L. (n.d.). Analysis and synthesis of image patterns by spatial interaction models. In *Progress in Pattern Recognition.* New York: Elsevier North-Holland.

Katende, J. (2004). *Linear systems theory*. (Unpublished Master's Thesis). Bayero University, Kano, Nigeria.

Kemal, N. A. (2003). *Control of magnetic suspension system using state feedback, optimal, and neural network controllers*. (Unpublished Master's of Engineering Thesis). Bradley University, Maribor, Slovenia.

Khan. (2009). *LTE for 4G mobile broadband: Air interface technologies and performance*. Cambridge CB2 8RU. Cambridge, UK: Cambridge University Press.

Kilin, S. Y., Nizovtsev, A. P., & Horoshko, D. B. (2007). *Quantum cryptography: Ideas and practice*. Minsk, Belarus: Belaruskaya Nauka.

Kirk Nordstrom, D. (2012). Models, validation, and applied geochemistry: Issues in science, communication, and philosophy. *Applied Geochemistry*. doi:10.1016/j.apgeochem.2012.07.007.

Klaue, J., Rathke, B., & Wolish, A. (2003). EvalVid-A framework for video transmission and quality evaluation. In *Proceedings of the 13th International Conference on Modelling Techniques and Tools for Computer Performance Evaluation*. Urbana, IL: IEEE.

Klienrok, L. (1979). *Computing systems with queuing*.

Knoche & McCarthy. (n.d.). Mobile users' needs and expectations of future multimedia services. *Wireless World Research Forum*.

Knopp, R., & Humblet, P. (1995). Information capacity and power control in single-cell multiuser communications. In *Proceedings of IEEE International Conference on Communication*. Seattle, WA: IEEE Press.

Knox, S., Coyle, L., & Dobson, S. (2010). Using ontologies in case-based activity recognition. In *Proceedings of 23rd Florida Artificial Intelligence Research Society Conference*. St. Pete, FL: AIRSC.

Koeppl, G. W. (1982). *Putnam's power from the wind*. New York: Van Nostrand Reinhold.

Kolias, C., Kolias, V., & Anagnostopoulos, L. (2004). *A pervasive wiki application based on voiceXML*. Retrieved from http://www.icsd.aegean.gr/publication_files/conference/275294916.pdf

Kolkeri, V. (2008). *Error concealment techniques in H.264/AVC for video transmission over wireless network*. Arlington, TX: The University of Texas at Arlington.

Kondratova, I. (2009). Multimodal interaction for mobile learning. In Proceedings *of the 5th International Conference (UAHCI '09)*. San Diego, CA: UAHCI.

Konikow, L. F., & Bredehoeft, J. D. (1992). Ground-water models cannot be validated. *Advances in Water Resources*, *15*(1), 75–83. doi:10.1016/0309-1708(92)90033-X.

Korolenko, P. V., Maganova, M. S., & Mesniankin, A. V. (2004). *Innovation methods of the analysis of stochastic processes and structures in optics: Fractal and multiracial methods, wavelet-conversions: The manual*. Moscow, Russia: MSU, Nuclear Physics, Scientific Research Institute.

Kotenko, V. V., & Rumiantsev, K. E. (2009). *Information theory and telecommunication security*. Rostov-on-Don, Russia: SFedU publishers.

Koutsakis, P., & Paterakis, M. (2004). Call-admission-control and traffic-policing mechanisms for the transmission of videoconference traffic from MPEG-4 and H.263 video coders in wireless ATM networks. *IEEE Transactions on Vehicular Technology*, *53*(5), 1525–1530. doi:10.1109/TVT.2004.833639.

Krasheninnikov, B. P. (2003). *Fundamentals of the image processing theory*. Ulyaniovsk, Russia: UlGTU Publ.

Kravchenko, V. F., Perez-Meana, H. M., & Ponomaryov, V. I. (2009). *Adaptive digital processing of multidimentional signals with applications*. Moscow, Russia: Fizmatlit.

Krishna, P., Jens, S., & Ralf, S. (2004). Network calculus meets queuing theory: A simulation-based approach to bounded queues. In *Proceedings of the 12th IEEE International Workshop on Quality of Service (IWQoS 2004)*, (pp. 114-118). Montreal, Canada: IEEE.

Krunz, M., Sass, R., & Hughes, H. (1995). Statistical characteristics and multiplexing of MPEG streams. In *Proceedings of IEEE INFOCOM*. Boston: IEEE.

Krunz, M., & Tripathi, S. (1997). Exploiting the temporal structure of MPEG video for the reduction of bandwidth requirements. *Proceedings - IEEE INFOCOM*, *1*(1), 67–74. doi:10.1109/INFCOM.1997.635115.

KSL. (2005). *KSL software and network services*. Retrieved from http://www.ksl.stanford.edu/sns.shtml

Kulman, N. K. (1961). Nonlinear filter for telegraph signal filtering. *Radio Engineering and Electronics*, *1*(9), 67–79.

Kumar, A. B. R., Reddy, L. C., & Hiremth, P. S. (2008). Performance comparison of wireless mobile ad-hoc network routing protocols. *International Journal of Computer Science and Network Security*, *8*(6), 337–343.

Kusagur, K., & Ram, S. (2010). Modeling, design, & simulation of an adaptive neuro-fuzzy inference system (ANFIS) for speed control of induction motor. *International Journal of Computers and Applications*, *6*(12), 29–44. doi:10.5120/1123-1472.

Kuznetsov, S. P. (2000). *Dynamic chaos (lecture course)*. Moscow, Russia: Nauka.

Lakshman, T., Ortega, A., & Reibman, A. (1998). VBR video: Tradeoffs and potentials. *Proceedings of the IEEE*, *86*(5), 952–973. doi:10.1109/5.664282.

Langton, C. (2004). *Orthogonal frequency divisional multiplexing tutorial*. Retrieved from www.complextoreal.com

Larson, J. (2000). *Introduction and overview of W3C speech interface framework*. W3C Working Draft. Retrieved from http://www.w3.org/TR/2000/WD-voice-intro-20001204/

Le Boudec, J., & Thiran, P. (2004). *Network calculus: Theory of deterministic queuing systems for the internet*. Berlin: Springer.

Lebedev, A. I., & Sherniavskovo, E. A. (1986). Probability method in computing texnika: Educational manual for institutes of higher learning on special. *Computer*.

Lee, J. B., & Kalva, H. (2008). *The VC-1 and H.264 video compression standards for broadband video services*. Berlin: Springer. doi:10.1007/978-0-387-71043-3.

Lee, J. S., & Miller, L. E. (1998). *CDMA systems engineering handbook*. Norwood, MA: Artech House.

Lemmon, J. (2002). Wireless link statistical bit error model. NTIA Report. 02-394. Washington, DC: US Department of Commerce.

Lerlerdthaiyanupap, T. (2008). *Speech-based dictionary application*. (MSc Thesis). University of Tampere, Tampere, Finland.

Lezin, Y. S. (1969). *Optimal filters with pulse signal accumulation*. Moscow, Russia: Sovetskoe Radio Publishing.

Lilly, M. T., Obiajulu, U. E., Ogaji, S. O. T., & Probert, S. D. (2007). Total-productivity analysis of a Nigerian petroleum-product marketing company. *Applied Energy*, *84*, 1150–1173. doi:10.1016/j.apenergy.2007.04.003.

Lima, A., & Menezes, L. (2005). *Motley-Keenan model adjusted to the thickness of the wall*. Paper presented at the SBMO/IEEE MTT-S International Microwave and Optoelectronics Conference. Brasilia.

Lin, W. J., Yueh, H. P., Liu, Y. L., Murakami, M., Kakusho, K., & Minoh, M. (2006). Blog as a tool to develop e-learning experience in an international distance course. In *Proceedings of the Sixth International Conference on Advanced Learning Technologies (ICALT'06)*. ICALT.

Liu, X., Chong, E., & Shroff, N. (2001). Opportunistic transmission scheduling with resource-sharing constraints in wireless networks. *IEEE Journal on Selected Areas in Communications*, *19*, 2053–2064. doi:10.1109/49.957318.

Lobinger, S. Jansen, & Balan. (2010). Load balancing in downlink LTE self-optimizing networks. In *Proceedings of IEEE 71st Vehicular Technology Conference 2010*. Taipei, Taiwan: IEEE Press.

Lott, M., & Forkel, I. (2001). *A multi wall and floor model for indoor radio propagation*. Paper presented at the IEEE Vehicular Technology Conference (VTC 2001-Spring). Rhodes Island, Greece.

Lottor. (1992). Internet growth (1981-1991). *RFC 1296*.

Lui, Z., Nain, P., Towsley, D., & Zhang, Z. L. (1999). Asymptotic behavior of a multiplexer fed by a long-range dependent process. *Journal of Applied Probability*, *36*, 105–118. doi:10.1239/jap/1032374233.

M. of WINNER. (2005). Assessment of advanced beamforming and MIMO technologies. *WINNER, IST-2003-507581*.

MacLeod, H., Loadman, C., & Chen, Z. (2005). *Experimental studies of the 2.4-GHz ISM wireless indoor channel.* Paper presented at the Annual Communication Networks and Services Research Conference (CNSR 2005). Halifax, Canada.

MagiQ Technologies, Inc. (2004). QPN 5505. *Reference Manual.*

Mallat, S. (2005). *A wavelet tour of signal processing: The sparse way* (3rd ed.). New York: Academic Press.

Mandelbrot, B. (1982). *The fractal geometry of nature.* San Francisco, CA: Freeman.

Mann, R., & Terplan, K. (1999). *Network design: Management and technical perspectives. New-York.* CRC Press.

Mao, W. (2003). *Modern cryptography: Theory and practice.* Upper Saddle River, NJ: Prentice Hall.

Marpe, D., Wiegand, T., & Sullivan, G. J. (2006). The H.264/MPEG4 advanced video coding standard and its applications. *IEEE Communications Magazine, 44*(8), 134–143. doi:10.1109/MCOM.2006.1678121.

Martin, S., Minet, P., & George, L. (2005). End-to-end response time with fixed priority scheduling: Trajectory approach versus holistic approach. *International Journal of Communication Systems, 18*, 37–56. doi:10.1002/dac.688.

Mathur, R., Klepal, M., McGibney, A., & Pesch, D. (2004). *Influence of people shadowing on bit error rate of IEEE 802.11 2.4 GHz channel.* Paper presented at the International Symposium on Wireless Communication Systems (ISWCS 2004). Port-Louis, Mauritius.

Mathwork Inc. (2011). *Fuzzy logic toolbox user guide version 2.2.14.* Retrieved from www.mathworks.com

Mathworks. (1998). Retrieved from http://www.mathworks.com

Matloff. (2000). *Some utilization analyses for ALOHA and CSMA protocols.* Davis, CA: University of California at Davis.

Mayers, D. (2001). Unconditional security in quantum cryptography. *Journal of the ACM, 48*, 351–406. doi:10.1145/382780.382781.

McGill, W. J. (1954). Multivariate information transmission, transactions PGIT. In *Proceedings of Symposium on Information Theory.* PGIT.

Meyer, Y. (1997). *Wavelets, vibrations, and scalings.* Montreal, Canada: Universite de Montreal.

Micheal, D., & Richard, R. (2003). *Computer communications and data networks for computer scientists and engineers.* Essex, UK: Pearson Prentice Hall.

Minaev, A., Bashkov, E., Anoprienko, A., Kargin, A., Teslia, V., & Babasyuk, A. (2002). Development of internet infrastructure for higher education in Donetsk region of the Ukraine. In *Proceedings of ICEE 2002 Manchester International Conference on Engineering Education.* Manchester, UK: ICEE.

Ming-Yang, X., Rong, L., & Huimin, C. (2004). Predicting internet end-to-end delay: An overview. In *Proceedings of the IEEE 36th South Eastern Symposium on Information Systems Theory,* (pp. 210 – 214). IEEE.

MIT Lincoln Laboratory. (2012). *1999 DARPA intrusion detection evaluation dataset.* Retrieved from http://www.ll.mit.edu/mission/communications/ist/corpora/ideval/data/index.html

Modestino, J. W., & Zhang, J. (1993). A Markov random field model-based approach to image interpretation. In *Markov Random Fields: Theory and Applications.* Boston: Academic Press, Inc..

Motiwalla, L. F. (2009). A voice-enabled interactive services (VòIS) architecture for e-learning. *International Journal on Advances in Life Sciences, 1*(4), 122–133. Retreived from http://www.iariajournals.org/life_sciences/lifsci_v1_n4_2009_paged.pdf

Motiwalla, L. F., & Qin, J. (2007). Enhancing mobile learning using speech recognition technologies: A case study. In *Proceedings of the Eighth World Congress on the Management of eBusiness (WCMeB'07).* WCMeB.

Murai, M. & Tanaka, M. (2000). Magnetic levitation (maglev) technologies. *Japan Railway & Transport Review,* (25), 61–67.

Murali, K., Leung, H., & Yu, H. (2003). Design of noncoherent receiver for analog spread-spectrum communication based on chaotic masking. *IEEE Journal*, *50*(3), 432–441.

Muzy, J. F., Bacry, E., & Arneodo, A. (1994). The muitifractal formalism revisited with wavelets. *International Journal of Bifurcation and Chaos in Applied Sciences and Engineering*, *4*, 245. doi:10.1142/S0218127494000204.

Muzy, J. F., Bacry, E., & Arneodo, A. (1999). Wavelets and multifractal formalism for singularity signals: Application to turbulence data. *Physical Review Letters*, *67*(25), 3515–3518. doi:10.1103/PhysRevLett.67.3515.

Nagle. (1984). Congestion control in IP/TCP internetworks. *RFC 896.*

Nahi, N. E., & Franco, C. A. (1972). Application of Kalman filtering to image enhancement. In *Proceedings of IEEE Conference on Decision and Control.* IEEE Publishing.

Nanda, S. K., & Balachandran, S., & Kumar. (2000, January). Adaptation techniques in wireless packet data services. *IEEE Communications Magazine*. doi:10.1109/35.815453.

Nanere, M., Fraser, I., Quazi, A., & D'Souza, C. (2007). Environmentally adjusted productivity measurement: An Australian case study. *Journal of Environmental Management*, *85*, 350–362. doi:10.1016/j.jenvman.2006.10.004 PMID:17129666.

National Research Council. (2007). *Models in environmental regulation decision making*. Washington, DC: The National Academies Press.

News. (n.d.). Retrieved from http://www.gap-optique.unige.ch

Ngala, G. M., Alkali, B., & Aji, M. A. (2007). Viability of wind energy as a power generation source in Maiduguri, Borno state, Nigeria. *Renewable Energy*, *32*(13), 2242–2246. doi:10.1016/j.renene.2006.12.016.

Nicopolitidis. (2003). *Wireless networks*. London: Wiley.

Niels, O. B. (2000). *Draft position paper for discussion at the ELSNET brainstorming workshop*. Retrieved from http://www.elsnet.org/dox/rM-bernsen-v2.pdf

Nisbet, P. D., & Wilson, A. (2002). *Introducing speech recognition in schools: Using dragon natural speaking*. Edinburgh, UK: University of Edinburgh.

Norros, I. (1994). A storage model with self-similar input. *Queueing Systems*, *16*, 387–396. doi:10.1007/BF01158964.

NS-2 Documentation. (n.d.). Retrieved from http://www.isi.edu/nsnam/ns/ns-documentation.html

NUC. (2004). The state of Nigerian universities. *Nigerian University System Newsletter*, *2*(1).

Oboko, R., Wagacha, P. W., & Omwenga, E. (2008). Adaptive delivery of an object oriented course in a web-based learning environment. In *Proceedings of 3rd International Conference on ICT for Development, Education, and Training*. Accra, Ghana: IEEE.

Ogata, K. (2002). *Modern control engineering*. New Delhi: Prentice-Hall.

Olifer, V. G., & Olifer, N. A. (1999). Principles of technologies, protocols–SPB. *Computer Networks*.

Ondas, I. S. (2006). VoiceXML-based spoken language interactive system. In *Proceedings 6th PhD Student Conference and Scientific and Technical Competition of Students of Faculty of Electrical Engineering and Informatics Technical University of Košice*. Košice, Slovakia: IRKR. Retrieved from http://irkr.tuke.sk/publikacie/_vti_cnf/Prispevok_eng.pdf

Onwugbolu, C. A., & Oloruniwo, F. (1988). *Measuring maintenance productivity. (Presented paper.)*. Cincinnati, OH: The Computer Aided Manufacturing Conference.

Oppenheim, A., & Schafer, R. (1989). *Discrete-time signal processing*. Upper Saddle River, NJ: Prentice-Hall.

Ozerdem, B., & Turkeli, M. (2003). An investigation of wind characteristics on the campus of Izmir Institute of Technology, Turkey. *Renewable Energy*, *28*, 1013–1027. doi:10.1016/S0960-1481(02)00155-6.

Pakucs, B. (2003). SesaME: A framework for personalised and adaptive speech interfaces. In *Proceedings of EACL-03 Workshop on Dialogue Systems: Interaction, Adaptation and Styles of Management*. Budapest, Hungary: EACL.

Parida, A., & Kumar, U. (2009). *Maintenance Productivity and performance measurement. Handbook of Maintenance and Engineering*. London: Springer-Verlag Ltd..

Park, K., & Willinger, W. (Eds.). (1999). *Self-similar network traffic and performance evaluation*. New York: Wiley-Interscience.

Parsons, J. D. (2000). *The mobile radio propagation channel*. Hoboken, NJ: Wiley Interscience. doi:10.1002/0470841524.

Paul, D. (2003). *Speech recognition for students with disabilities*. Edinburgh, UK: University of Edinburgh.

Pauli, D. (2009). Aussie govt considers quantum leap in secure comms. *Computer World*. Retrieved from http://www.computerworld.com.au/article/278658/aussie_govt_considers_quantum_leap_secure_comms/

Pecora, L. M., & Carroll, T. L. (1990). Synchronization in chaotic systems. *Physical Review Letters*, *64*, 821–824. doi:10.1103/PhysRevLett.64.821 PMID:10042089.

Peter, Y., Vantroys, T., & Lepretre, E. (2008). Enabling mobile collaborative learning through multichannel interactions. In *Proceedings of 4th International Conference on Interactive Mobile and Computer Aided Learning (IMC'08)*. IMC.

Petersen & Davie. (2000). *Computer networks: A systems approach*. San Francisco, CA: Morgan Kaufmann.

Petrov, E. P., & Trubin, I. S. (2007). Mathematical models of video-sequences of digital half-tone images. *Achievements of Modern Radio Electronic,* (6), 3-31.

Petrov, E. P., Smolskliy, S. M., & Kharina, N. L. (2007). Synthesis of models of multi-dimensional multi-valued Markov processes. *Vestnik of MPEI,* (1), 147-152.

Petrov, E. P., Trubin, I. C., & Butorin, E. L. (2002). The spatial-time model of digital Markov images. In *Proceedings of VIII Conference: Radar Technology, Navigation, and Communications,* (vol. 1, pp. 371-380). Voronezh, Russia: RTNC.

Petrov, E. P., Trubin, I. C., & Butorin, E. L. (2003). The spatial-time model of digital Markov images. In *Proceedings of IX Conference of Radar Technology, Navigation, and Communications*, (vol. 1, pp. 330-337). Voronezh, Russia: RTNC.

Petrov, E. P., Trubin, I. S., & Chastikov, I. A. (2007). Nonlinear filtering of video-sequences of digital half-tone images of Markovian type. *Achievements of Modern Radio Electronic,* (3), 54-88.

Petrov, E.P., Trubin, I.S., & Tikhonov, E.P. (2003). Nonlinear digital filtering of half-tone images. *Radio Engineering,* (5), 7-10.

Petrov, E. P. (2006). The spatial-time mathematical model of the sequence of digital half-tone image of Markov type. *Problems of Information Processing*, *1*(6), 46–52.

Petrov, E. P., & Chastikov, A. V. (2001). Method of adaptive filtering of binary pulse correlated signals. *Radio Engineering and Electronics*, *46*(10), 1155–1158.

Petrov, E. P., & Kharina, N. L. (2006). *Simulation of digital half-tone images of Markovian type with discrete arguments*. Vyatka, Russia: Vyatka State University Publishing.

Petrov, E. P., & Prozorov, D. E. (n.d.). Filtering of Markov processes with several states. *Radar, Navigation, and Communications*..

Petrov, E. P., Trubin, I. S., & Butorin, E. L. (2005). Nonlinear filtering of the sequence of digital half-tone images. *Radio Engineering and Electronics*, *50*(10), 1265–1270.

Petrov, E. P., Trubin, I. S., & Harina, N. L. (2006). *Modeling of multi-dimensional multi-valued Markov processes*. Radio Engineering.

Petrov, E. P., Trubin, I. S., & Harina, N. L. (2006). Problems of information processing. *Vestnik*, *1*(6), 41–46.

Phuah, J., Lu, J., & Yahagi, T. (2005). *Chattering free sliding mode control in magnetic levitation systems*. Chiba, Japan: Chiba University. doi:10.1541/ieejeiss.125.600.

Pisarevsky, A. N., & Chernyavsky, A. F. (1988). *Systems of technical vision (principal fundamentals, hardware and software support)*. Leningrad, Russia: Mashinostroenie Publishing.

Politis, D. N. (1994). Markov chains in many dimensions. *Advances in Applied Probability*. doi:10.2307/1427819.

Portet, F., Reiter, E., Gatt, A., Hunter, J. R. W., Sripada, S., Freer, Y., & Sykes, C. (2009). Automatic generation of textual summaries from neonatal intensive care data. *Artificial Intelligence*, *173*, 789–816. doi:10.1016/j.artint.2008.12.002.

Postel, J. (1980). User datagram protocol. *RFC 768.*

Postel, J. (1981a). Internet protocol. *RFC 791.*

Postel, J. (1981b). Transmission control protocol. *RFC 793.*

Priel, V. Z. (1974). *Systematic maintenance organisation.* London: MacDonald & Evans Ltd..

Project P905-PF EURESCOM. (2000). *Aquavit-Assessment of quality for audio-visual signals over internet and UMTS.* EURESCOM.

Prudnikov, A. P., Brychkov, Y. A., & Marichev, O. I. (1992). Integrals and series: *Vol. 4. Direct laplace transforms.* Boca Raton, FL: CRC Press.

Qasim, Said, & Aghvami. (2009). Mobile ad hoc networking protocols evaluation through simulation for quality of service. *IAENG International Journal of Computer Science, 36*(1), 10.

Qi, Q., Pei, Y., Modestino, J. W., & Tian, X. (2004). Source-adaptive FEC/UEP coding for video transport over bursty packet loss 3G UMTS networks: A cross-layer approach. In *Proceedings of 60th IEEE Vehicular Technology Conference (VTC'04),* (vol. 5, pp. 150-3154). IEEE.

Raghuraman, M. B. (2004). *Design and implementation of V-HELP system–A voice-enabled web application for the visually impaired.* (Unpublished Master Thesis). University of Nebraska, Lincoln, NE.

Rahman, S. D. & Fitzek. (2004). OFDM based WLAN systems. *Technical Report R-04-1002.* Denmark: Aalborg University.

Rajagopalan & Shen. (2006). What does using TCP as an evaluation tool reveal about MANET routing protocols. In *Proceeding of the 2006 International Conference on Wireless Communications and Mobile Computing.* Newark, DE: University of Delaware.

Raju, Jitendranath, & Mungara. (2010). Performance evaluation of ZRP over AODV and DSR in mobile ad hoc networks using qualnet. *European Journal of Scientific Research, 45,* 658–674.

Ramirez, P., & Carta, J. A. (2006). The use of wind probability distributions derived from the maximum entropy principle in the analysis of wind energy: A case study. *Energy Conversion and Management, 47,* 2564–2577. doi:10.1016/j.enconman.2005.10.027.

Rappaport, T. (1999). *Wireless communications: Principles & practice.* Upper Saddle River, NJ: Prentice Hall.

Rappaport, T. (2002). *Wireless communication: Principles and practice.* Upper Saddle River, NJ: Prentice Hall.

Ravi, K., Hussain, & Tirupathi. (n.d.). A new paradigm for the next generation wireless optimization cross layer design. *International Journal Computer Technology Applications, 2*(3), 475-484.

Reiser, M. (1982). Performance evaluation of data communications systems. *Proceedings of the IEEE, 70*(2), 171–194. doi:10.1109/PROC.1982.12261.

Ribordy, G., Gautier, J.-D., Gisin, N., Guinnard, O., & Zbinden, H. (2000). Fast and user-friendly quantum key distribution. *Journal of Modern Optics, 47,* 517–531.

Richard, C. D. (2004). *Magnetic levitation: A straightforward and fast information guide to magnetic levitation.* Retrieved from www.clearlyexplained.com

Richardson. (2003). IH264 and MPEG-4 video compression: Video coding for next-generation. In *Multimedia.* Hoboken, NJ: John Wiley & Sons.

Riedi, R. H., Crouse, M. S., Ribeiro, V. J., & Baraniuk, R. G. (1999). A multifractal wavelet model with application to network traffic. *IEEE Transactions on Information Theory, 45*(3). doi:10.1109/18.761337.

Rodriguez, E. (2008). *Robust error detection methods for H.264/AVC videos.* (Master's thesis). Universitat Politecnica de Catalunya, Vienna, Austria.

Rohling, M. Bruninghaus, & Grunheid. (1999). Broadband OFDM radio transmission for multimedia applications. *Proceedings of the IEEE, 87*(10), 1778–1789.

Romer, M. (2004). *MPEG-4 video quality analysis.* Ft. Lauderdale, FL: Florida Atlantic University.

Rumyantsev, K. E. (2010). Quantum communication: Theory, experiments, applications. *Info-Telecommunication and Computer Technology, Equipment, and Systems in South Federal University.* Rostov-on-Don, Russia: SFedU Publishers.

Sagias, N. C., Lazarakis, F. I., Tombras, G. S., & Datsikas, C. K. (2008). Outage analysis of decode and forward relaying over Nakagami-m fading channels. *IEEE Signal Processing Letters, 15*, 41–44. doi:10.1109/LSP.2007.910317.

Salatian, A. (2003). Interpreting historical ICU data using associational and temporal reasoning. In *Proceedings of 15th IEEE International Conference on Tools with Artificial Intelligence*. Sacramento, CA: IEEE.

Salatian, A., & Taylor, B. (2004). An agglomerative approach to creating models of building monitoring data. In *Proceedings of 8th IASTED International Conference on Artificial Intelligence and Soft Computing*. Marbella, Spain: IASTED.

Salatian, A., & Taylor, B. (2011). ABSTRACTOR: An expert system for fault detection in buildings. In *Proceedings of 1st International Conference on Intelligent Systems & Data Processing*. Vallabh Vidya Nagar, India: IEEE.

Salatian, A. (2010). A software architecture for decision support of building sensor data. *International Journal of Smart Home, 4*(4), 27–34.

Salatian, A., & Hunter, J. R. W. (1999). Deriving trends in historical and real-time continuously sampled medical data. *Journal of Intelligent Information Systems, 13*, 47–74. doi:10.1023/A:1008706905683.

Salatian, A., & Oriogun, P. (2011b). A software architecture for summarising and interpreting ICU monitor data. *International Journal of Software Engineering, 4*(1), 3–14.

Salatian, A., & Taylor, B. (2008). ABSTRACTOR: An agglomerative approach to interpreting building monitoring data. *Journal of Information Technology in Construction, 13*, 193–211.

Salo, J., Vuokko, L., El-Sallabi, H. M., & Vainikainen, P. (2007). An additive model as a physical basis for shadow fading. *IEEE Transactions on Vehicular Technology, 56*(1), 13–26. doi:10.1109/TVT.2006.883797.

Saltzberg, B. (2000). Performance of an efficient parallel data transmission system. *IEEE Signal Processing Magazine*, 17.

Sani, D. S. (2004). *Design and development of a magnetic levitation system*. (Unpublished Master's of Engineering Thesis). Bayero University, Kano, Nigeria.

Sanneck, H., Mohr, W., Le, L., & Hoene, C. (2002). *Quality of service support for voice over IP over wireless*. Wireless IP and Building the Mobile Internet.

Sarnoff Corporation. (2002). *Jndmetrix-iq software and JND: A human vision system model for objective picture quality measurements*. Sarnoff Corporation.

Sauro, J., & Kindlund, E. (2005). A method to standardize usability metrics into a single score. In *Proceedings of CHI'05*. Portland, OR: ACM.

Scarani, V. (2006). *Quantum physics: A first encounter: Interference, entanglement, and reality*. Oxford, UK: Oxford University Press.

Schulzrinne, H., Casner, S., Frederick, R., & Jacobson, V. (1996). RTP: A transport protocol for real-time applications. *RFC 1889.*

Schulzrinne, H., Rao, A., & Lanphier, R. (1998). Real time streaming protocol (RTSP). *RFC 2326.*

Sesay, Yang, Qi, & He. (2004). Simulation comparison of four wireless ad hoc routing protocols. *Information Technology Journal,* 219-226.

Sesia, Toufik, & Baker. (2009). *LTE-The UMTS long term evolution: From theory to practice.* New York: Wiley & Sons, Ltd.

Seybold, J. (2005). *Introduction to RF propagation*. Hoboken, NJ: Wiley Interscience. doi:10.1002/0471743690.

Shakkottai, Rappaport, & Karlsson. (2003). Cross-layer design for wireless networks. *IEEE Communications Magazine*. doi:10.1109/MCOM.2003.1235598.

Shalizi, C. R. (2003). Optimal nonlinear prediction of random fields on networks. In *Proceedings of Center for the Study of Complex Systems*. University of Michigan.

Shannon, R. E. (1998). Introduction to the art and science of simulation. In *Proceedings of the Simulation Conference* (Vol. 1, pp. 7-14). IEEE.

Shannon, C. E. (1948). A mathematical theory of communication. *The Bell System Technical Journal, 27*, 379–423, 623–656.

Shata, A. S. A., & Hanitsch, R. (2006). Evaluation of wind energy potential and electricity generation on the coast of Mediterranean Sea in Egypt. *Renewable Energy, 31*, 1183–1202. doi:10.1016/j.renene.2005.06.015.

Shaw, M., & Garlan, D. (1996). *Software architecture: Perspectives on an emerging discipline*. Englewood Cliffs, NJ: Prentice Hall.

Sheluhin, O. I., & Atayero, A. A. (2012). Detection of DoS and DDoS attacks in information communication networks with discrete wavelet analysis. *International Journal of Computer Science and Information Scurity, 10*(1), 53–57.

Sheluhin, O. I., Atayero, A. A., & Garmashev, A. V. (2011). Detection of teletraffic anomalies using multifractal analysis. *International Journal of Advancements in Computing Technology, 3*(4), 174–182. doi:10.4156/ijact.vol3.issue4.19.

Sheluhin, O. I., Smolskiy, S. M., & Osin, A. V. (2007). *Self-similar processes in telecommunications*. New York: John Wiley & Sons. doi:10.1002/9780470062098.

Shen, J. (2002). H^{∞} control and sliding mode control of magnetic levitation system. *Asian Journal of Control, 4*(3), 333–340. doi:10.1111/j.1934-6093.2002.tb00361.x.

Shor, P. W., & Preskill, J. (2000). Simple proof of security of the BB84 quantum key distribution protocol. *Physical Review Letters, 85*, 441–444. doi:10.1103/PhysRevLett.85.441 PMID:10991303.

Simon, M. K., & Alouini, M. S. (2005). *Digital communication over fading channels*. New York: John Wiley & Sons.

Simulink™. (2000). *Design and simulate continuous and discrete time systems*. Retrieved from http://www.mathworks.com/products/Simulink™

Singh, S. (2000). *The code book: The secret history of codes and code breaking*. London, UK: Forth Estate.

Smart, N. (2004). *Cryptography: An introduction*. New York: McGraw-Hill College.

Soifer, V. A. (2003). *Methods of computer image processing*. Moscow: FIZMATLIT Publishing.

Song, Y. (2001). Time constrained communication over switched ethernet. In *Proceedings IFAC International Conference on Fieldbus Systems and their Application,* (pp. 152-169). Nancy, France: IFAC.

Song, G. (2005). *Cross-layer resource allocation and scheduling in wireless multicarrier networks*. Atlanta, GA: Georgia Institute of Technology.

Soon-Duck, K. (2010). Uncertainty analysis of wind energy potential assessment. *Journal of Applied Energy, 87*, 856–865. doi:10.1016/j.apenergy.2009.08.038.

Spasic, I., Ananiadou, S., & Tsujii, J. (2005). *MaSTerClass: A case-based reasoning system for the classification of biomedical terms*. Retrieved http://qr.net/jzsU, accessed 2005.07.05

Spector, A. A. (1985). Multi-dimensional discrete Markov fields and its filtering at the presence of the non-correlated noise. *Radio Engineering and Electronics*, (5): 512–523.

Spector, A. A. (1987). Two-stage filtering of random fields at interference presence. In *Methods of Processing of Digital Signals and Fields under Condition of Interference*. Novosibirsk, Russia: IEEE Publishing.

Speigel, M. R., Lipschutz, S., & Liu, J. (2009). *Mathematical handbook of formulas and tables*. New York: McGraw Hill.

Square D® ethernet switch model SDM 5DE 100 installation and illustration bulletin . (n.d.). Retrieved February 03, 2009 from www.us.squareD

Sripada, S., Reiter, E., & Davy, I. (2003). SumTime-mousam: Configurable marine weather forecast generator. *Expert Update, 6*(3), 4–10.

Srivastava, V., & Motani, M. (2005, December). Cross-layer design: A survey and the road ahead. *IEEE Communications Magazine*. doi:10.1109/MCOM.2005.1561928.

Sterman, J. D. (2000). *Business dynamics – Systems thinking and modeling for a complex world*. New York: Irwin McGraw-Hill.

Stevens, W.R. (1997). TCP slow start, congestion avoidance, fast retransmit, and fast recovery algorithms. *RFC 2001.*

Stevens, W. R. (1998). *The protocols* (*Vol. 1*). TCP/IP Illustrated.

Stratonovich, R. L. (1959). Optimal nonlinear systems providing the extraction of the signal with constant parameters from noise. *Radiophysics, 11*(6), 892–901.

Stratonovich, R. L. (1960). Application of the Markovian process theory for signal optimal filtering. *Radio Engineering and Electronics, 11*, 1751–1763.

Stucki, D., Gisin, N., Guinnard, O., Ribordy, G., & Zbinden, H. (2002). Quantum key distribution over 67 km with a plug&play system. *New Journal of Physics, 4*, 41.1– 41.8.

Stuhlmuller, K., Farber, N., Link, M., & Girod, B. (2000). Analysis of video transmission over lossy channels. *IEEE Journal on Selected Areas in Communications, 18*(6), 1012–1032. doi:10.1109/49.848253.

Sulaiman, M. Y., Akaak, A. M., Wahab, M., Zakaria, A., & Suradi, J. (2002). Wind characteristics of Oman. *Energy, 27*, 35–46. doi:10.1016/S0360-5442(01)00055-X.

Sun, J.-T., Shen, D., Zeng, H.-J., Yang, Q., Lu, Y., & Chen, Z. (2005). Web-page summarization using clickthrough data. In *Proceedings of 28th Annual International ACM SIGIR Conference on Research and Development in Information Retrieval.* ACM.

Sven, U., Ales, F., & Stanislav, H. (2008). Quantification of traffic burstiness with MAPI middleware. In *Proceedings 2008 CESNET (Czech Educational and Scientific Network) Conference,* (pp. 13-22). Prague, Czech Republic: CESNET.

Takagi & Sugeno. (1985). Fuzzy identification of systems and its application to modelling and control. *IEEE Transactions on Systems, Man, and Cybernetics, 15*, 116–132.

Tanenbaum, A. (2003). *Computer networks.* Upper Saddle River, NJ: Prentice Hall.

Tar, K. (2007). Some statistical characteristics of monthly average wind speed at various heights. *Renewable & Sustainable Energy Reviews, 12*(6), 1712–1724. doi:10.1016/j.rser.2007.01.014.

Tedeschi, L. O. (2006). Assessment of the adequacy of mathematical models. *Agricultural Systems, 89*(2), 225–247. doi:10.1016/j.agsy.2005.11.004.

Telatar, I. (1999). *Capacity of multi-antenna gaussian channels, 10*(6), 585-595.

TellMe Voice Portal. (2002). Retrieved from http://www.tellme.com

The Network Simulator. (n.d.). *NS-2.* Retrieved from http://www.isi.edu/nsnam/ns/ns-build.html#allinone

Tikhonov, V. I. (1966). *Statistic radio engineering.* Moscow: Sovetskoe Radio Publishing.

Tikhonov, V. I. (1970). Nonlinear optimal filtering and the quasi-coherent signal reception. *Radioelectronics, 13*(2), 152–169.

Tikhonov, V. I., & Mironov, M. A. (1977). *Markov processes.* Moscow: Sovetskoe Radio Publishing.

Tomashevsky, A. I., & Kapranov, M. V. (2006). Fractal properties of chaotic dynamic processes in reverse time. *Nonlinear World,* (4-5), 214–237.

Torab, P., & Kanem, E. (1999). Load analysis of packet switched networks in control systems. In *Proceedings 25th Annual Conference of the IEEE Industrial Electronics Society,* (pp. 1222-1227). San Jose, CA: IEEE.

Triantafyllidou & Al Agha. (2007). *Evaluation of TCP performance in MANETs using an optimized scalable simulation model.* Paper presented at International Conference of Modeling, Analysis, and Simulation of Computer and Telecommunication Systems. Istanbul, Turkey.

Trubin, I. S., & Butorin, E. L. (2005). Spatial-time Markov model of digital half-tone images. *Radio Engineering,* (10), 10-13.

Trubin, I. S. (2004). Mathematical model of two statistically correlated video-sequences.[). St. Petersburg, Russia: SP Technical University Publishing.]. *Proceedings of Universities in Communications, 171*, 90–97.

Trubin, I. S. (2004). *Methods of digital signal processing.* Vyatka, Russia: Vyatka State University Publishing.

Trubin, I. S., & Butorin, E. L. (2004). Mathematical model of the digital image sequence. In *Proceedings of Russian NTO Popov Society: Digital Processing of Signals and its Application* (*Vol. 2*, pp. 166–169). Moscow: NTO.

Trulove, J. (2000). *Broadband networking*. Boca Raton, FL: CRC Press.

Tse, D., & Viswanath, P. (2005). *Fundamentals of wireless communication*. Cambridge, UK: Cambridge University Press. doi:10.1017/CBO9780511807213.

Turner, R., Sripada, S., Reiter, E., & Davy, I. (2008). Using spatial reference frames to generate grounded textual summaries of georeferenced data. In *Proceedings of 5th International Natural Language Generation Conference*. Salt Fork, OH: IEEE.

Tzes, A., Chen, J. C., & Peng, P. Y. (1994). Supervisory fuzzy control design for a magnetic suspension system. In *Proceedings of the 30th IEEE Conference on Fuzzy Systems,* (vol. 1, pp. 138-143). IEEE Press.

Van Nee, R. (2002). New high-rate wireless LAN standards. *IEEE Communications Magazine*, 40.

Vasiliev, K. K. (1995). *Applied theory of random processes and fields*. Ulyanovsk, Russia: UlGTU Publishing.

Vasiliev, K. K. (2002). Representation and fast processing of multi-dimensional images. *New Scientific Technologies,* (3), 4-24.

Vasiliev, K. K. (1995). Digital processing of image sequences in global monitoring problems of the Earth surface, the medicine, the air motion control, radar systems and hydro-location. In *Conversion of Military Complex, Double-Application Technologies*. Moscow: RIA Publishing.

Vasiukov, V.N. (2002). New approaches to solution of the image recognition and processing. *New Scientific Technologies*, (3), 44-51.

VCDemo Software. (n.d.). Retrieved from http://www.ict.ewi.tudelft.nl/vcdemo

Vehel & Sikdar. (2001). A multiplicative multifractal model for TCP traffic. In *Proceedings of IEEE ISCC'01*. IEEE. Retrieved from http://citeseer.ist.psu.edu/vehel01multiplicative.html

Velten, K. (2009). *Mathematical modeling and simulation: Introduction for scientists and engineers*. Weinheim: Wiley-VCH Verlag GmbH..

Venkataraman, P. (2009). *Applied optimisation with MATLAB programming*. New Jersey: John Wiley & Sons, Inc..

Vinkler, G. (2002). Image analysis, random fields, and dynamic methods of Monte-Carlo. In *Mathematical Fundamentals*. Novosibirsk, Russia: Siberian Division of RAS Publishing.

VirtualDub Software. (n.d.). Retrieved from http://www.virtualdub.org

Vishnevsky, V. M. (2003). *Theoretical bases of computer network design*. Moscow: Technosphere Publishing.

Viswanath, P., Tse, D. N. C., & Laroia, R. L. (2002). Opportunistic beamforming using dumb antennas. *IEEE Transactions on Information Theory*, *48*, 1277–1294. doi:10.1109/TIT.2002.1003822.

Viterbi, A. (1995). *CDMA: Principles of spread spectrum communication*. Boston: Addison Wesley Longman, Inc..

Voice, X. M. L. (2007). *VoiceXML application development life cycle*. Palo Alto, CA: Hewlett Packard Development Company. Retrieved from staff.washington.edu/benroy/ivr/vx_devlifecycle.pdf

Voxeo. (2003). *Voice voice server*. Retrieved from http://community.voxeo.com

Walker, E., Zepernick, H. J., & Wysocki, T. (1998). *Fading measurements at 2.4 GHz for the indoor radio propagation channel*. Paper presented at the International Zurich Seminar on Broadband Communications. Zurich, Switzerland.

Walsh, P., & Meade, J. (2003). Speech enabled e-learning for adult literacy tutoring. In *Proceedings of the 3rd IEEE International Conference on Advanced Learning Technologies (ICALT'03)*. IEEE. Retrieved from http://i-learn.uitm.edu.my/resources/journal/j1.pdf

Wang. (2005). Neuro-fuzzy modeling for microarray cancer gene expression data. *First Year Transfer Report*. Oxford, UK: Linacre College, Oxford University, Computing Laboratory.

Wang. (2010a). Dynamic load balancing in 3GPP LTE multi-cell networks with heterogeneous services. In *Proceedings of ICST Conference*. Beijing, China: LNCIST.

Wang. (2010b). *Dynamic load balancing and throughput optimization in 3GPP LTE networks (IWCMC 2010)*. Caen, France: IWCMC.

Wang, H., & Moayeri, N. (1995). Finite state Markov channel-A useful model for radio communication channels. *IEEE Transactions on Vehicular Technology*, *44*(2), 163–171. doi:10.1109/25.350282.

Wang, Y., Ostermann, J., & Zhang, Y.-Q. (2001). *Video processing and communications*. Upper Saddle River, NJ: Prentice Hall.

Warrier, Le, & Rhee (n.d.). *Cross-layer optimization made practical*. Raleigh, NC: Department of Computer Science, North Carolina State University.

Wenger, S. (2003). H264/AVC Over IP. *IEEE Transactions on Circuits and Systems for Video Technology*, *13*(7), 645–656. doi:10.1109/TCSVT.2003.814966.

Wenger, S., Stockhammer, T., & Hannuksela, M. M. (2003). *RTP payload format for H.264 video*. Internet Draft.

Wiegand, T., Sullivan, G. J., Bjntegaard, G., & Luthra, A. (2003). Overview of the H.264/AVC video coding standard. *IEEE Transactions on Circuits and Systems for Video Technology*, *13*(1), 560–576. doi:10.1109/TCSVT.2003.815165.

Williamson, K., Wright, S., Schauder, D., & Bow, A. (2001). The internet for the blind and visually impaired. *Journal of Computer Mediated Communication*. Retrieved from http://jcmc.indiana.edu/vol7/issue1/williamson.html

Windump.polito.it. (n.d.). Retrieved from http://www.windump.polito.it

WireShark Software. (n.d.). Retrieved from http://www.wireshark.org

Wolf, S., & Pinson, M. (1999). Spatial-temporal distortion metrics for in-service quality monitoring of any digital video system. In *Proceedings of SPIE International Symposium on Voice, Video, and Data Communications*. Boston: SPIE.

Wolf, S., & Pinson, M. (2002). Video quality measurement techniques. *Technical Report 02 392*. Washington, DC: US Department of Commerce, NTIA.

Wolfram Functions Site. (2011). Retrieved from http://functions.wolfram.com/GammaBetaErf/Gamma2

Wong, E. (1978). Recursive causal linear filtering for two-dimensional random fields. *IEEE Transactions on Information Theory*, *24*, 50–59. doi:10.1109/TIT.1978.1055818.

Wong, T. (1986). Design of a magnetic levitation system. *IEEE Transactions on Education*, *29*, 196–200. doi:10.1109/TE.1986.5570565.

Woods, J. W. (1972). Two-dimensional discrete Markov fields. *Information Theory*, *22*, 232–240. doi:10.1109/TIT.1972.1054786.

Wornell, G. (1996). *Signal processing with fractals: A wavelet-based approach*. London, UK: Prentice-Hall International.

Wu, D., Hou, Y. T., Zhu, W., Lee, H.-J., Chiang, T., Zhang, Y.-Q., & Chao, H. J. (2000). On end-to-end architecture for transporting MPEG-4 video over the internet. *IEEE Transactions on Circuits and Systems for Video Technology*, *10*(6), 923–941. doi:10.1109/76.867930.

Xylomenos, G. C., & Polyzos. (n.d.). Internet protocol performance over networks with wireless links. *IEEE Network*, *13*(4), 55–63.

Yang, G., Du, Y., & Chen, M. (2008). Computer aided investigation towards the wind power generation potentials of Guangzhou. *Computer and Information Science*, *1*(3), 13–19.

Yang, T. (2004). A survey of chaotic secure communication systems. *International Journal of Computational Cognition*, *2*(2), 81–130.

Yang, Z., Miyazaki, K., Kanae, S., & Wada, K. (2004). Robust position control of a magnetic levitation system via dynamic surface control technique. *IEEE Transactions on Industrial Electronics*, *51*(1), 26–34. doi:10.1109/TIE.2003.822095.

Yarlykov. (1980). *Application of Markovian theory of nonlinear filtering in radio engineering*. Moscow: Sovetskoe Radio Publishing.

Yindi, J., & Jafarkhani, H. (2009). Single and multiple relay selection schemes and their achievable diversity orders. *IEEE Transactions on Wireless Communications*, *8*(3), 1414–1423. doi:10.1109/TWC.2008.080109.

Zaiane, O. R. (2005). Recommended systems for e-learning: Towards non-intrusive web mining. *Data Mining in E-Learning, 2.*

Zaykovskiy, D. (2006). Survey of the speech recognition techniques for mobile devices. In *Proceedings of Speech and Computer (SPECOM'06).* St. Petersburg, Russia: SPECOM.

Zhang, Liu, Zhang, Jia, & Duan. (2011). A two-layer mobility load balancing in LTE self-organization networks. In *Proceedings of IEEE Internal Conference on Communication Technology.* Beijing: IEEE Press.

Zhou, N. (2008). *Novel batch dependant cross-layer scheduling for multiuser OFDM systems.* Washington, DC: IEEE Press. doi:10.1109/ICC.2008.728.

Zyren & McCoy. (2007). Overview of the 3GPP long term evolution physical layer. (White Paper) *Document number:3GPPEVOLUTIONWP Rev. 0: Freescale semiconductor.*

About the Contributors

Aderemi A. Atayero graduated from the Moscow Institute of Technology (MIT) with a Bachelor's of Science Degree in Radio Engineering and a Master's of Science Degree in Satellite Communication Systems in 1992 and 1994 respectively. He earned a Ph.D. in Telecommunication Engineering/Signal Processing from Moscow State Technical University of Civil Aviation, Russia in 2000. He is a member of a number of professional associations including: the Institute of Electrical and Electronic Engineers (IEEE), the International Association of Engineers (IAENG), and a professional member of the International Who's Who Historical Society (IWWHS) among others. He is a registered engineer with the Council for the Regulation of Engineering in Nigeria, COREN. As a two-time Head of the Department of Electrical and Information Engineering at Covenant University in Nigeria, he was also the coordinator of the School of Engineering at Covenant University. Dr. Atayero is widely published in International peer-reviewed journals, proceedings, and edited books. He is on the editorial board of a number of highly reputed International journals. Atayero is a recipient of several awards including the 2009/10 Ford Foundation Teaching Innovation Award. His current research interests are in Radio and Telecommunication Systems and Devices; Signal Processing, and Converged Multi-Service Networks. Atayero is a Full Professor of Communication Engineering and the current Vice-Chancellor (Academic) at Covenant University, Nigeria.

Oleg I. Sheluhin was born in 1952 in Moscow, Russia. In 1974 he graduated from the Moscow Institute of Transport Engineers (MITE) with a Master of Science Degree in Radio Engineering. After that he entered the Lomonosov State University (Moscow) and graduated in 1979 with a Second Diploma of Mathematics. He received a Ph.D. (Techn.) at MITE in 1979 in Radio Engineering and D.Sc. (Techn.) at Kharkov Aviation Institute in 1990. The title of his PhD thesis was "Investigation of Interfering Factors Influence on the Structure and Activity of Noise Short-Range Radar." His Doctorate of Science thesis is titled, "Synthesis, Analysis and Realization of Short-Range Radio Detectors and Measuring Systems." Sheluhin is a member of the International Academy of Sciences of Higher Educational Institutions. He has published 15 scientific books and textbooks for universities and more than 250 scientific papers. Since 1990 he has been the Head of the Radio Engineering and Radio Systems Department of Moscow State Technical University of Service (MSTUS). He is also the Chief Editor of the scientific journal, *Electrical and Informational Complexes and Systems*, and a member of Editorial Boards of various scientific journals. In 2004 he was awarded the title "Honored Scientific Worker."

* * *

Alatishe S. Adeyemi was born in Lagos, Nigeria in 1986. He graduated from Covenant University (CU) with a B.Eng. Degree in Information and Communication Technology in 2008 and a Masters of Engineering (M.Eng.) in Information and Communication Technology at Covenant University in 2012. He currently lecturers in the Department of Electrical and Information Engineering, Covenant University, Nigeria. Alatishe Adeyemi is a member of a number of professional associations including: the Institute of Electrical and Electronic Engineers (IEEE), the International Association of Engineers (IAENG), among others. His current research interests are in Satellite communications, Digital signal processing and control systems, E-learning and Operations research.

Oluseyi Olanrewaju Ajayi holds a B.Sc., M.Eng., and Ph.D. in Mechanical Engineering. His research area includes Energy systems, Design, and Production Technology. Professionally, Ajayi is a registered member of the Council for the Regulation of Engineering profession in Nigeria (COREN) as well as the Nigerian Society of Engineers (NSE).

Alexander Lakovlevich Anoprienko is the Dean of Computer Science and Technology at Donetsk National Technical University, the Director of the Technopark DonNTU UNITECH, a specialist in Computer Systems, Network Information Technology, and Computer Modeling, the initiator and administrator of the portal Masters DonNTU, and the author of a number of original scientific concepts. His research interests include the generic code-logical basis, integrated modeling environment, and cognitive computer simulation.

Mehrdad Ardebilipour was born in Iran, on February 1954. He received B.Sc. and M.Sc. Degrees in electrical engineering from K.N. Toosi University of Technology, Tehran, Iran, in 1977 and Tarbiat Modarres University, Tehran, Iran, in 1989, respectively. He has also been awarded the degree of Ph.D. by the University of Surrey, Guildford, England, in 2001. Since 2001, he has been assistant professor at K.N. Toosi University of Technology and is directing the Communications Engineering Department and the Spread Spectrum and Wireless Communications research laboratory. His current research interests are cognitive radio, cooperative communication, ad-hoc and sensor networks, MIMO communication, OFDM, game theory, and cross-layer design for wireless communications.

Charles K. Ayo holds a B.Sc., M.Sc. and Ph.D in Computer Science. His research interests include: mobile computing, Internet programming, E-business, government, and object oriented design and development. He is a member of the Nigerian Computer Society (NCS) and Computer Professional Registration Council of Nigeria (CPN). He is currently the Head of Computer and Information Sciences Department of Covenant University in Ota, Ogun state, Nigeria. Dr. Ayo is a member of a number of international research bodies such as the Centre for Business Information, Organization, and Process Management (BIOPoM), University of Westminister, the Review Committee of the European Conference on E-Government, and the Editorial Board of *Journal of Information and Communication Technology for Human Development.*

A. A. Azeta earned his Bachelor's of Science degree in Computer Science at the University of Benin in Benin City, Nigeria from 1989 to 1992 with a second class (Hons) upper division. Thereafter, he got admitted to the University of Lagos, Nigeria to work for his Master's in Computer Science between 1998 and 1999. He has worked as a consultant in so many Information and Communications Technology (ICT) companies in Nigeria, among them Compumetrics Solutions Limited, a technology research company based at Ikoyi Lagos, between 2001 and 2005. Mr. Azeta Joined Convenant University in 2005 as an Assistant Lecturer in the Department of Computer and Information Sciences, College of Science and Technology. He is currently a Ph.D. student in the Department of Computer and Information Sciences Covenant University, Nigeria. His current research interests are on Software Engineering, Mobile Computing and Algorithm Design. He is a member of the Nigerian Computer Society (NCS), and Computer Professional Registration Council of Nigeria (CPN). He has attended and presented papers in conferences. He is married with four children.

Oshin Babasanjo is a seasoned Network Consultant, with years of experience and currently working for a Cisco Partner in Milan, Italy. His research area includes wireless technology, networking and telecommunications. Oshin Babasanjo is a member of the Institute of Electrical and Electronic Engineers (IEEE). He holds various industry certifications from Cisco, Juniper, and ITSM. He currently holds a 1st degree and a Masters degree in Information and Communication Technology from the prestigious Covenant University, Ogun State, Nigeria.

Eduard Babulak is an international scholar, researcher, consultant, educator, professional engineer, and polyglot with more than thirty years of teaching experience and industrial experience as a professional engineer and consultant. His academic and engineering work was recognized internationally by the Engineering Council in UK, the European Federation of Engineers, and credited by the Ontario Society of Professional Engineers and APEG in British Columbia in Canada. He is a Mentor, Elite Group Member, and Chartered Fellow of British Computer Society, Fellow of Royal Society RSA, Nominated Fellow of the Institution of Engineering and Technology, Mentor and Senior Member of IEEE, Senior Member of ACM, Member of American Society for Engineering Education. Professor Babulak speaks 14 languages and his biography was cited in the *Cambridge Blue Book*, Cambridge Index of Biographies and number of issues of *Who's Who.*

Panos S. Bakalis received his B.Sc. in Electrical Engineering in Athens in 1975, and his PG Diploma in Electronics and Control in 1980, at CLP London. He received his M.Sc. in Systems Engineering 1982, and his Ph.D. in Control Engineering both at City University London. From 1986-92 he was Senior Lecturer at Thames Polytechnic, London and from 1992-96 became Senior Lecturer in the School of Computing at the University of Greenwich. Since then, he moved to the Department of Computer and Communications at the Medway School of Engineering, University of Greenwich where he has worked as a Senior Lecturer in Computer Networking. His research interests are in computer process control and optimization of large-scale systems. He has published papers in international Control Conferences and Journals. From 2008 he has widened his research interests to include the field of Ad Hoc Wireless

Computer Networks Protocols (MANET) using OPNET Modeler. He has published several papers in International Communications Conferences and Journals. As M.Sc. Programme Leader in Computer Networking he is supervising students for MSc projects and PhD thesis, in the capacity of MANET field.

Lawal Bello received his B.Sc. degree in Computer Science in 2004 from Usmanu Danfodiyo University in Sokoto, Nigeria and M.Sc. degree in Computer Networking Engineering from University of Greenwich, United Kingdom. He is currently a Ph.D. student with the Mobile and Wireless Research Centre at the School of Engineering, University of Greenwich, United Kingdom. His research interest includes Wireless Communications, design and performance, evaluation of routing protocols in mobile ad hoc wireless networks, and Power Management in MANET.

Christian Bolu, who is presently the Acting Head of the Department of Mechanical Engineering at Covenant University in Nigeria holds a Ph.D. in Industrial & Systems Engineering from University of Wales, United Kingdom, M.Eng. in Industrial Engineering from University of Toronto, Canada, and a B.Sc. in Mechanical Engineering from University of Nigeria, Nsukka. He has several years of university teaching experience from Covenant University, University of Nigeria, Nsukka, University of Ibadan, and University of Toronto. A Fellow of the Nigerian Society of Engineers, Dr Bolu has several SAP Solution Consultant and Solution Architect certifications. He has worked as Chief Executive Officer, Technical Manager and Technical Consultant in several companies in Nigeria, Kenya, and Ghana. His current research interest includes plant maintenance total productivity measurement, mechatronics adaptations, cutting stock problems, digital asset management and fibre optics network optimization.

Theofilos Chrysikos was born in Patras, Greece in 1982. He received his Engineering Diploma from the Department of Electrical and Computer Engineering of the University of Patras in 2005 and obtained his PhD in 2012 on Wireless Channel Characterization with emphasis on path loss modeling, shadowing, RF propagation mechanisms, channel modeling and measurements, and wireless information-theoretic security (physical layer security). Other topics of academic interest and research include ad-hoc networks, emergency services, roadside networks, MIMO fading channels, QoS in wireless networks, Cellular Mobile Telephony (2,5G/3G), Next Generations Networks, and migration issues. He is a member of the Technical Chamber of Greece.

Monday Ofori Eyinagho obtained a Bachelor's of Science Degree in Electronic and Electrical Engineering from the Obafemi Awolowo University in Ile-Ife, Nigeria in 1988. He also holds a Post-Graduate Diploma in Computer Science from the University of Lagos in Lagos, Nigeria (1991), an M.B.A. (General Management) Degree from the River State University of Science and Technology in Port-Harcourt, Nigeria (2003), a Master's of Science Degree in Computer Engineering, from the Federal University of Technology in Owerri, Nigeria (2004), and a Ph. D. in Computer Engineering from Covenant University in Ota, Nigeria (2011). Dr. Eyinagho has had extensive industrial work experience in a number of corporate organizations. He is currently a lecturer in the Department of Electrical and Information Engineering at Covenant University in Ota, Nigeria. Dr. Eyinagho has published scholarly papers in international journals. He is a member of The Nigerian Society of Engineers, a COREN Registered Electronics Engineer, and a member of the Nigeria Computer Society. His principal researches are in the areas of developing and implementing microprocessor-based systems and performance optimization of local area networks.

Richard Olayiwola Fagbenle (BSME (Illinois), MSME (Iowa State), Ph. D (Illinois)) is a Professor of Mechanical Engineering. He currently lectures at the Mechanical Engineering Department, Obafemi Awolowo University, Ile-Ife, Osun State, Nigeria. Equally, He is an adjunct Professor of Mechanical Engineering Department, Covenant University, Ota, Ogun State, Nigeria and a retired Professor and Adjunct Professor of Mechanical Engineering, University of Ibadan, Ibadan, Nigeria. Professionally, Prof. Fagbenle is a member of the Council for the Regulation of Engineering profession in Nigeria (COREN) and also a Fellow of the Nigerian Society of Engineers (NSE).

Samuel Oluwole Falaki is a Professor of Computer Engineering at the Federal University of Technology in Akure, Nigeria. He holds a Master's of Engineering Degree in Electrical Engineering from Leningrad University, a Master's of Science Degree in Computer Science from UCLA, and a Ph.D in Electrical Engineering from the University of Lagos in Lagos, Nigeria. His research interests are in the areas of Computer Architecture, Computer Communications and Networking, Network Security and Digital Signal Processing. He is a Fellow of the Nigeria Computer Society, a Member of the Nigerian Society of Engineers, a Member of IEEE, and a Member of ACM.

Artem V. Garmashev was born in Electrostal, Russia in 1986. He graduated from the Moscow Technical University of Communication and Informatics in 2011 with a Master's of Science Degree in IT. Later he began his Ph.D. program at the same university and continues study at present. His current research interests are information security, signal processing, and time series analysis.

D. Golubchikov was born in 1984 in Sochi, Russia. He graduated from Taganrog State University of Radio Engineering (TSURE) with a diploma of Engineering in Protected system of communication in 2006. He has been working in Taganrog Institute of Technology, South Federal University as assistant professor and writing his Candidate of Science (Ph.D.) dissertation on the methodology of efficiency estimation of quantum key distribution systems. D. Golubchikov is an author more than 30 scientific works. He is head of quantum cryptography research laboratory and head of student research group. The most significant papers are Golubchikov D. M., Rumyantsev K. E. "Quantum cryptography: principles, protocols, systems". Moscow, 2008 and Golubchikov D. M., Rumiantsev K. E. "Estimation of influence of error correction and privacy amplification on keys generation rate in QKD systems", Taganrog, 2010. His research interests include quantum cryptography, information security of telecommunication systems.

N.A. Ikhu-Omoregbe, has a B.Sc. degree in Computer science from the University of Benin, in Benin City, a M.Sc. degree in Computer Sciences from the University of Lagos, and a Ph.D. in Computer Science from Covenant University in Ota, Nigeria. His research interests include: Software Engineering, Mobile Computing, Mobile Healthcare and Telemedicine Systems, and Soft Computing. He currently lectures at Covenant University. He is a member of the Institution of Electrical and Electronics Engineers (IEEE).

Yury A. Ivanov was born in Moscow, Russia in 1985. He obtained a M.Sc. degree in Systems, network and devices in telecommunications from Chuvash State University in 2007. He obtained a Ph.D in Telecommunication Networks and Systems in 2011 from Moscow State University of Communication and Informatics. Ivanov has published over 35 scientific papers and his current research interests include Radio and Telecommunications Systems and Devices, transmission of multimedia data across telecommunication networks, assessment of the quality of video sequences. Ivanov is a member of a number of professional associations including: the Institute of Electrical and Electronic Engineers (IEEE) and the International Association of Engineers (IAENG).

Samuel Ndueso John is a Senior Lecturer in the department of Electrical and Information Engineering at Covenant University, Ota, Ogun State, Nigeria since December, 2007 to date. He obtained his Ph.D. degrees in Computer Systems and Network Engineering, from Donetsk National Technical University, Ukraine. He is a registered Computer Engineer by the Council for the Regulation of Engineering in Nigeria (COREN), a member of Nigeria Society of Engineering (MNSE), and a member of the Institution of Engineering and Technology (MIET). John has attended several conferences and published many technical papers in major professional journals. His areas of research interest are: The Effect of Latency on Quality of Service (QoS) in Voice over Internet Protocol (VoIP), Convergence of ICT: Prospects and Challenges as the new Emerging Technology & Network efficiency in data exchange (LAN & WLAN), and Surveillance Security Systems.

Ashkan Kalantari was born in Iran, on 1987. He received the B.S. in electrical engineering, communication from K. N. Toosi University of Technology, Tehran, Iran, in 2009. From September 2009 he has been a M.S. student at the faculty of electrical engineering, K. N. Toosi University of Technology. His current research interests are cooperative communication, and multi-user communication.

M. Kapranov graduated Radio Engineering faculty of the Moscow Power Engineering Institute (MPEI) in 1952. In 1957, in MPEI, he has defended a Ph.D thesis on a subject "Phase Self-tuning of Frequency". In 1961, he became an associate professor of the department of Radiotransmitting Devices MPEI. Since 1992 Kapranov is a professor and in 2009 he has received a title of "Honorary professor of MPEI." In 1986 as a part of a group of authors he was awarded the State Prize of the USSR in the field of a science for a cycle of publications "Phase Lock in Communication and Control." M. Kapranov is an expert in the field of the theory of nonlinear oscillations, dynamic chaos, fractals, and secure communications. He has prepared more than 15 doctors of philosophy. He is the author and the coauthor of about 160 scientific publications, among which 5 monographs, and some manuals under the theory of nonlinear oscillations, phase lock, and dynamic chaos.

James Katende was born in 1954 at Kampala, Uganda. He received the B.Sc., M.Sc., and Ph.D. degrees in Electrical Engineering, from the University of Lagos, in 1978, 1982, and 1987, respectively. He is Professor and Founding Dean of the College of Engineering & Technology, Botswana International University of Science & Technology. Formerly Professor and Dean, College of Science & Technology, Covenant University, Ota, Nigeria, Professor of Electrical Engineering, Bayero University, Kano, and Lecturer of Electrical Engineering, University of Lagos, Nigeria. He specializes in automatic controls and robotics.

A. Khandurin was born in 1985 in Zhukovsky, Moscow region, Russia. He graduated Radio engineering faculty of the Moscow Power Engineering Institute (MPEI) in 2008. In 2011, in MPEI, he has defended a Ph.D. thesis on a subject "Signals with an Additive Fractal Structure." A. Khandurin works in the Department of Fluctuations and Signals Generation of MPEI as a principal engineer. His research interests are in the study of dynamical chaos and fractals, controlling and synchronization of nonlinear circuits and systems, and secure information transmission.

Stavros A. Kotsopoulos received his B.Sc. in Physics from the Aristotle University of Thessaloniki (1975) and got his Diploma in Electrical and Computer Engineering from the University of Patras (1984). Moreover, he is an M.Phil and Ph.D. holder. Prof. Kotsopoulos is a member of the academic staff of the Department of Electrical and Computer Engineering of the University of Patras and holds the position of Professor. Since 2004 he is the Director of the Wireless Telecommunications Laboratory and develops his professional life teaching and doing research in the scientific area of Wireless Telecommunications. He is the (co)author of the book titled "mobile telephony" and (co)author of the "Handbook of Research in Heterogeneous Next Generation Networking: Innovations & Platforms". Professor Kotsopoulos directs a research team and has been the leader of several National and European research projects. He is a member of the Greek Physicists Society and of the Technical Chamber of Greece.

Matthew Kwatri Luka hails from Adamawa state, Nigeria. He received his B.Eng. in Electrical and Electronics Engineering from Federal University of Technology, Yola in 2009 and a M.Eng. (ICT) in the department of Electrical and Information Engineering, Covenant University Ota in 2012. His research interests are in Mobile communication networks, satellite communications and Artificial Intelligence.

Elena V. Medvedeva in 2012 had got the scientific degree of Doctor of Technical Sciences. She is Professor of State Educational Institution of Higher Professional Education "Vyatka State University." She is the author of over 100 scientific publications. Her research interests include multidimensional Markov fields in image processing.

Mustapha Muhammad was born in Kano, Nigeria on the 24th July 1977. He received the Bachelor of Engineering and the Master of Engineering degrees from Bayero University, Kano, Nigeria in January 2001 and February 2007 respectively. In March 2004, he joined Department of Electrical Engineering, Bayero University, Kano, Nigeria as a Graduate Assistant and rose to the rank of Lecturer I in 2012. He was on Study fellowship since 2010, as Ph.D. student in the Department of Mechatronics and Robotics, Faculty of Electrical Engineering, Universiti Teknologi Malaysia. His research interests include the areas of artificial neural networks, fuzzy modeling and control, intelligent control theories and mobile robots.

Charles Ndujiuba holds a Ph.D. in Electrical & Electronics Engineering from the University College London (University of London); Mastere Specialise (Masters with Specialisation) in Radio Communications from Ecole Superieure d'Electricite (SUPELEC) France; M.Sc. in Electrical Engineering from the University of Lagos; B.Sc. in Electronics & Communications Engineering from the London Metropolitan University. He is a Chartered Electronics Engineer (CEng) and a highly skilled wireless professional. He has more than 25 years RF, Microwave, Fixed-line (SDH and PDH), and PMR experience, with considerable international exposure. Ndujiuba has attended several conferences and published many technical papers in major professional journals of IEEE and IET. Prior to his present position as Senior Lecturer at Covenant University in Ota, Nigeria, Ndujiuba was the Technical Director in Globe Trunk Ltd in UK. His research interests include: Ultra-Low Noise Amplifiers, Active Devices and Circuits, UWB Transmitter, Modelling & Simulation, and Dielectric Resonator Antennas.

Eugeny P. Petrov is Dr.Sci (Techn.), professor of State Educational Institution of Higher Professional Education "Vyatka State University," the Head of Radio Electronic Means Department of the said University. He has coordinated numerous Russian research projects in the field of radio communications and digital image processing. He was a scientific supervisor of many researches fulfilled on the basis Governmental Order. E. Petrov has made a large contribution in the development of mathematical theory of image processing with Markov chains application. He is author of more than 300 scientific publications, books and conference proceedings. He is Academician of Russian Academy of Natural Sciences and Honored Employee of Higher Professional Education of Russian Federation. He has prepared of 4 Doctors of Sci (Techn.) of his University Department.

K. Rumyantsev was born in 1951, Taganrog, Rostov Region, Russia. He graduated from Taganrog State University of Radio Engineering (TSURE) with a diploma of Electrical Engineering in 1974. He worked in the Leningrad Institute of Electronic Technology and defended his Candidate of Science (Ph.D.) dissertation on the problems of receiving optical signals in the harsh noise environment from 1974 to 1978. He defended his second (doctoral) dissertation at the Leningrad Institute of Precise Mechanics and Optics, which was dedicated to the development of the theory of space-time approach to search and detection of optical radiation sources in 1988. K. Rumyantsev has worked in the TSURE as an Assistant Professor, Associate Professor, Full Professor, and Vice-Rector for Research since 1979. He was Head of the Department of Receiver and TV System of the TSURE from 1989 to 1997. He has been Head of the Department of Information security of telecommunication systems of the Southern Federal University since 1997. He is a holder of 290 scientific papers, 17 books, and 40 patents. His research interests include principles of construction, theory of analysis, algorithms of functioning, and models of the registrations of weak light signals.

Apkar Salatian (B.Sc., Ph.D.) obtained a B.Sc. Second Class Honors Upper Division in Computer Science from University Of Strathclyde, Glasgow, UK in 1991. He then obtained a Ph.D. in Computer Science from University Of Aberdeen, Aberdeen, UK in 1997. After working as a university lecturer in the UK for 12 years he is now a lecturer of Information Technology and Communications at the American University of Nigeria, Yola, Nigeria. His research interests are in the areas of time series analysis of high frequency, voluminous and noisy data, telemedicine, data mining, and software engineering and computing for development.

Sergey M. Smolskiy is Dr. Sci. (Techn.), professor of the National Research University Moscow Power Engineering Institute (MPEI). He has participated in various researches and coordinated many Russian projects in the field of communication, radar technologies, theory of nonlinear oscillations, radio monitoring, electrodynamics, quantum radio physics etc. He was a scientific supervisor of many researches fulfilled on the basis of Governmental Order. He is a member of editorial board of different scientific national and international journals and author of more than 250 scientific publications, books and conference proceedings. He is the co-author of eight large scientific books printed in English in USA, UK, Germany. He is Academician of three International Academies of Sciences, Honored Doctor of three foreign universities, member of IEEE.

Ehsan Soleimani-Nasab obtained the B.Sc. in Electrical Engineering from the Iran University of Science and Technology, Iran in 2006. He then received the M.Sc. and Ph.D. in Communication Systems from the K. N. Toosi University of Technology, Iran in 2009 and 2013, respectively. From April through October 2012, he was with the Department of Signals and Systems, Chalmers University of Technology, Sweden working as a Visiting Researcher. His research interests span signal processing for wireless communications, cooperative communications, MIMO systems, and cognitive radio networks.

Igor S. Trubin is Dr. Sci. (Techn.), professor of State Educational Institution of Higher Professional Education "Vyatka State University." He has participated in the few Russian research projects in the field of communication and digital image processing. He is author of more than 100 scientific publications, books and conference proceedings.

Index

3GPP LTE 343-344, 358-359

A

abstraction 2-3, 11, 53, 136, 138-145, 148, 170
Adaptive Neuro-Fuzzy Inference System (ANFIS) 343, 345, 358
Additive White Gaussian Noise (AWGN) 172-173, 178, 180, 186-188, 278, 401, 404
algorithmic simulation method 134
a priori data 279, 283-284, 287-288, 291
arrival curve 52-53, 62
Artificial Neural Network (ANN) 345, 361-362, 367, 369-373
axioms 8

B

ball mass variation 369
BB84 protocol 317-320, 322, 326, 333
bit binary images
  elements 210, 212-219, 221-222, 224-230, 232-234, 236-237, 241, 282-283, 285-286, 288-291, 293-297, 300, 302
bit error probability (BER) 168
breakdown 151, 153-162
BT-45 144
burstiness 53-55, 61, 69, 132

C

Carrier Sense Multiple Access with Collision Detection (CSMA/CD) 49-50, 70, 122, 133
Case-Based Reasoning (CBR) 73, 76, 79-80, 82, 85, 91, 95-96, 180, 305-311, 313, 347, 349-350
channel characterization 257-259, 273-274, 277
clean waves (CW) 98
Company MagiQ Technologies 317
confidential data 315-316
congestion collapse 117, 119, 134
constant
  bit rate 305-306, 308
  delay line 55-56, 58-60
convex optimization 252, 255
cooperative communication 242, 253, 255
cross-layer
  design 390-392, 407-410
  optimization 390-392, 396-397, 400-401, 405-406, 408-410

D

data
  streaming 169
  transfer 116-120, 122-123, 126, 128, 130-131, 134, 168, 180, 316, 323
  transmission 117, 119-120, 125-126, 134, 173, 175, 183, 315-316, 396, 407-408, 410
decode-and-forward 242, 244, 250-251
delay packet 47, 58, 60, 65
Destination Sequenced Distance Vector (DSDV) 307, 311-312
Digital Half-Tone Images (DHTI) 207-212, 219-222, 227-229, 234-238, 241, 278-279, 283-288, 291-296, 300, 302-303
  nonlinear filtering 278
  video sequences 207-210, 228, 234-238, 302
direct task 7
Donetsk National Technical University 116, 130
Dynamic Source Routing (DSR) 305-308, 311-313

E

effective bandwidth capacity 118-119, 122-125, 127, 131, 134
e-learning 71-80, 82, 86-87, 90-96
endogenic variables 5
end-to-end delay 47-49, 51, 53, 65, 67, 69, 305-306, 308, 311, 313
eNodeB 343, 347-351, 353-357

Erlang distribution 155
error packetization 194, 196-197, 202
Evolved Packet System (EPS) 344-345
exogenic variables 5

F

fading channel 172, 188, 242, 253-254, 275-276, 394-396
fast fading 395
feed forward network 367-368
filter 136-138, 141-144, 148, 211, 241, 283, 285-287, 292, 294-295, 301, 303
Finding Content Suitability (FCS) 71, 79, 90
First-Come-First-Served (FCFS) 56, 58-59, 61
    multiplexer 56
    queue 56, 61
flat fading 393, 395
formalized schematics 6-7
fractal 16-21, 24, 32-35, 42-46, 97-100, 103-106, 108-115
    function 98-99, 108, 114
    masking 109-113
    traffic 33
Fractional Brownian Motion (FBM) 24, 34-35, 37
frame collision 123, 134
Free Open Source code Software (FOSS) 178-179
frequency
    compression 97, 105-107, 110-112
    selective fading 395
Friis formula 260
functional model 4
fuzzy logic 343, 345-346, 358, 362

G

gamma distribution 155, 244, 376
Gilbert-Elliot model 173
Gilbert Model 172
Graphical Models (GM) 4

H

H.264/AVC 167, 170, 174, 183, 202-205
Hausdorff dimension 17, 19-21, 30, 115
HOST unit 120-122
hysteresis 343, 353-358

I

id 3000 Clavis system 321-322, 341
IEEE 802.3 49-50
industrial organization 149
Information Communication Systems and Networks (ICSN) 1, 16, 149
Intensive Care Unit (ICU) 136-137, 140-141, 146
    monitor data 137, 146
Internet meltdown 117, 119, 134
interpretation 4, 12, 54, 98, 103, 135-138, 140-141, 143-145, 148, 239, 279, 322, 386
INTERPRETOR software 135-137, 141, 144-145
isomorphism 1-3

K

key rate 331, 334

L

Lagrange formulation 363
leaky bucket algorithm 53-54
learning algorithm 347
Learning Management Systems (LMS) 72
Legendre transform 24-25, 30, 43
Lena 221-222
Line-of-Sight (LOS) 260-261
load balancing 343-344, 347, 350-353, 355-359
Local Area Networks (LANs) 47-51, 58, 65-67, 69-70, 118, 120, 122, 127, 131, 391, 408-409
    switched 47, 49, 51, 69

M

Mach-Zehnder interferometer 318-320
Magnetic levitation 361-365, 367-371, 373-374
markov chain
    BBI formation 218
    Digital Half-Tone Images (DHTI) 227-228
Markov chain 149-150, 161, 167, 194, 197, 210-215, 217-218, 221, 224-225, 227, 229, 236-241, 279
Markovian Process (MP) 170, 177, 184, 186, 207-210, 232-233, 236, 241, 278, 280-283, 285
    discrete value 279
Mathematical Models (MM) 3-4, 207-211, 213-215, 221, 227, 231, 236, 238, 241, 288, 302-303

matrix of transition probability (MTP) 241, 279, 281-282, 285-286, 292, 294
Maximal a posteriori probability (MAP) 241
maximum
 delay model 48, 57-60, 65
 weighted capacity 390-391, 399
Mean opinion Score (MOS) 176, 181-182, 184, 187-191, 193, 201-202
meteorological stations 379
m-learning 72, 74-76, 78-79, 86, 91, 96
Mobile Ad Hoc Network (MANET) 305-308, 311-313
moment generation 242, 244, 252
Monte-Carlo simulations 242
multi-antenna 205, 242, 244, 252-255
multifractal 16-25, 28, 30, 32-35, 37-38, 40, 42-45, 132
 traffic 32
multipath 178, 257, 276-277, 393-395, 397
multiplexing 59, 204, 348, 390-391, 393, 407-408, 410
Multi-Wall-Floor (MWF) model 265-270

N

Nakagami-m fading channels 242-244, 247, 249-250, 252-255
network
 calculus 48, 52, 54, 68
 layer 16, 43, 117-119, 130, 166, 187
Network Adaptation Layer (NAL) 170-171
Network Simulator 2 (NS-2) 178
neural network 93, 343, 345-346, 351, 361-362, 367, 370-371, 373-374, 388
noise immunity 278, 285, 287, 293, 295
nonlinear filtering 210, 221, 240, 278-279, 282, 285-288, 291, 295, 297, 300, 302-304
Non-symmetric half-plain (NSHP) 241

O

One-sided Markov random field (OSMRF) 241
optical fiber 316, 321, 332, 334, 341
Orthogonal Frequency Division Multiplexing (OFDM) 390-394, 396-401, 404-410
oscillations 24, 97-99, 108-112
outage probability 242-244, 247-253, 255, 263-264, 270

P

path loss 256-262, 264-268, 270, 273-276
 indoor 257, 259, 262, 273
pattern mining 135, 144-145, 148
phase coding 314, 316-317, 320, 322-323, 326, 331, 341
photons 316-321, 323, 326-328, 331-332
physical layer 62, 68, 118-120, 133, 171, 173-174, 187, 331, 358-359, 391-392, 396-401, 406
probability
 density function 182, 245, 262
 distribution 3, 7, 33, 161, 182, 377-378
productivity 13, 33, 117, 119, 130, 149-153, 156-158, 162-164
PSNR value 181-182, 187-189, 191, 193
purelin 373

Q

Quality of Service (QoS) 33, 36, 51-52, 70, 166, 168, 171-172, 175-176, 182-183, 203, 343, 347, 390-391, 396-397, 399-404, 406-410
 traffic 390, 401, 404, 406
quantum
 cryptography 314, 316-317, 319, 331-332, 338-339, 341-342
 key distribution 314, 316-317, 323, 327, 331-332, 334, 341-342
queue
 performance 16-17, 32-35, 37-38, 43-44
 tail 35-37
 theory 52, 68, 149, 152-154, 162, 164
Quintessence Labs Pty Ltd 317

R

Radio Receiver Devices (RRD) 241, 278-281, 283-287, 292-293, 295, 301-302
Real-Time Control Protocol (RTCP) 171
Real-Time Streaming Protocol (RTSP) 171, 205
Real-time Transmission protocol (RTP) 170-171, 186-188, 193, 200, 205
receiver buffer 56, 58
relay networks 242, 244, 252-255
renewable energy 376, 388-389
Resource Reservation Protocol (RSVP) 171
reverse task 8
Root Mean Square Error (RMSE) 181, 380, 386

S

schematic model 4
selection combining 253, 255
Self-Organizing Networks (SON) 343-344, 409
shadow fading 256, 262-264, 270, 274-277, 347-348
shadowing 244, 251, 257-258, 262-266, 268-275, 277
    deviation 257, 263, 265-266, 268-273
sight-impaired learner 71
Signal-to-Noise-Ratio (SNR) 206, 242-245, 249-250, 252, 255, 272, 401-406, 410
SIMUL8 157-160, 163
SIMULINK 119-120, 122-123, 132, 361-362, 365, 367, 373
single-photon avalanche detector (SPAD) 318
sinusoidal input 361, 371-372
slow fading 396
soft computing 146, 343, 359
software architecture 92, 135-137, 141, 144-148
state feedback controller 361-362, 364, 366-367, 373
stealthiness transmission 98, 109
step input 361, 367, 370
stochastic breakdown 149-150
streaming traffic 167-168, 202
structural model 4
subcarrier allocation 398, 400-401
switched Ethernet 50, 52, 66-70
symbol error probability 247, 255

T

tansig 373
TCP/IP protocol 116, 118, 124, 131
telecommunication 16-17, 25, 32-33, 43, 166, 176, 258, 274, 312, 316, 341-342, 376
temporal
    inferencing 138, 148
    interpolation 138, 148
traffic
    model 306-308, 311
    stream 54, 61
Transmission Control Protocols (TCP) 116-119, 122, 124, 127-128, 131-134, 171, 180, 305-308, 310-313, 390-391, 409-410
transport layer 118-120, 122, 124, 170-171, 187
truncation 103

V

variable bit rate 305-308
Vehicular Ad Hoc Network (VANET) 305-308, 311, 313
vicinity 211-214, 216-218, 221-227, 229, 232, 234, 236-238, 293, 297, 301
Video Coding Layers (VCL) 170-171
video-sequence 174, 177, 184, 194, 202-203, 209, 222, 224, 227, 229, 234, 237-238, 241, 295-296, 300-303
video streaming 14, 166-167, 175, 186, 201-203, 409
visually impaired learner 79
Voice-enabled Framework for Recommender and Adaptation (VeFRA) 71, 73, 75, 79-87, 89-90
Voice eXtensible Mark-up Language (VoiceXML) 71-74, 76, 84-85, 89, 91-94, 96
voice messages 97-98, 109, 112
Voice User Interface (VUI) 72

W

Wavelet Transform Modulus Maxima (WTMM) 16, 23-24, 26, 30
Weibull distribution 35, 155, 377, 388
Weierstrass function 97, 99-100, 103, 106, 115
wideband signals 97, 113
wind
    profile 375, 377, 381, 387
    speed 376-382, 384, 386-388
wind energy 375-377, 380-384, 386-389
    flux density 377, 380, 384, 387
    Nigeria 375
wireless broadband 166, 194, 392
    error models 171, 202
workload 34-35, 117-118, 122-129, 134, 151, 162